Jacob Youde William Lloyd

The History of the Princes, the Lords Marcher

And the Ancient Nobility of Powys Fadog....: Vol. III.

Jacob Youde William Lloyd

The History of the Princes, the Lords Marcher
And the Ancient Nobility of Powys Fadog....: Vol. III.

ISBN/EAN: 9783337170455

Printed in Europe, USA, Canada, Australia, Japan

Cover: Foto ©ninafisch / pixelio.de

More available books at **www.hansebooks.com**

THE HISTORY

OF

THE PRINCES, THE LORDS MARCHER,

AND THE

ANCIENT NOBILITY

OF

POWYS FADOG,

AND

THE ANCIENT LORDS OF ARWYSTLI, CEDEWEN, AND MEIRIONYDD.

BY

J. Y. W. LLOYD, OF CLOCHFAEN, ESQ.,

M.A., K.S.G.

VOL. III.

LONDON:

T. RICHARDS, 37, GREAT QUEEN STREET, W.C.

1882.

CONTENTS.

	PAGE
MANOR OF ESCLYS OR ESCLUSHAM—	
Cristionydd Cynwrig	3
Cefn y Fedw	5
Cefn y Carneddau, or Tir y Cellach	6
Plâs Kunaston and Woodhouse	7
Jones of Pen y Bryn	9
Lloyd of Coed Cristionydd	13
Puleston of Plâs Uchaf	14
Puleston of Plâs Isaf	15
Wynn of Tref Fechan	16
Roberts of Esclusham	17
Bersham of Bersham	18
John Wynn ab William ab Madog Goch of Fron Deg	19
Wynn of Bers	20
Tudor of Bettws y Mhers and Bersham	23
Roberts of Ty Cerrig	25
Power of Plâs Power	25
Lloyd of Bers	26
Puleston of Plâs y Mhers	27
Rhys ab Tudor ab Goronwy of Tref Gaian	29
Wynn of Bodfel	29
Thomas of Coed Helen	30
Trafford of Treffordd	31
Lloyd of Esclys	32
Gruffydd ab Dafydd Goch of Nant Conwy	33
Gruffydd of Bryn Bwa and Plâs y Bold	36
Jones of Croes Foel	38
Plâs Cadwgan	40
Roberts of Hafod y Bwch	41
Lloyd of Hafod Unnos	43
Parry of Tref Rhuddin, Llwyn Yn, and Nant Clwyd	45
Pryse of Llwyn Yn	48
Holland of Hendref Fawr	50
MANOR OF EGLWISESGLE—	
Description of the Manor	51
Hughes of Llanerch Rugog	55

Lloyd of Plâs Uwch y Clawdd . . . 58
Lloyd of Pentref Clawdd and Llwyn Owain . . 59
Edisbury of Erddig 60
Erddig of Erddig 62
Plâs ym Machymbyd 63
Maes Maen Cymro 65
Jones of Fron Dêg 66
Ellis of Y Groes Newydd. (*See also* Addenda.) . 68
Jeffreys of Acton 68
Edwards of Stansti 80
Maredydd of Stansti 82
Tegin of Fron Dêg 83

MANOR OF IS Y COED—

Description of the Manor, with those of Hoin and Cobham
   Isgoed 84
Hafod y Bwch 90
De Weild of Borasham 91
Brereton of Borasham 92
Ipstone of Ipstone 99
Plâs Llaneurgain 100
Cantref of Rhôs 103
Powel of Glan y Pwll 104
Mynachlog Rhedyn 105
Borasham of Borasham 106
Davies of Erlys 108
Erlys of Erlys 109
Roydon of Is y Coed 111

MANOR OF WREXHAM—

Description of the Manor 115
Puleston of Hafod y Wern . . . 119
Bady of Rhiwabon and Stansti . . . 123
Jones of Fron Deg 124
Elis of Maelor Gymraeg 125
Martyrdom of Mr. Richard Gwyn, *alias* White, of Llan-
   idloes 128
Religious persecutions by Jews and Christians . . 165
Theism 168
Description of the Wrexham Gentry . . . 171
The True Gentleman 172

MANOR OF BURTON—

Description of this Manor, and the Manors of Pickhill and
   Seswick 173
Sutton of Sutton and Gwersyllt . . . 185
Robinson of Gwersyllt Uchaf . . . 188
Trevalun 192

Trevor of Trevalun . . 196
Langford of Trevalun . . . 208
Plâs yn Horslli 214
Lloyd of Yr Orsedd Goch . . . 215
Aylmer of Almer and Pant Iocyn . . 217
Puleston of Trevalun . . . 219
Alunton of Alunton or Tref Alun . . 220
Trefalun of Trefalun . . . 221
Jones of Derlwyn 221
Griffith of Trefalun 222
Davies of Trefalun 222
Symon of Coed y Llai . . . 223
Maredyth of Trefalun 224
Wynn of Y Groesffordd . . . 226
Sanddef of Mortyn 227
Burton and Lewys of Burton . . . 228
Billott of Burton 231
Morton of Morton 233
Papers relating to Bromfield and Iâl . . 234

COMOT OF MERFFORDD—

Penarth Halawg or Hawarden . . 237
Ewlo Castle 241
Stanley of Ewlo Castle . . . 242
Lloyd of Pentref Hobyn . . . 243
Plâs yn Horslli, Powel of . . . 248

ANCIENT BRITISH RACES AND MONUMENTS —

Cromlechs and Tumuli . . . 257
Ancient Inhabitants of Britain . . 258
Ancient Kings of Hereford and Gloucester . 264
Cowydd i Sion ab Rhys ab Maurice o Llangurig 265
Meini Hirion . . . 270
Huw Arwystli . . . 270
Ancient Camps . . . 271

THE LEGEND OF ST. CURIG—

Curig Llwyd 271
St. Curig and St. Julitta . . . 273
Martyrdom of SS. Curig and Julitta . . 275
Welsh Poems in praise of St. Curig . . 283
Maelgwn ab Rhyswallawn, King of Arwystli . 287, 292
Llanelidan 288
Llangurig, Description of the Parish of . . 289
Martyrdom of St. Curig, Description of the . 291

ANCIENT WELSH ETHNOLOGY—

Caves at Cefn and Perthi Chwareu . . 295

The Ancient Iberians or Basques . . . 297
The Celts . . . 298

FIFTY MILLION YEARS AGO . 300

RELIGIOUS PERSECUTIONS . 304
The Law of Nations and Egypt . 306

LORDSHIP OF MAELOR SAESNEG —
Bangor Is y Coed . . 309
Pelagius, the Doctrines of . 310
Christianity . . . 313
Egyptian Records . . 317
Religion of the Jews . . 318
Theism . . . 320
The Ashera or Grove . . 323

GENEALOGIES—
Eyton of Eyton Isaf . . 324
Broughton of Broughton . . 332
Ellis of Alrhey . . . 335
Powel of Alrhey . . 338
Kenrick of Nantclwyd and Plâs Cerniogau . 339
Parry of Tref Rhuddin and Llwyn Yn . 345, 349
Lloyd of Bryn Lluarth . . . 345
Pryse of Llawesog . . . 345
Jones, Wilson of Gelli Gynon . 346
Pryse of Derwen Anial . . • . 347
Powel of Henllan . . 349
Lloyd of Plâs Llanynys . . 350
Hughes of Ystrad and Segroid . 350
Gethin of Plàs Cerniogau . . 353
Eyton of Maes Gwaelod . . 355
Castle of Overton Madog . . 355
Wynn of Gwern Haulod . . 356
Wynn of Llwyn . . . 358
Lloyd of Halchdyn . . . 359
Lloyd of Bryn Halchdyn . . 362
Lloyd of Halchdyn . . . 365
Fowler of Llys Bedydd and St. Thomas's Abbey . 366
Lloyd of Tal y Wern . . . 369
Bodylltyn in Rhiwabon . . 373
Lloyd of Willington . . . 374
Yonge of Sawerdeg . . 376
Pennant Family . . 377
Davies of Dungrey . . 379

LORDSHIP OF Y DREF WEN OR WHITTINGTON—
Description of the Lordship . . 381
Goronwy ab Tudor ab Rhys Sais, and his Descendants . 381

The Castle of Whittington . . 384
Sir Fulk Fitz Warine . . . 384
Gutyn Owain of Traian . . . 385
David ab Ienan ab Iorwerth, Abbot of Valle Crucis . 385
Fulk Fitz Warine of Whittington . . . 387
Llanerch Banna in Maelor . . . 389
Llanerch Banna, Penley 391
Dymock of Penley in Maelor Sacsneg . . 392
Goch of Maelor 396
Sir Matthew Goch, a Poem in Praise of . . 398
Eyton of Pentref Madog . . . 401
Wynn of Pentref Morgan . . . 403
Lloyd of Ebnall . . . 404
Powel of Whittington Park . . 405
Lloyd of y Dref Newydd . . . 406

ADDENDA—

Holt Castle . . 408
Ellis of Croes Newydd . 409
Fowler of Abbey Cwm Hir 409
Grant of the Abbey . 409
Tref Gaian . . 411
Arms of Gervys of Rhuddin 411
Wrexham . . 411
Llangurig . . 411
Cantref Meirion . 411

MANOR OF FABRORUM.

Harl. 3696, *fo.* 236.

FABRORUM MANERIUM TENENTES P' DIMISSIONES, ETC.

	Acres.			Value.			Rent s.		d.
ates, Hugh (Morton Ang') . .	17	0	6	7	0	0	1	0	0
romfield, Edward . .	0	0	5	0	6	8	0	0	6
roughton, John d'd (Coed Xpion-eth)	24	0	0	13	6	8	0	16	8
avid ap John ap Roger (Coed Xpioneth. . . .	4	2	6	2	0	0	0	3	10
avid ap Owin (Morton Ang') .	7	1	0	3	6	8	0	5	8½
avid, Will'm (Coed Xpioneth) .	8	0	6	4	13	4	0	5	8
avid, Kenrick (Morton Ang') .	13	3	0	6	0	0	1	2	4
dward ap David ap Edw' (Coed Xpioneth) . . .	3	3	0	2	3	4	0	3	8
dward ap John (Coed Xp'). .	14	2	20	7	0	0	0	16	0
dward ap John David Goz (Coed Xpioneth) . . .	15	1	20	7	0	0	0	17	6
dward ap John ap Edw' (Morton Ang')	19	0	0	8	10	0	1	2	8
dward ap Randle . .	1	0	0	1	3	4	0	0	8
dward ap Will'm (Mor' Ang') .	6	0	0	2	16	0	0	4	7
dwards, John, gen' (Coed Xpio-neth)	28	1	20	16	0	0	0	16	8
dwards, Jo' de Keuen y Werne (Thos' ap d'd Walker) Coed Xpioneth. . . .	4	0	0	1	14	4	0	0	9
llis, Dorathe vid' (Mor' Ang') .	2	3	16	1	4	0	0	3	7
yton, Edward (Coed Xpioneth) .	11	0	0	5	0	0	1	0	2
yton, Gerrard, esq. .	15	2	0	8	0	0	0	16	0
yton, Roger, gen' (Coed Xp') .	17	2	0	6	0	0	0	9	4
ouldsmith, Thos' (Morton Ang')	6	2	0	3	6	8	0	10	4
ope, Edw' (Morton Ang') .	5	3	0	2	13	4	0	9	6
ope, Thomas . .	12	0	0	6	13	4	0	5	4½
u'n ap Ho'ell (Coed X'p') .	20	0	0	10	0	0	0	18	4
u'n, Richard (Mor' Ang') .	12	3	20	5	0	0	no rent given		

	Acres.			Value.			Rent s.		d.
John ap Hugh ap d'd et d'd ap John filius eius	8	3	0	4	10	0	0	10	8
John ap Ieu'n	1	3	0	1	0	0	0	1	4½
John ap John Wynn iur' ux' (Coed X'pioneth)	25	2	0	13	0	0	1	0	2
John, Roger ap d'd lloyd (Coed X'pioneth)	3	0	0	1	13	4	0	1	3
John, Samuell	1	3	20	1	3	4	0	0	8
Johnson, John (Coed X'p')	3	0	0	2	0	0	0	2	2
Jones, Emanuell (Mor' Ang')	6	1	0	3	0	0	0	11	9
Lewis, Rob't (Coed X'p')	6	0	20	3	0	0	0	8	0
Lloyd, John ap Richard (Coed X'pioneth)	59	2	0	19	6	8	0	18	4
Lloyd, Watkyn (Coed X'p')	2	0	0	1	13	4	0	1	10
Manley, Cornelius, gen' (Morton Ang'l)	16	1	0	6	13	4	0	18	0
Richard ap d'd lloyd (Coed X'pioneth)	3	1	0	2	0	0	0	3	8
Richard ap Robert (Mor' Ang')	13	1	0	5	0	0	0	16	0
Robert ap d'd ap W'm ap d'd (Coed X'pioneth)	11	0	0	5	0	0	0	8	4
Robert ap John Rob't (Coed X'p')	22	0	0	9	0	0	1	1	2
Roger ap d'd ap lle'n (Mor' Ang').	6	1	20	3	6	8	0	4	10
Roger ap Will'm (Coed X'p')	14	0	0	8	0	0	0	17	2
Thelwall, Bevis, esq. (Morton Ang')	10	0	0	1	4	10	0	10	0
Thomas ap d'd Walker	*Vide.* Jo' Edwards.								
Thomas ap Edw' (Morton Ang')	11	2	0	5	0	0	0	12	0
Thomas, John (Coed X'p')	3	0	0	2	0	0	0	0	8½
William ap John Edw'	0	0	10	0	6	8	0	0	3
William, W'm	1	5	0	1	0	0	0	1	10
Williams, Margaret vid' (Coed X'pioneth)	19	1	0	10	0	0	0	4	6
S'ma Redd' .							22	18	2

MANOR OF ESCLUSHAM OR ESCLYS.—TOWNSHIP OF CRISTIONYDD CYNWRIG.

Harl. MS. 4181; Add. MS. 9865.

THE township of Cristionydd Cynwrig lies in the parish of Rhiwabon, of which it constitutes the third part, and is divided into the parochial townships or hamlets of Coed Cristionydd, Y Dref Fawr or Tref Cristionydd Cynwrig, and Y Dref Fechan or Tref Cristionydd Fechan.

Hoedliw, Lord of Cristionydd, fifth son of Cynwrig ab Rhiwallawn.⇌ Lord of Maelor Gymraeg. *Ermine*, a lion rampant *sable*, armed and langued *gules*.

Cynwrig ab⇌Gwladys, dau. and co-heir of Gruffydd, third son of Meilir Eyton,
Hoedliw | Lord of Eyton, Erlys, and Bwras or Borasham. *Ermine*, a
of Cris- | lion rampant, *azure*.
tionydd. | Her mother was Angharad, dau. and heiress of Llywelyn
ab Meurig ab Caradog ab Iestyn ab Gwrgant, Prince of
Glamorgan. *Gules*, three chevronells, *argent*.

Cynwrig Fy-⇌Margaret, dau. of Howel ab Moreiddig ab Sanddef Hordd or
chan of Cris- | the handsome, Lord of Morton or Burton and Llai. *Vert*,
tionydd. | semé of broomslips, a lion rampart, *or*.

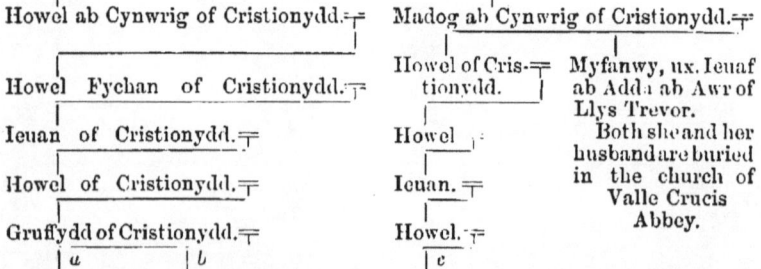

Howel ab Cynwrig of Cristionydd.⇌   Madog ab Cynwrig of Cristionydd.⇌

	Howel of Cris-⇌ Myfanwy, ux. Ieuaf
Howel Fychan of Cristionydd.⇌	tionydd. ab Adda ab Awr of
	Llys Trevor.
Ieuan of Cristionydd.⇌	Howel ⎮ Both she and her
	husband are buried
Howel of Cristionydd.⇌	Ieuan. ⇌ in the church of
	Valle Crucis
Gruffydd of Cristionydd.⇌	Howel. ⇌ Abbey.
⎮ a ⎮ b	⎮ c

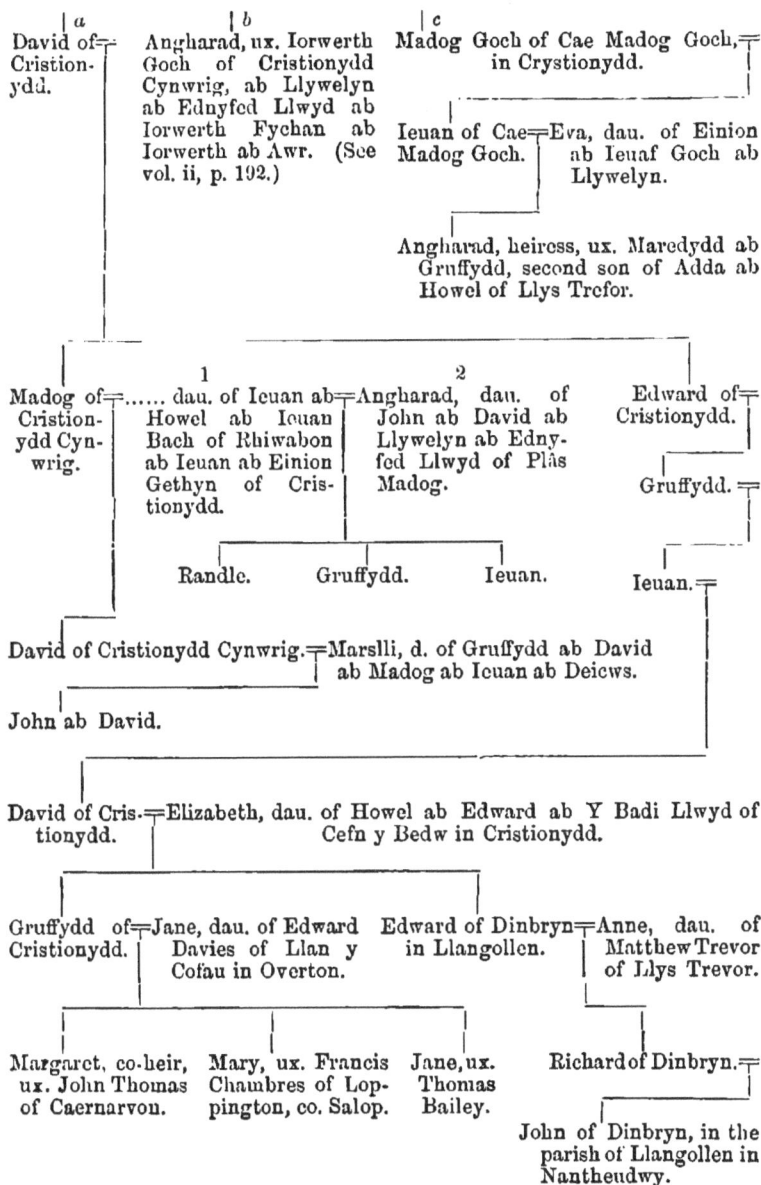

a	*b*	*c*
David of= Cristion- ydd.	Angharad, ux. Iorwerth Goch of Cristionydd Cynwrig, ab Llywelyn ab Ednyfed Llwyd ab Iorwerth Fychan ab Iorwerth ab Awr. (See vol. ii, p. 192.)	Madog Goch of Cae Madog Goch,= in Crystionydd.

Ieuan of Cae=Eva, dau. of Einion
Madog Goch. | ab Ieuaf Goch ab
| Llywelyn.

Angharad, heiress, ux. Maredydd ab
Gruffydd, second son of Adda ab
Howel of Llys Trefor.

	1	2	
Madog of= Cristion- ydd Cyn- wrig.	...... dau. of Ieuan ab= Howel ab Ieuan Bach of Rhiwabon ab Ieuan ab Einion Gethyn of Cris- tionydd.	Angharad, dau. of John ab David ab Llywelyn ab Edny- fed Llwyd of Plâs Madog.	Edward of= Cristionydd.

Gruffydd. =

Randle.   Gruffydd.   Ieuan.

Ieuan. =

David of Cristionydd Cynwrig.=Marslli, d. of Gruffydd ab David
| ab Madog ab Ieuan ab Deicws.

John ab David.

David of Cris-=Elizabeth, dau. of Howel ab Edward ab Y Badi Llwyd of
tionydd. | Cefn y Bedw in Cristionydd.

Gruffydd of=Jane, dau. of Edward	Edward of Dinbryn=Anne, dau. of
Cristionydd.	Davies of Llan y	in Llangollen.	Matthew Trevor
	Cofau in Overton.		of Llys Trevor.

Margaret, co-heir,	Mary, ux. Francis	Jane, ux.	Richard of Dinbryn.=
ux. John Thomas	Chambres of Lop-	Thomas	
of Caernarvon.	pington, co. Salop.	Bailey.	

John of Dinbryn, in the
parish of Llangollen in
Nantheudwy.

ESCLUSHAM.—TOWNSHIP OF CRISTIONYDD CYNWRIG CEFN Y BEDW.

Harl. MS. 2299.

Einion Gethyn of Cristionydd, ab Einion ab Ieuan ab Gruffydd ab⹀
Cynwrig Efell, Lord of Y Glwyscgl. *Gules,* on a bend *argent,* a lion
passant, *sable.*

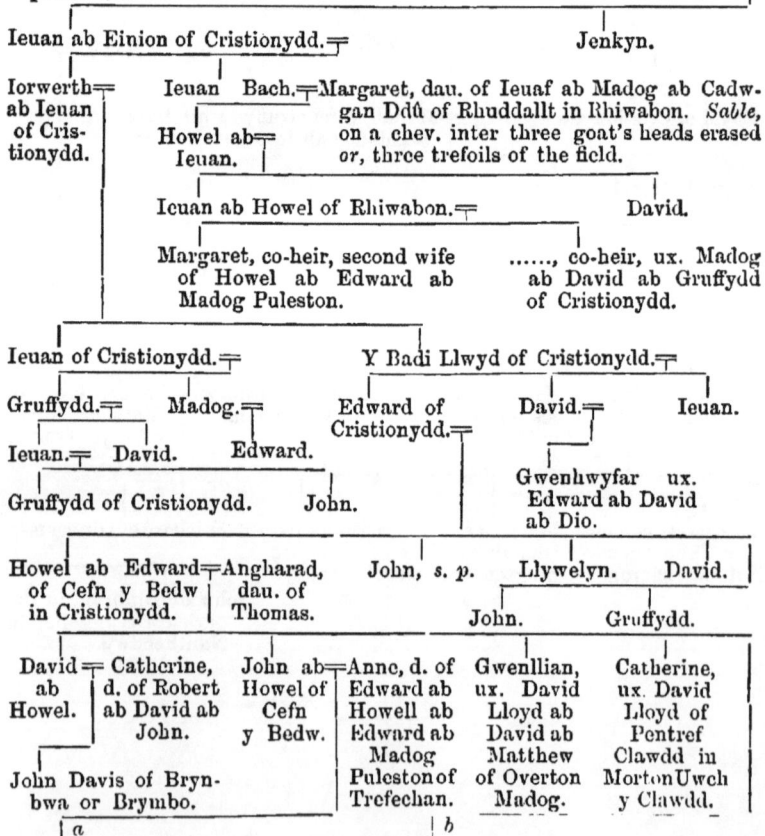

Ieuan ab Einion of Cristionydd.⹀   Jenkyn.

Iorwerth⹀   Ieuan   Bach.⹀Margaret, dau. of Ieuaf ab Madog ab Cadw-
ab Ieuan   gan Ddû of Rhuddallt in Rhiwabon. *Sable,*
of Cris-   Howel ab⹀   on a chev. inter three goat's heads erased
tionydd.   Ieuan.   *or,* three trefoils of the field.

Ieuan ab Howel of Rhiwabon.⹀   David.

Margaret, co-heir, second wife   ......, co-heir, ux. Madog
   of Howel ab Edward ab   ab David ab Gruffydd
   Madog Puleston.   of Cristionydd.

Ieuan of Cristionydd.⹀   Y Badi Llwyd of Cristionydd.⹀

Gruffydd.⹀   Madog.⹀   Edward of   David.⹀   Ieuan.
               Cristionydd.⹀
Ieuan.⹀ David.   Edward.   Gwenhwyfar   ux.
Gruffydd of Cristionydd.   John.   Edward ab David
                          ab Dio.

Howel ab Edward⹀Angharad,   John, *s. p.*   Llywelyn.   David.
   of Cefn y Bedw   dau. of
   in Cristionydd.   Thomas.   John.   Gruffydd.

David ⹀ Catherine,   John ab⹀Anne, d. of   Gwenllian,   Catherine,
ab   d. of Robert   Howel of   Edward ab   ux. David   ux. David
Howel.   ab David ab   Cefn   Howell ab   Lloyd ab   Lloyd of
     John.   y Bedw.   Edward ab   David ab   Pentref
                      Madog   Matthew   Clawdd in
John Davis of Bryn-   Puleston of   of Overton   Morton Uwch
bwa or Brymbo.   Trefechan.   Madog.   y Clawdd.
   | *a* | *b*

a	b
Catherine, ux. John ab John ab Madog ab Ieuan ab Madog of Rhuddallt.	Elizabeth, ux. David Ieuan ab Gruffydd, ab Edward ab David ab Gruffydd of Cristionydd. *Ermine*, a lion ramp., *sable*.

CEFN Y FEDW.

Cae Cyriog MS.

David Lloyd of Cefn y Fedw.⚯

Edward Lloyd of Cefn y Fedw.⚯

1	2
William Lloyd⚯ of Cefn y Fedw.	Edward Lloyd⚯Jane, dau. of John ab Roger of Nant of Hafod in Cristionydd. She married secondly, Matthew ab Randle ab John of Y Coedladd.

Edward Lloyd⚯ of Cefn y Fedw.

Samuel Lloyd⚯ of Hafod.

Jane, ux. John ab Randle ab John ab David ab Llywelyn ab John of Pen y Bryn.

Lydia, heiress of Hafod, which she sold to Ellis Lloyd of Pen y lan, 1690.

Thomas Lloyd of Cefn y = Elizabeth, dau. and heiress of John ab Randle, Fedw. He sold a great ab Richard of Acre Fair. Her mother was part of his lands to Ellis Jane, dau. of Randle ab John ab David ab Lloyd of Pen y lan. Llywelyn ab John of Pen y Bryn.

ESCLUSHAM.—TOWNSHIP OF CRISTIONYDD CYNWRIG.

CEFN Y CARNEDDAU *alias* TIR Y CELLACH.

Cae Cyriog MS.

Roger Eyton of Cefn y Carneddau, *alias* Tir y Cellach, second son of Edward Eyton of Bodylltyn and Fferm, ab Roger Eyton of Bodylltyn, ab John ab Elis Eyton of Rhiwabon. *Ermine*, a lion rampant, *azure*.

| 1c | | 2d |

Catherine, co-heir. She had Cefn y Carneddau, and married Roger Kynaston, attorney at Ludlow, ab Humphrey Kynaston, second son of Roger Kynaston of Morton, co. Salop, second son of Humphrey Kynaston of Hordley, ab Sir Roger Kynaston, Knight, ab Gruffydd Kynaston of Stoke. Roger Kynaston, the husband of Catherine, built the house at Cefn y Carneddau, now called Plâs Kynaston.

Mary, co-heir. She married Gruffydd ab John of Gaerddin, who purchased land there from John ab John of Gaerddin, who was the possessor of it in the time that Norden's Survey was taken in 1620. Gruffydd ab John afterwards sold this land to Sir Thomas Myddleton of Chirk Castle, Knight.

The above-named Gruffydd of Gaerddin was the son of John ab Ieuan ab Edward ab Rhys.

PLAS KYNASTON.

Harl. MS. 2299.

Roger Kynaston, attorney at the Court of Marches at Ludlow; second son (by Jane, his wife, dau. of Oliver Lloyd of Llai) of Humphrey Kynaston, second son of Roger Kynaston ab Humphrey Kynaston of Morton. *Ermine, a chevron, gules.* = Anne, dau. and co-heiress of Roger Eyton of Cefn y Carneddau.

John Kynaston of Plâs Kynaston and *jure uxoris* of Bryngwyn. = Elizabeth, dau. and heiress of Oliver Lloyd[1] of Bryngwyn in Llanfechain, and Ffrances his wife, dau. of Sir Richard Hussey of Crugion.

| Roger Kynaston, *ob. s. p.* | Humphrey Kynaston of Bryngwyn and Plâs Kynaston, 1760. = Martha, d. and eventual heiress of Robert Owen of Woodhouse, co. Salop. | Richard Kynaston of London. | John Kynaston. | Charles Kynaston. |

Martha Kynaston, heiress of Bryngwyn and Plâs Kynaston, married William Mostyn ab John Mostyn ab William Mostyn, third son of Sir Roger Mostyn of Mostyn and of Llys Pengwern in Nanheudwy, Knight.

[1] Oliver Lloyd of Bryngwyn, in the parish of Llanfechain, ab David Lloyd ab John Lloyd ab Robert Lloyd ab David Lloyd ab Howel ab John ab Ieuan Fychan of Bryngwyn, ab Howel ab Maredydd ab

PLAS KYNASTON AND WOODHOUSE.

Sir Roger Mostyn of Mostyn=Mary, dau. of Sir John Wynn of Gwydir in Tegeingl, and Llys | in Llanrwst, Knight; she died about 1657, Pengwern in Nanheudwy. | and was buried at Llanrwst. *Vert,* three | eagles, displayed in fess, *or.*

1	2	3
Sir Thomas Mostyn of Mostyn and Llys Pengwern, Knight. His son, Sir Roger Mostyn, was created a Baronet Aug. 3, 1660.	John Mostyn, *ob. s. p.*	William Mostyn,=Anne, dau. and heir Rector of of John Lewys of Chrysleton, Bodowyr in the Archdeacon of parish of Llanidan Bangor. in Cwmwd Menai in Môn.

1	2					
Thomas Mostyn, *ob. s. p.*	John = Mostyn, M.A., Rector of Castell.	Owain Mostyn.	Henry = Cather Mostyn ine, of Dol dau. of Ynys.		Elen, ux. Thomas Pryse of Gwern Eigron.	Grace, ux. Morris Lewys of Forys Cillwyn.

John Mostyn of Segrwyd=Jane, dau. and co-heir of John Dolben of Segr and Capel Gwyddelwen, | wyd in the Comot of Ceinmeirch. *Sable,* a High Sheriff for co. Den- | helmet closed, inter three pheons pointed bigh in 1749. | to the centre, *argent.*

John Mostyn=Anna Maria, daughter and co-heiress of Meurig Meredith of of Segrwyd. | Pengwern Llanwnda and Llewesog in Ceinmeirch, and Jane, | his wife, daughter and co-heiress of Ffoulke Lloyd of Bryn | Lluarth in Cynmeirch and Cilen in Edeyrnion.

John Meredith = Cicilia Margaret, Mostyn of dau. of Henry Segrwyd and Thrale of Bach Llewesog. y Graig.		Anna Maria, ux. Colonel John Lloyd Salusbury of Gallt Faenan; she died 8th Dec. 1846, and was buried at Henllan.

a

Gruffydd ab Tudor ab Madog ab Einion ab Madog ab Gwylawg ab Eginir ab Lles ab Idnerth Benfras, Lord of Maesbrwg. *Argent,* a cross flory engrailed *sable,* inter four Cornish choughs, ppr., on a chief *azure,* a boar's head couped of the field, tusked *or,* and langued *gules.* —*Add. MS.* 9865.

a

William Mostyn, *jure uxoris* of⹀Martha, dau. and heiress of Humphrey
Bryngwyn and Plâs Kynaston. | Kynaston of Bryngwyn and Plâs Ky-
 | naston.

William Mostyn of Bryngwyn and Plâs Kynaston.⹀Rebecca, daughter of
He took the name and arms of Owen on succeeding | Thomas Crewe Dod
to the Woodhouse estate; M.P. for co. Mont.; ob. | of Edge, co. Chester.
11 March 1795.

1

William Owen of Woodhouse and Plâs Kynaston.⹀Harriet Elizabeth,
Argent, a lion rampant and canton, *sable*. He sold | dau. of Major T.
Bryngwyn | Cumming of Bath.

2	1	1	2	3
Edward Henry = Elizabeth, dau. of	Rebecca,	Frances	Harriet,
Mostyn-Owen, Rev. Henry	ux. John	Maria, ux.	ux. John
Rector of Hinchcliffe of	Humphries	Richard	Mytton
Cound, co. Barthomly, co.	of	Noel,	of
Salop. Chester.	Llwyn.	Lord	Halston.
		Berwick.	

4	5	6
Sobieski, ux.	Eloisa, ux. Rev. Henry Cotton	Laura.
R. B. Deane.	of Great Ness.	

1	2	3	4	5	1
William Mos-	Arthur	Charles	Francis	Henry	Sarah Harriet,
tyn Owen of	Mostyn	Mostyn	Mostyn	Mostyn	ux. Edward
Woodhouse	Owen.	Owen.	Owen.	Owen.	Hosier Williams
and Plâs					of Eaton
Kynaston.					Mascott.

2	3	4	5
Frances, ux. Colonel Robert Myddle-	Eloisa.	Emma.	Sobieski.
ton Biddulph of Chirk Castle.			

ESCLUSHAM.—TOWNSHIP OF CRISTIONYDD. PEN Y BRYN.

Cae Cyriog MS.[1]

John ab David ab Llywelyn[2] ab John, of Pen y Bryn,
married, in 1587, Angharad, daughter of John ab David

[1] This pedigree was kindly sent to me by the Rev. William Madog
Williams. [2] Llywelyn was a son of John ab David of Plas Madog.

ab Edward ab Maredydd of Fron Dêg, by whom he had issue, one son Randal, his successor, and three daughters, Catherine, Alice, and Elizabeth.

Randal ab John ab David of Pen y bryn, married, first, in 1605, Margaret Lloyd, daughter and co-heiress of Gruffydd Lloyd of Ty Cerrig, and sister of Gwenhwyfar Lloyd, the mother of John Lloyd of Coed Cristionydd, (from whom Ty Cerrig came to him), by whom he had issue one son, Edward, of whom presently, and two daughters, Jane and Catherine. Randle ab John, married, secondly, Anne, relict of William ab Matthew of Rhiwabon and daughter of Edward ab John ab David, whose son and heir was Edward ab William ab John ab David[1] of Pen y lan in Dinhinlle Isaf, whose daughter and heiress married Ellis Lloyd, previously an Attorney at Ludlow, son of the Rev. Edward Lloyd, who in his latter days had the living of Llangower. By this second marriage, Randal ab John had issue two sons, John and Matthew, and two daughters : 1, Angharad, ux. Richard Evans ab Evan ab David ab Morgan ab Rhiwabon, and 2, Mary, ux. Hugh ab William ab Hugh of Cyssylltau.

Jane, the eldest daughter of Randal ab John ab David, married John ab Randal ab Richard of Acre Fair, by whom she had issue one only daughter and heiress, Elizabeth, who married Thomas Lloyd of Cefn y Fedw (son and heir of Edward Lloyd of Cefn y Fedw, ab William ab Edward ab David Lloyd of Cefn y Fedw), who sold much of his land to Ellis Lloyd of Pen y lan.

Catherine, the second daughter of Randal ab John ab David, married Robert ab Randal of Dinhinlle Uchaf in Cristionydd. They had a daughter and heiress, Anne, who married Richard Jones, son and heir of John ab John ab Edward of the Nant in Dinhinlle Uchaf, who sold his own lands as well as his wife's to Ellis Lloyd of Pen y lan.

John, the second son of Randal ab John ab David, married Jane, daughter of Edward Lloyd (brother of William Lloyd ab Edward ab David Lloyd of Cefn y Fedw), and by her had issue four sons : 1, Randal ; 2, Edward ; 3, Matthew ; and 4, David ; and two daughters, Mary and Margaret,

Matthew, the third son of Randal ab John ab David, was of Rhôs Sion ab Madog, and married, first, Mary, daughter of Antony Griffith of the said Rhôs, by whom he had issue, John, William, Mary, and Anne. He married, secondly, Anne, daughter of John ab Hugh ab Edward of Rhiwabon, and sister of Thomas Hughes, of Pennant y Belan, 1697.

Edward of Pen y Bryn, the eldest son of Randal ab John ab David, married Margaret, daughter of the above-named William ab Matthew of Rhiwabon, by whom he had issue one son, John ab Edward, and three daughters : 1, Anne, who died young ; 2, Cicily, ux. Thomas Twna of Clai in Bangor parish ; and 3, Elizabeth, ux. John Roberts, ab Robert ab Edward of the Caeau.

John Edwards of Pen y Bryn, son and heir of Edward ab Randal ab John, married, in 1669, Sarah, daughter and heiress of John ab Richard Francis of Cristionydd Cynwrig, and Margaret his wife, daughter of Richard ab David (and sister of Robert ab Richard, the father of Richard Roberts of Dinhinlle Uchaf) by whom he had issue four sons : 1, Randal Jones ; 2, Edward ; 3, John ; and 4, William ; and two daughters, Margaret and Sarah. The Cae Cyriog MS. ends here, and the following portion of the pedigree was compiled by the Rev. William Maddock Williams, late Rector of Llanfechain.

Randal Jones of Pen y Bryn, Attorney-at-Law, Re-corder of the Lordship of Bromfield and Iâl, son and heir of John ab Edward, married, first, in 1703, Elizabeth Wynn, natural and adopted daughter of Sir John Wynn of Watstay, Bart., by whom he had issue seven sons : 1, John Jones ; 2, Thomas ; 3, William ; 4, Robert ; 5, Edward ; 6, Elis ; 7, Randal. He married, secondly, Martha, daughter of —— Jones of Pont Twthil, Wrex-ham (grandfather to the late Longueville Jones of Oswes-try), by whom he had no issue.

John Jones of Pen y bryn, eldest son of the above

Randal, married Barbara, eldest daughter of Edward Hughes of Coediog and Plâs Draw in Dyffryn Clwyd, and by her had issue, three sons : 1, Randle, *ob. s. p.*; 2, John ; and 3, David ; and three daughters, Margaret, Elizabeth, and Catherine.

John Jones of Pen y Bryn, the second son, succeeded his father, and married in 1770, Mary, sole daughter and heiress of Roger Maddocks of Prees Henlle and Daywell in Whittington, co. Salop, and was High Sheriff for co. Denbigh in 1788. He had issue one son, John Maddock, who succeeded him, and five daughters : 1, Eleanor, of whom presently ; 2, Mary ; 3, Barbara ; 4, Elizabeth ; and 6, Henrietta.

John Maddock Jones of Pen y Bryn, Major of the Royal Denbigh Militia, married Margaret Maria Isabella, eldest daughter of Major-General Robert D'Arcy, Royal Engineers, by whom he had no issue. He dissipated and sold all the estates of his father and mother, excepting the property left to his father at Penley in Flintshire, which was left him by his kinsman, Roger Hanmer of Maes Gwaelod, and a tenement in Pen y Bryn, bought from Mostyn Owen of Plâs Kynaston, which he, John Maddock, was not permitted to enjoy, but was entailed on William Maddock Williams, his nephew.

Eleanor, the eldest daughter, and eventual heir of blood of John Jones of Pen y Bryn, married William Williams, Canon of St. Asaph, and Rector of Ysgeifiog, by whom she had issue, William Maddock Williams, Rector of Llanfechain, and two other sons, who died in their infancy, and two daughters: 1, Henrietta Maria, ux. Rev. H. W. O. Jones of Wepra Hall, co. Flint, and 2, Eliza, ux. Thomas Murhall Griffith of Wrexham and Ash Magna, co. Salop.

ESCLUSHAM.—COED CRISTIONYDD.

Cae Cyriog MS.

John Lloyd=Gwenhwyfar, third daughter and co-heiress of Gruffydd
ab Richard | Lloyd of Ty Cerrig in Cristionydd Cynwrig; she had Ty
of Coed | Cerrig in Pen y Bryn, and "rhan o faing yn gafell Eglwys
Cristionydd, | Rhiwabon". By her Will, dated in 1641, she left 7
living | acres, 0 roods, 36 perches, for the poor of Cristionydd
1620. | Cynwrig and Coed Cristionydd, at three shillings each,
| to be distributed at Christmas by her son John Lloyd
| ab Richard, then by the Vicars and Churchwardens. In
| 1737, some lands adjoining were purchased with Poor's
| money for £140, consisting of 9 acres, 2 roods, 2 perches.
| Both are now let in one farm under the name of Tai Nant.

1	2			
Edward Lloyd=Dorothy, d.	John Lloyd[1] of=Elizabeth, dau.	Gruffydd
of Rhiwabon,	of George	Coed Cris-	of Edward	Lloyd, Clk.,
a wise and	Moor of	tionydd (called	Lloyd of Plâs	Parson of
prudent man.	Wrexham,	John Lloyd	Madog ab	Ludlow.
	Merchant.	ab Richard).	William Lloyd.	

1	2	3		4	5
John =Elizabeth, d.	Simon	Peter = ... d. of	Cornelius	Elizabeth,
Lloyd of	of Edward	Lloyd.	Lloyd	Thomas	Lloyd of	ux. Roger
Coed	Dymoke of		of	Davies of	Oswestry,	Davies of
Criston-	Sonlli. Her		Wrex-	Wrex-	married	Rhiwabon
ydd,	brother Joseph		ham,	ham.	Mary	ab David
living	sold his inherit-		living		Kynas-	ab Robert
1697.	ance to Joshua		1697.		ton,	ab Stephen
	Edisbury of				1698.	of Bryn y
	Erddig.					Wiwair.

John Lloyd.	Elizabeth,	Phœbe.	Other children.

1	2	3	4	
Edward	Joseph =.... .. d.	Owain Lloyd[2]=	Simon Lloyd.	...... ux.
Lloyd,	Lloyd	of	went to Ireland	He had lands	John
ob. s. p.	of Cae	....	and returned to	in Rhiwabon	William
	Einion,	of	Rhiwabon and	Parish near	of Fron
	mar.	Castle	died at Wrex-	Rhos Llanerch	y Fien.
	and	Lyons	ham, 1698.	Rugog, which	
	died	in		he sold to Sir	
	in Ire-	Ire-	Alice, ux. Ieuan	John Wynn of	
	land.	land.	Evans of Y	Watsay, Knt.	
			Glwysegl.	and Baronet.	

a	b		c

---

[1] He left, by his will dated in 1670, £20 for sixteen of the poorest
in the parish of Rhiwabon, to be distributed by the Vicar and Churchwardens at Christmas.

[2] By his will dated 1684, he left £20, to be distributed at Christmas to the poor of Rhiwabon.

a	b	c
Joseph Lloyd had lands in Ireland, and was living in 1697.	William Lloyd in Rhiwabon parish, and some in Ireland. He built the house now called Plas Beinion, at the end of the field called Cae Einion, in 1685, but there had been an old house there before. His will is dated in 1707, in which he left £10 to the poor of the parish of Rhiwabon.	He had his father's lands = Anne, d. of Edward Lloyd of Plas Madog ab Edward ab Edward ab William Lloyd. Buried at Rhiwabon, March 21, 1708.

Edward Lloyd, ob. s. p.	Mary, heiress of Plas Beinion and Trefynant. = George Mears of Pennar, co. Pembroke.	Anne Lloyd, b. 1697, = Edward Lloyd ob. Sept. 23, 1745, of Plâs Madog buried at Rhiwabon. ab Samuel By her Will, date un- Lloyd ab known, she charged Edward Lloyd a small farm called ab Edward Caer Llwyn, in the ab Edward parish of Gwytherin, ab William with the yearly pay- Lloyd. ment of £1, to be dis- tributed to the poor on St. Thomas' Day. The proprietor of Caer Llwyn is now Mr. Fitz Hugh of Plas Tower, near Wrexham.[1]

Arthur Mears of Pennar, co. Pembroke and Plas Bennion, mar. Margaret, second daughter and co-heiress of Thomas Lloyd of Trevor Hall, and relict of Edward, son and heir of Edward Lloyd of Plas Madog, Esq., ob. s. p.

Hugh Mears, ob. s. p.

ESCLUSHAM.—CRISTIONYDD CYNWRIG. Y PLAS UCHAF.

Cae Cyriog MS.; Harl. MS. 2299.

Madog Puleston of Bers, second son of Robert = Angharad, dau. of David Puleston ab Richard Puleston ab Sir Roger Puleston of Emeral in Maelor Saesneg. *Argent*, on a bend *sable*, three mullets of the field.	ab Goronwy ab Iorwerth of Burton and Llai. *Vert*, semé of broomslips, a lion rampant, *or*.

2c

1d

---

[1] *Report of the Charity Commissioners.*

2c		1d
Edward Puleston=Isabel, dau. of Sir Randle Brere-		John Puleston of
of Cristionydd.	ton of Malpas, Knight. *Argent,*	Bers and Hafod
	two bars, *sable.*	y Wern.

1		2
John Puleston =Maud, dau. of David Lloyd		Howel ab Edward Pule-
of Plâs Uchaf	ab Tudor Lloyd ab Ieuan	ston of Plâs Isaf in
in Cristionydd.	of Bodidris yn Iâl.	Cristionydd.

David Llwyd of=Janet, dau. of John Eyton ab Elis Eyton of Rhiwabon.
Plâs Uchaf. | *Ermine,* a lion rampant, *azure.*

1 co-heir.	2 co-heir.	3 co-heir.
Catherine. She had Plâs	Elizabeth, ux. John	Elen, ux. Richard
Uchaf and married John	Wynn ab Edward	Tegin ab Edward
Sonlli[1] of Sonlli ab Robert	of Trefechan ab	Tegin of Fron
Sonlli of Sonlli. *Ermine,*	Howell ab Edward	Dêg.
a lion rampant, *sable.*	ab Madog	
They had 13 children.	Puleston.	

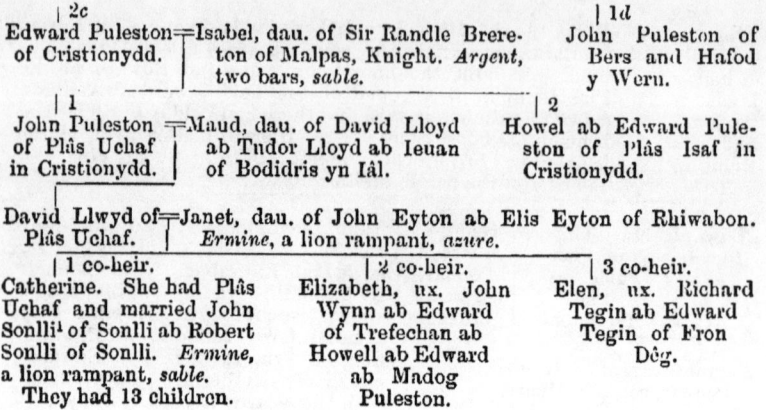

Y PLAS ISAF IN CRISTIONYDD.

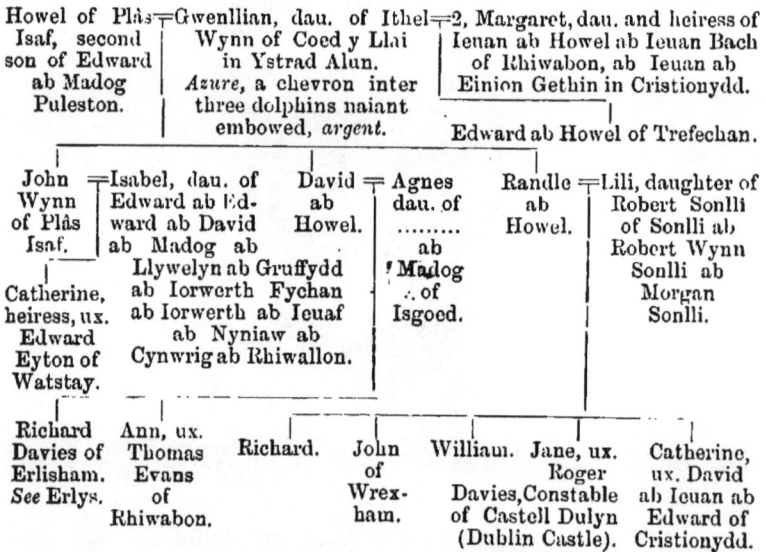

Howel of Plâs=Gwenllian, dau. of Ithel=2, Margaret, dau. and heiress of
Isaf, second | Wynn of Coed y Llai | Ieuan ab Howel ab Ieuan Bach
son of Edward | in Ystrad Alun. | of Rhiwabon, ab Ieuan ab
ab Madog | *Azure,* a chevron inter | Einion Gethin in Cristionydd.
Puleston. | three dolphins naiant |
           | embowed, *argent.* | Edward ab Howel of Trefechan.

John	=Isabel, dau. of	David = Agnes	Randle =Lili, daughter of
Wynn	Edward ab Ed-	ab dau. of	ab Robert Sonlli
of Plâs	ward ab David	Howel.	Howel. of Sonlli ab
Isaf.	ab Madog ab	ab	Robert Wynn
	Llywelyn ab Gruffydd	Madog	Sonlli ab
Catherine,	ab Iorwerth Fychan	∴ of	Morgan
heiress, ux.	ab Iorwerth ab Ieuaf	Isgoed.	Sonlli.
Edward	ab Nyniaw ab		
Eyton of	Cynwrig ab Rhiwallon.		
Watstay.			

Richard	Ann, ux.	Richard.	John	William.	Jane, ux.	Catherine,
Davies of	Thomas		of		Roger	ux. David
Erlisham.	Evans		Wrex-		Davies,Constable	ab Ieuan ab
See Erlys.	of		ham.		of Castell Dulyn	Edward of
	Rhiwabon.				(Dublin Castle).	Cristionydd.

---

[1] John Sonlli died in 1576, and was buried in Oxford. (See vol. ii, p. 144.)

TREFECHAN IN CRISTIONYDD.

Cae Cyriog MS.; Harl. MS. 2299.

Y Drefechan, *alias* Cristionydd Fechan. Note that this part of the parish of Rhiwabon is called Cristionydd, and contains Y Dref Fawr or Cristionydd Cynwrig, Y Dref Fechan or Cristionydd Fechan, which is now called Dinhinlle Uchaf, and Coed Cristionydd. Cristionydd contains about a third of the whole parish.

Edward ab Howel ab Edward=Alice, dau. of John ab Ieuan ab Deicws
of Trefechan, ab Madog | ab Deio of Lanerch Rugog. *Ermine*, a
Puleston. | lion rampant, *sable*.

| 1 | | 2 | |

John Wynn of Trefechan,=Elizabeth, dau. and   Edward.   Anne, ux. John
1563. He had with his wife | co-heiress of David   ab Howel ab
two portions of lands in | Llwyd ab John   Edward of
Cristionydd Cynwrig, | Puleston of Plâs   Cefn y Fedw.
which he called Plâs | Uchaf.
Ty Mawr.

Richard of=Mary, dau. of   Anne Wen, ux. David ab   Catherine
Trefechan. | William Edis-   Ieuan ab John ab   Wen,
           | bury of   Ieuan Llwyd of Pentref   *ob. s. p.*
           | Marchwiail.   Cristionydd.

Robert =Margaret, d.   Gruffydd =Elizabeth, dau. of John   Richard
Wynne | of Richard   Wynn | Sonlli of Cord in the parish Wynn,
of Tre- | Hughes of   of Bryn | of Wrexham, fourth son of went to
fechan, | Llanerch   yr Owen. | John Sonlli of Fron Deg.   Kent.
1620. | Rugog. | Her mother was Elizabeth,
                             | d. of Edward ab Rhys of Rhiwabon.

John   Robert   Thomas   Elizabeth,ux.Richard   Jane, ux. Joseph
Wynn,   Wynn,   Wynn,   Holland of Wrexham,   Bromfield of
ob.   went   went to   son of William   Wrexham, son
s. p.   abroad.   Mary-   Holland of Armstrie   of ...... Bromfield
                        land.   in Lancashire.   of Eglwys Wen.

Robert =Jane, dau. of Owain   John Wynn,   Matthew Wynn   William
Wynn | Lloyd of Plâs y   married   of Pentref Cris- Wynn,
of | Drain in the town-   Elizabeth,   tionydd, married *ob.*
Plâs | ship of Morton   dau. of Roger   Catherine, dau.   *s. p.*
Isaf in | Uwch y Clawdd,   ab David   of John ab
Tre- | son of David Lloyd   Goch of   Richard of Y
fechan. | of Pentref Clawdd   Pentref   Glewysegl ab
        | in the same town-   Crystionydd,   Ieuan ab Owain
        | ship, ab John ab   and died   of Pen y lan in
        | Robert ab David.   *s. p.* 1683.   Dinhinlle
        | Des. from Ithel   Uchaf.
        | Felyn.

| a | b | | c | | d |

a	*b*	*c*	*d*
	Dorothy, mar. John, second son of John ab Edward of Bryn Lleweni, by whom she had a daughter, Jane, ux. John Williams of Bryn.	Elen, single in 1697.	Jane, married John ab Edward ab William of Pentref Cristionydd, by whom she had three sons, James, Samuel, and William.

Richard Wynn of Trefechan, 1697.

Barbara Wynn, ux. Thomas Andrews of Overton Madog, ab John Andrews of Wern in Maelor Saesneg.

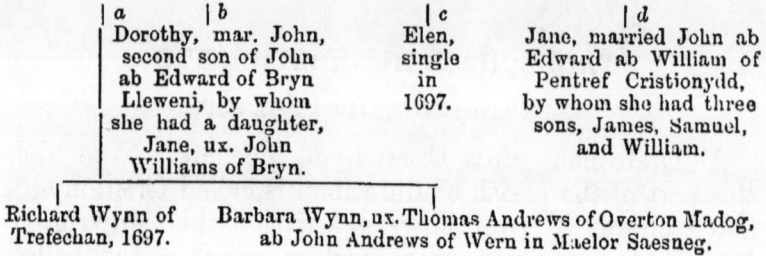

DINHINLLE UCHAF. PEN-Y-LAN.

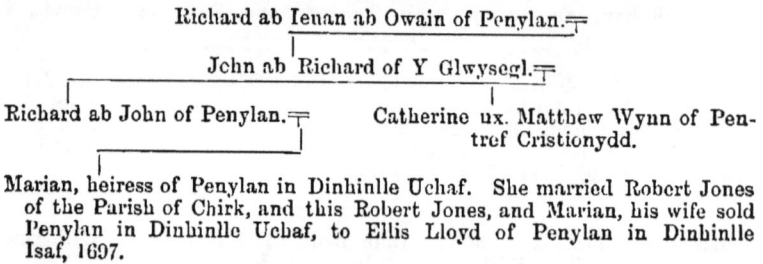

Richard ab Ieuan ab Owain of Penylan.

John ab Richard of Y Glwysegl.

Richard ab John of Penylan.

Catherine ux. Matthew Wynn of Pentref Cristionydd.

Marian, heiress of Penylan in Dinhinlle Uchaf. She married Robert Jones of the Parish of Chirk, and this Robert Jones, and Marian, his wife sold Penylan in Dinhinlle Uchaf, to Ellis Lloyd of Penylan in Dinhinlle Isaf, 1697.

ROBERTS OF ESCLUSHAM.

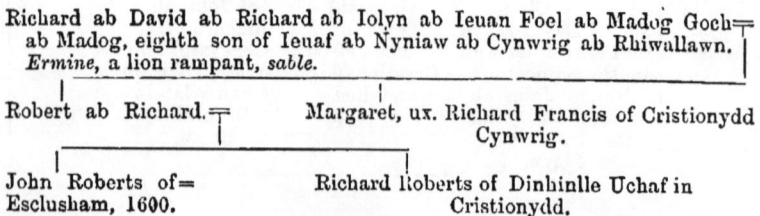

Richard ab David ab Richard ab Iolyn ab Ieuan Foel ab Madog Goch ab Madog, eighth son of Ieuaf ab Nyniaw ab Cynwrig ab Rhiwallawn. *Ermine,* a lion rampant, *sable.*

Robert ab Richard.

Margaret, ux. Richard Francis of Cristionydd Cynwrig.

John Roberts of Esclusham, 1600.

Richard Roberts of Dinhinlle Uchaf in Cristionydd.

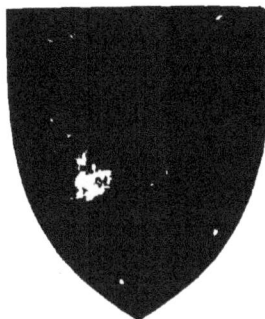

MANOR OF ESCLYS OR ESCLUSHAM, BERSHAM OF BERSHAM, AND WYNN OF FRON DEG.

Harl. MSS. 1972, 2299, 4181.

Gruffydd of Bers or Bersham,=Efa, dau. and heiress of Bledrws ab Ed-
second son Ieuaf ab Nyniaw | nowain Bendew. *Argent*, a chevron, *gules*,
ab Cynwrig ab Rhiwallawn. | inter three boar's heads couped, *sable*.

Iorwerth ab Gruffudd of Bersham.=Margaret, d. of Cynwrig   Howel.=
Gules, two lions passant in pale | Fychan ab Cynwrig ab
argent | Hoedliw of Cristionydd.

Hwfa ab=Janet, dau. of Ithel Dalfrith ab Trahaiarn   Iorwerth= Gruffydd.
Iorwerth | Goch of Lleyn. *Azure*, a chev. inter three   Fychan. |
of | dolphins naiant embowed, *argent*.
Bersham. | Hwfa.=

Howel ab Hwfa.   Madog yr Athro. See vol. ii, p. 130.
(*Harl. MS.* 4181.)   (*Harl. MS.* 4181.)

Howel ab= Madog y=Angharad, d. and   Gruffydd yr Athro, after=
Hwfa | Athro   heiress of Howel   his wife's death he became |
of | (*Harl.*   Grach ab Llywelyn   a Priest and was Parson |
Bersham. | MS.   ab Gruffydd of   of Llangedwyn. where he |
           2299.)   Eyton.   was buried.

Hwfa ab Gruffydd.=   ...... ux. Owain Fychan ab Owain ab Goronwy
                        ab Owain ab Edwyn, Prince of Tegeingl.

Gruffydd ab Hwfa.=

Llywelyn ab=Margaret, dau. of Llywelyn ab Rotpert ab Ieuan ab
Gruffydd. | Rhirid ab Iorwerth ab Madog ab Ednowain Bendew.

Margaret, ux. Ieuan Gethin, 1470.

1	2	3	4
Agnes, first wife of Iorwerth Fychan ab Iorwerth ab Awr.	Margaret, ux. Ithel Llwyd ab Ithel Gam, Lord of Mostyn in Tegeingl ab Maredydd ab Uchdryd ab Edwyn ab Goronwy.	Cicilia, ux. Sir Roger de Powys.	Alice, ux. Iorwerth ab Gruffydd ab Heilin ab Ieuan.

| a | b

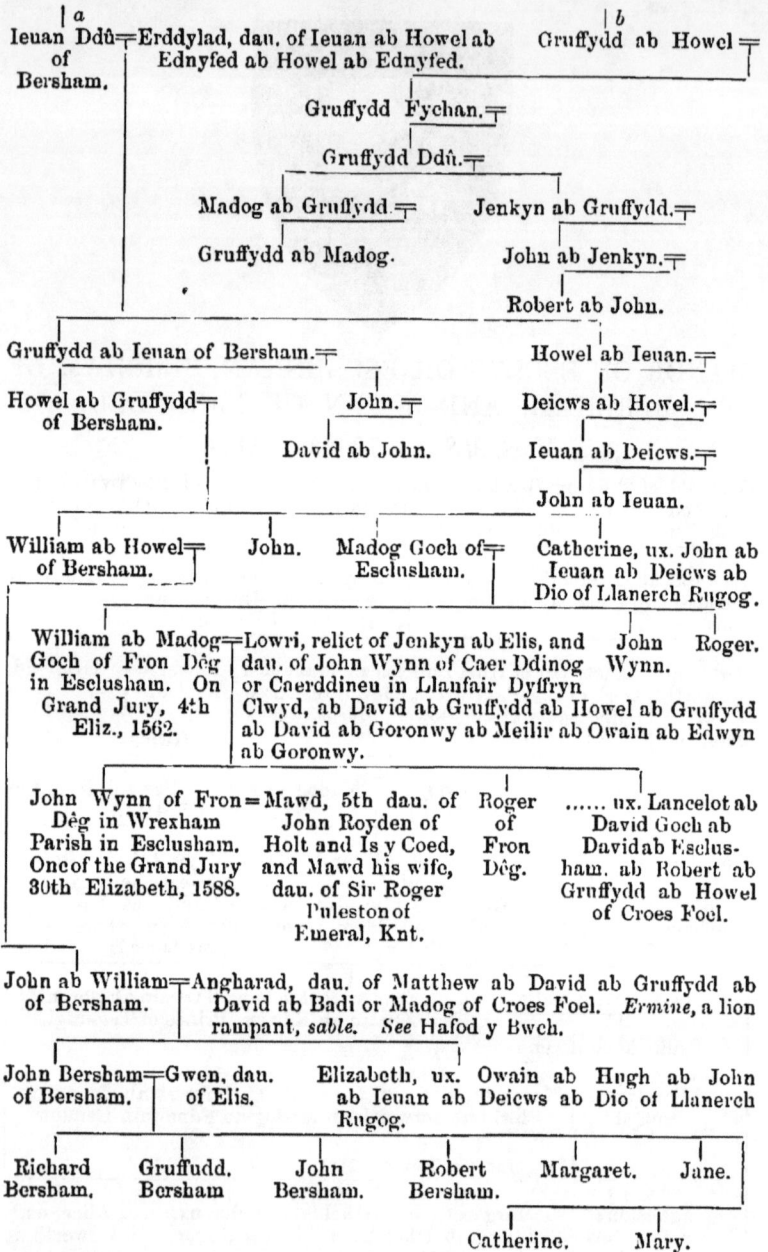

| a |
Ieuan Ddû=Erddylad, dau. of Ieuan ab Howel ab | b
of   Ednyfed ab Howel ab Ednyfed.   Gruffydd ab Howel =
Bersham.

Gruffydd Fychan.=

Gruffydd Ddû.=

Madog ab Gruffydd.=   Jenkyn ab Gruffydd.=

Gruffydd ab Madog.   John ab Jenkyn.=

Robert ab John.

Gruffydd ab Ieuan of Bersham.=   Howel ab Ieuan.=

Howel ab Gruffydd=   John.=   Deicws ab Howel.=
of Bersham.

David ab John.   Ieuan ab Deicws.=

John ab Ieuan.

William ab Howel=   John.   Madog Goch of=   Catherine, ux. John ab
of Bersham.   Esclusham.   Ieuan ab Deicws ab
           Dio of Llanerch Rugog.

William ab Madog=Lowri, relict of Jenkyn ab Elis, and   John   Roger.
Goch of Fron Dêg   dau. of John Wynn of Caer Ddinog   Wynn.
in Esclusham. On   or Caerddineu in Llanfair Dyffryn
Grand Jury, 4th   Clwyd, ab David ab Gruffydd ab Howel ab Gruffydd
Eliz., 1562.   ab David ab Goronwy ab Meilir ab Owain ab Edwyn
      ab Goronwy.

John Wynn of Fron=Mawd, 5th dau. of   Roger   ...... ux. Lancelot ab
Dêg in Wrexham   John Royden of   of   David Goch ab
Parish in Esclusham.   Holt and Is y Coed,   Fron   David ab Esclus-
One of the Grand Jury   and Mawd his wife,   Dêg.   ham. ab Robert ab
30th Elizabeth, 1588.   dau. of Sir Roger   Gruffydd ab Howel
     Puleston of   of Croes Foel.
     Emeral, Knt.

John ab William=Angharad, dau. of Matthew ab David ab Gruffydd ab
of Bersham.   David ab Badi or Madog of Croes Foel. *Ermine*, a lion
    rampant, *sable*. *See* Hafod y Bwch.

John Bersham=Gwen, dau.   Elizabeth, ux. Owain ab Hugh ab John
of Bersham.   of Elis.   ab Ieuan ab Deicws ab Dio of Llanerch
    Rugog.

Richard   Gruffudd.   John   Robert   Margaret.   Jane.
Bersham.   Bersham   Bersham.   Bersham.

Catherine.   Mary.

ESCLUSHAM.—TOWNSHIP OF BERS.

Harl. MS. 4181.

Gruffydd ab Einion ab Ednyfed ab Cynwrig ab Rhiwallawn.⹋Angharad, dau.
  Ermine, a lion statant gardant; *gules*, for Ednyfed ab │ of Thomas ab
  Cynwrig, Lord of Broughton.   Y Gwion.

Gruffydd⹋Jane, dau. of Henry de Laci, Earl of Lincoln, and Lord of Den-
Fychan. │ bigh, by Joanna, his wife, dau of William Martin, Baron of
        │ Cemaes in South Wales. (*Harl MS.* 1972.) Henry de Laci, died
        │ in 1310. Jane was the relict of Cynwrig ab Iorwerth ab Cas-
        │ wallawn ab Hwfa ab Ithel Felyn, Lord of Iâl.

Cynwrig.⹋Eva, dau. of Llywelyn ab Cynwrig Efell, Lord of Y Glwysegl.
         │ *Gules*, on a bend, *argent*, a lion passant, *sable*.

Ednyfed⹋Gwen, dau. of Cadwgan Goch ab Y Gwion   Goronwy.   Madog.
Goch of │ ab Hwfa ab Ithel Felyn, Lord of Iâl.
Bers.   │ *Sable*, on a chev. inter three goat's heads
        │ erased, *or*, three trefoils of the field.

Madog ⹋	...... dau. of Iorwerth⹋	Margaret, d. of Lly-	Sidan	Gruffydd⹋
Pabo	ab David ab Goronwy	welyn ab Gruffydd ab	or	Goch
of	of Burton and Llai.	Cadwgan, Lord of	Ithel,	of
Bers.	*Vert*, semé of broom-	Eyton. *Ermine*, a lion	see	Bers.
	slips, a lion rampant,	rampant, *azure*.	p. 22.	
	or.			Ieuan of⹋
		Gruffydd.		Bers.

Gruffydd ⹋Margaret, d. of Llewelyn   Gwenllian, ux.   Gwenllian, ux.
ab   │ of Halchdin in Maelor   Llywelyn   Goronwy ab Ieuan
Madog.   │ Saesneg, eldest son of   ab Iorwerth ab   ab David Llwyd
         │ Ednyfed Gam of Llys   Gruffydd of Llwyn   of Hafod y Bwch
         │ Pengwern in Nanheu-   On. *Ermine*, a   and Borasham.
         │ dwy. Party per bend   lion rampant   *Ermine*, a lion
         │ sinister. *Ermine* and   *sable*.   rampant *azure*.
         │ *ermines*, a lion rampt.
         │ *or*.

a │   b │

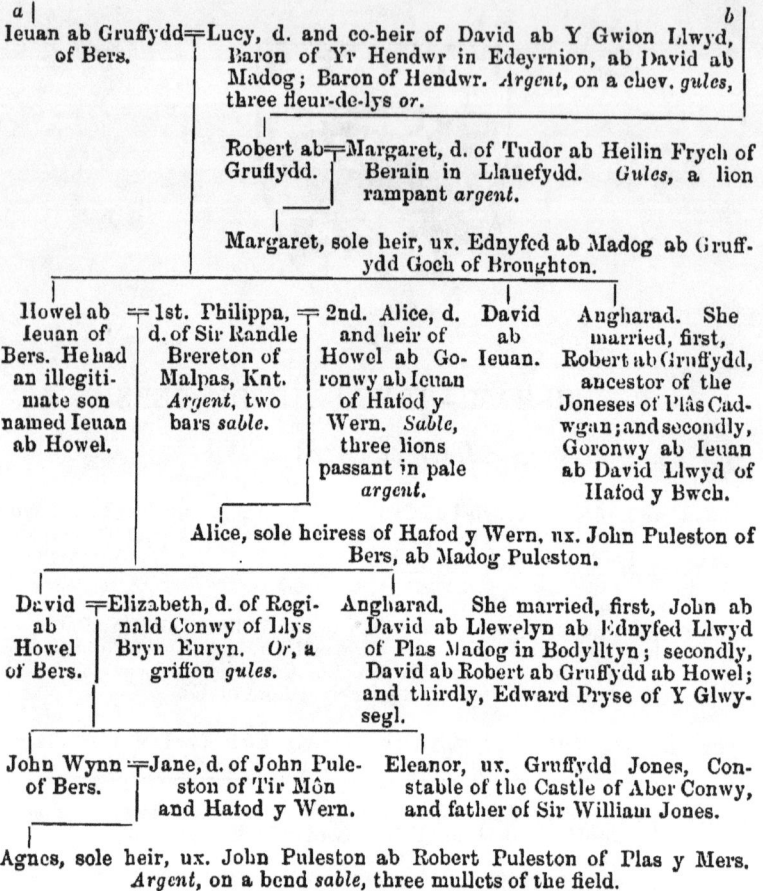

a |
Ieuan ab Gruffydd=Lucy, d. and co-heir of David ab Y Gwion Llwyd,
of Bers. | Baron of Yr Hendwr in Edeyrnion, ab David ab
Madog; Baron of Hendwr. *Argent*, on a chev. *gules*,
three fleur-de-lys *or*.
b |

Robert ab=Margaret, d. of Tudor ab Heilin Frych of
Gruffydd. | Berain in Llanefydd. *Gules*, a lion
rampant *argent*.

Margaret, sole heir, ux. Ednyfed ab Madog ab Gruffydd Goch of Broughton.

Howel ab = 1st. Philippa, = 2nd. Alice, d. David Angharad. She
Ieuan of | d. of Sir Randle and heir of ab married, first,
Bers. He had | Brereton of Howel ab Go- Ieuan. Robert ab Gruffydd,
an illegiti- | Malpas, Knt. ronwy ab Ieuan ancestor of the
mate son | *Argent*, two of Hafod y Joneses of Plâs Cad-
named Ieuan | bars *sable*. Wern. *Sable*, wgan; and secondly,
ab Howel. | three lions Goronwy ab Ieuan
passant in pale ab David Llwyd of
argent. Hafod y Bwch.

Alice, sole heiress of Hafod y Wern, ux. John Puleston of
Bers, ab Madog Puleston.

David =Elizabeth, d. of Regi- Angharad. She married, first, John ab
ab | nald Conwy of Llys David ab Llewelyn ab Ednyfed Llwyd
Howel | Bryn Euryn. *Or*, a of Plas Madog in Bodylltyn; secondly,
of Bers. | griffon *gules*. David ab Robert ab Gruffydd ab Howel;
and thirdly, Edward Pryse of Y Glwy-
segl.

John Wynn =Jane, d. of John Pule- Eleanor, ux. Gruffydd Jones, Con-
of Bers. | ston of Tir Môn stable of the Castle of Aber Conwy,
and Hafod y Wern. and father of Sir William Jones.

Agnes, sole heir, ux. John Puleston ab Robert Puleston of Plas y Mers.
Argent, on a bend *sable*, three mullets of the field.

BERS.

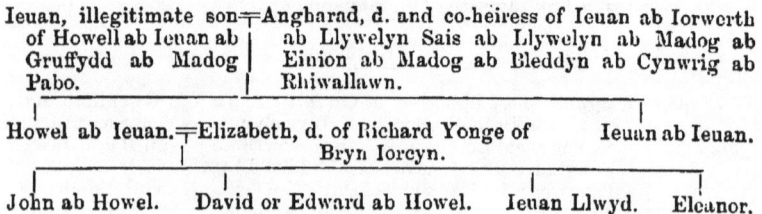

Ieuan, illegitimate son=Angharad, d. and co-heiress of Ieuan ab Iorwerth
of Howell ab Ieuan ab | ab Llywelyn Sais ab Llywelyn ab Madog ab
Gruffydd ab Madog | Einion ab Madog ab Bleddyn ab Cynwrig ab
Pabo. | Rhiwallawn.

Howel ab Ieuan.=Elizabeth, d. of Richard Yonge of Ieuan ab Ieuan.
Bryn Iorcyn.

John ab Howel. David or Edward ab Howel. Ieuan Llwyd. Eleanor.

Harl. MS. 4181.

Sidan *alias* Ithel, son of Ednyfed Goch of Bers,
married Alice, daughter of Maredydd Dhû of Mwssoglen
in Cwmwd Menai ab Goronwy ab Maredydd ab Iorwerth
ab Llywarch ab Bran, Lord of Cwmwd Menai (*argent*, a
chev. *sable* inter three Cornish choughs, with spots of
ermine in their bills ppr.) by whom he had issue three
sons ; 1, David, of whom presently ; 2, Ieuan, who had
a daughter, who married Gruffydd ab David Llwyd of
Bers, by whom she had a son Ieuan Deccaf, whose
daughter and heiress, Marsli, married Thomas Sutton ab
David ; and 3, Llywelyn ; and seven daughters,

1. Alice, ux. 1st, Robert ab Howel of Abyntbury ; and
2ndly, Ieuan ab David y Rhug.

2. . . . . . . ux. David Llwyd ab Madog ab Llywelyn ab
Gruffydd of Hafod y Bwch and Borasham.

3. . . . . . . ux. Howel Fychan ab Howel Wyddel ab
Einion ab Ithel ab Eunydd, ancestor of the Lloyds of Yr
Orsedd Goch.

4. . . . . . . ux. Madog ab Iorwerth Goch.

5. . . . . . . ux. Edmund Holland, son of Sir John Holland, Lord High Admiral of England, temp. Henry IV.

6. . . . . . . ux. . . . . . . Sheriff of London, by whom she
had four daughters ; one of whom married . . . . . . Abbot
of Westminster, another married . . . . . . Lieutenant of
the Tower of London ; . . . . . . married a captain in
France, and . . . . . . married, first, a captain that was a

companion of her brother, and, secondly, Captain Matthew Goch of Maelor.

David ab Sidin, the eldest son, married Margaret, daughter of David ab Ithel ab Goronwy, by whom he had a son and heir,

Richard ab David, who married Margaret, daughter of Madog ab Llywelyn ab Iorwerth ab Gruffydd, by whom he had an only daughter and heiress, Eva, who lived with John ab Elis Eyton of Rhiwabon, who fought in the army of King Henry VII at the battle of Bosworth in 1485, and by him had a son, Roger Eyton, who married Gwenhwyfar, daughter and heiress of Edward ab Madog ab Deio ab Madog Llwyd of Bodylltyn, ancestor of the Eytons of Bodylltyn.

ESCLUSHAM.—TOWNSHIP OF BERS OR BERSHAM. TY BELOTS. BETTWS Y MHERS.

Harl. MSS. 1972, 2299, 4181.

Madog ab Einion ab Madog ab Bleddyn ab Cynwrig ab Rhiwallawn,⊤

Llywelyn ab Madog.⊤......, d. of Iorwerth ab Y Code Blawd.   Ieuan.

Ithel Goch.⊤   Llywelyn Sais.

Llywelyn ab Ithel Goch.⊤Angharad, d. of David ab Ieuan ab Iorwerth ab David ab Goronwy of Burton and Llai.

Jenkyn ab Llywelyn.⊤Gwenllian, d. and heiress of Ieuan of Rhuddallt in Rhiwabon, ab Madog Llwyd ab Gruffydd of Maelor Saesneg, second son of Iorwerth Foel, Lord of Chirk.

| *a*

| a

Ieuan ab Jenkyn.⫟

Tudor ⫟Constans, d. of Gruffydd ab Lly-   David ab   Thomas ab   Madog.
ab | welyn ab Ednyfed Llwyd ab   Ieuan.   Ieuan.
Ieuan. | Iorwerth Fychan ab Iorwerth
     | ab Awr. See vol. ii, p. 192.

John ab Tudor.⫟   Margaret, ux. David Goch ab David of Esclusham,
                ab Robert ab Gruffydd of Croes Foel.

Edward Tudor of Ty Belots in Bettws y Mhers. = Mary, d. of John Guttyn.
     Ty Belots is now called Plas Power.

BERSHAM.

David ab Ieuan ab Jenkyn ab Llywelyn ab Ithel Goch.⫟

Edward ab David.⫟   Howel ab David.⫟Margaret, d. of Robert.

John ab Edward.⫟Angharad, d. of Edward ab Morgan   John ab Howel.⫟
          ab David ab Madog of Brymbo.
                                   John ab John.

Richard⫟Deili, d. of Robert ab Edward ab   Gruffydd married—1st, Mawd
ab | Howel ab Madog ab Howel ab   Wen, d. of John Wyn ab
John. | Ieuan ab Madog ab Einion ab   David, and relict of John
     | Madog ab Bleddyn ab Cyn-   Wynn Sanddef; 2nd, Mary,
     | wrig ab Rhiwallawn.   d. of Maredydd ab Elis.

John ab⫟Sibil, d. of Morgan ab   John   Fychan   married
John. | Robert ab Gruffydd   Gwenllian, d. of Hugh
     | Fychan.   ab David Goch.

Hugh = ..., d. of   Elizabeth,   Sibil, ux. Hugh   Margaret,
Jones Hugh ab   ux.   ab David Goch   ux.
of   Robert   Richard   ab David ab   Llywelyn.
Bers- of   Lloyd ab   Robert ab
ham. Wrex-   Hugh ab   Gruffydd of
     ham.   John.   Croes Foel.

John ab Richard = Catherine, d. of John Puleston   Sarah, ux.   John   ab
of Bersham.   of Plas ym Mhers ab Robert   Hugh ab   John ab
          Puleston.   Howel.

Maud, ux. Hugh ab Llywelyn   Anne, ux. Hugh ab Robert   Angharad.
ab Guttyn of Bers.   ab Howel of Mwyng-   Gwenllian.
                lawdd.   Joan.
                     Elizabeth.
                     Margaret.

TY CERIG IN RHIWABON.
Harl. MSS. 1972, 4181.

Thomas of Rhiwabon ab Ieuan ab Jenkyn ab Llywelyn ab Ithel Goch.⟤

Ieuan ab⟤ Robert ab Thomas   Margaret, ux. Geoffrey Bromfield of
Thomas | of Aberconwy.   Bryn y Wiwair.

Robert ab ⟤Margaret, d. of John   Alice, ux. William   Lili, ux. Ieuan ab
Ieuan. | Erddig Hen of Erddig.   ab Ieuan.   Randle.

John Roberts of Ty Cerrig, 1632.

ESCLUSHAM.—TOWNSHIP OF BERS.
PLAS POWER, FORMERLY CALLED TY BELOTS.
Cae Cyriog MS.

1		2
Sir Henry Power of Bers,═ Grissel, d. of Sir Richard		John ═Elizabeth,
Knight Mareschal of Ire- Bulkely of Baron Hill,		Power d. of Sir
land, Constable of the Beau Maris in Môn;		of Bers, George
Castle of Maryborough. and Agnes, his wife,		*ob.* 27th Gunter of
Created Viscount Valen- d. of Thomas Need-		March Racton,
tia, 1st March 1620, 18th ham of Cheshire. Gris-		1659. co. Sussex,
James I. *Ob. s.p.*, 25th sel died 8th Sept. 1641,		Knt.
May 1642. *Gules*, a and was buried at St.		
crescent *or*, on a chief Patrick's in Dublin.		
argent, three mullets		
pierced *sable*.		

Robert Power of Bers and Plâs War-═Dorothy, d. of Sir Cynwrig Eyton of
ren, co Salop, *ob.* 26th Dec. 1675. | Eyton, Knt. *Ermine*, a lion rampt. *az.*

John ═..., d. of Captain John	Robert	Cynwrig	1 Eleanor.	2	3 Mary.	4
Power	Manley of Wrex-	Power.	Power.	Elizabeth.		Susannah.
of Bers,	ham, brother of Sir					
1697.	Francis Manley of					
	Yr Bistog, Knt.					

Many Children. (See Burke's *Landed Gentry*.)

INSCRIPTION IN WREXHAM CHURCH.

"Here lieth the body of Sir Henry Power of Bersham, Knight, created Viscount Valentia in Ireland by patent dated 1st March 1620, Anno Jacobi Regis decimo octavo, who married Gressel, daughter of Sir Richard Bulkeley of Beaumaris in Anglesey, and deceased without issue 26th May 1642."

John Power, his brother and heir, was twice married, first, to Elizabeth, daughter of Sir George Gunter of Racton, co. Sussex, Knight, by whom he had issue; secondly, to Catherine, daughter of ...... Harden of Bedfordshire, who survived him. He died 27 March 1659.

Robert Power of Bersham, in the county of Denbigh, Esq., son and heir of the aforesaid John Power, married Dorothy, daughter of Kenrick Eyton of Eyton, Esq., by whom he had issue three sons and four daughters, viz., John, Robert and Kenrick; Eleanor, Elizabeth, Mary, Susannah. He died 26th Dec. 1677.

LLOYD OF BERS.

Harl. MSS. 1972, 2299.

Richard, natural son of Lewys Lloyd of Moelfré, second son of David Lloyd of Bodlith, ab Howel ab Maurice Gethin ab Ieuan Gethin ab Madog Cyffin. $=$ Elizabeth, d. of David ab John ab Maredydd of Lledrod.

| a

| a |
| Gruffydd=Elen, d. of Thomas Jones of Yscawennant.

| Humphrey Lloyd of Bers,=1st. Elizabeth, d. of Foulke=2nd. ..., d. of |

Humphrey Lloyd of Bers,	1st. Elizabeth, d. of Foulke	2nd. ..., d. of
Attorney-at-Law, and one of the Council for the Court of the Marches, 28th Oct. 1641.	Myddleton of Bodlith, High Sheriff for co. Denbigh in 1619. Seventh son of Richard Myddleton, Governor of Denbigh Castle.	Captain Roger Myddleton of Plâs Cadwgan.

| Ffoulke Lloyd, aged 13 in 1641. | Margaret, ux. .. Chambers of Plâs Chambers; ob. Nov. 1671. |

ESCLUSHAM.—TOWNSHIP OF BERS. PLAS Y MERS.

Cae Cyriog MS.; Lewys Dwnn, vol. ii, p. 359.

Madog Puleston of Bers (*argent*, on a bend *sable*, three mullets of the field), was the second son of Robert Puleston of Emeral in Maelor Saesneg, ab Richard ab Sir Roger Puleston. He married Angharad, daughter of David ab Goronwy of Burton and Llai, who, as well as his daughter Angharad, was living in 1415 ; by this lady, Madog had, besides a daughter, Angharad, the wife of Elis Eyton of Rhiwabon, a son and heir,

John Puleston of Bers. He married Alson, daughter of Howel ab Ieuan ab Gruffydd ab Ednyfed Goch of Bers (*ermine*, a lion statant gardant, *gules*) ; and Alson, his second wife, daughter and heiress of Howel ab Goronwy of Hafod y Wern (*sable*, three lions passant, in pale *argent*), by whom he had issue a son and heir,

John Puleston of Bers and Hafod y Wern, who married, first, Elen, daughter of Robert Whitney ab Sir

Robert Whitney, Knight, ab Sir Robert Whitney, Knight;
and, secondly, Alice, daughter of Hugh Lewys of Tir
Môn, by whom he had a son, John Puleston of Tir Môn,
who had Hafod y Wern, and was High Sheriff for co.
Denbigh in 1544. By his first wife, Elen Whitney,
John Puleston had issue five sons ; 1, Sir John Puleston,
of whom presently ; 2, Robert Puleston, Parson of Gresford ; 3, Huw Puleston, Vicar of Wrexham, and Parson
of Llanrhaiadr in Mochnant ; 4, Richard Puleston, who
had lands about Croes Madog ab Llywelyn ; and 5,
Lancelot ; and three daughters ; 1, Elizabeth, ux. Sir
Roger Salusbury, of Lleweni, Knight ; 2, Jane, who
married, first, Robert ab Maredydd ab Hwlkyn Llwyd of
Glyn Llufon, in the parish of Llandwrog, in the comot
of Uwch Gwyrfai, and, secondly, she married Sir William
Gruffydd of Penrhyn, Knight, Chamberlain of Gwynedd ;
and 3, ... who married, first, John Eyton Fychan
of Rhiwabon, and, secondly, John Erddig of Erddig.

Sir John Puleston of Bers, Knight, the eldest son, was
Chamberlain of Gwynedd, and Constable of the castle of
Caernarvon, and died in 1551. In the *Cambrian
Quarterly Magazine*, vol. v, p. 276, is a curious in-
ventory of the stores in Caernarvon Castle, taken after
his death, on the 25th February 5th Edward VI. He
married, first, Gainor, daughter of Robert ab Maredydd
ab Hwleyn Llwyd of Glyn Llufon, in the parish of
Llandwrog, in the comot of Uwch Gwyrvai, descended
from Cilmin Droctu, Chief of one of the Noble Tribes,
who lived at Glyn Llufon in the time of Mervyn Frych,
King of the Isle of Man (Mervyn was slain in 843),
being his brother's son. He bore, quarterly, 1st and 4th,
argent, an eagle displayed, with two heads *sable* ; 2nd
and 3rd, *argent*, three fiery ragged sticks *gules*, over all,
on an escutcheon *argent*, a man's leg, coupé à la cuise of
the second. Sir John married, secondly, Janet, daughter
of Maredydd ab Ieuan ab Robert of Cesail Gyvarch, who
purchased Gwydir, where he subsequently resided (*vert
three eagles, displayed in fess or*), by whom he had issue,
besides one son, Hugh, who married Margaret, daughter

and co-heir of Hugh Llwyd of Llwyn y Cnotiau, and
was ancestor of the Pulestons of that place, three
daughters; Jane, ux. Rhys Wynn; Ann, ux. Edward
Conwy; and Margaret, ux. ... Royden.

By his first wife Gainor, Sir John Puleston had issue
five sons; 1, Robert, of whom presently; John and
William, who died *s. p.*; 4, Rowland Puleston of Caernarvon, High Sheriff for Caernarvonshire in 1575; and
5, John, ob. *s. p.*; and five daughters; 1, Elizabeth,
ux. John Wynn[1] ab Hugh of Bodfel in Lleyn, Lord of
Ynys Enlli, High Sheriff for Caernarvonshire in 1551
and 1560, *sable*, a chevron inter three fleurs-de-lys,
argent, quartering also; 2, *or*, a lion rampant regardant
sable, for Nêst, daughter and co-heiress of Gruffydd ab
Adda ab Gruffydd ab Madog ab Cinillin ab Cadivor
ab Gwaethfoed; and 3, *gules*, a lion rampant inter
three helmets, *argent*, with the difference of a crescent,
gules, for Gwerfyl or Gwenhwyfar, the daughter and
heiress of Rhys ab Tudor ab Goronwy of Tref Gaian, ab
Tudor ab Goronwy ab Ednyfed Fychan (see Tref Gaian);
2, Sibil, ux. Elis ab William Lloyd; 3, Elen, ux. Maurice
ab Elis; 4, Jane, who married, first, Edward Gruffydd of

---

[1] The following notice of John Wynn, Esq., occurs in *Memoirs,
by Sir John Wynn of Gwydir, of several of his Contemporary Countrymen.* "The memorable services of John Wynn ab Hugh, born at
Bodfel, in Lleyn, whereof he was Lord, now in this tract are not to
be forgotten. He was standard-bearer to John, Earl of Warwick, and
afterwards Duke of Northumberland, in the great field fought between him and Kett and the rebels of Norfolk and Suffolk, near Norwich in Edward VI's time (in August 1549); his horse was slain
under him, and himself hurt, and yet he upheld the great standard
of England. There is mention of this (the) shot made at the great
standard of England in the Chronicles of that time, for which service
the Duke of Northumberland bestowed upon him two fine things in
Lleyn, viz., the Isle of Bardsey (Ynys Enlli) and the demesne house
of the Abbot of Bardsey, near Aberdaron, called the Cwrtwith. The
honourable mention made of his service in the grant, which I have
seen and read: a rare matter to find so good a master." John Wynn
was the son of Hugh ab John ab Madog ab Howel ab Madog ab Ieuan
ab Einion ab Gruffydd ab Howel ab Maredydd ab Einion ab Gwgan
ab Merwydd ab Collwyn ab Tangno, Lord of part of Lleyn, Eivionydd,
and Ardudwy.—See vol. ii, p. 136.

Penrhyn, ab Sir William Gruffydd, Chamberlain of Gwynedd ; and, secondly, Rhys Thomas of Coed Helen,[1] co. Caernarvon, High Sheriff for Caernarvonshire in 1574 (*argent*, on a cross sable, five crescents *or*, in the dexter chief, a spear's head erect, *gules*, for Sir Gruffydd ab Elidir, Knight of Rhodes); and 5, Margaret, ux. William Lewys of Persaddfed, in the parish of Bod Edeyrn, descended from Hwfa ab Cynddelw of Presaddved or Persaddved, one of the fifteen Noble Tribes of Gwynedd (*gules*, a chev. inter three lions rampant, *or*).

Robert Puleston of Bers, the eldest son, married Elen, daughter of William Fychan ab William of Cwchwillan in Llechwedd Uchaf, descended from Heilin ab Sir Tudor ab Ednyfed Fychan o Vôn, by whom he had issue five sons; 1, John ; 2, Rowland ; 3, Huw ; 4, Edward ; and 5, Richard ; and two daughters ; 1, Mary, ux. Edward Gruffydd, and 2, Anne.

John Puleston of Bers, living 1583, married Anne, only daughter and heiress of John Wynn ab David ab Howel ab Ieuan ab Gruffydd ab Madog ab Ednyfed Goch ab Cynwrig of Bers (*ermine*, a lion statant gardant *gules*), by whom he had issue two sons ; 1, Roger ; 2, John, who was living in 1604, and six daughters ; Catherine ; Jane ; Mary ; Dorothy ; Elizabeth ; and Anne.

[1] Rhys Thomas of Coed Helen, was the son of Sir William Thomas of Aberglasney, Knight Banneret, High Sheriff for Caermarthenshire in 1539, ab Thomas ab Rhydderch ab Rhys ab Gruffydd ab Llywelyn Voethys ab Llywelyn Ddû ab Owain ab Sir Gruffydd, Knight of Rhodes, ab Elidir ab Owain ab Idnerth ab Llywelyn, Lord of Buallt, ab Cadwgan ab Elystan Glodrhudd, Prince of Fferlis.--See vol. ii, p. 323 ; and Burke's *Landed Gentry*, art. "Hughes of Plâs Coch".

ESCLUSHAM.—TRAFFORD OF TREFFORTH.

Harl. MS. 4181.

Iorwerth Fychan ab Iorwerth ab Ieuaf ab Ninio ab Cynwrig ab Rhiwallon.⹋
Ermine, a lion rampant, *sable*.

Gruffydd ab⹋Lleuci, dau. of Ieuaf ab Llywelyn ab Cynwrig Efell,
Iorwerth. | Lord of Y Glewysegl. *Gules*, on a bend, *argent*, a lion
| passant, *sable*.

Llywellyn ⹋Eva, dau. of | Madog ⹋Annest, d. | David Goch, | Howel of
ab | David ab | Ddu. | of Ieuaf ab | ancestor | Croes Foel,
Gruffydd. | Ieuan ab | | Hwfa ab | of the | ancestor of
| Iorwerth ab | | Madog yr | Robertses | the Joneses
| David ab | | Athro. | of Hafod | of Croes
| Goronwy of | | See vol. ii, | y Bwch. | Foel and
| Burton and | | p. 139. | | Plâs
| Llai. | | | | Cadwgan.

Iorwerth ⹋Gwenllian, dau. of | Jenkyn ⹋Gwladys Moel, d.
ab | Llywelyn Fychan | Deccaf. | of Howel ab David
Madog. | ab Llywelyn ab | | Llwyd of Llech-
| Goronwy Fychan | | wedd.
| ab Goronwy ab |
| Ednyfed Fychan. | Margaret, ux. | Gwerfyl
| | Madog ab | ux.
David ab ⹋Catherine, dau. and | Marredydd ab | Ieuan
Iorwerth. | heir of David ab | Llywelyn Ddû | ab
| Gruffydd Fychan ab | ab Madog Llwyd | Howel
| Gruffydd of Rhiwlo, | ab Gruffydd of | Pickhill.
| son of Hwfa ab | Maelor Saesneg
| Iorwerth of Hafod | ab Iorwerth Foel | Erddylad
| y Wern. | Lord of Chirk. | co-heir.

Llywelyn. | Margaret, ux. Gwyn ab | Gwen, co-heir, ux.
| Goronwy ab Gwilym ab | David ab Gruffydd
| Maredydd of Yr Hôb. | Fychan ab Madog.

Madog ab⹋Margaret, dau. of Gruffydd | Ieuan ab Llywelyn, ancestor
Llywelyn. | of Rhuddallt. | of the Erddigs of Erddig.
a

David ab=Gwenhwyfar, dau. of Llywelyn ab Adda ab Howel ab Ieuaf ab
Madog. | Adda ab Awr of Llys Trevor in Nanheudwy.

Edward ab=Lleuci, dau. and heir of Madog ab Ieuan ab Einion of
David. | Is y Coed.

	1		2	3		1		2	3
Edward.=Margaret, d. and	Reignallt.		Margaret, ux. Ieuan	Catherine.
	heir of David ab	Maredydd.		ab Robert ab Gruf-	Gwenllian.
	Jenkyn ab Madog			fydd ab Howel ab	
	ab Ieuaf.			Gruffydd ab Iorwerth Fychan ab	
				Iorwerth ab Ieuaf ab Niniaw.	

Robert =Jane, dau.	David = Isabel, dau. and	Isabel, ux.	...... ux.
ab	of Randle	ab	heiress of Ieuan ab	John Wynn	John
Edward.	Brereton	Edward.	Llywelyn ab Howel	ab Howel	Gethin.
	of		of Coed y Llai ab	ab Edward	
	Borasham.		Iorwerth Fychan	of Plas Isaf in	
			ab Iorwerth ab	Cristionydd.	
			Awr. Vol. ii, p. 191.	

Edward =Jane, dau. of	Lancelot.	Elizabeth, mar., 1st, John
Trafford.	George Kynas-	William.	Wynn of the Tower, 2nd,
	ton of	James.	John ab Ithel Wynn of
	Oteley.	Hugh and Francis.	Coed y Llai.

Thomas Trafford, Receiver=Alice, dau. of Roger Bady of Rhiwabon, and
of North Wales. | Jane, his wife, dau. of Edward Brereton of
Ob. A.D. 1644. | Borasham. *Add. MS.* 9864.

| James. | Edward. | Mary. | Jane. |

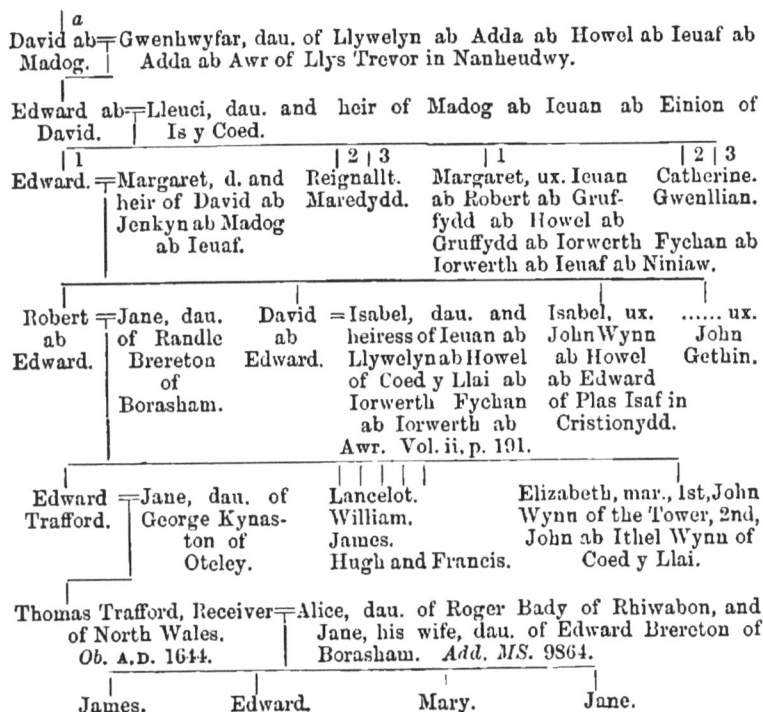

ESCLUSHAM.—TOWNSHIP ESCLYS. LLOYD OF
ESCLYS. (See vol. i, p. 192.)

David Goch of Pen Machno, in Nant Conwy, who
bore, *sable*, a lion rampant, *argent*, in a border engrailed
or, was the natural son of David, Lord of Denbigh and
Frodsham, whose trial and cruel death at Shrewsbury in

1283 has been already related in a previous chapter. David Goch married Angharad, daughter of Heilin ab Sir Tudor ab Ednyfed Fychan, by whom he had issue a son and heir,

Gruffydd ab David of Nant Conwy. It appears from the Extent of Nant Conwy, in the *Record of Caernarvon*, or *Great Extent of North Wales*, as it is also called, taken 26 Edward III (1352), that Gruffydd was the foreman of the jury for taking that Extent. He was buried in the Church of Bettws Wyrion Iddon, or Bettws y Coed, where his tomb is to be seen, with his effigy recumbent in armour, with the following inscription : " HIC IACET GRUFUD AP DAVID GOCH. AGNUS DEI MISERERE MEI." A full description of this tomb has been given by Mr. Bloxham, in the *Arch. Cambr.* for 1874, p. 128. He left a son and heir,

Gruffydd Fychan of Nant Conwy, who was the father of two sons, Howel Coetmor and Rhys Gethin ; 1, Howel Coetmor, commonly called the Baron Howel Coetmore, who bore *azure*, a chevron inter three fleurs-de-lys *argent*. He owned Gwydir and other large estates in the parish of Llanrwst, but generally resided at Castell Cefel Ynghoedmor, in the parish of Llanrwst ; this castle, according to Gruffydd Hiraethog, formerly belonged to Peredur ab Efrawg. He was buried at Llanrwst, and his tomb still remains, on which his sepulchral effigy is represented recumbent, in plate armour, with a tabard of his arms, with this inscription : " HIC IACET HOEL COETMORE AP GRVFF VYCHAN AMN" (see *Arch. Cambr.*, April 1874, pp. 128-131). He was the ancestor of the Wynns of Clynog Fawr ; Owens of Talwrn in Eivionydd ; Lloyds of Pen Machno ; and the Wynns of Glyn Llugwy.

Rhys Gethin, the second son of Gruffydd Fychan, lived at Hendref Rhys Gethin, in the parish of Bettws Wyrion Iddon, or Bettws y Coed. He was the father of Howel, the father of Rhys Goch, the father of

Robert ab Rhys of Pen Machno, who married Elizabeth, daughter of Owain ab Meurig ab Llywelyn ab

Hwlcyn of Bodcon, in the parish of Llan Veirian in
Cwmwd Malldraeth, descended from Hwfa ab Cynddelw
of Presaddved, in the parish of Bod Edeyrn (*gules*, a
chev., inter three lions rampant, *or*), by whom he had a
son,

Howel Lloyd of Pen Machno, who married Jane,
daughter and heiress of Robert ab Howel ab David
Fychan ab David Goch ab Ieuan Tegin of Dulassau in
Caernarvonshire, who was living in the time of Edward
III, and descended from Ednyfed Fychan, who bore,
gules, a chev. ermine inter three Englishmen's heads,
couped at the neck ppr. ; by whom he had issue two sons,
1, Evan Lloyd, of whom presently ; and 2, Richard
Lloyd.

The second son, Richard Lloyd, D.D., Vicar of Rhiw-
abon, Justice of the Peace and Quorum, 1614, married
Jane, daughter of Roderick Hughes, son of Richard
Hughes of Maes y Pandy, in the parish of Tal y Llyn
Meingul, in Meirionydd, descended, through Einion
Sais, from Caradog Freichfras, King of Brycheiniawg,
(quarterly 1st and 4th *argent*, three cocks, *gules*, for
Einion Sais, 2nd and 3rd *sable*, a chevron inter three
spear's heads, *argent*, imbrued *gules*), by whom he had
issue, besides a daughter Elizabeth, who married Peter
Ffoulkes of Eriviad, in the parish of Henllan (*gules*,
three boar's heads erased in pale *argent*), eight sons ; 1,
Samuel Lloyd, Vicar of Gresford ; 2, Evan Lloyd, Vicar
of Tref Ffynnon ; 3, Humphrey Lloyd, D.D., Vicar of
Rhiwabon 1653, and Dean of St. Asaph in 1663, who
married Jane, daughter of John Gruffydd of Lleyn, and
relict of Edward Brereton of Borasham, who died 8th
July 1644—Jane died 10th Oct. 1689 ; 4, John Lloyd,
Vicar of Marchwiail ; and Rhys, Edward, Thomas, and
Gerard, who all went to London.

Evan Lloyd of Dulassau, the eldest son of Howel
Lloyd, married, and had issue, besides a daughter
Barbara, who married William Wynn of Melai and
Maenan Abbey, Colonel in the army of Charles 1st, who
was slain at Wem, in the thirty-seventh year of his age,

two sons; 1, Sir Richard Lloyd, of whom presently, and 2, Howel Lloyd of Croes Iocyn, the father of Ieuan Lloyd of Croes Iocyn, who was living unmarried in 1697. 1368307

Sir Richard Lloyd of Esclys, in the Lordship of Maelor Gymraeg or Bromfield, and of Dulassau, in the county of Caernarvon, Knight, Chief Justice of the Brecon Circuit, and afterwards Chief Justice of North Wales, Governor of Holt Castle during the time of the Great Rebellion, and a faithful subject of King Charles I, whom he received at Bryn y Ffynnon in Wrexham in 1642. In connection with the King's visit to Wrexham at that time, the following anecdote appears in Ormerod's *Cheshire*, General Introduction, vol. i, p. 35 :

"Upon October 7, 1642, the King, having come over from Shrewsbury to Wrexham to meet a commission from the city of Chester, and intending to return the same day, appears to have taken up his quarters at Sir Richard Lloyd's house, who is said to have urged the length of the day's journey, and the unseasonableness of the weather, and to have pressed his royal guest to stay till the next day at Wrexham; and the King to have dismissed him and the other gentlemen with these pathetic and simple words: 'Gentlemen, go you and take to your rests, for you have homes and houses to go to, and beds of your own to lodge in; and God grant that you may long enjoy them! I am deprived of these comforts; I must attend my present affairs, and return this night to the place whence I came.''

Sir Richard Lloyd married Margaret, daughter of Ralph Snead of Bradwall and Keele in Staffordshire, by whom he had issue one son, Robert, and three daughters.

Robert Lloyd of Esclys and Dulassau, the only son of Sir Richard, married Frances, daughter of Sir Robert Williams of Penrhyn, in the county of Caernarvon, Knight and Baronet, and heiress of her brother, Sir Gruffydd Williams, Bart.; by whom he had issue a son and heir, Richard, who was one year old at the time of his father's death, which occurred Nov. 4th, 1675; and the son Richard died 9th April 1683. Frances, his mother, married, secondly, in 1688, Lord Edward

Russell, son of William, Duke of Bedford, and died *s. p.*
30 June 1714, aged 72.

Jane Lloyd, the eldest daughter of Sir Richard,
married Lewis Owen of Peniarth, in Meirionydd, and is
now represented by W. W. E. Wynn of Peniarth, Esq.

Mary, the second daughter, married Sir Henry Conwy
of Bodrhyddan, in Tegeingl, Knight and Baronet.

Anne, the third daughter, married, first, Edward
Ravenscroft, son and heir of Thomas Ravenscroft of
Bretton in Merffordd, Esq., and, secondly, John
Grosvenor, third son of Roger, son and heir of Sir
Richard Grosvenor of Eaton, co. Chester, Bart.

Sir Richard Lloyd died the 5th of May 1676, in the
71st year of his age, and was buried in lead under a
monument in his own chapel in Wrexham church.[1]

The crest of this family is a demi-lion rampant, *argent*,
issuing from a coronet.

MANOR OF ESCLUSHAM.—GRUFFYDD OF BRYNBWA OR BRYMBO.

Harl. MS. 2299; *Add. MS.* 9864.

David Goch of Mortyn, seventh son of David Hên=Gwenllian, dau. of John ab Goronwy ab Iorwerth of Mostyn (Burton) and Llai. *Vert*, semé of broomslips, a lion rampant, *or*, armed and langued *gules*.	ab Morgan ab Llywelyn, Lord of St. Clears.
a	

---

[1] *Harl. MS.* 2180.

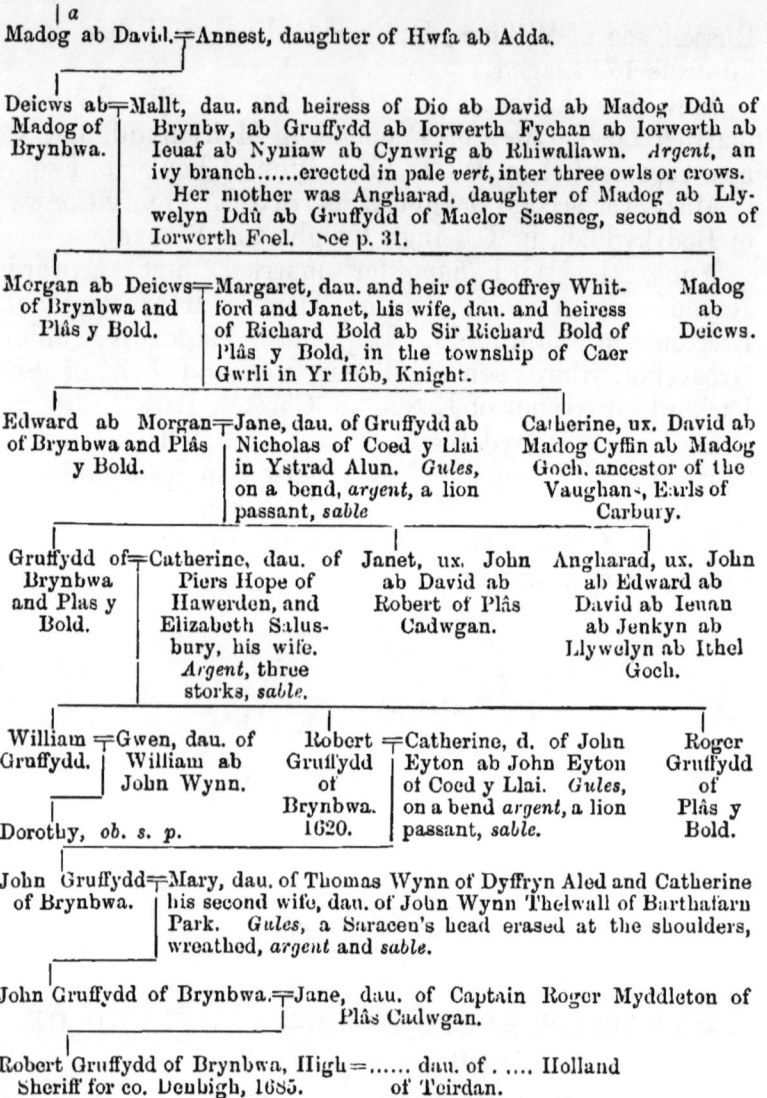

| a

Madog ab David.=Annest, daughter of Hwfa ab Adda.

Deicws ab=Mallt, dau. and heiress of Dio ab David ab Madog Ddû of
Madog of | Brynbw, ab Gruffydd ab Iorwerth Fychan ab Iorwerth ab
Brynbwa. | Ieuaf ab Nyniaw ab Cynwrig ab Rhiwallawn. *Argent*, an
ivy branch......erected in pale *vert*, inter three owls or crows.
Her mother was Angharad, daughter of Madog ab Llywelyn Ddû ab Gruffydd of Maelor Saesneg, second son of
Iorwerth Foel. See p. 31.

Morgan ab Deicws=Margaret, dau. and heir of Geoffrey Whit-   Madog
of Brynbwa and | ford and Janet, his wife, dau. and heiress   ab
Plâs y Bold. | of Richard Bold ab Sir Richard Bold of   Deicws.
Plâs y Bold, in the township of Caer
Gwrli in Yr Hôb, Knight.

Edward ab Morgan=Jane, dau. of Gruffydd ab   Catherine, ux. David ab
of Brynbwa and Plâs | Nicholas of Coed y Llai   Madog Cyffin ab Madog
y Bold. | in Ystrad Alun. *Gules*,   Goch, ancestor of the
on a bend, *argent*, a lion   Vaughans, Earls of
passant, *sable*   Carbury.

Gruffydd of=Catherine, dau. of   Janet, ux. John   Angharad, ux. John
Brynbwa | Piers Hope of   ab David ab   ab Edward ab
and Plas y | Hawerden, and   Robert of Plâs   David ab Ieuan
Bold. | Elizabeth Salus-   Cadwgan.   ab Jenkyn ab
bury, his wife.   Llywelyn ab Ithel
Argent, three   Goch.
storks, *sable*.

William =Gwen, dau. of   Robert =Catherine, d. of John   Roger
Gruffydd. | William ab   Gruffydd | Eyton ab John Eyton   Gruffydd
| John Wynn.   of | ot Coed y Llai. *Gules*,   of
| Brynbwa. | on a bend *argent*, a lion Plâs y
Dorothy, *ob. s. p.*   1620. | passant, *sable*.   Bold.

John Gruffydd=Mary, dau. of Thomas Wynn of Dyffryn Aled and Catherine
of Brynbwa. | his second wife, dau. of John Wynn Thelwall of Barthafarn
Park. *Gules*, a Saracen's head erased at the shoulders,
wreathed, *argent* and *sable*.

John Gruffydd of Brynbwa.=Jane, dau. of Captain Roger Myddleton of
| Plâs Cadwgan.

Robert Gruffydd of Brynbwa, High=...... dau. of ...... Holland
Sheriff for co. Denbigh, 1685.   of Teirdan.

JONES OF CROES FOEL.

Harl. MS. 4181.

Howel of Croes Foel, ab Gruffydd ab=Dygws, dau. of Madog Llwyd ab
Iorwerth Fychan ab Iorwerth ab | Gruffydd of Maelor Saesneg, second
Ieuaf ab Niniaw ab Cynwrig ab | son of Iorwerth Foel, Lord of Chirk,
Rhiwallawn. *Ermine,* a lion ram- | Maelor Saesneg, and Nanheudwy.
pant, *sable.*

Gruffydd ab=Angharad, dau. and heiress of Robert ab Howel ab Hwfa ab
Howel of | Gruffydd of Rhiwlo, third son of Hwfa ab Iorwerth of Hafod
Croes Foel. | y Wern. *Sable,* three lions passant in pale *argent.*

Robert ab=Elen, dau. of Gruffydd ab Gruffudd=Angharad, d. of Ieuan ab
Gruffydd | ab Llywelyn Sais ab Gruffydd ab | Gruffydd ab Madog Pabo
of Croes | Madog ab Ednyfed ab Urian. | ab Ednyfed Goch of
Foel. | | Bersham.

David, ancestor of the Joneses of   Ieuan.
Plâs Cadwgan.

John of =Catherine, dau. of   Madog. =......... dau. of   Gwenhwyfar,
Croes Foel.| Robert Lloyd ab | Howel ab Ieuan   ux. Edward
| David ab Bleddyn | ab Llywelyn   ab Howel ab
| ab Gruffudd of | ab Gruffydd   Llywelyn of
| Ffern in Glyn | ab Iorwerth   Llys Trevor.
| Berbrwg in Ystrad | Fychan.
| Alun.

Margaret, sole heir, ux. John Lloyd ab David Lloyd of Plas
y Bada in the township of Morton Anglicorum in the
Manor of Fabrorum.

Alice, ux. David ab Ieuan ab   Catherine, ux. William ab
David of Bryn Lluarth.   David Eyton.

John ab John of=Marslli, dau. of John ab Ieuan ab Deicws ab Dio of
Croes Foel. | Llanerch Rugog.

| a | b | c | d | e | f

a	b	c	d	e	f
Hugh Jones⨿ of Croes Foel.	David ab John.	=Margaret, d. of Thomas ab John ab Ieuan ab David of Gwinnlon.	Gwenllian, ux. Edward ab Howel of Wrexham.	...... ux. Nicholas Tresswell.	Anne. Jane.

Richard Jones.

Robert ab Gruffydd ab Howel ab⫧Angharad, dau. of Ieuan ab Gruffydd
   Gruffydd of Croes Foel. | ab Madog ab Ednyfed Goch of Bers-
                ham; second wife.

Ieuan ab Robert.⫧Margaret, dau. of Edward ab David ab Madog ab Lly-
         welyn ab Gruffydd ab Iorwerth Fychan.

Howel ab Ieuan.⫧Janet, dau. of Richard Yonge of Bryn Iorcyn yn Yr Hob,
         ab Maurice ab Jenkyn.

Margaret, heiress, ux. Robert ab David ab Gruffydd of Croes Foel, ancestor
     of the Robertses of Hafod y Bwch.

Robert ab Gruffydd ab Howel of⫧Angharad, d. of Ieuan ab Gruffydd ab
    Croes Foel. | Madog of Bersham.

David ab Robert⫧Catherine, d. and co-heir of Ieuan ab Iorwerth ab Lly-
of Esclys or | welyn Sais ab Llywelyn ab Madog ab Einion ab Madog
Esclusham. | ab Bleddyn ab Cynwrig ab Rhiwallon.

John.   David⫧Margaret, d. of Tudor ab Ieuan ab Jenkyn of Bettws y
     Goch. | Mhers, ab Llywelyn ab Ithel Goch ab Llywelyn ab Ma-
          dog ab Einion ab Madog ab Bleddyn.

        Edward.⫧Gwen, d. of Madog ab   Margaret, ux. Edward
              Gruffydd ab Ieuan   ab Howel ab Madog
              ab Adda ab Awr.   of Bersham.

        John.=Elizabeth, d.   Sir David, Vicar of   Elizabeth.
            of Madog.   Rhiwabon.

Lancelot ab⫧..., d. of William ab Madog Goch of Fron Deg, ab Howel ab
David Goch. | Gruffyd ab Ieuan Ddu of Bersham. *Gules*, two lions
         passant *argent*.

    Hugh ab—Isabel, d. of John ab Catherine, ux. Annest,
     David   Edward ab David David Brogdyn ux. Ma-
     Goch.   ab Ieuan ab Jen-   ab Robert   dog ab
           kyn ab Llywelyn ab Fychan.   Robert
           Ithel Goch.   Fychan.

John.

PLAS CADWGAN.

John ab David of Es-=Janet, d. of Edward ab Morgan of Brynbwa or Bryn-
clys or Esclusham, | bo, and of Plas Bold in Caer Gwrli, ab David ab
ab Robert ab Gryff- | Madog, second son of David Goch, ab David ab
ydd ab Howel of | Goronwy ab Iorwerth ab Howel ab Moreiddig ab
Croes Foel. | Sanddef Hardd, Lord of Burton and Llai.

Edward = Jane, d. and co-   Robert =Gwenllian, d. of   Eleanor,
Jones of | heiress of John Wynn Jones. | John Eyton ab   ux. Bar-
Plâs Cad- | Deecaf of Rhwyton in | John ab Elis Ey-   tholo-
wgan. | the Manor of Rhiw- | ton of Rhiwabon.   mew
         | abon.   Totti.
                                          |
                                        Hugh.

William Jones= Susanna, ux. Humphrey Pipe   Dorothy, ux. Humphrey
of Plas | ab Sir Richard Pipe, Lord   Ellis of Alrhey. She
Cadwgan. | Mayor of London.   died 23rd Nov. 1632;
                                            buried at Bangor.

Edward Jones of Plas Cadwgan, High Sheriff for co. Denbigh,=Margaret,
1576. Executed by Elizabeth in London, Sept. 21, 1586, for | d. of —
joining with Babbington in trying to place Mary, Queen of | Wilson.
Scots, on the throne. The estates were forfeited, but the
house and some of the lands were given to his daughter and
heiress, Anne, by Elizabeth.

Anne Jones,=Captain Roger Myddleton, second son of Richard Myddleton
heiress of | of Llansilin, eldest son of Richard Myddleton, Governor of
Plâs Cad- | Denbigh Castle in the time of Edward VI, Mary, and
wgan. | Elizabeth. *Argent, on a bend vert, three wolf's heads
           | erased* of the field. The mother of Captain Roger Myddle-
           | ton was Jane, daughter and heiress of John ab Rhys ab
           | Edward ab Bel of Wepra.

Elizabeth, =Ffoulk Myd-   Anne, co-   ..., co-heir, ux. Humphrey Lloyd
heiress of | dleton of   heir, ux.   of Bers, Attorney, and one of
Plas Cad- | Gwannynog   Ellis Mare-   the Council for the Court of the
wgan. | ab John ab   dydd of Pen- Marches; son of Gruffydd ab
           | William   tref Bychan. Richard, illegitimate son of
           | Myddleton.   Lewys ab David Lloyd, of Bod-
                                        lith; living 28th Oct. 1641.

a

Timothy Myddleton of ⊤ Anne, d. and heiress of — Cooke? of Stepney,
Plâs Cadwgan, 1660. | near London, merchant. She married secondly,
He bought Pant Iocyn. | Sir Thomas Powel of Plâs yn Horsli, Bart.

Anne, only child, heiress of Plâs ⊤ John Robinson of Gwersyllt, High Sheriff
Cadwgan and Pant Iocyn. | for co. Denbigh, 1690, M.P. for co. Den-
bigh, 1705-1707.

John Robinson of Gwersyllt, Plas Cadwgan, = Elizabeth,   William.
Pant Iocyn and Acton. Married 1708. His   eldest daughter
trustees sold Pant Iocyn and Acton to Ellis   and heiress of
Yonge of Bryn Iorcyn, and in 1783 these   Sir Gruffydd
estates were purchased from Mr. Yonge's   Jeffreys of
trustees, by Sir Foster Cunliffe, Bart.   Acton.

ROBERTS OF HAFOD Y BWCH.

Harl. MS. 4181.

David ab Bady or Madog ab David Goch ab Gruffydd of Croes Foel ab ⊤
Iorwerth Fychan ab Iorwerth ab Ieuaf ab Niniaf ab Cynwrig ab Rhiwallon. *Ermine*, a lion rampant, *sable*.

Gruffydd ⊤ Margaret, dau. and co-heir of Ieuan Fychan ab   Deicws of
of | Ieuan ab Howel y Gadair of Cadair Benllyn,   Llanerch
Croes | ab Gruffydd ab Madog ab Iorwerth ab Madog   Rugog.
Foel. | Rhirid Flaidd, Lord of Penllyn. *Vert*, a chev.,
inter three wolf's heads erased, *argent*, langued *gules*.

David of ⊤ Margaret, dau. and co-heir of Madog ab Llywelyn ab Ednyfed
Croes | ab Gruffydd ab Einion Goch of Sonlli. *Ermine*, a lion ram-
Foel. | pant, *sable*.

Robert ⊤ Margaret, dau. and heiress of Howel ab Ieuan, second   Matthew.
of | son of Robert ab Gruffydd ab Howel ab Gruffydd of
Croes | Croes Foel ab Iorwerth Fychan ab Iorwerth ab
Foel. | Ieuaf ab Niniaf ab Cynwrig ab Rhiwallon. See p. 39.

b

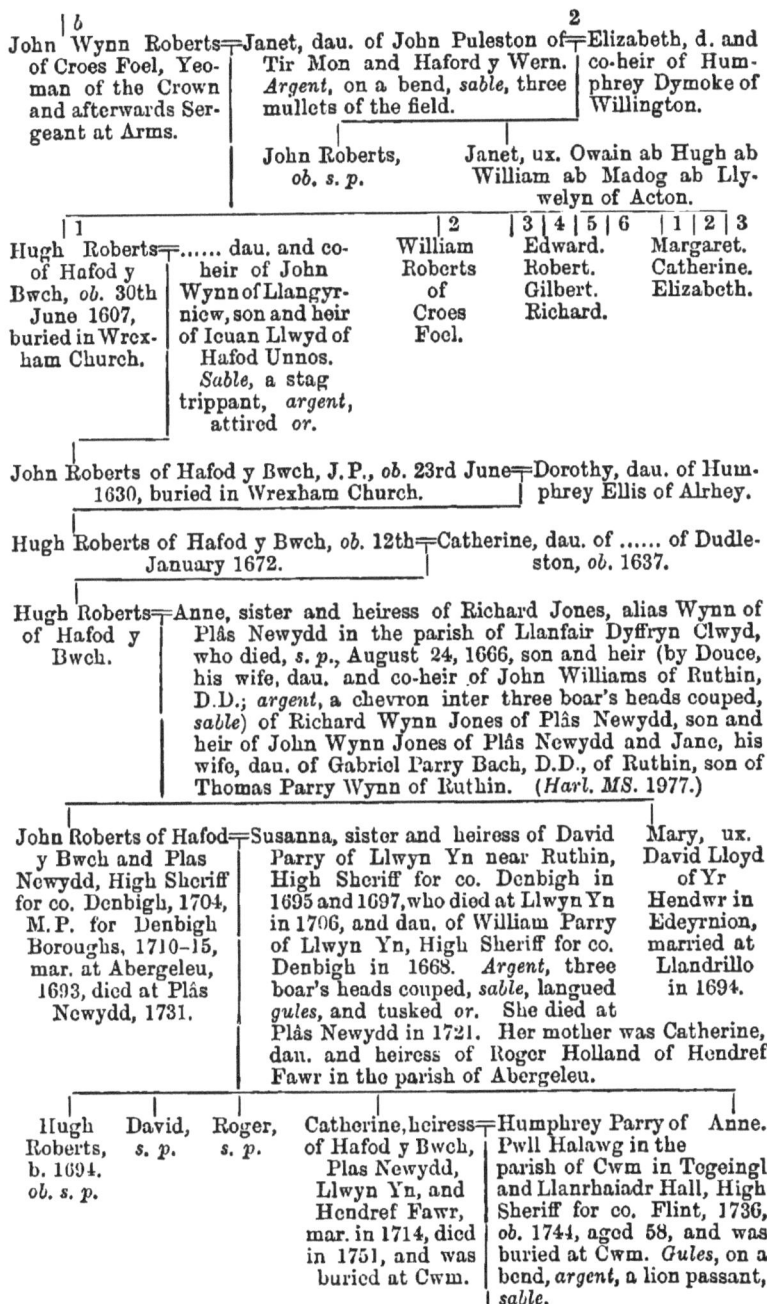

b		2
John Wynn Roberts=Janet, dau. of John Puleston of=Elizabeth, d. and		
of Croes Foel, Yeo- | Tir Mon and Haford y Wern. | co-heir of Hum-		
man of the Crown | *Argent*, on a bend, *sable*, three | phrey Dymoke of		
and afterwards Ser- | mullets of the field. | Willington.		
geant at Arms.		

John Roberts,　　　　Janet, ux. Owain ab Hugh ab
ob. s. p.　　　　　William ab Madog ab Lly-
　　　　　　　　　welyn of Acton.

1		2	3 | 4 | 5 | 6	1 | 2 | 3
Hugh Roberts=...... dau. and co-	William	Edward.	Margaret.
of Hafod y | heir of John	Roberts	Robert.	Catherine.
Bwch, *ob.* 30th | Wynn of Llangyr-	of	Gilbert.	Elizabeth.
June 1607, | niew, son and heir	Croes	Richard.	
buried in Wrex- | of Icuan Llwyd of	Foel.		
ham Church. | Hafod Unnos.			
| *Sable*, a stag			
| trippant, *argent*,			
| attired *or*.			

John Roberts of Hafod y Bwch, J.P., *ob.* 23rd June=Dorothy, dau. of Hum-
1630, buried in Wrexham Church.　　　　　| phrey Ellis of Alrhey.

Hugh Roberts of Hafod y Bwch, *ob.* 12th=Catherine, dau. of ...... of Dudle-
January 1672.　　　　　　　　　| ston, *ob.* 1637.

Hugh Roberts=Anne, sister and heiress of Richard Jones, alias Wynn of
of Hafod y \| Plâs Newydd in the parish of Llanfair Dyffryn Clwyd,
Bwch. \| who died, *s. p.*, August 24, 1666, son and heir (by Douce,
\| his wife, dau. and co-heir of John Williams of Ruthin,
\| D.D.; *argent*, a chevron inter three boar's heads couped,
\| *sable*) of Richard Wynn Jones of Plâs Newydd, son and
\| heir of John Wynn Jones of Plâs Newydd and Jane, his
\| wife, dau. of Gabriel Parry Bach, D.D., of Ruthin, son of
\| Thomas Parry Wynn of Ruthin. (*Harl. MS.* 1977.)

John Roberts of Hafod=Susanna, sister and heiress of David	Mary, ux.
y Bwch and Plas | Parry of Llwyn Yn near Ruthin,	David Lloyd
Newydd, High Sheriff | High Sheriff for co. Denbigh in	of Yr
for co. Denbigh, 1704, | 1695 and 1697, who died at Llwyn Yn	Hendwr in
M.P. for Denbigh | in 1706, and dau. of William Parry	Edeyrnion,
Boroughs, 1710–15, | of Llwyn Yn, High Sheriff for co.	married at
mar. at Abergeleu, | Denbigh in 1668. *Argent*, three	Llandrillo
1693, died at Plâs | boar's heads couped, *sable*, langued	in 1694.
Newydd, 1731. | *gules*, and tusked *or*. She died at	
| Plâs Newydd in 1721. Her mother was Catherine,	
| dau. and heiress of Roger Holland of Hendref	
| Fawr in the parish of Abergeleu.	

Hugh	David,	Roger,	Catherine, heiress=Humphrey Parry of	Anne.
Roberts,	*s. p.*	*s. p.*	of Hafod y Bwch, | Pwll Halawg in the	
b. 1694.			Plas Newydd, | parish of Cwm in Tegeingl	
ob. s. p.			Llwyn Yn, and | and Llanrhaiadr Hall, High	
			Hendref Fawr, | Sheriff for co. Flint, 1736,	
			mar. in 1714, died | *ob.* 1744, aged 58, and was	
			in 1751, and was | buried at Cwm. *Gules*, on a	
			buried at Cwm. | bend, *argent*, a lion passant,	
				sable.	

| *c*

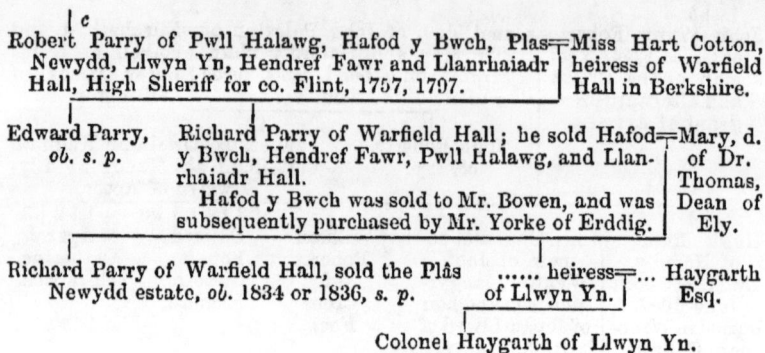

c

Robert Parry of Pwll Halawg, Hafod y Bwch, Plas=Miss Hart Cotton,
Newydd, Llwyn Yn, Hendref Fawr and Llanrhaiadr | heiress of Warfield
Hall, High Sheriff for co. Flint, 1757, 1797. | Hall in Berkshire.

Edward Parry,   Richard Parry of Warfield Hall; he sold Hafod=Mary, d.
ob. s. p.   y Bwch, Hendref Fawr, Pwll Halawg, and Llan- | of Dr.
     rhaiadr Hall.   Thomas,
     Hafod y Bwch was sold to Mr. Bowen, and was | Dean of
     subsequently purchased by Mr. Yorke of Erddig. | Ely.

Richard Parry of Warfield Hall, sold the Plâs   ...... heiress=... Haygarth
Newydd estate, ob. 1834 or 1836, s. p.   of Llwyn Yn. | Esq.

Colonel Haygarth of Llwyn Yn.

HAFOD UNNOS AND LLANGERNIEW.

Harl. MS. 2288.

Bleddyn Llwyd Hên ab Bleddyn Fychan ab Bleddyn ab Y Gwion ab Rad-=
vach ab Asar ab Gwrgi ab Hedd Moelwyog, one of the Fifteen Noble |
Tribes of Gwynedd. *Sable*, a stag *argent*, attired *or*.

2		1

Cynwrig ab Bleddyn of Hafod Unnos, in the=   Meurig Llwyd of Llwyn y
parish of Llangerniw. | Maen.

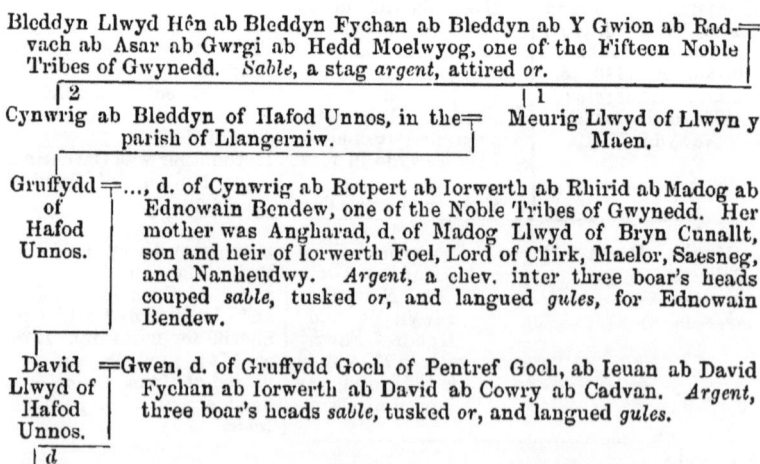

Gruffydd =..., d. of Cynwrig ab Rotpert ab Iorwerth ab Rhirid ab Madog ab
of | Ednowain Bendew, one of the Noble Tribes of Gwynedd. Her
Hafod | mother was Angharad, d. of Madog Llwyd of Bryn Cunallt,
Unnos. | son and heir of Iorwerth Foel, Lord of Chirk, Maelor, Saesneg,
     and Nanheudwy. *Argent*, a chev. inter three boar's heads
     couped *sable*, tusked *or*, and langued *gules*, for Ednowain
     Bendew.

David =Gwen, d. of Gruffydd Goch of Pentref Goch, ab Ieuan ab David
Llwyd of | Fychan ab Iorwerth ab David ab Cowry ab Cadvan. *Argent*,
Hafod | three boar's heads *sable*, tusked *or*, and langued *gules*.
Unnos. |

d

| d

Mared- =Morfydd, d. of Howel ab Rhys Gethin of Hendref Rhys Gethin,
ydd of | in the parish of Bettws Wyrion Iddon, or Bettws y Coed, ab
Hafod | Gruffydd Fychan ab Gruffydd[1] ab David Goch of Nant Conwy,
Unnos. | illegitimate son of David, Lord of Denbigh, son of Gruffudd ab
| Llywelyn ab Iorwerth Drwyn Dwn, Prince of Wales. *Sable,*
| a lion rampt. *argent,* in a border engrailed *or,* for David Goch
| of Nant Conwy.

David of =Mallt, d. and co-heir of Gruffydd ab Madog ab Llywelyn Fychan
Hafod | of Llwyn Dyrus in Lleyn, ab Gruffydd ab Ieuan ab Sir Gruffydd
Unnos. | Llwyd of Tref Garnedd and Tref Nant Bychan in Môn, Knt.
| *Gules,* a chief *ermine,* and chevron *or.*

| 1 | 2
Lowri, d. of Howel=Ieuan Llwyd[2] of Hafod Unnos.=Alice, d. of Robert ab
ab David ab Meu- : | John ab Meurig.
rig ab Howel Selyf,
Lord of Nannau. | 6 | 7
Or, a lion rampt. Henri, of Hafod=Jane, d. and co-heir of Ieuan,
azure. Her mother   Unnos. | Roger ab Howel ab   *ob. s.p.*
was Elen, d. of | Rhys ab Maredydd.
Robert Salusbury Roger Lloyd, an-   *Gules,* a lion rampt.
of Llanrwst.   cestor of the   *argent.*
                   Lloyds of Hafod
                   Unnos.
                   | 8
                   Geoffrey Lloyd of Dyff- Mallt, ux. John ab Rhys
                   ryn Erethlyn, Bard   Wynn of Ffynogion in Llan-
                   and Antiquary, an-   fair Dyffryn Clwyd. *Gules,*
                   cestor of the Lloyds   a chev. inter three stag's
                   of Palau.   heads cabossed *argent.*

e | f | g | h | i :

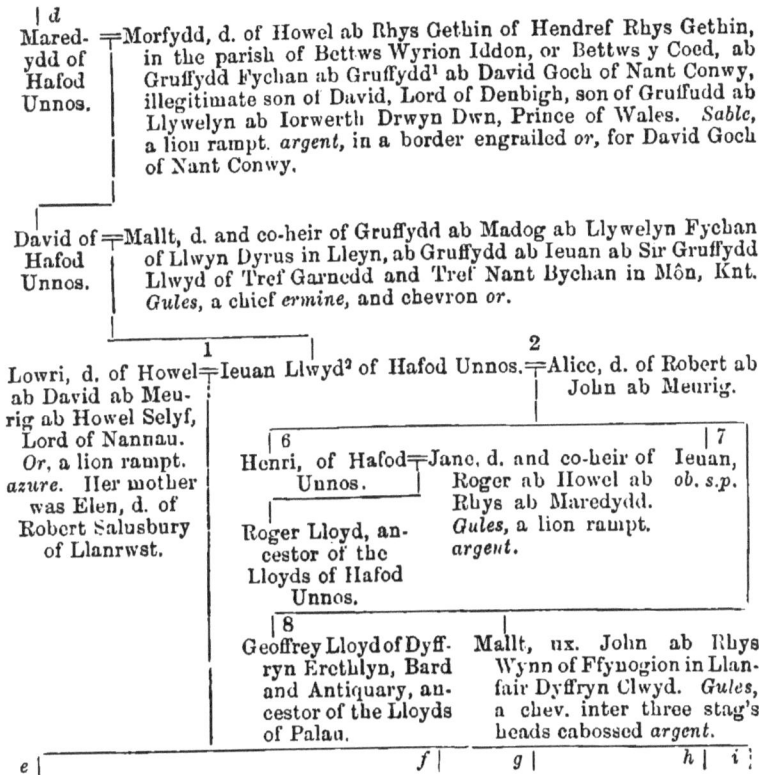

[1] Gruffydd ab David Goch is at Bettws y Coed, where his effigy is
still to be seen recumbent, in armour, with the following inscription :
"HIC IACET GRUFUD AP DAVID GOCH. AGNUS DEI MISERERE MEI." A
full description of this tomb has been given by Mr. Bloxham, *Arch.
Cambr.,* 1874, p. 128. It appears, from the Extent of Nant Conwy,
in the *Record of Caernarvon,* or *Great Extent of North Wales,* as it is
also called, taken on the next Monday after the translation of St.
Thomas the Martyr, 26th Edward III (1352), that Gruffydd was the
foreman of the jury for taking that Extent. David Goch, his father,
was a natural son of David, Lord of Denbigh, who was tried at
Shrewsbury, and brutally murdered by Edward I, the King of the
English in 1283. See p. 33.

[2] Besides these five sons enumerated above, Ieuan Llwyd had six
daughters :—1. Mallt, ux. Robert ab Richard ab Maredydd ; 2. Annesta, ux. Robert ab Maredydd ; 3. Elizabeth, ux. John Wynn Salusbury of Ruthin, son of Parson Ffoulk Salusbury, third son of Piers
Salusbury of Rûg and Bachymbyd ; 4. Gwenhwyfar, ux. John Panton,
ob. s. p. ; and 6. Catherine, ux. Humphrey ab Thomas.

e | 1
John Lloyd = Catherine, d. of Mare-
of Llan-   dydd ab Goronwy ab
gerniw,   Gruffydd Gethin[1] of
ob. v.   Dyffryn Aled in Llan-
patris.   sannan.

f | 2
Hugh
Lloyd.

g | 3
William Lloyd,
ancestor of the
Lloyds of Erw
Gwyddel.[2]

h | 4 i |
David
Lloyd,
Vicar of
Llanger-
niw.

| 5
Richard Lloyd, jure = Agnes, d. and heiress of John ab
uxoris of Bach   Gruffydd Llwyd of Bach Eirig, in
Eirig.[3]   Llanfair Dyffryn Clwyd.

Alice, co-heir,
ux. Robert
Vaughan ab
Richard of
Llanfair.

Jane, ux. John
ab David
Llwyd ab John
of Llangwm.

Catherine, ux.
John ab Howel
Fychan of Y Per-
kin in Eivionydd;
descended from
Collwyn ab
Tangno.

Elen, ux.
William ab
Richard
of Plas
Isaf.

Lowri, ux.
Hugh
Roberts of
Hafod y
Bwch.

TREF RHUDDIN AND LLWYN YN.
Harl. MSS. 2299, 4181.

David Fychan of Ceinmarch, ab David ab Iorwerth ab David of Ceinmarch, ab Cowryd ab Cadvan, Lord of Ceinmarch (Gwehelaeth Ceinmarch), ab Gaelawg Gawr ab Iddig, lineally descended from Cadell
Deyrnllwg, King of Powys. *Argent*, three boar's heads couped, *sable*,
tusked *or*, and langued *gules*, for Cowryd ab Cadvan. See *Archæologia
Cambrensis*, July 1876, p. 170.

| j

---

[1] Gruffydd Gethin ab David Llwyd ab Ednyfed ab Tudor ab
Dwywg ab Gwilym ab Rhys ab Edryd ab Enathan ab Siaffeth ab
Carwed ab Marchudd Lord of Uwch Dulas, Abergeleu, and Bryn
Ffanigl, Chief of one of the Noble Tribes. *Gules*, a Saracen's head
erased proper, environed about the temples with a wreath *argent* and
gules. He was the ancestor of Piers Wynn of Dyffryn Aled, whose
daughter and heiress, Diana, built the present mansion, and was the
mother of Piers Wynn Yorke of Dyffryn Aled.

[2] See *Archæologia Cambrensis*, January 1877, p. 35, note.

[3] *Ibid.*, January 1877.

j

Ieuan of⸗Eva, dau. of Madog ab Gruffydd, or, according to others, Eva,
Cein-   dau. of David ab Philip Goch of Faenor in Aber Rhiew in
march.   Cydewaen, ab Howel ab Llywelyn ab Meilir Grûg, Lord of Tref
             Gynon and Westbury. *Sable*, three horse's heads erased,
             argent.

Gruffydd Goch of Pentref Goch near⸗Gwladys or Mallt, dau. of Ieuan ab
Rhuddin. He built the Church of | Llywelyn ab Gruffydd Llwyd of
Gyffylliog, in the Comot of Llan- | Bodidris yn Iâl. Her mother was
erch as a Chapel-of-case to Llan- | Malli, dau. of Tudor ab Gruffydd
ynys. | Llwyd ab Heilin Frych of Berain
                                   | in Llanefydd.

Sir John, Parson of Llanynys.⸗Margaret, dau. of Cynwrig ab Einion
                               Gethin.

Harri of Tref Rhuddin.⸗Janet, dau. of Richard ab Jenkyn ab Gruffydd
                        ab Rhys.

John ab Harri of⸗Janet, dau. of Edward Thelwall ab Eubule Thelwall,
Tref Rhuddin.   of Plas y Ward.

1		2	3	4

Thomas Parry Wynn[1]⸗Margaret, dau. of | Richard ⸗Margaret, | Harri
of Tref Rhuddin. He | John Gruffydd of | Parry   d. of John | Parry.
married, first, Mar- | Chichli in Tin- | of Tref Pryse of | John
garet, dau. of John ab | daethwy, son of | Rhuddin. Derwen. | Llwyd
Harri Gervys ab John | Sir William | *Argent*, | Wynn.
Gervys ab Gerard | Griffith of Pen- | six bees |
Goch of Tref Rhuddin, | rhyn, Knight. | ppr. 3, 2, 1. |
Esq., who bore, *sable*, | | |
an arming sword, | | |
argent, hilt and pomel | John Parry Wynn = Elizabeth, d. of John Wynn
or, a buckle of the | of Llanbedr.   Ffoulkes of Eriviad. *Gules*,
second. She died *s. p.* | three boar's heads erased in
                      | pale *argent*, first wife *ob.* May
                      | 5, 1622. buried at Rhuddin.

k		*l*		*m*

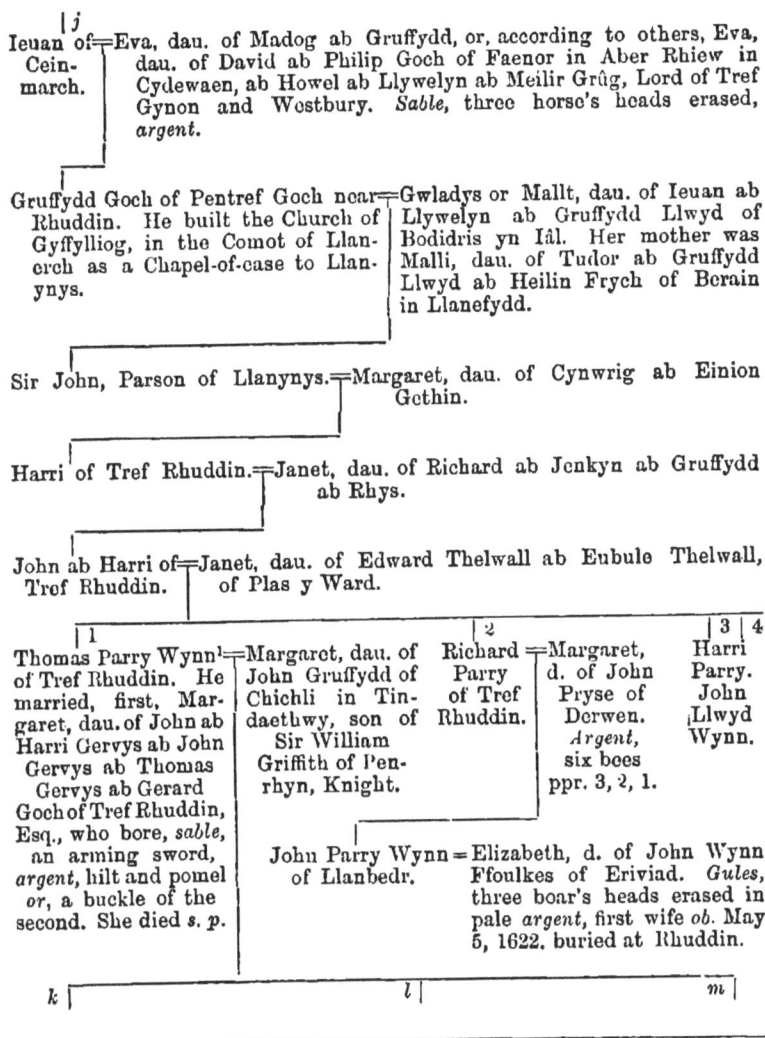

[1] Thomas Parry Wynn had issue by his second wife, besides the
three sons mentioned above, three daughters: 1. Elizabeth, ux.
Richard Langford of Trefalun and Tref Rhuddin, High Sheriff for co.
Denbigh in 1640. She died at Chester, 12th December 1657, and
was buried at Gresford, aged 78 years, having had twenty children.
2. Dorothy, ux. Robert Lloyd ab Richard Lloyd of Bach Eirig, in the
parish of Llanfair Dyffryn Clwyd, fifth son of Ieuan Llwyd of Hafod
Unnos; and 3. Grace, ux. Piers Mul of Rhuddin. *Sable*, two lions
rampant in fess *argent*.

k | 1

Simon Parry of⸺Jane, dau.
Gray'sInn,Barris- | of John
ter-at-Law. He | Thelwall of
bought Pont y | Llanrhudd.
Gof or Nantclwyd |
from Peter Ellis. |
Ob. July 7, 1627.

Thomas⸺Grace, dau. of Robert
Parry of | Lloyd a.b Edward
Pont y | Lloyd of Plas is y
Gof. | Clawdd yn Y Waun.

l | 2

Gabriel Parry Bach,⸺Mary, eldest
D.D., Head Mas- | daughter of
ter of Ruthin | Edward Pryse
School, 1607; S.R. | of Llwyn
Llanrhaiadr in | Yn, High
Mochnant, 1608; | Sheriff for
Vicar of Henllan, | co. Denbigh,
1609; V. of Aber- | 1627, and
geleu, 1613; S.R. | co-heir of
Llansannan,1616; | her brother
S.R. Llansant- | John Pryse
ffraid yn | of Llwyn
Mechain, 1617; | Yn.
R. Llangynhafal
and Precentor
of Bangor, 1632.

m | 3

Daniel
Parry.

William Parry of Pont y Gof or⸺Martha, d. of Simon
Nant Clwyd.[1] | Thelwall of theCourt
| of Arches, and son
Mary, ux. Eubule Thelwall, | of John Wynn Thel-
Barrister of Gray's Inn. | wall of Llanrhudd.

William Parry of⸺Catherine, dau. and heiress of Roger   Jane, ux. John
Llwyn Yn and | Holland of Hendref Fawr in the Parish   Wynn Jones of
Llanrhudd, High | of Abergelen, High Sheriff for co.   Plâs Newydd
Sheriff for co. | Denbigh in 1634, son and heir of Daniel   in Llanfair
Denbigh, 1668, | Holland of Henref Fawr. She died in   Dyffryn
married 1643. | 1705, and was buried in Abergelen   Clwyd.
| church, where a monument is erected
| to her memory. *Azure*, semé of fleur-
| de-lys, a lion rampant gardant, *argent*.

David Parry of Llwyn   Susanna, heiress of Llywn Yn and Hendref Fawr;
Yn, High Sheriff for   married, in 1693, John Roberts of Hafod y Bwch,
co.Denbigh in 1695 and   and Plâs Newydd. She died at Plâs Newydd
1697; *ob.* at Llyn Yn,   in the parish of Llanfair Duffryn Clwyd in
1706, *s. p.*   1721.

---

[1] His daughter and heiress, Mary, married Eubule Thelwall, the second son of John Thelwall of Bathafarn Park and Plâs Coch in the parish of Llanrhudd, by whom she had a son and heir, Thomas Thelwall of Nantclwyd, the father of Eubule Thelwall of Nantclwyd, whose daughter and heiress, Martha, married Andrew Kenrick of Woor Manor in Shropshire, Esq., ancestor of the Kenricks of Nantclwyd and Mertyn.

LLWYN YN IN THE TOWNSHIP OF TREF EYARTH IN LLANFAIR DYFFRYN CLWYD.

Harl. MS. 1969

Edwin, ab Goronwy, Prince of Tegeingl. *Argent*, a cross flory engrailed *sable*, inter four Cornish choughs ppr. Slain 1073. = Ewerydd, sister of Bleddyn ab Cynfyn, Prince of Powys, and dau. of Cynfyn ab Gwrystan ab Gwaethfoed. *Vert*, a lion rampant, *argent*, head, feet, and tail, embrued, for Gwrystan, Lord of Powys.

Owain ab Edwin, Prince of Tegeingl, elected Prince of North Wales in 1096. Died of consumption in 1103. *Gules*, three men's legs conjoined at the thighs, in triangle, *argent*. = Morfydd, dau. of Goronwy, son of Ednowain Bendew, of Llys Coed y Mynydd in Bodvari, Chief of one of the Noble Tribes. *Argent*, a chevron inter three boar's heads, *sable*, tusked *or*, and langued *gules*.

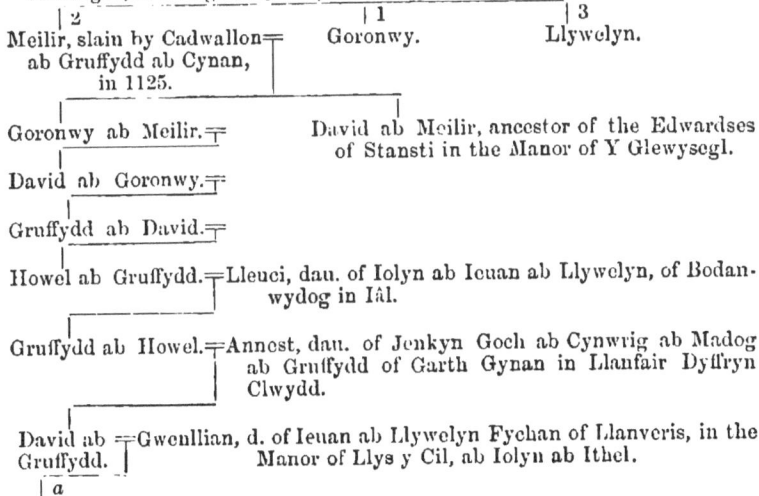

| 2 Meilir, slain by Cadwallon ab Gruffydd ab Cynan, in 1125. = | 1 Goronwy. | 3 Llywelyn. |

Goronwy ab Meilir. =   David ab Meilir, ancestor of the Edwardses of Stansti in the Manor of Y Glewysegl.

David ab Goronwy. =

Gruffydd ab David. =

Howel ab Gruffydd. = Lleuci, dau. of Iolyn ab Ieuan ab Llywelyn, of Bodanwydog in Iâl.

Gruffydd ab Howel. = Annest, dau. of Jenkyn Goch ab Cynwrig ab Madog ab Gruffydd of Garth Gynan in Llanfair Dyffryn Clwydd.

David ab Gruffydd. = Gwenllian, d. of Ieuan ab Llywelyn Fychan of Llanveris, in the Manor of Llys y Cil, ab Iolyn ab Ithel.

| a

| a

John Wynn. ⊤ Janet, d. and co-heir of David ab Gruffydd, one of the sons of Ieuan ab David ab Cynwrig ab Ieuan ab Gruffydd ab Madog Ddu of Copa'r Golenni in Tegeingl, ab Rhirid ab Llywelyn ab Owain ab Edwyn ab Goronwy. Palii of six pieces, *argent* and *sable*, for Madog Ddû.

| Rhys. He bore his mother's coat of arms in the first quarter instead of his father's. See *Lewys Dwnn*, vol. ii, p. 349, "Y Kaerddinog". ⊤ Elizabeth, d. of Piers Salisbury of Bachymbyd, and also of Rûg, in right of his wife, Margaret Wen, daughter and sole heir of Ieuan ab Howel ab Rhys ab David, Lord of Rûg. | Edward, married Margaret, d. of Gruffydd ab Twna of Tref Eyarth. | Lowri. She married first, Jenkyn ab Elis; and secondly, William ab Madog Goch of Fron Deg, near Wrexham. |

John ab Rhys of Caerddinog or Caerddineu. ⊤ Mary, d. of the Baron Lewys ab Owain of Cwrt Plâs yn Dref, Dolgellau, who was murdered at Dugoed Mawddwy, 11th Oct. 1555.

| 1

Edward Pryse of Llwyn Yn, High Sheriff for co. Denbigh in 1627. ⊤ Susan,[1] sister of Godfrey Goodman, D.D., Bishop of Gloucester, and d. of Godfrey Goodman, third son of Edward Goodman ab Thomas ab Edward ab Thomas ab Edward ab John Goodman of Rhuddin. Party per pale *ermine* and *erminois*, an eagle displayed with two heads *or*, on a canton *azure*, a martlet of the third. | 2 | 3 | 4 Rhys. John. Thomas. | Annest, ux. Robert ab Morgan ab Robert ab Morgan of Llanaber. |

| Gwen, ux. Richard Parry, D.D., Bishop of St. Asaph. | Joan, ux. Hugh Jones. | Jane, ux. John Davies, D.D., Vicar of Mallwyd, author of the Welsh Dictionary. He was a native of the parish of Llanveris. | Catherine, ux. Evan Morgan, B.D., Parson of Llanveris, 1616. | Margaret, *ob. s. p.* |

| John Pryse of Llwyn Yn, *ob. s. p.* ⊤ Elen, d. of Thomas Goodman, Esq. | Mary, heiress of Llwyn Yn, ux. Gabriel Parry Bach, D.D. | Anne. She was the 2nd wife of Charles Goodman[2] of Glanhespin, High Sheriff for co. Denbigh in 1666, who died 14th August 1693. Anne died 8th December 1684. | Martha, ux. Richard Yonge of Bryn Iorcyn. She died Dec. 18, 1654, and was buried at Corwen. |

[1] Susan was the niece of Gabriel Goodman, D.D., Dean of Westminster, the founder of Christ's Hospital and the Grammar School at Ruthin.—See *Hist. of the Diocese of St. Asaph.*

[2] Charles Goodman married first, Rebecca, daughter of Richard Langford of Trefalun, High Sheriff for co. Denbigh in 1640, by whom he had a daughter and heiress, Penelope, who was married to John Lloyd of Drefnewydd, co. Salop. Charles was a younger son of

HOLLAND OF HENDREF FAWR, IN THE PARISH OF ABERGELEU.

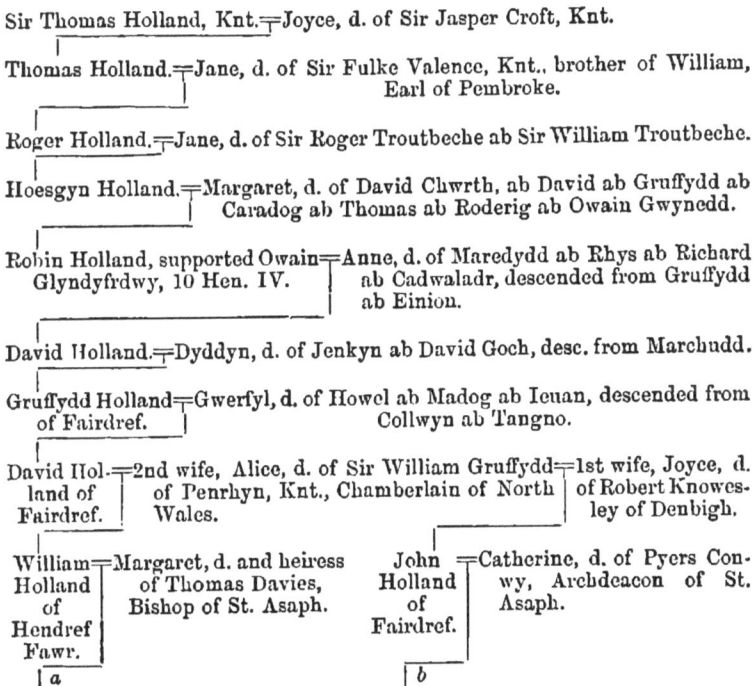

Sir Thomas Holland, Knt.=Joyce, d. of Sir Jasper Croft, Knt.

Thomas Holland.=Jane, d. of Sir Fulke Valence, Knt., brother of William, Earl of Pembroke.

Roger Holland.=Jane, d. of Sir Roger Troutbeche ab Sir William Troutbeche.

Hoesgyn Holland.=Margaret, d. of David Chwrth, ab David ab Gruffydd ab Caradog ab Thomas ab Roderig ab Owain Gwynedd.

Robin Holland, supported Owain=Anne, d. of Maredydd ab Rhys ab Richard Glyndyfrdwy, 10 Hen. IV. | ab Cadwaladr, descended from Gruffydd ab Einion.

David Holland.=Dyddyn, d. of Jenkyn ab David Goch, desc. from Marchudd.

Gruffydd Holland=Gwerfyl, d. of Howel ab Madog ab Ieuan, descended from of Fairdref. | Collwyn ab Tangno.

David Hol-=2nd wife, Alice, d. of Sir William Gruffydd=1st wife, Joyce, d. land of | of Penrhyn, Knt., Chamberlain of North | of Robert Knowes- Fairdref. | Wales. | ley of Denbigh.

William=Margaret, d. and heiress　　John　=Catherine, d. of Pyers Con-
Holland | of Thomas Davies,　　Holland | wy, Archdeacon of St.
of | Bishop of St. Asaph.　　　of | Asaph.
Hendref | 　　　　　　　　　　　Fairdref. |
Fawr. |
| a 　　　　　　　　　　　　　　| b

Thomas Goodman of Plâs Uchaf in Llanfair Dyffryn Clwyd, High Sheriff for co. Denbigh in 1613, who died in 1623, second son of Gawen Goodman ab Edward ab Thomas ab Edward ab Thomas ab Edward ab John Goodman of Rhuddin. By his second wife, Anne, Charles Goodman had issue a daughter and co-heiress, Susan, who married Gabriel Goodman of Rhuddin, a lawyer, son of Edward Goodman ab Gabriel Goodman ab Edward, eldest son of Gawen Goodman of Rhuddin.

a	
Pyers Holland ⊤ Sioned, d. of	
of Hendref ⏐ Holland.	
Fawr. ⏐	

Daniel Holland of ⊤ Elizabeth, d. of
Hendref Fawr. ⏐ Maurice Kyffin.

Roger Holland of Hendref Fawr, High ⊤ Jane, d. of Richard Parry, Bishop
Sheriff for co. Denbigh 1634. *Ob.* ⏐ of St. Asaph; buried at Abergeleu,
1642, and buried at Abergele. ⏐ 1641.—*Harl. MS.* 2180.

Catherine, heiress of = William Parry   Roger, *ob. s. p.*   Anne, ux. Richard
Hendref Fawr, *ob.*   of Llwyn Yn.   *Harl. MS.* 2180.   Parry of Coed Mar-
1700.   chan.—*Harl. MS.*
                                                                            2180.

b	
Pyers ⊤ Catherine, d. and heiress of	
Holland ⏐ Richard ab Ieuan ab David	
of Kin- ⏐ ab Ithel Fychan, by Alice,	
mael. ⏐ d. and heiress of Gruffydd	
ob. 1552. ⏐ Lloyd of Kinmael.	

David Holland   Humphrey Holland
of Kinmael.   of Teirdan, *ob.* 1612.

COM. DENBIGH, MANERIU' DE EGLVISEGLE.

Harl. 3696, *fo.* 223, *et seq.*

NOMINA JURATORU'.

Edwardus ap d'd lloyd.   Edwardus ap d'd ap Edw'.
Gr. ap John ap Edward.   Will'mus Erthig.
Hugh Gwyn ap Jo. Rob't.   Griffith ap Hugh.
Johannes ap Edward.   Robertus Griffith.
Will'us david Madock.   Johannes Broughton.
David ap John ap Ma'd'd.   Johannes Lloyd.
Johannes Bromfield.

To the first article they say they are altogether ignorant touchinge the boundes of the said mannor, for that it is inter-mixt in and amongst other mannors.

To the second they say they have no demesnes within the said mannor.

To the third article they referre themselves to their booke of entries both for landes and rents (except Mr. Jenkyn Lloyd), whose lands and rents are to them unknown. And as for fee-fermors within ye said mannor there are none to their knowledge.

To the fourth article they likewise referre themselves to their bookes of entries both for lands and rents.

To the fift article, as touchinge custumary tennantes, they have none but such as holde by lease.

To the sixt article as touching their commons, they are enter commons with other mannors within the Lordshipp of

Bromfield in a common called Myndd vcha, as for ye quantity they are not able to express it.

To the seaventh article they say they have no woode w'in that mannor, onlie vpon their ffreeholdes.

To the eight article they say they have no parke w'in the mannor, nor never had to their knowledge.

To the ninth article, as touching incrochements, they say they have none to their knowledge.

To the tenth article they p'sent that they have no copie or customarie landes within that mannor, but they are helde from fortie yeares to fortie yeares, and they are els where sett downe.

To the eleaventh article as touching quarries of stone they have but vpon their freeholdes. As for mynes of cole and leade they are graunted in lease vnto S'r Richard Grosvenor, knight; and as for chalke or marle they haue none.

To the twelveth article they say that they have no ffree-holdes that hath died without heire generall or speciall within that manor to their knowledge.

To the 13th article they say they have no towne corporate, etc.

To the 14th article they knowe none yt have exchaunged copie or leased landes for free to their knowledges.

To the fifteenth they say that they have no customarie mill within yt mannor.

To the sixteenth article they say that they have within that mannor vppon the high moore, peate, turfe, furse, and ffearne. And that the ffreeholders and leaseholders have them for their several uses, not paying anything for them, or ever did to their knowledge.

To the seaventeenth article they say that they have no viewe of ffranckpledge, leete, or lewsday, within that mannor, but they are to doe their service both at leete and Court Baron, vizt., at the Court leete twice in ye yeare, where it shall please ye Steward to appoint it; and at the Court Baron as often as they are required. As for com'on ffyne, etc., they pay none.

To the eighteenth article they say they knowe of noo howses that are fallen downe or decayed.

To the nyneteenth article they say that for ought they knowe or hath hearde, the Prince hath all waifes, estraies, etc., within that mannor.

To the twentieth article wee say that they have no ffishing, etc.

To the one and twentieth article they say that they have neither markett nor ffaires.

To the twoe and twentieth they knowe of none.

To the three and twentieth article they pay nothing to any other manor.

To the twenty ffowreth article they say they have onely a baylie to receave ye Princes rents, by whose appointm't is to vs vnknowne.

To the ffyve and twentith article they can say nothing.

To the six and twentith article they have the pole or perch to the custom of ye countrie.

LIBERI TENENTES.	ACRES.		£ s. d.
Allington, John (Jo' Randall and heirs to pay the rent) . . .	3 0	...	no rent given
Bady, Owen . . .	72 0	...	0 15 0
Bellot, Edward . . .	12 0	...	0 2 4
Bromfield, Edward . . .	50 0	...	0 8 10
David, John . . .	6 0	...	0 0 6
Davies, Edward (Rob't Lloyd de Ruabon).	20 0	...	0 10 0½
Davies, Richard . .	120 0	...	0 12 2
Davies, Rob't . . .	6 0	...	0 0 12
Edward ap John Mathew . .	8 0	...	0 0 10
Edward ap Richard Phillip .	8 2	...	0 1 5
Edward ap William . .	15 0	...	0 1 9
Edwards, Ralph and John .	39 0	...	0 3 0
Erthig, William . .	50 0	...	0 5 6
Goodman, Gabriell . .	38 0	...	3 3 8
Griffith ap Hugh . .	64 0	...	0 3 8
Griffith, Robert . .	60 0	...	0 5 3
Griffith, Robert, of Brimbo .	10 0	...	0 1 0
Griffith, Roger, of Eyton .	3 0	...	0 0 4
Howell ap Edward . .	5 0	...	0 1 4
Howell ap Howell . .	2 0	...	0 0 6
Hugh ap Robert . .	5 0	...	0 1 6
Hughes, Richard, heres .	290 0	...	0 16 0
Hughes, Thomas . .	4 0	...	0 0 2
John ap Hugh ap Edward .	10 0	...	0 2 0
John ap John ap Edward .	30 0	...	0 0 10
John ap John d'd Lloyd .	not given.	...	0 1 2
John ap John ap John llc'n .	12 0	...	0 0 5
John ap John Madock .	10 0	...	0 0 8
John ap Richard ap llc'n .	1 2	...	0 0 2
John David ap John Thomas .	8 0	...	0 2 0
Jones, Emanuell . .	4 0	...	0 2 4
Jones, Michaell et Katherine, vid' .	3 0	...	0 0 10
Jones, Owin (late the lands of Ieuan D'd)	24 0	...	0 1 8
Jones, Roger . .	4 0	...	0 1 4
Lewis, John and D'd (late the lands of Edward ap Randall) .	36 0	...	0 2 4

	ACRES.	£	s.	d.
Lloyd, D'd	43 0 ...	1	4	5
Lloyd, Gabriell, esq. .	257 0 ...	1	7	8
Lloyd, Robert	343 0 ...	1	6	10
Lloyd, Thomas	160 1 ...	0	6	7
Mathew, D'd	4 0 ...	0	0	1
Mathewes, Griff'	22 0 ...	0	1	0
Mereddeth, Edward .	1 0 ...	0	0	1
Mereddeth, Hugh	30 0 ...	0	2	3
Mereddeth, W'm, esq.	286 0 ...	2	8	0
Pate, Thomas	3 0 ...	0	1	6
Powell, Thomas	7 0 ...	0	3	8
Puleston, Edw', esq. .	30 0 ...	0	3	2
Randle ap Ellis de Knowlton (heres)	8 0 ...	0	1	8
Randle, John, jun'r .	8 0 ...	0	0	2
Randle, John, sen'r .	8 0 ...	0	0	10
Robinson, Will'm, esq.	32 2 ..	0	12	1½
Salsbury, Roger, esq.	30 0 ...	0	6	8
Soulle, Rob't, esq. .	300 0 ...	1	1	0
Trafford, Tho's, esq. .	4 tent' etc. ...	1	0	10
Warburton, Richard (late the lands of D'd Mathew)	20 0 ...	0	2	0
Wilkinson, John	2 0 ...	0	0	3
Wynn, Tho's	19 0 ...	0	1	10
Sm' Redd' laboru' tenen' .	0 0 ...	16	10	1
4° Eliz'	0 0 ...	17	16	1¼

There wanteth the rent of W'm Meredith for 46 acres of land.

		VALUE.			RENT.		
TENENTES PER DIMISSIONES	ACRES.	£	s.	d.	£	s.	d.
Bady, Owin	. 15 0 ...	4	0	0 ...	0	11	0
Breerton, Owin	. 14 0 ...	6	6	8 ...	0	6	2
Edward, John	. 18 2 ...	8	10	0 ...	0	1	5
Edwards, John	. 62 0 ...	30	0	0 ...	0	3	6
Gouldsmith, Thomas	. 2 0 ...	0	15	0 ...	0	2	0½
Goz, John	. 3 0 ...	1	3	0 ...	0	2	0
Hughes, Richard .	. 4 0 ...	1	10	0 ...	0	2	0
Lloyd, John	. 21 3 ...	11	0	0 ...	0	1	0
Mereddith, W'm, esq.	. 11 0 ...	4	0	0 ...	0	0	5
Powell, Thomas .	. 2 0 ...	0	16	0 ...	0	1	10
Trevor, Rich' Kn't, and Thos. Trafford, esq. .	. 60 0 ...	9	0	0 ...	1	13	4

(Sir Ric' holdeth 2 thirds, and Thomas 1 third part.)

Sm' redd' tenen' ad volunt' et p' dimiss'   .   64s. 8½d.

With the rent of Hanody Wirger.

In toto   ·   .   .   .   £19 14s. 9½d.

Y GLWYSEGL.—MORTON UWCH Y CLAWDD, LLANERCH RUGOG.

Cae Cyriog MS.

Dio of Llanerch Rugog, second son of David ab Madog ab David Goch of Croes Foel, married Angharad, daughter of Maredydd ab Llywelyn Dhû ab Gruffydd ab Iorwerth Foel ab Iorwerth Fychan, second son of Iorwerth ab Ieuaf of Llwyn On, by whom he had issue a son,

Deicws ab Dio of Llanerch Rugog, who married Lleuci, daughter of Tegin ab Madog ab Iorwerth Goch ab Frondeg ab Ednyfed Foel ab Ieuaf Fychan ab Ieuaf Nyniaw, by whom he had issue three sons; 1, Ieuan; 2, Madog; and 3, David ab Deicws of Cae Cyriog.

Ieuan ab Deicws of Llanerch Rugog, the eldest son, married Gwenhwyfar, daughter of Ieuan ab Llywelyn ab Gruffydd, second son (by Lleuci, his wife, daughter and co-heiress of Ieuan ab Philip ab Maredydd ab Gruffydd ab Madog Danwr, Lord of Llangurig), of Ednyfed ab Gruffydd ab Iorwerth ab Einion Goch ab Einion, Lord of Soulli and Eyton Uchaf, by whom he had issue a son and heir,

John ab Ieuan of Llanerch Rugog, who married Catherine, daughter of Howel ab Gruffydd ab Ieuan Ddû of Bers, ab Howel ab Hwfa ab Iorwerth ab Gruffydd of Bers or Bersham, second son of Ieuaf ab Nyniaw ab Cynwrig ab Rhiwallawn (*gules*, two lions passant in pale *argent*, for Iorwerth ab Gruffydd of Bersham), by whom he had issue a son and heir, Hugh, and four daughters ; 1, Elizabeth, ux. William Lloyd of Plas Uwch y Clawdd (*argent*, a lion rampant *sable*, armed, langued, and crowned *gules*); 2, Angharad, ux. Randle ab John ab David ab Llywelyn of Plâs Madog; 3, Marsli, ux. John ab John ab Robert ab Gruffydd ab Howel of Croes Foel ; and 4, Alice, ux. Edward ab Howel of Tref Fechan in Cristionydd, second son of Edward ab Madog Puleston.

Hugh ab John ab Ieuan of Llanerch Rugog, married Catherine, daughter of John Eyton of Watstay, ab John ab Elis Eyton, by whom he had issue four sons ; 1, John ab Hugh, of whom presently ; 2, Roger ab Hugh, who married Myfanwy, daughter of John, second son of Edward ab Maredydd of Fron Deg, in the parish of Wrexham, son of Gruffydd ab Adda ab Howel of Llys Trevor, by whom he had issue, David,[1] Charles, Alice, Elen, and Catherine ; 3, Owain ab Hugh, who married Elizabeth, daughter of John Bersham of Bersham, ab William ab Howel ab Gruffydd ab Ieuan Ddû of Bersham (*gules*, two lions passant in pale *argent*), by whom he had a daughter and heiress, Marsli, who married John Sonlli ab John Sonlli of Fron Dêg, fourth son of Robert Wynn Sonlli of Sonlli ; and 4, Richard ab Hugh, who married, first, Elizabeth, daughter of John ab Edward, by whom he had issue John and Gwen ; he married, secondly, Alice, daughter of Randle ab David, by whom he had issue three sons, Edward, Thomas, and George, who were all living in 1607, and six daughters, of whom Margaret, the eldest, married Lancelot Lloyd of Yr Orsedd Goch (*azure*, a lion salient *or*). Hugh ab John ab Ieuan of Llanerch Rugog, had likewise two daughters ; 1, Catherine, ux. Edward Erddig of Erddig, ab John Erddig ; and 2, ... ux. Hugh Wynn of Bryn Owain,

---

[1] David married and had issue two sons: 1, Edward of Cristionydd, who sold his estate to Ellis Lloyd of Penylan ; 2, Robert of Cristionydd ; and two daughters : 1, Elizabeth, ux. Edward ab Hugh of Cristionydd, and 2, Catherine ux. William Herbert.

third son of David Eyton of Eyton Uchaf (*ermine*, a lion rampant *sable*).

John ab Hugh of Llanerch Rugog, the eldest son, married Gwenhwyfar or Gwenllian, daughter of John Erddig ab David Goch of Erddig, by whom he had issue one son, Richard Hughes, and four daughters ; 1, Catherine, ux. Randle Davies ; 2, Elen, ux. Walter Panton, Vicar of Tirveccan, in Ireland ; 3, Mary, married, first, John ab Edward, and, secondly, Gruffydd ab Edward ; and 4, Jane, ux. Richard Lloyd, third son of William Lloyd of Plâs Madog.

Richard Hughes of Llanerch Rugog, married Jane, daughter of David ab Matthew Wynn ab David of Llys Trevor in Nanheudwy, by whom he had, besides two daughters—1, Elizabeth, and 2, Margaret, ux. Lancelot Hughes of Gorsedd Goch—a son and heir,

Edward Hughes of Llanerch Rugog, who married his cousin, Jane, daughter of Richard Hughes of Cadwgan Fechan, by whom he had issue two sons ; 1, Roger Hughes, who died *s. p.* ; and 2, Richard Hughes, and one daughter, Parnel, the heiress of her brother.

Richard Hughes, the second son, went to Virginia, and on his return succeeded to the Llanerch Rugog estate. He was living in 1620, and married Maig, daughter of Lancelot Lloyd of Yr Orsedd Goch, living in 1604, ab Thomas Lloyd, and relict of John Rathbone of Chester, by whom he had no issue ; and at his death he was succeeded by his only sister,

Parnel Hughes of Llanerch Rugog. She married John Payne of Morton, in Flintshire, attorney-at-law, and, dying in 1696, left an only son and heir,

John Payne of Llanerch Rugog. He married a lady in London, by whom he had an only daughter and heiress, Mary Payne, who married William Higgons of Shropshire, by whom she had an only daughter and heiress, Elizabeth Higgons of Llanerch Rugog, who died without issue and unmarried, April 19th, 1811. The Hugheses of Llanerch Rugog are therefore extinct ; but the estate now belongs to a family of the name of Jones, who came

from Chilton Hall in Shropshire; but whether they became possessed of Llanerch Rugog by purchase or by
gift is not known.—(*Cae Cyriog MS.*)

Y GLWYSEGL.—MORTON UWCH Y CLAWDD.
PLAS UWCH Y CLAWDD.

Cae Cyriog MS.; Harl. MS. 1969; *Add. MS.* 9864.

Ednyfed ab Gruffydd ab David ab Rhys Fychan ab Rhys Grûg,⹌Arddun, d.
Lord of Llanymdoferi, ab Yr Arglwydd Rhys, Prince of South │ of Ieuaf ab
Wales. *Argent*, a lion rampant *sable*, armed, langued and │ Cynwrig
crowned *gules*. See p. 324, note.   │ ab Rhiw-
                                                             │ allawn.

Ithel ab ⹌Joice, d. of Llywelyn ab Madog Foel, Lord of Y Glwysegl ab
Ednyfed. │ Ieuan ab Llywelyn ab Cynwrig Efell, Lord Y Glwysegl, and
         │ Ystrad Alun. *Gules*, on a bend *argent*, a lion passant *sable*.

Madog ab Ithel.⹌

Deicws.⹌Angharad, d. of John Puleston ab Robert Puleston ab Richard
        │ Puleston of Emeral. *Sable*, three mullets *argent*.
        │   Her mother was Gwenllian, d. of David ab David ab Ieuan ab
        │   Iorwerth ab David ab Goronwy ab Iorwerth ab Howel ab Morei-
        │   ddig ab Sanddef Hardd or the Handsome, Lord of Morton or
        │   Burton and Llai.

2   1
David ⹌Angharad, d. and co-heiress of Madog, son of Lly- John Wynn of
Lloyd. │ welyn ab Ednyfed of Soulli. Madog died in   Esclusham.
       │ 1481. *Ermine*, a lion rampant *sable*.

William Lloyd of Plâs Uwch⹌Elizabeth, d. of John ab   John Lloyd of Plâs
y Clawdd. A twin with his │ Ieuan ab Deicws of   y Bada. A twin.
brother John Lloyd.   │ Llanerch Rugog.

a

| a

John Lloyd of Plâs Uwch=Elizabeth, d. of Sir Thomas Hanmer of Hanmer,
    y Clawdd.   Knt., ab Richard Hanmer.

Thomas Lloyd of Plâs=Dorothy, d. of Robert Lloyd of the Bryn, in the
    Uwch y Clawdd.   parish of Hanmer, one of the Guard to Queen
         Elizabeth.

John Lloyd of Plâs Uwch y Clawdd;=Jane, d. of Richard Thelwall of Plâs
    living in 1620.   Coch, Warden of Ruthin.

Thomas Lloyd, died young,   Elen, died young,   Elizabeth, died young,
    s. p.   *s. p.*   *s. p.*

1		2	3	4
Jane, heiress of Plâs Uwch y Clawdd.	= Thomas Jones, younger brother of Richard Jones of Westyn Rhyn.	Elizabeth, ux. John Wynn, Parson of Llanganhafal, ab David Wynn ab Thomas ab John Wynn.	Elen, ux. Richard ab John ab David ab Edward of Westyn Rhyn in Selattyn and Llanfarthen.	Anne, married 1st, ... Wynn of Overton; 2nd, .. Wilde, brother of Ralph Wilde of Wrexham.

These four daughters of Thomas Lloyd sold Plâs Uwch y Clawdd
to Sir Thomas Myddleton Hên of Chirk Castle.

Eleanor, married Ffrancis Edisbury of Hafod y Bwch, 1680, second son of
    Richard Edisbury of London, second son of Cynwrig Edisbury, *alias* Wilkinson of Marchwiail.

Y GLWYSEGL.—MORTON UWCH Y CLAWDD.
PENTREF CLAWDD.

Cae Cyriog MS.

Robert ab David ab John of Pentref Clawdd, descended from Ithel Felyn,=
    Lord of Iâl.

John ab Robert of Pentref Clawdd.=
| a

a	
David Lloyd of Pentref Clawdd, which place he sold to Kenrick Edisbury of Street yr Hwch in Marchwiail, and it now belongs to Mr. Yorke of Erddig.	Catherine, d. of Howel ab Edward ab Y Badi Llwyd of Cefn y Fedw in Cristionydd, ab Madog ab Owain ab Gruffydd ab Cynwrig Efell, Lord of Y Glwysegl. *Gules*, on a bend *argent*, a lion passant *sable*.

Owain Lloyd of Plas y Drain, afterwards called Llwyn Owain, in the township of Morton Uwch y Clawdd. Buried at Rhiwabon July 19th, 1671. *Wynnstay MS.; Harl. MSS.* 1969, 4181.	Barbara, d. of Henry Williams of Cochwillan, and Jane, his wife, d. and heiress of Thomas Salusbury of Denbigh, third son of Sir John Salusbury of Lleweni, Knt. Henry Williams, who sold Cochwillan to the Earl of Pembroke, was the son and heir of William Williams of Cochwillan, co. Caernarvon, and Barbara, his wife, daughter of George Lumley, and sister and heir of John, Lord Lumley, and relict of Humphrey Llwyd.—*Harl. MS.* 4181; *Wynnstay MS.*

EDISBURY OF ERDDIG AND WREXHAM.

This family derives its name from Edisbury Hall in the hundred of the same name in Cheshire, where there was once an ancient castle, built by Ethelfleda, Queen of Mercia.

The next we learn of this family is from two monuments in Chatham Church in Kent. The first is to the memory of Robert Wilkinson Edisbury, Gent., of Marchwiail, co. Denbigh, who died Sept. 1610. The second monument is to his son, Kenrick Edisbury of Bedwal, in the parish of Marchwiail, who was Surveyor of His Majesty's Navy. He died Aug. 27, 1638, leaving issue by his wife Mary (daughter and heiress of Edward Peters, *alias* Harding, of Rochester, Gent.), two sons; 1, John, of whom presently; and 2, Richard, who was one of the persons afterwards taken prisoner with Sir Gerard Eyton, Knight Banneret, at Eyton, by Colonel Mytton in 1643. This Richard, who was of London, was father of Francis Edisbury of Hafod y Bwch, who married Eleanor, daughter of Thomas Johnes of Plàs Uwch y Clawdd, in the township of Morton Uwch y Clawdd, or Morton Wallicorum, younger brother of Richard Jones of Weston Rhyn, by whom he had three children, Richard, John, and Anne.

John, the eldest son of Kenrick Edisbury, was born at Chatham in 1601. At his father's death in 1638 he came to Wales, and settled at Pentref Clawdd, in the township of Morton Uwch y Clawdd, which place his father had bought from David Lloyd ab John ab Robert ab John, who was descended from Ithel Felyn, Lord of Val. Soon afterwards, John Edisbury bought the Erddig estate. His eldest son, Joshua, who was Churchwarden of Rhiwabon in 1661, built the present house at Erddig in 1678, and was High Sheriff for co. Denbigh in 1682. He resided at Erddig till his death. In 1715 the estate was sold under a decree of Chancery to John Mellor, a Master in Chancery, of the family of Mellor's Chapel in Derbyshire, who bequeathed it to his nephew (son of his eldest sister), Simon Yorke, Esq., first cousin to the Lord Chancellor, the Earl of Hardwicke.

The Edisburys, who were ardent Royalists, lost their estates in the Great Rebellion in the seventeenth century.

Joshua's eldest son managed to retain Bersham Hall (built by his father in 1698), and resided there. He died, leaving it to James, born Nov. 16th, 1735, and he, dying Nov. 4th, 1792, left it to his son Charles, who was born in 1772, and died in 1848, and was succeeded by his son James, born Feb. 7th, 1803, who dying Sept. 29th, 1859, left it to his son James Fisher Edisbury, the present owner, who was born Oct. 13th, 1837; and married, in 1867, Minnie, second daughter of T. C. Jones, Esq., M.P. for the Borough of Wrexham, and has issue two daughters, Minnie Adeline, born Aug. 3, 1868, and Phillis May, born Sept. 27, 1870.

MANOR OF Y GLWYSEGL.—TOWNSHIP OF ERDDIG.
ERDDIG OF ERDDIG.

PARISH OF GRESFORD.

Iorwerth Fychan ab Iorwerth ab Ieuaf ab Niniaf ab Cynwrig ab⊤
   Rhiwallon, Lord of Maelor Cymraeg. See Llwyn On.

Gruffydd ab Iorwerth⊤Lleuci, d. of Ieuaf ab Llywelyn ab Cynwrig Efell,
   Fychan. | Lord of Y Glwysegl. *Gules*, on a bend *argent*, a
              | lion passant *sable*

Llywelyn.⊤Eva, d. of David   David Goch, an-   Howel of Crocs   Madog
     | ab Ieuan ab Ior-   cestor of the   Foel, ancestor   Ddu.
       werth ab David   Robertses of   of the Joneses
       ab Goronwy of   Crocs Foel and   of Crocs Foel
       Burton and   Hafod y Bwch.   and Plas Cad-
       Llai.   wgan.

Ieuan.⊤Angharad, d. of Madog ab Iorwerth Goch ab Ior-   Madog, ances-
       werth Fychan of Maen Gwynedd, descended   tor of the
       from Idnerth Benfras, Lord of Maesbrwg. Her   Traffords of
       mother was Gwenllian, d. of Y Teg Fadog, Senes-   Esclusham.
       chal of Gruffydd, Lord of Glyndyfrdwy, and son
       of Madog ab Gruffydd ab Owain Brogyntyn.

Howel. ⊤Lleuci, d. of Ieuan ab Madog ab Gruffydd ab Madog of Y Plâs
       Ymachymbyd (Bachymbyd), ab Maredydd ab Llywelyn ab
       Madog ab Einion ab Maredydd ab Uchdryd, Lord of Cyfeiliog,
       son of Edwyn ab Goronwy, Prince of Tegeingl. *Argent*, a cross
       flory engrailed *sable*, inter four Cornish choughs, ppr.

David Goch,⊤Angharad Wen, d. of Morgan ab Llywelyn ab Ednyfed of
   s. p.   Soulli.

John Erddig of Erddig,⊤Deuli, d. of David Lloyd ab Tudor of Gelli Gynan
    1570. | and Bodidris in Iâl.

Edward⊤...., d. of Hugh ab John ab Ieuan ab   Gwenllian, ux. John ab
 Erddig | Deiews of Llanerch Rugog. *Ermine*,   Hugh ab John ab Ieuan
  of | a lion rampant *sable*.   ab Deiews of Llanerch
 Erddig. | Rugog.
   | *a*

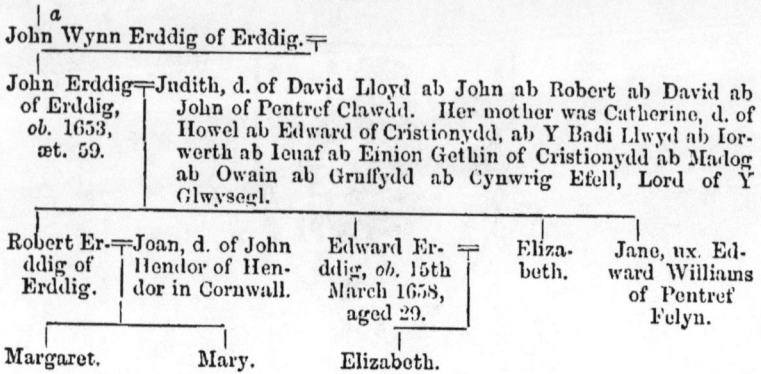

| a
John Wynn Erddig of Erddig.⊤

John Erddig⊤Judith, d. of David Lloyd ab John ab Robert ab David ab
of Erddig, | John of Pentref Clawdd. Her mother was Catherine, d. of
ob. 1653, | Howel ab Edward of Cristionydd, ab Y Badi Llwyd ab Ior-
æt. 59. | werth ab Ieuaf ab Einion Gethin of Cristionydd ab Madog
 | ab Owain ab Gruffydd ab Cynwrig Efell, Lord of Y
 | Glwysegl.

Robert Er-⊤Joan, d. of John   Edward Er- ⊤ Eliza-   Jane, ux. Ed-
ddig of | Hendor of Hen-   ddig, *ob.* 15th | beth.   ward Williams
Erddig. | dor in Cornwall.   March 1658,   of Pentref
 | aged 29.   Felyn.

Margaret.   Mary.   Elizabeth.

BACHYMBYD.

IN THE COMOT OF CYNMEIRCH IN THE CANTREF OF YSTRAD, AND
IN THE PARISH OF LLANYNYS.[1]

Myvyrian MS. 15,045.

Llywelyn ab Madog of Plas ym Machymbyd, ab Einion ab Maredydd ab⊤
Uchdryd ab Edwyn ab Goronwy, Prince of Tegeingl. This Llewelyn ab |
Madog owned Y Plas ym Machymbyd, and the greatest part of Tref Maes
Maen Cymro, and Tref Bryn Caredig, and he had lands also in Gyffy-
lliog and Derwen Anial.

Maredydd of Plâs ym Machymbyd.⊤   Madog.
| a | b | c

---

[1] The parish of Llanynys contains six townships: Tref Maes Maen
Cymro, Tref Bryn Caeredig and Tref Fechan in the comot of Llanerch
in Dyffryn Clwyd, Rhydonen in the comot of Dogfeilin in Dyffryn
Clwyd, and Bachymbyd and Ysgeibion in Cynmeirch.

a	*b*	*c*
Madog of Plâs⊤ ym Machy- mbyd.	David⊤	Einion.⊤

These two shared the lands in Gyffylliog,
Bryn Caredig, and Maes Maen Cymro.

Ithel.⊤ David, *ob. s.p.*, and his lands went to
Edward ab Ithel, his nephew.

Edward ab Ithel, *ob. s. p.*, and his lands went by
escheat to the Lord, from whom they passed to
Sir John Holland, who levied fines upon them, and
sold the same and David ab Einion's part to John
Salusbury.

Gruffydd, of Y Plâs⊤ ym Machymbyd.	Howel, had lands in Tref= Maes Maen Cymro.	David, had lands= in Tref Maes Maen Cymro.

Madog of Y Plâs ym Machymbyd. ⊤

Ieuan of Y=Angharad, d. of Howel Coetmor ab Gruffydd Fychan of Nant
Plâs ym   Conwy, ab Gruffydd, son of David Goch, Lord of Denbigh,
Mach-   illegitimate son of David, Lord of Denbigh, second son of
mbyd.   Gruffydd ab Llewelyn, Prince of Wales. Arms, quarterly,
         1st and 4th, *azure*, a chev. inter three fleurs-de-lys *argent*, for
         the Baron Howel Coetmor; 2nd and 3rd, *sable*, a lion rampant
         argent, in a border engrailed *or*, for David Goch, Lord of
         Denbigh.

Madog of Y Plâs=Catherine, d. of Gruffydd ab ym Machymbyd.	Llewelyn ab Gruffydd.	Lleuci, ux. Howel ab Ieuan ab Llywelyn ab Gruffydd ab Iorwerth Fychan of Erddig.

2 David Lloyd.⊤	1 Hugh ab Madog. He sold Plâs ym Machymbyd to Mr. John Salus- bury.

Richard Lloyd.⊤

Harri Lloyd.=Margaret, d. of Richard Wyrrall.   Margaret.

John Lloyd of Gwern y To.⊤..., d. of Tudor ab Robert of Segrwyd.

The township of Bachymbyd contains eight hundred
and forty acres, three roods and a half of land, wood, and
waste, in the holding of free tenants. Thereof Ralph ab
Maredydd and Ieuaf ab Maredydd held the third part of
the township, which third part fell "entire" to the lord,
as so much escheat, because all the tenants rose contrary
to the peace in two wars. And the sixth part of the
township was in the tenure of the descendants of Gruf-

fydd ab Maredydd. And thereof one-half fell to the lord as escheat, by reason of the aforesaid insurrections.

And there are also sixty-two acres of land and wood of which the lord takes no profit.

And there is a certain water-mill there, rendering thirty-four shillings and fourpence annually in season. Extenta Castri et Honoris de Denbeigh, facta per Hugonem de Beckele, 1334.

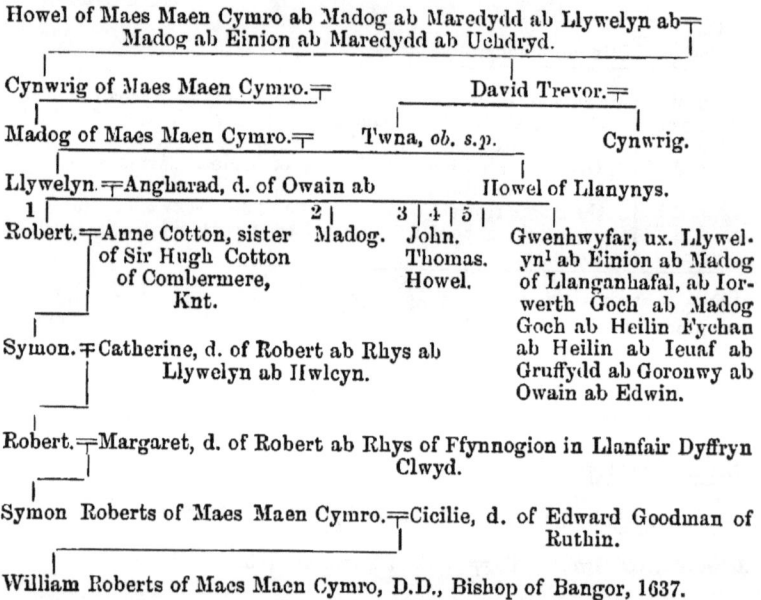

MAES MAEN CYMRO.

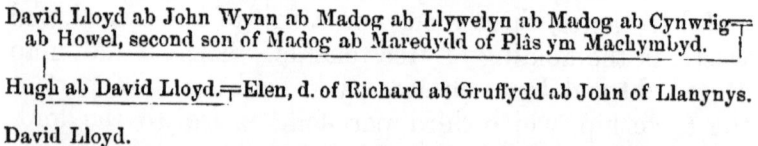

Harl. MS. 1969.

Howel of Maes Maen Cymro ab Madog ab Maredydd ab Llywelyn ab⹀ Madog ab Einion ab Maredydd ab Uchdryd.

Cynwrig of Maes Maen Cymro.⹀   David Trevor.⹀

Madog of Maes Maen Cymro.⹀   Twna, *ob. s.p.*   Cynwrig.

Llywelyn.⹀Angharad, d. of Owain ab   Howel of Llanynys.

1 Robert.⹀Anne Cotton, sister   **2** Madog.   **3** John. **4** Thomas. **5** Howel.   Gwenhwyfar, ux. Llywel-
     of Sir Hugh Cotton   yn[1] ab Einion ab Madog
     of Combermere,   of Llanganhafal, ab Ior-
     Knt.   werth Goch ab Madog
                                          Goch ab Heilin Fychan
Symon.⹀Catherine, d. of Robert ab Rhys ab   ab Heilin ab Ieuaf ab
     Llywelyn ab Hwlcyn.   Gruffydd ab Goronwy ab
                                         Owain ab Edwin.

Robert.⹀Margaret, d. of Robert ab Rhys of Ffynnogion in Llanfair Dyffryn Clwyd.

Symon Roberts of Maes Maen Cymro.⹀Cicilie, d. of Edward Goodman of Ruthin.

William Roberts of Maes Maen Cymro, D.D., Bishop of Bangor, 1637.

MAES MAEN CYMRO.

David Lloyd ab John Wynn ab Madog ab Llywelyn ab Madog ab Cynwrig⹀ ab Howel, second son of Madog ab Maredydd of Plâs ym Machymbyd.

Hugh ab David Lloyd.⹀Elen, d. of Richard ab Gruffydd ab John of Llanynys.

David Lloyd.

[1] Llywelyn of Llangynafal had a son named Gruffydd, the father of Robert, the father of John Wynn, whose son Richard was father of Richard Wynn of Llanganafal.

MAES MAEN CYMRO.

David, third son of Madog ab Maredydd of Plâs yn Machymbyd. ⊤

Gruffydd. ⊤ Lleucy, d. of Madog ab Gruffydd Fychan.

David. ⊤

Gruffydd Goch, who killed Ednyfed ab Y Dai. ⊤

Morgan. ⊤ Lleucu Llwyd.

Edward = Margaret, d. of Gruffydd ab	Sir Thomas Mor- = Mary, sister of
Morgan	Thomas ab John ab Belyn	gan, Clk., Vicar	John Gruffydd
of Maes	ab .... ab Goronwy ab	of Cilcain.	ab Thomas of
Maen	Einion of Cilcain.		Tre'r Cefn in
Cymro.			Cilcain.

John of	Thomas = Catherine,	John = Grace,	Harri = Gwenhwyfar, d.
Maes	Morgan.	d. of John	Morgan	d. of	Mor-	of Robert Mor-
Maen		ab Rhys ab	Vicar of	Rich-	gan,	gan of Llana-
Cymro.		Harri of	Nann-	ard	Vicar	ber (ab Robert
		Maes y	erch.	Mostyn	of	Morgan), by
		Groes.		of Pen	Cil-	Annest, d. of
				y Gelli.	cain.	John Pryse of
						Llwyn Yn.

MANOR OF Y GLEWYSEGL.—TOWNSHIP OF BROUGHTON.—JONES OF FRON DEG.

Cae Cyriog MS.; Harl. MS. 4181.

Gruffydd, second son of Adda ab ⊤ Angharad Fechan, d. of Llywelyn ab
Howel ab Ieuaf ab Adda ab Awr of | Owain ab Gruffydd ab Owain, son
Llys Trevor in Nanheudwy. | of Bleddyn ab Owain Brogyntyn,
                         | Lord of Dinmael.

a | 1   *b* | 2   *c* |

a | 1
Maredydd ab ⊤ Angharad, d. of Ieuan ab Madog
Gruffydd. | Goch of Cae Madog Coch in Cris-
| tionydd. *Ermine*, a lion rampant
| *sable*.

b | 2
Edward. He went
from Trevor to
Llanfair Dyffryn
Clwyd.

c |

| 3 | | 4 | | 1 | | 2
Robert of Pentref | Ior | Gwen,ux.Maredydd | ..., ux.
Cuhelyn in Llan- | werth. | ab Ieuan Llwyd, | Ieuan ab
fair Dyffryn | | ancestor of the | Gwyn
Clwyd. ancestor | | Pryses of Derwen | Llwyd.
of the Lloyds of | | Anial. *Argent,* six
Berth and | | bees, ppr. 3, 2, 1.
Rhagad.

Edward of Fron Dêg, near Wrex- ⊤ Myfanwy, d. of Rhys ab Ieuan ab Mare-
ham, and of Cristionydd; living | dydd, *alias* Y Goch ab Ieuan Ddu.
20th Henry VII. | *Gules*, a lion rampant *argent*.

| 1 | | 2
Howel ⊤ Angharad, d. of Howel ab | John of Y Coedladd | ..., ux. Ralph
of Fron | David ab Gruffydd of Mar- | in Rhiwabon. | ab Robert.
Dêg. | chwiail. *Ermine*, a lion | See vol. ii, p. 395.
| rampant *azure*.

David of Fron Dêg. ⊤ Janet, d. of Roger Deccaf of Rhwytyn. *Ermine*, a lion
| rampant *azure*.

Edward ab David of ⊤ Margaret, d. of Elis ab David ab Robert of Gnoltyn in
Fron Dêg, *ob.* 13th | Overton Madog, *ob.* 13th January 1622.
March 1655.

| 1 | | 2 | 1 | | 2
John ab ⊤ Mary, d. of Ralph | Roger ab = ..., d. of | Roger ab = Elen, d. of
Edward | Wynn ab David | Edward, | William ab Madog | John
of Fron | Wynn ab Edward | *s. p.* | Goch of Fron | Brereton.
Dêg. | of Wrexham. | | Dêg.

Edward ⊤ Alice, d. of Gruffydd Lloyd | Rondle | Elizabeth, ux. | Sarah,
Jones of | of Llanarmon yn Iâl. | Jones, | Edward Wil- | ux.
Fron Dêg. | *Sable*, on a chev. inter | *ob. s. p.* | liams of Fron | Ed-
| three trefoils of the field, | | Dêg. | ward
| three goat's heads erased | | | Jones.
| *or*.

Mary Jones, heiress of Fron Dêg, married her cousin Gruffydd Lloyd, eldest
son of Gabriel Lloyd of Llanarmon yn Iâl, ab David ab Thomas ab David
Lloyd ab David ab Rhys ab Gruffydd ab Gwilym ab Ithel ab Y Gwion
Gam ab Ieuaf ab Howel Foel or Hwfa Foel of Cymo in the parish of Llan-
dysilio in Iâl, ab Hwfa ab Ithel Felyn, Lord of Iâl and Ystrad Alun.
Mary Jones died young in 1690, and her husband, Gruffydd Lloyd, also died
young the same year, leaving two children, Edward Lloyd of Llanarmon
in Iâl and Fron Dêg, and one daughter, Margaret Lloyd. The above-
named Edward Lloyd married Barbara, daughter of Edward Elis of Coed
y Cra.

ELLIS OF GROES NEWYDD.

Elis ab Gruffydd ab Gwyn ab Goronwy ab Gwilym ab Maredudd of Yr Hob⊤
   ab Gruffydd ab Llywelyn ab Howel ab Moreiddig ab Sanddef Hardd, |
   Lord of Morton.

Richard ab Elis of Hope.⊤Gwenhwyfar, d. of John Ithel Wynn of Coed y Llai.

Elis ab Richard.⊤Anne, d. of Hugh Vychan ab David ab William.   Her
          mother was Catherine, d. of Thomas Griffith of Pant y
          Llongdu.

Gruffydd Elis of Fron Dêg.⊤   Peter Elis of Wrexham, 1636.

Peter Ellis of Groes Newydd,   Thomas Ellis, Governor of the Island of
   near Wrexham.   of Barbadoes.

— — —

Y GLWYSEGL. — TOWNSHIP OF ACTON.
JEFFRIES OF ACTON.
Cae Cyriog MS.

Richard ab Ieuan, third son of Adda ab Howel ab Ieuaf ab Adda ab Awr⊤
           of Trevor.

Robert Fychan ⊤Margaret, d. of John Eyton.
 | a

| a

Hugh ab ⊤ Janet, d. and co-heir of Madog Llwydd ab Llywelyn ab Iolyn ab
Robert. | David ab Deicws ab Ieuaf ab Iolyn Foel ab Madog Goch ab
| Madog ab Ieuaf ab Nyniaw ab Cynwrig ab Rhiwallawn. *Er-
| mine*, a lion rampant *sable*.

Jeoffrey ⊤ Catherine, d. of Richard ab Richard ab Howel, second son of
ab | John ab Einion ab Iolyn ab Iorwerth of Borasham, fourth son
Hugh. | of Llywelyn ab Gruffydd ab Cadwgan, Lord of Eyton, Erlys,
| and Borasham. *Ermine*, a lion rampant *azure*.

John Jeffreys of Wrexham, one ⊤ Margaret, d. of William Lloyd of Halchdyn,
of the Judges of North Wales, | in the parish of Hanmer. She married
ob. 19th May 1621; buried | secondly, Thomas Ireland, Chamberlain
in Wrexham Church. | of Chester; and thirdly, Sir Edward
| Trevor of Bryn Cunallt, Knt.

John Jeffreys of Acton, High Sheriff ⊤ Margaret, d. of Sir Thomas Ireland
for co. Denbigh, 1655. He out- | of Bewsey in com. Lancaster, Knt.,
lived all his sons. | ab Thomas Ireland.

1	2	3	4	5	6
John Jeffreys, ⊤ Dorothy, d.	Ed-	Thomas.	Charles.		Sir George
died in his of Sir Gruff-	ward.				Jeffreys, Knt.
father's life- ydd Wil-			William.		and Baronet.
time, 1670, liams of					
aged 34. Penrhyn,					
Bart.					

7	8	
Jeffrey Jeffreys	James Jeffreys,	Margaret, ux. Robert
of Y Glwysegl.	D.D.	Betton of Shrews-
		bury.

Sir Gruffydd Jeffreys of Acton, Knight, High Sheriff ⊤ Dorothy, sister of Ro-
tor co. Denbigh, 1683, in which year he was mar- | bert Pleydell of Am-
ried. He built a new house at Acton in place of | ney Holyrood, Esq.,
the old one. He was knighted in 1687, and died | High Sheriff for co.
4th March 1694, and buried at Wrexham.[1] | Gloucester in 1682.

	1
Robert Jeffreys of Acton,	Elizabeth, heiress of her brother Robert, mar-
ob. s.p.	ried John Robinson of Gwersyllt ab William
	Robinson.

2	3
Margaret, *ob. s. p.*	Frances, married to Philip Egerton of Acton, *ob. s. p.*

Ellis Yonge of Bryn Iorcyn purchased the Acton
estate from the trustees of the said John Robinson; and
in 1785 Acton was purchased from Mr. Yonge's trustees
by Sir Foster Cunliffe, Bart.

Thomas, the third son of John Jeffreys, the High
Sheriff for Denbighshire in 1655, resided for a long time
in Spain as British Consul at Alicant and Madrid. He
was made a Knight of Alcantara, and for the honour of

[1] His will was dated March 6th, 1694, and proved May 30th, 1696.

the descendants of Tudor Trevor, from whom the
Jeffreys are sprung, the proofs of his descent were ad-
mired even by the proud Spaniards. He rendered
himself so acceptable to the Spanish ministry as to be
recommended to our Court to succeed Lord Lansdowne
as British Envoy ; but the revolution put a stop to his
promotion. Fine full-length portraits of him and his
brother George were removed from Acton to Erddig.[1]

George, the sixth son of the above named John Jeffreys, was born at Acton in the year 1548, and educated at
Shrewsbury, St. Paul's, and Westminster. He was entered
of the Lower Temple, May 19th, 1663, was Recorder of
London at the age of thirty, and was appointed solicitor
to the Duke of York. He was made a Welsh judge in
1680, knighted and made chief justice of Chester, and
in 1681 obtained a baronetcy. In 1683 he was appointed Lord Chief Justice of the King's Bench, and on
the accession of James II in 1685, was raised to the
peerage by the title of Baron Jeffreys of Wem, in the
county of Salop. After the defeat of the Duke of Monmouth he was placed at the head of the special commission appointed to try the rebels, and his ready zeal
in carrying out the sanguinary directions of the king,
obtained for him a notorious celebrity not soon forgotten
by the reader of Lord Macaulay's account of the " Bloody
Assize". ·In 1685 he was appointed Lord Chancellor,
and in 1689 (1st William and Mary) was committed to
the Tower on a charge of high treason, and died there
April 19th, 1690, at the early age of forty-two.[2] He
married first,[3] Mary, daughter of Thomas Needham, M.A.,

[1] Pennant's *Tours in Wales*, i, 406, 408.

[2] The details of his life may be found in his *Memoirs*, by Woolrych;
Lord Campbell's *Lives of the Chancellors*; Fosse's *Judges*; and Macaulay's *History*.

[3] Pennant thus describes the manner in which this marriage was
contracted : "About this time he made clandestine addresses to the
daughter of a wealthy merchant, in which he was assisted by a young
lady, daughter of a clergyman. The affair was discovered, and the *con-
fidante* turned out of doors. Jeffreys, with a generosity unknown to
him in his prosperous days, took pity and married her. She proved
an excellent wife, and lived to see him Lord Chief Justice."

by whom he had issue—besides two daughters: 1,Margaret, married to Sir Thomas Stringer, and 2, Sarah, married to Captain Harnage of the Marines—a son and heir, John, Lord Jeffreys, who succeeded to the title and the estates, but dying in 1703, without male issue, the title became extinct. By his wife, Lady Charlotte Herbert, daughter and heiress of Philip, Earl of Pembroke, he had issue an only daughter and heir, Henrietta Louisa, who was married to Thomas, first Earl of Pomfret.

George, Lord Jeffreys, married secondly, Anne, daughter of Sir Thomas Blodworth, Knight, and relict of Sir John Jones of Furman in Gloucestershire.

James, the seventh son of John Jeffreys, the High Sheriff in 1655, was a Canon of Canterbury, and grandfather of Dr. Jeffreys, Rector of Whitford, and Residentiary of St. Paul's. The Canon died of a broken heart, at the sad conduct and character of his brother.[1]

DAME DOROTHY JEFFREY'S WILL.

From WILLIAM TREVOR PARKINS, ESQ.

Dame Dorothy Jeffreys of Acton, whose good deeds entitle her to be remembered in Wrexham and the adjoining parishes, was the widow of Sir Griffith Jeffreys, eldest son of John Jeffreys—eldest brother of the Chancellor—and his wife Dorothy, daughter of Sir Griffith Williams of Penrhyn, in Carnarvonshire. Sir Griffith Jeffreys was knighted by James the Second at Whitehall, on the 13th of May 1687, and died in 1693. He rebuilt the house at Acton, and his name appears in the list of Sheriffs for Denbighshire in 1683.

Lady Dorothy did not long survive the execution of her will, which was proved in the Prerogative Court of Canterbury by the two daughters, Mrs. Robinson and Mrs. Egerton, on the 29th of December 1729. Mrs. Egerton had no children, and, in consequence of the deaths of William, the only son of Mrs. Robinson, and his daughter Elizabeth, who died in infancy, the five daughters of Mrs. Robinson became even-

---

[1] Pennant makes this youngest son to be a Dean of Rochester, and states that his death occurred "on his road to visit his brother, the Chancellor, when under confinement in the Tower."

tually the only representatives of Sir Griffith Jeffreys and Lady
Dorothy. The three youngest of these ladies died unmarried.
Dorothy, the eldest, married Ellis Yonge, and succeeded to
the estate of Acton, but left no children to inherit it; while
Anne, the second one, became the wife of Cawley Humberston Cawley of Gwersylt, whose descendants have resumed
their original name of Humberston.   W. T. P.

"*In the Name of God Amen.*

"I Dame Dorothy Jeffreys of Acton in the County of Denbigh widow being in health of body and of perfect mind and
memory (thanks be to God) do make this my last will and
testament in manner following First and principally I commend
my soul into the hands of Almighty God my Creator in hopes
of Eternal Salvation through the merits and intercession of my
only Saviour and Redeemer Jesus Christ my body I commit to
the Earth to be decently buried at the discretion of my Executrixes herein after named and as for that worldly estate
wherewith it hath pleased God to bless me I give devise and
dispose thereof as followeth First I will that my debts and
funeral expences be paid and satisfyed And whereas my late
daughter Margaret Jeffreys by her last will and testament
dated the thirtieth day of September one thousand seven hundred and eleven did bequeath to the poor of the parish of
Wrexham in the said County of Denbigh the sum of one hundred pounds and also the sum of twenty pounds for the School-
ing of Poor Children my mind and will is that the said legacies shall be paid and discharged as by the said will is directed
And whereas by my deed dated the second day of September
one thousand seven hundred and fifteen I have obliged my
heirs executors and administrators to pay or cause to be paid
the sum of four thousand pounds in such manner as by the
said deed is directed being part of the marriage portion of my
daughter Frances Egerton wife of Philip Egerton of Acton
aforesaid Esquire whereas alsoe I have by my deed dated the
ninth day of May one thousand seven hundred and twenty
eight further obliged my heirs executors and administrators to
pay or cause to be paid the sum of four thousand pounds as
an additional fortune to my daughter Elizabeth Robinson wife
of John Robinson of Gwersilt in the said County of Denbigh
Esquire as by the said deed is directed Now I do hereby
ratifye and confirm my said several acts and deeds and my
mind and will is that the same shall be duly paid according to
the true intent and meaning thereof by my Executrixes hereafter named out of my personall estate and in deficiency thereof

out of my Real Estate (by mortgage sale or otherwise) which I do hereby charge with the payment of my said debts and also the several bequests and legacies hereafter mentioned vizt. I give devise and bequeath unto the parish of Bangor in the said County of Denbigh the sum of five hundred pounds to be raised out of my said estate within six months after my decease and laid out to interest on land security and the interest thereof to be applyed yearly for ever for the teaching to read and write and instructing in the Catechism according to the Church of England set forth and also for the putting out apprentices such and soe many poor children of the said parish of Bangor and in such manner as my said sons in law John Robinson and Philip Egerton and their heirs successively for ever shall direct order and appoint but in default of such direction and appointment by them or any of them then such nomination direction and appointment of such children as aforesaid shall be by the rector or minister and churchwardens of the said parish of Bangor for the time being. Item I doe give and bequeath unto the said parish of Wrexham the sum of four hundred pounds (over and above the said legacies before mentioned to be bequeathed by my said daughter Margaret) to be raised within six months after my decease and laid out to interest on land security and the interest thereof applied for the teaching and instructing and putting out apprentices such and soe many poor children of the said parish of Wrexham in such manner as my said sons in law and their heirs successively shall direct and appoint and in default thereof in such manner as the Vicar or Minister and Churchwardens for the time being of the said Parish of Wrexham shall direct and appoint. Item I bequeath unto the parish of Gresford the sum of fifty pounds to be raised within six months after my decease and laid out to interest and the yeo (*sic*) interest thereof yearly for ever applyed for the teaching and instructing such and so many poor children of the said Parish of Gresford in the Charity School there settled (over and beside the children that are or shall be appointed to be taught by virtue of the said Benefaction) and in such manner as my said sons in law and their heirs shall appoint and in default thereof in such manner as the Vicar or Minister and Churchwardens for the time being of the said parish of Gresford shall appoint Item I give unto the parish of Holt the sum of Thirty Pounds to be raised within six months after my decease and laid out to interest and the interest thereof yearly for ever applied for the teaching and instructing such and so many poor children of the said parish of Holt in such manner

as my said sons-in-law and their heirs shall appoint and in
default thereof in such manner as the Minister and Churchwardens for the time being of the said parish of Holt shall
direct and appoint   Item I leave unto the parish of Marchwiel
the sum of Twenty Pounds to be raised within six months
after my decease and laid out to interest and the interest
thereof yearly for ever distributed to such most necessitous
poor of the said parish (exclusive of such as are or shall be in
the Poors booke) and in such proportions as my said sons in
law and their heirs shall order and appoint and in default
thereof in such manner as the Rector or Minister of the said
Parish of Marchwiel and the Churchwardens for the time
being shall order and appoint   Item I do further leave unto
such poor house keepers as my executrixes shall order and appoint who shall be living at the time of my decease on or
about Rhosnesuy in the said parish of Wrexham the sum of
twenty pounds to be paid them within one month after my
decease in such proportions and shares as my said Executrixes
shall direct.

" Item   My mind and will is and I do hereby order that
my said Executrixes shall pay to such Churchwardens of the
said parish of Wrexham as shall be in such office at the time
of the erecting a new Church in the said Parish for the per-
forming Divine Service and Sermon in Welch the sum of one
hundred pounds towards the erecting the said Church provided the same shall be built within the space of seven years
after my decease otherwise this my said bequest to be void.

" Item   I give and bequeath unto my said son in law John
Robinson the sum of fifty pounds and to my said son in law
Philip Egerton fifty pounds to my Grandson William Robinson ten broad pieces of gold and to my niece Elizabeth Hughes
five broad pieces of gold to be paid them severally within one
month after my decease   Item   I do hereby give and bequeath unto my said daughter Elizabeth Robinson all my plate
belonging to my Dressing Table as also my Crimson velvet
Twilight   Item   I bequeath unto my said daughter Frances
Egerton my diamint buckle and my gold watch with the
chain and what thereto belongs and I commonly use therewith I also give unto her my Chariot Harnesses and Mares
Item   I give devise and bequeath unto my servant Sarah
Hughes the yearly sum of ten pounds to be paid her quarterly
during her life   Item   I give devise and bequeath unto the
several persons hereafter named the several sums hereafter
mentioned to be paid them severally within twelve months
next after my decease (vizt.) To Mr. Price late Vicar of

Wrexham aforesaid twenty guineas To Mr. Jones present
Vicar of Wrexham aforesaid twenty guineas To such Curate of
the said Parish of Wrexham as shall be officiating there at the
time of my decease five guineas To William Jones the present
Clerk of the said Parish of Wrexham two guineas To my god
son Charles Hughes eldest son of my Nephew Robert Hughes
of Trostry in the county of Monmouth Esqre twenty guineas
To my god daughter Jane Jones the daughter of William
Jones Esqre three guineas To Mrs Mary Yeude widow of Mr
Thomas Yeude deceased three guineas To my godson Thomas
Yeude eldest son of the said Mary Yeude five guineas To
James Yeude the younger son of the said Mary Yeude one
guinea To Alisha Yeude daughter of the said Mary Yeude one
guinea To my Cousin Beata Hudson spinster three guineas
To my Cousin Clipsome two guineas To Mrs Price of Derwen
one guinea to buy her a ring To my God daughter Dorothy
Price daughter of John Price late of Wrexham deceased two
guineas To my Coachman John Aston five guineas if living
with me at the time of my decease To my Servant Elizabeth
Wright two guineas To William Howell and Hannah Wright
servants of my said son and daughter Egerton and to each of
them one guinea and to such other servants of my said son
and daughter Egerton as shall be living with me at the time
of my decease forty shillings to be divided among them in
such proportions and shares as my Executrixes shall think fit.

"Item   I give devise and bequeath after the payment of
my debts legacies and funeral expences the one moiety or
halfe part of all my messuages lands tenements and hereditaments with their and every of their appurtenances in the
several Parishes of Wrexham Bangor Gresford Holt and
Marchwiel in the said County of Denbigh or elsewhere in the
Kingdom of England and Dominion of Wales and all my
right interest and title thereto to my said daughter Elizabeth
Robinson for the term of her life and from and after her decease to my Grandson William Robinson son of the said John
Robinson and Elizabeth Robinson and the heirs of his body
lawfully issuing and in default of such issue to the second third
and all other sons of the body of the said Elizabeth Robinson
by the said John Robinson begotten or to be begotten successively and the heirs of such sons lawfully issuing and for
default of such issue To the eldest daughter of the said Elizabeth Robinson by the said John Robinson and the heirs of
such eldest daughter lawfully issuing and for default of such
issue to the second third and all other the daughters of the
said Elizabeth Robinson by the said John Robinson succes-

sively and the heirs of such daughters lawfully issuing and in
default of such issue to the heirs of the body of the said Elizabeth Robinson and in default thereof to the said William
Robinson and his heirs for ever.

" Item I give devise and bequeath after the payment of my
debts legacies and funeral expences as aforesaid the other
moiety or one halfe of all my said messuages lands tenements
and hereditaments and all my right interest and Title thereto
to my said daughter Frances Egerton for and during the term
of her naturall life and from and after her decease to the first
son of the body of the said Frances Egerton begotten or to be
begotten and the heirs of such first son lawfully issuing and
in default of such issue to the second third and all other the
sons of the said Frances Egerton successively on her body begotten or to be begotten and the heirs of such sons lawfully
issuing and in default of such issue to the eldest daughter of
the said Frances Egerton and the heirs of such eldest daughter
lawfully issuing and in default of such issue to the second
third and all other the daughter and daughters of the said
Frances Egerton successively and the heirs of such daughters
lawfully issuing and in default of such issue to the said William Robinson my Grandson and his heirs for ever.

" And lastly I do hereby nominate and appoint my said
daughters Elizabeth Robinson and Frances Egerton Executrixes and residuary Legatees of this my last will and Testament revoking and disannulling all former wills by me heretofore made and I doe hereby publish and declare this to be my
last will and testament In witness whereof I have hereunto
put my hand and seal this third day of October in the second
year of the Reigne of George the Seconde of Great Britain
&c. King Defender of the Faith &c. Anno que Domini 1728
                                       " DOROTHY JEFFREYS."

" Signed sealed published and declared by the Testatrix to be
her last will and Testament contained in two sheets of paper
in presence of us who have subscribed our names as witnesses
hereto in the said Testatrix presence.

" FRANCES EGERTON.   " MARY EGERTON.
                               " THO. DAVIES."

Much curiosity has been expressed about this Lady, who is
deservedly remembered as the founder of several charities in
Wrexham and the adjoining parishes. She died in 1729,
having survived her husband, Sir Griffith Jeffreys of Acton,
for a long period, and her will was printed in *Bye-gones* for

April 1876. Her maiden name is omitted in the notice of Sir Griffith in Le Neve's *Knights*, and is not given in the *Cae Ceiriog Book*. Questions as to her family have been asked frequently, but have never, I believe, been answered.

I have now before me a copy of Sir Griffith's will which effectually clears up this uncertainty about "Dame Dorothy". I send it as likely to be interesting to many of those who read *Byegones*. And the following short statement of her parentage, for which I am indebted to the kindness of a friend, will shew exactly who she was, and explain several portions of both wills :—

Robert Pleydell of Holyrood Amney, co. Gloucester, Esq., *ob.* anno. 1675, *ætat.* 58.	=	Elizabeth, dau. of John Saunders, M.D., Provost of Oriel College, Oxon.	
Elizabeth, wife of Charles Hughes of Trostry, co. Monmouth, Esq.	Dorothy, wife of Sir Griffith Jeffreys of Acton, co. Denbigh, Kt.	Robert Pleydell, only son and heir, Justice of the Peace, and D.L., co. Monmouth.	= Sarah, dau. of Philip Shephard of Minching Hampton, co. Gloucester, Esq.

I may add that this branch of the widely-spread family of Pleydell is now represented by Lord Downe. The brother of Lady Dorothy Jeffreys was succeeded at Amney Holyrood by his only son, who was also Robert; and Charlotte Louisa, daughter and heir of this Robert Pleydell, married in 1724 John Dawnay, eldest son of the 2nd Viscount Downe. Henry Pleydell Dawnay, and John Dawnay, the sons of this marriage, were successively 3rd and 4th Viscounts; and the title still continues in the family of the latter. "Pledwell" the spelling of the name in Sir Griffith's will, is most probably the mistake of a lawyer or his clerk. W. T. P.

Extracted from the Principal Registry of the Probate, Divorce, and Admiralty Division of the High Court of Justice.

In the Prerogative Court of Canterbury.

" In the name of God Amen this ninth day of March Anno Domini One thousand six hundred and ninety four and in the seventh yeare of the reigne of our sovereigne Lord King William over England etc. I Griffith Jeffryes of Acton in the County of Denbigh Knight being weake in body but of perfect memory (thankes bee to God) Doe make this my last Will and Testament revoking all other Wills heretofore by mee made. First I bequeath my soul into the hands of Almighty God my heavenly Father by whom of his meere grace I trust to bee saved through the meritts and death of

my only Saviour and Redeemer Jesus Christ And my body to
be buried in Christian buriall att the discretion of my overseers and Trustees hereafter named and touching the dispo-
sition of my worldly estate with which it hath pleased God to
bless me I dispose thereof in manner following   My debts and
funerall expences being first paid and deducted And first
whereas by certain marriage articles bearing date the twenty
sixth day of July in the thirty fifth yeare of the reigne of our
late Sovereign King Charles the Second Anno Domini one
thousand six hundred eighty three I covenanted agreed and
promised to make a Settlement of Four hundred pounds per
ann. if the said Marriage took effect cleare and free from all
taxes and impositions whatsoever (public taxes only and always
excepted) upon ' Dorathy Pledwell' (*sic*) my then intended
wife which said marriage was afterwards compleated and
whereas by the said Settlement accordingly made it is men-
ton'd and declared that the intent and meaning thereof is only
for the setling and securing to my deare Wife the yearly rent
of Three hundred and fifty pounds per annum during her life
in lew and recompense of her dower joynture and meaning
faithfully to fulfil keep and perform the said Articles I doe
hereby will devise and bequeath unto my said dear Wife Fifty
pounds yearly out of such part of my estate as is unsettled to be
clearly and yearly paid her during her life as a rent charge by
my executor hereafter named (publick taxes only excepted) to
the intent that the said Articles may bee fully compleated and
performed Item I give and bequeath unto my three daughters
Elizabeth Margaret and Frances or if more bee liveing at
the time of my decease the sum of six thousand pounds to be
equally divided among them and two or more survivors of
them or in case there happen to bee but one daughter then my
will is that shee have the sum of Five thousand pounds only
paid her   And touching the time of payment of the said
porc'ons my will is that my Executor doe pay the said portons
to my said daughter or daughters as they shall respectively
attaine the age of eighteen years or at the day of marriage
which shall first happen Provided always that such marriage
shall bee contracted by and with the consent of their Guardians
hereafter named or the major part of them.   And as touching
my said daughters my will is that immediately from and after
my decease towards their present maintenance and education
my said executor shall pay yearly and every yeare the sum of
Fifty pounds per ann. to each of them till such time as tho
porc'ons before mentioned shall be paid and my further will is
that if my said Executor shall marry without the consent of

his Guardians hereafter named and the major part of them
that then he shall stand charged with the payment of Ten
thousand pounds porc'on for my said daughters or daughter to
bee payable to and devided among them as aforesaid and the
better to enable my executor hereafter named to pay my debts
discharge my funeral expenses and the legacyes hereby bequeathed (or which shall bee mentioned and expressed in a
schedule or codicil to this my Will annexed and subscribed
with my hand)   I doe hereby give grant devise and bequeatho
to my said executor all the Rest and Residue of my estate reall
or personall within doores or without (other than such part of
my estate as by the said articles or settlement are already disposed of) whether it bee houses lands tenements hereditaments leases mortgages rents arrearages of rent estates of inheritance or purchased in the County of Denbigh or Elsewhere
and all my household goods chattells and Cattell Whatsoever
and all bills bonds and debts due to mee by law and equity
from any person or persons whatsoever   To have and to hold
all the said houses lands tenements and hereditaments and
other the premises to my said executor and the heires males of
his body lawfully begotten and for want of such issue the remainder thereof to my right heirs for ever   Item I give devise and bequeath to my Cosen Thomas Gardner late Fellow
of All Souls Colledge in Oxon the sum of Twenty pounds
yearly dureing his life to bee paid by my executor desireing him
Joyntly with my Wife to take care of the tuic'on education
and government of him dureing his minority   Item I bequeath
to Mr. John Price Vicar of Wrexham the sum of twenty
pounds   Item I give and bequeath to my mother and to Dr.
Jeffreyes's widow and her son each of them Ten pounds to buy
them mourning   Item I give devise and bequeath to Mrs.
Judith Matthews of Acton the yearly sum of Twenty pounds
during her life if she live with my children after mine and my
wife's decease or else but ten pounds per annum   And I doe
hereby nominate and appoint my son Robert Jefferyes sole
Executor of this my last Will and Testament   And I doe
make order and ordaine my said Wife and my brother in law
Robert Pledwell (sic) of Holyrood Amney in the County of
Gloucester Esqr Doctor Jonathan Edwards Principall of Jesus
Colledge Oxon Peter Ellis of Crosnewydd in the County of
Denbigh Esqre and the said Thomas Gardner Trustees of this
my Will   And I nominate my said Wife together with the
said Peter Ellis Esqre and the said Thomas Gardner to be
guardians to my said Executor Robert Jeffreys and to my said
daughters Elizabeth Margaret and Frances until they severally

attaine the age of one and twenty yeares or bee married.   In witness whereof I have to this my last Will sett my hand and seal the day and year first above written

" GRIFFITH JEFFREYS

" Signed scaled and published in presence of us   .
" THO BRADSHAW   " WILLIAM BEAVAN
JONATH STANTON   EDWARD WILLIAMS

" Tricesimo die mensis Maii an'o dom' mill'mo sexcen'mo nonagesimo sexto emanavit Com'o D'næ Dorotheæ Jeffreys viduæ Petro Ellis Armiger' et Thomæ Gardner Gen' gardianis sive tutoribus Testamentariis in Test'em'n'o nominatis D'ni Griffith Jeffreys Militis defuncti habentis &c   Ad administrand' bona jura et credita dicti defuncti juxta tenorem et effectum Test'm'i ipsius def'ci in usum et beneficium et donec et quousque Rob'tus Jeffreys Ar minor filius dicti defuncti et Executor in d'c'o Testamento nominatus vicesimum primum ætatis suæ ann' compleverit de bene et fideliter administrando eadem ad Sancta Dei evangelica (vigore Comconis juratis)."

Y GLWYSEGL. — STANSTI VILLA.   EDWARDS OF
STANSTI.

Edwin ab Goronwy, Prince of Tegeingl. *Argent*, a cross flory engrailed *sable*, inter four Cornish choughs ppr.   Slain in 1073. = Bwerydd, sister of Bleddyn ab Cynfyn, Prince of Powys, and daughter of Cynfyn ab Gwrystan ab Gwaethfoed. *Vert*, a lion rampant *argent*, head, feet, and tail embrued.

Owain ab Edwin, Prince of Tegeingl, and elected Prince of Gwynedd in 1096.   Died of consumption in 1103. *Gules*, three men's legs conjoined at the thighs in triangle *argent*. = Morvydd, d. of Goronwy ab Owain Bendew of Llys Coed y Mynydd in the parish of Bod Vari in Tegeingl. Chief of one of the Noble Tribes. *Argent*, a chev. inter three boar's heads couped *sable*, tusked *or*, and langued *gules*.

| *a* | 2 | *b* | 1 | *c* | 3 | *d* | 4 |

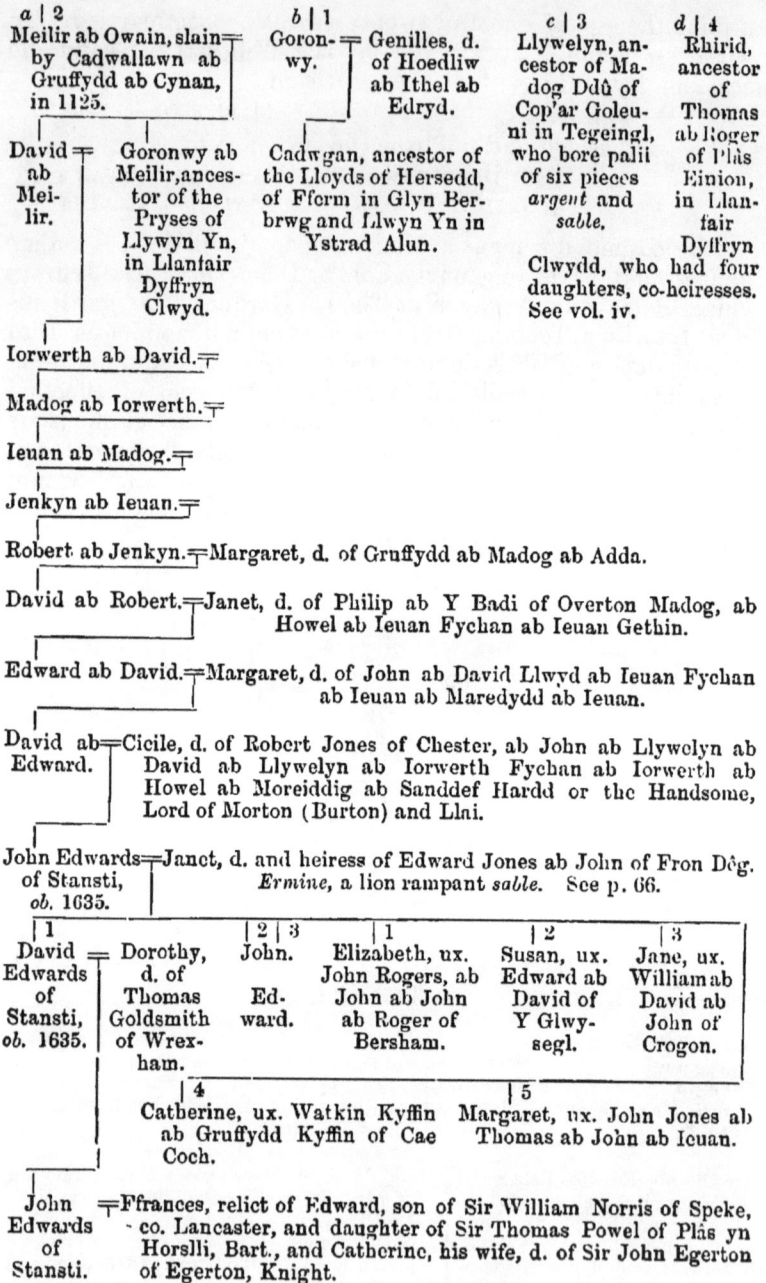

a | 2
Meilir ab Owain, slain⫤
by Cadwallawn ab
Gruffydd ab Cynan,
in 1125.

David ⫤ Goronwy ab
ab   Meilir, ances-
Mei-   tor of the
lir.   Pryses of
        Llywyn Yn,
        in Llanfair
        Dyffryn
        Clwyd.

b | 1
Goron- ⫤ Genilles, d.
wy.   of Hoedliw
         ab Ithel ab
         Edryd.

Cadwgan, ancestor of
the Lloyds of Hersedd,
of Fferm in Glyn Ber-
brwg and Llwyn Yn in
Ystrad Alun.

c | 3
Llywelyn, an-
cestor of Ma-
dog Ddû of
Cop'ar Goleu-
ni in Tegeingl,
who bore palii
of six pieces
argent and
sable.

Dyffryn
Clwydd, who had four
daughters, co-heiresses.
See vol. iv.

d | 4
Rhirid,
ancestor
of
Thomas
ab Roger
of Plâs
Einion,
in Llan-
fair

Iorwerth ab David.⫤

Madog ab Iorwerth.⫤

Ieuan ab Madog.⫤

Jenkyn ab Ieuan.⫤

Robert ab Jenkyn.⫤Margaret, d. of Gruffydd ab Madog ab Adda.

David ab Robert.⫤Janet, d. of Philip ab Y Badi of Overton Madog, ab
Howel ab Ieuan Fychan ab Ieuan Gethin.

Edward ab David.⫤Margaret, d. of John ab David Llwyd ab Ieuan Fychan
ab Ieuan ab Maredydd ab Ieuan.

David ab⫤Cicile, d. of Robert Jones of Chester, ab John ab Llywelyn ab
Edward.   David ab Llywelyn ab Iorwerth Fychan ab Iorwerth ab
            Howel ab Moreiddig ab Sanddef Hardd or the Handsome,
            Lord of Morton (Burton) and Llai.

John Edwards⫤Janet, d. and heiress of Edward Jones ab John of Fron Dêg.
of Stansti,   *Ermine*, a lion rampant *sable*. See p. 66.
ob. 1635.

1	2	3	1	2	3
David Edwards of Stansti, *ob.* 1635.	Dorothy, d. of Thomas Goldsmith of Wrexham.	John. Edward.	Elizabeth, ux. John Rogers, ab John ab John ab Roger of Bersham.	Susan, ux. Edward ab David of Y Glwysegl.	Jane, ux. William ab David ab John of Crogon.

4	5
Catherine, ux. Watkin Kyffin ab Gruffydd Kyffin of Cae Coch.	Margaret, ux. John Jones ab Thomas ab John ab Ieuan.

John   ⫤Ffrances, relict of Edward, son of Sir William Norris of Speke,
Edwards   co. Lancaster, and daughter of Sir Thomas Powel of Plâs yn
of   Horslli, Bart., and Catherine, his wife, d. of Sir John Egerton
Stansti.   of Egerton, Knight.

MAREDITH OF STANSTI.

Burke's Extinct Baronetage.

Richard Maredith of Pentref Bychan, second son of John Maredith ab Rawlyn Maredith of Trefalun, married Jane, daughter of Morgan ab David ab Robert, by whom he had three sons, 1, John Maredith, 2, Sir William, of whom presently, and 3, Hugh Maredith of Pentref Bychan.

Sir William Maredith of Stansti and Leeds Abbey in Kent, knight, treasurer, and paymaster of the army, *temp.* Elizabeth and James I. He married Jane, daughter of Sir Thomas Palmer of Wingham, Bart., and by this lady (who married, secondly, John, Earl of Carbury), he had issue two sons, 1, Sir William, his successor, and 2, Thomas, *ob. s. p.* ; and two daughters, 1, Anne, who married, first, Sir Robert Bassett, and, secondly, Francis, Lord Cottington, and 2, Jane, ux. Sir Peter Wyche.

Sir William Maredith of Stansti and Leeds Abbey, created a baronet 13th August 1622. He married Susanna, daughter of Francis Barker of London, by whom he had issue, besides a daughter Elizabeth, ux. Sir Henry Oxenden of Dean, in Kent, two sons; 1, Sir Richard ; and 2, Roger Maredith, one of the Masters in Chancery, who married Anne, daughter of Sir Brocket Spencer of Offley, co. Herts, Bart.

Sir Richard Maredith, second baronet, of Stansti and

Leeds Abbey.   He married Susanna, daughter of Philip Skippin of Tobsham, co. Norfolk, a Major-General in Cromwell's army ; by whom he had issue six sons.

I. Sir William Maredith, third baronet, of Stansti and Leeds Abbey, *ob. s. p.* 1682.

II. Henry Maredith, a colonel in the army, who married Mary, daughter and heir of Walter Attwood of Hackney, co. Middlesex, by whom he had an only daughter and heiress, Susan, of Leeds Abbey, which she inherited on the death of her uncle, Sir Roger.   She died *s. p.*, and Leeds Abbey was sold in 1765-6 to John Calcraft of Ingress.

III. Sir Richard, fourth baronet, *ob. s. p.* 1723.

IV. Thomas, M.P. for co. Kent, *ob. s. p.*

V. Philip, *ob. s. p.*

VI. Sir Roger Maredith, fifth baronet, of Leeds Abbey, M.P. for co. Kent, 1727.   He married Mary, daughter of Francis Tyssen of Shacklewell, and died *s. p.* 1739.

ESCLYS UWCH Y CLAWDD.   TEGIN OF FRON DEG.

Harl. MSS. 1972, 4181.

Iorwerth Goch ob Madog ab Ieuaf ab Nyniaw ab Cynwrig ab Rhiwallawn.⊤

Madog ab⊤..., d. of Sidan ab Ednyfed Goch ab Cynwrig ab Gruffydd Fychan
Iorwerth. | ab Gruffydd ab Einion ab Ednyfed, Lord of Brochdyn or
| Broughton.   *Ermine*, a lion statant gardant *gules*.

Tegin ab Madog.⊤
| *a* | *b*

a		b
David ab Tegin.=		Lleuci, ux. Deiews ab Dio of Llanerch Rugog.

Robert Tegin=Agnes, d. of Tudor ab Howel ab	Madog ab David.=
of Fron Deg. Ieuan ab Ednyfed Gam.	Edward ab Madog.

Richard Tegin, = Catherine, d. of David ab Gruffydd Fychan of Burton, ab
Sergeant-at-   Madog ab Iorwerth Fychan ab Iorwerth ab David ab
Arms.   Goronwy of Burton and Llai. *Sable*, three roses *argent*.

MANERIUM DE ISCOYD.

Harl. 3696, *fo.* 262.

LIBERE TENENTES.

		Acres.				£	s.	d.
Allington, John .	.	10	0	0	...	0	3	2
Barker, Hugo ap Robt' (Ru' ap Hugh)		4	0	0	...	0	0	8
Billet, Edw' .	.	18	0	0	...	0	1	0
Brereton, Owen .	.	385 & 1 mess's...				2	13	3
Broughton, Edw' miles varia mess'		105	0	0	...	2	2	5½
Broughton, Randall, gen' .	.	not given			..	0	1	3
Calveley, John .	2 mess', 2 tent'	96	0	0	...	0	19	8
Chester, mayor & citizens .	1 tent'	54	0	0	...	1	7	0
Davis, John .	2 mess'	212	0	0	...	1	16	8
Dodd, Gwyne .	1 mess'	3	0	0	...	0	0	10
Dodd, Will'm .	.	4	0	0	...	0	2	0
Edgeburye, John	.	2	0	0	...	0	2	0
Edward ap David	.	1	0	0	...	0	0	2½
Edward ap John de Etton .		3	0	0	...	0	1	10
Edward ap Ile'n .	1 mess'	6	0	0	...	0	1	10
Edward ap Rondell	1 mess'	10	2	10	...	0	1	9
Ellice, Dorothye	.	1	0	1	...	0	0	2
Eyton, Edw' .	varia tent', etc.	440	0	0	...	0	11	8
Eyton, Gerrard .	.	not given			...	1	10	2
Eyton, John, gen'	.	57	0	0	...	0	9	0
Goldsmith, Tho's	.	6	0	0	...	0	5	8
Griffith, John .	.	0	0	1	...	0	0	0½
Griffith, John ap John de Garthen 1 tent'	50	0	0	...	0	0	10
Griffith, Tho's (Joh'es ap Ieu'n Maddock)	12	0	0	...	0	0	10
Hugo ap Will'm .	.	12	0	0	...	0	3	0
Humfrye, John .	1 mess'	4	0	0	..	0	1	0
Jefferyes, John .	1 tent', 1 mess'	55	0	0	...	0	7	3
John ap Edw' ap Ieu'n .	.	40	0	0	...	0	0	10
John ap Rob't ap John ap Ieu'n (Sir E. Broughton) .	1 mess'	20	0	0	...	0	2	2
Jones, Owen .	1 mess'	34	0	0	...	0	4	7
Kenrick, John .	.	per terris lib'is...				0	0	2

	Acres.	£ s. d.
Kenrick ap Rob't et d'd (Sir E. Broughton) . . .	not given ...	0 0 10
Langford, Richard . 1 mess'	20 0 0 ...	0 5 2
Lewes, Richard . . 2 mess'	60 0 0 ...	0 10 0
Leighton, Richard (Sir E. Broughton)	4 0 0 ...	0 8 0
Lloyd, David . . .	12 0 0 ...	0 5 7
Lloyd, John (Sir E. Broughton) .	2 0 0 ...	0 0 4
Lloyd, John ap Richard . 1 mess'	11 0 0 ...	0 16 4
Lloyd, Rice . . .	not given ...	0 3 0½
Lloyd, Robert . . 1 tent'	12 0 0 ...	0 3 7
Maddock, John Will'm . .	2 0 0 ...	rent not given
Margaret, v' Robert . 1 mess'	5 0 0 ...	0 2 4
Parry, Ric' ep'us Asaphen'. .		
1 mess', 4 cott	110 0 0 ...	1 4 9
Payne, Oliver John . .	4 0 0 ...	0 3 4
Phillip, Will'm . . 1 mess'	1 0 0 ...	0 0 2
Price, Samuell . . 1 mess'	20 0 0 ...	0 2 0
Puleston, Edw' . . 3 mess'	28 0 0 ...	0 7 4
Randall, John . . 1 mess'	6 0 0 ...	0 3 4
Richard ap John ap Edw' . .	70 0 0 ..	0 2 6
Richard ap Robert . .	12 0 0 ...	0 1 10
Richard ap Will'm . .	8 0 0 ...	0 1 3
Robert ap d'd . . .	4 0 0 ...	0 2 0
Roger ap Roger (Gerrard Eyton) .	not given ...	0 0 7
Roydon, Roger . . 6 mess'	181 0 0 ...	1 19 7
Santhye, al's Sandy, Rob'. .	1 2 0 ...	0 0 6
Soulley, Rob' . . .	18 0 0 ...	0 4 2½
Sutton, Roger . . .	2 0 0 ...	0 0 8
Taylor, John . . 1 mess'	26 0 0 ...	0 3 8
Taylor, Thomas . . .	1 0 0 ...	0 0 4
Thomas, David (Will'm Patc) 1 mess'	0 2 1 ...	0 0 2
Thomas ap d'd ap Ieu'n ap Ilc'n .	not given ...	0 1 3½
Thomas ap John ap Edward .	40 0 0 ...	0 0 10
Vaghan, Will'm . . .	not given ...	0 6 8
Warburton, Sir Peter . 1 mess'	17 0 0 ...	0 3 6
Wells, Lawrence . .	50 0 0 ...	0 18 8
William, Henry . . 1 mess'	20 0 0 ...	Sr. H.Salesbury payes the rent.
William ap·Hugh . .	7 0 0 ...	0 1 7
William, John ap John Griffith .	1 0 0 ...	0 0 2½
Wright, Edw' . . .	50 0 0 ...	1 16 7
S'ma Redd' lib'oru tenen'		25 1 5½
4o Eliz'		25 7 4½
Thomas Powell por terr' lib'is		0 0 6

TENENTES P' DIMISSIONES.

	Acres.			Value.			Rent. £	s.	d.
Broughton, Edw., miles	45	0	0	16	19	8	2	12	6½
Broughton, John, d'd, Ruyton	24	0	0	13	0		0	16	0
Breerton, Edw' Owen, Cackadutton	44	0	0	13	6	8	1	6	5
Caucley, John, Sutton	3	0	0	1	6	8	0	0	10
Chester, Villa de, Cackadutton	2	0	0	1	0	0	0	2	9
David ap John Roger, Ruyton	6	0	0	2	13	4	0	3	10
Davies, John de Erlirs or Erlist,									
Byeston Iscoyd	6	0	0	2	6	8	0	5	0
Cackadutton	1	2	0	1	6	8	0	3	2
Eton	1	2	0	0	15	0	0	2	10
Davies, John, gent., Cackadutton	4	0	0	1	10	0	0	3	2
Dodd, Owen, Sutton	0	0	3	0	3	4	0	0	2
Dodd, Wm. and Owen, Sutton	2	0	0	0	13	4	0	0	8
Edgebury, John, Eton	diversas terr'						0	8	0
Edward ap d'd, Cackadutton	10	0	0	4	13	4	0	10	6
Edward ap John ap Edward, Sutton	1	0	0	0	6	8	0	1	4
Ruyton	0	1	0	0	2	6	0	0	6
Eton, Edward, Ruabon	0	2	0	0	4	0	0	0	6
Eton, Jerrard, Eton	6	2	0	2	0	0	0	8	0
Eton, Thomas, Sutton	1	0	0	0	10	0	0	1	0
Fletcher, Hugh, Cackadutton	1	0	0	0	7	6	0	2	4
Griffith ap Tuder, Ruyton	2	2	0	1	6	8	0	2	0
Goldsmith, Thos., Cackadutton	1	0	0	0	8	0	0	1	0
Gough, John, Cackadutton	1	2	0	0	13	4	0	2	10
Heres of John ap Edw' ap d'd ap Mad', Ruyton	3	0	0	1	3	4	0	2	0
Heres of Meredeth ap Ellice (Will'm Launcelot), Ruyton	4	0	0	2	6	8	0	3	4
Heres of Thomas ap Will'm ap John, Cackadutton	0	2	0	0	6	8	0	2	8
Howell ap Ile'n, Eton	1	2	0	1	6	8	0	1	8
Hugh ap Thomas, widow of, Sutton	3	1	0	1	13	4	0	4	8
Jerrard, Jane, Cackadutton	3	0	0	1	6	8	0	4	0
Ieu'n ap Shone, Christ K.	2	2	0	1	10	0	0	1	8
John ap Edw. ap John, Ruyton	7	1	0	3	0	0	0	6	4
John ap Edw. ap D'd ap Mad' Eyton	3	0	0	1	10	0	0	2	0
John ap Edw' ap d'd ap Mad', vide *heres.*									
John ap Robt', Sutton	5	0	0	2	12	8	0	5	1
John, Robert, Sutton	0	0	2	0	5	0	0	0	2
John, William, ap Jo' Griffith, Sutton	13	3	20	6	15	10	0	9	4
Jones, Hugh, Erlisham.	10	2	0	3	10	0	0	7	0
Jones, Owen, Byeston Iscoyd	22	0	0	8	5	1	1	9	8
Gowrton Iscoyd	8	3	0	3	0	0	0	5	1

	Acres.			Value.			Rent.£	s.	d.
Leighton, Rich', Sutton .	6	1	10	3	6	8	0	4	2
Lewes ap Edw', Sutton . .	0	0	3	0	4	0	0	0	2
Lloyd, John, ap Ric., Cackadutton	7	0	0	2	13	4	0	13	4
Lloyd, Hugh, Eton . .	4	0	0	1	13	4	0	3	0
Lloyd, Hugh, ap Mad', Eton .	3	0	0	1	10	0	0	4	4
Madock, Sara, Sutton .	Cott', &c.						0	0	4
Margaret, v' Robt., Eton .	4	0	0	2	6	8	0	4	2
Margaret, v' Robt' ap d'd ap Grono, Iscoyd Abimbery .	13	0	0	12	0	0	0	15	0
Meredeth, widow of Lewes, Cacka-dutton . . .	1	2	20	1	0	0	0	3	9
Mynshaw, John, Sutton .	1	0	0	0	6	8	0	1	0½
Pierce, Wm', Cackadutton .	2	2	0	1	0	0	0	3	4
Pierce, Wm' et Tho's, Cackadutton	0	2	20	0	8	0	0	0	8
Powell, John ap John, d'd, Cacka-dutton . .	2	0	0	1	6	8	0	5	6
Powell, Tho's, Cackadutton .	5	2	0	2	13	4	0	9	0
Puleston, Edw', Cackadutton .	26	3	0	12	10	0	1	18	8
Sutton .	2	0	0	0	13	4	0	1	8
Randall, John, Ruyton .	2	2	0	1	6	8	0	1	4
Randle, Agnes, v' Christioneth Kenrick . .	4	1	0	2	0	0	0	3	2
Richard ap Edw', Christioneth Kenrick . .	1	3	0	1	6	8	0	1	1
Richard ap Ellis, widow of (Thomas Evans), Ruyton .	5	0	0	3	6	8	0	3	4
Richard ap Rob't .	29	3	10	16	12	4	2	1	1
Roydon, Roger .	51	3	30	24	10	0	1	6	3
Salisbury, Henry, Cackadutton .	12	3	0	6	0	0	0	7	3
Sutton Inhabitants, Sutton .	6	0	0	1	16	0	0	4	0
Taylor, Jo' et Kenrick Eyton, Sutton	8	1	0	3	0	0	1	6	5
Thelwale, Benis, Ruyton .	20	0	0	10	0	0	0	16	9
Thomas ap d'd ap John, Ruyton .	5	0	0	1	13	4	0	3	0
Thomas ap John Griffith, Beyeston Iscoyd .	6	0	0	2	6	8	0	5	4
Thomas ap Maddock, Byeston Iscoyd	0	0	4	0	6	8	0	0	6
Vernon, Ric', Cackadutton .	1	0	0	0	7	0	0	0	7
Wells, Lawrence, Byeston Iscoyd .	Tent, &c.			No value given			0	5	0
William ap Hugh ap Griffith, Sutton	9	0	20	4	0	0	0	11	0
Wright, Edw. Sutton .	12	2	20	5	10	0	0	13	6
Wynn, assign of Robt', Ruyton .	1	0	0	0	16	0	0	1	1
Wynn, Robt', Sutton .	0	2	0	0	4	0	0	0	·6½
S'ma Redd' tenen' ad volunt' et p' demiss' .							27	17	4
4o Eliz' . . .							26	6	3
Redd' in toto .							52	18	9

HEIN MANERIUM.

LIBER TENENS.

COMES DE BRIDGEWATER (RIC'US TREVOR, MILES) 80 ACRES £7 10s. 6¼d.

TENENTES PER DIMISSIONEM.	Acres.			Value.			Rent. £	s.	d.
Hugo ap Will'm	3	1	0	1	6	8	0	4	7
Jones, Edw' .	2	2	0	1	10	0	0	5	6
Jones, Hugo .	10	3	20	6	0	0	0	5	6
Kenrick, William	12	0	20	8	0	0	0	13	3
Mottershed, Eliz'	3	3	0	1	13	4	0	3	9
Richard, ap Will'm	6	3	16	3	13	4	0	8	11
S'ma Redd' ten' ad volunt' et p' demiss'							2	0	9½
4o Eliz'							27	6	5

The rest is conveyed away in fee simple vt
dicitur.

COBHAM.

Harl. 3696, *fo.* 290.

The presentment and verdict of the Jurie for the Manor
of Cobham Iscoyd whose names are herevnder written, viz. :—

George Bostock, esq.
Dauid Speed, gent.
Thomas Calcott, gent.
Thomas Pate, gent.
William Wyld, gent.
Frauncis Pickering, gent.
John Yardley, gent.
John Wilkinson.
Randolph Hutchins.

Thomas Wilkinson.
Thomas Palford.
Roger Edgworth.
John Wright.
William Batha.
George Wright.
Richard Vernon.
Roger Greene.

The said jury vppon their oathes do p'sent that ye persons
vnder named are his highnes customarie tennants or tenaunts
by leases for ffortie yeares within ye said mannor, and pay for
the landes in their severall tenures and occupations. The
rents vpon their names appearinge, and doe further pay and
perfourme all other duties, payments, and services specified in
their said leases, and due and accustomed to be aunswered,
paid, and perfourmed for landes of yt nature, which landes in
anncient tymes, in ye begining of ye raigne of the late Queene
Elizabeth of famous memorie, and long since before were helde
by the tennants thereof and their auncestors as their inherit-

aunce, and claymed by them as discendible to them and their heires. As well by coppies of court rolles as by ye custome of ye countrey, and so by them hold and enioyed vntill ye ffourth yeare of the said late Queene Elizabeth her raigne, as in the pr'amble for ye mannor of Howlington more perticulerlie is meuconed and more plainly appeareth.

	Acres.			Value.			Rent. £	s.	d.
Bostock, George .	13	0	0	6	0	0	1	3	7
Brewerton, Owen, esq. .	13	2	0	4	3	4	1	3	8
Broughton, Edw', miles .	42	2	0	18	10	0	5	4	8
Calcott, Thos. .	14	0	1	6	0	0	1	16	8
Caluerley, John .	16	0	0	5	16	8	2	1	4
Chester, Mayor, &c., of .	6	2	0	3	5	4	0	10	2
Crue, Edw' .	1	0	0	0	10	0	0	2	0
Davies, John, of Erchlisham, gen' .	4	2	0	2	8	0	0	9	0
Edwardes, John .	0	1	0				0	0	2
Fletcher, Hugh .	3	0	0	1	6	8	0	6	3
Gettyn, Humfrey .	4	0	0	2	3	4	0	7	2
Goldsmith, Thomas .	1	0	0	0	10	0	0	1	0
John ap John Gethin .	3	0	0	1	10	0	0	5	2
Jones, Hugh .	3	&c.		1	6	8	0	2	2
Jones, Owen .	1	1	20	0	18	0	0	2	8
Jonet v' Hugh . 1 mess'	2	0	0	1	10	0	0	2	1
Lloyd, John .	8	0	0	3	16	8	0	14	2
Meredeth, heres of Jo' .	6	0	0				0	13	4
Mynshaw, Jo' .	2	0	0	1	0	0	0	2	1
Pate, Tho's .	12	0	1	5	0	0	1	5	9½
Puleston, Edw' .	1	0	0	0	15	0	0	2	2
Puleston, Rob' .	6	0	0				0	13	4
Read, John .	3	0	0	1	13	0	0	1	2
Richard ap Robert .	5	2	20	3	8	6	0	13	4
Trevor, Jo', miles .	1	1	20	0	18	0	0	2	8
Wilkinson, Jo' .	2	0	0	1	0	0	0	2	8
William ap Hugh .	3	0	0	1	10	0	0	5	2
Wright, Edw' .	2	1	20	2	0	0	0	4	10
Wyn, Robt. .	3	1	0	1	3	4	0	8	3

	£	s.	d.
The rent of Cobham Iscoyd and Cobham Almer was 40 Eliz' . . .	22	15	4½
Now, as the tennantes sworne have gyven it in by the p'ticulars, it comes but vnto .	18	5	1½
Shorte of the former .	4	10	3

But I find the landes belonging vnto one manor to lie generally within another, so as the baylie of one manor gathers rentes in dyuers manors. So that thowgh the rentes come shorte in one it is payde in some other, as will appear in the total.

		£	s.	d.
Cobham Iscoyd demisable is	.	16	11	$4\frac{1}{2}$
demean	.	0	33	8
S'ma	.	17	5	$0\frac{1}{2}$
S'ma redd' ad h'mic diem	.	19	7	$6\frac{1}{2}$
4° Eliz'	.	22	15	$4\frac{1}{2}$

The rest is soulde.

MANOR OF ISGOED.—TOWNSHIP OF BWRAS.
HAFOD Y BWCH.

Harl. MS. 4181.

David Llwyd of Hafod y Bwch and Bwrasham, second son of Madog=Lleuci, ab Llywelyn ab Gruffydd ab Cadwgan, Lord of Eyton, Erlisham, d. of and Borasham. *Ermine,* a lion rampt. *azure.* See vol. ii, p. 157.

Ieuan ab David Llwyd=Eva, d. and heir of Gru- Howel ab Gwladys.
of Hafod y Bwch. His ffydd ab Gruffydd Ddû David
estates were forfeited ab Gruffydd Fychan ab Llwyd. His Lleuci.
to the king for his Gruffydd ab Howel ab estates were
having joined Owain Hwfa ab Iorwerth ab forfeited to Angba-
Glyndwr. He had a Gruffydd ab Ieuaf ab king in con- rad.
natural daughter mar- Nyniaf. *Gules,* two sequence of
ried to David ab Ieuan lions passant *argent,* his having
Painod. for Iorwerth ab Gruff- joined Owain
ydd of Bersham. Glyndwr.

Goronwy ab =Gwenllian, d. of Ieuan ab Gruffydd Goch of Bers, ab Madog
Ieuan of Pabo ab Ednyfed Goch (*ermine,* a lion statant gardant
Hafod y *gules*), and relict of Robert ab Gruffydd ab Howel ab Gruff-
Bwch. ydd of Croes Foel.

Mallt, sole daughter=David Lloyd ab Tudor Lloyd of Bodidris yn Iâl.
and heiress of Hafod V *Gules*, three pales *or*, in a border of the third, semé
y Bwch. of ogresses.

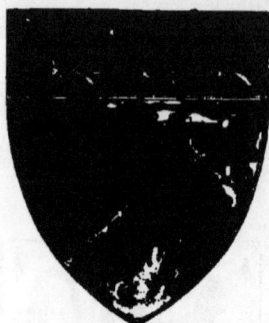

MANOR OF ISGOED.—DE WEILD OF BORASHAM.

John de Weild or Wylde of Holt. *Argent*, a chevron *sable*, on a chief of the second, three martletts of the field.

Richard de Weild of Holt.—Margaret, d. of John Lowther of Holt. *Or*, seven annulets *sable*.

David de Weild of Holt.—Margaret, d. of John Maredydd ab Rowland ab Maredydd of Trefalun. *Azure*, a lion salient *or*.

Richard de Weild of Holt.—Angharad, d. and co-heir of Jenkyn ab Ieuan Llwyd of Allt Llwyn Dragon, now called Plâs yn Iâl, ab Llywelyn ab Gruffydd Llwyd of Bodidris yn Iâl, ab Maredydd ab Llywelyn ab Ynyr of Iâl. *Gules*, three pales *or*, in a border of the third semé of ogresses.

Jenkyn de Weild of Holt.—Lleuci, d. and heiress of David Llwyd of Crew, ab David Llwyd ab Thomas ab Rhys ab Hwfa Grûg ab Hwfa ab Sanddef ab Elidir ab Rhys Sais. *Ermine*, a lion rampant in a border *azure*.

Thomas de Weild or Wylde of Borasham. He purchased from the Lord of Bromfield the house and lands in Borasham, after the attainder of Howel and Ieuan, the sons of David Llwyd of Hafod y Bwch and Borasham.—Tibot, ux. David Thelwall of Plâs y Ward.

1. Catherine, 1st co-heir, ux. William Brereton, *jure uxoris* of Borasham, second son of Sir Randle Brereton of Malpas, Knight.

2. Margaret, 2nd co-heir. She married first, William Alunton ab David ab Gruffydd of Alunton; and secondly, Edward ab Howel of Llwyn On.

MANOR OF IS Y COED.—BRERETON OF BORASHAM.

Ormerod's *Hist. of Cheshire*; *Cae Cyriog MS.*

William de Brereton, Lord of Brereton, in the County Palatine of⚊
   Chester, 1125. *Argent, two bars sable.*

William de Brereton, Lord of Brereton.⚊

Sir Ralph de Brereton, Knt., Lord of Brereton.⚊Cicilie, d. of Sir George St.
             George, Knt.

Sir William de Brereton Knt , Lord of⚊Margaret, d. of Randle de Thorn-
   Brereton.   ton, son of Peter de Thornton.

Sir Ralph or Randol-⚊The Lady Ada, fourth daughter and co-heiress of
phus de Brereton, David, Earl of Huntingdon in England, son of
Knt. He married, Henry,[1] Crown Prince of Scotland, son of David,
secondly, Margaret, first King of Scotland, and relict of Henry de
daughter and co- Hastings. Her mother was Maud, d. of Hugh
heiress of Sir Rhy- Cyfeiliog, Earl of Chester. It was in the suite of
dderch Groes, Knt. the Princess Maude that Sir Randolph de Brere-
        ton went to Scotland.

Sir William de Brereton, Knt., Lord⚊Cicilie, d. of Sir Richard de Sandbach,
   of Brereton.   Knt.

a

[1] Henry, Crown Prince of Scotland, married Adeline, daughter of
William de Warrenne, Earl of Warrenne and Surrey, by whom he
had issue three sons ; 1, Malcolm, King of Scotland, who died *s. p.*
in 1165 ; 2, William, surnamed the Lion, King of Scotland, and
father of Alexander II, King of Scotland ; and 3, David, Earl of
Huntingdon, who married Maud, daughter of Hugh Cyfeiliog, Count
Palatine of Chester, by whom he had four daughters, co-heirs ; 1,
Margaret, who married Adam, Lord of Galloway, by whom she had
two daughters, co-heirs, Devorgila, ux. John de Baliol, and Mar-
jory, ux. John the Black Comyn, Lord of Badenoch ; 2, Isabel, ux.
Robert Bruce ; 3, Maud ; and 4, Ada.

| a

Sir William de Brereton, Knt., Lord=Roesia, d. of Sir Ralph de Vernon,
    of Brereton. | Knt., Baron of Sheproc.

William de Brereton, *ob. vita patris.*=Margaret, d. of Richard Bosley.

Sir William de=1st, Elen, sister and co-heir of David Eger-=2nd, Marga-
Brereton, Knt., | ton, Baron of Malpas, son and heir of Sir | ret, d. of Sir
Lord of Brere- | Philip de Malpas, Knt., and Elen, his | John Done
ton. He had | wife, d. of John de Sancto Petro, son of | of Utkinton,
the moiety of | Urien de Sancto Petro, by Idonea, his | co. Chester,
the Barony of | wife, d. and co-heir of David le Clerk, | Knt.
Malpas. | Baron of Malpas.

Sir William de Brereton, Knt., Lord   Sir Randle=Alicia, Lady of Ipstones,
of Brereton. He served in Nor-   Brereton,   d. and heiress of Wil-
mandy. He died, and was buried   of Malpas,   liam Ipstones, Lord of
there. His tomb, with his arms   Knt.   Ipstones, son and heir
quarterly on it, is to be seen in   of Sir John Ipstones,
the church where he was buried,   Knt., Lord of Ipstones
to this day, says Lewys Dwnn.   in Cheshire.
He left £10 to be paid yearly for
the repairs of the church and his   1. *Argent,* a chev. inter
tomb, that it might be a memorial   three crescents *gules.*
of him. He married Andella, dau.   2. *Or,* two ravens ppr.
of Sir Hugh Venables, Baron of   for Corbet of Wattles-
Kinderton (*azure,* two bars *argent*),   borough.
and was the ancestor of Sir William   3. *Sable,* an Escarbuncle
Brereton, Knt., Lord of Brereton,   of eight rays *or,* for
1591.   Tirret.

| 2

William Brereton=Catherine, d. and co-heir of Thomas de Wyle of Bora-
of Borasham,   sham. *Argent,* a chevron *sable,* on a chief of the second
1450.   three martletts of the field.

Edward=1st, Elizabeth, d. of John Roydon of Pulford,=2nd, Dorothy, second
Brere- | and Maude, his wife, d. of Sir Roger | wife, d. of Richard
ton of | Puleston of Emrall, Knt. *Vert,* three | Hanmer of Hanmer,
Bora- | roebuck's heads erased in bend *or,* in | and Margaret, his
sham. | dexter chief a rose of the second, Roydon. | wife, d. of Sir Roger
                                                 Kynaston, Knt.

Thomas Bre-=Margaret, d.   Elizabeth,   Joanna,   Cathe-
reton, Rector | of Ithel ab   ux. James   ux. Cyn-   rine, ux.
of Llaneur- | Gruffydd ab   Eyton of   wrig ab   Launce-
gain, 1539; | Belyn of   Eyton.   Richard   lot Lloyd
V. of Llan- | Nerewys.   *Ermine,* a   of Pen-   of Yr Or-
drinio, 1557; | Palii of six   lion rampt.   achlech.   seddGoch
V. of Gres- | pieces *argent*   *azure.*   in Trefa-
ford, 1566. | and *sable.*   lun.

Peter Brere-= Jane, d. of   Hugh,   Dorothy,   Mary.
ton, M.A., | Owain ab John   *s. p.*   ux. William
Vicar of | ab Howel   John.   Lewys of
Llanfihan- | Fychan.   Ran-   Wrexham.
gel, 1597.   dolph.

| 1a | 2b

1a		2b	
Randolph Goch=Margaret, d. of Elis ab		John = Margaret, d. and	
Brereton of	Elis Eyton of Rhiwa-	Brere-	heiress of Richard
Borasham.	bon. Her mother was	ton of	ab Ieuan ab David
	Berrenet, d. of Thomas	Boras-	ab Ithel Fychan
	Bulkeley. *Ermine*, a	ham.	of Llaneurgain.
	lion rampant *azure*.		*Argent*, a chevron
			inter three boar's
Jane, daughter and heiress, married Robert ab Ed-		heads couped *sable*.	
ward ab Edward ab David ab Madog ab Llywelyn,		See p.	
ancestor of the Traffords of Treffordd. (She was			
also the wife of Robert, son of Edward Puleston			
of Esclusham.) *Ermine*, a lion rampant *sable*.			

Margaret,	Jane, married 1st,	Owain	Elizabeth. She married 1st,
ux.	Edward Bwras;	Brereton	John Caurden, by whom
Thomas	2nd, Cynwrig ab	of	she was mother of Richard
ab John.	Howel of Glan y	Borasham.	Caurden, Dean of Chiches-
	Pwll, in Borasham.		ter; 2nd, John ab Madog
			ab Ieuan ab David; 3rd,
			Robert Wynn ab Morgan of
			Sonlli.

The above named Owain Brereton of Borasham, was High Sheriff for the county of Denbigh in the years 1581 and 1588. He married, first, Elizabeth, only daughter of John Salusbury of Llyweni, Chamberlain of Denbigh, and M.P. for Denbigh in 1554, and Catherine, his wife, daughter and heiress of Tudor ab Robert Fychan of Berain, in Llannefydd. He married, secondly, Catherine, daughter of Harri Goch Salusbury of Llywesog, in the parish of Llanrhaiadr, and relict of John Lloyd of Bodidris yn lâl.

By his first wife Elizabeth, Owain Brereton had issue nine sons and five daughters.

1. Edward Brereton, of whom presently.

2. John Brereton of Esclusham, who married Margaret, relict of Robert Empson of London, and daughter of Hugh Wynn of Wigfair, in Meriadog, *vert*, three eagles displayed in fess *or*, by whom he had four daughters, co-heirs; 1, Elizabeth, *ob*. Feb. 26th, 1656, ux. Thomas Bulkeley of Coedan, in Anglesey; 2, Jane, who married, first, John Ffachnallt of Ffachnallt in Tegeingl, by whom she had a daughter Jane, who married Richard Evans, Parson of Cilcain; and, secondly, she married Owain Lloyd, second son of William Lloyd of Plâs Madog, in Rhiwabon; 3, Dorothy; and 4, Elen. John Brereton, died 24th Jan, 1622, and was buried at Wrexham.

3, Thomas ; 4, William, a Captain in the army ; 5, Owain, a Captain in the army ; 6, Edward ; 7, Randle, a Lieutenant in the army ; 8, Andrew, a Lieutenant in the army ; and 9, Roger.

The five daughters were ; 1, Mary, who married, first, Cynwrig Hanmer of Caer Fallwch, in Llaneurgain, ab Pyers Hanmer, ab Richard Hanmer, ab Howel ab David ab Ithel Fychan,[1] and, secondly, she married Harri Jones ; 2, Elen, ux. George Kywr of Plâs Cadwgan ; 3, Dorothy, ux. Robert Trevor of...... ; 4, Catherine, ux. William Lloyd of Plâs Madog, in Rhiwabon ; and 5, Sarah, *ob. s. p.*

Edward Brereton of Borasham, the eldest son of Owain Brereton, held an Eisteddfod in 1597, and was High Sheriff for Denbighshire in 1598, in which year he died. He married Anne, daughter of John Lloyd of Bodidris, in Iâl, High Sheriff for Denbighshire in 1551, and Catherine, his wife, daughter of Harri Goch Salusbury of Llanrhaiadr, by whom he had issue three sons ; 1, Owain, of whom presently ; 2, Edward ; and 3, Roger ; and three daughters ; 1, Catherine, ux. John Lloyd of Ar Ddwyfaen, in Dinmael ; 2, Jane, ux. Roger Bady of Stansti ; and 3, Margaret.

Owain Brereton of Borasham, married Sarah, daughter and heiress of Edward Eyton of Eyton, who had all her father's lands, except Park Eyton. She married, secondly, Ralph Egerton, Esq. Owain Brereton died in 1603, leaving issue a son and heir,

Owain Brereton of Borasham, who died in 1648. He had a son and heir,

Edward Brereton, who died on the 8th of July 1645, in his father's lifetime. He married Jane, daughter of John Gruffydd of Lleyn, co. Caernarvon (*azure*, a chev. inter three dolphins, naiant, embowed *argent*), which lady married, secondly, Humphrey Lloyd, Vicar of Rhiwabon and Dean of St. Asaph, and died 10th October 1689. By his wife Jane, Edward Brereton had issue two sons.

---

[1] Ithel Fychan of Llaneurgain ab Cynwrig ab Rotpert ab Iorwerth ab Rhirid ab Iorwerth ab Madog ab Ednowain Bendew.

1. .... Brereton of Borasham, who died without issue in December 1657.

2. Edward Brereton, who succeeded to the Borasham estates on the death of his brother. In 1689 he was chosen to represent Denbigh and its contributory Boroughs in Parliament; and, after a contested election with Mr. Williams, son of Sir William Williams, the Speaker of the House of Commons, was again elected in 1690. He was appointed Alderman of Denbigh Aug. 11, 1693, and re-elected member for the Boroughs in 1698.

In 1701 Thomas Cotton contested the Boroughs with Mr. Brereton, but the latter was again successful.

He married a daughter of Sir Thomas Lake of Cannons, in Middlesex, Knt., by whom he had issue two sons; 1, Edward; and 2, John Brereton.

Humphrey Brereton of Borasham, Esq., died between the years 1725 and 1735, in which last year his sister, Madam Anne Brereton, was assessed for the estates.

John Robinson Litton was assessed for these estates from 1748 to 1764. Mrs. Robinson Litton's name appears in 1764, and she was succeeded in 1765 by John Twigge, Esq., who was High Sheriff for Denbighshire in 1785.

Lord Kenyon bought the Borasham estate from John Twigge about 1790.

———

John ab Howel Brereton, by his will dated 18th March 1537-8, proved 28th April 1539, desires that his body may be buried at St. Margaret's, Westminster, and leaves to his nephew, John Wynn ab David, all lands, etc., within Bromfield, the town of Wrexham, Iâl, Edeyrnion, Maelor Gymraeg, Maelor Saesneg, "rents of Llangerniw due to me, Vaynor Dymeirchion, my farmours of Baklonds, my farmours of my vicarage of Long Stanton (in Cambridgeshire)".

I have not been able to discover who this John ab Howel Brereton was; but there was a John Brereton, Canon of the Royal Chapel of St. Stephen's, Westminster, who was living in 1536.

Elizabeth Brereton, daughter of John Brereton, Esq. Her will was dated 24th March 1543, and proved in 1545. She appears by her will to have married, first, John Courden ; secondly, John ab Madog ab Icuan ab David ; and, thirdly, Robert Wynn ab Morgan of Soulli.

CYWYDD I MAISTYR OWAIN BRYRTWN O FWRAS.

SION TUDYR AI CANT.

Y mae genyf ym ganwyl
Y Maelor wen ym lêr wyl
A lle i ynill llawenydd
A lles y rhawg a llys rhydd
A llys hynod lle i sonion
A llew sydd yn a llys hon
Owain gwr enw a gerir
Ymwras ail Emrys hir
Barwn o Frywtwn[1] ai fraint
Barwn henfro brenhinfraint
Bu wirflawd heb i orffen
Bu rad Duw 'n nhac Bryrtwn hen
Awn ŷ gler enwowglew oedd
At Owain yn fihteioedd
At lew Ifainc teulufaidd
O ryw o gras rywiog glan
Rhodd i'r aur rhydd ar Arian
Y carw Ifanc arafwych
Ar fedd gwr arafiad gwych
Siriol glew sy reiol glan
Sadrwydd yn pwyso oedran
Gwr o waed yw goran y del
Gwraidd iachau pob gradd uchel
A myng o radd Mynwair aur
Ir mwnygl acrwg manaur
Dun hael da iawn i helynt
Dwyn iawn gwrs Ednowain[2] gynt
Dysgod i feilch dasg hyd fedd
Dyn a rhediad o anhrydedd
I iach oll uwch i llaw
Y llwybr oedd lle i bu'r eiddaw

---

[1] Brereton.   [2] Ednowain Bendew.

Iddo i rhoed da i gwedd ŷ rhawg
Orau enerch wyr y enarchawg
Elsbeth[1] air odieth rydeg
Lan doeth o Lyweni deg
Nid yw hael onid ŷ hi
Nid iselbris nod Salbri[2]
A gwaed Penrhyn[3] yn unwedd
Gadwynawg waed o Wynedd
Merch hên Sion[1] ymraych hwn sydd
Merch Ann Mawr yw i chynydd
Seren yw sy oran yn wir
Salbri[2] waedol sel brodir
Olwen ddyn law ddiannael
Eigr a Sion ai gwr sy hael
Duw ai gwyddiad da i gweddau
Da ddawn lys a denddyn lan
Cyd euro cerdd cyd roi i caid
Cyd gynal cadw i gweiniad
Cyd wych wrthel cyd chwerthin
Cyd lawgwr cyd lenwi gwin
Cyd talu brig gwaed dilyth
Cyd euro beirdd cyd roi byth
I glod aeth ef ai wraig lan
Dros led dagar sy lydan
Da dros dadl di drawst ydyw
Dryd ar Sais di rodres yw.
   Owain sydd eineoes iddo
Uchaf yw i iachau fo
Teg waed Maelor waed digoll
Teg Angel waed Tegeingl oll
Ais gref Ysgwier Ifainc
A bery draw ef awr drainc
Iw lys gwrol is gorallt
Ymwras draw ymrest yr allt
Yno fydd iawn yw i fod
......ndd Ifanc o iawn ddefod.

---

[1] Elizabeth was the daughter of John Salusbury, Esq., heir of Llyweni, and Catherine, his wife, daughter and heiress of Tudor ab Robert Fychan of Berain in Llannefydd.   [2] Salusbury.

[3] Sir Thomas Salusbury of Llyweni, Knt., who died, and was buried in the chapel of the Carmelites at Denbigh, in January 1505, married Janet, only daughter by his first wife of Gwilym Fychan of Penrhyn, Chamberlain of North Wales, ab Gwilym ab Gruffydd ab Gwilym ab Gruffydd ab Heilin ab Sir Tudor ab Ednyfed Fychan.

IPSTONE OF IPSTONE, IN THE COUNTY PALATINE OF CHESTER.[1]

Harl. MSS. 1396 ; 5529, fo. 31 ; 6128, fo. 60.
Lewys Dwnn, vol. ii, p. 353.

Sir John de Ipstone, Lord of Ipstone, Ipstones, or Ipstanes, *ob.* A.D. 1394. = Elizabeth, dau. and heiress of Thomas Corbet of Wattlesborough, eldest son and heir of Sir Robert Corbet of Morton Corbet and Wattlesborough, Knight. Thomas Corbet died A.D. 1375. He had two younger brothers, Fulke, whose only daughter and heiress married John Lord of Mawddwy, son and heir of William Lord of Mawddwy, fourth son of Gruffydd ab Gwenwynwyn, Prince of Upper Powys ; and Sir Roger Corbet of Morton Corbet, Knight, ancestor of the Baronet family of Corbet of Morton Corbet.

William Ipstone, Lord of Ipstone, *ob.* 1 H. IV, A.D. 1399. = Maude, d. and heir (by Elizabeth, his wife, d. and heir of Sir Nicholas de Becke, Knight) of Sir Robert de Swinnerton, Knight, son and heir of Sir Robert de Swinnerton, in com. Stafford, Knight. Maude married, first, Sir John Savage of Cheshire, Knight ; secondly, Sir Piers Leigh ; thirdly, William de Ipstones ; and fourthly, Richard Peshall.

William Ipstone, died issueless.

Christian.

Alice, Lady of Ipstans or Ipstones. = Sir Ranulph or Randulphus Brereton de Malpas, Knt., second son of Sir William Brereton de Brereton, Knt., Lord of Brereton. *Argent,* two bars *sable.*

2nd son, William Brereton of Borasham, Esq., 1450. = Catherine, d. and co-heir of Thomas de Wylde of Borasham, Esq. *Argent,* a chev. *sable,* on a chief of the second, three martletts of the field.

Edward Brereton of Borasham, Esq. = 1st wife, Elizabeth, d. of John Roydon of Pulford, Esq., and ..., his wife, d. of Thomas Hanmer of Llys Bedydd or Bettisfield, Esq. *Vert,* three roebuck's heads erased in bend *or,* in dexter chief a rose of the second. = 2nd wife, Dorothy, d. of Richard Hanmer and sister of Sir Thomas Hanmer, who was knighted at the taking of Terwin and Tourney.

a	*b*		*c*	*d*	*e*

---

a	b	c	d	e
	Thomas Brere-—Margaret, ton, Rector of d. of Ithel Northope, 1539; ab Gruff- of Llandrinio, ydd ab 1557; and of Belyn.[1] Gresford, 1566.	Eliza- beth, ux. James Eyton of Eyton, Esq.	Joanna, ux. Cyn- wrig ab Richard of Penach- lech.	Cathe- rine, ux. Lancelot Lloyd of Tref Alun.

John Brere-=Margaret, d. and heiress of Richard ab Ieuan ab David ab ton of Bora- Ithel Fychan of Llaneurgain, Esq., descended from Ed-
sham, Esq. nowain Bendew, Chief of one of the Noble Tribes of Wales.
Argent, a chev. inter three boar's heads couped *sable*.

Owain Brere-=1st wife, Elizabeth, dau. of John=2nd wife, Catherine, d.
ton of Bora- Salusbury, Esq., heir of Lleweni, of Harri Goch Salus-
sham, High M.P. for Denbigh, 1554; and bury of Llewesog, Esq.,
Sheriff for co. Catherine, his wife, d. and heir- and relict of John Lloyd
Denbigh, ess of Tudor ab Robert Fychan of Bodidris, Esq.
1580 and of Berain, Esq.
1588.

1	2
Edward Brereton of Borasham, High Sheriff for co. Denbigh, 1598, in which year he died.	John Brereton of Esclu-sham. See p. 273.

PLAS LLANEURGAIN IN TEGEINGL.

Lewys Dwnn, vol. ii, p. 325.

Ednowain Bendew, Chief of one of the Noble=Gwerfyl, d. of Lluddocaf, ab
Tribes. He lived at Llys Coed y Mynydd Tudor Trevor, Lord of Chirk,
in the parish of Bodvari in Tegeingl. Whittington, Oswestry, Nan-
Argent, a chev. inter three boar's heads heudwy, and Maelor Saesneg.
couped *sable*, tusked *or*, and langued *gules*.
| a

[1] Belyn settled at Nercwys in Ystrad Alun, and was one of the sons of David ab Cynwrig ab Ieuan ab Gruffydd ab Madog Ddu of Copa'r Goleuni in Tegeingl, who bore palii of six pieces, *argent* and *sable*. Madog Ddu was the son of Rhiryd ab Llewelyn ab Owain ab Edwin, Prince of Tegeingl.

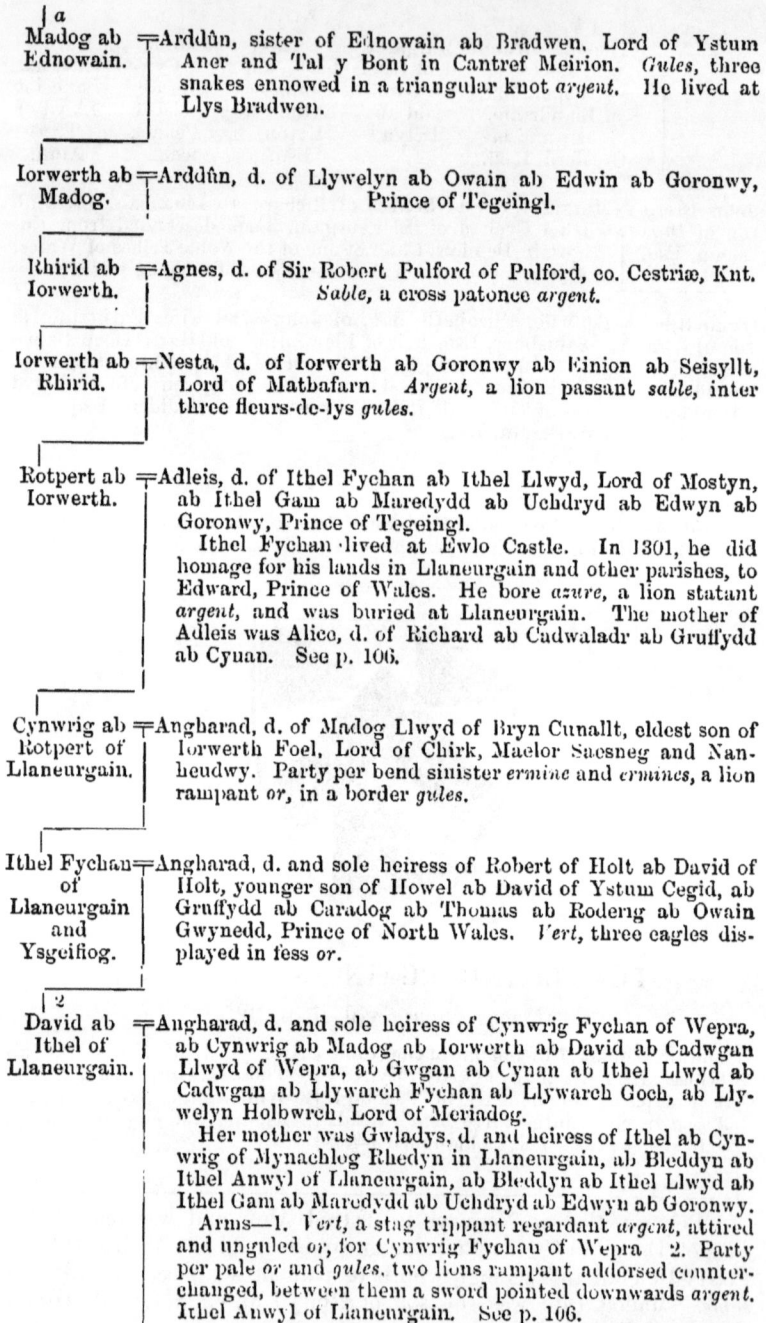

| a

Madog ab Ednowain. =Arddûn, sister of Ednowain ab Bradwen, Lord of Ystum Aner and Tal y Bont in Cantref Meirion. *Gules*, three snakes ennowed in a triangular knot *argent*. He lived at Llys Bradwen.

Iorwerth ab Madog. =Arddûn, d. of Llywelyn ab Owain ab Edwin ab Goronwy, Prince of Tegeingl.

Rhirid ab Iorwerth. =Agnes, d. of Sir Robert Pulford of Pulford, co. Cestriæ, Knt. *Sable*, a cross patonce *argent*.

Iorwerth ab Rhirid. =Nesta, d. of Iorwerth ab Goronwy ab Einion ab Seisyllt, Lord of Matbafarn. *Argent*, a lion passant *sable*, inter three fleurs-de-lys *gules*.

Rotpert ab Iorwerth. =Adleis, d. of Ithel Fychan ab Ithel Llwyd, Lord of Mostyn, ab Ithel Gam ab Maredydd ab Uchdryd ab Edwyn ab Goronwy, Prince of Tegeingl.
Ithel Fychan lived at Ewlo Castle. In 1301, he did homage for his lands in Llaneurgain and other parishes, to Edward, Prince of Wales. He bore *azure*, a lion statant *argent*, and was buried at Llaneurgain. The mother of Adleis was Alice, d. of Richard ab Cadwaladr ab Gruffydd ab Cynan. See p. 106.

Cynwrig ab Rotpert of Llaneurgain. =Angharad, d. of Madog Llwyd of Bryn Cunallt, eldest son of Iorwerth Foel, Lord of Chirk, Maelor Saesneg and Nanheudwy. Party per bend sinister *ermine* and *ermines*, a lion rampant *or*, in a border *gules*.

Ithel Fychan of Llaneurgain and Ysgeifiog. =Angharad, d. and sole heiress of Robert of Holt ab David of Holt, younger son of Howel ab David of Ystum Cegid, ab Gruffydd ab Caradog ab Thomas ab Roderig ab Owain Gwynedd, Prince of North Wales. *Vert*, three eagles displayed in fess *or*.

| 2

David ab Ithel of Llaneurgain. =Angharad, d. and sole heiress of Cynwrig Fychan of Wepra, ab Cynwrig ab Madog ab Iorwerth ab David ab Cadwgan Llwyd of Wepra, ab Gwgan ab Cynan ab Ithel Llwyd ab Cadwgan ab Llywarch Fychan ab Llywarch Goch, ab Llywelyn Holbwrch, Lord of Meriadog.
Her mother was Gwladys, d. and heiress of Ithel ab Cynwrig of Mynachlog Rhedyn in Llaneurgain, ab Bleddyn ab Ithel Anwyl of Llaneurgain, ab Bleddyn ab Ithel Llwyd ab Ithel Gam ab Maredydd ab Uchdryd ab Edwyn ab Goronwy.
Arms—1. *Vert*, a stag trippant regardant *argent*, attired and unguled *or*, for Cynwrig Fychan of Wepra 2. Party per pale *or* and *gules*, two lions rampant addorsed counterchanged, between them a sword pointed downwards *argent*. Ithel Anwyl of Llaneurgain. See p. 106.

| c | d

b		c	d
Ithel ab=Margaret, d. of David Lloyd		Gruff- =Marjory or Mar-	Ieuan.
David of	ab Bleddyn of Herscdd in	ydd ab	slll, d. of John	See p.
Llaneur-	Ystrad Alun, ab Gruffydd	David.	aer Conwy IIen	104.
gain.	ab Heilin ab Bleddyn ab		of Bodrhyddan	
	Madog ab Rhirid ab Einion		ab Jenkyn	
	ab Cadwgan ab Goronwy		Conwy.	
	ab Owain ab Edwin ab			
	Goronwy, Prince of Tege-	David.=	Pyers Gruffith of Caer-	
	ingl.		wys.	

Harri. He had two wives and thirty children, one of whom
was Dr. William Parry, M P. for Queensborough, who was
executed for high treason by Queen Elizabeth in 1584.

Ieuan ab Ithel = Margaret, d. of James Conwy of Sychdin in Llaneurgain,
of Llaneur- and Rhuddlan, son of John Aer Conwy of Bodrhyddan ab
gain. John ab Jenkyn Conwy. *Sable*, on a bend *argent*, cottised
by two bendletts *ermine*, a rose between two annulets
gules.

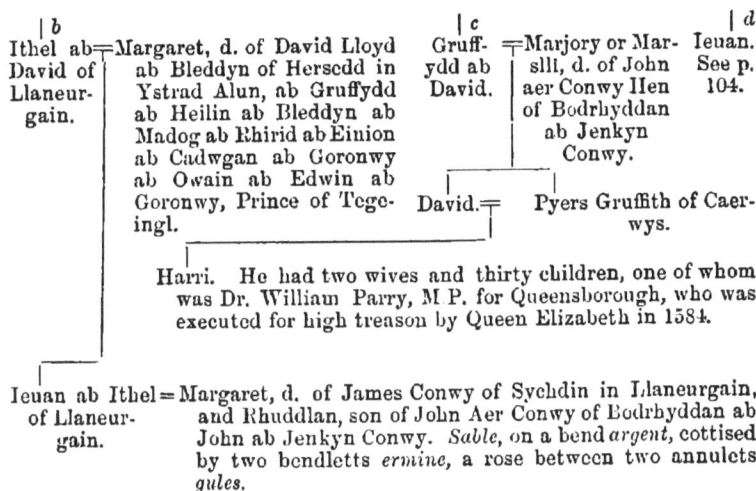

Ieuan ab Ithel of Llaneurgain, had issue by his wife
Margaret, besides three sons, two daughters ; 1, Catherine,
ux. John Wynn of Llwyn Egryn ; and 2, Elizabeth, ux.
John ab Rhys ab David. The three sons were :—

1. Elis Evans of Plâs Llaneurgain, who married
Gwenhwyfryd, daughter and co-heir of Thomas Hack-
luit, and ......, his wife, daughter and co-heir of Thomas
Latchett, Esq., by whom he had a son and heir, Thomas
Evans of Plâs Llaneurgain, who by Jane his wife, daugh-
ter of John Mytton of Rhuddlan, son of Pyers Mytton,
Sergeant-at-Arms, had a son and heir—Thomas Evans of
Plâs Llaneurgain, who was High Sheriff for co. Flint in
1624, and married Joan, daughter of Richard Puleston,
Clk. This family is now represented by Edward Pryse
Lloyd of Glanscvin, Esq.

2. Sir James, Vicar of Boduan.

3. Richard ab Ieuan of Llaneurgain. He married
first, Jane, daughter and heiress of William Glegg of
Gayton, in Cheshire, Esq. (*sable*, two lions counterpassant
argent, collared *gules*), and Margaret, his wife, daughter
and heiress of William ab Madog ab Llywelyn ab Madog
Foel of Marchwiail (*ermine*, a lion rampant, in a border
azure), by whom he had an only daughter and heiress,

Margaret Wen, who married John Brereton of Borasham, Esq.

Richard ab Ieuan married, secondly, Alice, only daughter and heiress of Gruffydd Lloyd of Cinmael, son and heir of Ieuan ab Rhys ab Gruffydd Llwyd ab Robert ab Rhys ab Rotpert, ab Gruffydd of Cinmael, in the comot of Is Dulas and cantref of Rhôs, ab Sir Howel, Knight, ab Gruffydd of Henglawdd, ab Ednyfed Fychan of Môn, Baron of Bryn Ffanigl, in the parish of Bettws Wyrion Wgan, in Is Dulas, and General and Prime Minister of Llywelyn ab Iorwerth, Prince of Wales. Arms—1, *sable*, a chevron inter three mullets *argent*, for Rhys ab Rotpert ; 2, *gules*, a chevron inter three mullets *or*, for Rotpert ab Gruffydd of Cinmael ; 3, *gules*, a chevron *ermine*, inter three Englishmen's heads, couped in profile, ppr., for Ednyfed Fychan ; and 4, *gules*, a Saracen's head erased, gardant, bearded ppr., wreathed about the temples *argent* and *azure*, for Marchudd of Bryn Ffanigl, Lord of Uwch Dulas, in the cantref of Rhôs.[1] By this marriage Richard ab Ieuan had a daughter Catherine, heiress of Cinmael, who married Pyers Holland of Fairdref, in the parish of Abergelen, High Sheriff for co. Denbigh in 1578, son of John Holland ab David ab Gruffydd Holland.

---

[1] The cantref of Rhôs contains the comots of Uwch Dulas, Is Dulas, and Creuddyn. The parishes of Llanddulas and Llanelian are in Uwch Dulas. The parishes of Abergelen, Cegidog, and Bettws Wyrion Wgan, are in Is Dulas.

IS Y COED.—TOWNSHIP OF BWRAS. POWEL OF GLAN Y PWLL.

Cae Cyriog MS.; Lewys Dwnn, vol. ii, p. 311.

David ab Ithel Fychan of Llaneurgain. See p. 101.

| Ieuan ab David. | Gruffydd, ancestor of the Griffiths of Caerwys. | Lewys. | John, ancestor of John Lloyd of Ysgeiviog. | Ithel of Llaneurgain. |

Howel ab Ieuan.=Margaret, d. of Richard ab Howel ab Ieuan Ychan.

1		2		3	4
John Wynn, eldest son.	=Annest, d. of Hyw ab Rhys ab Howel.	Robert Wynn.	=Annest, d. of Robert ab Maurice.	Thomas ab Howel.=Catherine, d. of Thomas ab Ieuan.	Hyw.

1		2	3	4	5	6	7
Cynwrig Powel of of Glan y Pwll ym Mwras.	=Jane, dau. of John Brereton of Bwras.	Harri Powel.	Richard Powel.=Jane, dau. of Jenkyn ab Jenkyn of Llanelwy.	Randal. John. Thomas. Edward.			

John Powel of Kilystryn.=Margaret, d. of Edward Puleston of Trefalun.

| Catherine, ux. Harri Griffith. | Margaret, ux. William Jones. | Elizabeth, ux. Ffachnallt. | Rhys Ffachnallt of Ffachnallt. *Argent*, a chev. inter three boar's heads couped *sable*. |

MYNACHLOG RHEDYN.

Harl. MS. 1969.

Goronwy, Prince of Tegeingl, second son of Einion,═Ethelfleda, d. and heir-
ab Owen ab Howel Dda, King of Wales. He | ess of Edwin, Earl of
obtained the cantref of Tegeingl, which contains | Mercia, and relict of
the comots of Cynsyllt, Prestatyn and Rhuddlan, | Edmund Ironside,
through his marriage. | King of England.

Edwyn ab Goronwy, Prince of Tegeingl, Chief of═Ewerydda, sister of
one of the Noble Tribes. He lived at Llys Edwin, | Bleddyn ab Cynfyn,
in the parish of Llaneurgain, and at Castell Ed- | ab Gwrystan, Prince
win, in the parish of Llanasaph. He was slain by | of Powys. *Or, a lion
Rhys ab Rhydderch ab Owain in 1073, and was | rampant gules.*
buried at Llaneurgain. Rhual, near Mold, was
the residence of Edwin when he died, for it is recorded that "Edwin of Rhual was buried at Llaneurgain in 1073". *Argent, a cross flory engrailed
sable,* inter four Cornish choughs ppr.

2 | 1

Uchdryd. Cadwgan ab Ble-═2, Angharad, | Owain, Prince of Tegeingl.
ddyn, Prince of Powys, | d. of Mared- | In 1196 he was elected
gave him the cantrefs of | ydd ab Bledd- | Prince of North Wales by
Mirion, Penllyn, and the | yn, Prince of | Hugh Lupus, Earl of Ches-
comots of Mawddwy and | Powys. | ter. He died of consump-
Cyfeiliog. He married first, | | tion in 1103. *Gules,* three
Nesta, d. of Llywelyn Eur- | | men's legs conjoined at the
dorchog, Lord of Iâl and | | thighs in triangle *argent.*
Ystrad Alun.

Maredydd ab Uchdryd.═Janet, d. of Ithel ab Eunydd, Lord of Trefalyn and
Y Groesffordd. *Azure, a lion salient or.*

Ithel Gam, Lord═ | Einion. He had | Madog. He | Goronwy of Tre-
of Mostyn and | Bachymbyd and a | had lands in | fryd, ancestor of
Llaneurgain, | great part of Maes | Maes Maen | the Edwardses
living in 1237. | Maen Cymro. | Cymro. | of Caer Fallwch.

a

| a

Ithel =Margaret, d. of Hwfa ab Iorwerth of Bersham (*gules*, two lions
Llwyd,   passant in pale *argent*), ab Gruffudd ab Ieuaf ab Niniaf ab Cyn-
Lord of   wrig ab Rhiwallawn.
Mostyn.

| 2 | 1

Bleddyn. =Gwenllian, d.   Ithel Fychan, Lord of Mostyn. =Alice, dau. of
      of Ieuan ab   He did homage for his lands   Richard ab
      Gruffydd ab   in Llaneurgain and other   Cadwaladr ab
      Madog Ddû   parishes to Edward, Prince of   Gruffydd ab
      of Copa'r   Wales, at Chester in 1301.   Cynan.
      Goleuni.   *Azure*, a lion statant *argent*.

Ithel Anwyl. He lived at Ewlo Castle, and was one=   Bleddyn   David ab
    of the captains of Tegeingl, to prevent the English   Fychan.   Bleddyn,
    from invading the country. He was buried at   Bishop
    Llaneurgain. He bore party per pale *or* and *gules*,   of St.
    two lions rampant addorsed, counterchanged, be-   Asaph.
    tween them a sword pointed downwards *argent*,
    hilt and pomel *or*.

Bleddyn Llwyd. =

Cynwrig ab Bleddyn of My-=Angharad, d. of Maredydd   Ithel of Myna-
   nachlog Rhedyn. He died   of Yr Hob ab Gruffydd ab   chlog Rhedyn,
   in Harlech Castle, aiding   Maredydd ab Llywelyn ab   in Llaneurgain.
   David ab Ieuan ab Einion.   Ynyr of Iâl.

Ithel. He had two natural sons=Lowri, d. of Ieuan ab Gruffydd ab
   named Cwnnws and Y Dai.   Madog ab Iorwerth ab Madog ab
                          Rhirid Flaidd.

Gwladys, sole heiress, ux. Cynwrig Fychan ab Cynwrig ab Madog ab Iorwerth ab David ab Cadwgan Llwyd of Wepra. See p. 101.

See p. 101.

IS Y COED.—TOWNSHIP OF BORASHAM.

Harl. MSS. 1972, 2299, 4181.

Llywelyn ab Gruffydd ab Cadwgan.= Gwenllian (second wife), d. of Owain
   Lord of Eyton, Erlisham, and   ab Trahaiarn ab Ithel ab Eunydd
   Borasham. *Ermine*, a lion rampt.   ab Gwernwy, Lord of Tref Alun
   azure. See vol. ii, p. 156.   and Y Groesffordd.

| a

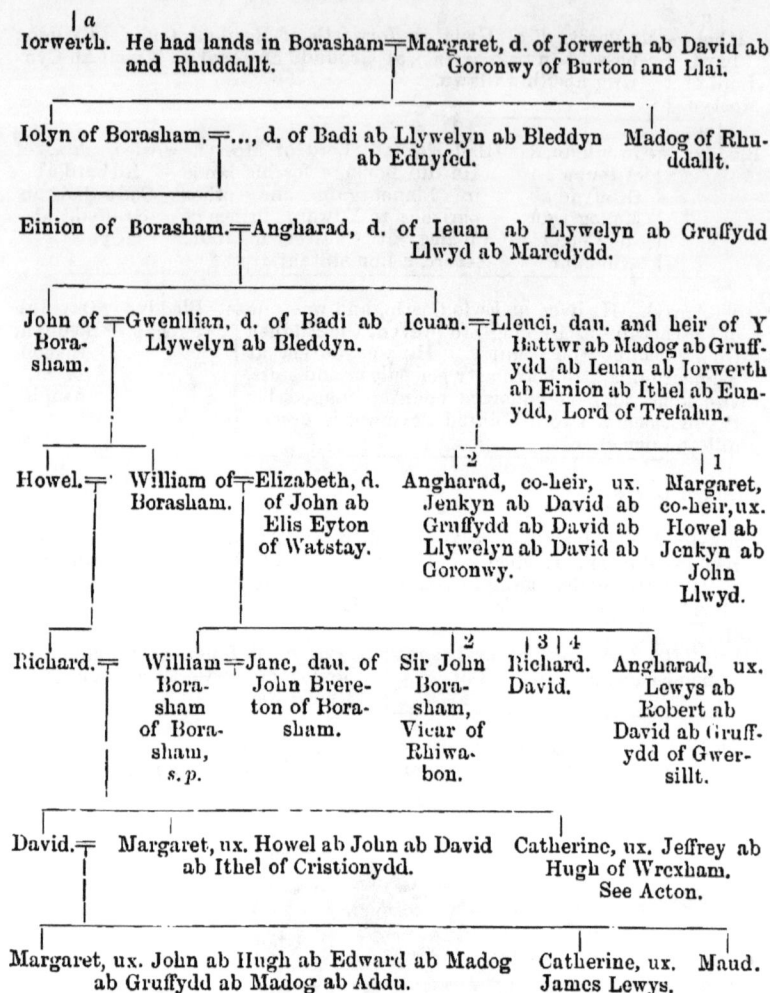

| a

Iorwerth. He had lands in Borasham=Margaret, d. of Iorwerth ab David ab
and Rhuddallt.   Goronwy of Burton and Llai.

Iolyn of Borasham.=..., d. of Badi ab Llywelyn ab Bleddyn   Madog of Rhu-
                        ab Ednyfed.   ddallt.

Einion of Borasham.=Angharad, d. of Ieuan ab Llywelyn ab Gruffydd
                        Llwyd ab Maredydd.

John of =Gwenllian, d. of Badi ab   Ieuan.=Llenci, dau. and heir of Y
Bora-   Llywelyn ab Bleddyn.   Rattwr ab Madog ab Gruff-
sham.   ydd ab Ieuan ab Iorwerth
                                              ab Einion ab Ithel ab Eun-
                                              ydd, Lord of Trefalun.

                                              | 2 | 1
Howel.= William of=Elizabeth, d.   Angharad, co-heir, ux.   Margaret,
        Borasham. of John ab   Jenkyn ab David ab   co-heir, ux.
                   Elis Eyton   Gruffydd ab David ab   Howel ab
                   of Watstay.   Llywelyn ab David ab   Jenkyn ab
                                    Goronwy.   John
                                                               Llwyd.

                                    | 2 | 3 | 4
Richard.= William=Jane, dau. of   Sir John   Richard.   Angharad, ux.
          Bora-   John Brere-   Bora-   David.   Lewys ab
          sham   ton of Bora-   sham,   Robert ab
          of Bora- sham.   Vicar of   David ab Gruff-
          sham,   Rhiwa-   ydd of Gwer-
          s. p.   bon.   sillt.

David.= Margaret, ux. Howel ab John ab David   Catherine, ux. Jeffrey ab
         ab Ithel of Cristionydd.   Hugh of Wrexham.
                                                 See Acton.

Margaret, ux. John ab Hugh ab Edward ab Madog   Catherine, ux.   Maud.
    ab Gruffydd ab Madog ab Addu.   James Lewys.

MANOR OF IS Y COED.—TOWNSHIP OF ERLYS.
DAVIES OF ERLYS.

Madog Puleston of Bers, second son of Robert=Angharad, d. of David ab
Puleston of Emeral, ab Richard Puleston, | Goronwy of Burton, ab
who was Seneschal of the Lordships of Maelor | Iorwerth ab Howel ab
Gymraeg and Maelor Saesneg, 47 Edward III, | Mareiddig ab Sanddef
son of Sir Richard Puleston of Emeral, Knt. | Hardd, or the Handsome,
Argent, on a bend *sable*, three mullets of the | Lord of Morton or Bur-
field, for Madog Puleston. | ton and Llai.

| 2
Edward Puleston of Cris-=Isabel, d. of Sir Randle Bre- John Puleston of
tionydd, in the Manor | reton of Malpas, Knight. Bers and Havod
of Esclys or Esclu- | *Argent*, two bars *sable*. y Wern.
sham. |

| 2
Howel ab=1st, Gwenllian, dau. of Ithel=2nd, Margaret, d. and heiress
Edward of | Wynn of Coed y Llai or Lees- | of Ieuan ab Howel ab Ieuan
Plâs Isaf | wood. Bach of Rhiwabon, ab Ieuan
in Cris- | ———————————— ab Einion Gethin of Cristion-
tionydd. | | 4 ydd, ab Einion ab Ieuan ab
| Edward ab Howel of Gruffydd ab Einion Efell,
| Trefechan Lord of Y Glwysengl. *Gules*,
| in Cristionydd. on a bend *argent*, a lion
| passant *sable*.

| 1 | 2 | 3
John Wynn=Isabel, d. of Edward David=Agnes, Rondle=Lily, daughter
of Plas | ab Edward ab David ab | d. of ab | of Robert Sonlli
Isaf. | ab Madog ab Lly- Howel | ... ab Howel. | of Sonlli ab
 | welyn ab Gruffydd ab | Madog | Robert Wynn
Catherine, | ab Iorwerth Fy- Ed- | of Is- | Sonlli. *Ermine*,
heiress ux. | chan ab Iorwerth ward. | goed. | a lion rampant
Edward | ab Ieuaf ab Niniaf | | *sable*.
Eyton of | ab Cynwrig ab | |
Watstay. | Rhiwallon. *Ermine*, | 1 | 2 | 3 |
 | a lion rampant Richard, Janet, ux. Catherine,
 | *sable*. John of Roger ux. David
 | Wrex- Davies, ab Ieuan
 | ham. Constable ab Ed-
 | William. of Castle ward of
 | Dulyn. Cris-
 | tionydd.

| a | b

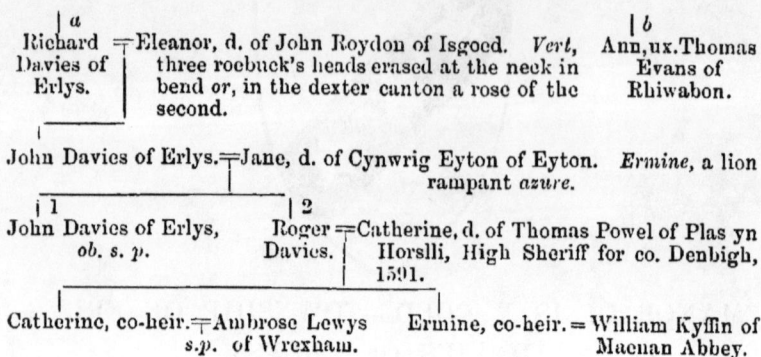

a		b
Richard Davies of Erlys. =Eleanor, d. of John Roydon of Isgoed. *Vert*, three roebuck's heads erased at the neck in bend *or*, in the dexter canton a rose of the second.		Ann, ux. Thomas Evans of Rhiwabon.

John Davies of Erlys.=Jane, d. of Cynwrig Eyton of Eyton. *Ermine*, a lion rampant *azure*.

1	2
John Davies of Erlys, *ob. s. p.*	Roger Davies. =Catherine, d. of Thomas Powel of Plas yn Horslli, High Sheriff for co. Denbigh, 1591.

| Catherine, co-heir.=Ambrose Lewys *s.p.* of Wrexham. | Ermine, co-heir. = William Kyffin of Macnan Abbey. |

MANOR OF IS Y COED.—TOWNSHIP OF ERLYS.

ERLYS OF ERLYS.

Harl. MS. 2299.

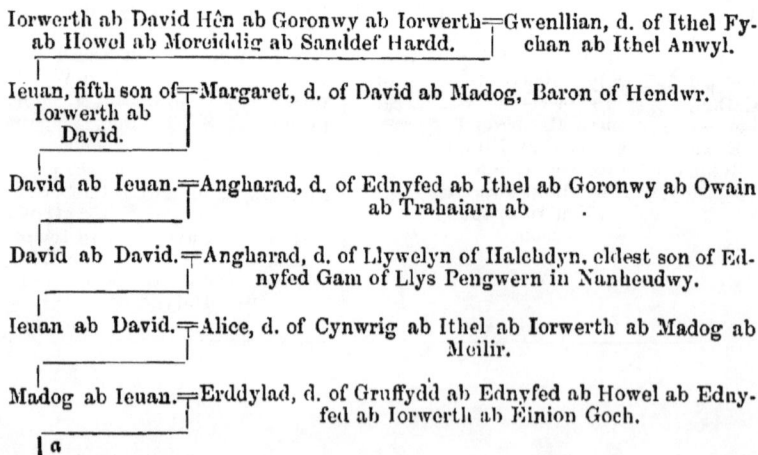

Iorwerth ab David Hên ab Goronwy ab Iorwerth=Gwenllian, d. of Ithel Fyab Howel ab Moreiddig ab Sanddef Hardd. | chan ab Ithel Anwyl.

Ieuan, fifth son of=Margaret, d. of David ab Madog, Baron of Hendwr.
Iorwerth ab
David.

David ab Ieuan.=Angharad, d. of Ednyfed ab Ithel ab Goronwy ab Owain ab Trahaiarn ab .

David ab David.=Angharad, d. of Llywelyn of Halchdyn. eldest son of Ednyfed Gam of Llys Pengwern in Nanheudwy.

Ieuan ab David.=Alice, d. of Cynwrig ab Ithel ab Iorwerth ab Madog ab Meilir.

Madog ab Ieuan.=Erddylad, d. of Gruffydd ab Ednyfed ab Howel ab Ednyfed ab Iorwerth ab Einion Goch.

a

| a

Edward ab Madog ⊤ ..., d. of Llywelyn ab David ab Llywelyn ab Madog Foel
of Erlys. | of Marchwiail.

John of Erlys. ⊤ Margaret, d. of Robert ab Iorwerth ab Howel of Llwyn
           On. *Ermine, a lion rampant sable.*

John Erlys of Er- ⊤ Catherine Llwyd, d. of William ab Gruffydd ab Iolyn
lys. | Llwyd of Gresford, descended from Eunydd ab Gwernwy.

Edward Erlys of = Margaret, d. of Robert ab Howel ab David ab Gruffydd
Erlys.   ab Llywelyn ab Madog Foel of Marchwiail.

– – – –

MANOR OF IS Y COED.—TOWNSHIP OF ERLYS.
ERLYS OF ERLYS.

Cae Cyriog MS.

Llywelyn Foel of Marchwiail ab Madog Foel ab Iorwerth ab Hwfa Fychan ⊤
ab Hwfa Grûg ab Sanddef of Marchwiail, fourth son of Elidir ab Rhys
Sais, Lord of Eyton, Erlisham, and Borasham. *Ermine, a lion rampant*
in a border azure.

David ab Llywelyn, ⊤ Gwenllian, d. and heiress of Madog ab Ieuaf of Erlys,
jure uxoris of | fifth son of Hwfa ab Iorwerth of Havod y Wern.
Erlys.   *Sable,* three lions passant in paie *argent.* Her mother
           was Eva, d. of Madog Gloddaeth of Creuddyn.

Ieuan ab David of Erlys. The ⊤   Llywelyn ab David ⊤ Nesta, dau. of Y
Harl. MS. 2299 states that this   of Erlys. | Ffawis Hardd-
Ieuan was the son of David ab   lech.
David ab Ieuan ab Iorwerth ab
David Hen ab Goronwy ab Ior-   David of = ..., ux. Edward ab Madog
werth ab Howel ab Moreiddig   Erlys.   ab Ieuan ab David ab
ab Sanddef Hardd, Lord of   David ab Ieuan ab Ior-
Burton and Llai.   werth ab David Hen ab
                                         Goronwy.

Madog ab Ieuan of Erlys. ⊤

| a

| a
Edward ab Ma-⊤Margaret, d. of William ab Gruffydd ab Robert of Cwch-
dog of Erlys. | willan.

John Erlys of Er-⊤Margaret, d. of Robert ab Edward ab Howel ab Gruffydd
lys. | of Llwyn On. *Ermine, a lion rampant sable.*

John Erlys of Er-⊤Catherine Llwyd, d. of William Llwyd ab Gruffydd ab
lys. | Iolyn Llwyd of Yr Orsedd Goch in Gresford, ab David
| ab Ieuaf Llwyd ab Howel Fychan ab Howel Wyddel
| ab Iorwerth ab Einion ab Ithel ab Eunydd ab Gwer-
| gygwy ab Gwaeddgar.

Edward Erlys of⊤Margaret, d. of Robert ab Howel ab David of Marchwiail,
Erlys, 1599. | ab Gruffydd ab Llywelyn ab Madog Foel of Marchwiail.
| *Ermine, a lion rampant in a border azure.*

1			2	3	4	5		6
John =Elizabeth, d. of			Owain	Robert	David	William		Hugh
Erlys	James Eyton		Erlys.	Erlys.	Erlys.	Erlys.		Erlys.
of	of Eyton. *Er-*							
Erlys,	*mine,* a lion	Catherine, ux. John ab			Margaret, ux. John			Ann.
1599.	rampant *azure.*	John ab Gruffydd.			ab Robert Fychan.			

Richard Erlys.   Edward Erlys.

MANORS OF IS Y COED AND HOLT.
ROYDON OF IS Y COED.

Harl. MS. 1971, fo. 65B.

Richard Roydon, who was a native of Kent, came to
Bromfield, or Maelor Gymraeg, with the Commissioners
of the Lord Abergavenny, Lord of the moiety of Bromfield, *temp.* Henry VI.

By Isabel his wife he had issue three sons : 1, Hugh,
of whom presently ; 2, William Roydon, Receiver of
Bromfield, who was father of John Roydon of Talwyn,

father of William Roydon of Talwyn, who had, besides a
daughter Elen, ux. Roger Wynn Sanddef of Mortyn,
and a younger son Ralph, a son and heir, Roger Roydon
of Talwyn, whose daughter and co-heir Alice married
Thomas Yale of Plâs yn Iâl, who was living in 1598.

Hugh Roydon of Holt and Is y Coed in Maelor Gymraeg, married Catharine, daughter and heir of Gruffydd
ab Madog ab Ieuaf Llwyd ab Howel Ddû ab Madog ab
Heilin ab Einion Goch ab Ithel ab Eynydd, Lord of
Trefalun and Y Groesffordd (*azure*, a lion salient *or*), by
whom he had issue three sons : 1, John, of whom presently, 2, Sir William Roydon, Parson of Gresford, and,
3, Sir Hugh Roydon, a priest ; and two daughters,
Catherine, ux. Gruffydd ab Madog ab John Deckaf of
Sutton, and Elizabeth.

John Roydon of Holt and Is y Coed, Sergeant-at-
Arms. He married Gwenhwyfar, daughter of Richard
Tegan ab David of Is y Coed, and had issue a son and
heir, John Roydon, and four daughters : 1, Jane, ux.
Hugh Eyton of Eyton (*ermine*, a lion rampant *azure*) ;
2, Gwen, ux. Gilbert Malavery ; 3, Sibyll, ux. William
Woodhall of Holt ; and, 4, Catherine, ux. David Sutton.
By his will, dated 1513, he leaves certain " copy landes
and tenementes of fee simple, the which I have within
the Lordship of Bromfield, except the copy landes in the
town of Wrexham, to my wife Roos, Catherine Roden,
my sister". He likewise mentions John Roden, his
son ; Maude, his son's wife ; his daughters, Elizabeth,
Sibill, and Catherine : and his brother, Sir William
Roden.

John Roydon of Holt and Is y Coed, married, first,
Mary, daughter of Richard Hanmer of Llys Bedydd, and
Jane, his wife, daughter of Tudor Fychan, by whom he
had no issue. He married, secondly, Mawde, daughter
of Sir Roger Puleston of Emrall, Knt., by whom he had
issue three sons : 1, Roger, *ob. s. p.*; 2, John, of whom
presently ; and, 3, Thomas, *ob. s. p.*; and seven daughters :
1, Elizabeth, who was the first wife of Edward Brereton
of Borasham (*argent*, two bars *sable*) ; 2, Jane, who

married, first, Richard Jones of Drithwys, and, secondly John Davies of Middleton; 3, Dorothy, ux., first, Roger Eyton, and, secondly, she married Bartholomew Fitton of Carden; and, 4, Alice, ux. John Maredydd of Trefalun (*azure*, a lion salient *or*); 5, Joanne, ux. John ab William ab Madog Goch; 6, Elizabeth, ux., first, John Davies of Erlisham, and, secondly, Thomas Trence of Holt; and, 7, Sibill, contracted to John Langford of Rhuddin.

John Roydon of Holt and Is y Coed, married, first, Anne, daughter of Richard Chambres of Sussex, by whom he had issue three sons: 1, Roger, his successor; 2, Thomas, *ob. s. p.*; and, 3, John, who died *s. p.*; and three daughters: 1, Joanne, ux. Edward Crewe of Holt; and Rose and Elizabeth, who both married in London. He married, secondly, Margaret, daughter of Morgan Broughton, by whom he had four daughters: Dorothy, ux. Thomas Forster of Trefalun, Margaret, Alice and Anne.

Roger Roydon of Holt and Is y Coed, a Captain in the Royal Army. He married Jane, daughter of Thomas Powel of Plâs yn Horslli, by whom he had issue, besides three daughters, 1, Anne, ux. Richard Deane of Wyrral, 2, Dorothy, ux. Edward Alton of Golborn Bellew, and, 3, Elizabeth, who died young, seven sons—1, John, his successor; 2, Thomas Roydon, who married Catherine, daughter of Roger Wynn of Purley, by whom he had a son, John; 3, Samuel, *ob. s. p.*; 4, Pauleyn, *ob. s. p.*; 5, Roger Roydon of Bristol, who married and had issue seven children; 6, James, who went to the Low Countries; and, 7, William Roydon, who married Jane, daughter of John Lancelott of Wrexham, by whom he had issue two children, Samuel and Margaret.

John Roydon of Holt and Is y Coed, *ob.* 20th March 1666. He married Eleanor, daughter and heir of Edward Maurice[1] of Lloran Uchaf in Cynllaith, and relict

---

[1] Edward Maurice of Lloran Uchaf, ab Maurice ab Maredydd ab Ieuan ab Rhys ab Howel ab Gruffydd of Lloran Uchaf, ab Ieuan Gethin ab Madog Cyffin ab Madog Goch of Lloran Uchaf and Moeliwrch, ab Ieuaf ab Cuhelyn ab Rhun ab Einion Efell of Llwyn y Main, Lord of Cynllaith.

of Daniel Maurice of Lloran, ab Hugh Maurice, second son of Maurice ab Maredydd ab Ieuan of Lloran Uchaf (party per fess *sable* and *argent*, a lion rampant counter-changed). The mother of Eleanor was Blanche, daughter of Thomas Corbet of Lee. By this lady he had issue five sons: 1, John, of whom presently; 2, Roger; 3, Maurice of Wolverhampton; 4, Charles of London; and, 5, Arthur; and four daughters: 1, Jane; 2, Dorothy, *ob. s. p.*; 3. Anne, ux. John Lloyd of Goban in Sutton; and 4, Eleanor.

John Roydon of Is y Coed married Mary, daughter of —— Hanmer of Kenwick in Com. Salop, by whom he had issue two sons, 1, John, and 2, Charles, who married Elizabeth, daughter of William Speed of Holt; and three daughters, Catherine, Frances, and Dorothy.

John Roydon of Is y Coed married Elizabeth, daughter of —— Whitehall of —— in Com. Derby; she died 13th February 1674, leaving issue one son, John, aged one year in 1674.

Other members of this family were, William Roydon, Collector Antiquaru' Eschet de Englefeld, 24 Henry VI. Idem, Will'm, Eschetor, 25 et 38 Henry VI. This Englefeld is now called Eglwyegl. (See p. 66.)

Richard Roydon of Holt married Anne, daughter of Thomas Powell of Horslli, Esq., by whom he had six daughters—Dorothy, Maud, Mary, Anne, Alice, and Jane, ux. Lancelot Bostock of Holt.

The arms of the Roydon family were *vert*, three roebuck's heads erased at the neck in bend *or*, in dexter chief a rose of the second.

WREXHAM MANOR.

Harl. 3696.

SUPERUISUS MANERII DE WREXHAM IN COMIT' DENBIGH PER JOHANNEM NORDEN SENIOREM.

NO'I'A JURATORUM.

Hugo Meredith, armiger.	Dauid Thomas.
Robertus Puleston, armiger.	Joh'es Jones.
Nicolaus ap Jon. Edward.	Richardus Beniamin.
David ap Jon. Robert.	Radulphus ap Ellis.
Hugo Griffith.	Rogerus ap Richard.
Dauid ap Dauid.	Will'us Griffith Smyth.
Joh'nes ap John.	Owen's ap Robert.
Joh'es Dauid Thomas.	Richardus Hall.

Qui dicunt super sacramenta sua vt sequitur, vizt.:

To the first article they say that the mannor or towneship of Wrexham is bounded from Wrexham churchyard to the foote bridge south of the said church, leauing the landes of the right honourable the Lord Wootton vpon the right hand of the lane to the barnes in pen y bryn westward, and thence along the lane to the westend of Glyn parke[1] (excepting one field called Owen, w'ch is parcell of the Court farme belonging to the mannor of Valle Crucis, and two closes, one of Mr. Jeffreys, and thother of Thomas Lloyd). And so from the said westend of Glyn Park along eastward to the landes of Robert Puleston, Esquire, neere the Prince his highness water mill called the Velyn newydd or newe Mill. And we doe further say and present that so much of the said Glyn Park as extendeth from the said westend thereof along to the river Clewedog, w'ch runneth through the said parke eastwards to the said landes of Robert Puleston, neere the said Mill, to be within this mannor of Wrexham, for that being conuerted into arrable land, the tithe thereof is gathered w'th the towneship of Wrexham; and that the tenaunts there doe their seruice w'th the tenants of Wrexham. Then from the eastend of the said parke along the River to the bridge called Pont Yuelin newydd; and thence a brooke called Gwen fro, and compasseth

---

[1] A plan of Glyn Park is here given. The manor of Wrexham Abad was granted to the Abbey of Valle Crucis by Madog ab Gruff-ydd Maelor, Prince of Powys Fadog, in A.D. 1200, and was subsequently the property of the Lord Wootton. See Iâl.

the lands of Robert Puleston northward to the Mores called
Gwern dunck, and so along northward by Bryn Tunck and the
Kae Mawr, and thence to the furthest end of Kae wad, by the
towneship of Acton, and so along by Gwern Acton westwards
to Gwayn y tecuyn by the towneship of Acton, neere the house
of Jo'n ap Hugh ap Ed. Stantie; and then compassing Gwayn
y tecuyn and the lane to Tal y geifer, along by the towneship
of Stanstie, to a place called Clawdd Wad, westward; and so
along Clawdd Wad to the brook Gwenfro southward; then
along the said brooke, Bryn y ffynnon; and then to a garden of
Robert Soullye, Esq.; and by the gardens of Ed. Crewe, gent.,
and Edward Danies; and so by Danid ap Hughe, silkweaver,
and so into Streete yr Abad; then ouer the way to the house
of Robert ap Hughe, butcher, being the Lord Woottons land;
and so through the gardens, westwards, to the stile of Bryn y
Fynon; and thence along the brooke, leauing it on the right
hand; and so to the west stile againe, to the churchyard of
Wrexham, where we began, and nowe doe end.

M'd' that there is a smithie and a litle parcell of ffreehold
land of Robert Puleston in Pentre yr velin Abad belonging to
this manno' of Wrexham, and also certeine cottages and a
crofte in Lampyat, w'ch is the landes of Thomas Trafford,
Esq., and out of this manno'; and one cottage and barne in
th'east end of the Beaste markett, and two parcells of land in
Kae pants and in bron pull yr vwd, w'ch are also out of this
manno', w'ch are the lands of Margarett Verch Robert, widowe.

To the second article this Jury sayeth that there is no
demesne land in this manno' to their knowledge, saue that
Parke of Glyn Park, as they thinke, w'ch is sett downe in the
boundes of this manno'.

To the 3, 4, and 5 articles the said Jurie say that the ffreeholders names w'thin this manno' are sett downe in this booke,
their landes and rentes, to their knowledge; and that there
are leaseholders and customary tenants from 40 yeares to 40,
and likewise their names and what they holde, and their rentes,
as neere as they could learne and sett out, sett downe also at
large in the booke of the surueyours perambulac'on.   And
that the customary tenaunts to the Prince his highnes doe pay
at the taking of newe leases for 40 yeares, and so from 40 to
40, two yeares rent of their said customary landes for a ffine,
according to the composition made betweene the late Queene
of famous memorie and the tenauntes of Bromfield and Yalle.
The effect of w'ch composition is sett downe more at large in
the presentments of the Juries of Hoult, Burton, Ruabon, and
others, whereunto this Jurie referre themselves.   And this

Jurie doe not knowe of any ffine paid or due to be paid by the said tenauntes at the marriage of their daughters.

To the 6, 7, and 8 articles they say that there is no common of waste within this mannor, and that there is neither woods nor vnderwoodes in the said manno', but a fewe vnderwoods in Glyn Park of hasell, alders, withie, and thornes, and such like, w'ch the tenants there doe take and vse for tinsell as need requires; and that there were some oakes in the said l'arke, as it seemes, but gone many yeares agoe, and now a few scrubbs standing. And that there is no parke of deare or warren of conies w'thin the said mannour.

To the 9, 10, and 11 articles the said Jury say that there is no incrochment within this manno', but about one acre called l'ull yr Vwde, w'ch was taken by lease dat' xviii° Martii a° Eliz. 23, graunted to Robert Sonlley, Esq., as this Jury is informed, and nowe in the occupac'on of Margarett ve' Robert, widd'. And that the landes holden from 40 yeares to 40 yeares are sett downe in the book of presentment by this Jurie, as also by the surveyo'; and that there are not quarrs of stone, mines of cole, leade, marle, or chalke, to their knowledge.

To the 12, 13, and 14 articles they say that they doe not knowe of any ffreeholder that died without heire, and that they do not heare of any bastard or alien that doe enioy any landes within this mannour; and that there is no towne corporate or burrowe within this manno', to their knowledge; and that they doe not knowe any copieholder or leaseholder of 40 yeares that have exchaunged or vnlawfully incerted any landes for freehold, or have incerted any such into their customary land.

To the 15 and 16 articles they say that the Prince his Highness hath a custome water mill in this mannour, called y vellyn Newydd, or Newe Mill, whereat the tenauntes and inhabitantes of this manno' of Wrexham and of other towneships are bounde to grinde; and that Roger Bellot, gent., hath a lease of the same mill (amongst other thinges) vnder the great scale of England, for three liues in being, at the rate of ten poundes, six shillings, eight pence, p' ann', and nowe in the tenure of Robert Puleston, Esquire, who had the same at the hands of the said Roger Bellot, and is kept in very good reparac'on; and that there is neither pete, turfe, furze, or such like, in this mannor, save in the fields by the hedge-side there bee some fearne w'ch poore people doe gather.

To the 17 article they say that this manno' is a member of the lordshipp of Bromefield, and that the tenauntes doe serue at the Leete and Lawe days of the said Lordshipp, as they are bound to doe; and that they pay no fines, headsiluer, or king-siluer; but they pay their rentes, ffines of alienac'ons, amer-ciamentes of courtes mizes, and all such paymentes as other the inhabitantes of the said lordship doe, as often as the same are due and required.

To the 18 article they say and present that Hughe Mere-dith, Esquire, hath two houses of the Prince his landes out of reparac'on, and say that the said Hughe hath timber brought into the said towne readie to build, amend, and repayre the said house. And they further present that Owen Brereton, Esquire, hath a house fallen downe in Hope Street within the said mannor; and that Edward Dauies, gent., hath a house in the tenure of Mary Treuor a litle out of reparac'on; and Henry Salisbury, Knight, hath one house of the Prince his landes a litle out of reparac'on, adioyning to the house of Edward Bailie.

To the 19 and 20 articles they say that they knowe not whether wayfes, estraies, and other casualties menc'oned in this article, be due to the Prince his highness or to the Kinges Ma'tie, as they happen; and that there is neither ffishing nor fowling in this manour, to their knowledge.

To the 21 they say that vpon Mundays and Thursdays mar-ketts are kept within the towne of Wrexham; and that there are three ffayres kept in the said towne yerely, viz., upon the xijth of March, the fifte of June, and the viijth of September; and that Roger Bellot, gent., hath the toule, pickage, and stallage of the same by lease, but what it is worth they knowe not.

To the 22 and 23 they say that they know not of any rent or land concealed or w'thheld w'thout right in this mannor, nor of any reprises or payments to issue out of this mannor; but that the Bayliff of the said mannor, for gathering the rentes thereof, hath a certaine ffee from the Prince his Highnes.

To the 24 article they say that there are presented and made at Mich'as Leete yerely, by the Jurie of this mannor, two cunstables w'ch doe serue the yeare following. And that the chief Steward of this mannor and the whole lordshipp of Bromfield and Yale (as this Jurie haue credibly heard) is the right honourable John Earle of Bridgewater; and that John Jeffreys, Esquire,[1] John Dauies, and Thomas Foster, are his

---

[1] John Jeffreys of Acton, Esq. *Ermine*, a lion rampant *sable*, armed and langued *gules*.

deputies; and that Thomas Trafford, Esquire, Receauour.[1] But what ffees they or either of them haue, this Jurie knoweth not.

To the 25 they say they knowe not of any aduousons or beneficies that the Prince his Highnes hath or ought to have within this mannor.

To the 26 they say that, as farre as they can learne or finde out, that the olde and accustomed acre vsed in theise partes conteyneth a CLX pertches, and that every perche conteyneth 24 foote.

MANOR OF WREXHAM.—HAFOD Y WERN.

Harl. MS. 4181.

Iorwerth of Llwyn On, ab Ieuaf ab Niniaf ab Cynwrig ab Rhiwallon.
Ermine, a lion rampant *sable*.

Hwfa ab Iorwerth of Hafod y Wern, *Sable*, three lions passant in pale *argent*.

He married, secondly, Tangwystl, d. of Owain, Lord of Mechain Is y Coed, son of Madog ab Maredydd, Prince of Powys, by whom he had a daughter Generus, who married, first, Bleddyn Llwyd ab Bleddyn Fychan of Havod Unnos; and secondly, Goronwy Fychan ab Goronwy.

Hwfa ab Iorwerth married, thirdly, Eva, d. of Llywelyn ab Ynyr of Iâl, by whom he had four sons, 1, Madog y Athro of Yr Bistog; 2, Gruffydd of Rhiwlo; 3, David of Yr Bistog; and 4, Ieuaf of Erlys or Erlisham; and two daughters, Lleuci and Myfanwy.

Margaret, d. of Cynwrig ab Hoedliw of Cristionydd Cynwrig in the Manor of Esclys or Esclusham, fifth son of Cynwrig ab Rhiwallon, Lord of Maelor Gymraeg. *Ermine*, a lion rampant *sable*.

The mother of Margaret was Gwladys, d. and co-heir of Gruffydd, third son of Meilir Eyton, Lord of Eyton, Erlys, and Bwras or Borasham. *Ermine,* a lion rampant *azure*.

{ *a*

---

[1] Thomas Trafford of Treffordd in Esclusham, Esq. *Ermine*, a lion rampant *sable*, armed and langued *gules*.

| a

Goronwy ab Hwfa=......, d. and co-heir of Ieuan ab Howel ab Maredydd of
of Hafod y Wern. | Ilenllys in Cefn y Ffarm in Lleyn, descended from
    Collwyn ab Tangno, Lord of Eivionydd and Ardudwy.

Ieuan ab Goron-=Erddylad, d. and heiress of Iorwerth Goch, fourth son of
wy of Hafod y | Madog ab Llywelyn ab Gruffydd, Lord of Eyten, Erlys
Wern. | or Erlisham, and Borasham. *Ermine,* a lion rampant
    azure.

Goronwy ab Ieuan=Alise, d. of Cynwrig ab Maredydd Ddû of Môn.
of Hafod y Wern. |

Howel ab Goron-=Nest, d. of Ieuan ab Iorwerth ab Madog Maelor, ab
wy of Hafod y | Thomas ab Owain ab Bleddyn ab Tudor ab Rhys
Wern. | Sais.

Alice, co-heir.=Howel ab Ieuan ab Gruff-   Gwerfyl, co-heir, ux. Tudor, ab
She had Hafod | ydd of Bersham, ab Ma-   Robert *alias* Hob y Dili of Caer
y Wern, and | dog Pabo ab EdnyfedGoch   y Drudion, ab Tudor ab Einion
was the second | ab Cynwrig ab Gruffydd   ab Cynwrig ab Llywarch ab
wife of Howel | Fychan ab Gruffydd ab   Heilin Gloff ab Tegid Farffog
ab Ieuan. | Einion ab Ednyfed, Lord   ab Tangno, *alias* Cadwgan ab
    of Broughton or Brogdin,   Ystrwyth ab Marchwystl ab
    second son of Cynwrig ab   Marchweithian of Llys Lly-
    Rhiwallon. *Ermine,* a lion   warch, Lord of Is Aled, and
    statant gardant *gules,* for   Chief of one of the Noble
    Ednyfed, Lord of Brough-   Tribes. *Gules,* a lion rampant
    ton.   *argent.*

Alice, sole heir-=John Puleston of Bers, eldest son of Madog Puleston of
ess of Hafod y   Bers.
Wern.

PULESTON OF HAFOD Y WERN.

Madog Puleston of Bers, second son of=Angharad, dau. of David ab
Robert Puleston of Emeral in Maelor | Goronwy of Burton and Llai,
Saesneg, ab Richard Puleston ab Sir | ab Iorwerth ab Howel ab
Roger Puleston of Emeral, ab Sir Rich- | Moreiddig ab Sanddef Hardd
ard Puleston ab Sir Roger Puleston of | or the Handsome, Lord of
Emeral, Knight, who was slain by the | Morton or Burton and Llai.
Welsh in 1294. *Argent,* on a bend *sable,* | *Vert,* semé of bromslips a
three mullets of the field. | lion rampant *or.*

| a   2b

1a		2b
John Puleston of=Alice, d. of Howel ab Ieuan ab Gruff-		Edward Pules-
Bers, and *jure*	ydd of Bers, and heiress of her	ton of Cristion-
uxoris of Hafod y	mother Alice, daughter and co-heir-	ydd in Esclu-
Wern.	ess of Howel ab Goronwy of Hafod y	sham.
	Wern.	

John Puleston of=1st, Elen, dau. of=2nd, Alice, d. of Hugh ab Lly-
Bers and Hafod y   Richard Whitney   welyn ab Hwlcyn ab Howel ab
Wern. See Plâs   ab Sir Robert   Iorwerth Ddu of Presaddfed in
ym Mhers.   Whitney, Knight.   the parish of Bod Edyrn in
   Môn ab Iorwerth ab Gruffydd
John Puleston of=Catherine, dau. of   ab Iorwerth ab Maredydd ab
Tir Mon and Hafod   Piers Stanley of   Mathusalem ab Hwfa[1] ab Cyn-
y Wern, High   Ewlo Castle.   ddelw, one of the Fifteen Noble
Sheriff for co. Den-   Tribes. *Gules*, a chev. inter
bigh, 1544.   three lions rampant *or*.

2		3	
Richard =Jane, d. of Gruffydd ab		Roger of El-=Dorothy, dau. of	
Pules- Edward ab Morgan of		tham. Thomas Cowel.	
ton. Brynbw.			

1	2	4	6	7
Emma, ux. 1st,	Jane, ux. John	Eliza-	Emeline, ux.	Cathe-
John Lewys of	Wynn ab David	beth, ux.	John Wynn of	rine, ux.
Gwersyllt;	ab Howel ab	Robert	Gresford, ab	Owen
2ndly, John Bre-	Ieuan ab Gruff-	Sonlli of	David ab	Rose of
reton; 3rdly,	ydd ab Madog	Sonlli.	Robert ab	Malpas.
Wm. Hooker.	Pabo of Bers.		David Sutton.	

1		5	3	
Piers =Catherine, d. of Sir		Lili, ux. Roger	Janet, ux. John Wynn	
Puleston	Thomas Hanmer	Deccaf of Rhwy-	Roberts of Croes Foel.	
of Hafod	of Hanmer,	tyn.	*Ermine*, a lion rampant	
y Wern.	Knight.		*sable*.	

John =Jane, d. and	Rich- =Jane, d. of	Edward.	Elen,	Mar-
Pules-	co-heir of	ard	Gruffydd	Nicholas.	ux.	garet.ux.
ton of	John Almor	Pules-	ab Edward	Roger, *s. p.*	Wil-	Rhys ab
Hafod	of Almor, ab	ton.	ab Morgan	John, *s. p.*	liam	Richard.
y	John Almor		of Osryn-	Harri, *s. p.*	Al-	
Wern.	ab John Al-		bw.	William,	mor.	
	mor ab Ieuan			*s. p.*		
	ab David of					
	Almor.					
	Azure, a lion					
	salient *or*.					

Dorothy, ux. John Wynn Lloyd of Plas y Bada, in the   Jane.
township of Morton Anglicorum in the Manor of Fabrorum. *Argent*, a lion rampant *sable*, armed, langued,
and crowned *gules*.

a		b	c	d	e

---

[1] Rowlands, in his *Mona Antiqua*, says, "that Hwfa ab Cynddelw
of Presaddved, held his estate in fee, by attending on the Prince's
coronation, and bearing up the right side of the canopy over the
Prince's head at that solemnity", and cites the following extract, from
a MS. of one Lewys Dun, out of the Gloddaith Library: "Yr Hwfa

| a | | | b | c | d | e |

Robert =Susann, d. of Hugh Mare-   Ermine.   Elen.   Alice.   Catherine.
Puleston | dydd of Pentref By-
of Hafod | chan, near Wrexham, second son of Sir Richard Maredydd of
y Wern. | Pentref Bychan ab Rowland Maredydd of Trefalun.   *Azure, a*
              lion salient or.

Robert Puleston of=Jane, d. of John Wynn of Copa'r Goleuni in Tegeingl.
Hafod y Wern. | Palii of six pieces *argent* and *sable.*

John Puleston of Hafod y Wern.=Helen, d. of Sir Cynwrig Eyton of
  Born 1603, and appointed to be | Eyton, Knt., ab Sir Gerard Eyton[1]
  one of the Knights of the Royal | of Eyton, Knight Banneret. *Er-*
  Oak, *ob.* 1674. | *mine, a lion rampant azure.*

John Puleston of Hafod y=Dorothy, d. and co-heir, by Dorothy his wife, of
  Wern. Born 1658; mar- | John Lloyd of Ferm, co. Flint, ab Rhys Lloyd;
  ried 1692; *ob.* 1722. | *ob.* Sept. 1741. *Sable, a lion rampant argent,*
                         | *in a border engrailed or.*

Richard Puleston=Mary, d. of Rev. Philip Egerton, D.D.,   John =Dorothy,
  of Hafod y Wern; | third son of Sir Philip Egerton of   Pules-   third d. of
  ob. Dec. 9th, | Oulton, co. Chester, Knight; *ob.*   ton.   Eubule
  1745. | Nov. 2nd, 1764. *Argent, a lion*   Thelwall
         | *rampant gules, inter three pheons*   of Nant-
         | *sable.*   clwyd.

Philip Puleston of=Mary, youngest sister and co-heir of   Ffrances, *ob.*
  Hafod y Wern. | John Davies of Gwysanneu and   Nov. 14th,
  Born 1742; buried | Llanerch Park. Buried in Wrexham   1804, aged 69.
  in Wrexham | Church, Sept. 22nd, 1802, aged 63.
  Church, April 10th |
  1776, aged 34. |

Ffrances Puleston, sole=Bryan Cooke of Owston, co. York, Lieutenant in
  heir of Hafod y Wern. | the Royal Horse Guards, Colonel of the 3rd
  Married 18th Dec. 1786; | West York Militia, M.P. for Maldon; *ob.* 1820;
  buried in the chancel of | son of Anthony Cooke of Owston, son of Henry
  Owston Church, 8th Jan. | Cooke of Owston, third son of Sir Henry Cooke
  1818. | of Wheatley, co. York, Bart.

Philip Davies Cooke of Hafod y Wern, Gwy-=Lady Helena Caroline
  sanneu and Owston, J P. and D.L., F.L.S., | King, d. of George, third
  F.G.S., F.Z.S. Born 1793; *ob.* 20th Nov. 1853. | Earl of Kingston.

Philip Bryan Davies Cooke of Hafod y Wern, Owston, and Gwysanneu.
            Born 2nd March, 1832.

hwn a'i Etifeddion hynaf a wiscant y Dalaith am ben y Twysog gyda
Esgob Bangor, ac y dydd cyntaf y cyssegrid y Twysog yn y Dalaeth
yr oedd i Hwfa, y par dillad a fai am y Twysog wrth wisgo y Dalaith
am ei ben. A hyn oedd wasanaeth Hwfa ab Cynddelw."—*Cambrian
Register*, vol. i, p. 145.
   [1] Sir Gerard Eyton of Eyton, was a zealous and distinguished
Royalist in the time of the Civil Wars, and was in arms against the
Commonwealth in the Castle of Denbigh when it surrendered to the
Parliamentary forces. He compounded for his property, which was
sequestered. See vol. ii.

BADY OF RHIWABON AND STANSTI.

Harl. MSS. 1972, 1481, 2299.

John ab David ab Ieuan ab Bady ab Ieuan Foel ab Madog Goch ab Madog,══
eighth son of Icuaf ab Nyniaw ab Cynwrig ab Rhiwallawn.

Robert Bady══Margaret, d. of Roger Deccaf ab David Deccaf of Rhwytyn,
of Stansti. in the Manor of Rhiwabon and parish of Bangor Is y Coed.
Ermine, a lion rampant *azure.*

Roger Bady of Stansti and══Jane, d. of Edward Brereton of Borasham, High
Plas yn y Delff, in Sheriff for co. Denbigh in 1598.
Rhiwabon, 1600.

Owain Bady of Rhiwabon, 1630. Sold Plas yn══Jane, d. of Edward Lloyd of
y Delff to Sir Thomas Myddleton Hen. Plâs Madog.

Robert Bady of the parish══..., d. of John Edwards of Plâs Newydd in the
of Chirk, 1697. parish of Chirk.

Timothy Bady.   Edward Bady.   John Bady.

JONES OF FRONDEG.

Harl. MS. 1972.

Iolyn ab David ab Deicws ab Ieuaf ab Iolyn Foel ab Madog Goch ab Madog⹋
ab Ieuaf ab Nyniaw ab Cynwrig ab Rhiwallawn.

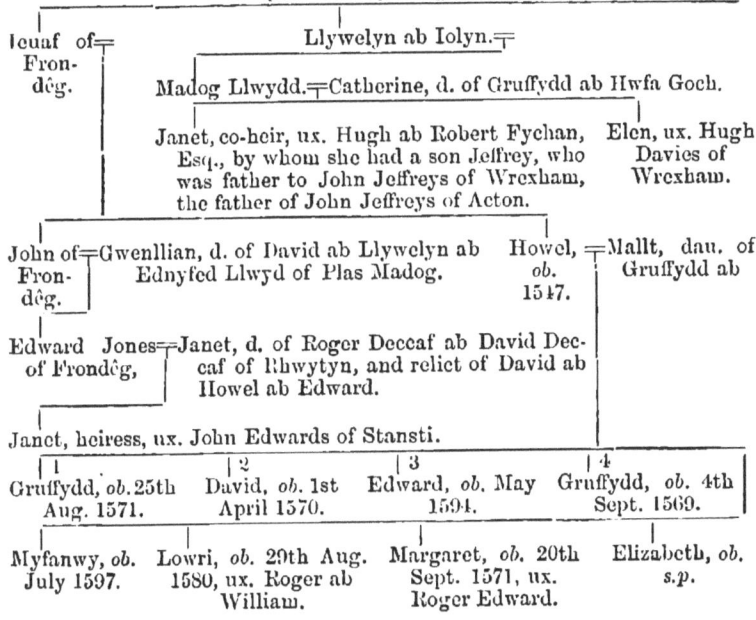

Ieuaf of⹋   Llywelyn ab Iolyn.⹋
Fron-
dég.

Madog Llwydd.⹋Catherine, d. of Gruffydd ab Hwfa Goch.

Janet, co-heir, ux. Hugh ab Robert Fychan,   Elen, ux. Hugh
Esq., by whom she had a son Jeffrey, who   Davies of
was father to John Jeffreys of Wrexham,   Wrexham.
the father of John Jeffreys of Acton.

John of⹋Gwenllian, d. of David ab Llywelyn ab   Howel, ⹋Mallt, dau. of
Fron-   Ednyfed Llwyd of Plas Madog.   *ob.*   Gruffydd ab
dég.   1547.

Edward Jones⹋Janet, d. of Roger Deccaf ab David Dec-
of Frondég,   caf of Rhwytyn, and relict of David ab
           Howel ab Edward.

Janet, heiress, ux. John Edwards of Stansti.

1	2	3	4
Gruffydd, *ob.* 25th Aug. 1571.	David, *ob.* 1st April 1570.	Edward, *ob.* May 1594.	Gruffydd, *ob.* 4th Sept. 1569.
Myfanwy, *ob.* July 1597.	Lowri, *ob.* 29th Aug. 1580, ux. Roger ab William.	Margaret, *ob.* 20th Sept. 1571, ux. Roger Edward.	Elizabeth, *ob.* *s.p.*

ELIS OF MAELOR GYMRAEG.

Harl. MS. 4181.

Ieuaf Fychan ab Ieuaf ab Nyniaw ab Cynwrig ab Rhiwallawn. *Ermine, a* lion rampant *sable*.

Ednyfed Foel.

Angharad, ux. Iorwerth ab Ednyfed ab Meilir.

Iorwerth Goch.

Madog ab Iorwerth. — Agnes or Annest, d. of David ab Ieuan ab Iorwerth ab David ab Goronwy of Burton and Llai.

Ieuan Foel. | David, Vicar of Rhiwabon. | Tegyn ab Madog. | Angharad, ux. Ieuaf ab Llywelyn ab Gruffydd ab Iorwerth Fychan of Erddig.

David. | Richard.

Bady or Madog. | Iolyn ab Ieuan.

Iolyn ab Bady. | Ieuan ab Bady. | Gruffydd ab Bady. | David ab Iolyn. | Richard ab Iolyn.

Iorwerth ab Iolyn. | David ab Ieuan.

Gruffydd ab Iorwerth. — Margaret, d. of Gruffydd ab David ab Howel.

Elis ab Gruffydd — Margaret, d. of Maredydd ab Edward or Iorwerth.

Owain ab Elis. — Anne, d. of Robert Atnery of Chester. | Maredydd ab Elis, married, and had two daughters, co-heirs. | Edward. Simon. John. Roger. John. | Catherine. Gwen. Elizabeth.

1
William Elis. = Rose, d. of Richard Ross. | 2
John Elis. | 3
David Elis. | Elizabeth. | Anne.

Harl. MS. 4181.

David Llwyd ab Iorwerth Ddû ab⟂Eva, d. of Gruffydd ab Gryffydd Ddû,
Iorwerth ab Howel ab Ieuaf ab | and relict of Ieuan ab David
Nyniaw ab Cynwrig ab Rhiwall- | Llwyd ab Madog ab Llywelyn ab
awn. | Gruffydd.

Ieuan ab David.⟂Gwenllian, d. of Ieuaf ab Einion ab Ieuaf ab Llywelyn ab
Cynwrig Efell.

Jenkyn Llwyd. =

MAELOR.
Harl. MSS. 1972, 4181.

Ieuaf ab Madog ab Bledrws, twelfth son of Cynwrig ab Rhiwallawn.⟂

Ieuaf Ddû.⟂Efa, d. of Ieuaf ab Adda ab Awr of Trevor.

Howel Maelor.⟂Gwenllian, d. of Einion ab Iorwerth ab Einion Goch of
Sonlli.

Angharad, heiress, ux. Madog ab David ab Ednyfed. Descended from Sanddef Hardd, Lord of Burton and Llai.

Howel ab Icuan ab Madog ab Einion ab Madog ab Bleddyn ab Cynwrig═╤═
　　　　　　　　ab Rhiwallawn.

Madog ab Howel.═╤═

Howel ab Madog.═╤═..., d. of Maredydd ab Rhys ab Gruffydd of Rhiwabon.

Edward ab Howel.═╤═Margaret. d. of David ab Robert ab Gruffydd ab Howel.

Robert ab Edward.═╤═

1			2		
John ab═Gwenllian. d. of Howel			Hugh ═	Robert	John Roberts
Robert.	ab Ieuan ab Rhys of		Roberts.	Roberts.	Sidanwyn.
	Y Glwysegl.				

David ab Hugh.

Deili, ux. Richard ab John ab Edward ab David ab Icuan ab
　　　　Jenkyn ab Llywelyn ab Ithel Goch.

Sibyl, ux.	Mary, ux.	Eliza-	Jane, ux.	Annie,	Margaret, ux.
Robert ab	Hugh Ey-	beth, ux.	John	ux.	John Lloyd of
Edward ab	ton of Bryn	Peter	ab John	Row-	Stansti ab John
Edward.	yr Onen.	Fowler.	ab Roger.	land.	Lloyd.

Deili, ux. John ab David ab Howel　　　Catherine, ux. Robert ab Gruffydd
　of Brymbo or Brynbwa.　　　　　　ab Gruffydd ab Edward ab Morgan.

A TRUE REPORT OF THE LIFE AND MARTYRDOM OF MR. RICHARD WHITE,

SCHOOLMASTER,

Who suffered the 15th day of October, an. Dom. 1584.[1]

I have received your letters, my dear friends, dated the 17th day of November, wherein you renew your old suit unto me to lay down in a brief discourse the lingering martyrdom of Mr. Richard White, the which had been done before this day, had I not hoped that some other man of greater skill and experience would take in hand so good a matter, answerable to the weight and worthiness thereof; but understanding that those who are better able than myself to do it are either employed to other business of greater importance that they can have no leisure, or else hindered by the iniquity of the time that they can have no opportunity, I have presumed here, as it were with a coal, rudely to draw the portraiture of his great patience and constancy, rather than that the memory of so glorious a martyr should perish, referring the polishing and painting thereof in colours to a more cunning workman.

Therefore you shall understand that he was born at Llanydlos in Montgomeryshire, and descended of honest parentage, bearing the surname of Gwin; but after his coming to the University, some of his acquaintance, perceiving the Welsh word to signify *White* in English, termed him White, by the which name he was ever afterward known and called. Of his younger years there is nothing memorable, saving that he was twenty years of age before he did frame his mind to like of good letters; at which years, following the counsel of the wise philosopher (who saith), *Quod nunquam sera est ad bonos mores via,* he gave his mind to repair to such places as he knew most famous for learning.

First he travelled to Oxford, where he made no great abode; from thence he resorted to Cambridge, and there

---

[1] The following is printed from a contemporary MS. that was found some time ago in the Mission House of the Catholic Chapel, Holywell. It agrees in the main with the long account of the death of the "Protomartyr of Wales" given by Dr. Bridgewater (from which Dr. Challoner drew up his brief memoir), but is an independent production, entering into many more details than are given in the published account.

made choice of St. John's College, where he lived by the charity of the said College, and chiefly of Dr. Bullock, then head of the household, his very good benefactor. But when alteration of religion compelled sundry principal men of both Universities to leave their rooms and livings, the said Dr. Bullock, amongst the rest, left also his house and country. Afterwards, a new governor being placed in his stead "who knew not Joseph", need and poverty compelled this young man to become a teacher before he could perfectly lay the foundation to be a learner; and when he had bestowed some few years in the University, God put in his mind, by persuasion of friends, to return towards his own country; and so he placed himself in Maelor,[1] where he bestowed his poor talent among the youths of that country, and, in the end, his life and blood for their further benefit. A happy return to the whole country, if the miserable blind people would consider of it; much they are beholden unto him for the offices of his life, but much more for his glorious death and martyrdom.

The whole time he remained there was about sixteen years, the which he so divided that all Maelor and every part thereof might fare the better by him. First, he placed himself in Orton Madock,[2] where he spent most of these years; from thence he removed to Wrexham (where he spent his life as you shall understand hereafter), and so he went to Gresford, then to Yswyd, and last of all to Orton again; by reason of which public charge in all these places he was greatly acquainted, his company of the better sort much desired, and of the people generally loved for his diligence in teaching and other good parts known to be in him. His moderation and temperance in his life and conversation were such, that his adversaries could never to this day charge him with any notable crime, or any other fault than the following of his faith and conscience (which now-a-days is accounted madness), for testimony whereof I appeal to those places where he hath conversed. During this while he so profited by his own private study in knowledge of good literature, that it was wonder to them that knew him before to see in the man so great ripeness from so late a beginning. He was not unskilful in most of the seven liberal sciences, and in histories very well seen; but now, in his latter time, he gave his time wholly to the study of divinity. As for his knowledge of the Welsh tongue, he was inferior to none in his country, where he hath left to the posterity some precedent in writing, eternal monuments

---

[1] Bromefield in Denbighshire.   [2] Overton Madog.

of his wit, zeal, virtue, and learning. A little before his coming
to Orton this latter time, he married thence a young girl by
whom he had six children, whereof he sent three to heaven before him in their infancy, the other three he left with their
mother. And so being the second time placed in Orton among
his wife's friends, Mr. Downam, the named Bishop of Chester,
and his officers, began to molest him for refusing to receive
at their communion-table. In the end, after some troubles, he
yielded to their desires although greatly against his stomach, by
the earnest persuasion of a gentleman (Roger Puleston), who
had then, and hath now, a great part of that country at command; and lo, by the providence of God, he was no sooner
come out of the church but a fearful company of crows and
kites so persecuted him to his home that they put him in great
fear of his life, the conceit whereof made him also sick in
body as he was already in soul diseased; in the which sickness he resolved himself (if God would spare his life) to become a Catholic, the which good purpose, afterward having
recovered his health, he performed accordingly.

But the enemy of mankind, envying his well-doing, and
fearing lest the example of so good a man, being a public
person, would do much harm to his cause, incited the minds
of such as were (in the parish) before infected with heresy to
molest him, who never gave over their malice until they had
banished him out of the country and diocese. From thence
he went over the river of Dee unto Erbistock, where, in an
old barn, he exercised still his former profession of teaching;
but the spiteful heretics made means to expel him thence
also, and to despatch him at length out of the whole country;
for, indeed, they were unworthy to have among them so
blessed a man.

Then he travelled abroad to seek relief and comfort among
strangers which was denied him by his own countrymen at
home, who were most beholden unto him. In the end it
pleased God to deliver him to the hands of his adversaries, in
that town where he afterwards suffered. The next day after
his apprehension being Thursday, the justices of the peace
met him in the said town to determine of him; in the mean
time the prisoner escaped, for that Thursday was not yet come
wherein, in the same place, he should glorify God by his constant death. And before two years were expired (July 1580)
he was apprehended again by one David Edwards, a mercer,
not far from the place whence he had made the escape, who
laid violent hands on him in the highway, having neither
commission from superior magistrates nor any special quarrel

to the party himself but of a foolish blind zeal, being a hot
Puritan, and of spiteful hatred to the man's religion.   Now
the servant of God having the second time fallen into the
hands of his enemies, was first carried to the mercer's house
(who took him), and both his legs were loaded with heavy
bolts.   Afterward conveyed to the black chamber (Siambar
ddu), a vile and filthy prison, where he lay on the cold ground
two days and two nights, fed, etc., thence brought before
Robert Puleston[1] to be examined, who (being an enemy to the
Catholic religion) returned his commitment for vehement sus-
picion of treason; so he was sent to Ruthin (for there the
gaol remained), both arms being made sure with strong hand-
bolts, where, at his first coming, the gaoler entertained him
with a huge pair of bolts on both heels, the which continued
the first quarter.   Marry, towards the second quarter, the
gaoler, being now better acquainted with the man's behaviour and innocency, remitted some part of his former rigour
towards him.   And here I may not omit to tell you a strange
accident which chanced to a gentleman (John Salusbury of
Rûg) of good account in the country a little after the prisoner's
coming to town, who, passing by the gaol in company with
one Goodman, Dean of Westminster, and perceiving the
prisoner to stand in the door, first paused a while beholding
him, then shook his head upon him, saying, " Oh, White,
White, thou art an unprofitable member of the commonwealth!" the which words he spake in hearing of this preacher,
to maintain a little credit he was in with him and other heretics,
but plainly against his own conscience and knowledge ; for all
the country knew him to be inclined in mind unto the same religion for the which the other man sustained imprisonment and
irons even in his presence.   But see what followed : the gentleman returned home sick, and was never seen abroad after
this word until he came to be buried ; a sore word to the man
himself, and a good example to all dissemblers, especially in
credit and authority, to take heed what they say or do against
their own conscience.   Another chance happened, no less
strange than the former; unto a preacher, one Ithel Thelwell,
son to Simon Thelwell (who afterward, as you shall hear, pronounced sentence of death upon the martyr).   This minister,
being Master of Arts and a preacher of no small account,
having entered unto his sermon (before the judges and all the

---

[1] This gentleman was a continual enemy to the prisoner, and
busy at his indictment, but never lived to see his death, ending his
own life miserably.

worship of the shire, in the assize week, which no doubt
he had provided against the Catholic religion and this holy
confessor), suddenly fell dumb, that the judges themselves
were fain to call him out of the pulpit with shame enough;
whereupon there wanted not some who affirmed that Mr.
White had bewitched him; but many reported that this good
man's imprisonment was the cause of the preacher's dumb-
ness.   But what think you? were the magistrates moved at
the sight hereof to take compassion on their prisoner?
Nothing less: "Induratum enim erit cor Pharaonis ne demit-
terit Israel,"—Israel should not depart.   (Exod. x.)

In this first assize, kept at Ruthin about Michaelmas A.D.
1580, he had not much said to him, saving that the judges
were earnestly in hand with him to accuse his benefactors and
forsake his religion, wherein God so assisted him that they
could not prevail.   Towards Christmas, the gaol was removed
unto Wrexham, where a new gaoler received him with a great
pair of shackles, the which he was compelled to wear both day
and night all the year following, by the special commandment
of the sheriff (Owen Brereton), an enemy to all good men, and,
namely, to this man of God, even to his last breath and after.

Now, the second assize being kept at Wrexham, in May
A.D. 1581, the adversaries were busy to make him relent, so
far, at the least, as to hear an heretical sermon, for they did
imagine that his fall would give the Catholic religion a sore
blow, especially in Maelor, where the people depended much
upon his virtue and learning.   But when the magistrates saw
that fair means and gentle persuasions could take no place,
they began to extend towards him plain violence; for, presently, six of the sheriff's men were commanded to carry him
unto the church, who took the servant of God upon their
shoulders, with his heels upward, and so bare him in proces-
sion-wise round about the font (a very strange spectacle to the
beholders), laying him along under the pulpit, where a preacher
was ready to welcome the poor man with a railing sermon.
But all this while he so stirred his legs that, with the noise of
his irons, the preacher's (Thomas Jones) voice could not be
heard; whereat the judges and sheriff were in a great rage,
commanding to carry him thence into the stocks.   But he
told them that it needed not, for he offered to go with them
quietly to any punishment for his conscience—yea, to the gallows, if they would have it, but to their schismatical assem-
blies, he told them, he would never go or come quietly.   And
thus he was locked in the stocks, both legs, from ten o'clock
before noon until eight at night, vexed all the space with a
rabble of ministers.

In the end he was turned loose toward his gaol, halting all
the way as he went by reason of stiffness in his legs over-
charged with stocks and fetters, which rueful spectacle the
mercer beholding, brake forth into a great laughter; a lewd
nature of a malicious heretic, to feed himself in such wicked
malice upon the cruel affliction of the poor man.   In the mean
time the magistrates, consulting how they might collect matter
enough out of that day's work to make him away, caused a
jury to be impanuelled, men for their own purpose, haters of
the Catholic faith, to whom was no store made of his demeanour in the church, and words to the justices.   But the jury,
perceiving that the evidence against him did not bear weight,
found a bill for the disturbance of divine service, and, thereupon, he was fined by Judge Bromley in a hundred marks;
a most wicked verdict and sentence against all law of God
and man, and a pretty stratagem, first, to do open violence to
his body, and then to bring him under the danger of their law
—I dare say contrary to the intention of the law-makers themselves, who could not conceive a man in his case violently
carried to their church upon men's shoulders.   Well, howsoever
they conceive, I am sure that many who were present at this
device complained of the injustice done unto him that day, the
which even God Himself, to the honour of His servant, showed
presently before the bar, by an evident miracle; for when
James Garm, the pronotary or primitary, should have read the
bill of his indictment, he was stricken blind, as we read of
Elymas the sorcerer to have been by the sentence of St. Paul
(Acts xiii), and whereas the judge called upon him twice or
thrice to read the bill, the said pronotary, opening his breast
in great rage, confirmed with an oath that he was stark blind;
whereunto Sir George replied, " Speak softly, lest the Papists
make a miracle of that."   And thus the bill was turned over
to be read by another clerk that stood by.

The assize being kept at Denbigh in September following, there was no great matter done against him, saving
that Sir George Bromley caused him to be indicted in seven
score pounds for not coming to church, upon the penal statute
of twenty pounds a month, then lately enacted; a ridiculous
thing that a poor man lying close prisoner many years together, and at the command of his gaoler, should, notwithstanding, be guilty of the statute before it was devised.   But
equity and conscience can have no place where corrupt and
blind affection reigneth.   After that he was fined in this
double mulct, viz., at the assizes before in a hundred marks
for coming to church, and, at this assize in two hundred

marks for not coming. It pleased Mr. Justice to play and
sport with his prisoner (as the cat doth with the mouse before
she devour it), pleasantly demanding of him what he had to
discharge himself of his debt. Whereunto Mr. White, very
devoutly making low obeisance, answered, "I have somewhat
towards it." "What hast thou?" sayeth the justice. "I
have", sayeth he, "sixpence;" the which answer did set Sir
George in such a rage that nothing might cool the same until
he beheld the poor man's legs well charged with two pair of
irons, for fear belike of running away, now being so much in
the Queen's debt. Some which were present at this talk re-
proved the prisoner for crossing Mr. Justice, being he knew
well that the man could never abide to be crossed; some were
of a contrary mind, allowing his answer as proceeding from
the wise man's counsel, who biddeth answer a fool according
to his foolishness, that he may not seem wise in his own conceit. To tell you mine opinion, I think that the demand was
beside all wit and discretion, to ask a poor prisoner, who, depended on the devotion and charity of others, what he had to
discharge 300 marks and odd money.

At this assize, John Hughes and Robert Moris, his fellows,
were first committed to prison with him, who had long before
his apprehension sustained irons for the same cause at the
council in the Marches, and were now removed to their own
country, no doubt by the special providence of God, to receive
mutual comfort one of the other, and especially to learn of
this blessed confessor the rules of perfect charity, patience,
devotion, and all other acts of virtue.

The next assize, kept at Wrexham in the year 1582, the
adversaries having learned the experience in the same place a
twelvemonth before, that forced haling of the prisoner to sermons could take no good end, devised another stratagem
more cunning than the former, but with as ill success; for
upon Friday in the assize week, at about four of the clock in the
afternoon, the prisoners were sent for to the bar, where, beside their expectation, a minister was ready to entertain them
with an heretical sermon, of the which wrong they ceased not
to complain to the judges, telling them that they came not
thither to hear sermons, but to receive law and justice.
Marry, their complaint taking no place they turned their
speech to the preacher, the one in Latin, the other in English, and the third in Welsh, so fast that the magistrates
were not a little offended with them, threatening them, if they
would not give over, heavy bolts, whips, stocks, dungeons,
and pillory; to be short, the prisoners were removed in no

small displeasure, and the preacher made an end of his lying sermon with small grace.

In this assize, certain pedlars and tinkers, who then bare some sway in the town, hot Puritans and full of the gospel, complained upon the sheriff[1] that he was not so sharp to his prisoners as they required; yea, moreover, in plain terms, that he relieved them[2]—an heinous offence, if it were true, and worthy punishment, that a magistrate should give such an open example as to do a deed of charity, if it be a deed of charity to relieve poor Papists for, except I mistake, the Protestant preachers have found out of late in their new divinity that Christian men are bound to relieve felons and murderers in prison, or any other malefactors, but not Papists; and this Christopher Goodman teacheth and practiseth at West Chester, where he taketh special order that the poor Catholics in the castle may reap no benefit by the poor man's box, and other relief which is in the city gathered for prisoners; whereby may appear that all is not the word of the Lord (whereof these fellows brag so much) that cometh out of their mouths, but they are glad now and then to drop among it some of their own words and inventions: and this by the way; now to our matter.

Upon this complaint, presently order was laid down by the judges that Mr. Sheriff must have four overseers to assist him, who so narrowly looked to their charges that all access of their friends unto them was barred, except of their wives only; and they were not suffered to bring them any relief at all but these honest men must oversee it; the which strange dealing did drive into the people's heads such a mutiny, that every man affirmed how their adversaries did mean to despatch the poor men by famine whom they could not make away by any colour of law. And here I may not forget to tell you the notable malice that David Edwards, the mercer before named, one of the said overseers, bare this man of God; who, being on horseback ready to take his journey and beholding the prisoner to stand at the gaol-door in his irons, with his little child in his arms, suddenly the spiteful wretch, as one in some frantic mood, crossed the way towards him, and, in a great rage, overthrew him backwards on the stones, leaving the print of his nails in his face, putting also the babe in no small hazard of his life. But what think you? durst he com-

---

[1] Edward Hughes of Holt, Esq.

[2] At Easter, none was admitted to the communion-table but such as had a token from one of the two tinkers.

plain hereof to the judges? Or could he hope to find any remedy at their hands? Nothing less. The good man laid up this injury among others more to be remedied by a more indifferent Judge, who would no doubt one day, and could, remedy the same. Another like token of a malicious heart this desperate heretic showed about the same time, causing his wife and daughter to depose before Ievan Lloyd of Yale that the prisoner was seen two flight-shots from the gaol (naming the place, Coytmor); the which his gaoler disproved to their faces, affirming that one Ievan Lewis was the man, and not he. Where you may see what malice can do in a wicked mind, void of God's fear, conscience, religion, and all goodness. Verily, if justice might have taken place, the pillory, which was a little before threatened (as you have heard) to the innocent man and his fellows, should have been the reward of these perjured women, for whom and for such it was chiefly ordained.

The Michaelmas following our prisoners were removed to the Holt (where the assize was kept), to be there indicted of high treason, as appeareth by a letter that Mr. White wrote himself to a friend of his, the copy whereof I have laid down *verbatim* as followeth:

The copy of Mr. White, his letter, reporting the indictment of the three prisoners at the Holt, and the manner of their adversaries' proceeding against them.

After my hearty commendations, these are to certify you of our estate. Upon Friday, in the assize week, we were indicted of high treason by the great inquest, Owen Brereton being foreman, by the procurement of David Edwards, Sir Hugh Soulley the apostate, David Powell Goch, Vicar of Ruabon, who did follow the bill against us (as far as I could understand); for Mr. Justice Townshend demanding who followed the bill, the clerk of the indictment gave answer, David Powell, and he then stood at the bar. Sir Hugh Soulley and David Edwards had gotten one Lewis Gronow, of Miriadock in this county of Denbigh (who was prisoner with us for an execution of debt), to bear witness against us, the which Lewis had been on the pillory at Denbigh by the procurement of Mr. Tudur Probert. This honest man, being examined before the two judges, Ievan Lloyd of Yale, Roger Puleston, Owen Brereton, and others, deposed that we three had persuaded him and divers others to abstain from the church, and to acknowledge the Pope's authority; and that he had to prove this sundry witnesses, whom he named to them: as David Penrhun, Peter Roydon, John Roberts Barker of Ruthin, and Edward Erles, who were all in our gaol at several times. David Penrhun did not appear; the rest were deposed, who, upon their oaths cleared us, and proved our adversary perjured.

Moreover, one Robert Clarke, minister of Wrexham, deposed that he heard John Roberts Barker, before named, report how David Penrhun did tell him that I did call the church *domum diaboli;* the which John Roberts denied upon his oath, and so the minister was foresworn. Again, there was two gentlemen in our gaol for an execution, Mr. Thomas Price Winne of Llanarmon in Yale, and Thomas Lloyd of Abergeley, who offered to depose that Lewis Gronow was in hand with them to bear false witness against me; but they cried on him in these words, " Fie on thee, fie on thee ! thou, being an old man ninety years of age, and wouldst thou have us bear false witness with thee against any man ?" In the afternoon, the second inquest was called, which went upon life and death. In the mean time, John Hughes his wife was examined strictly, to get more evidence for the last inquest; but nothing could be gotten. Here the gaoler had a great charge given him by Sir George to look well unto us three ; and so he bound our arms behind our backs with cords, and watched us in the shire-hall all the day fasting, that we looked for present death the next day after. At length the second inquest came in far in the night with their verdict, and said nothing of us. And this is all I can certify at this time. What shall become of us God knoweth, unto whom we commit ourselves and you, with commendations from my fellows, desiring the assistance of your prayers and other good friends for us. Wrex., the 12 of October Anno Dom. 1582. Your daily beadsman, RICH. WHITE.

At this assize a lamentable chance happened unto a gentlemen of good calling (John Edwards of Cherk), who had been a Catholic and a great benefactor to these prisoners, and was now brought by infirmity and importunity of carnal friends to renounce his faith before the bar, with open protestation ; a pitiful example never heard of in Wales before, and no small discomfort to the poor prisoners. But what followed ? The gentleman returned home, his soul loaded with sin, his conscience with desperation, his body with punishments so strange and fearful that my tongue doth tremble to utter them, my heart doth bleed to think upon them ; but the country doth remember them, and the posterity will talk of them. How far better had it been for him to fall into the hands of men, from whom many ways he might have escaped, at least by death, than to fall into the terrible hands of Almighty God, from whose fingers he might neither dead nor alive escape. Alas, that the constancy of his poor beadsmen could not stay him from so foul a deed, whom he beheld chained and bound hand and foot, ready to offer their lives and blood for that cause which he came to renounce and forsake. But I pray God that his poor soul may not now answer for this dissimulation before that seat where all our actions must be discussed, where dissimulation can take no place, nor friendship prevail; and that his example may be a warning to other gentlemen to take heed of the like attempt.

At Christmas, after this assize, the new sheriff (Ievan Lloyd of Yale, 1583) entering into his office, first removeth from the prisoners their overseers, being able of himself to oversee them sufficiently; then chargeth them with great irons, for the great good will he bare to them.

At the assize in May 1583, order was taken for their removing to the council of the Marches, the which was done with great solemnity, binding their arms fast behind them, *tanquam latrones cum fustibus et gladiis* (Matt. xxvi), as their Master and Captain was sometimes brought before the high priest. They hoped by torments to wrest from them some evidence against themselves, that they might after with more colour despatch them. Thither was brought to meet these prisoners two young men, prisoners also, from Flint gaol, to be tortured likewise for the same cause, Mr. John Benet and Harry Pue, the one a priest the other a layman, both right virtuous and constant Catholics; who were all five in November following, at Bewdley and Bridgnorth, laid in the manacles (a kind of torture at the council, not much inferior to the rack of the Tower of London), whereof there is written a special treatise, collected out of divers letters from the said confessors to their friends, of which letters I have selected so much as concerneth our martyr, whereof this is the copy.

A Copy of a Letter sent from one of the Catholic prisoners to a friend of his, wherein he showeth the torturing of himself and of his fellows at Bewdley, in Nov. anno Dom. 1583.

Being so often called upon to lay down particular notes of the council's dealings towards us during the time of our trial and torments, I have collected such things as my fellows and myself could remember to satisfy your request, and conferred diligently therein with them again, lest any untruth had escaped us by overmuch haste in writing. Therefore you shall understand, that Sir George Bromley sent for John Huges and Robert Moris before him, upon Tuesday, in the morning about eight of the clock, being the 26th of November, etc. The 27th day following, being about eight of the clock in the morning, Mr. Richard White and Harry Pue were brought to Atkins's chamber, the Queen's attorney, and all the way as they passed, the people lifted up their hands after them, saying, "God save you! God stand with you!" When they were come before the attorney, he examined them awhile together, and, being separated, the said attorney turned him to Mr. White, and said as followeth.

Atkins. I protest before God, that the principality of Wales is the third part of the realm wherein no punishment at all hitherunto hath been used towards such lewd, obstinate, and disobedient persons; upon whom (as Mr. Justice sayeth) no more mercy ought to be had than on a mad dog, for all Papists be the Queen's professed enemies.

White. You slander them, they are not; and, for my part, I do acknowledge her to have full authority in all temporal causes within her own dominions, and so we are taught by our superiors.

A. You are contrary to your fellows herein, for Benet calleth the Pope *rex regum,* and he sayeth himself, in his own style, *si non valeat verbum Domini valeat gladius Petri.*

W. As for Mr. Benet you have forthcoming, let him answer for himself; and, as touching the Pope's style, I know it not, but this that I have told you I believe to be true.

A. Wilt thou swear it?

W. Will you enlarge me if I do?

A. If thou wilt answer directly to such questions as we are to demand of thee upon thy further reformation, although thou be indicted of treason, yet I will be a suitor for thee to the council, who shall be a means for thee to her Majesty to procure thy pardon. We will not charge thee with any point of religion, but of treason; we will not demand of thee how many sacraments there be, as the Papists did our men in Queen Mary's time, but we will demand of thee when thou hast been first reconciled, by whom, in what place, where last confessed, how often, and whether thou hast been in confession with Benet or no, sithence he came to the country.

W. Do not you know that confession is a point of religion, and one of the chiefest; and, in demanding of me such a question, you break promise?

A. It is no point of religion at all, but the very invention of the Pope to draw subjects thereby from their prince to promise obedience to him, that he may displace the prince to enrich his own coffers. What thinkest thou, may he lawfully displace any prince of his kingdom?

W. He doth displace none.

A. Now, how say you to the Bull of Pius Quintus against our most gracious Queen?

W. Notwithstanding that Bull (the which I never saw), I believe and confirm that she is our lawful Queen.

A. Doth not the Pope grant pardons and plenaries to such as will kill our Queen?

W. I deny that; for he neither doth so, nor yet will do so, nor can if he would.

A. He cannot indeed, but it is his common practice so to do; for the late rebels in the north, and Saunders in Ireland, had a Bull from the Pope to invade the realm, to murder the Council and the Queen's royal person; and he hath to this end directed seminaries (as nurseries for all disobedient persons to run into), from whence do come those lewd runagate priests, who labour to seduce the people from their obedience to their prince, and to cause an uproar within the realm if it be not prevented in time.

W. As for the rising in the north, I was not privy thereto, neither to Dr. Saunders going to Ireland, being prisoner at the very same time; therefore you do me wrong to charge me with other men's actions. And, as touching the seminaries, I heard it reported that they have the Queen's arms upon their college at Rome, and that they use in both colleges a daily prayer for her Majesty.

A. They have the arms of England, but they do not mean the Queen of England; and, as for their prayer, they pray, after their seditious manner, that she may be either converted or confounded, and so dost thou.

W. When I pray for her Majesty, I make her of no higher degree than a neighbour; for a man is bound to love God above all things, and his neighbour as himself; and I place her under the highest degree of neighbourhood, contained in the commandment, Honour thy father and mother, etc., but I will not make her my God.

A. She is indeed *pater patriæ*. But to let these words pass, how say you to the premises? Will you answer us directly concerning your reconciliation and confession with Benet within these three weeks, as some of your own fellows do witness?

W. Doth not the Scripture say that the Pharisees and Sadducees came to St. John, confessing their sins and to be baptised?

A. Yes; but that was not auricular confession. Peradventure thou wouldst recite another place in the 19th of the Acts (this place Mr. Benet had taught the attorney before), where it is said that the believers confessed their deeds to the Apostles.

And so in the end Mr. White was turned to the manacles about nine of the clock in the morning, upon which torture he was strictly examined by the aforesaid attorney upon the former interrogatives about his reconciliation and confession, who promised him that he should not be delivered from the torments until he would confess the truth. And, moreover, he willed him to have regard to himself, being an old man, and not so able to endure the pains as some of his fellows were; and that some had confessed already, and were at ease, as he should be also, if he would do the like. But all these charming words could not prevail against the resolute soul of this constant confessor, who bestowed all the time of his torments in continual prayer, by craving of God for his tormentors mercy and forgiveness, and for himself safe deliverance from their malice by the merits of Christ Jesus His passion; and this he did with a loud voice. But the persecutors seemed to be tormented with his words, as if they had been possessed, for they never ceased running in and out all the while, muttering one to another he knew not what. Then he fell to prayer in silence, and so continued until dinner time without any answer to their demands; whereat the pitiful men, moved no doubt with compassion, supposing the man to be speechless, took him down, and so left him to remain with his manacles until their coming again.   Immediately after dinner came to visit the prisoner Mr. Justice Bromley, Mr. Townsend, Mr. Phillips, Mr. Leighton of the Plash, Mr. Thelwall, being all of the council ; Mr. Atkins, the attorney ; Mr. Sherrer, Thomas Evans, deputy solicitor ; and divers others. Then Sir George Bromley, as one in a great rage, uttered these words.

Bromley. There is no more pity to be had on thee than on a mad dog ; and it were better that all such wretches were hanged, than that the state of the realm should be troubled with the like.   For it standeth us upon to look unto such, and we are so commanded by the Queen and the council ; yea, if we had no authority from above, yet we might do it of ourselves.

W. Sir, if you have authority, either of yourselves or from others, I pray you put me to death out of hand, and therein you shall do me greater pleasure than to kill me continually in these torments, the which I have felt all this day for my conscience.

B. Nay, thou shalt first be tormented, and then hanged afterwards ; for thou art indicted of high treason, and I cannot help thee, unless upon thy reformation I stay the verdict of the quest, or else reprieve thee ; and if thou wilt do no service to the Queen, if the quest refuse to cast thee, I will have them all to London ; but if thou wilt detect and bewray such treasons as are to be asked of thee, we will do for thee, and if thou fear to lose thy benefactors, we will provide that thou shalt live as well as thou dost now ; nay, not so neither, but thou shalt have a competent living to live withal.   And if thou tell more than Robert Moris hath done, thou shalt be better looked unto ; for he hath confessed already, and is now at ease.

W. Etiam innocentes cogit mentiri dolor.

Sherrer. Sir, he can work well in a garden ; he hath sometimes been my man, and now he hath wife and children.

Phillips. If he will forsake his religion, he shall be my man and gardener too.

A. Indeed, I must say that he is more sensible, and can yield better reason for himself than Benet, who calleth the Pope *rex regum,* for he sayeth that the Pope hath a temporal sword in England.

B. Yea, that Benet, he had rather dispense with the Pope's laws, which are so far, than with the Queen's laws, which be so nigh.

W. The Pope is a priest, and he meddleth not with the temporal sword, which belongeth to kings and princes ; for priests may not fight with the sword.

B. We are all kings and priests.   Well, the time passeth away ; if thou answer not directly about thy reconciliation and confession with Benet, etc., thou must needs go to the tortures again.

W. Where did you read in all the Scriptures that Christians did compel any by tortures to be of their religion ; but we read that Christ whipped the unworthy out of the Temple.

B. It is written in the Gospel, " Go out into the highways, and compel them to come in", and so we do the like.

P. I pray, sir, to pardon him this time from the manacles until the morning.

B. Well, I am content; and now I pray thee, White, what didst thou give for thy wife?

W. Sir, that question is no point of religion.

And so the council laughing, departed, and Mr. White was turned over to confer with Sherrer.

E. Sir, this man hath been confessed with Benet the priest within these three weeks, and there are witnesses against him of his own fellows, and yet he will not confess it.

S. What, dost thou deny a truth? he that denyeth a truth denyeth Christ, for Christ is the truth; thou denyest the truth, *ergo*, thou denyest Christ!

W. I deny neither Christ nor the truth, because I say nothing.

S. To say nothing or conceal a truth, is the denying of the truth.

W. Then this post denyeth the truth, for it saith nothing.

S. I am sorry with all my heart that I have spoken for thee, and make full account thou shalt to the tortures again.

And so Sherrer departed, and Mr. White remained in the same place with his manacles two long hours after, expecting when he should be laid in them again; but God protected him from any further cruelty at that time.

After that the council had proved these happy men, and found in them no refuse metal, but pure gold, they sent them towards their own country again, with the like pomp wherewith they were brought thence before, *Christi signata in corpore ferentes* ("Bearing the marks of Christ Jesus in their bodies", Gal. vi.). Thus it pleased God by the weak to confound the strong, and by the simple to overcome the prudent; for whereas their adversaries purposed through tortures to increase their own credit, and to quench the faith of these blessed confessors, behold their tortures turned to the foil of the enemy, to the eternal praise of the men afflicted, to the honour of God, and to the good example of their dear country. *A Domino factum est istud et est mirabile in oculis nostris* (Psalm cxvii).

And being now returned home, at the first assize they had nothing said unto them, but two of the witnesses were bound to appear at the next assize following to bear evidence against them as they should be instructed. At which time three of the prisoners were arraigned in manner and form following.

The arraignment of Mr. Richard White, John Hughes, and Robert Moris, at Wrexham in Denbighshire, upon Friday, being the 9th of October, and the feast of St. Denis, anno Dom. 1584, Sir George Bromley, Chief Justice; Simon Thelwall, Deputy Justice; Piers Owen, Sheriff of the Shire;[1] Dr. Ellis, Roger Puleston, Ievan Lloyd of Yale, and Owen Brereton, with others, assistants.

As the prisoners were coming to the bar, Mr. White, in the way before all the assembly, blessed himself, whereat a young gentleman (Francis Bromley) there present made no little pastime, often crossing his body in derision, and casting withal mocks and mowes with his head and mouth towards the poor man; but scornful youth is to be borne with, for he had forgotten that the same holy sign of the cross which he scorned was made on his forehead when he was christened, and ho had not read that Christ foreshowed it would appear one day before all the world in glory (Matt. xxv), at which time he shall be forced to behold it unto his everlasting confusion, if he do not prevent here God's wrath by daily penance. With like scorn he and his fellows derided the good man's answers to the judges, namely, when he said in Latin, *Christianus sum* ("I am a Christian"); a thing to be lamented with tears of blood, and a matter for posterity to marvel at, that men bearing the names of Christians could grow to such impiety and height of paganism as to sport at their own profession.

The prisoners, now standing before the bar, first were commanded to hold up their hands; then the pronotary informed them that they stood indicted of high treason, and that they should have their trial. And so he read the bill of their indictment, viz., that they had offended against the statutes of supremacy and persuasion; hereupon the judges demanded how they would be tried. To the which demand Mr. White answered in the name of himself and his fellows, "We will be tried by you, who are the justices of the bench; for you are wise and learned, and better able to discern the equity of our cause than the simple men of our own country, altogether unacquainted with such matters." But their desire taking no place, a jury was impanuelled, and the witnesses examined, Lewis Gronow, Edward Erles, Howell David. Gronow deposed that the said three prisoners were in hand with him on a Sunday in July, an. Dom. 1582, to become a Papist; secondly, that he heard them also to acknowledge the Bishop of Rome to be supreme head of the Church; thirdly, that he heard Richard White in plain terms to affirm the Pope now living to have the same authority which Christ gave unto Peter.

Erles deposed that he heard White rehearse certain rhymes

---

[1] Piers Owen, Esq., of Garth y Medd, in the parish of Abergele.

of his own making against married priests and ministers; secondly, that he called the Bible a bubble; thirdly, that he termed Justice Bromley *ustus y fram*; and, fourthly, that he defended the Pope's supremacy.

Howell David, against Mr. White, deposed that he heard him complain of this world; and, secondly, affirm that it would not last long; thirdly, that he hoped to see a better world; and, fourthly, that he confessed the Pope's supremacy.

The said Howell David deposed against his cousin John Hughes, that, meeting with him at a place called Rhud y Ceirw, in Ruabon parish, he sought to persuade him unto the Roman religion, adding the churches of Protestants to be full of wicked spirits, and the Pope supreme head of the Catholic Church; moreover, that he sent one John Griffith, a priest, unto him after this conference between them, who tendered to bind him by oath unto his Roman faith. And all this talk both the prisoners denied not to have been before their apprehensions.

Thus the examination of the witnesses being received, the judges demanded of the prisoners what they had to say against the evidence for their own defence; the prisoners took exception against the witnesses, and with many circumstances showed their depositions not to be allowed. That Lewis Gronow had been on the pillory for perjury by the procurement of Mr. Tudur Probert, and was not therefore to be admitted as a lawful witness, referring themselves for the truth of this matter to the knowledge of Mr. Simon Thelwall himself. Thelwall answered, if he had committed perjury, he hath had his punishment; it may be he telleth truth in this point. John Hughes his speeches to the justice were these. "Now they have made an end, Mr. Justice, and said what they can against us, I trust we shall be also heard what we can say for ourselves. I am able to prove that two of these witnesses have been bribed to bear false evidence against us." Whereat Thelwall started, saying, "What, what dost thou say? that they have been bribed?"

Hughes. And am able to prove it.

Thelwall. How much had they?

H. Thirty-two shillings.

T. Who gave it them?

H. They had it.

T. How canst thou prove it?

H. Mr. John Wynne ap William Madock Goch (see p. 19), a gentleman of this parish, told my fellows and me, that one Peter Royden, entering into speech of us, informed him how Lewis

Gronow and Ed. Erles received xvis. a piece to bear this false witness; and that Royden himself was offered xvis., but he refused it.[1]

The gentleman was called before the bar and deposed, the prisoners' report declared unto him, the which he reiterating before all the hall justified to be true; whereat the assembly were greatly astonied, and the judges themselves not a little daunted.   Nevertheless, having before laid down the plot, whom they purposed to kill and whom to save, it was not for their purpose to yield unto the truth; but they went to cast a mist over the eyes of the inquest, that they might not see their legerdemain, for Thelwall, turning to the jury, answered the gentleman's deposition in these words.

"It is not likely that any man should give any money to bear witness against them; for what advantage should any man have by their deaths?   As touching Howell David, his reward was not with the least; for he had the benefit of a bond of two hundred pounds, which he had forfeited to his cousin John Hughes; he had also his lands from him, by the friendship of Sir George Bromley, who, in consideration of this his good service, denied the prisoner justice and law against him." The words that the poor afflicted man used to the justice concerning the said Howell his cousin were these.   "This man hath taken away my house and lands from me and my children, beside all law and conscience, and now he seeketh my life and blood.   I appeal to you, Mr. Justice, whether he be an indifferent witness against me; moreover, he committed perjury in deposing before the council that I did not receive one pennyworth of harm by him at what time he kept forcible possession in my house, whereas I can prove that he and his people consumed divers gallons of butter and cheeses of mine, and spoiled me of a blanket and other stuff; and Mr. Ievan Lloyd of Yale, there sitting, knoweth well what man of conversation Howell David is, and hath been; and as I am certain that he hath forged these matters against me, so may I also take upon my soul that he belieth Mr. Griffith, for it is well known that Catholic priests do not use to tender oaths unto any person to be of their religion."

And thus this part of the tragedy finished.

The prisoners, excepting against the witnesses (as is before declared), denied the evidence to be true.   "Therefore, Mr.

---

[1] This money was given by Ievan Lloyd of Yale the year he was Sheriff, but he knew not that so much money should be paid for his own grave.

Justice (said the prisoners), we beseech you to consider that
we are falsely accused by foresworn men, borne to that purpose." Whereunto Thelwall answered, " Well, well, you are
likely to feel the smart of it ;" and so, turning to the jury, he
read the statute of persuasion, repeating often such words as
seemed to make against the prisoners ; then preparing himself
to give the charge, as a preamble he discoursed before upon
the evidence, extolling the witnesses, dispraising the prisoners,
Mr. White by name, remembering in particular his behaviour
at a sermon in the church, and another sermon before the
bar, where he and his fellows stamped with their feet, and
because their stubbornness might appear more manifestly to
the inquest, Mr. Thelwall demanded of them such questions
as he knew they could not answer with safe conscience affirm-
atively. The first question was, whether they would come to
the church ? The prisoners answered, that they were in the
Catholic Church, and from thence would not be removed ;
the second, whether the Queen ought to be supreme head of
the Church ? and, turning to Mr. White, urged him to answer
plainly and to utter his conscience; the prisoner acknowledged
to the Queen as much authority as Edward the Confessor and
Queen Mary had. Dr. Ellis[1] replied, " There is no reason,
White, but thou shouldst confess the Queen head of the
Church within her own dominions." He answered that
he did acknowledge her to have as much authority as his
father and elders did grant to their princes, and withal he
asked Mr. Dr. in Latin, *Quid est ecclesia?* The which question being a deep point of divinity, and besides his profession
was too high for Mr. Dr. his capacity. Here Mr. White was
charged by some of the company to have spoken words to
Lewis Gronow his accuser, directly approving the Pope's
supremacy, viz., that he affirmed Christ to have twelve Apostles, and that of them He chose one to be head, whom He
named Peter ; and that unto him He gave power to bind and
to loose, and in him to his successors : the prisoner answered
that these were not his words, but St. Chrysostom's. John
Hughes likewise, to this question of the supremacy, said in effect
as his fellow had done before him ; and Robert Moris being
demanded also this point, answered that this question was to

---

[1] This Dr. Ellis is a fit man to sit in judgment upon the servants
of God, who is known to be of as profane a life as any in the world.
He hath had children by his own sister, and long kept his sister's
daughter, and was naught with his own daughter, as the report
goeth.

be learned in schools by divinity, and not before the bar by compulsion or penal statutes. Mr. Thelwall demanded again, what if the Pope came with a power to invade the realm, and to fight against the Queen, whose part would he take? Moris answered that he was well assured that the Pope would not come to fight against the Queen. Then Mr. Thelwall, having wrested from these men so much treason as would serve his turn to despatch them, turned to the jury and said, "Now you may see the stubbornness of these fellows; demand what you will, they will answer nothing directly. It standeth the Queen upon to look unto such lewd companions as these are and their like, for by such kind of people the Queen and the realm have been divers times in danger." And so he roved over the insurrection in the north, the excommunication of Pius V, Story and Felton, Dr. Saunder's coming into Ireland, Campion and his fellows, Arden and Sommerfield, Francis Throckmorton; aggravating the prisoners to be of one religion with the persons before named and recited. At the upshot of this conflict the poor men requested the jury, for the love of God and safeguard of their own souls, to have regard unto their consciences; and Mr. White said, "For my part, I have as much wrong as any can have, and am as guiltless of this indictment as any here, I take God to witness." Hughes also said, "Judge you whether I would make my cousin Howell David privy to any secret matter, and especially touching my life, for we have been at variance about lands this ten years and above. Yonder are sitting on the bench Mr. Puleston and Mr. Ievan Lloyd of Yale, who do know this to be true. And, moreover, they know what truth and honesty is in the said Howell my cousin, therefore, I beseech you, to consider of him." But the gentlemen held their peace. Furthermore he said to the jury, "Demand of the judges whether their commission be to hang us, because we refuse to go to church, and to answer to the question of the supremacy, and then find us guilty according to your law; or else, for the love of God, weigh and consider of the witnesses what manner of men they be, and how falsely they have foresworn themselves; have regard unto your consciences for the safeguard of your own souls, or else our blood shall be required at your hands." Finally, Moris protested, saying, "I take God to witness, I call heaven and earth to record, I appeal unto the last day of judgment, that I am as innocent of this indictment as the child that was born yesternight. Lay, therefore, God's fear before your eyes, for we are not so much afraid of our own lives as we are careful for your souls."

Here Mr. Justice Bromley appointed the pronotary to read
the commission from the Privy Council, to the which had
subscribed Sir Thomas Bromley, Lord Chancellor; Sir Harry
Sydney, Lord President of the Marches; Sir Francis Wal-
singham, the Queen's principal Secretary; Sir James Crests,
and others.   In the end, being ready to dismiss the jury, both
judges gave them a new charge again, terrifying the simple
men with the sight of the commission from the higher powers.
So the jury departed to the church, where they remained all
the night following with their keeper, saving that two of
them, about an hour after their coming, were sent for to
confer with the judges, to know of them whom they should
acquit and whom they should find guilty, as it is reported.
The next day after, being Saturday, about eight of the clock
in the morning, they returned with their verdict, and found
Mr. Richard White and John Hughes guilty of felony and
treason, but Robert Moris they discharged; whereupon Mr.
Thelwall said that some favour was showed Moris although he
deserved none, being no less guilty than the rest.   Marry, the
prisoner took it for no favour to be separated from his dear
companions, the faithful confessors of Jesus Christ, for he
made great lamentation and wept bitterly in the sight of the
whole court, saying, "The worse luck I."   Whereby, as-
suredly, God's holy name was glorified in him, the Catholic
religion honoured, many of the audience confirmed by his example, and the justice of God satisfied for the offence he had
committed in his manacles, by the compulsion of those men before whom he was now arraigned.   Finally, as Mr. Thelwall was
ready to give the judgment (for Sir George Bromley could not
find in his heart to sit himself that day), John Hughes said,
"Come let us have it; we are as ready to die for our consciences as you are to pronounce judgment against us."   So
the justice commanded the clerk of the assize to lay down
that Moris was acquitted and Hughes reprieved.   Then he
turned to Mr. White, and said as followeth, "Richard White,
thou art accused of treason and found guilty by the country;
what hast thou to say why thou mayest not die according to
the laws of the realm?"   "If I had (said Mr. White) I should
not be heard, do you make of it what you will.   Only this I
say, that I am no more guilty than you are a true Christian
man; and, if I be a traitor, your father and grandfather, and
yourself, in Queen Mary's time, were traitors."   But Mr. Thelwall regarding little the prisoner's words, proceeded to the
sentence in this manner following: "Richard White shall be
brought to prison from whence he came, and thence drawn on

a hurdle to the place of execution, where he shall hang half dead, and so be cut down alive, his members cast into the fire, his belly ripped into the breast, his bowels, liver, lungs, heart, etc., thrown likewise into the fire, his head cut off, his body parted into four quarters. Finally, head and quarters to be set up where it shall please the Queen. And this execution to be done on a Thursday; we will appoint you the day before we go. And so the Lord have mercy upon him."

At which sentence the condemned person was nothing dismayed, neither changed countenance, but resolutely gave answer, saying, "What is all this? Is it any more than one death?" After this good work was brought to an end, Mr. Thelwall said to Robert Moris, "Thou art here indicted for abstaining from the church the space of twenty-seven months, contrary to the peace of the Queen's majesty, her crown, and dignity. What sayest thou, art thou guilty?" Moris answered, "I cannot deny but the bill is true, marry, I have been in prison all the while and before." Thelwall replied, "Thou mightest have had leave to go into the church if thou hadst been willing."

Moris. I might have bought that better cheap five years ago.

Thelwall. Hast thou money to pay the Queen?

Moris. I hope her majesty hath no need of my money; and, if I had money, I would be more willing to pay it than to lie in prison as I do.

Thelwall. Wilt thou now go to church?

Moris. No; I do not fear your gallows so much as I did your tortures.

At which words Mr. Thelwall started as if he had been stung with a wasp, and, in great rage, said that if such stubborn fellows as he was were cut off it were no great matter. And so he charged him with a fine of five hundred and forty pounds, charging the sheriff to look well unto him, as he would answer the fine at his own peril.

Last of all, the wives of the two condemned persons appeared, carrying on their arms two little infants, whom Mr. Thelwall solicited in courteous manner to reform themselves, and not to follow the ways of their disobedient husbands. But the wives refused to follow his counsel; and Mr White's wife said unto him, "If you lack blood, you may take my life as well as my husband's; and if you will give the witnesses a little bribe, you may call them; they will bear evidence against me as well as they did against him." But the poor woman was quickly commanded to silence, and together with her

companion committed to the gaol, where they made no long
abode, for the pitiful gentleman before his departure, upon
better advisement, took sureties of them for their appearance
another day, and so turned them loose whiles he went about
to hang their husbands; and thus ended this day's action.
The which was the last day of appearance unto our blessed
confessor in this world, and the eighth assize in number from
the beginning of his imprisonment—a number mystical in
Holy Scripture, as St. Augustine noteth: *Septem sunt* (saith
he) *quæ perficiunt, octavus clarificat, et quod perfectum est de-
monstrat* ("The number of seven doth make perfect, the number of eight clarifieth, and showeth the perfection of the
rest.")[1]   For in this eighth assize appeared to the world how
much the good man had profited in the school of Christ, and
what perfection continual patience can work in a resolute
soul, who, notwithstanding his intolerable calamity, behaved
himself all the time of his arraignment so pleasantly that he
moved the people sundry times to laughter, an evident argument of his guiltless conscience, either towards his prince or
country.

At his first coming to the bar, Lewis Gronow was asked
whether he knew the prisoners; to the which question the
disciple of Judas, answering in the Welsh tongue said, *Adwen
yn dda*, that is to say, "I know them well."   Mr. White replied, *A nineath adwenon dithe yn ddrwg* ("And we know
thee bad"); whereat the company laughed, because of the
equivocation those two words, "good" and "bad", have in
that language.   At the same time some of the assistants, perceiving the said Gronow to be hard of hearing, desired Mr.
Justice to speak louder unto him; the prisoner answered, he
should better hear than any in that assembly, having so many
holes in his ears.   And when the jury brought in their verdict
finding him guilty of that felony and treason whereof they
were in their hearts as guilty themselves, he said, *Non audent
aliter dicere propter metum Judæorum* ("They dare not otherwise say for fear of the Jews"), alluding to a place in the
Gospel of certain fearful disciples that durst not openly profess
their belief in Christ.   Many other like speeches he had this
while to the inquest and others, the which for brevity I omit;
and so he continued to the last breath, that his own fellows
reported they never knew him more pleasantly disposed than
he was after his condemnation.   And the very day of his execution, understanding that the executioner was in hand to

---

[1] Aug. lib. 1, "De Sermone Do. in Monte."

bargain the doublet he had on his back, he changed it for a
worse that one of his fellows gave him, and told the company
how he had deceived the hangman; yea, at the hour of his
death, as the executioner was putting the rope about his neck,
he smiled and said, "Good William, I would advise thee to
leave off this occupation, use it not much, for it is but a simple
office;" so little was this resolute man daunted with the fear
of death, of whose cup he was sure presently to taste. But I
stay too long in these merry conceits, having so lamentable a
matter in hand of greater importance concerning this blessed
confessor, especially considering that I must over-pass many
things in particular, as his behaviour and speeches to his fellows after his condemnation, to his wife, to the ministers, and
others, which would require a large volume; and I see this
rude treatise is waxen already larger than I purposed at the
beginning. Likewise, taking the cloth in his hands wherewith his eyes should have been covered, he lapped it about his
head, and, perceiving that it was not well, he called to the
hangman for help, and smiling said, "Put it on, William, as
thou art accustomed to others; thou knowest better than I,
for I am not very skilful in this occupation." Another merry
proceeding was at his first coming to the bar after that his
trial was referred to a jury. Sir George Bromley, for a show
of justice and indifferency, commanded the sheriff to return a
substantial jury to pass upon him and his fellows, who accordingly returned William Almar, Esq., to be the foreman, and all
the rest men of worship and credit, which, being called, not
one of them would appear, although they were threatened to
be fined in a 10l. a piece; the which Mr. Justice perceiving,
he charged the sheriff to return a *tales de circumstantibus*,
which is another jury of such as were present in the hall.
And so he returned John Rogers (of Brintanor, was drowned)
to be foreman, a bankrupt who had sold and mortgaged all
his lands, and the rest of the jury simple fellows of small
value and less credit. But when Mr. White saw what poor
company they were, he said, with a loud voice, "Is this your
tales?" (making as if he had not known what the word *tales*
did mean until he saw the jury appear); and then he said,
"This is indeed a *tales, quales* non est in *Wales*, neque usque
ad *cales;*" which moved the hall to laughter, whereat Sir
George being offended, said very churlishly, "A little more of
your Latin will cost your hanging." Now to our matter.

The Martyrdom of Mr. Richard White, upon Thursday after his
   condemnation, being the 15th of Oct., anno Dom. 1584.

Now the servant of Christ, having passed through many
calamities, and drawing towards an end of all his sorrows,
was, together with his fellows or companions, the space of ten
days before his death, viz., from the first day of the assize to
the time of his execution, coupled fast and chained with an
huge iron chain and horse-lock, and warded diligently day
and night with a band of men, the which cruelty he took to be
a preface to death, and a plain warning to make himself ready.
The Tuesday before his execution, a gentleman in the sheriff's
name offered to discharge him of all his troubles if he would
acknowledge the Queen supreme head of the Church within
her own dominions; but, the man being constant, refused to
purchase his own liberty so dear, and the same day, being
ready to meat, he called for his knife, telling the gaoler how
he needed be so scrupulous as to keep his weapon from him,
as though he feared lest he should spill himself, being offered
his life if he would recant his religion.

The Wednesday following, he had provided two dozen of
silk points, the which he blessed and kissed one after another,
appointing his wife to bestow the one dozen (which was of
colour white, answerable to his name) upon twelve priests, and
the other dozen upon twelve gentlemen to whom he was greatly
beholden. Then he bended a single penny, and blessed, etc.,
to be delivered his ghostly father, to whom he was beholden
himself. Lastly, he caused his garters to be given two priests
of his familiar acquaintance; and the day before he had sent
his signet or seal of brass off his finger to a gentleman, his
very familiar friend. All the which tokens the said parties do
keep reverently, as a treasure in value more worth than thousands of gold and silver, assured monuments of the good will
he bare them in this world, and pledges of the care he would
take over them in heaven.

The Thursday morning his wife, espying David Edwards
the mercer to pass by the gaol, moved at the sight of him,
said, "God be a righteous judge between thee and me."
But Mr. White understanding the matter, rebuked her, saying
that if they did not forgive now freely all their labours would
be lost.

About ten of the clock in the morning, the time approaching
wherein he must taste with Christ of his last draught, the
gaoler came to separate the prisoners and to set them at some

liberty. This while, Mr. White, hearing a great noise in the backside of the gaol, demanded what it was, and being told that the gaoler's wife made lamentation for him, he turned to his wife and said, "I pray thee, Catharine, go and comfort her." Coming down the stairs to the common gaol, he found the house full of people weeping and lamenting, among whom were divers children, on whose heads, one after another, laying his hands, he prayed God to bless them. Then beholding a number without the gaol, attending opportunity to bid him farewell, he reached them his hands out of the window, and so took his leave of them all; the like he did also with many in the gaol; and whereas one of them, a gentleman who had formerly been his scholar, made great lamentations, he comforted him in these words: "Weep not for me, for I do but pay the rent before the rent day." Last of all, he bestowed five shillings in small pieces of silver to the poor at the prison door, the which money a Catholic had sent him to be distributed with his own hands. At his passing to the execution, he gave his wife eleven shillings and his beads, the which was in effect all the wealth he left her. And so, being disburdened of worldly cares, all his care was for heavenly joys, whither the happy soul made haste, groaning with St. Paul to be loosed from the lump of clay (Phil. i), and thirsting with the holy prophet to be with God, the fountain of life—as the hart, when she is chased, thirsteth after the fountain of water (Psalm xli). The hour at length drawing on wherein God had ordained to render unto His good and faithful servant a just reward of all his labours, the sheriff[1] being then entered into the gaol, said, "White, make thee ready; and you women" (meaning his wife and John Hughes's wife), "if you have taken your leave, depart, and let him prepare himself to die." The prisoner answered, "Good Mr. Sheriff, have patience awhile, and I will despatch out of hand;" and so he kissed the wives and blessed his little infant (who was not above one month old), making a cross in his forehead. Here his two companions requested Mr. Sheriff to see the execution, but it would not be granted; whereupon they kneeled down, and the wives together with them, for his benediction. The martyr, pointing with his hand unto them, desired God to stand with them; and so went toward the stade which was provided for him instead of a hurdle, saying, "In the name of Jesus", as he went out of the prison door. When he was come to the

---

[1] Piers Owen of Garth y Medd in the parish of Abergele, High Sheriff A.D. 1584.

place he blessed himself; then his arms were tied behind his
back, and so the man of God was laid on the stade before
named, and drawn through the town to the place of execution,
leaving behind him in the gaol his wife and little child, therin
declaring himself to be the true disciple of Christ, who had laid
a law before in the Gospel that, if any man come unto Him,
and did not hate his father and mother, and wife and children,
and brother and sister, yea, and his own life too, he could not
be His disciple (Luke xii). All the way along as he was
drawn, he said the rosary, using the end of a string wherewith
he held up his irons instead of beads. And that the merits of
so holy a man might appear to the world, God vouchsafed to
honour his death by a manifest sign; for the elements being
clear and the weather dry all that morning, as soon as he was
laid on the hurdle the sky waxed cloudy over the town that he
suffered in, and a shower of rain poured down abundantly
until body and soul were parted, at which instant inconti-
nently the rain ceased. Whereby appeareth that the death of
His saints is precious in our Lord's sight, and the promise
made in Holy Scripture performed too, in that the elements
should fight for His servants against senseless people. For
the truth hereof I refer me to all those who were present that
day at this pitiful spectacle, who never ceased long after to talk
of the strange event. Finally, the servant of God being come
to an end of his journey, first the sheriff caused a proclamation
to be made (as the custom is) that none should approach near
the gallows. His arms were loosed, wherewith he turned to
the people, and said, "God is merciful unto us; behold the
elements shed tears for our sins." After this, the gaoler
caused him to climb up the ladder, and the executioner kneeled
to ask him forgiveness. The martyr gave answer, "I do forgive thee before God, and I wish thee no more harm than I
wish mine own heart." This while the sheriff and Owen
Brereton whispered together, and first Owen Brereton demanded of him whether he would have a priest. The prisoner
answered, "Yea, with all my heart; but I will have no minister." "White", said the sheriff, "thou hast committed
heinous treason against the Queen's majesty, the which hath
brought thee to this end. Art thou sorry for the same, and
dost thou ask her forgiveness?" Mr. White answered, "I
never committed any treasons against her more than your
father and grandfather have done, unless it be a treason to
fast and to pray." Owen Brereton replied, "Yes, that thou
hast; for they have been manifestly proved against thee in
open court." The prisoner gave answer, "Well, I pray God

forgive the witnesses who foresware themselves against me; and I pray God forgive you, Mr. Brereton, for I never gave cause that you should be so mine enemy." "It is true", said Mr. Brereton, "thou never gavest me cause; but for that thou hast been an ill member of the commonwealth, and not worthy to live." Last of all, the Vicar of Wrexham[1] spake: "Dost thou acknowledge the Queen to be supreme head of the Church?" The prisoner answered, "I acknowledge her to be lawful Queen of England, and otherwise I never said; and I beseech you all to bear witness hereof, that they belie me not when I am dead." Sonlley replied, "Why wouldst thou not confess so much before the bar?" Mr. White said, "The question was not asked me; but I told the council at another time that I was her poor subject, and that I prayed for Her Majesty. Mine examinations are to be seen, and my hand to the same; search the records, and you shall find this to be true. Moreover, that I offered to go out of the realm to pleasure them, or into rocks and deserts; yea, if it were possible, under the ground, to use my conscience in the least offensive manner I might, or into what place soever it would please my prince to send me; but nothing will serve." Again, Sonlley demanded whether he would forgive David Edwards, his apprehender. He gave answer, "Yes, with all my heart, I pray God forgive him, and grant that we may both meet in heaven. I forgive also his wife, and all those who were any way guilty of my death; and I desire all the world to forgive me, and you who are here present to pray for me, and especially all those who are members of the Catholic Church, whereof the Pope is the head; and to bear me witness that I die in the old Catholic faith, and that I am innocent of all treasons wherewith I have been charged by perjured persons, the which I take upon my death." "Well, well", said the sheriff, "no more of that. Despatch, hangman." Here the company kneeled to pray for him, and prayed himself all the while; then, turning to the people, he spake again, saying, "My dear countrymen, I beseech you for God's sake to have regard unto your souls, and to reconcile yourselves unto the Catholic Church, for I fear you are led astray unto everlasting damnation, except you take heed betimes. Remember your souls, and lose not that for this vile transitory muck which Christ hath so dearly bought. This is but one hour's pain to me, and what is that in respect of the torments

---

[1] Sir Hugh Sonlley, son of Robert Sonlley of Sonlley, Esq., near Wrexham. See vol. ii, p. 144.

in hell, which shall never have an end?" Thus he continued his speech a long while, repeating the same over twice or thrice, until the sheriff and others, being offended with his talk, commanded the executioner to climb up the ladder and to despatch him; who, preparing himself to execute their bloody wills, asked the prisoner forgiveness the second time; whereupon the martyr, taking him by the hand, kissed it, saying, "I do forgive thee with all my heart, God and our Blessed Lady and St. Michael forgive thee; it is all one to me that thou do this deed as another." Finally, as the executioner offered to put the rope about his neck, he smiled, advising him to leave the occupation, for it was but simple; again he smiled as he went to cover his own face with a cloth and could not. He called to the hangman for help, telling him that he was not cunning in the occupation, the which as he was in doing, the prisoner requested him to deliver the kerchief to his poor wife, although he demanded double the price. So the executioner came down, and the sheriff commanded the gaoler to bid him turn the ladder, at which words Mr. White lifted up the kerchief, and said, "I have been a jesting fellow, and if I have offended any that way, or by my songs, I beseech them for God's sake to forgive me." In the end, as he was saying the prayer of the publican, *Deus propitius esto mihi peccatori* ("O God be merciful to me a sinner"), the executioner turned the ladder, and so he hanged awhile, knocking his breast continually with both hands until his senses were taken from him. In the mean time the hangman leaned upon his shackles of purpose to despatch him out of his pains the sooner; but the sheriff, doubting he should die too soon, commanded to cut him down. At which words the people desired him to take compassion upon the poor prisoner and to let him die, the same also two or three gentlemen which were present requested, by whose earnest entreaty he was stayed yet a little longer. In the end, the rope was cut, and the prisoner carried to the hurdle, on the which being laid along, as the executioner was busy to remove the irons and to cut off his secret parts, the man revived and recovered his senses again. And although thieves and murderers were well acquainted with the hangman's office, yet he wanted skill to do this execution answerable to the bloody wills of the magistrates, by reason of which he put the martyr to double pains, and exceeded in cruelty the bloody sentence pronounced against him. For, having made a little hole in his belly, he pulled out of the same his guts by piecemeal; the which device taking no good success, he mangled his breast with a butcher's axe to the very chine, most pitifully; then tearing his entrails he threw them into the fire before his face, whereat the servant of God never shrunk, nor once showed any sign of impatience, but still continued knocking his breast, until the sheriff's men held his arms back by force. Finally, being ready to lift up the last gasp he lifted up his head and shoulders over the hurdle, and beholding so cruel a slaughter, he said in the Welsh tongue, " O Duw gwyn pybeth y diw hun," *i.e.*, " O good God, what is this?" The gaoler answered, "It is an execution for the Queen's majesty;" whereunto the martyr replied, saying, " Jesus have mercy upon me !" and so, at the striking off his head, he died.

If it may be called a death, and not rather a change into a better life to die for Christ, a happy change from the temporal calamities of this world to the eternal joys of heaven,— from sorrow and pain to rest and solace, from weeping to singing, from misery unto felicity, from the company of sinful men to be conversant with saints and angels, from the sight of the gallows, of the burning fire, of the boiling pan, of the bloody axe, of the cruel hangman, to the sight of God, who now with His own holy hands wipeth away all tears from his eyes, who now rewardeth His good and faithful servant with a crown of life (the case of all martyrs), for his constant faith ; a crown of justice, for suffering innocently (the case of Abel); with a crown of glory, for the shame he sustained by the accusation of wicked men (the case of Naboth). Now the good man from heaven laugheth to scorn the folly of his persecutors, whose wicked malice God converteth to the eternal good of his friend. O glorious martyr, which hath washed and made white his robe in the blood of the Lamb ! O holy arms, which were so often lifted up before the bar for the name of Christ! O blessed prisons, which were sanctified so many times with the presence of his body ! O happy fetters, wherewith his feet were tied, and his soul loosed from the band of sin ! O precious wood, which was the instrument of his glorious martyrdom ! O sacred ground, which is hallowed with the martyr's blood ! from whence it crieth unto heaven for vengeance, by so much more forcible than Abel's blood by how much his cause was more honourable, and his torments greater. And the soul from heaven prayeth for his benefactors and friends on earth, by so much the more effectually by how much they draw nearer his steps in life and conversation. The body was locked in prison, but the soul was made free ; the dungeon was dark and loathsome, but the mind was illuminated with light from God. The members were replenished with wounds and wallowed with blood. But although the outward man was corrupted, yet the inward man was renewed from day to day; the lump of earth was betrayed to the hands of the wicked men, and they have executed their malice upon it; for what else could be expected at their hands, being his disciples who was a murderer from the beginning? But his spirit, purified with the fire of tribulation, as gold in a furnace, from all earthly dross, returned to Him that made him.

Therefore, I may truly conclude of our martyr with the words of St. Cyprian : The enemy locked his feet and made fast those happy legs with infamous fetters, as though his soul might also with his body be fettered, or that gold with the rust of this iron be corrupted. These fetters and locks are no bands, but an ornament to the servant of God and confessor of His name; the feet of Christians are not tied to their rebuke, but clarified to their renown. O happy feet, born in a good hour, which are not by the smith, but by the Lord of glory, set at liberty! O happy feet, bound in a good hour, which have run so blessed a race to paradise ! O happy feet, bound for a while in this world that they may always be free with God! O happy feet, made heavy and slow with bolts and horse-locks, but light and swift in their journey unto Christ, for the expectation of our felicity promised is secure and certain (as learned Leo telleth us) where is participation of our Lord's Passion. What shall we, then, think of this constant man who hath fought a good fight, who hath consummated his course, who hath kept his faith ? What else, but that our Lord hath rendered unto him his crown of justice, a just judge, and that he resteth from all his labours, for his works do follow him ? Whereby the Catholic reader may understand and learn that it is not an easy matter to be made worthy of the crown of martyrdom, beholding so blessed and perfect a man to pass into the same hardly through shame and rebukes, banishment from his country, displeasure of his friends, persecution of enemies, need and poverty, imprisonment, dungeon, stocks, fetters, chains, bolts, horse-locks, manacles, false evidence of witnesses suborned, wicked verdict of false juries, cruel sentence of wicked judges, rope and gallows, the bloody axe of the butcher, the barbarous hands of the hangman ;—that man must have a resolute soul who purposeth to vanquish all these afflictions; but this man hath vanquished : and how ? By following the advice of his Captain, who biddeth us first sit down and reckon the charges before we lay the foundations. The want of which consideration is the true cause of the miserable return of so many cold and inconstant Catholics into their old vomits again. This is the way to heaven, this is the ladder of Jacob, these are the steps to martyrdom; we must not think that any thing chanceth to the servants of God without His consent and providence, of whom He hath said, "He that toucheth you, toucheth the apple of mine eye:" nothing can be done against them by men on earth but it is before by the premeditate council of God concluded in heaven. Pilate had no power over Christ but as it was given him from above, nor any tyrants in their days over the holy martyrs without God's permission. Whom He purposeth to crown He suffereth the enemy to rack, not accepting redemption that they might find a better resurrection. And though the simple people are borne in hand in printed books, published with privilege and authority, that no man suffereth for his conscience, yet the innocency of this man is apparent to God, before whose eyes the subtle enemy can cast no mist nor colour of treason against him; and the same one day will be apparent to the world, when this blast of heresy will be blown down to hell again from whence it had root. And neither was our glorious martyr at all discouraged with the name of traitor, for he had read that St. Stephen was accused to have spoken words against God and Moses; St. Paul to be a seditious fellow; and Christ our Saviour a subverter of His own nation and an enemy to Cæsar. Yea, it was the common practice of old paynim tyrants to feign that they punished in holy men, not religion, but treason; and this they were not ashamed to publish, envying the confessors of truth the name and honour of martyrs. And, I pray you, is it any marvel, for what participation hath justice with iniquity? Or what society is there between light and darkness? Or what agreement between Christ and Belial? Or what part hath the faithful with the infidel? The light of the sun, which is a friend to all the world, is yet an enemy to weak eyes; but he that is in filth let him be filthy still. Our holy confessor is past their malice, his soul in glory, his memory in benediction, his ashes and relics in veneration. The sun when it riseth clear, pierceth not more bright from east to west than the fame of his death pierced the hearts of all Wales from north to south; the wiser sort lamenting to see justice trodden under foot, the simple people honouring his patience and constancy for the faith of the old Britons, their dear progenitors. Yea, I dare say, that among so great a multitude as were beholders of this cruel tragedy, there were not a score present but they believed him at that instant (notwithstanding

all his external miseries) to be in far better case than themselves; for that nation, although the terror of laws driveth it
to dissemble with the world, yet cannot be brought generally
to believe this new deceit of lying masters to be true, nor to
persuade themselves the faith of their forefathers (from whom
they had received so many monuments and examples of virtue
and godliness) to be false. It is not the learning of ministers,
neither their good life, nor their great miracles, that can persuade a whole nation from the religion which it hath kept
since the Apostles' time to this unfortunate age inviolably.
And lest I be thought to forge this thing of my countrymen,
I refer me to those who were at this man's arraignment and
execution; they can report the demeanour of the people towards
him. I refer me to the executioner, who caused himself to be
shut up in a chamber close prisoner, for fear of his life, and
came forth at length with a timorous heart to execute this
cruel deed; he can resolve you with what countenance his
speeches were received of the multitude, when he lifted up the
martyr's head, and showed it to the people, saying, " This is
White's head, this is White's head;" being either not so bold
or not so shameless, as to name him traitor, according to
their accustomed manner in such a play. I refer me to
the gaoler, who can witness with what difficulty necessary
things for his execution were provided. The ladder he was
fain to steal at midnight, from the backside of a man's house.
The coals his servants were forced to carry on their backs
from the coal pits two long miles, for want of a horse, which
he could neither borrow nor hire. The axe he was glad to
take from the butcher's stall, because he might not entreat
any smith to defile his hands with such a work. What should
I speak of the pan wherein his quarters were boiled; of the
water, fire, rope, and other implements necessary to the
slaughter? How hardly the said gaoler came by these things
that day the town of Wrexham can testify. And is it any
wonder? The people knew his innocency, being well acquainted with the good man's conversation the space of twenty
years together; they knew his cause to be just and honest,
being directly for religion. They knew the example to be
rare, the like never heard of in Wales since the death of St.
Winifred, tracing therein the happy steps of his blessed coun-
tryman St. Alban, the first martyr of the ancient Britons, and
protomartyr of this island.

But it may be here marvelled why the gaoler showed himself more forward than his office required to spill the blood of
the good man whom a little before he greatly favoured. For-

sooth, the poor wretch was enjoined in penance by the judges to play the hangman for a fault that he had committed after the prisoner's return from the council, the which was this : having conceived a good opinion of him and his fellows, he was contented to set them at liberty, upon their only promise to return against the next assize following, wherein they should be arraigned, having lately been manacled and indicted of high treason. And although the prisoners at the time appointed kept promise, nevertheless the gaoler was shent and put in fear of his life ; but at this cruel murder he made the magistrates some parts of amends.

Now the execution being ended, Lewis Gronow, the good man's principal accuser, beholding such cruelty done to him, and knowing him to be innocent, repented with Judas for betraying innocent blood; but he brought not the money back again with Judas the which he had received for his life. For he came to Denbigh, where the next assize following was kept (his conscience moving him, no doubt, by the special providence of God, that the innocency of the martyr and his companions might be evident to the world and the adversaries' malice detected) ; before the gaoler and a great multitude of people (whose eyes glared to hear the discourse), he acknowledged his fault to the prisoners, as it may appear in a letter sent from the said prisoners to their friends of the same matter, whereof this is the copy.

A copy of a Letter sent from John Hughes and Robert Moris concerning Gronow his confession to them at the assize at Denbigh in May, after the execution of Mr. White.

After our hearty commendations, these are to let you understand that, in the assize week, a thing chanced unto us greatly beyond our expectation ; for Lewis Gronow, our principal adversary, came into our gaol, of whom we demanded why he did so wilfully cast his soul away by slandering us so shamefully. To the which Gronow answered that he never accused any of us both, but that all his speeches and doings were against Mr. White alone. We replied that his examination was read before the bar, wherein appeared how he bare witness against us all three. Gronow answered, " Whatsoever was read or spoken before the bar as proceeding from me, more than I tell you, they have belied me." And therewith he began to wring his hands and to sigh and groan, making great lamentation, and exclaiming against himself; further telling us that he was tormented in conscience for the offence he had committed against Mr. White, more than for any offence that ever he had done in his life. Here he told us that he was enticed to this wicked deed by the fair promises of Sir Hugh Sonlley, Vicar of Wrexham, and David Edwards, mercer, to see him enlarged out of prison and his debts discharged, the which was afterwards by them performed accordingly. Then he was sent to the Holt to bear witness against us, where we were indicted; and for his good service there, the vicar and mercer aforesaid wrote a letter in his behalf to Sir George Bromley to procure him by his friendship a placard. The man went to the council with his letter, caused his bill to be drawn, and tendered it to Sir George to be signed as he walked in the garden at Ludlow; the which Mr. Justice perusing, and finding therein no special matter specified why he should have a placard, refused to sign it; whereupon Gronow delivered him the letter from the vicar and mercer, wherein they signified that the bearer was the man which followed against the papists; the which when Sir George Bromley perceived, taking Gronow by the hand, demanded whether he was the man that followed against the papists. Gronow answered that he was the man that followed against Richard White, and no man else. Mr. Justice replied that he could not have his bill signed unless he would follow against all three. And so turning from him, he sent two of his gentlemen which attended on him in the garden, Thomas Puleston and Moris Jones, one after another, to persuade him to follow against us three, if he would have his bill signed, the which (as he said) he utterly refused to grant. This course failing, Mr. Justice was in hand with him to swear that he would at the least bear witness against Richard White, but he denied to swear; then he required him to put in sureties, and that also he denied to do. In the end, Gronow yielded to deliver his promise, and gave Sir George his hand thereupon, that he would meet him at the next assize following; and so his bill was signed and a placard procured from the council for him; by virtue whereof, and by friendship of the vicar and mercer before named, there was gathered for him at Wrexham thirty shillings; and, afterwards, returning home to his own country among his friends and kinsfolk, twenty marks. All this he protested to be true before Coytmor, our gaoler, and a great number of people then present at his speeches. This is all we can certify you at this time. From Denbigh, the 15th of May, anno Domini 1585.

Your daily beadsmen,

JOHN HUGHES and ROBERT MORIS.

Thus you may see the man's innocency confirmed every way, in his lifetime, at his death, and after his death, by the deposition of a gentleman[1] at his arraignment, by his own protestation at his last breath, by the adversaries' confession here, and by God's miraculous operation for him even in his lifetime (as it may appear by what has been said already); but much more after his martyrdom, through the just punishment which fell to both judges at once. For the one (Sir George Bromley) lost his credit, returned home from the bar

---

[1] John Wynn ab William ab Madock Goch of Frondeg in the parish of Wrexham. See p. 19.

and left his wits behind him, who yet liveth an idiot. The other judge[1] lost his credit with all his friends, and, within a while after, his life also, that he neither enjoyed office after this day's work nor good hour. The greatest part of the jury dropped away miserably, and never lived to see the next assize following. The crier[2] became a fool and a momme, and so lived a long time, and in the end died wretchedly. But the plague which chanced to David Edwards the mercer was notable, who, as his malice towards this servant of God exceeded, so his punishment was dreadful, God recompensing the wretch according to his works in weight and measure. For as he walked abroad with one of his neighbours about the beginning of Lent, in the same year wherein the holy man died, being now come to the place where he had taken him, suddenly was catched; for there he received his just hire, and thence returned home sick, was laid in a bed; finally, he ended his life in great repentance without fruit (not unlike to the death of Antiochus the tyrant), often naming the martyr and cursing the hour he took him. Of whom it is reported that no man, from the beginning of his sickness, might well approach near him, alive nor dead, for the horrible stink of his body. So his own foot was caught in the snare he had laid for his neighbour. By the which terrible examples the persecutors may learn to take heed how they anger the servants of God, lest withal He be also moved who dwelleth in them; for the apostle saith that holy men are the temple of God. And although the martyr hideth from their eyes the invisible sword wherewith He striketh, nevertheless it is manifest that he hath it always ready to draw out when God appointeth. Therefore, St. Gregory exhorteth to exhibit due fear and reverence to holy men, who when they are moved unto anger. who else is provoked but their Lord who possesseth them? Therefore, by so much the more careful we ought to be in avoiding the displeasure of God's saints by how much the more we are persuaded that our Lord doth inhabit in them, who is able to revenge their cause when He listeth. The which good Counsel of the holy father a gentleman of the country may do well to remember and follow, who for me shall be nameless, because I seek not his discredit, but the glory of God and conversion of his soul, whereof I pray our Lord Jesus Christ that he may have grace to consider.

---

[1] Simon Thelwall of Plâs y Ward was one of the Council for the Marches of Wales. He died A.D. 1586, aged 60, and was buried at Ruthin.　　　　　[2] Christopherson.

Marry, by this token you shall understand whom I mean, that it was his hap to ride on an ambling mare from his parish church upon a Sunday morning, and in the way the said mare received a great blow on her side, the sound whereof was heard by himself and all his people which then attended on him, but nothing seen. Forthwith the gentleman was forced to light, and a sledge sent for to carry the mare into the stable, and there she died shortly after, and, being flayed, the place on her side where the blow had been given appeared blue. The which accident I suppose to be a warning unto the gentleman that he should not imbrue his hands in the blood of this martyr. For the same chance fell out in An. Dom. 1578, a little before the apprehension of the man against whom he hath been a principal doer. The which miracle, and the rest that are here in this writing declared, were not showed to make our martyr of a more blessed life before God, but to signify unto us that he was a blessed man and his soul in high favour with God, and to stir in our souls that due reverence towards him which his virtues deserved; for God hath promised to honour them who will glorify Him. The like may be said by the manifold great and strange wonders that his blood, bones, ashes, and other holy monuments of his have done; the which in particular the incredulity of this time will not suffer to be published, but they shall be one day (God willing) made manifest to the glory of God, honour of His saint, confirmation of the Catholic faith, and confutation of heresy.

And here I will end, beseeching the blessed soul of this glorious martyr to bear with me where I have not expressed his heroical endeavours at large agreeable to the worthiness thereof; for he knoweth well that there was not in me want of good will, but of knowledge and cunning sufficient to set forth such a matter. Protesting that I have spoken but few things of much which might be said in the commendation of so holy a man, for I do not mean to add anything to his praise and honour. He needeth not our praise, neither desireth the same; it is enough for him that he hath eternal praise and honour with God and His angels in heaven. But I have bestowed my travail herein to signify the good will I bare him on earth, to procure his mediation for me in heaven, to give the Catholic reader an example of constancy, to bring the adversary into remembrance of his own madness and wickedness, and to let the world understand what open injustice and violence the poor afflicted Catholics sustain for their conscience and religion, under the visor of treason, at the hands of malicious heretics.

To oppose the progress of what the Christian Church called heresy, the Papal government established two institutions : 1. The Inquisition ; 2, Auricular Confession —the latter as a means of detection, the former as a tribunal for punishment.

In general terms, the commission of the Inquisition was, to extirpate religious dissent by terrorism, and surround heresy with the most horrible associations : this necessarily implied the power of determining what constitutes heresy. The criterion of truth was thus in possession of this tribunal, which was charged " to discover and bring to judgment heretics lurking in towns, houses, cellars, woods, caves, and fields". With such savage alacrity did it carry out its object of protecting the interests of religion, that between 1481 and 1808, it had punished *three hundred and forty thousand persons*, and of these nearly *thirty-two thousand had been burnt!* In its earlier days, when public opinion could find no means of protesting against its atrocities, " it often put to death, without appeal, on the very day that they were accused, nobles, clerks, monks, hermits, and lay persons of every rank". In whatever direction thoughtful men looked, the air was full of fearful shadows. No one could indulge in freedom of thought without expecting punishment. So dreadful were the proceedings of the Inquisition, that the exclamation of Pagliarici was the exclamation of thousands, " It is hardly possible for a man to be a Christian, and die in his bed."

In the thirteenth century, the Inquisition destroyed the Protestants of Southern France, and its unscrupulous atrocities extirpated Protestantism in Italy and Spain.

By the action of the fourth Lateran Council in the year 1215, the power of the Inquisition was frightfully increased, the necessity of private confession to a priest —auricular confession—being at that time formally established. This, so far as domestic life was concerned, gave omnipresence and omniscience to the Inquisition. Not a man was safe. In the hands of the priest, who, at the confessional, could extract or extort from them their most secret thoughts, his wife and his servants were turned into spies. Summoned before the dread tribunal, he was simply informed that he lay under strong suspicions of heresy. No accuser was named; but the thumbscrew, the stretching-rope, the boot, and the wedge, or other enginery of torture, soon supplied that defect, and, innocent or guilty, he accused himself!

In the first year of the operation of the Inquisition in Spain, 1483, two thousand Jews were burnt in Andalusia by Torquemada, a Dominican monk, the Confessor of Queen Isabella, and seventeen thousand were fined or imprisoned for life. Llorente, the historian of the Inquisition, computes that Torquemada and his collaborators, in the course of eighteen years, burnt at the stake *ten thousand two hundred and twenty persons*, and otherwise tortured *ninety-seven thousand three hundred and twenty-one*.

"As hitherto apprehended, religion can be said to have brought nothing but misery on the world at large. Deeds of a dye that shock humanity have been committed from first to last in its name. In the Old Testament it is said, "If thy brother, thy son, or thy daughter, the wife of thy bosom, or thy friend that is as thine own soul, entice thee saying: Let us go and serve other Gods (*i. e.*, differ from thee in thy creed and would have thee follow theirs), thou shalt not consent to him nor hearken to him : neither shalt thou spare him, but thou shalt surely kill him ; thy hand shall be first upon him, afterwards the hands of all the people, and thou shalt stone him with stones that he die."

In the 31st chapter of Numbers, we read that the Lord ordered Moses to avenge the Israelites of the Midianites, and when the Jewish army returned from their plundering and murdering excursion, Moses and Eleazer the Priest went out to meet them, and Moses said unto them, "Have ye saved all the women alive ? *behold these caused the children of Israel to commit trespass against the Lord.* Now, therefore, kill every male among the little ones, and kill every married

woman, but the women children that are virgins keep
for yourselves"; of these, we read in verse 35, besides
the other booty, " there were thirty and two thousand
women who were virgins." In Numbers, chap. xxv, we
learn the reason why Jehovah ordered Moses to vex the
Midianites, was because an Israelite named Zimri had
married a Midianitish woman, for doing which, Phinehas,
the son of Eleazer, the son of Aaron, the Priest of Jehovah,
rose up from among the congregation, and took a javelin
in his hand and went into Zimri's tent, and murdered
them both, by thrusting the javelin right through their
stomachs, in the way described in verse 8.   Here, then,
we have an order to butcher the boys, to massacre the
mothers, and to keep the little girls for themselves,
merely because the Jewish religion was different from
the religion of the Midianites.

Again, in the New Testament, Jehovah's son, Jesus
Christ, says, " Think not that I am come to send peace
on earth ; I come not to send peace but a sword.   For I
come to set a man at variance against his father, and the
daughter against her mother, and the daughter-in-law
against her mother-in-law; and a man's foes shall be they
of his own household."[1]

In later days, this religion instituted the Inquisition,
excavated the dungeon, built the torture-chamber and
furnished it with the rack, lighted the slow fire about
the stake to consume, drenched the battle-field with
blood, and has driven into exile the best and noblest of
their kind.

> " And are they in the right who, free from doubt,
>   Can sit in sweet abstraction from each thought
>   Of Earth, pondering the lives of those who fought
> The battles of Jehovah ; viewing the rout
> That Israel spread as God's own act, the shout
>   Upraised for victory, glorious most when fraught
>   With deepest ruin to the foe, as taught
> By the Creator ?   'T may not be !   Without

---

[1] Matthew x, v. 31.

The special faith that suffers me to view
  In one among the multitude of creeds,
Each by its advocates alone held true,
  The truth, or other of the pregnant seeds
Of discord among men, I take my flight
From blood-stained legends, Nature, to thy Light!"

Almost the only parts in the book called the Bible
that convey to us any idea of God are some chapters in
Job, and the 19th Psalm. Those parts are true *deistical*
compositions; for they treat of the *Deity* through his
works. They take the book of Creation as the word of
God, they refer to no other book, and all the inferences
they make are drawn from that volume.

I insert in this place, in proof of what is here stated,
the 19th Psalm, as paraphrased into English verse by
Addison.

" The spacious firmament on high,
  With all the blue ethereal sky,
  And spangled heavens, a shining frame,
  Their great Original proclaim.
  The unwearied sun from day to day,
  Does his Creator's power display,
  And publishes to every land
  The work of an Almighty hand.

" Soon as the evening shades prevail,
  The moon takes up the wondrous tale,
  And nightly to the listening earth
  Repeats the story of her birth;
  Whilst all the stars that round her burn,
  And all the planets in their turn,
  Confirm the tidings as they roll,
  And spread the truth from pole to pole.

" What though in solemn silence all
  Move round this dark terrestrial ball !
  What though no real voice, nor sound,
  Amidst their radiant orbs be found !
  In reason's ear they all rejoice,
  And utter forth a glorious voice,
  For ever singing as they shine,
  ' The hand that made us is Divine'."

What more does man want to know than that the hand, or power, that made these things is Divine, is Omnipotent? Let him believe this with the force it is impossible to repel, if he permits his reason to act, and his rule of moral life will follow of course.

The allusions in Job have all of them the same tendency with this Psalm, that of deducing or proving a truth, that would be otherwise unknown, from truths already known.

Two questions are asked in the book of Job that are applicable to this subject. "Canst thou by searching find out God? Canst thou find out the Almighty to perfection?"

First—Canst thou by searching find out God? Yes; because, in the first place, I know that I did not make myself, and yet I have existence, and by *searching* into the nature of other things, I find that no other thing could make itself, and yet millions of other things exist; therefore it is, that I know by positive conclusion, resulting from this search, that there is a power superior to all those things, and that power is God.

Secondly—Canst thou find out the Almighty to *perfection?* No; not only because the power and wisdom He has manifested in the structure of the Creation that I behold is to me incomprehensible, but because even this manifestation, great as it is, is probably but a small display of that immensity of power and wisdom by which millions of other worlds, to me invisible by their distance, were created, and continue to exist.

The two questions have different objects: the first refers to the existence of God, the second to His attributes; reason can discover the one, but it falls infinitely short in discovering the whole of the other.

The only passage in the New Testament that has any reference to the works of God, by which only His power and wisdom can be known, is related to have been spoken by Jesus Christ as a remedy against distrustful care. "Behold the lilies of the field, they toil not, neither do they spin."

That the universal law (says Dr. Conyers Middleton of Cambridge) revealed in the works of the Creation, was actually revealed to the heathen world long before the gospel was known, we learn from all the principal sages of antiquity, who made it the capital subject of their studies and writings.

"Cicero", says Middleton, "has given us a short abstract of it in a fragment still remaining from one of his books on government, which", says Middleton, "I shall here transcribe in his own words, as they will illustrate my sense of what I wish to state."

"The true law", says Cicero, "is right reason conformable to the nature of things, constant, eternal, diffused through all, which calls us to duty by commanding, deters us from sin by forbidding ; which never loses its influence with the good, nor ever preserves it from the wicked. This law cannot be over-ruled by any other, nor abrogated in whole or in part ; nor can we be absolved from it either by the Senate or by the people ; nor can there be one law at Rome and another at Athens —one now and another hereafter ; but the same eternal, immutable law, comprehends all nations, at all times, under one common master and governor of all—GOD. He is the inventor, propounder, enactor of this law ; and whoever will not obey it must first renounce himself and throw off the nature of man, by doing which he will suffer the greatest punishments, though he should escape all the other torments which are commonly believed to be prepared for the wicked."

"Our doctors", continues Middleton, "perhaps will look on this as pure Deism ; but let them call it what they will, I shall ever avow and defend it as the fundamental, essential, and vital part of all true religion."

WREXHAM GENTRY.

Thomas Churchyard, whose *Worthines of Wales*, dedicated to Queen Elizabeth, was published in 1587, found the Wrexham neighbourhood an extremely good one. He writes in honour of what he calls *A Generall Commendation of Gentilitie:*—

" Nere Wricksam dwels, of gentlemen good store,
  Of calling such, as are right well to live ;
  By market towne, I have not seene no more,
  (In such small roome) that aunoient armes doe give.
  They are the joy and gladness of the poor,
  That dayly feedes the hungrie at their doore ;
  In any soyle, where gentlemen are found,
  Some house is kept, and bountie doth abound.

" They beautifie both towne and countrie too,
  And furnish't are to serve at need in feeld ;
  And everything in rule and order do,
  And unto God and man due honour yeeld.
  They are the strength and suretie of the land,
  In whose true hearts doth trust and credit stand.
  By whose wise heads the neighbours ruled are,
  In whom the prince reposeth greatest care.

" They are the flowers of every garden ground,
  For where they want, there growes but wicked weeds ;
  Their tree and fruite in rotten world is sounde,
  Their noble mynds will bring foorth faithfull deedes.
  Their glorie rests in countries wealth and fame,
  They have respect to blood and auncient name ;
  They weigh nothing so much as loyall hart,
  Which is most pure, and clean in every part.

" They doe uphold all civill maners myld,
  All many acts, all wise and worthie waies ;
  If they were not, the countrey would grow wyld,
  And we should soone forget our elders daies.
  Wax blunt of wit, in speech grow rude and rough,
  Want vertue still, and have of vice enough,
  Showe feeble spreete, lack courage everywhere,
  Doubt many a thing, and our owne shadowes feare.

" They dare attempt, for fame and hye renowne,
  To scale the clowdes, if men might clyme the ayre ;
  Assault the starres, and plucke the plancts downe,
  Give charge on moone, and sunne that shines so fayre.
  I meane they dare attempt the greatest things,
  Fly swiftly ore high hilles if they had wings,
  Beate backe the seas, and teare the mountaines too.
  Yea, what dare not a man of courage do ?"

THE TRUE GENTLEMAN.

" He never speaks of himself except when compelled, never
defends himself by a mere retort; he has no ears for slander
or gossip, is scrupulous in imputing motives to those who interfere with him and interprets everything for the best. He
is never mean or little in his disputes, never takes unfair advantage, never mistakes personalities or sharp sayings for
arguments, or insinuates evil which he dare not say out.
From a long-sighted prudence, he observes the maxim of the
ancient sage that we should conduct ourselves towards our
enemy as if he were one day to be our friend. He has too
much good sense to be affronted at insults, and is too well
employed to remember injuries. He is patient, forbearing,
and resigned on philosophical principles. He submits to pain
because it is inevitable; to death because it is his destiny.
If he engages in controversy of any kind, his disciplined in-
tellect preserves him from the blundering discourtesy of better,
perhaps, but less educated minds, who, like blunt weapons,
tear and hack instead of cutting clean, who mistake the point
in argument, waste their strength on trifles, misconceive their
adversary, and leave the question more involved than they
find it. He may be right or wrong in his opinion, but he is
too clear-headed to be unjust; he is as simple as he is forcible,
and as brief as he is decisive. Nowhere shall we find greater
candour, consideration, indulgence. He throws himself into
the minds of his opponents, he accounts for their mistakes, he
knows the weakness of human reason as well as its province
and its limits. If he be an unbeliever, he will be too profound
and large-minded to ridicule religion or to act against it ; he
is too wise to be a dogmatist or fanatic in his infidelity. He
respects piety and devotion ; he even supports institutions as
venerable, beautiful, or useful to which he does not assent ; he
honours the ministers of religion, and it contents him to de-
cline its mysteries without assailing or denouncing them. He

is a friend of religious toleration, and that not only because
his philosophy has taught him to look on all forms of faith
with an impartial eye, but also from the gentleness of feeling
which is the attendant of civilisation."—*Cardinal Newman.*

SUPERUISUS MANERII DE BURTON.

Burton.   Harl. 3696, *fo.* 80.

NOMINA JURATORUM.

Will'us Robinson, armiger.

Thomas Langford, gen.	Randall Langford, gen.
Eduardus Gryffith, gen.	Will'us Jones, gen.
Georgius Powell, gen.	Eduardus ap Roger, gen.
Thomas Powell, gen.	Petrus Roberts, gen.
Jacobus Lewes, gen.	Ellis Allington, gen.
Johannes Santrey, gen.	Eduardus Williams, gen.
Joh'es Allington, gen.	Edwardus Meredith.
Joh'es Sutton, gen.	Edwardus ap Thomas.

Will'us Pulford.

Qui dicunt super sacramenta sua viz't ad primum articulum
quoad circuitum limitum manorii, viz't.

In primis, at a water called the ffrood falling into the
Brooke called Raegidog to the Riuer of Allyn, and along the
River to a gutter neere Dauid Maddockes house, thence along
that Gutter to a Com'on called Kaer Estyn, thence to a place
called the Talurn, thence to Porth y Llwyd Coed, and thence
to a place where the hoare wython did growe neere the common Moore, and from thence as it seemeth vnto the said Jury
by disposic'ons, that it extendeth streight through the said
com'ons to Morwall, the w'ch said Morwall doth part Denbighshire, Flintshire, and Cheshire, and from thence neere vnto
Whittells house, thence to Collops Pitt, thence to the south
end of Pulford Bridge, and so following the Brooke to the
river of Dee, and so up the river to the Reccauo'es bridge
vppon Deuen, thence through Marsley Parke along the gutter
w'ch parteth the Broad Land and Bushie Land from the said
parke, thence to the Bottome vnderneath Pen yr Allt Goch, so
to the vicars wood, thence to Pant Yockin house, then bordering upon Acton and to Stanstie Vcha, and then vppon
Broughton.   These last Towneships be in the manor of Eglwis
Egle, then bordering vppon Brombo and Gofnis, and thence
to the riuer of Raegidog, where we first began excepting the

lordships of Merford and Horsley, which lieth within the said Mannour.

2. We knowe no demeasne landes within this Mannour to our knowledge.

3. The ffreehould Tenaunts we doe present by booke their lands and rentes as farr as we are informed.

4. The names of the leasehoulders, their landes and Rentes, we haue likewise presented by book to our knowledge.

5. The names of the customary Tenaunts we do likewise present by themselues by a booke w'th a preamble in the beginning of the said booke, touching the composition and Covenant of the late Queene Elizabeth, of famous memory, of the said customary landes, in w'ch preamble the contents of this Article are fully answered.

6. The said Jury doth present but two wastes or Commons in this Mannour w'ch undergoe the names of wastes or com'ons called by the name of Keuen Guiersillt, conteyning by estimac'on   , and Gwern Gwrydey, being part of the common Moore, conteyning by estimac'on Threescore acres adioyning vpon the south parte thereof vppon the landes of Sir Richard Grosuenor, knight.

The said Jury, in their names and in the names of the rest of the Prince his Tenaunts of the said Mannour of Burton, doe humbly pray that they may be admitted and ordered to haue their auncient Com'on in the said Moore as auncient Tennaunts of the same Mannour haue formerly had therein.

There are, besides, highwayes and Crosswayes in some places larger then in others, w'ch we conceaue are not meant to be presented for wasts or Com'ons, and therefore we hauo omitted to sett downe such.

7. There are woods in Marsley Parke in the tenure of the Earle of Bridgewater, and woods in Llay called the Acre Newydd, in the tenure of Dame Susan Puleston, and also vnderwoods in Tithin Sidalles in the tenure of William Lewis, and also woods in Fron Ardreth in Allington or Cobham Almor in the tenure of Sir Richard Treuor, knight. Their quantities we referre to Mr. Norden. Besides, most of the Princes Tenaunts haue some Trees and hedgerowes, which are not wasted to our knowledge. But some haue fallen Trees and Woods vppon their lands as we conceaue it for their owne necessary vses, or to be imployed about their landes.

8. There is parte of Maresley Parke, als' Houlte Parke, within this Mannour of Burton, stored with deere, in the tenure of the Earle of Bridgewater, but no warren of Conies.

There are Incroachments as followeth in Burton viz't.

9. A certaine parcell of wast ioyning vppon the landes of Edward Williams, by estimac'on Thirtie yardes in length and sixe in breadth, in the occupac'on of Margaret Davies widowe.

Ite', an incrochm't ioyning to the lands of Nich'as dicus, in the tenure of William Dauid vichan, by estimac'on Thirty yardes in length, and in breadth eight.

Item, another parcell of incroachm't ioyning to the lands of Thomas Powell, by estimac'on 7 perches.

Item, an incrochment to the Cac Cadarne, cont' by estimac'on 8 yards square.

Item, another vnto the broade Gake, cont' 4 perches square.

Item, another to William Nicholas house, conteyning 3 perches.

Item, another to William Griffs house, conteyning two perches.

Item, another to Bartholomewe Williams house, conteyning two perches.

Item, another parcell of waste ioyning to the landes of Anthony Lewis, in th'occupac'on of Lewis Barton, by estimation in length fforty yardes, and in breadth eight yardes.

Item, a certaine parcell of waste ioyning to the lands of Anthony Lewis, conteyning in length Thirty yardes, and in breadth twelve yardes.

Item, a certeine parcell of incrochement ioyning to the landes of Edward Bellott, in th'occupac'on of Edward Trafford, cont' by estimac'on eight yardes square.

Item, a certaine parcell of incrochement ioyning to the lands of Richard Langford, conteyning by estimation Twenty yardes in length, and sixe in breadth.

10. These we present by booke.

11. Ffor quarries, Cole Mines, and lead, Sir Richard Grosvenor, knight, hath a grant thereof. Ffor Marle there is some within the landes of the said Tenantes, w'ch they vse for their owne profit, but what benefit it may be worth by the yeare we knowe not.

12. There is none to our knowledge.

13. There is none.

14. There is none to our knowledge.

15. There is a milne in the tenure of Sir Richard Treuor, knight, but howe he holds it we knowe not.

16. There is ffurze and fferne, w'ch the Tenaunts take for their use, but no benefite to the Prince to our knowledge.

17. We knowe none in this Mannour particularly.

18. We knowe none.

19. The Prince haue all to our knowledge.

20. The ffishing and the Rent is presented by booke, ffor ffowling there is none of profite.

21. There is none.

22. We knowe none.

23. We knowe not.

24. There is one Baylife belongeth to this manour of Burton, and no other officers that we knowe; but the Earle of Bridgewater highe steward, John Jeffries, esquier, and Thomas Foster, gent', Thomas Trafford, esquier, Receavour quere their patents.

25. None that we knowe.

26. Our customary acre conteyneth one hundred and sixty perches, each perch conteyning four and twenty foote.

27. There are such lands in Burton w'ch are graunted by customary lease, whose tithe Sir Richard Treuor holdeth.

LIBERE TENENTES.	£	s.	d.	Acres.			
Allington, Ellis, Gresford . .	0	0	2	7	0	0	0
Allington, John, Allington . .	0	18	0	48	0	0	0
Billott, Edw', esq. (John), Burton and Gresford . . .	3	10	9	50 and 2 mess'			
Billott, Edw', and Edw' Puleston .	3	5	4	70 and 2 mess'			
Bridge, Edward (John Johnson), Gresford . . .	0	0	1	4	0	0	0
David, Thomas, Allington . .	0	1	5½	18 and 1 mess'			
Dauies, Matild', included in the holding of Thomas, her son . .							
Dicus, Nicol (Will'us David Vaughan), Burton) . . .	0	9	6	11. 1 tent'			
Edward ap Robt' ap Howell, Llay. .	0	0	10	3	0	0	0
Edward ap Roger, Burton . .	0	4	3	30. 1 mess'			
Edward ap Will'm Griffith . .	0	17	4	32. 3 mess'			
Edwards, John, of Stansty, Gwersillt .	0	14	5	28	0	0	0
Egerton, Richard, kn't, Allington .	0	27	0	30	0	33	0
Ffoster, Thomas, Allington .	0	0	2	8	0	0	0
Griffith, Edward, Allington .	0	4	2	16. 1 mess'			
Griffith, Edward ap Will', Burton and Llay . . .	0	17	4	32. 3 mess'			
Griffith, Robert, Allington . .	0	5	11½	10	2	0	0
Grovenor, Ric', kn't . .	0	11	7	203	0	0	0
Hugh, John . .	0	0	6	6	0	0	0
Hugh ap John lle'n ap Edw' .	0	2	2	5	0	0	0
Jefferys, John, esq., jun., Gwersillt .	0	0	10½	5	0	0	0
Jerrard, Thomas (Ellis ap Hugh), Gwersillt . . .	0	0	11	Tent'			
Jeuan ap Edward, Burton . .	0	0	2	4	2	0	0
John lle'n ap Edward, Gwersillt .	0	7	11½	5. 1 tent'			

	£	s.	d.	Acres.
Jones, Edward (Ric'us Gregorye), Allington	0	1	9	4. 1 mess'
Jones, Will'm .	0	2	1	23. 1 mess'
Langford, John, Burton .	0	0	2	6. 1 mess'
Langford, Randall (Sir Tho' Trevor, kn't), Burton and Llay .	0	7	4	40. 1 mess',&c.
Langford, Ric', Allington and Gresford	1	14	9¾	5. 1 mess',1 tent'
Langford, Thos' (Ric'us Langford), Burton and Llay .	0	7	8	58.
Lewes, Anthony, Burton .	0	18	0	74. 1 mess'
Lewes, Thos', Io', and Joh'es Lewes, Burton .	0	0	2	30. 1 mess'
Lewes, Will' and James, Gwersillt .	0	19	0	122. 4 tenta'
Lloyd, D'd, Gresford .	0	16	4	53. 1 mess'
Lloyd, Richard .	0	8	5¾	221. 1 mess'
Lloyd, Thomas, Allington .	0	13	10½	40. 1 mess',&c.
Maddock, Edw', Allington .	0	1	0½	7. 1 mess'
Mereddeth, Edw', of London, Llay, and Burton .	0	5	9½	15. 1 mess',&c.
Mereddeth, Hugh, esq., Gwersillt .	0	1	8	36. 1 tent'
Meredeth, John, Allington, Gresford and Llay .	1	4	0	1 mess',&c.
Powell, George, Burton and Llay .	0	7	7	51. 1 mess'
Powell, Tho', of Brimbo .	0	9	11	91. 3 tenta'
Powell, Tho', of Horsley, Allington, Horsley and Gresford .	0	18	11¾	⎧ 11 mess' ⎩126 0 1 0
Powell, Tho', jun., Allington .	0	0	3	2 2 0 0. 1 mess'
Puleston, heredes Edward, Allington .	0	3	4	10. 1 tent'
Puleston, Georges, esq., Llay, Burton and Gwersillt .	1	0	0	⎧ 1 mess'. Cu' ⎩divers tentis et terris
Puleston, Margar' .	1	5	0	12. 1 mess'
Puleston, d'na Susanna, Llay and Gwersillt .	0	7	6	133. 7 mess'
Pulford, Will'm, Gresford .	0	0	1	1 2 0 0. 1 tent'
Ravenscroft, Tho', Burton and Llay .	0	4	11	11 2 0 0. 2 tenta'
Richardson, Robt', Burton .	9	17	3	
Roberts, Hugh, Gresford .	0	0	10½	9 cottages cu 'terr'
Robinson, Will'm, esq., Gwersillt and Llay .	1	10	6	⎧94 0 0 0 ⎩1 mess', &c.
Salsbury, Roger, Llay and Gresford .	0	8	4	18. 3 tenta'
Salsbury, Will'm, Burton .	2	0	0	40 0 0 0
Santhey, John, Burton .	0	4	3	44. 1 mess'
Santhey, Robt', Allington and Burton.	5	3	3	290. 2 mess'
Speede, D'd, Allington .	0	2	5	2 mess', &c.
Speede, Rich', Allington and Gresford.	0	2	10	19 0 0 0
Sutton, John, Gwersillt .	0	13	6½	154. 2 mess'
Sutton, Launcelot .	0	0	2	8. 1 mess'
Thomas ap Hugh (Powell) .	0	0	1	

	£ s. d.	Acres.
Thomas, Edw', Allington and Gresford	0 1 7	{15 2 0 0 (1 mess', &c.
Trevor, John, kn't, Burton and Gresford	1 1 11	42. 1 mess',&c.
Will'm ap Io' Tho' ap Ric', Burton .	0 1 0	{10 2 0 0 (1 mess', 5 tenta'
Williams, Edw', Gresford and Allington	0 1 0½	30. 1 mess'
Williams, Henry, Gwersillt .		8 0 0 0
Wright, John, of Pulford, Burton .	0 13 0	80. 1 mess',&c.

MANERIU' DE BURTON CUM MEMBRIS SUNT TENENTES ET PER DIMISIONEM ET AD VOLUNTAT'.

	A.	R.	P.	£	s.	d.
				Rent.		
Allington, Ellis, Hunckley . .	25	1	0	5	0	0
Allington, John, Burton Allington .	0	1	2	0	6	8
Billot, Edw', esq., Burton .	29	1	0	12	0	0
Billot, Edw', Burton Allington .	54	0	0	20	0	0
Edward ap Edw' Griff', Burton Allington .	2	0	0	1	6	8
Edwards, John, gen', Burton Allington .	0	3	0	0	5	0
Edwards, John, ap Howell ap Griff', Burton Allington .	14	1	20	3	6	8
Ffoster, Thomas, Burton .	17	28	0	7	13	4
" " Burton Allington .	23	2	20	10	13	4
Griffith, Edw', Burton Allington .	10	2	0	4	0	0
Griffith, Rob't, Burton .	27	0	0	13	0	0
Grosvenor, Ric', k't, Burton .	29	1	0	13	6	8
Inhabitants of Burton .	2	0	0	val. 3		4
James ap Hugh, Burton Allington .	3	0	0	0	16	0
Jarrard, Jane, Hunckley .	piscarium.			0	16	0
Jefferyes, John, esq., Burton Allington .	0	1	2	0	3	4
Jenkin, Tho' (heredes), Burton Allington .	6	1	0	3	6	8
John ap Mad' (heredes), Burton Allington.	22	2	0	12	0	0
Jones, Edw', Burton Allington .	21	2	0	9	0	0
Jones, Will'm, Burton .	0	3	20	0	6	8
Langford, Ric', Burton .	3	0	0	1	4	0
Langford, Ric', Burton Allington .	7	2	0	3	0	0
" " Hunckley .	9	0	0	3	3	4
Lewes, James, Burton Allington .	8	2	0	3	6	8
Lewes, Will'm, Burton Allington .	11	2	0	5	0	0
Lloyd, D'd, Hunckley .	10	0	0	2	6	0
Mereddeth, Edw', of London, Burton Allington .	8	0	0	4	0	0
Mereddeth, John, of London, Burton Allington .	13	0	0	5	10	0
" " Hunckley .	5	0	0	1	10	0
Mereddeth, John, gen', Burton Allington .	14	3	0	5	0	0
Owin, John Griffith, Hunckley .	7	0	0	2	0	0
Powell, Thomas, Burton Allington .	0	2	0	0	10	0
" " Hunckley .	1	2	0	0	8	0

	A.	R.	P.	£	s.	d.
				Rent.		
Powell, Tho', esq., de Allington, Burton Allington . .	0	1	0	0	6	8
Powell, Tho', of Brymbo, Burton Allington .	7	0	0	2	16	8
Powell, Tho', of Horsley, Burton .	2	3	0	1	6	8
„ „ Burton Allington	207	0	6	70	0	0
Puleston, Margar', Burton Allington .	4	0	0	1	8	0
Puleston, Margar', d. of Edw', Allington .	13	3	20	4	0	0
Puleston, dame Susan, Burton . .	17	0	2	6	0	0
„ „ Burton Allington .	159	2	0	22	13	4
Puliston, Robt', Burton Allington .	6	2	0	4	0	0
Pulford, Will'm, Hunckley .	0	2	0	0	13	4
Probin, Will'm, Burton Allington .	12	3	0	5	10	0
Randle, John, Burton Allington	3	3	0	1	10	0
Relew, Ant', Burton Allington .	0	2	0	0	5	0
Roberts, Peter, Burton Allington .	11	0	0	5	0	0
Robinson, Will'm, esq., Burton Allington .	8	1	0	3	0	0
Roger, John, Burton Allington .	0	3	0	0	13	4
Salsbury, Henry, Burton .	54	3	0	20	0	0
Sandy, John, gen', Burton .	18	3	20	7	10	0
Sandy, Robert, Burton .	2	2	0	0	13	4
Speede, Rich', Burton Allington .	10	2	0	4	0	0
Sutton, John, Burton Allington .	2	0	0	1	0	0
Tho' ap Hugh, Burton Allington .	2	0	0	1	10	0
Thomas, Edw', Burton Allington .	7	0	0	2	10	0
Trevallen, John, Burton Allington .	25	0	0	13	6	8
Trevor, John, kn't, Burton .	Mereford Mill.					
„ „ Allington .	0	0	24	0	6	8
Trevor, Ric', kn't, Burton .	4	0	0	1	14	0
„ „ Burton Allington .	7	3	20	2	8	8
„ „ Allington .	8	0	20	2	14	4
Edw' Will'ms ap W'm Griffith, Burton Allington . . .	2	0	0	1	10	0
Wynton, Deane and Chapter (Comes Bridgewater), Burton Allington .	1	0	0	0	6	0
Sum' of the freeholde Rentes of Burton p' ann' at this day is				44	15	6¾
It was 4 Eliz' but . . .				38	8	5¾
More than before . . .				6	7	0¼
The yearlie rent of the lease holde at will and in fee ferme is				87	2	6½
In 4 Eliz' it was but . . .				71	9	8½
Lesse then now by . .				15	12	10
Which may be by the fee fermes.						
The whole, rent free and lease, etc., is .				131	18	1½

MORTON ANGLICORU'.

Harl. 3696, *fo.* 123, *et seq.*

	A.	R.	P.	£	s.	d.
Bates, Hugh . . .	20	0	0	1	6	0
Breerton, Owin, esq. . .	4	0	0	0	3	2
David ap John ap Ieu'n Goz .	4	0	0	0	6	0
David ap Owin . .	Mess', &c., & 3 par' terr'.			0	5	6½
Davies, Edward (Robert Lloyd) .	52	0	0	2	19	8¾
Edward ap John ap Edward .	20	0	0	1	2	8
Eyton, Edw' . .	1	0	0	0	1	4
Ffortescue, Nicol' . .	48	0	0	2	1	0
Gouldsmith, Thomas . .	8	0	0			
Hope, Edward . .	5	0	0	0	7	6
Hope, Thomas . .	5	0	0	0	19	1
John, D'd Broughton . .	0	2	0	0	0	6
John, Roger Lle'n . .	0	2	0	0	0	10
Jones, Emanuel . .	10	0	0	0	9	9
Katherin v'z Edward . .	2	0	0	0	2	1
Kenricus ap David . .	15	2	0	1	5	8
Martin ap Ieu'n . .	1	2	0	0	1	4
Robert ap Randle . .	7	0	0	0	13	4
Robert ap Randle ap John Thomas .	17	0	0	0	10	6
Thomas ap Edward . .	10	0	0	0	15	0
Wells, Lawrence (land of Peter Roydon) .				0	0	6
Will'm ap John D'd . .	3	2	0	0	5	4
Will'm ap John Rob't . .	15	0	0	0	19	0
Williams, Richard . .	143	0	0	3	13	4
S'ma of the rentes of Morcton at this day is .				18	9	3½
4° Elizabeth . . .				17	0	9½

£1 8s. 11½d. lesse then now.

— — —

MINERA MANERIUM.

Harl. 3696, *fo.* 129, *et seq.*

	A.	R.	P.	£	s.	d.
Batha, John .	0	0	4	0	0	4
David, Morgan .	1	1	0	0	1	0
Edward ap d'd ap R's .	1	3	0	0	1	2
Edward ap Robert .	2	2	0	0	2	0
Griffith, Hugh .	2	0	0	0	1	3
Griffith, John .	Mynes Mill			2	15	8

	A.	R.	P.	£	s.	d.
				Rent.		
Gwenver d'd and Mary .v'z Edw' ap Rob't	0	2	10	0	0	11
Hugh ap D'd	9	0	20	0	3	7
Hugh ap D'd Richard	5	2	0	0	2	3
Hugh ap Richard	9	0	20	0	5	1
Hugh ap Rob't ap Ho'ell	34	1	3	0	18	4
Jeu'n ap D'd	0	2	32	0	1	0
John ap Edward	0	1	25	0	0	8½
John ap Hugh	0	0	5	0	0	3
John ap Hugh et Tho' ap Jo' Hugh	12	1	6	0	6	10
John ap Hugh ap D'd	0	2	0	0	0	4
John ap Hugh ap Hoe'll	7	0	0	0	4	0
John ap John ap Edward	3	2	0	0	0	7
John ap John Richard	0	0	2	0	0	2
John ap Richard ap W'm	4	0	0	0	1	4
John Robin ap Ho'ell	1	3	0	0	2	0
John Robert ap Ho'ell	4	0	0	0	3	9
Kenrick, Hugh	26	0	0	0	1	3
Middleton, Roger	4	0	0	0	2	0
Morgon ap Ho'ell	2	2	0	0	4	6
Nicholas ap Edward	0	1	0	0	0	6
Owin, John D'd	7	3	0	0	2	1
Richard ap Ho'ell	7	0	0	0	1	4
Richard ap Hugh	11	0	0	0	7	4
Robert ap Hugh	4	1	0	0	4	1
Robinson, W'm, esq.	26	0	0	0	1	8
Thomas, D'd	4	1	0	0	3	0
Vaughan, John	13	2	0	0	5	1
The Inhabitants	capellan.			0	0	4

The s'ma of the yearlie rentes of the lease land
and at will in the Manor of Minera now . | 7 | 1 | 4½

In 4° Eliz' but . . . | 6 | 15 | 5½

More by 5s. 10d.

MANERIU' DE PICKHILL ET SESWICK IN COM' DENBIGH.

Harl. 3696, *fo.* 202.

Qui dicunt super sacramenta sua, viz'.

Imprimis, to the first Article they say, that the Mannor of Pickhill and Seswick is bounded from a place called Croes Wladys, with the River Dee running along the south and east partes, and ye River Clymedog on the north, and likewise on the east to ye River Dee, with certaine landes belonging to ye

Mannor of Ruabon southwest, excepting certaine other landes within ye boundes of this Mannor belonging to the Earles of Derby.

There belongeth to the said Mannor as part and parcell thereof three parcells of landes, whereof one is called Gro Thomas, the other being two p'cells called Hile lying beyond the River Dee, and one tenement called Rhyd y Bont Vawr beyond Clywedoc, and divers other parcells beeing beyond the said river, all reputed to bee members of the said Mannor of Pickhill and Seswick.

To the second Article they say, that if there be any demesnes within that Mannor they do not know where it lyeth, neither in whose holding it is, and further, yt they never heard heretofore of any such landes to bee within that Mannour.

To the third Article they say, that the names of all ye freeholders, and what everie of them doth holde, and their Rents are particulerlie laide downe, and as for ffeeferm'ts they know of none in yt Mannor.

To the ffourth and ffifth Article they say, ye customary Tennants of this Mannor are his Prince his Highnes Tennants by Leases, and doe hold their Messuages, landes, and Tenementes vppon their severall names sett downe, and doe respectivelie pay for ye same the severall Rents vppon theire names appearing by their severall Leases for ffortie yeares, and soe from fortie yeares to fortie yeares forever, and doe pay two yeares Rent for a fyne vpon the taking of their Leases, according to the composition made between ye late Queene Elizabeth, of famous memorie, and ye Tenn'ts of Bromfield and Yale, in the ffowrth yeare of her late most happy Raigne, and this Jury doe not knowe of any thing paid or due to be paide by any of the said Tennants vppon ye marriage of their daughters.

To the sixt Article they say, that the Kings highwaies excepted, there is no waste or commons in ye said Mannor to their knowledge.

To the seaventh Article they say, that they have no great quantitie of wood or vnderwood within this Mannor, and all that is is well preserved to their knowledge.

To the eight Article they say, that there is no parke or Warren within this Mannor.

To the nynth they say as to the sixt, that they have no Common or Wast to their knowledge, and therefore no encrochment.

To the tenth they say, that the landes held from fortie yeares to forty in ye holding of theis Tennants, are ye cus-

tomarie lands of this Mannor, and that there is no escheat
lands within this Mannor other then what is hold by lease.

To the elcaventh they say, that there are no mynes of cole,
lead, chalk, nor quarries of stones, but for marle, some quantitie there is, but no great use made of it, the benefitts whereof
they doe not knowe.

To the twelveth and thirteenth they say, that they doe not
knowe that any ffreeholder died without heire, either generall
or speciall, and that there is not any towne corporate, bou-
rough towne, or other, within ye said Mannor.

To the ffourteenth and fifteenth they say, that they doe
not knowe of any such exchaunges or vnlawfull vnserting of
landes into Leases as are demaunded in yt Article. There bee
two milles in ye Townshipp of Pickell, now in the tenure of
Rog'r Ellis or Dorothie Ellis, and whether they bee custom'e
mills or noe, this Jury do not knowe.

To the sixteenth they say as to the sixt and ninth, that they
have no Commons or Waste, neither peate, turfe, etc.

To the seaventeenth they say, that the ffreeholders and Tenants of this Mannor, beeing a member of the Lordshipp of
Bromfield, doe serve at the leete and law daies of this Lordshipp, as they are bound to doe. And that they doe pay all
fynes of alienac'ons, amerciaments of courts, mizes, and all
other payments for their rate and proporc'ons as others the
Tennants of the foresaide Lo'ps doe, when and as often as ye
same are due, but no Kings silver nor head silver.

To the eighteenth they say, that there is no Coppeholde
Tenem't in decay within this Mannor to their knowledge.

To the nyneteenth they say, that they knowe not whether
the casualties menc'oned in this Article be due to the Prince
his Highnes, or to the Kings most excellent Ma'tie.

To the twentith they say, that there is no fishing nor fowling belonging to this Manor.

To the 21st they say, that they have no markets or faires
held w'hin this Manor.

To the two and three and twentith, that they knowe not of
any rents or lands concealed or withheld in this Manor, nor of
any Repriss or payments going out of the same.

To the fowre and twentith they say, that there are yearlie
made at the leete at Michaelmas by the Jurie of this Mannor,
theis officiers following, viz., Pettie Constable and Bayliffe,
to gather ye Princes his Rents, w'ch doe serve for ye yeare
following within ye said Mannor, and yt the Sheriffes Steward,
as this Jurie have credible heard, is the Right Honorable the
Earle of Bridgewater, and John Jeffreys, Esq., John Dauies

and Thomas Foster, Gent., are his deputies, and that Thomas
Trafford, Esq., is receavo'r, but what ffees they or eithor of
them have this Jury knoweth not.

To the five and twentith Article they say, there are no ad-
vowsons or benefices w'thin this Mannor.

To the six and twentith they say, that as farre as they can
learne and find out, the old and accustomed acre vsed in those
partes and in most of the countreys next adioyning, conteyneth one hundreth threescore perches in everie acre, and
everie of ye saide pearches conteyneth ffowre and twenty
foote to the pearch or pole.

PICKHILL & SESWICK.

LIBERI TENENTES.		A.	R.	P.	£	s.	d.
Bellot, Edw', esq., Pick' & Sesw'	.	37	0	0	0	7	8
Eyton, Humfrey, Pick'	.	15	0	0	0	2	0
Jefferyes, Jo', esq., Pick', Sesw' & Bed'	.	3	0	0	0	1	4
Mereddeth, Hugh, esq., Pick' & Ses'	.	4	0	0	0	1	0
Powell, John, gen', Pick'	.	3	0	0	0	1	0
Rogers, John, gen', Pick'	.	5	0	0	0	2	0
S'ma Redd' lib'oru' tenen' .	.				0	15	0

TENENTES PER DIMISSIONEM MANERII PREDICT'.

		A.	R.	P.	£	s.	d.
Breerton, Owen, esq., Bedwall	.	36	1	10	1	16	6
Browne, John, *Ibid.*	.	2	0	0	0	3	5
D'd ap d'd, *Ibid.*	.	2	0	0	0	3	7
D'd Lloyd ap Roger, *Ibid.*	.	17	0	0	1	14	1
Decka, John, Pick' & Sesw'	.	3	0	0	0	2	8
Decka, Thomas, *Ibid.*	.	52	0	6	3	5	11
Dymock, Will'm, *Ibid.*	.	9	3	20	0	10	5
Edgebery, Kenrick, gen', Bedw'	.	40	1	0	2	3	0
Edward ap John ap Rob't, Pick' & Sesw'	.	4	0	20	0	7	6
Ellice, Dorathe, Pick', Sesw' & Bed'	.	115	0	32	10	9	2
Ellice, Sidney, Pick' & Sesw'	.	141	0	22	11	5	6½
Eyton, Garrard, gen', Bedw'	.	37	0	0	1	13	7
Gamwell, Will'm, iur' vx', *Ibid.*	.	13	0	0	0	6	8
Goldsmith, Thomas, *Ibid.*	.	13	1	20	0	14	4
Griffith, Roger, gen', *Ibid.*	.	4	1	0	0	3	5
Hall, Thomas	.	100	0	0	4	19	10
Hope, Thomas	.	0	2	0	0	0	3
James, John, Pick' & Bed'	.	19	0	26	1	5	6
Jefferyes, John, esq.	.	61	0	30	3	1	4
John ap John Gwynn, Bedw'	.	11	0	20	0	13	0

	A.	R.	P.	£	s.	d.
				\(Rent.\)		
John ap John ap W'm ap Mad', Pic' & Ses'	4	0	0	0	3	4
John James ap D'd, Bed' . .	10	1	0	0	18	0
John ap Roger ap lle'n, *Ibid.* . .	3	2	0	0	3	0
John ap W'm ap Mad', *Ibid.* . .	8	1	0	0	9	0
Jones, Roger, *Ibid.* . . .	26	3	0	1	19	4
Mereddeth, Hugh, esq., Pick' & Sesw' .	0	0	20	0	0	4
Presland, Richard, Bedw' .	13	2	0	0	18	0
Price, Agnes, v, d'd ap, *Ibid.* .	3	0	0	0	5	6
Puleston, John, gen', Pick' .	58	1	6	3	16	3¾
Puleston, Mary, *Ibid.* .	9	2	0	0	19	11
Randall ap John, *Ibid.* .	1	2	20	0	3	8
Raulfe, Ellizens, *Ibid.* .	20	2	0	1	5	10
Rogers, John, gen', *Ibid.* .	4	2	0	0	3	4
Rowland, John, Bed' .	7	3	20	0	7	6
Soulle, Robt' et al', *Ibid.* .	12	2	0	1	0	10
Sutton, John, gen', Pick'	47	0	0	1	10	3
Thomas ap John, *Ibid.* .	8	0	20	0	17	2
Thomas, Roger, Bedw' .	17	2	0	1	14	1
William, John, Pick' . .	4	1	0	0	5	0
Wyn, Rob't, gen, Bedw'	29	1	10	2	10	2
Pickill s'ma redd' tenen' ad volunt' et per dimiss'				38	4	7
The last makes the rent uncertain.						
4° Eliz' Redd' in toto .				42	0	20¼
Bedwall s'ma redd' .				26	11	5
4° Eliz' . . .				25	13	7½

MANOR OF MORTYN OR BURTON.—TOWNSHIP OF GWERSYLLT.

Harl. MSS. 1972, 4181.

Morgan ab David ab Goronwy ab Madog Sytton or Sutton, Lord of Sytton in Isgoed, sixth son of Elidir ab Rhys Sais, Lord of Eyton. *Ermine,* a lion rampant *azure.* The said Madog Sutton paid £16 per annum to the Lord of Bromfield or Maelor Gymraeg for the Lordship of Sutton. He held lands in Is y Coed.

a

| a

David de Sutton in Is y Coed.=...d. of Richard Cotgrave of Cheshire.

David Sutton of Sutton and Gwersyllt, 35 Edward III=2nd, Lleuci, d. of
(1361). He married first, Marslli, d. and heir of | Iorwerth Fychan
Howel ab David Llwyd ab Cynwrig ab Iorwerth ab | ab Iorwerth ab
Ynyr of Iâl and Gwersyllt. Cynwrig ab Iorwerth | Awr ab Ieuaf ab
was living in 1292. By this marriage there was | Nyniaw ab Cyn-
issue a son, named Madog Sutton. | wrig ab Rhiwal-
| lawn. *Ermine*, a
| lion rampant *sable*.

Gruffydd of=Catherine, d. of Madog ab Iorwerth Fychan of Mortyn ab
Sutton and | Iorwerth ab David ab Goronwy ab Iorwerth ab Howel ab
Gwersyllt. | Moreiddig ab Sanddref Hardd, Lord of Mortyn (Burton) and
| Llai. *Sable*, three roses *argent*.

David of Sut-=Gwerfyl, d. of Gruffydd ab Bleddyn of Mortyn ab Robert ab
ton and | David Goch, ab David Hen ab Goronwy ab Iorwerth ab
Gwersyllt; | Howel ab Moreiddig ab Sanddef Hardd. *Vert*, semé of
living 3rd | broomslips, a lion rampant *or*.
Henry V, and
33rd Henry | Angharad, ux. Deicws ab Madog ab Adda Llwyd ab Adda
VI (1455). | ab Madog ab Llywelyn ab Madog ab Meilir Eyton of
| Eyton.

Robert of =Eleo, d. of David ab Gruff-   Thomas =Marsli, dau.   Gwerfyl,
Sutton and | ydd of Tref Alun, ab   Sutton. and heir of   ux. Jenkyn
Gwersyllt; | David ab Llywelyn ab   See p. Ieuan Dec-   ab Ieuan
living 8 | David ab Goronwy ab   188.   caf ab   of Stansti.
Hen. VII. | Iorwerth ab Howel ab   David
| Moreiddig ab Sanddef   Llwyd.
| Hardd. David ab Gruff-
| ydd died in 1476.

| 1 | 2 | 3 | 4 | 5 | 6 | |
David =Margaret, d. of John   Sir   Lewys John.   Catherine, Eliza-
Sutton | ab Richard ab Ma-   Howel.   Sutton, Gruff-   ux. Robert beth.
of Sut- | dog ab Llywelyn of Mor-   Vicar- ydd.   Fychan ab
ton and | Halchdyn in Mae-   gan.   General.   Robert ab
Gwers- | lor Saesneg, eldest   Ieuan ab
yllt. | son of Ednyfed Gam   David of
| of Llys Pengwern   Brochdyn.
| in Nanheudwy.

John Wynn Sutton of Sut-=Ermeline, d. of John Puleston of Hafod y Wern.
ton and Gwersyllt. | *Argent*, on a bend *sable*, three mullets of the
| field.

| 1 | 2 | 3 | 4 | 5 | 6 | 7 | 8 |
John =Margaret,   David   Hugh. Edward. Alice, ux. Rhys ab
Sutton | d. of Wil- Sutton. Wil- Pyers. David ab Rhys ab
of Sut- | liam   Lancelot liam. Roger. Ieuan ab Llywelyn
ton and | Hookes ab Sutton,   ab Howel ab Cyn-
Gwers- | Hugh   married   wrig ab Iorwerth
yllt. | Hookes of   Catherine,   Figill of Ystrad
| Aber-   d. of John   Alun.
| conwy.   Roydon.

b | 1   c | 2   d | 3   e |

b | 1		c | 2	d | 3	e
John Sutton = Morfydd, d. of Howel		William	Edward = Catherine, d. |	
of Sutton	ab Llywelyn ab	Sutton.	Sutton.	of Ralph Dar-
and Gwers-	Owain of Brynbw.			ling of March-
yllt.				wiail.

4
Captain Ellis Sut- = Jane, d. of Cadwaladr Wynn Pryse
ton, Constable of Rhiwlas, and relict of George
of Harlech Castle, Puleston of Llai. She died 8th March
1622. 1664.

John Sut- = Jane, d. of John Wynn Lloyd	Elis = ...,d. of Hugh	Jane.
ton of Sut- of Plas y Bada, which place	Sut- Owen of Caer	Anne.
ton and was sold by her brother Ro-	ton. Berllan.	Rose.
Gwersyllt, bert Lloyd to Sir Thomas		
1600. Myddleton Hen of Chirk		
Castle.		

Gwersyllt Isaf, which is situate on the banks of the
Alun, remained in the Sutton family till 1660, when it
was sold by Captain Ellis Sutton, an old Cavalier, who
was ruined in the Royal cause, to Colonel (afterwards
Sir Geoffrey) Shakerley, of Shakerley in Lancashire.

Colonel Sir Geoffrey Shakerley was a distinguished
Royalist in the time of Charles I, and commanded a regiment of Horse. It was out of regard for his old friend
and comrade Colonel Robinson of Gwersyllt Uchaf, that
he bought Gwersyllt Isaf, so that he might live near
him. George John, son of Sir Geoffrey Shakerley of
Gwersyllt, was baptised at Gresford, Sept. 18th, 1682.

Captain Ellis Sutton was churchwarden in 1662, and
was buried at Gresford, Dec. 18th, 1694.

Lewys Sutton, Vicar-General 3 and = Angharad, d. and heir of William ab
4 Henry VII, fourth son of Robert John ab Einion ab Iolyn of Bore-
Sutton ab David. sham or Bwras.

John Lewys. = Margaret, d. of William Alunton of Alunton or Trefalun.

William Lewys = Dorothy, d. of Thomas Brereton, Rector of Llandrinio and
of Wrexham. Vicar of Gresford, third son of Edward Brereton of Bora-
sham, and Dorothy, his second wife, d. of Sir Thomas
Hanmer of Hanmer, Knt.

James Lewys of = Catherine, d. and heir of David ab Richard ab Richard ab
Gwersyllt. Howel ab Iolyn.

1		2	3
John Lewys, = Sacay, d. of Richard Powel of Lon-		William	Lancelot
a Lawyer, don (descended from Elystan Glo-		Lewys.	Lewys.
1640. drudd), and Elizabeth, his wife, d.			
of David Offley of London.			

GWERSYLLT UCHAF.

Thomas ab David Sutton ab Gruffydd⹀Malli, d. and heir of Ieuan Deccaf ab
  ab David, 7th Henry VII, 7th │   David Llwyd.
  Henry VIII.

Robert Sutton of⹀Catherine, d. of   Lewys⹀Janet, d. of   Mallt, ux. David
  Gwersyllt.   │ Robert ab Ed-   Sut- │ Robert ab   Lloyd ab Bleddyn
───────────── │ ward ab Howel   ton. │ Edward ab   ab Jenkyn ab
Jane, d. and heir, │ of Llwyn On.   │ Howel of   Iorwerth ab
  ux. John Nor- │ *Ermine*, a lion   │ Llwyn On.   Gwilymo. Their
  bury of Frod- │ rampant *sable*.   │   son was Thomas
  sham.   Lloyd of Treu-
                                                        ddyn.

John Lewys of Gwersyllt⹀Emma, d. of John Puleston (Tir Mon) of Hafod y
          Uchaf.   │   Wern.

John Lewys of Gwersyllt, Uchaf.⹀   Jane, ux. John Peake of Caernarvon.

Edward Lewys sold the   John.= Margaret,   Elizabeth,   Margaret, *s.p.*
  lands of Gwersyllt   Lewys d. of Wil-   ux. ....   Elen, *s. p.*
  Uchaf to Bishop Robin-   liam   Holland,   Gwen, *s. p.*
  son. He died *s. p.*   Hookes.   *s. p.*

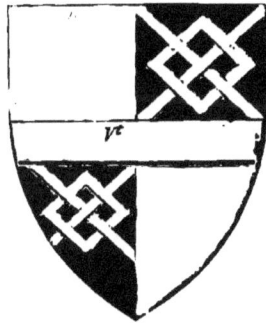

MANOR OF MORTYN OR BURTON.—ROBINSON OF
GWERSYLLT UCHAF.

Cae Cyriog MS.

Sir William Norris of⹀Annesta, d. of Maredydd ab Tudor ab Goronwy, and
  Cheshire, Knt.   │   sister of Owain Tudor.

Robin Norris.⹀Jane, d. of Sir Pyers Dutton, Knt.

Harri Robins.⹀Elen, d. of Sir William Stanley of Hooton, Knt.

| a

John Robins.=Elen, d. of William Brytall ab Jenkyn Brytall ab John Brytall ab John Brytall ab Ralph Brytall of Worrall.

| 2

Nicholas Robinson, D.C.L., Bishop of Bangor, and=Jane, d. (by Mary, his one of the Council for the Court of the Marches wife, d. of Sir William from 1566 to 1585, when he died. He alienated Gruffydd of Penrhyn, the Skerries and Mynachdy from the See of Ban- Knt.,: Chamberlain of gor in favour of one of his sons. He also bought North Wales) of Sir Gwersyllt Uchaf from Edward Lewys ab John Randle Brereton, Knt., Lewys ab John Lewys ab Lewys ab Thomas ab ab Randle Brereton. David Sutton of Gwersyllt. Nicholas Robinson She married secondly, died Feb. 15th, 1585. Arthur Price of Fae- nor in Cydewain.

William Robinson=Jane, dau. of John Humph- Hugh Ro- Marga- of Gwersyllt Uchaf, Pryce of Llanfair in rey. binson, ret, ux. and of Mynachdy in Cydewaun or New- Herbert. D.D., Head Edward Môn, which last town Hall, High Pyers. Master of Pryce of place is on the coast Sheriff for co. Mont. Winches- Faenor, opposite to the in 1586, descended ter School ab Arthur Skerries Light- from the Royal line and Arch- Pryce. house, High Sheriff of Elystan Glod- deacon of for co. Denbigh, rudd, Prince of Glouces- 1630, and for Angle- Fferlis. ter. sey, 1632.

John Robinson of Gwersyllt Uchaf and Mynachdy. Born in 1616.= Mar- Vice-Admiral of North Wales, and a Colonel in the Royal Army; garet, d. appointed to be one of the Knights of the Royal Oak in 1660; of Ed- M.P. for Beaumaris from 1601 to 1679. He went with Charles II ward to the Continent, and in his absence the Parliament confiscated Norris of his property, and gave it to a stranger, who built a new house Speke, there, and called it Plâs Newydd. The property was restored co. Lan- to him by the king on his return. He died in 1680, and was caster, buried in Gresford Church, where there is a monument erected Esq. to his memory.

William Robinson=Jane, only d. and heiress John. Margaret, Jane, of Gwersyllt Uchaf of Timothy Myddleton ux.]. =Sir ux. and Mynachdy, of Plâs Cadwgan and — Strode, John High Sheriff for co. Pant Iocyn, seventh son of Sir Knt.; 2. = Roy- Denbigh, 1690, and Thomas Myddleton of Chirk Charles don. M.P. for that Castle. Knt. *Argent*, on a bend Selby, Am- county 1705-7. *vert*, three wolf's heads erased herst. *argent*.

John Robinson of=Elizabeth, eld- William Robin-= Eliza- Frances. Gwersyllt Uchaf, est d. and heir- son Lytton. His beth, d. Mynachdy, Plâs ess of Sir Gruff- maternal cousin, and co-heir Cadwgan and Pant ydd Jeffreys of Lytton Strode of Giles Iocyn, and *jure* Acton, Knt. Lytton, devised Heyshon *uxoris* of Acton. *Ermine*, a lion to him the Kneb- of London. Married in 1708. rampant *sable*. worth estate.

b | c | d | e | f |

b		*c*	*d*	*e*	*f*
William Robinson of Gwersyllt Uchaf, Mynachdy, Plâs Cadwgan, Pant Iocyn, and Acton. He perished in a storm on his return from a sporting excursion on the Skerries. His trustees sold Pant Iocyn and Acton to Elis Yonge of Bryn Iorcyn, and in 1783 these estates were purchased from Mr. Yonge's trustees, by Sir Foster Cunliffe, Bart.	=Elizabeth, d. of William Robinson Lytton of Knebworth.	Dorothy, ux. Elis Yonge of Bryn Iorcyn and Acton, *ob. s. p.*	Anne=Robinson, married in 1731.	Cawley Humberston Cawley of Gwersyllt, High Sheriff for co. Denbigh in 1739.	Three other daughters, *ob. s. p.*

A child, *ob. infans.*

Elizabeth, *ob.* s. p. before 1752.

John Humberston Cawley of Gwersyllt.

John Robinson Lytton of Knebworth.	=..., d. of ...... Brereton of Borasham.	Elizabeth, ux., 1st, William Robinson of Gwersyllt Uchaf; 2nd, Lawrence Williams.	Barbara, ux. William Warburton of Yarrow, in the Queen's County in Ireland, and ancestor of Lord Lytton.

INSCRIPTION on the Monument erected in Gresford Church, to the Memory of John Robinson of Gwersyllt, Esq.

H. S. J.

Iohannis Robinson.

Qui

Tribunus Caroli Martyris, fortunas ejus (hoc est Ecclesiam Monarchiamque) sustenebat strenue.

Rege cadente

Carolum exulem non deseruit exul,

Cum reduce redux.

Apud   Gwersyllt,

Ubi omnia sua a rebelli manu direpta reliquerat, Ædificijs ab eadem eleganter constructis gavisus est.

Ab uxore Margarita, filia Edwardi Norris

De Speak in Com. Pal. Lancast. Arm.

Gulielmum, Johannem, Margaritam, et Janam.

Suscepit prolem.

Corpus e meliori licet luto compositum,

Vulneribus tamen pronis

Fractum pariter ac honestum,

Animam ad Cœlum aspirantem

Ultra Annum ætat. 65 retinere non valens

Martij 15° reddidit.   Ære Christianæ MDCLXXX.

EPITAPH OF JOHN ROBINSON IN GRESFORD CHURCH.

Gwyn eu Byd y Tangueffydd-wyn.
O vos intrantes respicite
Ut hic in pace quiescit
Inter vicinos semper Pacis arbiter
IOHANNES ROBINSON de GWERSYLLT,
Armigeri.
Vir quidem Egregius
Et amicis omnibus utilis.
ELIZABETAM
GRIFF'I JEFFREYS de ACTON, Militis
Filiam natu maximam˙
Duxit uxorem
Reliquit viduam,
Ex uxore meritissima Filium habuit unicum,
Filias quinque
Obiit 2da die Novr. 1732.
Ætat. ann. 45.

EPITAPH OF WILLIAM ROBINSON IN GRESFORD CHURCH.

In memory
of Anne, sole daughter and heir of
Timothy Myddleton of Pantiocyn,
Esq., who was married to
William Robinson of
Gwersyllt, Esq., and had issue
John, William, and Frances.
She died Aug. 23, 1693.
And in memory also of the
said William Robinson, Esq.,
who dyed Nov. 15,
1717, aged 49.

MANOR OF MORTYN (OR BURTON), TOWNSHIP OF TREFALUN.

Harl. MSS., 1969-2299 ; *Cae Cyriog MS.*

Eunydd, Lord of Dyffryn Clwyd, was the son of Morien ab Morgeneu ab Gwrystan ab Gwaethfoed of Powys, according to some authors ; but, according to others, he was the son of Gwergynwy ab Gwrgeneu, Chief of one of the Noble Tribes, ab Gwaeddgar ab Bywyn ab Biordderch ab Gwriawn ab Gwndan ab Gwylan ab Gwynfyw Frych ab Cadell Deyrnllwg II, King of Powys. The mother of Eunydd was Gwenllian, daughter and heiress of Rhys ab Marchan,[1] who was lord of seven townships in Dyffryn Clwyd, viz., Tref Pen y Coed, Y Fynechtid, Y Groes Lwyd, Pant Meugan, and three others ; and bore *azure*, a fess *or*, inter three horse's heads erased *argent*.

Eunydd, Lord of Dyffryn Clwyd, came into Powysland in the time of Bleddyn ab Cynfyn, Prince of Powys, and fought with him against the English. For his services, the Prince gave him the townships of Trefalun, Almor, Y Groesffordd in Maelor Gymraeg ; and Lleprog Fawr, Lleprog Fechan (Leadbrook), and Trefnant y Rhiw in Tegeingl. He married Eva, daughter and heiress of Llywelyn ab Dolffyn ab Llywelyn Eurdorchog. This Llywelyn ab Dolffyn was lord of seven townships,

---

[1] Marchan was the son of Cynwrig ab Cyddelw Gam ab Elgad ab Lles Ddeawr ab Ednyfed ab Gwynan.

viz., 1, Aelhaiarn ; 2, Llygadog ; 3, Ucheldref ; 4, Garth-aiarn ; 5, Llandderfel in Penllyn ; 6, Caer Gilor ; and, 7, Y Saeth Marchog. By this lady Eunydd had issue two sons, 1, Ithel, and 2, Heilin, and a daughter named Heunydd, the consort of Maredydd ab Bleddyn, Prince of Powys. He bore *azure*, a lion salient *or*.

Ithel ab Eunydd was Lord of Trefalun or Alunton, Y Groesffordd, Lleprog Fawr, Lleprog Fechan, and Tref-nant y Rhiw. He married Eva, or, according to others, Gwaladys, daughter and co-heiress of Gruffydd, third son of Meilir Eyton ab Elidir, Lord of Trefwy or Eyton, who bore *ermine*, a lion rampant *azure*. The mother of Eva was Angharad, the daughter and heiress of Llywelyn ab Meurig ab Caradog ab Jestyn ab Gwrgant, Prince of Glamorgan, who bore *gules*, three chevronells *argent*. By this lady, Ithel had issue, besides a daughter named Angharad, six sons ; 1, Einion ; 2, Trahaiarn ; 3, Ior-werth Sais ; 4, Rhirid Sais ; 5, Howel ; and, 6, Einion Goch.

These six sons gave land to build the church of Y Groesffordd, and Trahaiarn had the greatest share of land, as is well known by all that country, by old writings, says Lewys Dwnn. The sepulchres of the descendants of Ithel ab Eunydd are in the church of Y Groesffordd ; and the sepulchres of the descendants of Heilin ab Eunydd, Lord of Dyffryn Clwyd, are in the church of Llandderfel in Penllyn.

Einion ab Ithel, the eldest son, married Elen, daughter of Rhys Fychan ab Rhys ab David ab Meilir, by whom he had issue, besides Heilin, the ancestor of Sir William Maredydd of Stansti, Bart., which title is now extinct, and the Maredydds of Pentref Bychan, an elder son and heir,

Iorwerth ab Einion. He married twice ; by his first wife he had two sons, Iorwerth, and Iorwerth Chwith, and a daughter named Arddûn. By his second wife he had issue seven sons ; 1, Icuaf ; 2, Hwfa ; 3, Howel ; 4, David ; 5, Philip ; 6, Ednowain ; and 7, Cynwrig.

Ieuaf ab Iorwerth married, and had issue, besides two

daughters, Efa and Arddûn, three sons, 1, Icuaf Grach ; 2, Gruffydd ; and 3, Iorwerth. Gruffydd ab Ieuaf married, and had issue, besides a daughter named Annest, two sons, 1, Madog ; and 2, Cynwrig.

Madog ab Gruffydd married Alice, daughter of Maredydd of Yr Hôb, and had issue, besides a daughter named Gwenllian, five sons, 1, Y Batto; 2, Maredydd; 3, David ; 4, Hugh ; and 5, Gruffydd.

Y Batto ap Madog married Mallt, daughter of Ithel ab David ab Cynwrig ab Rotpert ab Iorwerth ab Rhirid ab Madog ab Ednowain Bendew, and had issue two daughters, co-heiresses, one of whom, named Janet, married John Almor of Almor or Aylmor, one of the Marshalls of the Hall to Henry VII. The other, named Lleuci, married Ieuan ab Einion ab Iolyn ab Iorwerth of Bwras or Borasham, younger son of Llywelyn ab Gruffydd ab Cadwgan, Lord of Eyton, Erlysh, and Bwras, by whom she had two daughters, co-heirs—

I. Margaret, ux. Howel ab Jenkyn ab Ieuan Llwyd, and

II. Angharad, co-heiress of Trefalun, ux. Jenkyn ab David ab Gruffydd of Trefalun ab David ab Llywelyn ab David Hên ab Goronwy of Mortyn (Burton) and Llai, by whom she had an only daughter and heiress named Mallt, who married Richard Trevor, fourth son of John Trevor ab Iorwerth or Edward ab David, third son of Ednyfed Gam of Llys Pengwern in Nantheudwy. By this alliance, the Trevors became possessed of Trefalun, which is still in the possession of their descendants.

TREFALUN.

Hengwrt MS. 110.

Llywelyn, fourth son of David Hen ab—Erddylad, dau. of Goronwy ab
Goronwy ab Iorwerth ab Howel ab More- | Llywelyn ab Cynwrig Efell.
iddig ab Sanddef Hardd, or the Hand- | *Gules*, on a bend *argent*, a
some, Lord of Mortyn and Llai. *Vert*, | lion passant *sable*.
semé of broomslips a lion rampant *or*.

David ab ═Gwenllian, d. of David Goch ab Heilin Fychan, descended from
Llywelyn. | Hwfa ab Ithel Felyn. Lewys Dwnn, vol. ii, p. 318, states
| that Gwenllian was the daughter of Madog Goch ab Heilin
| Fychan.

Gruffydd ═Janet, d. of Robert ab Bleddyn ab Robert. *Argent*, a chevron
ab David. | inter three boar's heads couped *sable*.

David ab Gruffydd of Trefalun.═Margaret, d. of Ieuan ab Howel ab Ieuan
ob. 1476. | ab Gruffydd.

Jenkyn ab David of═Angharad, d. and co-heiress of Ieuan ab Einion ab
Trefalun. | Iolyn ab Iorwerth of Bwras, ab Llywelyn ab Gruff-
| ydd ab Cadwgan, Lord of Eyton Erlys and Bwras.

Mallt, heiress of	William═..., d. of Howel ab	Gruff-	Elen, ux.
Trefalun, ux.	ab David	David ab Gruffydd	ydd of	Robert Sut-
Richard Trevor.	of Tref-	Fychan of Plâs yn	Llanest-	ton ab
	alun.	Horslli. *Sable*,	yn.	David of
		three roses *argent*.		Sutton and
				Gwersyllt.

Catherine, heiress of Trefalun, ux. John Langford of Rhuddin.

TREFALUN.

Cae Cyriog MS.; Harl. MS. 4181.

Iorwerth Foel, Lord of Chirk, Maelor Sacsneg, and Nanheudwy, married, as previously stated (vol. i, p. 313), Gwladys, daughter and co-heiress of Iorwerth ab Gruffydd ab Heilin of Fron Goch in Mochnant. This lady was buried in Hanmer Church, where her tomb yet remains, with this inscription round the lid of the stone coffin, " HIC IACET WLADYS VXOR IERWERTH VOYL. ORATE P. EA." In the space within the inscription is a very fine foliated cross, almost identical with that described by Camden, i, 12, as being at St. Burian's in Cornwall. By this lady, Iorwerth Foel had issue five sons, of whom the fourth was Ednyfed Gam, who had Llys Pengwern in Nanheudwy for his share of his father's territories.

David, the third son of Ednyfed Gam, married twice ; his first wife was Gwenllian, daughter and co-heiress of Adda Goch of Trevor, ab Ieuaf ab Adda ab Awr of Trevor. This Adda Goch bore the arms of Tudor Trevor in a border gobonated *argent* and *gules*, pellatée counterchanged. By this lady David had a son named Iorwerth, of whom presently. David married secondly, Morfydd, relict of Sir Richard Croft of Croft Castle in Herefordshire, Knt., and third daughter of Gruffydd Fychan, Lord of Cynllaith Owain, and Baron of Glyndyfrdwy, by whom he had a daughter Margaret, who married first, Robert Llwyd ab Gruffydd ab Goronwy ;

and secondly, Howel ab Llywelyn of Llwyn On in the manor of Tref Abynt or Abyntbury. See vol. ii, p. 120.

Iorwerth ab David, who, at his death, was buried in Valle Crucis Abbey, married Angharad, daughter of Robert Puleston of Emeral or Ember Hall in Maelor Saesneg, and Lowri, sister of Owain Glyndwr, and daughter of the above-named Gruffydd Fychan, Baron of Glyndyfrdwy, by whom he had issue five sons, and a daughter named Rose, who married Ottwel Worsley, Esq., by whom she had issue four daughters,

1. . . . . ux. . . . . Whetnall, by whom she had issue a son, Sir Richard Whetnall, and a daughter, who married Sir Edward Powys.

2. . . . . ux. Sir James Gainford, Knt., by whom she had issue two sons, James and Nicholas, and two daughters, of whom one married Sir William Courtney, Knt., and another married Sir William Fiennes, Knt.

3. . . . . ux. Lord . . . . Howard, brother of the Duke of Norfolk, by whom she had two sons ; she married, secondly, Sir John Ali, Knt.

4. . . . . ux. . . . . Lee, by whom she had issue Edward Lee, Archbishop of York, and two other sons.

The five sons of Iorwerth ab David were, 1. Robert Trevor ; 2, John Trevor ; 3, Richard Trevor, ancestor of the Trevors of Croes Oswald ; 4, Otwel Trevor, who married Catherine, eldest daughter of Howel of Glasgoed ab Maurice Gethin of Garth Eryr in Mochnant ; and 5, Edward Trevor, who married the Lady Tiptoft, Countess of Worcester.

Robert Trevor, the eldest son of Iorwerth ab David, was Steward of Denbigh, Sheriff of Flintshire, Justice and Chamberlain of North Wales. He married . . . . daughter of Gwilym ab Gruffydd, by whom he had no issue, but left at his death, which occurred in 1492, a natural son, Sir William Trevor, Chaplain to John ab Richard, Abbot of Llanegwystl, predecessor to David ab John ab Iorwerth ab Ieuan Baladr. Sir William Trevor had a natural son, John Trevor, who married and had issue a son, John Trevor, the father of Randal Trevor of Chester.

John Trevor Hên, the second son of Iorwerth ab David, married Agnes, daughter and co-heiress of Pyers Cambrey ab Perkin Camber of Trallwng, ab Sir Roger Camber, Knt. The mother of Agnes was the daughter and heir to Cumus and heiress to Llys Main in Llaneurgain. This Pyers Cambrey had two other daughters, one married to Mr. Blunt, and was mother to Sir Edward and Richard Blunt, Knts., and Peter and Thomas Blunt. She married, secondly, Mr. Welsh. The third daughter married Mr. Hopton, and had issue Edward Henry and several others. Agnes, the wife of John Trevor, died in 1484, and he died in 1493, leaving issue, besides two daughters, Elen, ux. John Llwyd ab John ab Deicws Vongam of Coed Abynt, or Llwyn y Cnotiau, and Catherine, ux. Howel ab Rhys ab Maredydd of Hiraethog, four sons,

i. Robert Trevor, who married Catherine, daughter and heiress of Llywelyn ab Ithel of Plâs Têg and Y Wyddgrûg. He died in September 1487, before his father, and was buried in Llanegwystl, or Valle Crucis Abbey. His widow married, secondly, Rhys ab Howel of Ystymllyn. See Yr Hôb.

ii. Edward Trevor, Constable of Whittington Castle, who died in 1537, and ancestor of the Trevors of Bryn Cunallt and Treflech.

iii. Roger Trevor of Pentref Cynwrig, ancestor of the Trevors of Pentref Cynwrig, Bodyn Foel, and Trawsgoed.

iv. Richard Trevor of Trefalun. He married Mallt, daughter and sole heiress of Jenkyn ab David ab Gruffydd of Trefalun, ab David ab Llywelyn, fourth son of David Hên ab Goronwy of Burton (Mortyn) and Llai (*vert*, semé of broomslips, a lion rampant *or*). See p. 195.

Richard Trevor of Trefalun died in 1534, leaving issue by his wife Mallt, besides a daughter, Annesta, who married first, Howel ab Rhys ab Howel of Cynllaith, and secondly, Rhys ab Ieuan of Trewen in Iâl, a son and heir,

John Trevor of Trefalun, who married Margaret, daughter and heir of David ab Rhys ab Cynwrig of

Cwm, by whom he had issue three sons, 1, John ; 2, Richard ; and 3, Edward ; and two daughters, Jane, ux. Edward ab John ab Nicholas of Llanfair, and Margaret.

John Trevor of Trefalun, the eldest son, married Anne, daughter of Randle Broughton of Broughton, in the manor of Y Gwrthymp in Maelor Saesneg (*ermine,* a lion statant gardant *gules*), by whom he had issue four sons, 1, John ; 2, Randolph Trevor, who married Elen, daughter of William Royden, and widow of Roger Wynn ; 3, David Trevor ; and 4, Edward Trevor ; and three daughters, 1, Margaret, ux. Roger Jones of Llwyn On, in Trefabynt or Abyntbury (*ermine,* a lion rampant *sable*) ; 2, Catherine, ux. David Alunton of Alunton (Trefalun) (*azure,* a lion salient *or*) ; and 3, Dorothy, who married, first, Lewys ab William ab Llywelyn of Mortyn or Burton, ab Madog Fychan ab Madog ab Deiews ab Madog ab David Goch ab David Hên ab Goronwy of Mortyn (Burton) and Llai, and, secondly, John Wynn ab William of Mortyn (Burton).

John Trevor of Trefalun, the eldest son, married Mary, daughter and heiress of Sir George Bruges of London, Knt., of the family of Bruges of Gloucestershire and Worcestershire. He built the present house of Trefalun, and died July 15th, 1589, and was buried at St. Bride's, Fleet Street, London. By his wife Mary he had issue, besides two daughters, 1, Gwenhwyffryd, ux. Edward Puleston of Trefalun, and 2, Ermine, ux. Robert Lloyd ab Edward of Hersedd in Ystrad Alun, five sons,

1. Sir Richard Trevor of Trefalun, Knt., Governor of Newry and the counties of Down and Armagh, and Vice-Admiral of North Wales, and High Sheriff for co. Denbigh in 1610. In the year 1638, when he was eighty years old, he erected his own monument in Gresford Church, representing himself in armour, kneeling ; and his wife Catherine by him. The inscription informs us that it was chiefly in memory of his lady that he caused this memorial to be erected. There is, however, another monument to his lady, who is placed kneeling with her five daughters. At Trefalun is a singular portrait of Sir Richard dressed in black. Above, hang his

arms, with the words "*So then*"; beneath are some me-
dicines, and "*Now thus*"; allusive to his former and
present state.[1] He lived, as he tells us, to see his
children's children's children. He married Catherine,
daughter of Roger Puleston of Emral, Esq. (*sable*, three
mullets *argent*), by whom he had issue five daughters,
co-heirs, 1, Magdalene, who married, first, Arthur, son
and heir of Sir Henry Bagnall, High Marshall of Ireland,
and secondly, Sir Arthur Tyrringham of Tyrringham,
Knight of the Bath ; 2, Mary, ux. Evan, son and heir of
Sir John Lloyd of Bodidris in Iâl, Knight-Banneret ;
3, Anne, *ob. infans ;* 4, Dorothy, ux. Sir John Hanmer
of Hanmer, Bart.; and 5, Margaret, ux. John Griffith of
Lleyn. She died in 1625.

ii. Sir John Trevor, knighted at Windsor in 1618,
Surveyor of the Navy and Comptroller of the Household. He bought Plâs Têg from David Trevor of that
place, and built the present house there, which he made
his residence. He died in 1629, and was buried at
Llanestyn in Yr Hôb, where there is a monument erected
to his memory ; of whom presently.

iii. Randle Trevor of Cornwall.

iv. Sir Sackville Trevor. He had the command of
one of the men-of-war, sent over to Spain in 1623, to
bring back the Prince of Wales, afterwards Charles I.
He subsequently distinguished himself greatly in the
war with France in 1626. He married, first, Eleanor,
daughter of Sir John Savage of Rocksavage in Cheshire,
Knt., and widow of Sir Henry Bagnall, Knight-Marshall
of Ireland, and secondly, Elizabeth, fourth daughter of
Cynwrig Eyton of Eyton, Esq., and Elizabeth his wife,
daughter of Sir Richard Brooke of Norton Priory, in the
county palatine of Chester, Knt.

v. Sir Thomas Trevor, born 1586, knighted in 1620,
Solicitor-General to Prince Charles, and Baron of the
Exchequer. He married[2] a daughter of William Her-

---

[1] Pennant's *Tour in Wales*, vol. i, p. 410.

[2] According to a note in *Lewys Dwnn*, vol. ii, p. 354, he married
Prudence, daughter of Henry Boteler, Esq. In 1641, he was, with
others impeached, but from which he was honourably acquitted.

bert, Esq., by whom he had a son and heir, Sir Thomas
Trevor, who was created a Baronet in 1641, and a
Knight of the Bath. As he died without male issue,
the Baronetcy became extinct.

Sir John Trevor of Plâs Têg, Knt., the second son of
John Trevor of Trefalun, Esq., married Margaret,
daughter of Hugh Trevanion of Carihays in Cornwall,
Esq., by whom he had issue four sons, 1, Sir John
Trevor; 2, Richard Trevor; 3, Charles; and 4, William;
and two daughters, 1, Anne, ux. Sir Charles Williams of
Llangybi Castle in Monmouthshire, Bart.; and 2, Jane,
ux. Sir Edward Fitton of Gosworth in Gloucestershire,
Bart.

Sir John Trevor of Plâs Têg, Knt., succeeded to the
Trefalun estate on the death of his uncle Sir Richard in
1638. He married Anne, daughter of Edmund Hampden, by whom he had issue three sons—1, Sir John; 2,
Richard Trevor of Merton College, Oxford, Doctor of
Physic of the University of Padua, who died in 1676,
and was buried in St. Dunstan's in the West, in London;
and 3, Ralph Trevor, a Hamburgh merchant, *ob. s. p.*
He married and had issue one son, Ralph Trevor, and a
daughter Elizabeth, who married, first, Hezekiah Burton,
S.T.P., Rector of Barnes and Prebendary of Norwich,
and, secondly, she married Edward Fowler, S.T.P.,
Bishop of Gloucester. Sir John Trevor had also five
daughters, 1, Elizabeth, ux. William, son and heir of Sir
William Masham of Oates in Essex, Bart.; 2, Susanna,
ux. John Morley of Glynde in Sussex. Their son, Sir
John Morley, married Elizabeth Clark, and left Glynde
to his cousin, John Trevor; 3, Margaret, ux. Colonel
John Fielder of Burrough Court in Hampshire; 4, Anna,
who married, first, Colonel Robert Wilding, and secondly,
Thomas Lane of Hackney. The daughter of Anna Trevor
and Colonel Wilding married, first, Sir Robert Barnard,
and secondly, Thomas, Lord Trevor; and 5, Jane, who
married, first, ... Elwes of Lilford, co. Northampton,
Esq., and secondly, the Hon. Sir Francis Compton, son
of the Earl of Northampton.

Sir John Trevor, Envoy Extraordinary to the Court of France. He was knighted by Charles II, and constituted one of his principal Secretaries of State; on his return from an embassy in France in 1668, he was made a Privy Councillor; which high offices he fulfilled until his decease in 1672, at the age of forty-seven. His father survived him rather more than twelve months. He married Ruth, daughter and heir of Edward Hampden of Great Hampden in Buckinghamshire, and co-heir of her uncle, Sir Alexander Hampden of Hartwell in Buckinghamshire, Knt., by whom he had issue five sons and three daughters.

i. John Trevor of Trefalun and Plâs Têg.

ii. Sir Thomas Trevor. He attained such high reputation at the bar, that he was, in 1692, made Solicitor-General, and received the honour of Knighthood; in three years afterwards he became Attorney-General, and, on the accession of Queen Anne, was made Lord Chief Justice of the Common Pleas. On December 31st, 1711, he was created Baron Trevor of Bromham; in 1725, he was made Lord Privy Seal, and, in 1727, Lord Chief Justice of Great Britain. In 1730, he was made President of the Privy Council, only six weeks before his death. He married, first, Elizabeth, daughter of John Searle of Finchley, by whom he had issue two sons and three daughters—1, Thomas, second Lord Trevor, who, by Elizabeth, his wife, daughter of Timothy Burrell of Cuckfield in Sussex, had a daughter Elizabeth, who married Charles Spencer, Duke of Marlborough; 2, John, third Lord Trevor, one of his Majesty's Judges for Wales. He married Elizabeth, daughter of Sir Richard Steele of Caermarthen, by whom he had an only daughter, Diana Trevor. The three daughters of Sir Thomas were, 1, Anne Trevor of Southgate in Middlesex; 2, Letitia, ux. Robert Cock of Camberwell, Surrey, Esq.; and 3, Elizabeth.

Sir Thomas Trevor married, secondly, Anne, daughter of Colonel Robert Wilding, and relict of Sir Robert Barnard of Brampton, Bart., by whom he had three other sons: 3, Robert, of whom presently; 4, Edward;

and 5, Richard Trevor of Glynde, Bishop of St. David's and of Durham.

Robert, the third son, succeeded as fourth Lord Trevor. He was Envoy Extraordinary Plenipotentiary to the States General, and Commissioner of the Revenue in Ireland. In 1775, he was created Lord Viscount Hampden. He married Constantia, daughter of the Baron de Huybert, Lord of Kruyningen, in Zealand, by whom he had issue, besides a daughter, Maria-Constantia, who married the Earl of Suffolk, two sons—1, Thomas Trevor, second Lord Viscount Hampden, and fifth Lord Trevor, who died in 1824, *s. p.*; and 2, John Trevor, third Lord Viscount Hampden, and sixth Lord Trevor, who died in 1824, *s. p.*, when all his honours became extinct.

iii. Hampden Trevor.

iv. Edward Trevor.

v. Richard Trevor, who by Mary his wife, daughter of . . . . . . Hornby of Chertsey, had issue one son, Richard Trevor, and a daughter, Mary Trevor.

The three daughters of Sir John Trevor and Ruth his wife, were, 1, Mary, Maid of Honour to Queen Katherine ; 2, Anne, ux. John Spencer of Maulin, in Sussex ; and 3, Elizabeth, ux. John Borrett of Shoreham, Prothonotary.

John Trevor of Trefalun and Plâs Têg, the eldest son of Sir John, married Elizabeth, daughter of . . . . Clarke, and relict of John Morley of Glynde, in Sussex, and who married, thirdly, Sir . . . . Cutts, by whom he had issue two sons, 1, John Morley Trevor, of whom presently ; and 2, Thomas Trevor of East Barnet, Barrister-at-Law ; and two daughters, 1, Elizabeth, ux David Pothill of Chepstead, in Kent ; and 2, Arabella, who married, first, Robert Heath of Lewes, in Sussex, and secondly, Brigadier-General Montague, brother of George, first Earl of Halifax.

John Morley Trevor of Trefalun, Plâs Têg, and Glynde, who died in 1719, married Elizabeth, daughter of Edmund Montague of Horton, in Northamptonshire, by whom he had, besides seven daughters, a son and heir,

John Trevor of Trefalun, Plâs Têg, and Glynde, Commissioner of the Admiralty. He married Elizabeth, daughter of Sir Thomas Frankland of Thirtleby, in Yorkshire, and died in 1743 *s. p.*, and devised his estates in North Wales to five of his six surviving sisters.

Of the seven daughters of John Morley Trevor, Ruth, Arabella, Mary, and Margaret, died unmarried; the three others were,

Lucy Trevor, who married Edward Rice of Newton and Dynevor Castle, by whom she had a son, the Right Hon. George Rice, who married, in 1756, Cecil, Baroness Dynevor, daughter of William Talbot, first Earl Talbot, created, in 1780, Baron Dynevor of Dynevor Castle, with remainder, failing his issue male, to his daughter, Lady Cecil, who succeeded her father, at his death in 1782, as Baroness Dynevor. By this lady, George Rice had a son and heir, George Talbot, Lord Dynevor, ancestor of George Rice Rice Trevor, fourth Baron Dynevor, who assumed the additional surname of Trevor, as inheritor of the estates of the Trevors of Glynde.

Anne Trevor, of whom presently. She married the Hon. Colonel George Boscawen, third son of the Lord Viscount Falmouth.

Gertrude Trevor, who married the Hon. Charles Roper, third son of Lord Teynham, and the Baroness Dacre, his second wife, by whom she had issue two sons, 1, Charles Trevor Roper, Lord Dacre, who died *s. p.* in 1794 ; and Henry Roper, who died *s. p.* in 1787 ; and one daughter, Gertrude, who succeeded to her brother as Baroness Dacre, and married Thomas Brand Holles of The Hoo, by whom she had issue Thomas (Lord Dacre) and Major-General the Hon. Henry Otway Trevor, who assumed the arms and name of Trevor, according to the will of the late Viscount Hampden.

Charles, Lord Dacre, married Mary, daughter and heiress of Sir . . . . Fludyer, Knt., and executed a will in favour of his widow, who eventually, partly under her husband's will, and partly by purchase from her sister-in-law, Gertrude, became the owner of a moiety of the estates so devised by John Trevor to his five sisters.

A partition of these estates was effected between Lady Dacre and George Boscawen of Trefalun, Esq., M.P. for Truro, son and heir of the above-named Anne Trevor, and the Hon. Colonel Boscawen, about the year 1790 ; and Plâs Têg fell to the lot of the Dowager Lady Dacre.

Anne Trevor, co-heiress of Trefalun, married, as before stated, the Hon. Colonel George Boscawen, by whom she had issue, besides two daughters, Anne Boscawen, Maid of Honour to Queen Charlotte, and Charlotte Boscawen, both of whom died unmarried, two sons,

I. George Boscawen of Trefalun, M.P. for Truro. He married Annabella, daughter of Sir William Bunbury, Bart., and died *s. p.*

II. William Boscawen, Barrister-at-Law. He married Charlotte, daughter of the Rev. James Ibbetson, D.D., Archdeacon of St. Alban's, by whom he had four daughters, co-heiresses.

I. Grace Trevor Charlotte Boscawen, who married William Fleming, Esq., and died *s. p.* 1781.

II. Anne Arabella Boscawen, who married the Rev. Christopher Parkins, by whom she had a son and heir, Wm. Trevor Parkins, M.A., Barrister-at-Law, who, by his wife, Margaret Annabella Jane, daughter of the Rev. William Lloyd of Blaen y Glyn in Merioneth, Rector of Llanfaethlu in Môn, and descended from Cadwgan of Nannau, Prince of Powys, has issue a son and heir, William Trevor Parkins, B.A., of Balliol College, Oxford, and two daughters—1, Arabella Margaret Trevor Parkins ; and 2, Mary Estelle Trevor Parkins. The first born son, William Trevor Parkins, died an infant.

III. Catherine Emily Boscawen, married, first, Henry Rowlands, Esq., and secondly, the Rev. Fletcher Fleming of Bayrigg, Westmoreland.

IV. Elizabeth Mary Boscawen, married T. Griffith, Esq., by whom she had a son and heir, Boscawen Trevor Griffith, Esq., who, by his wife, Helen Sophia, daughter of Vice-Admiral Norwich Duff, has issue two sons—1, Boscawen Trevor Griffith, and 2, Arthur Sackville Trevor Griffith, and two daughters—1, Helen Evelyn Trevor Griffith, and 2, Alice Catherine Trevor Griffith.

SPECIAL COMMISSIONS. DENBIGH, No. 3402.
WRIT OF REBELLION AGAINST JOHN TREVOR.
29 *Eliz.* (1587).

Elizabeth dei gra' etc. Dil'tis nobis Roberto Brock, Rob'to Whitby, Ric'o Woodfyne et Joh'i Okyle gen'o's sal't'm. Quia Joh's Trevor de Trevallin in com' Denbigh armiger cui p' publicas p'clamac'o'es p' vic' Denbigh et fflint in diu's ,locis cor'd'm com' virtute se'paliu' brui' eisd'm vic' direct ex p'te' n'ra p'ceptu' fuit' q'd id'm Joh'es Trevor sub pena ligeantie sue coram Baron de Scc'io n'ro apud Westm' ad certu' diem iam p'terit' p'sonaliter comp'eret, mandato tamen n'ro in ea p'te parere manifeste contempsit. Ideo vobis coniunctim vel diuisim mandam', q'd prefac' Joh'em Trevor vbicu'q' invent' fuit infra Regnu' Anglie tanq'm Rebellem et legis n're contempt' Attachiat' vel attachiari faciatis vel vnus v'r'm attach' vel attachiari faciat. Ita q'd eu' heab' vel h'er ifaciat' vel vnus v'r'm heab' vel h'eri faciat coram Baron de Scc'io n'ro apud Westm' a die pasche p'x' futuro in xv dies. Ad respondend' sup' hiis que sibi obiicient' tunc ib'm, ac ad faciend' vlterius et recipiend' quod Curia n'ra considerauit in hac p'te. Dam' enim vniu' sis et singulis vic maiorib' batt'. Constabular' et al' officiar' ministris et ligeis n'ris quibuscu'q' t'm infra lib'tat' q'm extra tenore pii'cu' firmit in mandat' q'd vob' et cuil't v'r'm in execuc'o'e p'missor' intenden' sint et assisten' in om'ib' diligent' p'ut decet. In cuius rei testimoniu' has l'ras n'ras fieri fecim' paten' T. Rogero Manwood milit' apud Westm' septimo die februarii anno r' r' 29° p' Rotliu' memorand' de eod'm Anno Regine hui' hillar' Commissionu' et l'rar' paten' Rot'lo'. Et p' quandam ordinac'o'em in Scc'io remanem' et in custod' Remem'atoris Regine ib'm existen'.

FFANSHAW'.

Responc' Rob'ti Brocke et Rob'ti Whitby duor' Com'issionar' infra no'i'ator'.

Virtute istius Com'issionis nobis et aliis direct' diligent' scrutati sumus infra no'i'at' Joh'em Trevor t'm' apud mansional' suam domu' in Trevallyn in com' Denbigh, q'm in diu's's aliis locis in p'd' com' Denbigh et in com' Flynte infra content'. Sed ip'm p'd'c'm Joh'em Trevor neque viuius invenire p' q'd ip'm Joh'em attachiar' nullo modo potuimus s'c'd'm tenorem Com'issionis p'd' p'ut interius nobis r'cipit'.

ROB'T BROCKE,
ROB'T WHITBY.

Libat' in Cur' 8° die Maii anno 19° Regine Elizabeth p' man' iufrano'i'at Rob'ti Whitby vnu' Com'issionar'.

INSCRIPTION ON THE MONUMENT OF JOHN TREVOR OF TREFALUN IN GRESFORD CHURCH.

Sion Trevor Trevalyn Ysgwier, y 19 o dad i dad o Tvdvr Trevor, a fy farw yn Lhvndain ymis Mchevin 1589, ci esgyrn ef ci vab ai aer S'r Richard Trevor a barodd ci mvdo ir Feddrod honn i orphwys gidai henafiaid, fal wrth ymado a'r byd i dvmvnodd. Blynyddoedd ei icincktid a dros-fwriodd ef yn rhyveloedd Frainck dann Frenhin Henry 8. Ei ganol-fyd a gyfoesodd ef yn llywodraeth a gwassanaeth ei anedigaethwlad. Ef a briododd Mary merch George Bridges, Yscwier; ac a fy iddo o honi bvmp o vcibion a dwy o verched. Sef 1. S'r Richard Trevor Marchog. Depvty-Lif'enant y Sir honn, yr hwn a briododd Katrin merch Rocsier Pvleston o Emral Yscwier, fab S'r Edward Pvleston, Marchog. 2. Sion Trevor Yscwier, Golygwr ar Lynges ardderchawg y Vrenhines, yr hwn a briododd Marged merch Hyw Trevanion, Carihays Ynghornyw Yscwier, vab S'r Hyw Trevanian, Marchoc. 3. Rondl Trevor, a fy farw yn cyfagos arol ci dad. 4. Sackvil Trevor, Capten yn awryw o Longav 'r vrenhines. 5. Thomas Trevor, Myfyriwr y Cyfraith. 6. Winiffred, a briodes Edward Pvleston o Al'ynton Yscwier T. ac Ermin a briodes Robert Lloid o Hersedd Yscwier.

LANGFORD OF TREFALUN AND RHUDDIN.

Harl. MS. 1971 ; *Lewys Dwnn*, vol. i, p. 325.

Henry (or Robert) Langford, co. Leicester.   *Gules*, a shoveler *argent*, membered *or*.

| a

| a

John Langford of Leicestershire, Constable of Rhuddin—Catherine, dau. of Castle, and Steward of Dyffryn Clwyd, 4 and 9 Henry IV (1403, 1412). As appears also by a record at Rhuddin, 7 Henry VI, a deed, granted to David Thelwall, of certain lands in Maes Maen Cymro, in 9 Henry IV. "Iliis testibus Jo'he' de Langford, tunc Constabulario de Ruthin D'no Edw'do tunc Receptore ib'm D'no Thoma de Thelwall." Sir John de Hopton granted the Manors of Hardborough; Woodcock, Palington, and Fulbroc, in the county of Warwick, to John, son of Henry Langford, Dat. 10, R. II, 1387.

A Court was held at Rhuddin before John Langford, Steward of Dyffryn Clwyd the next ..... after St. Martin, the Bishop. 1 Henry IV.

ThomasGervys of Rhuddin. *Sable*, a sword *argent*, pomel *or*, a Catherine wheel *argent*. for Gerard Goch.

Richard Langford, Constable of the—Alicia, dau. and heir of Howel ab Castle of Rhuddin, 19 Henry VI (1431). *Ob.* 12 July 1466. Edmund, Lord Grey[1] and Hastings, granted a patent to Richard Langford, and Edward his son, of the Constableship of the Castle of Rhuddin, dated at Wrest, 13 July, 25 Henry VI. The same Edmund gave the Receivership of the Lordship of Rhuddin to the said Richard Langford, at Torperley, 19 Henry VI.

Gruffydd ab Morgan ab Cynwrig ab Gwilym ab Thomas ab Einion ab Cadwgan ab Goronwy ab Owain ab Uchdryd ab Edwin, Prince of Tegeingl. She died 10th August, 4 Edw. IV, relict of John Wentall, *fil.* Ric'i. *Argent*, a cross flory engrailed *sable*, inter four Cornish choughs ppr.

Edward Langford, Constable of the—Elen, d. of John Dutton of Dutton, Castle of Rhuddin, *ob.* 10 Nov. 16 Henry VII (1447). Henry VI granted the Escheatorship and Attorneyship of Denbigh lands to Edward Langford for life, for his good services against Richard, Duke of York. Dated at Northampton, 4 Feb., 38 Henry VI.

ab Sir Pyers ab. Edmund ab Sir Thomas ab Sir Hugh ab Hugh ab Thomas ab Sir Hugh ab Hugh ab Hudard, by Dame Alice, Lady of Dutton; she died 5 Edward IV. Quarterly, 1st and 4th *argent*, a bend *sable*; 2nd and 3rd *gules*, a fret *or*.

John Langford=Catherine, d. and heir of William ab David of Trefalun of Rhuddin, and Mortyn (which David *ob.* 1476) ab Gruffydd ab *ob.* 26 Dec., 23 David ab Llywelyn ab David ab Goronwy ab Iorwerth Henry VIII. ab Howel ab Moreiddig ab Sanddef Hardd, or the Handsome, Lord of Mortyn. *Vert*, semé of broomslips, a lion rampant *or*.

Richard Langford of Trefalun and Rhuddin.

[1] The Greys became possessed of the Castle of Rhuddin and the Cantref of Dyffryn Clwyd, at the time of the conquest of Wales by the English. *Rotulus Wallie*, 10 Edw. I (1282): "Castrum de Rutthin, et Cantredum de Desfreneloyt, et terra Wenchelinæ de Lascy, confirmata Reginaldo de Grey, per Manum Regis. Apud Dinby, 23 Octobris."

Richard Langford of Trefalun and Rhuddin, 1586, married twice. His first wife was Margaret, daughter of John Almor of Almor, ab John ab Ieuan ab David Almor ab David Sant ab Ithel ab Goronwy ab Einion ab Owain ab Trahaiarn ab Ithel ab Eunydd, Lord of Trefalun and Y Groesford, by whom he had issue five sons and three daughters.

i. John Langford, of whom presently.

ii. Edward Langford, who married Catherine, daughter of Humphrey Lloyd of Llai or Leighton, High Sheriff for co. Montgomery in 1540 (*sable*, three horse's heads erased *argent*), by whom he had issue, besides two daughters, Pernel, and Ermine, ux. Richard ab John of Wysbock, a son and heir, William Langford, who married Elizabeth, daughter of Walter Hockleton ab John ab Walter ab William ab Walter ab William ab Walter ab William ab Walter de Hockleton, 34 Henry III, ab Hugh ab Hugh de Woderton (*argent*, a fess *sable*, fretty *or*, between three crescents of the second), by whom he had a son and heir, Thomas Langford, 1613.

iii. William Langford ; iv, Roger Langford ; and v, Mathey Langford.

The three daughters of Richard Langford were, 1, Katherine, ux. Morgan ab Thomas ; 2, Elizabeth, ux. Thomas Wyton ; and 3, Anne, ux. John Wynne ab Thomas, by whom she had two sons, Edward and John.

John Langford of Trefalun, died March 27th, 1606, and was buried in Gresford Church. He married Katherine, daughter of John ab Henry Gervys of Rhuddin (*sable*, a sword pointed downwards *argent*, hilt and pomel *or*, a buckle *argent*, and a Catherine wheel and border of the second), by whom he had a son and heir,

Richard Langford of Trefalun and Rhuddin, High Sheriff for co. Denbigh in 1640, *ob.* 1643. He married Elizabeth, daughter of Thomas Parry Wynn ab John ab Harri of Tref Rhuddin ab Sir John, Parson of Llanynys ab Gruffydd Goch[1] of Pentref Coch near Rhuddin, ab

---

[1] Gruffydd Goch built the church of Cyffylliog, in the comot of Llanerch, as a chapel-of-ease to Llanynys, which parish lies partly in

Icuan of Ceinmeirch ab David Fychan ab Iorwerth ab
David ab Iorwerth ab Cowryd ab Cadvan, Lord of Ceinmeirch (Gwehelaeth Ceinmeirch), ab Gaelawg Gawr ab
Iddig, lineally descended from Cadell Deyrnllwg, King
of Teyrnllwg, now called Powys (*argent*, three boar's
heads couped *sable*, tusked *or*, and langued *gules*), for
Cowryd ab Cadvan.[1] On an escutcheon at Trefalun
(General Townshend's), painted on wood, are the arms of
Langford (*gules*, a shoveler *argent*, impaling arms;
quarterly, 1st and 4th *argent*, three boar's heads couped
sable; 2nd and 3rd, *sable*, three horse's heads erased
argent), with this inscription : " Elizabeth, wife of
Richard Langford of Trevalyn, Esq., deceased on the
twelfth day of December, An' D'ni 1657, being aged
seventy-eight years, and having had twenty children."
She died at Chester and was buried at Gresford. By
this lady Richard Langford had issue twenty children,
sixteen of whom are as follow, and the remaining four
must have died infants.

1. John Langford, of whom presently ; 2. William
Langford, who married Hellen, daughter of . . . . Wood,
and sister of Owain Wood of Llangwyfan in Môn
(quarterly, 1st and 4th *argent*, a chevron inter three
owls *gules*--2nd and 3rd *azure*, three squirrels rampant
or); 3, Edward, *ob. s. p.* ; 4, Theophilus ; 5, George,[2] who
married Anne, daughter and heir of William Lloyd ab
John Lloyd of Rhuddin ; 6. Simon of Chester, a mercer ;
and 7, Richard, who died young.

The nine daughters of Richard Langford were, 1,
Mary, ux. William Ha...er of Couley Hall, co. Lancaster ;
2, Elizabeth, ux. Edward Sautry of Burton ; 3, Catherine, ux. Walter Caradog of Monmouth ; 4, Jane, ux.
Edward Pryse of Ffynogion in Llanfair Dyffryn Clwyd,

---

the comots of Llanerch and Dogfeilin, in the cantref of Dyffryn
Clwyd, and partly in the comot of Ceinmeirch, in the cantref of
Ystrad.

[1] See *Archæologia Cambrensis*, October 1876, p. 263.

[2] George Langford had issue by his wife two sons, John and William ; and three daughters, Katherine, Alice, and Mary.

io dda. *ob.* March 26th, 1659 ; three died young ; 8, Rebecca, ux. Charles Goodman of Glan Hespin, High Sheriff for co. Denbigh in 1613 (party per pale *ermine* and *erminois*, an eagle displayed with two heads *or*, on a canton *azure*, a martlet of the third); and 9, Elen, ux. Major Thomas Swyft, in Anglesey or Môn.

John Langford of Trefalun, the eldest son of Richard, married Elizabeth, daughter of Simon Thelwall of Plâs y Ward and Dorothy his wife, relict of Andrew Maredydd of Glan Tanad, by whom he had issue, besides a daughter, Dorothy, ux. William Mostyn of Rhyd, Esq., two sons, 1, Richard, who died *s. p.*, and 2, John.

John Langford, the second son, succeeded to Trefalun, and was High Sheriff for co. Denbigh in 1677.   He was living in 1681, and married Mary, daughter of Jonathan Green of Stapleford, Esq., by whom he had issue, besides a daughter, Mary, three sons, 1, Richard ; 2, Jonathan ; and 3, John.

Here the *Harl. MS.* 1971 ends.   The following information relative to the Langford family has been kindly sent me by William Trevor Parkins, Esq., of Glasfryn, to whom I am much indebted for a great amount of information relative to the families who possessed lands in the manors of Is y Coed and Mortyn, called in English Burton.

It is stated in Ormerod's *Cheshire*, vol. ii, p. 175, that John Langford of Trefalyn, Esq., married Mary, daughter of Jonathan Bruer of Bruer Stapleford, May 12th, 1760 (1660 ?).

In the Gresford Register I find as follows :—

1686.

" John ye son of Mr. John Langford, was buried December 1st."

" Mr. John Langford was buried January 2nd."

" Jonathan, ye son of Mr. John Langford, was buried January 14th."

1720.

" George Langford of Trevallin, Esq., buried the 28th day of May 1720."

This George Langford seems to have been succeeded at Trevalyn by a sister. I have a copy extract from the Pulford Register, which I transcribe.

" Bruer, Benjamin, of Hunley, in Waverton parish, and Mrs. Dorothie Langford of Trevallin, in Gresford, married by licence at Pulford, 3rd August 1723."

Benjamin Bruer appears to have lived at Trevalyn till 1747. Mrs. Dorothie Bruer, his wife, was buried at Gresford, March 10th, 1732.

In 1753, William Travers, Esq., how I do not know, appears to have become the owner of the Langford estate in Trevalyn. He died in 1765, as did Edward Travers, who succeeded him in 1777. Ursula, the widow of Edward Travers, died in 1796, and the Rev. Robert Twiss became the owner of the estate ; I think under her will. He called his eldest son Travers —he is the present Sir Travers Twiss, and sold the Trevalyn of the Langford's to General Townshend's father about sixty years ago.

There were other Langfords alive after the death of George Langford in 1720.

Simon Langford, " a Denbighshire man", is stated in Rowland's *Mona Antiqua* to have been instituted to the living of Rhoscolyn in Anglesey in 1709 ; and his name appears among the subscribers to that work in 1723.

John Langford of Oswestry, Clerk, joined Benjamin Bruer in a bond for the payment of a sum belonging to the parish charities in 1740.

There was also an Archdeacon of Merioneth of the same name.

TREVALUN.

Richard Langford of Trefalun and Rhuddin, whose first wife was Margaret, daughter of John Almer of Almer, married, secondly, Marslli, daughter of Ieuan ab Howel of Trefihywe (?) by whom he had issue three sons and four daughters.

   1. Thomas, of whom presently.

II. George Langford of Trefalun, who married, first, Alice, daughter of Roger Wynn Sandes of Mortyn, by whom he had issue, Randle, William, Nathaniel, and Elen. He married, secondly, Elen, daughter of John Dryhurst of Denbigh, by whom he had issue, John, Dorothy, Jane, and Grace.

III. Owain Langford of Rhuddin, who married and had issue a son, John Langford of Rhuddin.

The four daughters were, 1, Jane, ux. John Matthew of Yr Hôb; 2, Elen, ux. John ab Gruffydd ab John ab Madog of Yr Hôb; 3. Jane, ux. .... Jackson; and 4. Alice, ux. Thomas Lloyd of Pwll gallo dij (?) and had a son, Edward Lloyd of Rhuddin.

Thomas Langford, the eldest son of Richard Langford, by his second wife, Marslli, married Anne, daughter of John Trevor, by whom he had issue three sons and three daughters.

I. Richard Langford, of whom presently.

II. Edward Langford, *ob. s. p.*

III. Owain Langford, who married, first, Anne, daughter of Evan Griffith of Llai, by whom he had a daughter, Anne. He married, secondly, Frances, daughter of Sir Thomas Aston, Knt., and relict of John Sockwell and Richard Davies of Croughton. She died December 31st, 1632, *s. p.*

The three daughters were, 1, Jane, ux. William Middlehurst of Wrexham, by whom she had a daughter, Catherine; 2, Alice, *ob. infans;* and 3, Catherine.

Richard Langford of Trefalun, 1636. He married, first, Jane, daughter of Richard Lloyd ab Euyr of Wrexham, by whom he had a son, William, who died in 1632, aged thirteen, *s. p.* He married, secondly, Elizabeth, daughter and heir of John Sockwell of Hock, by Frances, daughter of Sir Thomas Aston, Knt., by whom he had issue two sons, James and Aston, and a daughter, Elizabeth, who married Thomas Hunt ab Richard, by whom she had a daughter, Mary, ux. John Fletcher of Chester.

PLAS YN HORSLLI.

Harl. MSS. 1969, 2299.

Gruffydd ab David Fychan of Trefalun, ab David ab Madog ab=Margaret,
Iorwerth ab Ieuaf ab Iorwerth ab Einion ab Ithel ab   d. of
Eynydd.   David.

Ieuan Llwyd=Gwerfyl, d. and heir of Ieuan ab =Gwenllian, d. and co-
jure uxoris   David ab Madog of Horslli,   heiress of Howel ab
of Plas yn   sixth son of David Hên of   Madog ab Ieuaf Llwyd
Horslli.   Goronwy ab Iorwerth ab Howel   of Trefalun, ab Howel
     Moreiddig ab Sanddef Hardd,   Fychan ab Howel
     or the Handsome. Lord of   Wyddel ab Iorwerth
     Mortyn and Llai. *Vert,* semé of   ab Ieuaf ab Iorwerth
     broomslips, a lion rampant *or.*   ab Einion ab Ithel ab
         Eynydd. See p. 215.

Margaret, co-heir and heiress of Plas   Annest,   Robert ab   Catherine,
yn Horslli. She married Howel   ux.   Ieuan   ux. Thomas
ab David ab Gruffydd Fychan ab   Madog   Llwyd,   Allington or
Madog ab Iorwerth Fychan of   Wynn.   *ob. s. p.*   Alunton.
Mortyn and Llai, ancestor of the
Powells of Horslli.

MANOR OF MORTYN OR BURTON.—LLOYD OF YR ORSEDD GOCH.

Cae Cyriog MS.; Harl. MSS. 1969, 2299.

Howel Fychan of Trefalun, ab Howel Wyddel (who was so called be-⊤ cause he could speak Irish) ab Iorwerth ab Ieuaf ab Iorwerth ab Einion ab Ithel ab Eynydd.

Ieuaf Llwyd.⊤Marslli, d. of Howel Pigot.

David ab Ieuaf, ⊤Gwenllian, d. and heiress of Goronwy Goch ab David Hen, ab Goronwy ab Iorwerth ab Howel ab Moreiddig ab Sanddef Hardd or the Handsome, Lord of Morton and Llai.   Madog ab Ieuaf⊤

Howel ab Madog.⊤

Thomas ab Howel, *ob. s. p.*   Gwenllian, co-heir, ux. Ieuan Llwyd ab Gruffydd ab David Fychan ab David ab Madog ab Iorwerth. See Plas yn Horslli, p. 214.   Eva, co-heir, ux. David ab Gruffydd Fychan ab Madog of Talwrn, by Croes Howel in Mortyn or Burton. *Sable,* three roses *argent.*

Iolyn Llwyd.⊤Lleuci, d. of Ieuan Llwyd ab Gruffyd ab Goronwy ab Howel ab Cynwrig ab Iorwerth ab Iarddur.   Gwenllian, ux. Gruffydd Fychan ab Madog ab Iorwerth Fychan of Talwrn by Croes Howel in Mortyn. *Sable,* three roses *argent.*

Gruffydd ab Iolyn.⊤ Witness to a deed 4th May, 8th Hen. VII.

| a

Jenkyn ab Iolyn.⊤

Howel.⊤Maud, d. of Ieuan ab Einion ab Iolyn.

| b

Madog ab Iolyn.⊤

Gwonhwyfar, ux. Ieuan ab Madog Ddû.

a			b	
William = ... d, of Howel ab			Lewys.=Gwenhwyfar, d. of John ab	
Lloyd of	David ab Gruffydd		Iolyn ab Madog ab Dio ab	
Gresford.	Fychan of Plas yn		David ab Howel ab David	
	Horslli. *Sable*, three		ab Rhirid Sais ab Ithel ab	
	roses *argent*.		Eynydd.	

John.=   Thomas. =   David. =

Thomas.

Lancelot Lloyd of Yr=Catherine, d. of Edward Brereton of   Catherine, ux.
   Orsedd Goch.   Bwras, High Sheriff for co. Den-   John Erlys
                         bigh, 1598.   of Erlys.[1]

Thomas Lloyd of Yr Orsedd=Margaret, d. of Lancelot Bostock ab Robert
   Goch.   Bostock of Churton.

Lancelot Lloyd of Yr=Margaret, d. of Richard Lloyd ab Hugh ab John ab
   Orsedd Goch, 1604.   Ieuan ab Deicws ab Deio of Llanerch Rugog.

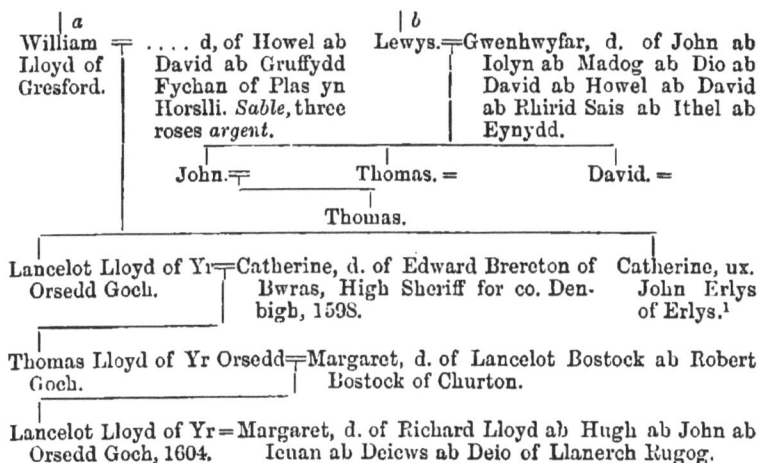

AYLMER, OR ALMOR, OF ALMOR AND PANT IOCYN.

Cae Cyriog MS.; Harl. MSS. 1969, 2299.

Trahaiarn ab Ithel ab Eynydd. He and his five brothers=Jane, d. of
gave land to build the Church of Gresford. He had the greatest | Ednyfed
share of land, as is well known by all in that country, by old | Gam.
writings, says Lewys Dwnn.

Owain ab Trahaiarn =

a	1	b	2		c	3	d		e		f	

[1] John Erlys of Erlys ab John ab Edward ab Madog ab Ieuan ab
David ab David ab Ieuan ab Iorwerth ab David Hen ab Goronwy of
Mortyn and Llai.—*Harl. MS.* 2299.

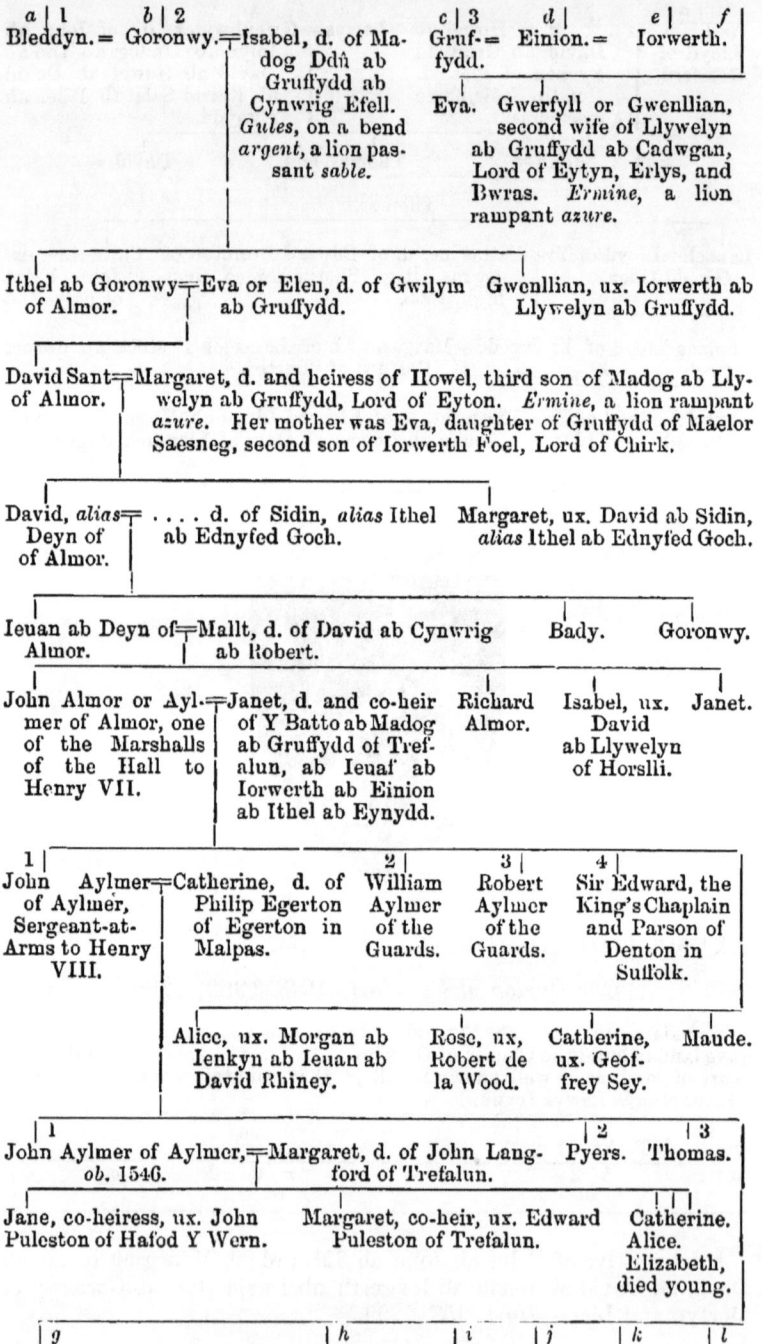

a | 1   b | 2   c | 3   d | e | f

Bleddyn. = Goronwy.⹀Isabel, d. of Ma-   Gruf-= Einion.= Iorwerth. |
              dog Ddû ab   fydd.
              Gruffydd ab
              Cynwrig Efell. Eva. Gwerfyll or Gwenllian,
              Gules, on a bend   second wife of Llywelyn
              argent, a lion pas-   ab Gruffydd ab Cadwgan,
              sant *sable*.   Lord of Eytyn, Erlys, and
                                Bwras. *Ermine*, a lion
                                rampant *azure*.

Ithel ab Goronwy⹀Eva or Elen, d. of Gwilym Gwenllian, ux. Iorwerth ab
  of Almor.   ab Gruffydd.   Llywelyn ab Gruffydd.

David Sant⹀Margaret, d. and heiress of Howel, third son of Madog ab Lly-
  of Almor. welyn ab Gruffydd, Lord of Eyton. *Ermine*, a lion rampant
           azure. Her mother was Eva, daughter of Gruffydd of Maelor
           Saesneg, second son of Iorwerth Foel, Lord of Chirk.

David, *alias*⹀ .... d. of Sidin, *alias* Ithel Margaret, ux. David ab Sidin,
  Deyn of   ab Ednyfed Goch.   *alias* Ithel ab Ednyfed Goch.
  of Almor.

Ieuan ab Deyn of⹀Mallt, d. of David ab Cynwrig   Bady.   Goronwy.
  Almor.   ab Robert.

John Almor or Ayl-⹀Janet, d. and co-heir Richard Isabel, ux. Janet.
  mer of Almor, one   of Y Batto ab Madog Almor.   David
  of the Marshalls ab Gruffydd of Tref-   ab Llywelyn
  of the Hall to   alun, ab Ieuaf ab   of Horslli.
  Henry VII.   Iorwerth ab Einion
             ab Ithel ab Eynydd.

1 | 2 | 3 | 4 |

John Aylmer⹀Catherine, d. of William Robert Sir Edward, the
  of Aylmer,   Philip Egerton Aylmer Aylmer King's Chaplain
  Sergeant-at-   of Egerton in of the   of the and Parson of
  Arms to Henry Malpas.   Guards. Guards. Denton in
    VIII.   Suffolk.

              Alice, ux. Morgan ab Rose, ux, Catherine, Maude.
              Ienkyn ab Ieuan ab Robert de ux. Geof-
              David Rhiney.   la Wood. frey Sey.

1 | 2 | 3

John Aylmer of Aylmer,⹀Margaret, d. of John Lang- Pyers. Thomas.
    ob. 1546.   ford of Trefalun.

Jane, co-heiress, ux. John   Margaret, co-heir, ux. Edward Catherine.
  Puleston of Hafod Y Wern.   Puleston of Trefalun.   Alice.
                                                        Elizabeth,
                                                       died young.

| g | h | i | j | k | l

	g		h		i		j		k		l
Edward=Dorothy, d. of Sir		Catherine,		Marga-		Elen, ux.		Jane,		Anne.
Aylmer.	George Calverley of	ux. Wil-		ret, ux.		Robert		ux.		
	the Lea in Cheshire,	liam		Rich-		Lloyd of		John ab		
	Knt., and relict of	Roydon of		ard		Plâs yn		Robert		
	.... Bostock of	of Mortyn		Lang-		Her-		ab Ior-		
	Churton, co. Ches-	or Burton.		ford of		sedd.		werth of		
	ter. *Argent*, a fess			Trefa-				Llwyn		
	gules, inter three			lun, ab				On.		
	calves *sable*.			John						
				Lang-						
				ford.						

William Aylmer of Aylmer and Pant=Elen, d. of Pyers Puleston of Hafod
Iocyn. This is the person men- | y Wern, and Catherine, his wife,
tioned by Churchyard in his *Wor-* | d. of Sir Thomas Hanmer of Han-
thines of Wales. | mer, Knt.

William Aylmer, according to the *Cae Cyriog MS.*=

Jane, heiress of Aylmer and Pant=Gilbert, son and heir of Sir William
  Iocyn | Gerard, Knt.

William Gerard,=	Thomas=	Emanuel	John	Mary, married, first, Eliza-
sold Pant Iocyn	Gerard.	Gerard.	Gerard	Thomas Wynn of	beth.
in 1613.				Plâs Newydd, and,	
				secondly, David Lloyd.	

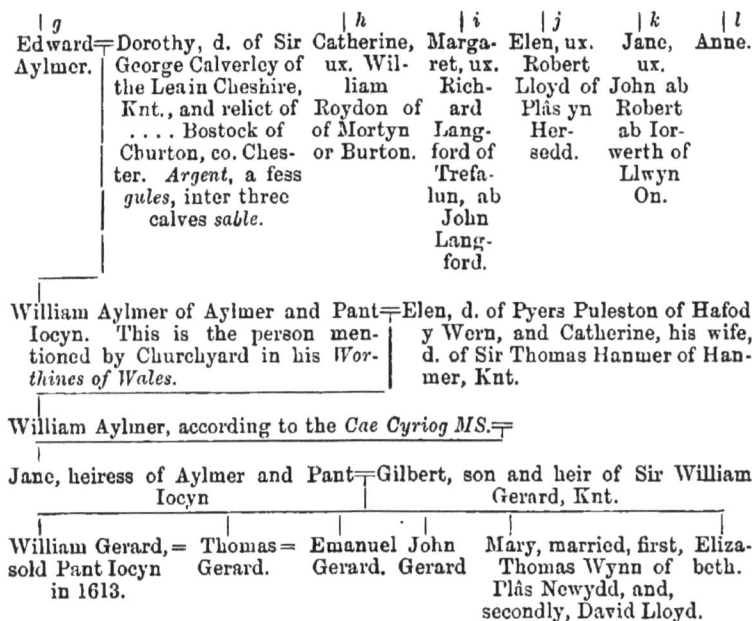

The Aylmer family removed from Aylmer to Pant
Iocyn, and removed the materials of the house at Aylmer
there. The estate was subsequently sold to the Trevors
of Trevalun, in whose family it still remains. Pant
Iocyn was formerly one of the principal gentlemen's
seats in the county of Denbigh, but for more than a
century it has been inhabited by farmers. Churchyard,
in his *Worthines of Wales*, printed in 1587, mentions
it as the residence of "Maister Aylmer". This person
was William Aylmer, whose son William left one only
daughter, Jane, who married Gilbert Gerard, Esq. Their
son, William Gerard, sold it in 1613 to Nathaniel Owen,
Esq. (*argent*, a lion rampant and canton *sable*), who
sold it to John Panton, Esq. (*gules*, three bars *ermine*,
in chief a cross crosslet *argent*), he consenting to pay
£10 per annum to Jane, the widow of Gilbert Gerard,
Esq. In 1615, John Panton sold it to George Lloyd,
Bishop of Chester (*sable*, a chev. inter three mullets
argent), whose family lived there till 1630, when it was
sold to Thomas Manley, Esq. (*argent*, a sinister hand

couped at the wrist in a border engrailed *sable*), who
made considerable improvements in the house. In 1634,
it was sold to William Jones, Esq. (Tudor Trevor, in a
border engrailed *or*), whose trustees sold it to Timothy
Myddleton of Plâs Cadwgan for £2,000. (See Plâs
Cadwgan and Gwersyllt Uchaf.)

PULESTON OF TREFALUN.

Sir Richard Puleston of Emeral=Ermine, d. of Richard Hanmer of Hanmer
in Maelor Saesneg, Knt.   in Maelor Saesneg.

Edward Puleston,=Margaret, d. and co-heir of John Almor of Almor or
jure uxoris of   Aylmer, and Margaret, his wife, d. of John Langford
Trefalun.   of Trefalun.

Edward Puleston=Gwenhwyfryd, d. of John Trevor of   Dorothy, ux. John
of Trefalun.   Trefalun and Mary his wife, d. of   Jones of Llwyn
     Sir George Bruges of London, Knt.   On, in Abynt-
           bury.

Edward Puleston of Trefalun. ⯗

Margaret Puleston,=John Powel, Esq., son and heir of Sir Thomas Powel
heiress of Tref-   of Plâs yn Horslli, Bart. John Powel died in his
alun.   father's lifetime, December 1642.

Sir Thomas Powel of Plâs yn Horslli, Bart.

ALUNTON OF TREFALUN OR ALUNTON.

Cae Cyriog MS.; Harl. MSS. 1969, 2299.

Howel ab David ab Rhirid Sais ab Ithel ab Eynydd of Trefalun.⹊

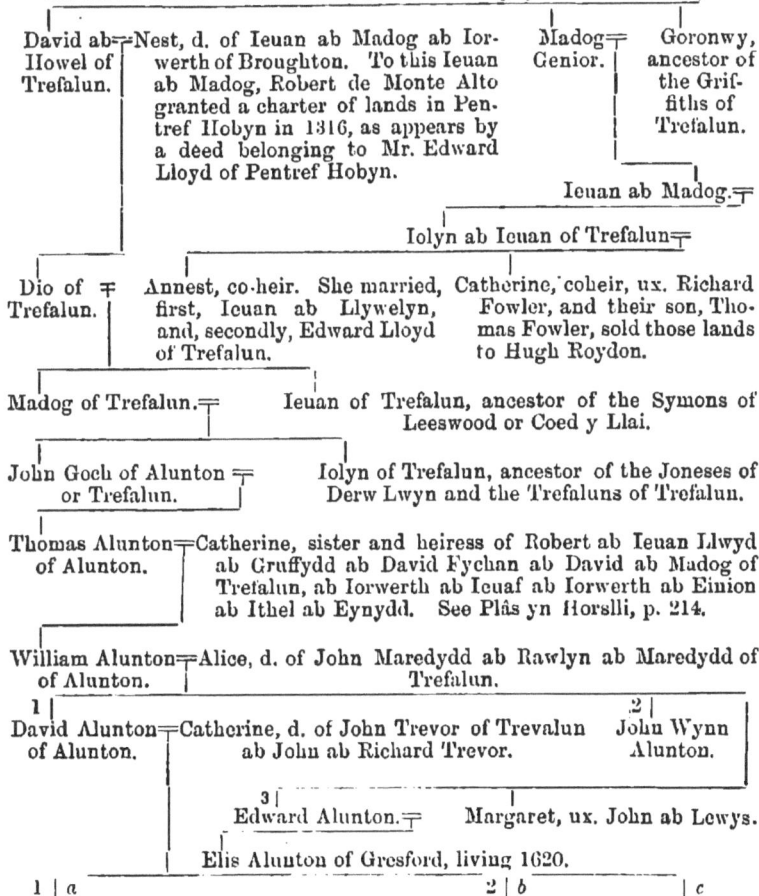

David ab⹊Nest, d. of Ieuan ab Madog ab Ior-   Madog⹊   Goronwy,
Howel of | werth of Broughton. To this Ieuan   Genior. | ancestor of
Trefalun. | ab Madog, Robert de Monte Alto | the Grif-
          | granted a charter of lands in Pen- | fiths of
          | tref Hobyn in 1316, as appears by | Trefalun.
          | a deed belonging to Mr. Edward |
          | Lloyd of Pentref Hobyn. |

                                        Ieuan ab Madog.⹊

                        Iolyn ab Ieuan of Trefalun⹊

Dio of ⹊   Annest, co-heir. She married, Catherine, coheir, ux. Richard
Trefalun. | first, Ieuan ab Llywelyn,   Fowler, and their son, Tho-
          | and, secondly, Edward Lloyd   mas Fowler, sold those lands
          | of Trefalun.   to Hugh Roydon.

Madog of Trefalun.⹊   Ieuan of Trefalun, ancestor of the Symons of
                              Leeswood or Coed y Llai.

John Goch of Alunton ⹊   Iolyn of Trefalun, ancestor of the Joneses of
  or Trefalun. | Derw Lwyn and the Trefaluns of Trefalun.

Thomas Alunton⹊Catherine, sister and heiress of Robert ab Ieuan Llwyd
  of Alunton. | ab Gruffydd ab David Fychan ab David ab Madog of
               | Trefalun, ab Iorwerth ab Icuaf ab Iorwerth ab Einion
               | ab Ithel ab Eynydd. See Plâs yn Horslli, p. 214.

William Alunton⹊Alice, d. of John Maredydd ab Rawlyn ab Maredydd of
  of Alunton. | Trefalun.
1 | 2 |
David Alunton⹊Catherine, d. of John Trevor of Trevalun   John Wynn
  of Alunton. | ab John ab Richard Trevor.   Alunton.

               3 |
              Edward Alunton.⹊   Margaret, ux. John ab Lewys.

              Elis Alunton of Gresford, living 1620.

1 | a   2 | b | c

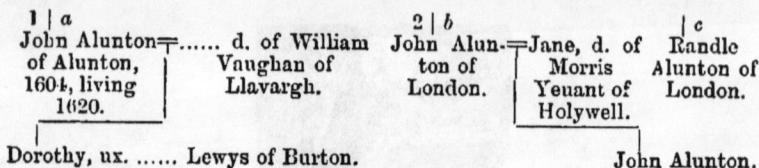

1 | a
John Alunton⊤...... d. of William
of Alunton, | Vaughan of
1604, living | Llavargh.
1620. |

Dorothy, ux. ...... Lewys of Burton.

2 | b
John Alun-⊤Jane, d. of
ton of | Morris
London. | Yeuant of
| Holywell.

| c
Randle
Alunton of
London.

John Alunton.

TREFALUN OF TREFALUN AND JONES OF DERLWYN.

Harl. MS. 1969.

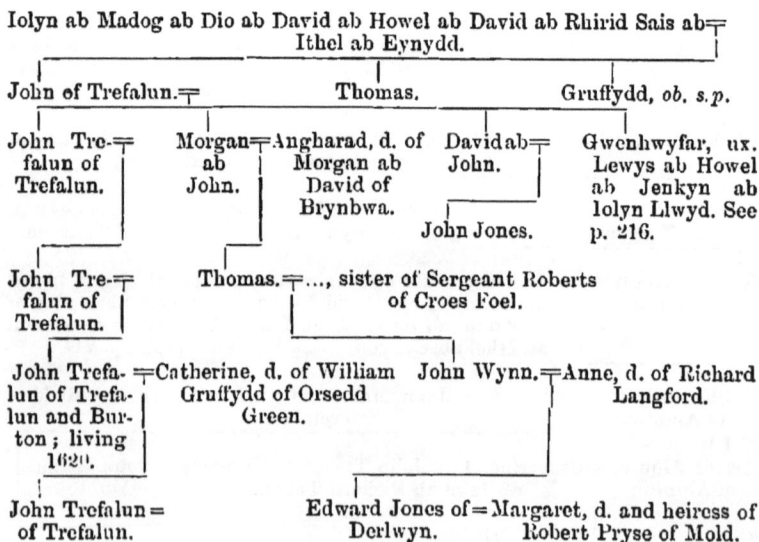

Iolyn ab Madog ab Dio ab David ab Howel ab David ab Rhirid Sais ab⊤
Ithel ab Eynydd. |

John of Trefalun.⊤   Thomas.   Gruffydd, ob. s.p.

John Tre-⊤   Morgan⊤Angharad, d. of   Davidab⊤   Gwenhwyfar, ux.
falun of | ab | Morgan ab   John. | Lewys ab Howel
Trefalun. | John. | David of | ab Jenkyn ab
           | Brynbwa. | Iolyn Llwyd. See
                        John Jones.   p. 216.

John Tre-⊤   Thomas.⊤..., sister of Sergeant Roberts
falun of | of Croes Foel.
Trefalun. |

John Trefa-⊤Catherine, d. of William   John Wynn.⊤Anne, d. of Richard
lun of Trefa- Gruffydd of Orsedd | Langford.
lun and Bur- | Green.
ton ; living |
1620. |

John Trefalun =   Edward Jones of=Margaret, d. and heiress of
of Trefalun.   Derlwyn.   Robert Pryse of Mold.

GRIFFITH OF TREFALUN.

Harl. MS. 2299.

Iolyn ab Madog ab Goronwy Fychan ab Goronwy ab⊤Gwenllian, d. of Deicws
  Howel ab David ab Rhirid Sais ab Ithel ab Eyn- | ab Madog of Trefa-
  ydd.   lun.

Gruffydd.⊤Margaret, d.   Edward.   John, ancestor of the   Madog.
     | of   Daviess of Trefalun.

Edward ab Gruffydd.⊤Jane, d. of John Maredydd ab Rawlyn ab Maredydd
                            of Trefalun.

Edward Griffith; living 1620.⊤Mary, d. of Robert Puleston.

Robert Griffith ;=   Edward=   Mary, ux. Robert Lloyd   Anne, ux. John
  living 1620.   Griffith.   of Cymo in Iâl.   Trefalun of
                                           Trefalun.

DAVIES OF TREFALUN.

Harl. MS. 2299.

Iolyn ab Madog ab Goronwy Fychan ab Goronwy⊤Gwenllian, d. of Deicws
  ab Howel ab David ab Rhirid Sais ab Ithel ab | ab Madog of Trefalun.
  Eynydd

| a | b | c | d

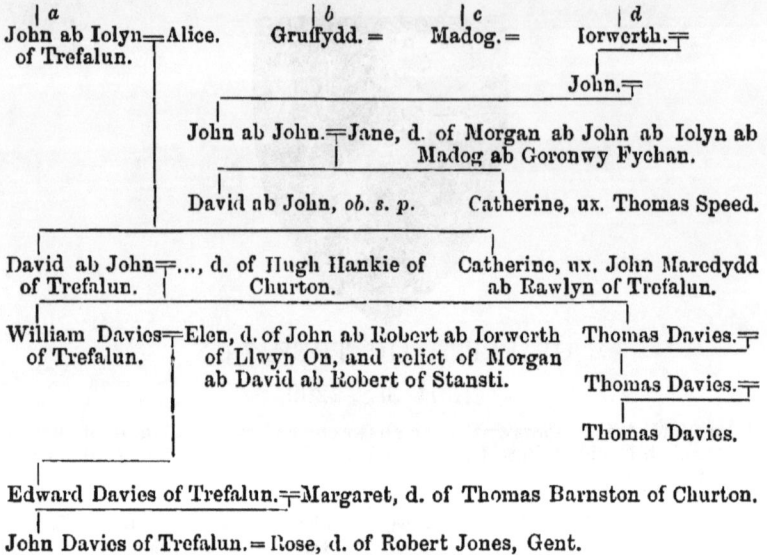

| a | b | c | d |
John ab Iolyn=Alice. of Trefalun. | Gruffydd. = | Madog. = | Iorwerth.=

John.=

John ab John.=Jane, d. of Morgan ab John ab Iolyn ab
Madog ab Goronwy Fychan.

David ab John, *ob. s. p.*   Catherine, ux. Thomas Speed.

David ab John=..., d. of Hugh Hankie of   Catherine, ux. John Maredydd
of Trefalun.   Churton.   ab Rawlyn of Trefalun.

William Davies=Elen, d. of John ab Robert ab Iorwerth   Thomas Davies.=
of Trefalun.   of Llwyn On, and relict of Morgan
     ab David ab Robert of Stansti.   Thomas Davies.=

Thomas Davies.

Edward Davies of Trefalun.=Margaret, d. of Thomas Barnston of Churton.

John Davies of Trefalun. = Rose, d. of Robert Jones, Gent.

SYMON OF COED Y LLAI.

Harl. MS. 1969.

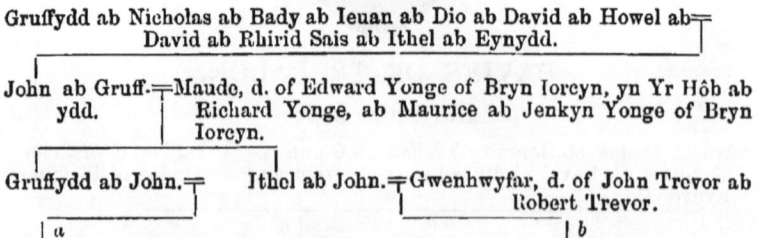

Gruffydd ab Nicholas ab Bady ab Ieuan ab Dio ab David ab Howel ab=
David ab Rhirid Sais ab Ithel ab Eynydd.

John ab Gruff-=Maude, d. of Edward Yonge of Bryn Iorcyn, yn Yr Hôb ab
ydd.   Richard Yonge, ab Maurice ab Jenkyn Yonge of Bryn
   Iorcyn.

Gruffydd ab John.=   Ithel ab John.=Gwenhwyfar, d. of John Trevor ab
     Robert Trevor.

| a | | b |

| a
John ab Gruffydd.⊤Gwen, d. of Howel ab Llywelyn
　　　　　　　　　of Maes Garmon, in Ystrad
　　　　　　　　　Alun.

| b
John ab Ithel.⊤
　　　　　　│
　　　　　John.

Symon of Coed y Llai.⊤..., d. of ...... Hanmer of Overton Madog in Maelor
　　　　　　　　　　　　　　　　　　　Saesneg.

Peter Symon of=Elen, d. of William Thomas　　Mary, ux. John ab John ab
　Coed y Llai.　　of Llanferis, in Iâl.　　　　Ieuan of Y Nercwys, in
　　　　　　　　　　　　　　　　　　　　　Ystrad Alun.

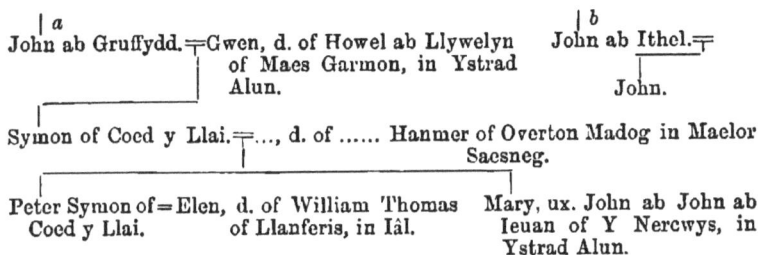

MAREDYDD OF TREFALUN.

Harl. MSS. 1969, 2299.

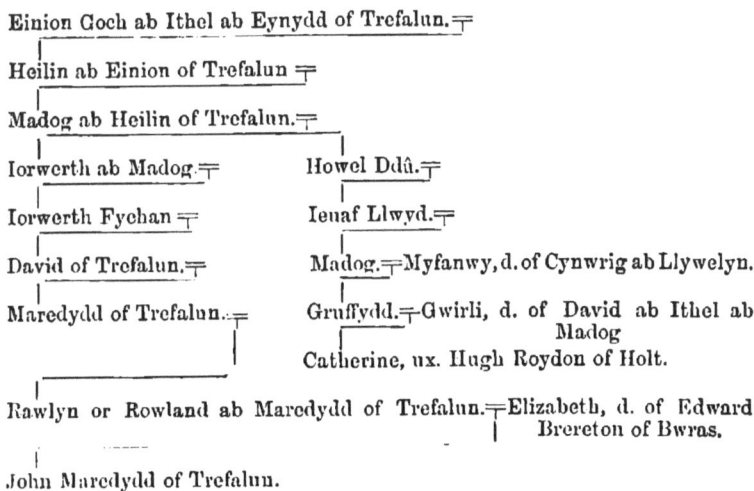

Einion Goch ab Ithel ab Eynydd of Trefalun.⊤
　│
Heilin ab Einion of Trefalun ⊤
　│
Madog ab Heilin of Trefalun.⊤
　│　　　　　　　　　　　　　│
Iorwerth ab Madog.⊤　　　　Howel Ddû.⊤
　│　　　　　　　　　　　　　│
Iorwerth Fychan ⊤　　　　　Ieuaf Llwyd.⊤
　│　　　　　　　　　　　　　│
David of Trefalun.⊤　　　　Madog.⊤Myfanwy, d. of Cynwrig ab Llywelyn.
　│　　　　　　　　　　　　　│
Maredydd of Trefalun.⊤　　Gruffydd.⊤Gwirli, d. of David ab Ithel ab
　　　　　　　　　│　　　　　　　│　　　　　　　　Madog
　　　　　　　　　│　　　　Catherine, ux. Hugh Roydon of Holt.

│
Rawlyn or Rowland ab Maredydd of Trefalun.⊤Elizabeth, d. of Edward
　　　　　　　　　　　　　　　　　　　　　　│　　Brereton of Bwras.
　│
John Maredydd of Trefalun.

The above-named John Maredydd of Trefalun married Catherine, daughter of John ab Jolyn ab Madog ab Dio ab David ab Howel ab David ab Rhirid Sais ab Ithel ab Eynydd, by whom he had issue five sons and four daughters.

I. John Maredydd ab John, his successor.

II. William Maredydd, ob. *s. p.*

III. Thomas Maredydd, who married Dorothy, daughter of Edward ab Madog, by whom he had issue, besides a daughter, Catherine, seven sons—1, John ; 2, Thomas ; 3, William ; 4, Edward ; 5, Roger ; 6, Owain ; and 7, Randle.

IV. Edward Maredydd, who married Margaret, daughter of Thomas ab David.

V. Richard Maredydd of Pentref Bychan.[1]

The four daughters were—1, Alice, ux. William Alunton of Alunton ; 2, Catherine, ux. Richard ab David ab Madog ; 3, Margaret, ux. David de Weild of Holt ; and 4, Jane, ux. Edward ab Gruffydd ab Gruffydd.

John Maredydd ab John of Trefalun, married twice ; by his second wife, Margaret, daughter of Thomas Morgan of Mortyn, he had an only daughter, Alice, ux. William Lloyd.

By his first wife, Margaret, daughter of Richard Manley[2] of Monkfield (*argent*, a sinister hand couped at the wrist in a border engrailed *sable*), he had a son and heir,

John Maredydd of Trefalun, who married Alice, daughter of John Roydon of Holt, by whom he had issue, besides a daughter Jane, who married Captain Anthony Lewys of Burton, two sons.

I. John Maredydd of Trefalun, who married Ermine, daughter of Edward Puleston of Trefalun.

II. Edward Maredydd, who married Catherine, daughter and heir of Edward Kenrick of Golftyn, by whom he had two daughters, Elizabeth and Alice, who both died *s. p.*

---

[1] See Burke's *Landed Gentry.*
[2] William Manley, *Harl. MS.* 1969.

WYNN OF Y GROESFFORDD.

Lewys Dwnn, vol. ii, p. 355.

Gruffydd ab Einion ab Gruffydd ab Llywelyn ab Cynwrig ab Osbern Wy- ⊤
ddel of Cors y Gedol. *Ermine,* a saltier *gules,* a crescent *or,* for difference. |

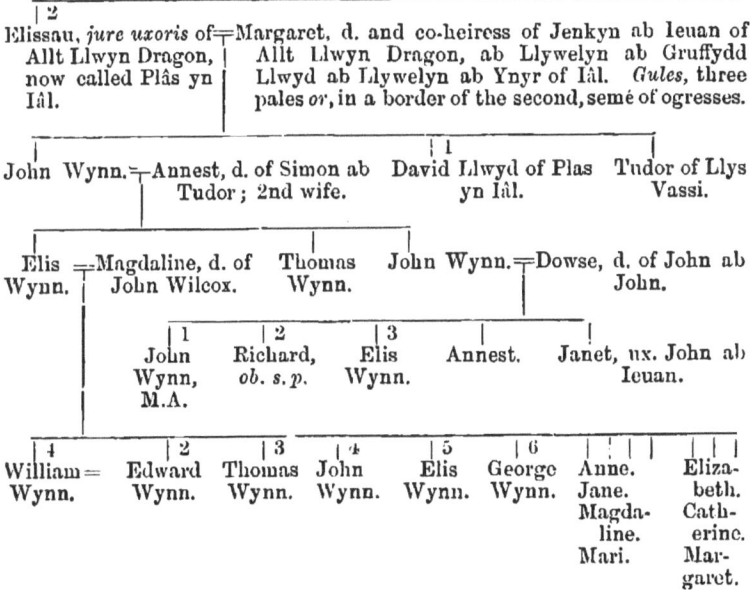

|2
Elissau, *jure uxoris* of⊤Margaret, d. and co-heiress of Jenkyn ab Ieuan of
Allt Llwyn Dragon, | Allt Llwyn Dragon, ab Llywelyn ab Gruffydd
now called Plâs yn | Llwyd ab Llywelyn ab Ynyr of Iâl.   *Gules,* three
Iâl.   pales *or,* in a border of the second, semé of ogresses.

John Wynn.⊤Annest, d. of Simon ab   David Llwyd of Plas   Tudor of Llys
    Tudor; 2nd wife.   yn Iâl.   Vassi.

Elis =Magdaline, d. of   Thomas   John Wynn.⊤Dowse, d. of John ab
Wynn. | John Wilcox.   Wynn.   John.

|1 John |2 Richard, |3 Elis   Annest.   Janet, ux. John ab
Wynn,   *ob. s. p.*   Wynn.   Ieuan.
M.A.

|4 William = |2 Edward |3 Thomas |4 John |5 Elis |6 George   Anne.   Eliza-
Wynn.   Wynn.   Wynn.   Wynn.   Wynn.   Wynn.   Jane.   beth.
    Magda-   Cath-
    line.   erine.
    Mari.   Mar-
    garet.

MANOR OF MORTYN OR BURTON.—TOWNSHIP OF MORTYN. SANDEV OR SANDDEF OF MORTYN.

Harl. MS. 1972; Lewys Dwnn, vol. ii.

David Goch, seventh son of David Hen ab⊤Gwenllian, dau. and heir of
Goronwy ab Iorwerth ab Howel ab Morei- | John ab Morgan ab Lly-
ddig ab Sanddef Hardd, or the Handsome, | welyn ab Ifor, Lord of St.
Lord of Mortyn and Llai. *Vert*, semé of | Clears and Tredeger in
broomslips, a lion rampant *or*. Living 10 | South Wales.
Edw. II.

| 1 | 2 |

Robert ab David Goch of⊤ Madog of Mortyn=Agnes, dau. of Hwfa ab
Mortyn. | see p. 228. Adda.

| 1 | |

Madog ab Robert of Mortyn.⊤ Iorwerth Foel of Mortyn. = Bleddyn.

Gruffydd ab Madog of Mortyn.⊤Janet, d. of Madog ab Gruffydd of Trefalun.
Azure, a lion salient *or*.

Madog ab Gruffydd⊤Lleuci, d. and heir of David Almer ab Madog ab Ior-
of Mortyn. | werth Fychan ab Iorwerth ab David ab Goronwy of
Mortyn and Llai. *Sable*, three roses *argent*.

Rawlin or Rowland⊤Margaret, d. of David Llwyd ab David ab Ieuan Fychan
ab Madog of Mor- | ab Ieuan of Llanuwchllyn, ab Gruffydd ab Madog ab
tyn. | Iorwerth ab Madog ab Rhirid Flaidd, Lord of Penllyn.
Vert, a chev. inter three wolf's heads erased *argent*,
langued *gules*.

John Wynn of Mor ⊤Elizabeth, d. of Pyers Hope ab Oliver Hope ab Robert
tyn; *ob*. 20th May | ab Jenkyn Hope ab Robert le Hope, of Broughton,
1544, 36 Henry | in the Lordship of Merffordd. *Argent*, three storks
VIII. | *sable*.

| 1 | | 2 | 3 |

Roger Wynn, sur-⊤Elen, d. of William Roydon of Talwyn or Tal- John.
named Sanddeff | wrn ab John Roydon of Talwyn ab Wil- Edward.
of Morton. | liam Roydon, Receiver of Maelor Gym-
raeg, second son of Richard Roydon of Kent. *Vert*,
three buck's heads in bend *or*, in dexter chief a rose
of the second.

a | 1   b | 2   c |

a | 1
Owain Sanddeff=Eleanor, d. of Roger Kynaston
  of Mortyn, | of Lechreche. She died 1st
  1611. | March 1613, and was buried
       | at Gresford.

b | 2
John
Sanddef.

c |
Alice, ux. George
  Langford of
  Trefalun.

John Sanddef;=Margaret, dau. of John Lloyd Rosendale of Foxhall or
  ob. 1604, | Foulk's Hall in the parish of Henllan. Quarterly or and
  v. patris. | azure, four roebucks passant counterchanged.

       | 2
Robert or Richard=Anna, d. of John
  (L. Dwnn) of Al- | Benyn, and
  lington and Bur- | relict of Edward
  ton; living 1620. | Puleston.

I .
Catherine, ux.
  Laurence Swet-
  tenham of ......

John Sanddef, son and heir
  apparent; living 1620.

| 1 | 2 | 3
Samuel.
John, 1651.
Nathaniel.

I   I
Margaret.
Elizabeth.

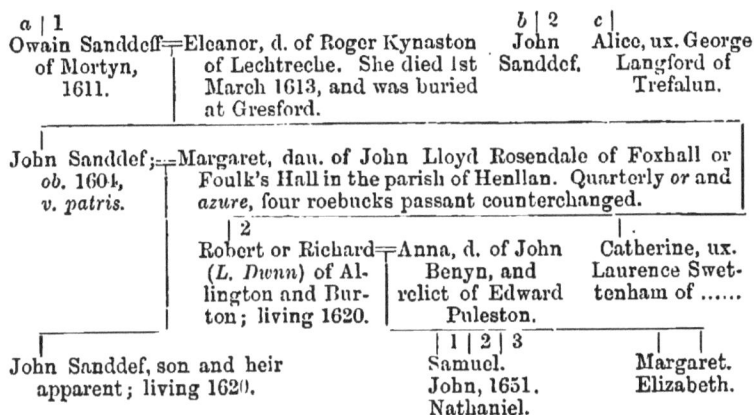

BURTON AND LEWYS OF BURTON.

Add. MS. 9864.

Madog Fychan ab Madog ab Deicws ab Madog ab David Goch, ab David⸗
Hen ab Goronwy ab Iorwerth of Burton and Llai. *Vert*, semé of broomslips, a lion rampant *or*, armed and laugned *gules*. See Brynbwa, p. 37.

Llywelyn ab Madog.=Janet, d. of Robert Grosvenor.

William ab Llywelyn of Burton.=Alice, d. of John ab Iolyn of Aylmor.

John Bur-=Margaret, d. of ...
ton of | Smallman of co.
Burton. | Salop.

Lewys ab Wil-=Dorothy, d. of John Trevor
liam of | ab John Trevor of Tref
Burton. | Alun ab Richard Trevor.

Roger Bur-=Jane, d. of Thomas
ton of | Yonge of Croxton
Burton. | in Maelor Saes-
      | neg.

Captain Anthony=Jane, d. of John Mare-
Lewys of Burton | dydd of Tref Alun,
Hall. | and Alice, his wife, d.
     | of John Roydon of Is
     | y Coed. *Azure*. a
     | lion salient *or*. She
     | died 9th Feb. 1632,
     | and was buried in
     | Gresford Church.

Richard Lewis, *ob. s. p.* in his father's lifetime.   Lewys Lewys, *ob. s. p.*

Captain Anthony Lewis of Burton Hall, by his will
dated August 1, 1634, which is stated to have been
" drawne up by himself praying it may be construed to
common sense, and not to be by Lawe wrested to nice
constructions", he devised his Mansion and real Es-

tates, charged with annuities, charitable rent charges, and Legacies for his numerous "Cosens", amongst whom was William Lewys, "Marchant", to his "loving Cosen Sir Sackville Trevor, Knt.", for life with remainder to "his most belovedst Cosen Sir Thomas Trevor, Knt., one of the Barons of His Majesties Exchequer", for life, with remainder to his "Cozen Thomas Trevor, Esq., sonne and heir apparent of the sayd Sir Thomas", for life, and his heirs in tail male. He was very specific in his bequests of armour, plate, rings, and arms; and left "to the Preacher that preached his funeral sermon £3", praying that he "would not there in his pulpit prayse nor yet disprayse the gonne life of the dead corps before him, as commonly most devines doe most grosly, too much of the one or other, nor yet shewe his witt in giving there a wipe concerning this my request, but follow his text to the profitt of the hearers, soe end and interr me". He also bequeathed, "to discharge his funeral, not meaning to have any blacks given, £120."

He died soon after the date of his will, and there is a monument to his memory above the door of the south porch in Gresford Church, with an inscription in Welsh, of which the following is a translation.

"This is in memory of Captain Anthony Lewis of Burton, in this Parish, who was a Benefactor to this Church by restoring its windows, pews, and roofs. Who also left a testimony of his love to the poor of the Parish for ever, by providing bread for them every week. This was erected by Sir Thomas Trevor, Knight and Baronet, as well from his own piety, in memory of his relative, as from an earnest desire to fulfil the wish of his dear and worthy Father, Sir Thomas Trevor, Knight, one of the Barons of King Charles's Exchequer, throughout the reign of the said King, the 31st day of August, 1659."

It is stated in a "Catalogue of Benefactors" that, in 1634, Anthony Lewis "bestowed towards glazing the Church windows, and building the seates, and paving the Church, in all £300", a sum of money which, in the days of King Charles I, must have been looked

upon as extremely large ; and, it is further stated, that
he charged his lands in Burton, " towards providing of
bread to be distributed among the Poor every Sunday at
Church", with the payment of £7 per annum.

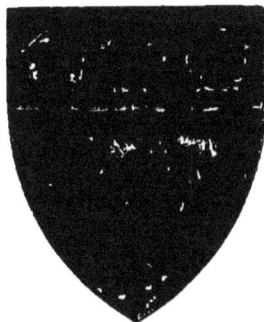

MANOR OF MORTYN OR BURTON.—TOWNSHIP OF BURTON. BILLOT OR BELLOT OF BURTON.

Harl. MS. 1971.

John Billott, descended as heir male from Sir Ingram
Billott of Thorpe Billott, in Com. Norfolk, married Catherine, daughter and heir of Thomas Morton, Lord of
Great Morton, in Com. Cestriæ, 24 Henry VI, by whom
he had a son and heir,

Thomas Billott of Great Morton, and Lord of that
Manor, 36 Henry VI. He married Margaret, daughter
of John Spencer of Congleton, who bore the coat of
Dutton, with a bend *azure,* by whom he had a son and
heir,

Thomas Billott of Great Morton, who married three
times : first, Catherine, daughter and co-heir of Thurstan
Gowan of . . . . in Com. Lanc. (*ermine*, on a cross saltier
azure, five cressets or five beacons *or*) ; secondly, he married Elizabeth, daughter of . . . Liversage of Macclesfield,
by whom he had issue, besides a daughter, Catherine, ux.
William Canton of Lancashire, a younger son, Thomas
Billott of Morton Alcumlow, who died 1 Edw. V.

He married . . . . daughter of Thomas Smethwick of Smethwick, by whom he had an only daughter and heiress, who married Ralph Brodhurst, whose daughter and heiress, Margery, married Nicholas Hobson of Over Alderley. Thomas Billott married, also, a daughter of Smethwick of Smethwick, by whom he had no issue. By his first wife, Catherine Gowen, he had issue a son and heir,

John Billott of Great Morton, who married Jane, daughter of Ralph Morton of Little Morton (*argent*, a greyhound *sable*, collared *gules*), by whom he had issue four sons and seven daughters, 1, Thomas, of whom presently; 2, William, who married Elen, daughter of . . . . Sandford; 3, Philip; and 4, Robert Billott, who married, and had issue, Richard and Robert, Jane and Mary.

The seven daughters were, 1, Margery, ux. Ralph Thornton of Chester; 2, Ursula, ux. Edward Vnwyn of Chaterley, co. Stafford; 3, ... , ux. Roger Greene of Congleton; 4, Elen, ux. John Somerford; 5, Blanche, ux. Roger Sparke, secondly, she married Richard, brother of Piers Pudston of Handymeme; 6, Elizabeth, ux. Robert Davenport of Chorley; and 7, Catherine, ux. John Creswall of . . . .

Thomas Billott of Great Morton purchased divers lands in the townships of Burton and Gresford in the manor of Burton, 5 Edw. VI, 1552. He was also Farmer of St. John's Hospital in Chester, and High Sheriff for co. Denbigh in 1556. He married Alice, daughter of William Roydon of Talwyn in Burton (*azure*, three roebuck's heads erased in bend *or*, in dexter chief a rose of the second), by whom he had issue ten sons and six daughters, 1, Edward, of whom presently; 2, Thomas; 3, Hugh Billott or Bellot, D.D., Bishop of Bangor, Dec. 1585, translated to Chester, June 25, 1595, *ob.* 1596, and was buried in the chancel of Wrexham Church; 4, John; 5, George; 6, Robert Billott of Beyham, of whom presently; 7, David; 8, Matthew, and 9, Owain.

The six daughters were, 1, Mary, ux. Richard Myn-
sule, and secondly, Arthur Starky of Wrenbury; 2,
Ermyn, ux. first, John Manley of Pulton, and secondly,
Thomas Maudsley of Lache, near Chester; 3, Dorothy,
ux. John Drinkwater of Chester; 4, Jane; 5, Elizabeth;
and 6, Susan.

The sixth son, Robert Billott of Beyham, 1580, married Dorothy, daughter of John Brereton of Coleston,
by whom he had, besides a daughter Catherine, a son
and heir, Roger Billott of Bers, who died March 30th,
1634.   He married . . . . , daughter of Arthur Starkey
of Wrenbury, by whom he had, besides two daughters,
Mary and Anne, three sons, 1, Arthur, of whom presently; 2, Robert Billott of Wrexham, who died March
7th, 1641. He married Jane, daughter of Edward Puleston
of Llwyn y Cnotiau, and relict of Thomas Goldsmith, by
whom he had no issue; and 3, Thomas Billott, who married the daughter and heir of Doctor Houghton.   Arthur
Billott, the eldest son, was a Lieutenant in the army in
Germany, and died *v. patris*.   He married Catherine,
daughter of . . . . Frogge of Whitby in Com. Cestriæ,
by whom he had issue one son, Roger, *ob. s. p.*, and
three daughters, 1, Margaret, ux. Henry Griffith of
Bromhal; 2, Elizabeth, *ob. s. p.*; and 3, Bridget, ux.
John Ravenscroft of Newall.

Edward Billott of Great Morton in Cheshire, and of
Burton in Maelor Gymraeg, 1597, married Ursula, daughter
of . . . . Vnwyn de Chaterley in Com. Staff., by whom
he had no issue.   He married also, Anne, daughter of
Pyers Mostyn of Talacre, Esq., by whom he had issue
four sons and three daughters, 1, Edward, of whom presently; 2, Thomas, *ob. s. p.;* 3, John; and 4, George;
the three daughters were, 1, Dorothy, ux. William Griffith : 2, Magdalene, ux. Pyers Wynn Ffoulkes of Eri-
fiad, in the parish of Henllan (*gules*, three boar's heads
erased in pale *argent*); and 3, Catherine, ux. John
Conwy of Rhuddlan, and secondly, Pyers Conwy of Yr
Hendref.   She died August 2nd, 1654.

Edward Billott of Great Morton and Burton was

living in 1613. He married Amy or Mary, daughter and co-heir of Anthony Grosvenor of Dudlyston, by whom he had issue three sons and four daughters, 1, John, of whom presently; 2, George; and 3, Thomas; the daughters were, 1, Susanna, ux. John Broughton of Broughton; 2, Frances; 3, Elizabeth, ux. Thomas Bromley of Hampt; and 4, Mary, ux. Thomas Gamul of Chester, *ob.* Dec. 23rd, 1631.

John Billott of Great Morton and Burton was born in 1594. He was High Sheriff for Denbighshire in 1642, and was living in 1649. He married a daughter of .... Bentley of Ashes in Com. Staff., by whom he had issue three sons, 1, Edward Billott, who married Sibyl, daughter of Sir Randle Egerton, by whom he had no issue; 2, Sir John Billott of Morton, Knt., High Sheriff of Cheshire in 1663. He married Anne, daughter of Roger Wilbraham of Darfold, by whom he had issue Thomas, John, and Anne; and 3, George Billott.

MORTON OF MORTON.

Randulphus de Venables, dominus de Magna Morton.
Robertus de Morton.
Robertus de Morton.
Roger de Morton, 21 Edward III. — Robert.
Stephen de Morton.
Robert de Morton = Sibill. Ralph de Morton, 9 Hen. IV. — Roger. John — Catherine, ux. Hugo Venables, Baron of Kinderton.
Thomas de Morton. Thomas de Morton.
Thomas de Morton.
Catherine, heiress of Morton, ux. John Billott, 24 Henry VI.

PAPERS RELATING TO THE LORDSHIPS OF BROMFIELD AND YALE.

Add. MS. 11,827, fo. 8.

Mynheer Benting, Earl of Portland, beggs of King William to him and his Heires for ever, the Lordships of Denbigh-land, Bromfield and Yale, in the County of Denby.

The Warrant coming to the Lords of the Treasury, the Gentlemen of the County, upon one or two days' notice, were heard against the Grant before the Lords of the Treasury, my Lord Godolphin, Sir Stephen Fox, Sir William Turnbull, and Mr. John Smith, on fryday the tenth May 1695.

Sir Wm. Williams (of Llanfordaf) said,

That this was part of the ancient Revenue of the Prince of Wales, and that the Welsh were never subject to any but to God and their King, and that none showed their Allegiance more than the Welsh. That in the Statute which granted fee farm Rents there was particular Exception of the Welsh revenue not to be Alienable, that there were mites of £500 payable out of those Lordshipps to the Prince of Wales, which shows that by tenure it belongs to the Prince of Wales, and altho' there was none now, yet he doubted but to see one of the present King's own body.

Sir Roger Puleston said,

That the Revenue of those Lordshipps do support the Government of Wales by paying the Judges and others their salaries, and if given away there would be a failure of Justice.

Mr. Robert Price.

That the Grant that was making was of a Large Dominion, being five Parts in 6 of one County, which was too great a Power for any foreign subject to have, and the People of the Country too great to be subject to him. That there were near fifty mean Lordshipps under those Mannors, that there were about 1500 free holders, that there were waste and Commons of many thousand acres, that there were Mines of Lead and Copper of great value, and the present rent reserved above £1500 per annum.

A hearing at the Treasury upon the intended Grant of the Lordships of Denbigh, Bromfield, and Yale, to the Earl of Portland, 10 May 1695.

That Courts were kept in all those Lordships in the King's name, that all or most of the Gent. in the Country were tenants to the King and suitors to his Courts, and thereby oblig'd to the King by a double Allegiance, their General Allegiance as subjects, and their Particular Allegiance as Tenants, and if the King gave away the one it was to be fear'd it would Lessen the Lands of the Other, since it is observable that interest and property have an ascendant over duty.

That these Lordships were formerly Lordships Marchers, which occasion'd thus when William the Conqueror had brought England into subjection, but could not subdue the Welsh Country, he gave to his normand Lords some neighbouring Lands to Wales, and furnished them with Men and Arms, and what Ground they could take from the Welsh by intrusion or Conquest, those Norman Lords were to hold as Lordships Marchers, of which were Barons or Palatinates, and what they got or usurped by their Power, they maintained by their severity and oppression, and under this Vassalage the Brittains continu'd untill 29th of Hen. 8th, which was since the statute of union was made, and they esteem'd it their happiness to be under the English Laws and Government, and so have continued to this day, none having more eminently signaliz'd their constant Loyalty to their Rightfull King than themselves.

But if his Majesty shall think fit to disunite from his Crown by this Grant, and put them under a foreign subject, it's putting them in a worse posture than in their former Estate when under Wm. the Conqueror and his Normand Lords.

The Brittains were always Men of Courage and Sincerity, and yet of resentment, tho' Henry 4th and 5th were Martial Princes, and had a hatred against the Brittains because they persever'd in their Duty to Richard ye second who was their Rightfull, tho' infortunate, King; and made scandalous and reproachfull Laws against them, yet it was worth remark that those Princes had never Peacefull or happy days till they reconcil'd themselves to that great People, not to tell the History of Owen Glindir, who was but an Inferior Person of the Long Robe, but when a Stranger wou'd have incroach'd upon the wast and Commons of his neighbours, his Law and Arms, with his Neighbours Assistance, became a Terror to the English Nation.

It is worth consideration what Title the King hath to grant it is a revenue that belongs to the Prince of Wales, and in case of the want of such it vestes in the Crown rather as a use fonctuary than Property, till a Prince be created to whose creation the Revenue is annexed by these, tho' unusuall words, in the Laws, to him and his Heirs, who shall be King of England.

By the Statute of 21 Jam. First in Cha. 29, in the Preamble of that Statute, it was doubted whether Charles, Prince of Wales and Duke of Cornwall, could grant Leases of the Dutchy Lands for 3 lives or any longer than his own Life, tho' the Statute said that he had an Estate of Inheritance under a speciall form of Limitation differing from the ordnary Rules of Inheritance at. the Common Law, and therefore necessary to have these Leases confirmed in Parliament.

The use that is made of that Statute in case is, if the Prince and Duke of Cornwall, who have an Inheritance in their revenue can't grant Estates without Parliament for any Longer than their Own Lives, how then can his present Majesty, who is our King by a Modern Contract, and hath but an Estate for Life in Possession in the Crown by the Act of Settlement, grant away the inheritance and absolute fee of the Principality of Wales, for it is a great absurdity in the Law to say that a Tenant for Life can grant a fee, as it is to say that a Tenant in fee cann't grant any more than for his own Life, and if the aid of Parliament was necessary to help in one case, it was more necessary in the other.

It is well known in former Reigns there have been of Resomption, which always pass'd when the People groan'd under the weight of heavy Taxes and the Nation engaged in a warr. If this was the Reason for the Legislative Power to pass a Bill of resumption, it is full as good Reason for his Majesty not to grant, since we are both in warr and under the most heavy Pressure of Taxes that ever History bore Testimony of. Let it be consider'd, can it be his Majesty's Honour or his interest, when his people hear this and understand it, that he dayly gives away the Revenue, and more, the Perpetuity of his Crown's Revenue, to his foreign subjects.

Good Kings, after a long and chargeable warr, were accustom'd to tell their people that they sorrow'd for the hardships the nation underwent by Long and heavy Taxes, and that now they would Live on their Own; but it is to be fear'd if Grants are made so large and so frequent, there will be nothing left for the King or his Successors to call their own or live upon.

It is to be hoped your Lordships will consider we have had but one Day's notice of this attendance, and must, therefore, come very much unprovided, but yet we doubt not but these Hints and broken thoughts we have offer'd to your Lordships will, by your great Judgment, be improv'd, whereby the ill consequence of this Grant may be Timely represented to his Majesty.

Lord Godolphin said,

Had not the Earl of Leicester these Lordships in grant to him in Queen Elizabeth's time?

Sir Robert Cotton of Chesh'e said,

I believe I can give the best Acc't in that case. The Earl of Leicester had but one of these Lordships, and that was Denbigh Land. He was so oppressive to the Gent. of the County that he occasion'd them to take up Arms to oppose him, for which three of my wife's family of the Salisburys were hang'd in that Quarrell, but it ended not there, for their Quarrel was still kept on foot, and the Earl of Leicester was glad to be in peace and to grant it back again to the Queen, and it hath been ever since in the Crown.

Lord Godolphin.

Gent., you have offer'd many weighty Reasons, and we shall represent them to his Majesty.

CANTREF UWCHNANT. COMOT OF MERFFORDD.

This comot contains the parish of Penarth Halawg or Hawarden, and part of the parish of Gresford, viz., the townships of Horslli and Llai.

The parish of Penarth Halawg contains the townships of Hawarden, Ewlo, Coed Ewlo, Pentref Hobyn, Broughton, Bretton, Aston, Banael, Broadlam, Mancott, Moor, Rake and Manor, Sealand, Shotton and Morffa Caerlleon of Saltney.

In this comot are the Castles of Hawarden and Ewlo.

PENARTH HALAWG OR HAWARDEN.

The Castle of Hawarden stands on a conical hill in the manor or township of Hawarden, which name seems to be formed from the word *garth*, a mountain or hill, and *din*, the root of *dinas*, a fortified city, generally situate on a hill.　As it is usual in Welsh to drop the initial letter *g*, *gardd-din* becomes *arth*, or *ardd-din*, and, aspirated, *harden*.[1]　In *Domesday Book* the name was written *Haordin*; at which time it was a lordship, and had a church; two carucæ or ploughlands, half of one belonging to the church; half an acre of meadow; a wood two leagues long and half a league broad.　The whole was valued at forty shillings, and the population then consisted of four villeyns, six boors and four slaves. At the Conquest, William the Conqueror granted this manor to Hugh Lupus, Earl of Chester.[2]　It afterwards devolved upon the Barons of Montalto, or Y Gwyddgrûg, which they held by stewardship of the Earls of Chester, and who made it their residence.[3]　Robert, Baron de Montalto, granted the Marsh of Saltney, or Morfa Caerllcon, to the monks of Basingwerk for pasturage.　He also gave them the same privilege in Hawarden, and the liberty of cutting rushes for thatching their buildings.[4]

　　Hawarden remained in the possession of the Barons de Montalto till 1327, 1 Edw. III, when Robert, the last Baron de Montalto (for want of issue) left this manor and his other great possessions to Isabel, the Queen mother, and from her it passed to the Crown.　Hawarden is called in old writings Penarddllech; this may be a contraction from Pen Garth y Llwch, "the summit of the hill by the quicksands or swamps", with which the Morfa Caerllcon, or Saltney Marsh, lying between this place and Chester, formerly abounded.　The epithet *halawg* (from *hâl*, salt, or *salt-marsh*) evidently refers to its situation on or near a *salt-marsh*.[5]

　　The inhabitants of Hawarden have been for many ages known by the name of "Hawarden Jews", the reason for which is supposed to be best explained by the

---

[1]　Carlisle's *Topographical Dict.*
[2]　Pennant's *Tour*, vol. i, pp. 122-4.
[3]　Camden, ii, 826.　　　　　[4]　Charters in Record Office.
[5]　*Arch. Camb.*, January 1873, p. 61.

following account preserved and current in the parish
from time immemorial, and said to be a translation of an
ancient Saxon MS.

"In the sixth year of the reign of Cynan ab Elis ab Anarawd, King of Gwynedd (which was in the year 946), there
was in the Christian temple, at a place called Hardin, in the
Kingdom of North Wales, a rood-loft, in which was placed an
image of the Virgin Mary, holding a very large cross in her
hand, called the 'holy rood'. About this time there happened a very hot and dry summer; so dry that there was no
grass for the cattle. Upon which most of the inhabitants besought the image, or holy rood, to send them rain; but to no
purpose. Among the rest the Lady Trawst, whose husband's
name was Seisyllt or Sitsyllt, a nobleman, and governor of
Hawarden Castle, went to pray to the said holy rood, and she,
praying earnestly and long, the image and holy rood fell down
on her head and killed her; upon which a great uproar was
raised, and it was concluded and resolved upon to try the said
image for the murder of the said Lady Trawst, and a jury was
summoned for the purpose, whose names were as follow :

"'Hincot of Hancot, Span of Mancot,
    Leach and Lach and Comberbach;
    Peet and Pate, with Corbin of the Gate,[1]
    Milling and Hughet, with Gill and Pughet.'

These, upon examination of evidences, declared the said Lady
Trawst to be wilfully murdered by the said holy rood, and
that the holy rood was guilty of the murder, and also guilty
in not answering the many petitioners. But whereas the said
holy rood was very old and decayed, she was ordered to be
hanged; but Span opposed that sentence, saying, that as they
wanted rain, it would be best to drown her. But that was
fiercely opposed by Corbin,[1] who answered that, as she was
the holy rood, they had no right to kill her, and he advised
them to lay her on the sands by the river Dee, below Hardin
Castle, from which they might see what became of her; which

---

[1] There was a descendant of this Corbin, believed to be in the
direct male line, living in 1811 at the house called "The Gate" (*i.e.*,
from its situation near the gate of the castle), and in possession of
part of the same freehold, with a family of three sons and four
daughters. The names of Leach, Milling, and Hewet, are still numerous in the parish; and those of Span, Pate, Comberbach, and Gill,
are frequent in the neighbourhood.

was accordingly done. Soon after which, the tide from the
sea came and carried the said image to some low land, being
an island, near the walls of a city called Caer Lleon (now
Chester), where it was found the next day, drowned and
dead ; and they erected a monument of stone over it with this
inscription,

> " 'The Jews their God did crucify,
> The Hardeners theirs did drown,
> Because their wants she'd not supply,
> And lies under this cold stone.'

"There is now (1811) the pedestal of an old cross, consist-
ing of three steps with a part of the column in it, of the red
sandstone of the neighbourhood, standing on the Rood Dee
or race course below the walls of Chester, on the very spot
probably where the holy rood was found."[1]

This Lady Trawst, who is thus stated to have been
killed by the fall of the holy rood in 946, appears to me
to be identical with the Lady Trawst, the daughter and
heiress of Elissau, who was the second son of Anarawd,
King of Gwynedd, who died in 913. She married
Seisyllt, Lord of Maes Essyllt, by whom she had two
sons, Cynan ab Seisyllt and Llywelyn ab Seisyllt, the
latter of whom married, at the age of fourteen, as previously stated, Angharad, the only daughter and heiress
of Maredydd ab Owain, King of Powys. See vol. i.

In 1651, Hawarden Castle fell into the hands of the
Commonwealth, and it was purchased from the agents of
sequestration by Serjeant Glynne, the ancestor of the
late Sir Stephen R. Glynne, Bart.

HAWARDEN.

Add. MS. 6032, fo. 140.

Tho' Dux Clarencie ten' Cast' et domin' de Harvarden cu'
o'ibus membris etc. de d'no Rege et Com' Cest' p' seruitiu'
Militare 9 H. 5.

Willielmus de Monte acuto nup' comes Sa : ten' coniunct'
feoffat' cum Eliz' Ux' sua Man' de Hawarden Senescall: Castri
et man' de Neston cu' p'tiis de d'no rege ut Com' Cest' p'
ser' Mil' 21 R. 2.

---

[1] Carlisle's *Topographical Dict.*

EWLO CASTLE.

This castle, which is situate in the township of Coed Ewlo, is now in ruins. It is memorable as the place where a detachment of the army of Henry II, then encamped on Morfa Caerlleon, sustained a check from the Princes David and Cynan, the sons of Owain Gwynedd, in 1156.

Leland speaks of it as "a ruinous castle or pile belonging to Hoele, a gentleman of Flintshire, that by auncient accustume was wont to give the bagge of the sylver harpe to the beste harpir of North Walys, as by a privilege of his auncestors". This gentleman is supposed to be Thomas ab Richard ab Howel, Lord of Mostyn, in whose family that privilege was long invested, and who was contemporary with Leland.[1]

The manor of Ewlo was reckoned an appurtenance to the manor of Montalto or Mold. It was in the Crown in the 26th Henry VIII, who granted a lease of it to Pyers Stanley, Esq., a gentleman of his household, with the tolls of the market of Flint.[2] This lease bears the date April 7th, 1535.

[1] Pennant's *Tour*, vol. i, p. 119.
[2] *Harl. MS.* 1968.

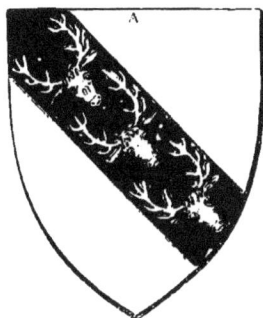

STANLEY OF EWLO CASTLE.

Lewys Dwnn, vol. ii.

Sir William Stanley of Hooton. Knight,⊤Margaret, d. and sole heir of Sir
Standard-bearer to Richard III at the │ John Helcij or Heighlegh,
battle of Boswerth.   │ Knight.

│

Pyers Stanley of Ewlo Castle, Esq., ap.⊤Constance, d. of Thomas Salus-
pointed Escheator and Sheriff of co. │ bury Hên of Llyweni.
Meirion., 22 Sept., 1 Henry VII (1485). │

1		2	3	4	5	6	7
Pyers ⊤Janet, d. of		Ffoulk.			Edward Stanley of Har-	Thomas.	
Stanley of │ SirThomas		John.			lech, M.P. for co. Meirion,	William.	
Ewlo │ Butler,		Harri.			1542; appointed Con-		
Castle. │ Knight.					stable of Harlech Castle,		
│					by letters patent, 26th		

Pyers Stanley of⊤Jane, d. of ......   March, 5 Edw. VI (1558).
Ewlo Castle.   │   Parker.

│

Edward Stanley of Ewlo Castle,⊤Margaret, d. of Sir James Stanley, Knt.
living 1597.   │

│

Robert Stanley of Ewlo⊤Alice, d. of Thomas Salusbury of Fflint, third son
Castle.   │   of Sir Thomas Salusbury of Llyweni, Knt.

│

Anne Stanley, heiress of Ewlo=John Mostyn of Coed On, of the House of
Castle.   Mostyn of Mostyn.

LORDSHIP OR COMOT OF MERFFORDD.—LLOYD OF PENTREF HOBYN.

OWAIN AB HYWEL DDA, who reigned over South Wales and Powys from 948 to 985, married, first, Angharad, daughter and heiress of Llywelyn ab Mervyn, Prince of Powys, who bore, *or*, a lion's gamb erased bendways *gules*, by whom he had a son, Maredydd, who succeeded to the kingdom of Powys, and bore his maternal arms. Owain married a second wife, by whom he had another son, called Einion, who succeeded his father in the Principality of South Wales. He married Nesta, daughter of the Earl of Devon, by whom he had two sons, 1, Tudor Mawr, ancestor of the Princes of South Wales; and, 2, Goronwy, who became Prince of Tegeingl in Gwynedd.

Prince Goronwy married Ethelfleda, daughter and heiress of Edwin, Earl of Mercia, and relict of Edmund Ironside, King of England, and doubtless by this match he obtained possession of the Cantref of Tegeingl, which contains the three comots of Cynsyllt, Prestatyn, and Rhuddlan. By his wife Ethelfleda, Goronwy had issue a son and heir, who was called Edwin, after his maternal grandfather.

Edwin ab Goronwy, who succeeded his father in the Principality of Tegeingl, bore, *argent*, a cross flory engrailed *sable*, inter four Cornish choughs ppr. He married Gwerydd or Ewerydda, sister of Bleddyn ab Cynfyn, Prince of Powys. He lived at Llys Edwin, in the parish of Llaneurgain, and at Castell Edwin, in the parish of Llanasaph. He was slain by Rhys ab Rhydderch ab Owain in 1073. Rhual, near Y Gwyddgrûg (Montalto or Mold), was the residence of Edwin when he died, for it is recorded that "Edwin of Rhual was buried at Llaneurgain in 1073". He left issue three sons—1, Owain, of whom presently ; 2, Uchdryd, Lord of Cyfeiliog and Meirion ; and, 3, Hywel, who, together with his brother Uchdryd, and the sons of Cadwgan ab Bleddyn, defeated the Normans in Ceredigion and Dyfed.

Owain ab Edwin succeeded his father as Prince of Tegeingl. He bore *gules*, three men's legs conjoined at the thighs in triangle *argent*. In 1096 he was elected Prince of North Wales by Hugh Lupus, Earl of Chester, but was soon afterwards deposed. He died of consumption in 1103. By his wife Morvydd, the daughter of Goronwy ab Ednowain Bendew, chief of one of the Noble Tribes, who bore *argent*, a chev. inter three boar's heads couped *sable*, he had five sons—1, Goronwy, who married Genilles, daughter of Hoedliw ab Ithel ab Edryd, by whom he had a son Cadwgan, who was the ancestor of the Lloyds of Hersedd, of Ffern in Glyn Berbrwg, and of Llwyn Yn in Ystrad Alun ; 2, Meilir, who was slain by Cadwallawn ab Gruffydd ab Cynan in 1125, and was ancestor of the Pryses of Llwyn Yn in Tref Eyarth in Llanfair Dyffryn Clwyd, and the Edwardses of Stansti in the manor of Y Glewysegl in Maelor Gymraeg ; 3, Llywelyn, of whom presently ; 4, Aldud, ancestor of Madog Ddû of Copa 'r Goleuni in Tegeingl ; and 5, Rhirid, who was the ancestor of Thomas ab Roger ab Llywelyn of Plâs Einion in Llanfair Dyffryn Clwyd, whose daughter and co-heiress Gwen conveyed that estate to her husband, John Lloyd, son of Roger Lloyd of Bryn Eglwys, fifth son of David Lloyd ab Elissau of Plâs yn Iâl.

PENTREF HOBYN.

Heilin Fychan ab Heilin ab Ieuaf ab Gruffydd ab Llywelyn ab Owain╤
ab Edwin ab Goronwy, Prince of Tegeingl.

David Goch.╤

Gruffydd ab╤
David.

Rheinallt ab╤
Gruffydd.

Madog Goch.╤

Bleddyn ab Madog.╤

Robyn of Rhydonen in the parish of Llanynys.╤

Simon of Rhydonen.╤

Lowri, heiress, ux. Richard ab Thomas of Caer
Fallwch ab Edward ab Ithel ab Goronwy Foel ab
Goronwy Fychan ab Goronwy ab Pyll ab Cynan
ab Llywarch Fychan ab Llywarch Goch, Lord of
Rhôs, ab Llywelyn Holbwrch, Lord of Meriadog,
vert a stag trippant *argent*, attired and unguled
or.

Rhys ab Rheinallt╤Mallt, d. of Cynan ab Ithel ab Cynwrig ab Bleddyn ab
of Coed y Llai in | Madog Goch ab Owain Fychan ab Owain Wynn ab
Ystrad Alun. | Rhys ab Iorwerth of Môn, descended from Ithel
Felyn. According to the *Cae Cyriog MS.*, Rhys
married Jane, d. of Ithel ab Cwmws of Llaneurgain,
a natural son of Ithel ab Cynwrig ab Bleddyn Llwyd
ab Ithel Anwyl, who lived at Ewlo Castle.

David ╤Elen, d. of Gruffydd Fychan ab Gruffydd
ab | ab Einion ab Gruffydd of Cors y Gedol.
Rhys. | *Ermine*, a saltier *gules*, a crescent *or.*
for difference.

Edward ab╤Mallt, d. of Robert
David of | Llwyd Hen of Plâs
Pentref | yn Hersedd.
Hobyn. |

Ieuan ab David
of Coed y
Llai.

Margaret, ux. Gruffydd
ab Heilin ab Cadwgan
Deccaf ab Iorwerth ab
Cadwgan ab Iorwerth
of Llwyn Egryn. *Sable,*
on a chev. inter three
goat's heads erased *or,*
three trefoils of the
field.

David Lloyd╤Jane, d. of Pyers ab William ab Ithel of Disserth in Tegeingl,
of Pentref | ab Cynwrig ab Bleddyn ab Madog ab Madog Goch, ab
Hobyn. | Owain Fychan ab Owain Wynn ab Rhys ab Iorwerth of
Môn, descended from Ithel Felyn, Lord of Iâl.

Edward Lloyd╤Margaret, dau. of Edward Morgan of Gwylgre (Golden
of Pentref | Grove) in the parish of Llanasaf, descended from Edny-
Hobyn, *Ob.* | fed Fychan. *Gules,* a chevron *ermine,* inter three English-
25th July 1620; | men's heads couped at the neck, in profile ppr. bearded
buried in Mold | and crined *sable.* *Ob.* 29th May 1631.
Church.

a   *b*   *c*

	a			b		c
Edward Lloyd of—Mary, d. of George Hope of		Thomas		Mary, ux. Ed-
Pentref Hobyn,	Broughton in the parish of	Lloyd,	ward Conwy[1]
High Sheriff for	Hawarden, *Argent*, three	M.A.	of Sychdyn
co. Fflint, 1679.	storks *sable*. She died 9th		in Llaneur-
	July 1628,		gain.

John Lloyd of Pentref Hobyn, High Sheriff for Co. Flint, 1700.—

Edward Lloyd=Dorothy, d. of John Eyton of Coed y Llai or Leeswood, and
of Pentref | Dorothy, his wife, d. of William Herbert of Ceri and
Hobyn. | Trefeglwys. *Gules*, on a bend *argent*, a lion passant *sable*.

Edward Lloyd of Pentref Hobyn.=..., d. of ...... Pennant of Baggillt.

Edward Lloyd of Pentref Ho-=Mary, eldest d. and co-heir of Thomas Lloyd
byn, and *jure uxoris* of Trevor | of Trevor Hall, Glanhavon and Valle
Hall, Glanhavon, and Valle | Crucis Abbey, High Sheriff for co. Mont-
Crucis Abbey, High Sheriff | gomery, 1749; and Mary, his wife, dau.
for co. Flint in 1763, and for | and heiress of Robert Trevor of Trevor
co. Denbigh in 1768. | Hall and Valle Crucis Abbey.

The above named Edward Lloyd and Mary his wife had
issue five sons and two daughters, 1, Robert Lloyd, *ob.
s. p.*; 2, Thomas Lloyd, *ob. s. p.*; 3, John Lloyd, *ob. s. p.*;
and 4, Trevor Lloyd of Trevor Hall, Pentref Hobyn and
Valle Crucis Abbey, High Sheriff for co. Mont. in 1787,
ob. s. p.

The two daughters were Mary and Margaret, co-
heiresses of their brothers. Mary, the eldest, was cut
out of all the estates, which went to the second
daughter, Margaret. Mary married Thomas Mather of
Ancoats in Lancashire, by whom she had issue, besides
a daughter, Dorothy-Pennant, who died *s. p.*, two sons,
Thomas Trevor Mather, who married his first cousin,
Margaret, the eldest daughter of Rice Thomas of Coed
Helen, near Carnarvon; she had Pentref Hobyn; but
both she and her husband died issueless, and Pentref
Hobyn reverted to the Thomases of Coed Helen. The
other son of Mary Lloyd and Thomas Mather, was
Samuel Lloyd Mather, who married Elizabeth, daughter
of Richard Spearman of Plymouth, by whom he had one
son, Thomas Mather, an officer in the Royal Navy, who

[1] Edward Conwy of Sychdyn was the son of Hugh Conwy ab Edward Conwy ab Harri Conwy of Sychdyn, ab James Conwy of Rhuddlan, second son of John Aer Conwy of Bodrhyddan.

died *s. p.*, and one daughter, Mary Palmer, who married Thomas Baldwyn Lloyd of Plâs Llanasaf in Tegeingl, by whom she had one son, Trevor Lloyd, and two daughters, Margaret Baldwyn Lloyd and Mary Lloyd.

Margaret, the youngest daughter of Edward Lloyd of Pentref Hobyn, had, as before stated, all the estates. She married Rice Thomas of Coed Helen, near Carnarvon, of the Royal House of Elystan Glodrudd, Prince of Fferlis (quarterly, 1st and 4th *argent*, on a cross *sable*, five crescents *or*, in the dexter canton a spear's head *gules*, for Sir Gruffydd ab Elidir, Knight of Rhodes; 2nd and 3rd *gules*, a lion rampant regardant *or*, for Elystan Glodrudd, Prince of Fferlis), by whom she had issue one son, Rice Thomas of Coed Helen, Trevor Hall, Glanhafon, and Valle Crucis Abbey, who died *s. p.*; and six daughters, 1, Margaret of Pentref Hobyn, ux. Thomas Trevor Mather, *ob. s. p.*; 2, Elizabeth, ux. Sir William Bulkeley Hughes of Plâs Coch in Anglesey, Knt. (*argent*, a chev. inter three Cornish choughs ppr., each holding an *ermine* spot in its beak); 3, Jane, *ob. s. p.*; 4. Anne, *ob. s. p.*; 5, Trevor, *ob. s. p.*; and 6, Pennant, who married William Iremonger of Wherwell Priory, co. Hants, Colonel of the Queen's Royal Regiment of Infantry, who died in 1582, leaving issue—besides three daughters, 1, Margaret Sophia; 2, Helen Frances; and 3, Elfrida Susanna Harriet, ux. Sir William Eden of West Auckland, co. Durham, and Maryland, Bart.—five sons, 1, William, of whom presently; 2, Thomas Lascelles, *b.* 1815; 3, Frederick Assheton, *b.* 1816; 4, Pennant Athelwold, *b.* 1821; 5, Henry Edward, *b.* 1826.

William Iremonger, Esq., of Wherwell Priory, born 1808, married in 1844 Mary Anne Widmore, only daughter of W. H. Kilpin of Longparish and King's Clere, by whom he had issue, William Henry, born at Florence, 1845; Mary Delicia; Elfrida Harriet; and Mildred Elen.

COMOT OF MERFFORDD.—PLAS YN HORSLLI IN
GRESFORD PARISH.

Harl. MSS. 1972, 2299.

Sanddef Hardd, or the Handsome, was Lord of the township of Mortyn (called Burton by the English) and of Llai
in Merffordd. He bore *vert*, semé of broomslips a lion
rampant *or*, armed and langued *gules*. He was the eldest
son of Caradog, or Cadrod Hardd, Lord of Tref Fodavon
in Môn,[1] who bore *argent*, two foxes countersalient, the
dexter surmounted by the sinister, *gules*, by his second
wife, Angharad, daughter of Brochwael ab Y Moelwyn of
Llwydiarth in Mon.

Caradog, or Cadrod Hardd, was the son of Gwrydr ab
Maelog Ddû ab Cwnws Ddû ab Cillyn Ynad ab Peredur
Teirnoedd ab Meilir Eryr Gwyr y Gorsedd ab Tydai ab
Tudredd ab Gwylfyw ab Marchudd ab Bran ab Pill ab
Cynfyr ab Meilir Meiliorn ab Gwron ab Cunedda
Wledig, King of Cumberland, 530.

Sanddef Hardd married Angharad, only daughter of
Gruffydd ab Cadwgan, Lord of Nannau (*or*, a lion rampant *azure*). By this lady Sanddef had, besides Gruffydd and other issue, a son and heir,

---

[1] *Lewys Dwnn*, vol. ii, p. 264.

Moreiddig, Lord of Mortyn and Llai, who married Tangwystl, daughter of Cadwgan ab Cadwaladr, second son of Gruffydd ab Cynan, King of Gwynedd (*gules*, three lions passant in pale *argent*). Cadwalladr was Lord of Ceredigion, and resided in the Castle of Aberystwyth. By this lady Moreiddig had issue three sons— 1, Howel; 2, Llywelyn of Mortyn, who married Cecilia, daughter and heiress of Llywelyn ab Dolphyn ab Llywelyn Eurdorchog, Lord of Iâl and Ystrad Alun, by whom he had a daughter and heiress, Sibyl, ux. Llywelyn ab Ithel; and 3, Gruffydd ab Moreiddig.

Howel ab Moreiddig, Lord of Mortyn and Llai, married, for his second wife, Gwenllian, relict of Ithel ab Eunydd, Lord of Trefalun, and daughter and co-heiress of Gruffydd, third son of Meilir Eyton, Lord of Eyton, Erlys, and Bwras (*ermine*, a lion rampant *azure*). Gruffydd ab Meilir married Angharad, daughter and heiress of Llywelyn ab Meurig ab Caradog ab Iestyn ab Gwrgant, Prince of Glamorgan (*gules*, three chevronells *argent*). By this marriage Howel had issue, besides a daughter, Margaret, ux. Cynwrig Fychan ab Cynwrig ab Hoedliw, Lord of Cristionydd (*ermine*, a lion rampant *sable*), three sons, 1, Iorwerth ab Howel; 2, Ynyr ab Howel, Lord of Gelli Gynan in Iâl, A.D. 1165; and 3, Ithel ab Howel, who married Clementia, daughter of Cadwgan ab Meilir Eyton, Lord of Eyton (*ermine*, a lion rampant *azure*), by whom he had a daughter and heiress, Dyddgu, ux. Cadwgan Goch ab Y Gwion, Lord of Iâl (*sable*, on a chev. inter three goat's heads erased *or*, three trefoils of the field).

Iorwerth ab Howel, Lord of Mortyn and Llai, married, first, Jane, daughter of Rhirid Foel of Blodwel (*argent*, three raven's heads erased ppr., their beaks *gules*). Rhirid Foel was the third son, by his second wife, Eweredda, daughter of Iago ab Gruffydd ab Cynan, Prince of Gwynedd, of Gruffydd, Lord of Cyfeiliog (*or*, a lion's gamb erased in bend dexterwise, *gules*), second son of Maredydd ab Bleddyn, Prince of Powys. By this match Iorwerth had issue a son and heir,

Goronwy ab Iorwerth, Lord of Mortyn and Llai, who, by Gwenllian, his wife, daughter of Rhys ab David ab Maredydd Hên ab Howel, natural son of Maredydd ab Bleddyn, Prince of Powys (or, a lion ramp. *gules*), had issue, besides a daughter, Mali, ux. Howel Goch ab Maredydd Fychan of Abertanad, ab Maredydd ab Rhys ab Maredydd ab Howel, natural son of Maredydd ab Bleddyn, Prince of Powys, a son and heir,

David Hên ab Goronwy, Lord of Mortyn and Llai. He married Angharad, daughter of Iorwerth Goch of Burgedin, according to some authors, but, according to others, she was the daughter of Iorwerth Goch ab Madog ab Maelion of Creuddyn, by whom he had issue eight sons and three daughters—1, Iorwerth ab David, of whom presently; 2, Gruffydd ab David; 3, Goronwy Goch ab David of Mortyn, whose daughter and heiress, Gwenllian, married David of Yr Orsedd Goch, ab Ieuaf Llwyd ab Howel Fychan of Trefalun; 4, Llywelyn, ancestor of the Matheys of Llanestyn in Yr Hôb, and Jenkyn ab David of Trefalun, whose line is now represented by the heirs of the Trevors of Trefalun; 5, David Goch of Mortyn, ancestor of the Sanddefs of Morton, the Griffiths of Brynbw, and Plâs Y Bold in Caer Gwrli; 6, Howel of Pickill in Maelor Gymraeg; and 7, Madog of Horslli.

Madog of Plâs yn Horslli, the seventh son of David Hên ab Goronwy, married, and had issue two sons,

I. David of Plâs yn Horslli, who was the father of Ieuan of Plâs yn Horslli, whose daughter and heiress, Angharad, married Ieuan Llwyd ab Gruffydd Llwyd ab Gruffydd Fychan of Trefalun. (See p. 214.)

II. Iorwerth of Horslli, who married and had issue one son, Ednyfed ab Iorwerth of Horslli, his heir, who died *s. p.*, and one daughter .... heiress of her brother, who married Ednyfed Llwyd ab Iorwerth Fychan ab Iorwerth ab Awr, ancestor of the Lloyds of Plâs Madog in the manor of Rhiwabon.

The three daughters of David Hên ab Goronwy of Mortyn were—1, Angharad, who married, first, Madog ab

Llywelyn ab Gruffydd ab Cadwgan, Lord of Eyton, Erlys and Bwras, who died in 1331, and was buried on the Feast of St. Matthias, in the north aisle of Gresford Church (*ermine*, a lion rampant *azure*). She married, secondly, Madog Foel of Y Glwysegl ; 2, Eva, ux. Gruffydd Grach ab Iorwerth ab Meilir ab Goronwy ab Gruffydd ab Llywelyn ab Cynwrig Efell, Lord of Y Glwysegl, ancestor of the Eytons of Coed y Llai or Leeswood ; and 3, Gwenllian.

Iorwerth ab David Hên of Llai and Mortyn, married Gwenllian, daughter of Ithel Fychan ab Ithel Llwyd ab Ithel Gam, Lord of Mostyn. Ithel Fychan bore *azure*, a lion statant *argent*, and did homage for his lands to Edward of Caernarvon at Chester, 29th Edw. I (1300). By this lady Iorwerth had issue, besides a daughter, Margaret, ux. Iorwerth of Bwras and Rhuddallt, fourth son of Llywelyn ab Gruffydd ab Cadwgan, Lord of Eyton, Erlys, and Bwras, and ancestor of the family of Bwras or Borasham of Bwras, six sons, 1, Goronwy ab Iorwerth, of whom presently ; 2, Madog Distain ; 3, Iorwerth Fychan, of whose line we have to treat ; 4, Gruffydd ab Iorwerth, who married Gwenllian, daughter of Howel Fychan ab Howel ab Einion, by whom he had a daughter and heiress, ux. Maredydd ab Llywelyn Ddu of Abertanad and Blodwel, second son of Gruffydd ab Iorwerth Foel of Maelor Saesneg ; 5, Ieuan ab Iorwerth, who married Margaret, daughter of David ab Madog, Baron of Hendwr in Edeyrnion ; and 6, Iorwerth Foel, who married Margaret, daughter of Maredydd ab Gruffydd Llwyd ab Llywelyn ab Ynyr of Iâl.

Goronwy of Llai, the eldest son of Iorwerth ab David, bore *argent*, on a bend *sable*, three mullets of the field, died and was buried in the Llai Chapel on the north aisle of Gresford Church. His tomb, on which he is represented recumbent in armour, with his mailed hand grasping his sword, still remains. The arms on his shield are a bend charged with three mullets, and there is also this inscription, "HIC IACET GRONW. F. IORWERTH. F. DD. CVI AIE DS ABSOLWAT." He married Gwenllian, daughter of Adda Goch ab Ieuaf ab Adda ab Awr of Trevor, by whom he had issue, besides two daughters, Margaret, ux. Madog ab Llywelyn of Halchdyn in Maelor Saesneg, eldest son of Ednyfed Gam of Llys Pengwern in Nantheudwy, and Angharad, ux. David of Rhiwlo, a son and heir,

David ab Goronwy of Llai, who married Angharad, daughter of Gruffydd ab Llywelyn ab Cynwrig ab Osbern Wyddel of Cors y Gedol (*ermine*, a saltier *gules*, a crescent *or*, for difference), by whom he had two daughters, co-heirs, 1, Eva, second wife of Sir Jenkyn Hanmer of Hanmer, Knt., ab Sir David Hanmer (*argent*, two lions passant gardant *azure*); and 2, Margaret, ux. Madog Puleston of Bers. This Madog Puleston took the arms of his wife's family, viz., *argent*, on a bend *sable*, three mullets of the field.

Iorwerth Fychan of Mortyn, the third son of Iorwerth ab David, bore *sable*, three roses *argent*, seeded *or*. He married Lleuci, daughter of Maredydd Llwyd ab Maredydd ab Rhys Goch, by whom he had a son and heir,

Madog ab Iorwerth of Mortyn, who married Gwenhwyfar, daughter of Rhys ab Ithel ab Maredydd, by whom he had issue, besides a daughter, Catherine, ux. Gruffydd ab David Sutton of Sutton and Gwersyllt, two sons, 1, David Almer, whose daughter and heiress, Lleuci, married Madog ab Gruffydd ab Madog ab Robert ab David Goch ab David Hên ab Goronwy of Mortyn and Llai (*vert*, semé of broomslips a lion rampant *or*); and 2, Gruffydd Fychan.

Gruffydd Fychan, the second son of Madog ab Iorwerth, was of Talwrn by Croes Howel in Mortyn. He married Gwenllian, daughter of David of Yr Orsedd Goch in Gresford Parish, son of Ieuaf Llwyd ab Howel Fychan ab Howel Wyddel of Trefalun (*azure*, a lion salient *or*), but, according to others, she was the daughter of David ab Ithel Llwyd ab Ithel Fychan, by whom he had issue three sons, 1, David Fychan, of whom presently ; 2, Madog ab Gruffydd ; and 3, Owain ab Gruffydd.

David Fychan of Mortyn married three wives—1, Gwen, daughter of David ab Iorwerth ab Madog Ddu of Abyntbury, ab Gruffydd ab Iorwerth Fychan ab Iorwerth ab Ieuaf ab Niniaf ab Cynwrig ab Rhiwallawn (*ermine*, a lion rampant *sable*), by whom he had one son, Gruffydd ab David, who died *s. p.*, and a daughter, Catherine, ux. Richard Tegyn of Fron Deg, Sergeant-at-Arms, son of Robert Tegyn ab David ab Tegyn ab Madog ab Iorwerth Goch ab Madog ab Ieuaf ab Niniaw (*ermine*, a lion rampant *sable*). He married, secondly, Eva, daughter and co-heir of Howel ab Maredydd ab Ieuaf Llwyd of Trefalun, ab Howel Fychan ab Howel Wyddel ab Iorwerth ab Einion ab Ithel ab Eynydd, Lord of Trefalun (*azure*, a lion salient *or*), by whom he had a son and heir, Howel, of whom presently ; and, thirdly, he married a daughter of Edward Stradlinge.

Howel ab David was the first of this branch of the family who settled at Plâs yn Horslli, which place he became possessed of in right of his wife Margaret, daughter and heiress of Ieuan Llwyd, Perchenwr Plâs yn Horslli, who was the son of Gruffydd Llwyd ab David Fychan of Trefalun, ab David ab Madog ab Iorwerth ab Ieuaf ab Iorwerth ab Einion of Trefalun, the eldest son of Ithel ab Eynydd, Lord of the townships of Trefalun, and Y Groesffordd. The above-named Ieuan Llwyd, who was originally of Trefalun, became possessed of Plâs yn Horslli by his marriage with Angharad, daughter and heiress of Ieuan ab David ab Madog of Horslli, seventh son of David Hên ab Goronwy of Mortyn and Llai (*vert*, semé of broomslips, a lion rampant *or*). By his wife, Margaret, Howel ab David had issue, besides a daughter .... the wife of William ab David ab Gruffydd ab David ab Llywelyn of Trefalun, a son and heir,

Thomas Powell of Plâs yn Horslli, Constable of Holt Castle. He married Catherine, daughter and heiress of Lancelot Lowther, Constable of Holt Castle, who bore *or*, six annulets *sable*, by whom he had issue four sons, 1, Thomas, of whom presently ; 2, John Lancelot ; 3,

George Anthony; and 4, Edward, who all, with the exception of Thomas, died *s. p.*; and five daughters, 1, Anne, ux. Richard Roydon of Holt; 2, Margaret, ux. William Howlstog; 3, Dorothy, ux. John Ffylkyn; 4, Wenhwyfrid, who had four husbands, first, John Norton; second, George Tormacon; third, Edward Gotley; and fourth, John Dod; and 5, Ursula, ux. Alexander Coates.

Thomas Powell of Plâs yn Horslli, died at a great age and was buried at St. Mary's, Gresford, April 26th, 1613, and his wife, Alice, died on December 25th, 1609, and was buried at Gresford. She was the daughter and co-heiress of Ralph Wortesley or Worsley of Berkett[1] in Cheshire,[2] by whom he had issue six sons and two daughters, 1, Thomas, of whom presently; 2, John; 3, William Powell of Chester, Deputy; 4, Ralph; 5, Alexander; and 6, George Powell, who was living in 1640, and married to a daughter of . . . . Lloyd of Hersedd in Ystrad Alun. The eldest daughter, Alice, married John Lloyd of Llys Vassi, and Joanna, the second daughter, married Roger Roydon of Holt and Is y Coed, Captain in the Royal Army.

Thomas Powell of Plâs yn Horslli, the eldest son, was High Sheriff for co. Denbigh in 1591. He married Dorothy, daughter of Maurice Wynn of Gwydir (*vert, three eagles displayed in fess or*), and died September 18th, 1629, and was buried at St. Mary's in Chester, having had five sons, 1, Sir Thomas, of whom presently; 2, John Powell, of whom presently; 3, Roger; 4, Richard Powell, M.A., who resided in Ireland; and 5, Worsley Powell; and four daughters, 1, Eleanor; 2,

---

[1] The arms of Worsley of Birkett were, ... a chevron inter three falcons *sable*, the leashes *gules*.

[2] Hugh Worsley, who was descended from Jordan Worsley of Worsley Manor, married a daughter of Standish of Standish, by whom he had a son, William Worsley of Berkett in Cheshire, who married Joanna, daughter of Adam Birkenhead of Huxley, by whom he was father of Ralph Worsley of Berkett, who married a daughter of Pick of London, by whom he had two daughters, co-heirs, Alice, ux. Thomas Powell; and Avisa, who married, first, Thomas Vandrey, secondly, Humphrey Davenport, and, thirdly, John Shakerley.

Margaret, ux. William Edwards of Eyton, High Sheriff
for co. Denbigh in 1654 ; 3, Catherine, ux. Roger Davies
of Erlys, ab John ab Richard Davies of Erlys, ab David
ab Howel ab Edward Puleston of Cristionydd, ab Madog
Puleston of Bers (*argent*, on a bend *sable*, there mullets
of the field) ; and 4, Sidney. (*Harl. MS.*, 2180.)

John Powell, the second son of Thomas Powell and
Dorothy his wife, was of Bodylltyn in the township and
parish of Rhiwabon, which place he acquired by his
wife, Jane, the daughter of John Mills of London, merchant, who purchased it from John Eyton. John Powell,
who was living in 1620, had issue three daughters, co-
heirs, 1, Jane, ux. Edward Williams of Hafod y Bwch,
son and heir of William ab David ab Ieuan Llwyd ;[1]
2, Catherine, ux. Maurice Matthew, Clk., Rector of Erbistog in 1660 (see Blodwel Fechan) ; and 3, ... who
sold her lands to the Rector of Erbistog.

Sir Thomas Powell of Plâs yn Horslli, son and heir
apparent of Thomas Powell and Dorothy his wife, was
created a Baronet by King Charles I in January 1628,
and was High Sheriff for co. Denbigh in 1639. He
married Catherine, daughter of Sir John Egerton of
Oulton in Cheshire, Knt., and Margaret his wife, daughter
of Sir Rowland Stanley of Hooton, Knt., by whom he
had issue two sons, 1, Thomas, who died in 1627 *s. p.*,
in his great grandfather's lifetime ; and 2, John, of whom
presently ; and one daughter, Ffrances, who married,
first, Edward Norreys of Speke Hall in Lancashire,
and secondly, John Edwards of Stansti in the manor of
Y Glwysegl, and died September 19th, 1655.

John Powell of Bakersed, the second son of Sir Thomas,
died in December 1642 in his father's lifetime. He
married Margaret, daughter and co-heiress of Edward
Puleston of Trefalun, ab Edward Puleston of Trefalun,
ab Edward Puleston, second son of Sir Richard Puleston
of Emrall, Knt. By his wife, Margaret, who died Nov.
23rd, 1663, John Powell had issue two sons, 1, Sir

---

[1] See Penylan.

Thomas, of whom presently; and 2, Worsley, who died in his father's lifetime; and four daughters, 1, Catherine; 2, Ffrances, ux. Thomas Reddendale of Wrexham; 3, Elizabeth, *ob.* July 5th, 1663, *s. p.*; and 4, Anne.

Sir Thomas Powell of Plâs yn Horslli, Bart., was High Sheriff for co. Denbigh in 1657. He married, first, Mary, daughter of William Conwy of Bodrhyddan in Tegeingl (*sable*, on a bend cottised *argent*, a rose between two annulets *gules*), by whom he had issue two sons, 1, Thomas, of whom presently; and 2, William, who died *s. p.* Sir Thomas married, secondly, Jane, daughter of Robert Ravenscroft of Bretton, and relict of Henry Hardware of Peele, by whom he had issue two daughters, 1, Elizabeth, ux. Thomas Eyton of Trimley and Coed y Llai, High Sheriff for co. Flint in 1684; and 2, Margaret. Sir Thomas died and was buried at Gresford, September 28th, 1706, aged seventy-five.

Thomas Powell of Plâs yn Horslli, Esq., was born in 1650. He was High Sheriff for co. Denbigh in 1684, and died April 9th, 1689, in his father's lifetime. He married, first, Anne, daughter and heiress of Walter Cookes of London, merchant, and relict of Timothy Myddleton of Pant Iocyn. By her, who was buried at Gresford in 1675, he had issue one son, William, *ob. s. p.*, and two daughters, Mary and Margaret. Thomas Powell married, secondly, Wenefrid, daughter and heiress of John Mitho of Crascombe in co. Somerset (*or*, three negro's heads ppr., wreathed *argent*), by her, who died and was buried at Gresford in 1701, he left issue a son, Samuel, and a daughter named Winefride.

The male line of the Baronet family of the Powells of Plâs yn Horslli is now extinct. In the Gresford Registers we find that Edward Lloyd of Horslli, Esq, was buried there in 1714.

In Gresford Church is a monument with the following inscription (*Harl. MS.* 2129, fo. 24) :

" Here lyeth the body of Thomas Powell of Horsley, Esq., son and heir of Sir Thomas Powell, Bart., who in his lyfe tyme married two wives; the first was Anne, dau. to Walter Cookes of London, merchant, by whom he had a son that died young, Mary and Margaret. The second wife was Winefred, dau. and heir to John Micho of Crascombe, in the county of Somerset, Esq., by whom he had two sons and two daughters. . . . . died 9 April 1689, aged . . . . years."

All the atchievments of the said Thomas Powell are hung on the pillar, viz., penon, helmet, and crest, etc.

ARMS.—*Sable*, three roses *argent*, with a label *or*, impaling *or*, three negro's heads couped *sable*, wreathed *argent*, for Micho.

CRESTS.—On a helmet in a ducal coronet *gules*, a . . . . head *argent*, beaked of the first with three pointed rays behind the head.

On a helmet, a negro's head couped ppr., wreath *argent*.

THE ANCIENT RACES AND MONUMENTS OF BRITAIN.

The oblong tumuli or long barrows that are found in almost all parts of the kingdom are the burial places of those inhabitants of the island who lived in the Neolithic Age. The most important remains of that period are the vast serpent mounds, the cromlechs, and the upright monoliths or Meini Hirion, and the oval tumuli. Of the cromlechs, Kit's Coedy House, near Aylesford in Kent, consists of four stones of great size and hardness standing upright in the ground, which remains to this day, but the top stone is gone. Aubrey, in the *Monumenta Britannica*, says: "About a mile from White Horse Hill, on the top of the hill, are a great many great stones, which were layed there on purpose, but as if tumbled out of a cart, without any order; but some of them are placed edgewise." He also says "that the sepulchre was 74 paces long and 24 broad", and was like the cromlech called Y Lech at Caer Gybi in Môn.

There are two long barrows made of large stones on the highest summit of the western extremity of Esgair Clochfaen, in the parish of Llangurig in Arwystli. It has been suggested to me by some of my friends, that the word Cloch-faen is a corruption of Goluch-Faen, or Stone of Worship. The bones found in these tumuli were those of a short dolicho-cephalic race, that is, a race whose skulls were long and narrow, and the implements buried with them were either of stone or flint.

" With regard to the ancient inhabitants of Britain", said Tacitus, "and whether they sprang from the soil or came from abroad is unknown, as is usually the case with barbarians. Their physical characteristics are various, and from this conclusions may be drawn. The red hair and large limbs of the Caledonians point clearly to a German origin. The dark complexion of the Silures, their usually curly hair, and the fact that Spain is the opposite coast to them, are evidence that Iberians of a former date crossed over and occupied those parts." For a corroboration of this statement of Tacitus, I refer the reader to the work entitled *Cave Hunting*, by Prof. Boyd Dawkins.

Professor Rolleston states, in the work on *British Barrows*, p. 679 : " As regards the earlier of the two prehistoric races, we have in this country dolicho-cephaly combined with low stature and dark complexion in a very considerable number of our population. The fact of the existence of this stock—or perhaps, we may say, of its survival and its reassertion of its own distinctive character, in the districts of Derby, etc.—was pointed out in the year 1848 by the late Professor Phillips, at a meeting of the British Association at Swansea.

From the sepulchral discoveries it appears that the Neolithic tribes occupied the whole of Britain themselves for perhaps many ages. Subsequently, however, they were invaded by men of a different race, whose remains we find buried in round barrows. From these remains we find that the invaders were a tall race of men with short round or brachi-cephalic skulls, and that all their weapons were made of bronze. These bronze weapons are always found buried with them, whether we find them buried with the Neolithic race, or separately in their round tumuli. Stonehenge is surrounded by a

vast number of long barrows, although there are many
round ones. Dr. Thurnam says that two of the round
barrows near Stonehenge appear to be contemporary, or
very slightly posterior, to the date of the temple itself.
"In digging down to their base, chippings and fragments, not merely of the Sarsens were found, but likewise of the blue felspathic hornstones, foreign to Wilt-
shire, which assist in the formation of the Megalithic
structure."

"We here see traces of at least two nations established
in these islands before the era of the Celtic settlements.
Some prefer to include in one wide description all the
fair tribes of high stature with red or golden hair, and
blue or grey-blue eyes ; and they count as true Celts all
of that kind who are neither Danes nor Germans. Some
class together in the same way all the short peoples
with black hair and eyes, whether pale-skinned or ruddy
in complexion, calling them Iberians on account of their
supposed affinity with the dark races remaining in the
south of Europe. All the tall, round-headed and broad-
headed men are described together as comprising "the
van of the Aryan army", with whom became intermin-
gled tall dark and red-haired men from Scandinavia,
and fair people of Low-German descent. All the short
and dark races, whether long-headed or round-skulled,
are treated as descendants of a primitive non-Aryan
stock, including "the broad-headed dark Welshman, and
the broad-headed dark Frenchman", and connected by
blood, not only with the modern Basque, but with the
ancient and little known Ligurian and Etruscan races.[1]

Diodorus Siculus, who lived in the first century after
Christ, when describing Britain says : "There is in that
island a magnificent temple of Apollo, and a circular
shrine, adorned with votive offerings, and tablets with
Greek inscriptions on the walls. The kings of that city
and rulers of the Temple are the Boreads, who take up
the government from each other according to the order

[1] *Origins of English History.* By Charles Elton, Esq. London :
Bernard Quaritch, 15, Piccadilly.

of their tribes. The citizens are given up to music, harping, and chaunting in honour of the Sun." This temple is generally supposed to be that of Stonehenge ; if that is the case, Stonehenge had not been destroyed in the first century after Christ.

If any person of importance were in peril from disease or the chance of war, a criminal or slave was killed or promised as a substitute. The Druids held that by no other means could a man's life be redeemed or the wrath of the gods appeased ; and they went so far as to teach that the crops would be fertile in proportion to the rich- ness of death.[1] It became a national institution to offer a ghastly hecatomb at particular seasons of the year. In some places the victims were crucified or shot to death with arrows ; elsewhere they would be stuffed into huge figures of wicker-work, or a heap of hay would be laid out in the human shape, where men, cattle, and wild beasts were burned in a general holocaust.

In the Bible we read of Jehovah requiring the human sacrifices of seven of Saul's sons, in order to remove a famine in the days of David ; and, after they were hung up, " God was entreated for the land". And later on we are told that Jesus, the son of the Virgin Mary, was offered up as a sacrifice to Jehovah to appease his wrath.

In the Highlands, even in modern times, there were May-day bonfires at which the spirits were implored to make the year productive. A feast was set out upon the grass, and lots were drawn for the semblance of human sacrifice ; and whoever drew the " black piece" of a cake dressed on the fire was made to leap three times through the flame. In many parts of France, the sheriffs or the mayor of the town burned baskets filled with wolves, foxes, and cats, in the bonfires at the Feast of St. John. " C'était en beaucoup d'endroits en France l'usage de jeter dans le feu de la Saint-Jean des mannes ou des paniers en osier contenant des animaux, chats, chiens, renards, loups. Au siècle dernier même dans plusieurs villes c'était le maire ou les échevins qui fai-

---

[1] *Strabo*, iv, 272. Cæsar, *De Bell. Gall.*, vi, 15.

saient mettre dans un panier une ou deux douzaines de
chats pour brûler dans le feu de joie. Cette coutûme
existait aussi à Paris, et elle n'y a été supprimée qu'au
commencement du règne de Louis XIV."[1]

It is said that the Basques burn vipers in wicker
panniers at Midsummer, and that Breton villagers will
sacrifice a snake when they burn the sacred boat to the
goddess who has taken the title of St. Anne.

The valley of the Wye and the beautiful broken hill-
country west of the Malvern range have one of the most
confused and uncertain histories among all the English
shires. Naturally a district of Gwent, in South Wales,
and still inhabited for the most part by a peasantry of
Welsh descent, many of whom even now employ their
ancestral Cymric tongue, it was yet early attached to
the English interest, and has been counted, in its eastern
half at least, as a part of England from the very first
days of the Teutonic conquest. Long before that period
Herefordshire, with several of the surrounding shires,
formed part of the old principality or kingdom of the
Silures, the British race that held out with fiercest
energy against the invading Roman legionaries. Modern
anthropological investigations have tended to show that
the Silurians were not a pure Celtic race, but a dark,
long-skulled, non-Aryan people, allied to the primitive
Neolithic inhabitants of Britain, and perhaps, also, to the
modern Basques of the Pyrenean region. To this day
the type of *physique* usually identified with the rem-
nants of the prehistoric Euskarian stock is exceptionally
common among the men of Hereford; and even the
casual visitor can hardly fail to be struck by the dark com-
plexions, oval heads, and prominent cheek-bones so frequently noticed in the country districts about Ross and
Monmouth. Be this as it may, however, it is at least
certain that the Silurians, even if originally Euskarian
by race, must have adopted the Celtic tongue at a very
early date, as their brethren, the so-called Black Celts,

---

[1] Gaidoz, *Esquisse de la Religion des Gaulois.* See also vol. i, pp.
40, 41, 42, 52, 266.

have long done in Ireland and Scotland. During the
Roman invasion these Celticized aborigines offered a
peculiarly sturdy resistance to the southern conquerors.
Herefordshire, indeed, is the classic country of Caractacus (Caradog), the land celebrated in the vigorous rhe-
toric of Tacitus as the last home of British freedom.
The great range of late pre-Roman earthworks which
caps the Malvern hills probably marks the first line of
defence thrown up by the Silurian chief against the advance of Ostorius, who had crossed the Severn to attack
him with all the troops collected from the numerous
stations that dot the surface of the Cotswolds. The
camps at Whitborne, Croft-Ambrey, Thornbury, and
Wapley, seem to belong to a later campaign, when the
line of the Malverns was abandoned, and Caractacus
was forced to fall back upon his secondary range of fort-
resses in the rear. Finally, Coxwall Knoll is held, with
great probability, to be the scene of the last desperate
defence, immortalised in the vague description of Tacitus.

The Silures, however, says Tacitus, induced the other
nations to revolt, and the Iceni broke out into open war,
but were defeated by Ostorius. " In this state of affairs
Ostorius dies, being quite spent with fatigue and trouble. The enemy rejoiced at his death as a general in no
way contemptible, and the rather because, though he did
not fall in battle, he expired under the burthen of that
war."[1]

After Frontinus had at length pacified the whole district from the Forest of Dean to the banks of the Usk,
we hear for the first time the name around which the
whole subsequent history of the country centres—that of
Ariconium. The important station so styled lay either
at Ross itself or at Weston-under-Penyard, two miles
distant. Just as the root-syllable of Uriconium, vari-
ously disguised, crops up over and over again in the
history of the Wrekin district, so the root-syllable of the
very similar Ariconium perpetually occurs in the history

[1] Tacitus, *Ann.*, xii, 39 (Camden).

of ancient and mediæval Herefordshire. Long after the Romans had left the country, the dubious Welsh writer, quoted as Nennius, speaks of this region under the name of Ercing, a word whose connection with Ariconium is not particularly clear until we recollect that the first was pronounced hard like Erking, while the second was a Latinised variation of some crude form, Aricon or Arcon. Geoffrey of Monmouth, a writer of local knowledge, calls it Hergin; and, indeed, the lively and romantic archdeacon is never very remarkable for correctness in the use of aspirates. In the *English Chronicle* and other Anglo-Saxon documents the name is converted into a typical Teutonic clan-title, as Ircingafeld; and from that corrupt form it has been finally modernised into Archenfield, a clear product of sound local etymological instinct, still preserving for us in a fairly recognisable shape the old root of Ariconium.

So much for the most primitive name of Herefordshire itself, regarded as a fixed unit of territory. The history of the folk who dwell in it is far more complicated. Very soon after the earliest West Saxon brigands had crossed the Cotswolds and settled down in the rich valley of the lower Severn around Gloucester and Worcester, a small outlying colony from this young parent state appears to have penetrated still further westward and conquered for itself from the Welsh of Gwent a petty principality in the hither half of Herefordshire. The men of the Worcestershire kingdom were called Hwiccas: those of the region beyond the Malverns became known as Magesætas—a name of the same type as the Dorsætas, the Somersætas, the Wilsætas, and the Defnsætas of southern Wessex, or as the Wroken-sætas and Pec-sætas of Shropshire and Derbyshire. The termination seems usually to imply a settlement of a few English overlords among a large conquered and servile Celtic population; and such was certainly the case in Herefordshire, where the number of slaves recorded in Domesday is unusually high. Perhaps the first syllable of the name may be derived from

the Roman station of Magna — or the Cymric word
which it represents—as that of the Dorsetæs is cognate
with Durnovaria, and that of the Wrokensætas with Uriconium. Another small English tribe of West Hecans seems
also to have inhabited old Herefordshire; yet Florence
of Worcester, who is usually remarkable for his accuracy
in dealing with his own district and its neighbourhood,
apparently identifies them with the Magesætas. When
the Mercian kings began to consolidate the petty principalities of the Midlands, and to drive the West Saxons
across the Thames and the Avon, they united the lands
of the Hwiccas and Magesætas to their own overlord-
ship, but left the native princes in possession as subject
kings or ealdormen. The town of Hereford, which had
acquired its present name in the exact modern form as
early as the days of Bede, was made into the see of the
Bishop of the Magesætas shortly after the conversion of
Mercia. But it must then have been a border fortress
of the Teutonic colonists; for the Wye remained the
boundary between Welsh and English long after the days
of Offa, and the portion of Herefordshire beyond that
river contains local names almost exclusively of the
Welsh type to the present day.[1]

THE BRITISH KINGS OF HEREFORD, GLOUCESTER, ERGING OR URKENFIELD, AND EWIAS.

Caenawg Gawr ab Iorwerth Hirflawdd ab Tegonwy ab Teon, etc.=
See vol. i, p. 360.

Caradog Ffreichfras, King of Hereford, Gloucester, Erging, and Ewias.=

Ilyfaidd, King of Hereford, Gloucester, Erging, and Ewias.=

Lluddocaf, King of Hereford, Gloucester, Erging, and Ewias.=

Rhiengar, sole=Ynyr ab Cadfarch, lineally descended from Vortigern,
heiress.   Prince of Erging and Ewias, and King of Britain.
| a

| a

Tudor Trevor, King of Hereford, Gloucester,⊤Angharad, d. of Hywel Dda,
    Erging, and Ewias; *ob.* 948.   King of Wales.

| 1 | 2 | 3

Goronwy died in his father's lifetime.⊤   Lluddoccaf. See   Dingad. Vol.
    See vol. i, p. 308.   vol. i, p. 310.   i, p. 309.

Rhiengar, sole heiress.⊤Cuhelyn ab Ifor ab Severus, Prince of Buallt.   See
                    vol. i, p. 308.

Elystan Glodrhudd, Prince of Fferlis, King of Hereford, Gloucester,⊤
    Erging, and Ewias. Born in Hereford Castle, and was living in the |
year 1010.

Cadwgan, Prince of Fferlis. He was defeated in battle by William the Con-
    queror, who took his kingdom of Hereford, Gloucester, Erging, and
    Ewias.

The history of some of his descendants is given in
vol. ii, p. 300, and their genealogy at p. 322. One
branch of this house settled in the parish of Llangurig.
The following is their descent, as far as I have been able
to trace it in the *Harl. MS.* 1969.

Maurice ab Madog ab Einion ab Howel of Mochdref and Ceri.⊤
                   Vol. ii, p. 225.

Rhys ab Maurice of Mochdref.⊤Eva, d. of Howel ab Owain ab Gruffydd ab
                   Ieuan ab Meilir ab Menwn.

John of Llan-=Dyddgu, d. of Jenkyn ab Llywelyn ab Howel ab   Richard.
   gurig.   Rhys ab David ab Howel Fychan of Cefn yr
          Hafodau in Llangurig. See vol. ii, p. 289, and
          History of Llangurig, by Mr. Edward Hamer.

COWYDD I SION AB RHYS AB MAURICE.[1]

Mae o Einion ymwanwr,
Mynnu'r gamp mae'n orcu gwr.
Mae hwy arfau'r mab hirfawr,
Mae llun gwych fal Lleon Gawr,
Y mae grym y gwr yma,
O dywaid, hwn ei dad da.
Mae gwayw Sion mwy a'i gâd ef,
Mynn ei waithdrafn mewn wyth dref.
Mae cledd du yn gyvru'n gwaith,
Mentr teilwng mewn tair talaith,

---

[1] From *Add. MS.* 14,901, No. 12, in the British Museum.

Er ffo dewrion lle bon' byth,
Na chwilio gwych wehelyth.
Ni ffŷ Sion, hoff yw ei swydd ;
Er gwarau gwr a gorwydd ;
Gwas dewrwych, a gais daraw,
A'i gweryl aeth gar ei law.
Gwr yr Sion a gurai saith,
Gwr dinam, garw, diweniaith,
Ni roi gefn er ei gyfarch,
Sein ar ŵr mai Sion yw 'r arth.
Gwr yw Sion gorau y sydd,
Arg ofion â 'r gwayw efydd ;
Llew glân o Elystan Llwyth,
Lle 'i daliodd llû á 'i dylwyth.
Lliw gwyn o Frochdyn a'i frig,
Lle mae arwydd llew Meurig.
Sarff yw gâs, Syr Ffŵg o ŵr,
Os am ynys ymmwanwr ;
Dyged o Gorbed y gair,
Draw Farwn, byth drwy fawrair.
Y Mochdref mae ef am waed
At ais a gwrdd t'wysogwaed.[1]
Trig ar f'wng trwy Geri fawr
Traws flin-walch teiroes flacnawr.
Nid enyll neb o'i dynion
Am droi swydd i'm daro, Sion :
Ni fyn Sion union anair,
E fyn â'r ffŷnn ofni'r Ffair ;
E fyn gael fo iawn i gyd ;
A fynodd, a fu enyd.
Ef yw'r bŵ i fawr a bach ;
Heb ochel ni bu weliach.
Dewr yw Sion, a dyrys yw,
Drwy gedyrn fel draig ydyw.
Oen diddig oni ddigier,
Obry'n mysg brawn a môr
Ei wraig a rydd rywiawg ran
O'r gorau aur ac arian.
Ei bwyd rhoes heb wâd yn rhydd
Odidawg, a'i diodydd.
Gwen, gu, lân, gan galeuig,
Gwen bûr-ddoeth, gwn, heb awr ddig.

---

[1] Mochdref, a parish adjoining Llandinam, and near Newtown.

Lloer Siancyn gwreiddin graddol,
Llirddynt had, llwy-ddiant i'w hol.
[Gwraig] Sion gŵyrael Llangurig
Lloer i bro, lliw aur i brig,
I gŷd hefyd gâd, Dofydd,
Gwen a Sion dau cân' oes hydd,
A'i gwr êl o'i gwerylon,
Ag y sydd gorau, Sion.
Ni bu Rys mynebwr well
Yn eich hoedl oedd na Chadell,
Na Morys yn ei mawredd,
Nag Einion wych, gwn, un wedd,
Nag Elystan aig lwys dad,
Na deunaw gynt yn y gâd.
Y Nudd yw Sion oedd i'w serch,
Addaw[1] rhoddion ail Rhydderch,
Nerth Einion wrth ei ynys,
A fu'm mhob braich Sion mab Rhys.
Nerth Dduw i Sion, wyrthiau'r Saint.
I'w dâl hynod êl henaint.

Sion Ceri a'i Cant

AN ODE ADDRESSED TO JOHN AB RHYS AB MAURICE[2] OF LLANGURIG.

By John, the Bard of Kerry.

A tilter comes of Einion's race,
None better loves the game,
A youth stout and tall—his arms are taller still,
Noble is his form, like that of Lleon Gawr :[3]
The strength of our hero
Is said to equal that of his doughty father.

---

[1] "Adaw" in MS.

[2] Maurice ab Madog ab Einion ab Howel of Mochdref, Esq., son of Tudor ab Einion Fychan, Lord of Cefn y Llys, descended from Elystan Glodrudd, Prince of Fferlis. He married Tangwystl, daughter and co-heiress of Gruffydd ab Jenkyn, Lord of Broughton, who bore *sable*, a chevron inter three owls *argent*. By this lady, Maurice had issue six sons—1, Ieuan Lloyd ; 2, Rhys ; 3, David ; 4, Llewelyn ; 5, Maurice Fychan, whose daughter and co-heiress, Catherine, married Jenkyn Goch of Clochfaen ; and 6, Ieuan Gwyn.

[3] A king of Britain, according to the *Bruts*, who built Chester, called to this day Caer Lleon Gawr, the Fortress of Lleon the Giant.
— Williams's *Eminent Welshmen*, p. 276.

Greater still hath the spear of John been proved,
In eight towns is the effect of its thrust desired.
In battle he drives his black sword
With a worthy daring in the three principalities.[1]
From where they stand to the last, though brave men fly,
His noble tribe will never yield their ground.
Fly will not John, his duty is dear to him.
In the play of horse and horseman[2]
A youth stout and mettlesome, who will strive to strike,
When his quarrel has come to his hand.
John is a hero who can beat seven,
A hero void of offence, rough, no flatterer,
Who, though he be courted, will not cringe—
The bear is the sign that the man is John.
A hero is John, possessed of the best
Reminiscences, with the brazen spear.
A pure-bred lion of Elystan's tribe,[3]
Where with his people he avenged himself on a host.
Of the white hue of Broughton and its branch[4]
Where is the symbol of the lion of Meurig?
He is a hateful serpent, a Sir Fulke of a man[5]
If called to combat for the Island.[6]
Derived from Corbet was the epithet,[7]
The Baron yonder, for a perpetual fame.
To Mochdref does he owe his blood—
The blood impulsive in the breast of princes.
For three generations there dwells a chieftain
To trouble the perverse and vain throughout the extent of
    Kerry.
Not one of its men shall be free
To strike me, John, for exercising my calling.[8]

---

[1] Of Gwynedd, Powys, and Dyfed.   [2] The tournament.
[3] Elystan Glodrydd.
[4] Perhaps an allusion to the family coat.
[5] Sir Fulke Fitzwarren.   [6] I.e., of Great Britain.
[7] Madog ab Einion ab Howel of Mochdref married Anne, daughter
of Piers Corbet, Lord of Lee or Leigh juxta Caus, descended from
Roger Corbet, Lord of Leigh, who bore _or_, two ravens ppr. in a border
engrailed _gules_, second son of Robert FitzCorbet, Baron of Caus.—
Harl. MS. 1396; _Lewys Dwnn_, vol. i, p. 314. Einion married Nest,
daughter and heiress of Adda ab Meurig ab Adda ab Madog ab
Maelgwyn, Lord of Kerry and Maelienydd.
[8] _I.e._, of a clerwr or minstrel. They were sometimes subjected to
legal measures in consequence of their erratic habits of life.

The upright John will not allow abuse :
He will have the fair awed by the staves (of the officers).
He will have justice done to every one,
And what he wills at once has come to pass.
He is a terror to great and small ;
Beware him those who would keep a whole skin !
John is both stout and formidable,
He is a dragon amidst the strong ;
A gentle lamb, if he be not angered ;
Then he descends upon them with his brawn and marrow.
A goodly share will his Wife bestow
Of the best of gold and silver.
Her provision she distributes without stint,
Which is excellent, as also her liquor.
She is fair, kindly, and pure, lavish in gifts,
Fair, and very wise, to my knowledge, and never angry.
Bright as the moon is she, sprung from the root of Jenkyn,
May her seed shoot forth, and may her posterity prosper.
The arched eyebrow of John's Wife is to Llangurig
As the moon to the land, radiant as gold o'er the hill.
On John and his Lady bestow then, O God,
To live together the hundred years of the Hart,
And may her husband John come forth
From his quarrels however is best ;
Rhys was no better opponent
In your lifetime, nor was Cadell,
Nor Maurice in his might,
Nor the noble Einion, I ween, in any way ;
Nor Elystan, the father of the pure race,
Nor twice nine of any of those of yore.
A very Nudd is John to those he loves,
He promises gifts like a Rhydderch,[1]
To his country Einion's strength
Is John the son of Rhys in both his arms.
May John gain strength from God, and miracles wrought
        by the saints,
To uphold him until he be old and full of renown.

---

[1] Rhydderch Hael, or the Generous.

MEINI HIRION.

Add. MS. 15,022, *folio* 108.

Maesmawr. Main hirion.

Mae man ar y Mynyd rhwng Ial ac Ystrad Alun uwchben
Rhyd y gyfarthfa a elwir y maes mawr lle bu y vrwdyr rhwng
Meilir ap   a Beli ap Benlli Gawr lle llas Beli ap Benlli
Gawr ag y gossodes Meirion dau faen yn y sefyll un ymhob
pen ir bed y rhain a fuant yno hyd ofewn y deugain Mlyned
yna y daeth dyn anraslon un Edwart ap Sion ap Llywelyn o
Ïâl pwid y dry'll tir a gaessid or Mynyd yn yr hwn oid y bed
ar main uchod yndo ac y codes y main ac y dodes tros bibell
odyn Galch ac o dra gwres ar pwys ar unwaith a gwedir ei
tarthi ef ai bwriod ac ai llosgod yn yr Odyn yn galch y rhai a
vuassent yno lawer cantoed oflynydoed a diwed drwg a daeth
ido yr hwn a diadurnod red y milwr marw ir hwn y canassai
y Bard ar Englynion bedeu Milwyr Ynys Brydein yr Euglyn
hwn.

> Pieu y bed yn maesmawr
> Balch i law ar i lafnawr?
> Bed Beli ap Benlli Gawr.

Mae ym mhlwy y Wydgrug o fewn Powys Vadawg yn gyvagos
ir Maesmawr yn agos lan afon Alan man a elwir Maes Garmon
lle y rhodis duw fal y tystia Beda y Vudugoliaeth ir Bryt-
taniaid diarfau ar y Saesson drwy diosg odiam y pennau a
dyrchaf i dwylo tu ar nefoed a dywedyd ar ol Garmon Aleliwia deirgwaith deir gwaith llefoes y Saeson i dorri gydfe au
bodi gan daflu eu harfau odiwithynt a chymryt y eu traed i
ffo ac hyd hedyw ydis yn coffhau y gair hwnnw Aleliwia
pan rodo un wasgar neu dinystr anesgorawl elyn, fe a dywedis
ef a roes Aleliwia ar ei elyn neu ei gasseion.

Mal y cafas Huw Arwystl ei awen un Huw Arwystl oed
Grupyl tlawd diystyr ac o eisieu lletty weithie arno y myny
chai ef fyned i gysgu i eglwys Llandinam yn sir Drefaldwyn
pan delei ef ar y hynt fford honno ac ef a damweiniod id
dyfod y fford honno ar nos Galanmai a chysgu yno y nosson
honno a phan oed yn ei drymyn gwsg ef a welei drwy e hun
un yn dyfod attaw ag yno dodi peth yn oi ben a thranoeth y
bore pan deffrod ef. efa damweiniod i forwyn dyfod heibio a
vuassen yn ceissio haf a choflaid haf genthi a dywed wrth y
rhai oed gida hi wrth fyned heibio yr ffenestr tan yr hon oed
Huw yn gorwed y geiriau hyn sef, ni ryd neb o honoch chwi

dym haf ir crypul yma, mi a rof haf ido ac a fwriod gangen o
ir goed ido trwyr fenestyr ac a diolchod ef ar gan idi yr hwn
ni chanasau benill o ganiad erioed or blaen ac ni medrai ar
gan a ganod ef idi syd yn diliu fal hyn yn yr Euglyn hwn.

Ac o hynny allan y dechreuod brydydu ac a wnaeth lawer o
gerd orchestol ac a fu gymmeradwy gida Bonedigion Cymry oll
amser y ei fowyd yn ol hynny a peth a welei ef dodi yn ei ben
drwy e hun oed yr awenyd a roes duw ido yr hon oed yu
rhagori rhag un awen oed yn un oes ag ef.

Am Gaer Rhydwyn, a chaer Berwyn a Chaer Myfyr.

Rhudwyn Gawr pioed Gaer Rhydwyn uwch ben Pentre yr
Gaer yn ymyl Croes Yswallt. Berwyn Gawr pioed Gaer Berwyn ym Mynyd Berwyn. Cadeir Berwyn yn y gaer. Myfyr Gawr
pioed Caer Myfyr ym mynyd Myfyr o fewn tref y clawd yn
sir Amwythic—tri brodyr oedynt.

Caer Gadfael; ne Dingad fael yn ymyl Llann nefyd yng
hwnawd   ynghantref Rhyfoniog yn sir dinbych y mae.

Caer dinhen groen, a thre Dinhengroen yn ymyl Abergele
yng Cwmwd yng Cantrev yn Sir Ddinbych y mae.

Llech yr ast, neu lech yfiliaist, ym plwy Caer run y mae.
Ricell Arthur yno y mae hefyd yn gyfagos ir Llech un o bob
tu ir fford syd yn myned o Daly Cafn i fwlch y deufaen yng
Cwmmwd   yng Cantref   yn sir Gaer yn Arfon
y maent.

Carned y Saesson a buarth merched Mafon y maent o bob
tu ir fford syd yn tywys o fwlch y dufaen i Aber.

Bed Ffrymden ym Llannewyd y mae ac ywen yn tyfu
trwydo o fewn wythlath ne deg at y fynwent.

Caer Drewyn yn ymyl Grug, a Glyndyfrdwy ymae o fewn.

Caer enni, ym plwy Llanfor ym Penllyn y mae.

Pabell Llywarch hen yn Llanfor ym Penllyn yn agos ir
Eglwys y mae.

THE LEGEND OF ST. CURIG.

At a period of great antiquity, not later than, and
possibly anterior to, the seventh century, a person of
foreign appearance, and habited in the garb of a pilgrim,
disembarked from a ship that had brought him to a spot
near to that on which stands the modern town of Aberystwyth. He tarried not at the point of landing, in the
vale of the Ystwyth river,—then, doubtless, a tangled

wild of marsh and thicket to the water's edge,—but
straightway bent his steps up the steep and pathless
ascent towards the heights of Plinlimmon.   Reaching at
length the summit, and weary with his walk, he sat on
a rock, and, scanning the surrounding prospect, he espied
on the bank of the Wye a spot which he deemed eligible
for his future resting-place.   There, the work doubtless
of his own hands, uprose first a humble hermitage and
chapel, and afterwards a church, which, though not of
spacious dimensions, became celebrated for the beauty of
its architecture and the elegant carving and design of
its massive oaken roof.   The rock whereon the pilgrim
sat bears to this day the name of "Eisteddfa Gurig", or
Curig's Seat.   The church on Plinlimmon, adjacent to
the highest point of the macadamised mail-road from
Aberystwyth to Hereford, still bears testimony to its
founder by its name of "Llangurig", the Church of St.
Curig.   Moreover, a crozier or pastoral staff, stated by
Giraldus to have belonged to him, and to have been endowed with a supernatural healing power, was for centuries preserved with a loving veneration for his memory
in the church of St. Harmon's on the Radnorshire border :
a proof that he became a bishop (perhaps of Llanbadarn
Fawr, hard by the scene of his landing), or else the abbot
of a religious community, which in that case must have
been founded by himself.

Such is the legend of Curig Lwyd, which has led to
the hypothesis adopted by Professor Rees, that he was
not only the original founder of the church of Llangurig, but also its patron saint ; an hypothesis to which
a certain additional colour would be given by the traditional appellation of "Curig Lwyd", or "the Blessed",
by which he was popularly known.   A wider investigation, however, of the subject will lead unavoidably to
the inference that the Professor, critically accurate and
cautious as he usually is in his surmises, was somewhat
premature in thus determining the question ; and this is
the more surprising, inasmuch as he has himself furnished us with a list of churches in Wales, the dedica-

tory titles of which alone might have led him to doubt the soundness of such a conclusion. In his *Essay on the Welsh Saints*,[1] he tells us that the churches of *Llanilid a Churig*, Glamorganshire, and *Capel Curig*, Caernarvonshire, are dedicated to Juliet and Curig together; and that Juliet is also the saint of Llanilid Chapel, under Defynog, Brecknockshire. There are also two other churches, those, namely, of Porth Curig, Glamorganshire, and Eglwys Fair a Churig, Carmarthenshire, of which the Professor states that it is uncertain to whom they are dedicated. The festival of Juliet and Cyrique, he adds, is June 16th. Leland says that "in the middle of Lerine Creek, on the coast of Devon, was a litle celle of Sainct Cyret and Julette longging to Montegue", a Priory of Black Monks, from which they were driven, but restored by Henry I (iii, f. 18). This little cell was on a small *pill*, or creek, on the E. side of the Fowey river estuary now called Penpole Creek, up which is still a place of the Wymonds called "St. Cadoc", in error, perhaps, as well as Leland's "Carac", for Ciric. The priory to which it pertained was Montacute in Somerset. There are indications that the devotion to these saints was widely extended over the West of England. The chapel within the donjon on the islanded part of the Castle of Tintagel, ascribed to King Arthur, was dedicated to St. Juliet, called by Leland (ii, 73) St. Ulette (cf. W. Ilid), *alias* Uliane, which was still standing in his time. The foundations of this chapel were visible only a few years ago, and the altar slab was removed by a "tourist" within living memory. In Leland's list of Cornish monastic foundations (viii, f. 91) is "Prior. S. Cyriaci. mon. nigri." The church of S. Cury (Curig?), near the Lizard, and also Menheniot, seem to have been his, and Curry Rivell, North Curry, and Curry Mallet, near Taunton. St. Helen's, one of the Scilly Isles, is called St. Elid's by Borlase; and in Leland's account of these islands, he speaks of "Saint Lides Isle where yn tymes past at her sepulchre was gret superstition."

[1] Page 307, and note, p. 82.

Lewys Glyn Cothi (*Works, Dosparth,* I, p. 21) describes a church dedicated to S. Curig as square in
shape :

> " Gwely 'n fraisg a'i liw'n ei frig,
> Gloew '*sgwar,* fal Eglwys Gurig."

He also ridicules friars, who had no love for the bards,
who carried about images of this Saint, among others,
made of glass or alder-wood, which they exchanged for
provisions or clothing.

If these churches were dedicated to the martyr St.
Cyricus or Quiricus, whether jointly or otherwise with
his mother Juliet, the probability would lie, *primâ facie,*
in favour of the hypothesis that Llangurig was so too.
Nor is there anything, in fact, to oppose to it, save the
existence of the legend, and the analogy of other
churches in Wales believed to have derived their names
from those who respectively founded them, and who,
from that act alone, were afterwards, in the popular estimation, honoured with the title of Saints. In such a
case, moreover, it would appear not a little remarkable
that one bearing the name of the infant martyr should
have landed on our island, and have devoted the remainder of his life in it to the special service of religion in so wild and remote a region therein, unless, indeed, a positive connection existed between the peculiar
devotion introduced by him and the saint whose name
he bore, and under whose patronage he may have held
himself to be, in virtue of that name—an early instance,
perhaps, of a practice which gradually became general
in the church. That this was really the case will appear
highly probable from a comparison of the history of the
saint and of his martyrdom with such notices as have
come down to us of the *cultus* actually rendered to him
in Wales during subsequent centuries ; and if we add to
this the narrative of the migration, so to speak, of that
cultus from the eastern to the western churches, the probability will be changed into certainty.

It is stated by Ruinart[1] and by the Bollandists that

---

[1] Ed. Ratisbon, 1869.

various "acts" of these saints had been published in ancient times, one of which, included in the list of apocryphal works of Pope Gelasius, is printed by the New Bollandists[1] in Greek and Latin. Another account, believed by them to be genuine, is also published by them, together with a statement as to its origin, from which it appears that Pope Zosimus (A.D. 417), who had seen an edition of their acts which appeared to him to be spurious, wrote to a bishop of Iconium named Theodorus, requesting to be furnished with such genuine particulars of the martyrdom of SS. Cyricus and Julitta as could then be obtained on the spot where it took place, during the tenth persecution of the Christians under Diocletian, somewhat more than a century before.

Francis Combefis, O. P., has published from the Greek records in the King's Library at Paris, among the select triumphs of illustrious martyrs of Christ, a letter of this Theodore, Bishop of Iconium, in which is set forth the martyrdom of the holy martyr Cericus, and his mother Julitta. It is entitled, " Θεοδώρου Ἐπισκόπου Ἰκονίου Ἐπιστολὴ, δηλοῦσα τὸ μαρτύριον τοῦ ἅγιου Μάρτυρος Κηρύκου, καὶ τῆς τουτοῦ μητρὸς Ἰουλίττης." This epistle is referred to by Allatius in *Diatriba de Simeonum Scriptis*, page 91. An ancient version of it is mentioned in the *Notes to the Martyrology*, by Baronius, and has been found in the Vatican and Vallicellanian Libraries by the editors. It runs as follows :—

A LETTER OF THEODORUS, BISHOP OF ICONIUM, SETTING FORTH THE MARTYRDOM OF THE HOLY MARTYR CERICUS AND OF HIS MOTHER JULITTA.

"1. Since thy Reverence has demanded, by thine honoured letters, of my miserable vileness, to be informed about the narrative of a martyrdom very widely noised abroad, I mean that of Cyricus and of his mother Julitta; whether in the city of the Iconians also, from whence, too, the glorious martyr Julitta is said to have sprung, and her noble son Cyricus, the same account of their martyrdom has been received, as being the land in which they were born and brought up; because of there being contained

---

[1] Ed. Paris, 1867.

in it certain over-boastful and inconsistent sayings and trivialities foreign to our Christian hope; and, if it be possible to
discover the true account of their martyrdom, that it be
sent to thy Perfection. Having received from thee these
sacred writings, and having been fully observant of thine in-
junction, and having taken into my hands with zealous ear-
nestness the narrative of the martyrdom of the holy Cericus
and his mother Julitta; and having opened and read it with
great attention, I have found you to be speaking the truth, O
most holy of Fathers, and most worthy of Priests; for these
one might justly call the croakings of frogs or of daws. For
they are manifestly, as I think, devices of Manichees, or, perhaps, other heretics of heterodox opinions, who mock at and
endeavour to bring into hatred and censure the great mystery
of godliness.

" 2. But when, after making much search and investigation,
according to our ability, we effected nothing more, we inter-
rogated the inhabitants of the district and those by birth most
noble among the Isaurians, so that we might be able to obtain
some consecutive account, if only from hereditary tradition,
setting forth the conflict of the holy martyrs. Whereupon
Marcianus, a Christ-loving man, who had been made Tribune
of the Notaries and Chancellor of Justinian the King, when
he held the command in chief of the army; and Zeno, a very
wise man, who was also at that time his Assessor, gave the
following narrative respecting the Saints. That they had
heard from persons of noble descent that the ever-memorable
martyr Julitta was a relative of theirs, being a flower of the
first blood of Lycaonia, of blameless life, so that they made a
commemoration of her every year, doing this especially because of their relationship to her.

" 3. Now this lady, descended from royal blood, when the
persecution raged against the Christians in the time of Dioele-
tian, Count of Lycaonia (a man most ferocious, and delighting
exceedingly in the shedding of the blood of martyrs), took to
flight with two female attendants and her son of three years
old, viz., the glorious martyr Cericus, from the city of Iconium, which was that of her birth. Having abandoned her
property, which was considerable, she reached Seleucia, and,
finding there the Christians in still greater trouble at the
hands of Alexander the Governor, in the city of Seleucia,
under the King Diocletian, from whom he had received a
royal edict, enjoining the infliction of every sort of punishment upon those who would not sacrifice to the idols (as they
ascribed the name of gods to those who were not gods), she,

reflecting on the passage in Holy Scripture, ' Give place to anger', in order that they might not put themselves in the way of dangers, having fled from thence also, went off to Tarsus, which is the metropolis of the first province of the Cilicians.

"4. Then, as though by commandment, Alexander, who had vastly outdone Domitian in ferocity and cruelty, having removed thither, the victorious martyr Julitta was arrested, clasping in her arms her son, who was quite an infant, viz., the glorious martyr Cericus. And while they were apprehending her, her two attendants abandoned her and took to flight, and became spectators from without of the things that were done to her. Then she, standing before the judicial tribunal, when Alexander enquired what was the charge against her, and her fortune, and her country, she boldly answered the judge by taking on herself the name of the Lord Jesus Christ our God, by saying, ' I am a Christian.' Then Alexander, inflamed with anger, commanded her son to be taken away from her, and to be brought to him, inasmuch as he was both fair, and had no predeterminate knowledge of anything. But her, completely adorned as she was, he ordered to be beaten unsparingly with undressed thongs. Now when the executioners forcibly tore from the arms of his noble mother the boy who kept wailing, and longing to go back to his mother, and gazing after her, and brought him to the Governor, while the officers wrought upon her what was enjoined them, by beating her unmercifully, she made no other answer than, ' I am a Christian, and sacrifice not to demons.'

"5. While she then, like a lifeless statue, was being striped terribly by the blows, and uttering loudly, without ceasing, the same cry, the Governor took the child by the hands and endeavoured to soothe him with caresses, so that he should not cry, and placed him upon his knees, and attempted to kiss him. But the child, gazing stedfastly on his mother, pushed the Governor away, and drew back his head from him, and struggling against him, he scratched the Governor's face with his nails, and, like the offspring of some chaste turtle, the holy Cericus uttered an imitative sound, loudly uttering the same declaration that was being spoken by his mother, and saying ' I am a Christian', and kicked the Governor in the side, for it is the nature of childhood to be violently excited; so that this wild beast was enraged, under such circumstances (for he ought not to be called a man, who would not forgive an innocent action), and caught the boy by the foot and dashed him to the ground from his lofty judgment-seat. With such a confession was the skull of the glorious martyr broken against the corner of the steps, and crushed by the sharpness of the blow, so that the platform of the tribunal was covered with blood. Thus the heaven-born infant rendered up his spirit into the hands of God: for '*the souls of the Just are in the hand of God* (Wisdom iii, 1).

"6. At this sight, the holy Julitta was, as it were, filled with joy, and said, 'I give Thee thanks, O Lord, because thou hast deemed my son worthy to be perfected before me, and to gain an unfading crown.' Whereupon the judge, also deploring the act, orders her to be suspended on a rack, and severely tortured, and the pitch to be drawn bubbling from the cauldron and poured upon her feet. The judge also commanded exhortation to be made to her by the herald, 'Julitta, take pity on thyself, and sacrifice to the gods, and deliver thyself from the tortures, lest thou suffer the fate of thy son.' But she persevered in enduring her torments with a noble courage, crying out and saying, 'I sacrifice not to deaf and dumb wooden idols of demons, but I worship Christ the only Son of God, by whom the Father made all things, and I hasten to overtake my son, that with him I may be made worthy of the kingdom of Heaven.' But when the judge, inhuman to the extreme of madness, saw her unfailing constancy, he pronounced sentence upon her, by ordering that her head should be cut off, and that the remains of her son should be cast into the place of condemned persons.

"7. The executioners then fixed the gag upon her mouth, and led her away to the accustomed place to execute the order. Now it was that Julitta entreated the executioners to wait a little until she had prayed to God the only Good. And the executioners were softened, and granted her a little time. Then she knelt down and prayed, saying, 'I thank Thee, O Lord, because Thou hast called to Thee my son before me, and hast deemed him worthy, for Thy holy and terrible Name, to quit this present worthless life, and to be united with Thy Saints in the life eternal. Receive me, also, Thine unworthy servant, and cause me to obtain this great blessing, that I may be numbered with the wise virgins who have been deemed worthy to enter into the heavenly and incorruptible marriage-chamber; and let my spirit bless Thy Father, the Almighty God and Maker of all things, and the Holy Ghost for ever. Amen.' And when she had finished the 'Amen', the officer, brandishing his sword, severed her noble neck, without the city, and cast her body into the place where lay the remains of the glorious martyrs. The victorious martyr Julitta, and her glorious son Cericus, were perfected in the grace of Christ on the 15th of the month of July.

" 8. On the night of the following day her two maid-servants carried off their bodies and hid them and laid them in the ground in a suburb of Tarsus. Afterwards, one of the maid-servants, having survived to the times of the pious Emperor Constantine, when the Truth was brought to light, and the Churches of God, by grace, took courage, made known the spot. Then all the Faithful made haste to go there, each one to obtain from the relics of the Saints somewhat for the sustenance of his own life, and for the glory of our good God. These things, therefore, in truth, were done, as I have declared them to thy devout mind; and do thou deliver them to faithful men, who shall be able also to instruct others in the certainty of them, that they be not carried away by writings manifestly fabulous, but may believe the truth itself; in Jesus Christ our Lord, with whom to the Father with the Holy Ghost be glory, honour, power, for ever and ever. Amen."

The above is from the Greek text with its Latin version by Combefis. There is, however, an older Latin version, which differs from it in some particulars, especially in giving the name of Zosimus. It is entitled *Epistola Theodori Ep. de passione SS. Quirici et Julittæ jam olim Latine reddita ex MSS. Romanis*, and begins thus, " Charissimo Fratri et sancto Coepiscopo Zosimo Theodorus annuente Domino Præsul, salutem in Domino."

From this time forward the devotion to these holy martyrs spread widely over the East. A panegyric is still extant in their honour, written by Metaphrastes, or more probably by Nicetas the rhetorician, as is supposed, in the ninth century, the facts in which were furnished by Bishop Theodore's letter. Offices in their honour were sanctioned by St. Germanus, and Anatolius, Patriarch of Constantinople, A.D. 449-58, while others are known to have existed at Byzantium and Mauroleum. A complete office, with canon, by Josephus the hymnographer, A.D. 883, contains some verses commencing thus :

Κηρίκον ὑμνῶ σὺν τεκούσῃ προφρόνως Ἰωσήφ.

Josephus speaks of their tomb as being bedewed with the grace of the Holy Spirit, and of cures being wrought there ; but is silent as to its locality. The reason for this, as we shall shortly see, was in all probability the circumstance that the bodies themselves had, at a much earlier period, been conveyed away, and treasured up as precious relics in certain churches of the West. The story of their removal is thus given in an ancient MS. discovered at Rome,[1] as related by Henschenius the Bollandist, in his commentary for the 1st of May, on the *Life of St. Amator*, a Bishop of Auxerre, who lived from A.D. 344 to 418, and was consecrated A.D. 388. This *Life* is said to have been written A.D. 580.

" After the lapse of many years from their gaining the crown of martyrdom, St. Amator, Bishop of Antissiodorum, accompanied by the most illustrious Savinus, travelling through the territory of Antioch, by the grace of Christ found their most holy bodies, and on his return brought them, with great devotion, to Gaul. On reaching the city of Autrice (Chartres) he so far yielded to the entreaties of Savinus as to bestow on him one of the boy's arms, which appears to have been deposited in the church at Nevers. The other remains he caused to be entombed a second time in the very house ' where the Bishop, powerful by the glory of his merits, is yet venerated by the faithful'. Whether the city of Antioch visited by St. Amator was that in Pisidia or in Syria, or more probably another of that name, near Tarsus, the scene of the martyrdom, is not stated. From the Nevernais the arm of St. Cyricus was removed by Abbot Hucbald to his monastery of Elno ' *in Hannonia*'."[2] In the *Gallican Martyrology*, by Saussaye, it is stated that considerable portions of the relics were distributed among different churches in Gaul, " whereby a great devotion was stirred up everywhere towards the martyrs themselves, so that many churches, monasteries, and other ' trophies' (as they were then called), were erected in

---

[1] The MS. commences thus : " Incipiunt miracula SS. Quirici et Julittæ, quæ Teterius Sophista, corum servus, edidit, de corporibus corum a S. Amatore Antiochiæ repertis."

[2] Perhaps St. Amand's in Flanders, of which Hainault is a province.

their honour. Among them Toulouse, Arles, Carnot, and Auvergne, are specially named. The devotion also extended itself to Spain, where, at Burgos, an office with nine lections is known to have been recited in their honour. In France, Cyricus became known indifferently by the names of St. Cyr and St. Cyrique; and the name of 'Cir Ferthyr', once attached to the site of a ruined chapel in Lleyn, Carnarvonshire, may possibly be a translation of the former."[1]

From the foregoing account it will not be difficult to explain how, in early times, a Gaul, inspired with the prevalent devotion to these martyrs, may have been called by the name of one of them; may have landed on the coast of Wales, bringing with him, mayhap, a small but treasured portion of the relics in his own country esteemed so precious; may have built in honour of this, his patron saint, a humble chapel, enlarged subsequently into a church, with its monastic establishment adjacent; and taken precautions for the preservation, after his death, of the memory of the acts and sufferings of one whom he himself held in such tender veneration, by translating some narrative of them in his own possession into the language of the people to whom he had been the means of introducing the knowledge and *cultus*, as saints, of himself and his martyred mother.

That such was actually the fact is not obscurely intimated in several scattered notices which are to be found in the manuscript works of Welsh bards and elsewhere. In a fragmentary poem on St. Curig in the *Llyfr Ceniarth MS.*, a *Book of his Life* is referred to as extant in the author's time. Other fragments of poems in the same MS., by Sion Ceri and by Huw Arwystli, relate also certain circumstances of the martyrdom, in all probability derived from this traditionary biography. And lastly, some curious "*emynau*", or hymns, in the Welsh language, are found in the volume of *Lives of Cambro-British Saints*, published by the Welsh MSS. Society, comprising a "Lectio" evidently intended for the in-

---

[1] Rees' *Welsh Saints*, p. 332; *Arch. Camb.*, 4th-Ser., v, p. 87.

struction of the people on the annual festival, together
with some collects, which leave no doubt as to the identity of the saints, whose actions are referred to, with those
whose acts were recorded by Bishop Theodore for the
information of Pope Zosimus.

With these fragmentary notices is connected another
question of no little interest, relative to the genuineness
and authenticity of the acts of these martyrs traditional
in the Principality.   Was the narrative contained in
them substantially identical with that furnished by the
Bishop of Iconium to the Pope ?   Or did it rather savour
of inspiration drawn from the spurious writings referred
to in the Bishop's letter as " containing overboastful
and inconsistent sayings, and trivialities foreign to our
Christian hope", and which are ascribed by him to the
" machinations of Manichees and other heretics who
make a mock of, and endeavour to create a contempt
for, the great mystery of godliness"?   It would be natural to suppose that, from the time of the publication of
the authentic *Acts*, the spurious ones would have speedily
ceased to obtain currency, and have fallen into oblivion.
So far, however, from this being the case, we find them
incurring the condemnation of Pope Gelasius (A.D. 492-6),
" having been brought, together with their relics, from
the East".   We are left to infer, therefore, that Bishop
Theodore's account, when forwarded to Rome, was either
not at all, or but partially, circulated in Asia : hence St.
Amator, when carrying away with him the bodies of the
martyred mother and son, must have taken with him
also the apocryphal account of their death.   And this
inference is confirmed by the fact that these apocryphal
Acts were edited by Hucbald, who, as we have seen,
was presented with the arm of St. Cyricus at Nevers,
and who died in the year 930.   And again, A.D. 1180,
they were edited by Philip, an abbot of the Premonstratensian Abbey of Bona Spes, for John, the abbot of the
church of St. Amandus at Elno.   John, it would appear,
furnished Philip, in the first instance, with a copy of the
apocryphal *Acts* together with Hucbald's work, for we

find him stating in a letter to John that he had made in them considerable corrections, and had omitted much that appeared to him profane, irrelevant or absurd.

If these were the *Acts* brought by St. Amator into Gaul, it would follow almost of course that they alone would have been known to Curig Lwyd, and by him disseminated in Wales. The Welsh fragmentary notices will be found amply confirmatory of this view; and as they and the foregoing account are reciprocally illustrative of one another, we propose now to allow them to speak for themselves. The first of these notices is that in the *Emynau Curig* (Hymns of St. Curig), as the devotions printed in the *Lives of the Cambro-British Saints*, already mentioned, are strangely called. The third of these is as follows : "The holy martyr Curig was discreet from his childhood. He suffered martyrdom, and was very wise, and a teacher of heavenly things, and opposed the cruel commandment of Alexander the king, and rejected a lordly life, from a pure heart and the wisdom of a perfect man. He desired not the vain things of this world, but that he might obtain the joys of Paradise ; and suffered for the Triune God and one Lord severe persecution from men ; and for love to Christ the King he endured the torments of fire on his body and on his arms ; and through faith in the Trinity he persevered in faith and in prayer to God, so that the faithful might escape the pains of Hell, and obtain the joys of the heavenly kingdom, by the words of the Catholic faith, and become no less perfect in Christ than that martyr. Therefore we piously call on the undefiled Curig, our helper in Heaven, that by his prayers we may obtain and deserve the very glorious reward which he is said to enjoy with the hosts of angels for ever and ever.[1] Amen."

This *Emyn*, or lesson, furnishes a remarkable coincidence with the apocryphal life published in the *Acta Sanctorum* of the Bollandists. It represents the martyr as speaking and acting as an adult, whereas the latter

[1] *Lives of the Cambro-British Saints*, pp. 276 and 610.

describes Cyricus, though an infant, as speaking with
the words of a full-grown man, and as reproving Alexander for his idolatry and cruelty, even challenging
him to inflict on him strange and unheard-of tortures of
his own devising, through which he passes in succession
unhurt, by the power of God.   With these, the allusions
obscurely thrown out in the following fragments of
Welsh poems, mainly agree.   The first is attached in
the MS. to a portion of Huw Cae Llwyd's poem on the
Four Brothers of Llangurig, who was born, and probably
passed his life, in the neighbourhood of that place, but
need not, therefore, be his.[1]

THE FIRST FRAGMENT.

Llurig fendigedig wyd,
Ceidwad [in] a'r Ffrainc ydwyd
Mae i'th wlad, fel y wnaeth [wedd]
Dy achau, a llyfr dy fuche[dd]
Mae'n rhan, o bedwar ban byd,
Dy wyrthiau, rhaid yw wrthyd !
Da fyd fu ar dŷ feudwy,
A'i leian gynt ar lan Gwy.
    Mael gad, pan geisiodd Maelgwn
Lunio hud i leian hwn,
Ei feirch, a'i gewyll efo,
A arwe[i] niodd wr yno ;
Trigo'r llaw wrth y cawell,
Ynglŷn ni wnai Angel well ;
A'i wŷr aeth ar ei ol
A lynant bawb olynol ;
Hwynthwy oedd[ynt] arnat ti
Yn dy guddigl di 'n gweddi ;
Drwy dy nerth, Gurig Ferthyr,
Y rhoddai yn rhydd ei wŷr ;
A'i gwyrthiau, 'n ael gorthir,
A wnaeth Duw o fewn i'th dir ;

---

[1] The language of Huw Cae Llwyd, in the opinion of the Rev.
D. S. Evans, proves that he was a South Wallian writer ; but Llangurig is on the borders.   The poems in the text, at least in the state
in which they are here presented, are not, he thinks, the production
of that accurate prosodian and mellifluous poet.

Delwau o gwyr, rhwng dwylaw Gwen,
A lunioedd lcian lanwen ;
Y rhith, ac nid anrheithwyd,
Dinbych [Llan] Elidan Lwyd :
A'i delw, nid o hudoliaeth,
Rhoi llef ar Dduw Nef a wnaeth ;
A'i gradd, fel y gweryddon,
Gydâ Sant a gedwais hon.
Maelgwn aeth, mal y gwn i,
Ei delwaith i addoli ;
Hwn a roddais, yn bresent,
Glasdir at glos, da ei rent,
Hysbys yw bod llys a llan,
A theml i chwithau y man.
Ni bu rwydd rhag Arglwyddi
Daro dyn wrth dy wyr di ;
Chwithau a fu'n dadlau 'n deg,
Ar Ustus gynt ar osteg :
Ar fraich deg oedd faich dy fam
Silits a roes hwyl . am
Holl feddiand Alexander
A fu megis gattiau gêr.
Pob cwestiwn gan hwn o hyd
Wrth ddadl di a gwrthodyd.

. . . . .

THE SECOND FRAGMENT.

Plwyf hardd sydd, brif ffordd a bryn,
Lle rhed Gwy 'r hyd dwfr a glyn ;
Plwy' heddyw aplaf hoywddyn,
Pa le ceir gwell, plwyf Curig Wyn ?
Curig, fab gwar, llafar, llen,
Yw'n tad, a'n porthiant, a'n pen.
Caru hwn, creda' i, cai radoedd mawlgerdd,
Y trwbl a ddug, teirblwydd oedd,
Bilain dordyn aeth i'w dwrdio,
Alexander oedd falch dro.
Silit ddinam, ei fam fo,
Wen a welad yn wylo ;
Ofer gwelad ! Na âd Gurig
Wr garw o'i ferth 'rolddig ;
Dewai 'n fyw, dyna alaeth,
Dewai 'n gnawd gwyn, ag nid gwaeth ;
Ni thyfodd, fe garodd gwr,
Ar ci dir erioed oerwr.

Nerthwr 'n yw 'r gwr a garwyd,
Gwych iawn, ac a chwyr addolwyd ;
Yma a thraw a wellhawyd
I garwr glân Gurig Llwyd.
Duw Lwyd cynhenwyd gwenwynig—i'w trais
Tros fy anwyled foneddig.
Chwerw i doe chwarae dig
Dichwerwedd Duw a Churig.

　　Tra dewr o natur ydwyd,
Trig ar y gair, trugarog wyd ;
Tremi'r dewr walch trymai ;
Tacr, dewr wyt, Duw, ar dy rai.

THE THIRD FRAGMENT.

Pwy a aned er poeni,
Pwy'n deirblwydd no'n Harglwydd ni ?
Curig bob awr y carwn,
Goreu help oedd garu hwn.
Poen oedd i'w wedd pan oedd iau,
Pen Merthyr poen a wethiau.
Pob gweinied pawb a geiniw
Bonedd Ffrainc beunydd a'i ffriw.
Perlen a glain parch naw gwlad,
Plwy' Curig, pa le fwy cariad ?

　　I rwydd Saint a roddais i
Anrheg arnom rhag oerni.

　　　.　　.　　.　　.　　.

THE FOURTH FRAGMENT.

Ni bu wan yn byw ennyd
Nid ofnai 'i groen boen o'r byd.
Alexander oedd herwr
Ar Dduw, ac oedd oerddig wr.
Iddew o'r fainge oedd ar fai
Amhorth oer a'i merthyrai.
Efo â llid, a'i fam lân,
I'r pair aeth, 'wr purlan ;
Ni ddarwena 'i ddwr annoer
Ar hwynthwy mwy na'r nant oer.
Teirblwydd a fu 'n arglwydd 'n hyn
Tri mis lai, Duw, a'i rwymyn' ;
Yn fab iach yn fyw y bu,
Ac â maen i'w gymynu.
Yn lludw ei ddaith a'n llwyddodd,
Ac yna fab gwyn i'n f' oedd.

Ag oerddrwg y gwr drwg draw
E fu asiaeth i'w feisiaw;
Troes Duw hwynthwy tros dyn teg
Trwy'r astell draw ar osteg;
Torrai Iddew trwy wddwg
Ni'm dorwn draw am dyn drwg.
O'i esgidiau nadau a wnaed,
Yno fal anifeiliaid.
Crist yw'n rhan, croeso Duw'n rhodd,
Curig a'i fam a'i carodd.
Saith angel rhag bodd oedd,
Sel at y saith Silits oedd.
Mab a fu'n gwledychu'n gwlad,
A merch ir, mawr o'i chariad,
        ......digariad gorynt
O lan Gwy, a'i leian gynt.
Ac arall, mab Rhyswallawn,
Feddwl oer, a fu ddwl iawn;
Meddylio, cyn dyddio'n deg,
Am oludau, em loywdeg;
A Churig [Wyn] ni charai,
Dwyllo neb un dull a wnai;
Ei addoli ef ar ddau lin,
Ar war bryn a wna'r brenin;
Cwympo yma, camp ammharch,
Colli o'i wyr a chylla ei farch;
A Churig, fab gwych hoywrym,
A ddiddigiodd wrth rodd rym:
A diddan nid oedd anodd,
A glowson' roi glas yn rhodd.
Tyredig swmp a roid seth
Mal eurdrefn, amal ardreth;
Tri thir, mal traeth euraid,
Tri yn un cylch, tri yn un caid.
Caer fy arglwydd, lle'i ceir fawrglod,
Cwmpas dy glai, er dy glod;
Llangurig, pob lle'n gywraint,
Llawer hyd braff, lle rhad braint;
Troell wen hardd, tri lliw'n hon,
Tir Curig at tair coron,
P'le well un plwy ni ellir,
Plwy Curig nid tebyg tir.

TRANSLATION.

A coat of mail art thou
To us, and to the French, too, a guardian.
Thy country possesses, as it made it, the form
Of thy descent and the Book of thy Life.
The portion of the four quarters of the world
Are thy miracles.　Great is our need of thee !
Happy has been the Hermitage,[1]
With its nun, of yore on the bank of the Wye.
　When Maelgwn, mailed for battle, sought
To practise a deception on the nun of this spot,
His coursers and his baggage
Were brought there by a man.
To a hamper his hand cleaved ;
It was held tight ; no angel could make it more so.
Also his men who followed him
Were held fast,—all, one after the other.
When these made earnest prayer
To thee in thy chapel,
By thy power, O martyr Cyricus,
He set his men free.
And God wrought, on the brow of the upland,
His wonders within thy territory.
The nun, pure and holy,
Fashioned figures of wax between her fair hands :
The likeness, and it was not disfigured,
Of blessed Elidan of the church of Denbigh ;[2]
And her image, by means of no deception,
Uttered a voice to the God of Heaven ;
And, like the youths, she maintained
Her position with the saint.
Maelgwn went, as well I know,
To the figure thus made to worship,
And for an offering he gave

---

[1] Curig Lwyd's Hermitage probably is meant, on the spot where the church was afterwards built.　The nun would seem, from the context, to have occupied it after his death.

[2] Llanelidan, five miles from Ruthin, in the uplands of the Vale of Clwyd.　In an English poem of the xivth century, Prince Horn is said to have entered the service of Elidan, a king who dwelt on Snowdon, in the vith century.　Mr. Stephens conjectured improbably that the name might be a corruption of that of Llywarch Hên's father, Elidyr Lydanwyn.—Haig's *Anglo-Saxon Sagas*, p. 68-9.

Pasture land of great price to the sacred enclosure.
Well known to fame are now
Your glebe house, churchyard, and temple.
Thy men are not free to strike a man
In presence (or for fear) of their lords.
Well hast thou pleaded also
Of yore, before a judge in open court,
When a burden on the fair arm of thy mother
Julitta, who gave thee example;
In whose eyes the possessions of Alexander
Were all but as worthless things.
By thee was each question of his
Refuted in disputation.

The resemblance to the apocryphal *Acts* in these last
lines is unquestionable. The preceding ones seem as
clearly to contain the substance of a tradition referring
the foundation of the church of Llangurig to Maelgwn
Gwynedd, whose repeated injuries to religion, and subsequent reparation of them, as told by his contemporary
Gildas, seem to have procured for him the privilege of
being made the typical representative of such legends:
at least he is found similarly figuring in the *Life of St.
Brynach* and others. The adoption of the legend by
the Welsh bard is valuable so far as it proves that the
foundation of the church of Llangurig was referred, in
or about the fifteenth century, to a period dating so
far back as the sixth; and that it could not, therefore,
have been built for the first time by the monks of Strata
Florida, to whom it seems afterwards to have appertained as a vicarage. The next is a fragment of a poem
by Sion Ceri, a bard certainly of the fifteenth century.

Beautiful is the parish, on highway and hill,
Where flows along the vale the stream of Wye,
The parish to-day of one energetic and powerful.
Than the parish of blessed Curig, where will you find a
    better?
Curig, a youth gentle, eloquent, and learned,
Is our father, our head and our support,
My belief is that to love him brings down graces; the
    trouble

He endured, when three years old, ought to be praised in
 song.
The tyrant Alexander, proud of temperament,
And of a high stomach, proceeded to menace him.
His guileless mother, the blessed Julitta,
Was seen to weep.
A fine spectacle ! It had no power to restrain
The murderous wrath of the cruel wretch towards Curig.
While he lived he held his peace,—therein lies the sorrow.
In his holy flesh he was silent[1] and unconcerned,
The man of cold heart who loves him not
Ne'er hath prospered in his territory.
It is our beloved saint who strengthens us ;
Highly exalted is he who is honoured with tapers of wax.[2]
Everywhere have favours been received
By pure lovers of the holy Curig :
On behalf of my beloved and exalted one
Was God aroused to wrath by violence stirred by venom.
Bitterness comes of bandying strife
With the loving-kindness of God and of Curig.
By nature thou art exceeding firm,
Dwell on the word—thou art merciful ;
Fury will weigh down the steadfastness of the brave :
Thou, O God, art merciful to thine own.

Defects in the metre, as well as the sense, prove the
corruptness of several of these lines. The identity of
its legend, however, with the apocryphal *Acts* is evinced
by the epithet of "eloquent" ascribed to the martyr,
when only three years old, whose deeds are magnified,
apparently at the expense of the mother, whose Christian heroism seems to be tacitly ignored. The remaining
fragments are from the pen of Huw Arwystli, who is
emphatically the poet of Llangurig, as shown by his
recently published poems on the principal families of
that place.[3] In these, notwithstanding the vexatious
mutilation of the text, some striking coincidences of

---

[1] This seems irreconcilable with the previous statement as to his
eloquence, but is to be understood of his patience under suffering.

[2] It is still a common custom in the Catholic Church to burn a wax
taper as an offering before the statue of any saint whose prayers are
desired to obtain some special favour from Heaven.

[3] In *Montgomeryshire Collections*, vol. iv, p. 54.

the Welsh legend with the apocryphal *Acts* are plainly discernible.

Who is it was born to suffer pain?
Who but our patron, when three years old?
Not a moment passes but we love Curig,
There is no better help than to love him.
Tortured was his frame in his infancy,
To the person of a martyr pain was befitting.
Illustrious is his merit, noble was his birth,
Gentle his demeanour; let all daily serve him.
Where does love exist, if not in the parish of Curig,
The pearl and the gem revered by nine lands?
To the beneficent saint have I given
Gifts to secure us against cruelty.

The beginning of the next is wanting.

Ne'er in the world for long hath lived a weak one,
Who dreaded not pain of body.
    Alexander was a despoiler of God,
When angered, a cruel man was he.
In guilt a very Jew—from the seat of judgment
With monstrous cruelty he martyred him.
He, with his pure mother, indignantly
Entered the cauldron—the pure and bright one.
The water heated for him bubbled not
More than would a cold stream.
Three months short of three years old
Was our patron when thus they bound him.
When a child, and in perfect health,
By a stone was he dashed to pieces.
His passage through ashes hath angered us,
To us, therefore, he is a blessed saint.
Through that wicked and cruel man,
A framework of boards was to be ventured upon;
These were turned by God to the advantage of the saint,
For, thro' the boards, in sight of all,
The Jew[1] fell, and broke his neck.
For that wicked man I feel no pity.
On the spot, from his shoes, issued
Yells, like those of brute beasts.
Christ is our portion, may God receive graciously our gift,
Curig and his mother loved Him,

---

[1] Jew is used here as a term of opprobrium.

Seven angels were filled with delight,
Julitta was a spectacle for the seven.
    A youth there was—one who ruled the land,
And a young maiden, greatly beloved,
[*hiatus*] were without affection
For the Wye's bank, and its nun of old time,
And another, the son of Rhyswallon,[1]
Was cold of heart, and dull of understanding.
Before the day dawned, his thoughts would run
Upon riches, and brilliant gems;
And he loved not holy Curig;
He would cozen any one in any way.
On both his knees is the king
Worshipping him on the slope of the hill;
Here a shameful mischance befals him,
He loses his attendants, his steed breaks away.
And Curig, a saint as generous as powerful,
Was appeased by virtue of an offering,
And was readily induced to console him.
We have heard that the gift of a close was given him,
An eminence, steep and towering, was bestowed,
Like a pile of gold, an ample tribute;
Three lands like a golden strand,
Three in one ring, three in one were obtained,
The enclosure, my patron, wherein thou art greatly honoured,
Of Llangurig, each spot exactly measured,
Encircles thy soil, for thine honour.
Many a good length is there, where there is free privilege,
A bright and beautiful circle,[2] wherein are three colours,
In the land of Curig, with a prospect of three crowns,
Better parish can there not anywhere be
Than the parish of Curig, no other land is like it.

There are three or four passages in these two fragments in striking conformity with the spurious *Acts*.
Such are the incident of the cauldron or *cacabus*, that of
the shoes out of which issued horrible yells, the seven
angels who descend from heaven, and the age of the
child, exactly two years and nine months. There is
some variation in the details. In the *Acts* the cauldron

---

[1] This may be a false reading for Caswallawn, the father of Maelgwn Gwynedd, who is the subject of the legend as told in the poem
attached to that of Huw Cae Llwyd.

[2] Or "wheel". Can this mean a *corona* or chandelier?

is filled with burning pitch; in the poem, with boiling water. In the former, the shoes, on the Governor's demanding a sign, become alive; nay, more, eat and drink; and, finally, are transformed into a bull, out of whose neck springs a he-goat, instead of being left, as in the nursery tale, after the dissolution of the Governor's body by fire; and the seven angels appear for the purpose of restoring to life a thousand persons, who embrace Christianity after being beheaded by the Governor's order. On the other hand, the martyr's death, by being dashed against a stone, would seem to have been derived from the genuine *Acts;* unless, indeed, the passage, which is certainly obscure, is rather to be referred to an incident in the spurious work, in which a space is scooped out of a large stone, capacious enough for the two martyrs to sit in, the sides of which are afterwards filled with molten lead. The whole, in fact, bears marks of an attempt to reduce the narrative of the spurious *Acts* within credible dimensions by the elimination of its absurdities; a theory borne out by the statement in the *Emynau,* that Cyricus was an adult who, from his childhood, had been distinguished for his piety and ability; and also by the statement that the *Life* published by Hucbald, and obtained, doubtless, by him from Nevers, underwent a similar process of castigation, first by himself, and a second time, subsequently, by his editor, Abbot Philip.

The most remarkable fact connected with the history of these *Acts* is perhaps this, that the genuine narrative furnished by Bishop Theodore to Pope Zosimus within a century after the event, never succeeded in superseding them in popular estimation. It affords a strange confirmation of the saying, which has almost passed into a proverb, " Give a falsehood a start of twenty-four hours, and the truth will never overtake it." Father Combefis, a Dominican, by whom Bishop Theodore's letter in the original Greek was exhumed from among the MSS. in the King's Library at Paris in 1660, expressed a hope that the public reading of the apocryphal *Acts* proscribed by Pope Gelasius, already suppressed at Nevers, might be put down by authority also at Ville Juif (a corruption of Villa Julittæ), a town six miles south of Paris, where they were read annually from a pulpit to a great concourse of people. And Father Porée, a Premonstratensian, writing in 1644, states that the use of these, which had thus usurped the place of the genuine *Acts*, was in his time widely disseminated throughout France. So difficult is it to eradicate a popular usage, especially when calculated to gratify the love of the marvellous, so deeply rooted in our nature. It is instructive, moreover, to learn from Bishop Theodore's letter, that these, and similar extravagancies in legendary saints' lives, do not necessarily owe their origin to motives of gain or self-interest on the part of those who may be made the unconscious means of handing them down to posterity, as has often been erroneously supposed. In this instance, we have seen that they were actually due to the malice of enemies of the Christian faith, on which it was sought to cast discredit by the substitution of false for true narratives of the deeds of those whose lives and deaths, if recorded simply and without such exaggeration, would have furnished the strongest testimony to the truth of their belief.

In conclusion, an anecdote may not be out of place which may possibly serve to illustrate the simple faith of the villagers of Llangurig in the power of their patron saint to obtain them favours from heaven. A traveller by the Shrewsbury and Aberystwyth mail, not many years back, while beguiling the tedium of the journey by careless gossip with the coachman, was informed by him, as an extraordinary fact, that the finest crops of wheat in the county of Montgomery were said to be grown in the parish of Llangurig, despite the apparently unsuitable nature of the land and climate for that object. Can this have been a remnant of the old belief, long after the memory of the saint, and the popular devotion to him, had faded from the popular mind? The apocryphal *Acts* of Cyricus close with a prayer by him for those who should honour him hereafter, that they might obtain their petitions according to their necessities, one of which was that they might be blessed in their wine, oil, corn, and all their substance. Whether attributable or not to this passage in his legend, the published Welsh poems in his honour teem with expressions of such a belief in the power of his prayers, and of belief also in the reception of tangible tokens, without number, of his protection and favour.

HOWEL W. LLOYD, M.A.

PROFESSOR BOYD DAWKINS ON "ANCIENT WELSH ETHNOLOGY."

Refer to pp. 257-264.

[*From the Oswestry Advertizer.*]

On the 7th of June 1882, Professor W. Boyd Dawkins, M.A., F.R.S., of Owens College, Manchester, delivered a lecture on "The Ancient Ethnology of Wales", before the Honourable Society of Cymmrodorion at the Freemasons' Tavern, Great Queen Street; Mr. C. W. Williams Wynn occupying the chair. Mr. Wynn briefly opened the meeting by saying that he and ethnological science had barely a bowing acquaintance, but under the auspices of so distinguished an ethnologist and antiquary as Professor Boyd Dawkins, whose researches in the neighbourhood of Cefn were well known to him, he hoped to become better acquainted with it.

Throughout his lecture, Professor Boyd Dawkins relied almost entirely on his memory for the facts in relation to the subject under consideration, the result being a prolixity and discursiveness which would have been prevented had his remarks been committed to paper in the manner usual with Cymmrodorion speakers. The lecture, however, was of very great interest, and was listened to throughout with marked attention by an appreciative audience. Premising that it would be of interest to lay before such a Society as that of the Cymmrodorion, which might be considered the Welch brotherhood in London, several points in connection with the ancient ethnology of Wales, Professor Boyd Dawkins pointed out that the claims of race were coming more and more to the front. As the most ancient, if not the most honourable, race in this island, he would deal with *Welsh* ethnology before the commencement of history, and in its special connection with the introduction of civilisation into Wales. By one of those

accidents that come to those who look for them, a few years
ago a series of ethnological discoveries were made on the
estate of Mrs. Wynn of Cefn.   Under a stone cairn were found
a number of flat stones overlapping one another, and forming
the roof of a large stone chamber, which turned out to be an
ancient family vault containing a number of human skeletons,
together with a few flint flakes, and the remains of various
domestic animals, including specimens of the small Welsh
cattle, the goat, the dog, the horse, and that other animal
which plays an important part in civilisation—the pig.   These
remains undoubtedly proved that the people who had been
buried in the sepulchral chamber thus found were in the agri-
cultural phase of civilisation and well acquainted with domestic animals.   Another discovery of bones was made at a
place called Perthi Chwareu, where a sepulchral cavern was
found literally crowded with skeletons.   The two discoveries
were of the greatest interest as bearing on each other, for the
skeletons and the animal remains in each instance proved to
be of the same type.   Examination showed the human bones
to be those of a short people with long skulls, prominent
noses (in one series a family oddity in the shape of a *nez
retroussé* was well preserved), and small features.   The polished
stone implements found near them showed that they belonged
to the neolithic age.   These chamber tombs had been found
throughout Wales, in various parts of the United Kingdom,
and also on the Continent, all containing the remains of the
same kind of people.   ·

The lecturer next proceeded to deal with the civilisation
of the people thus discovered.   In this country there are evidences that their civilisation was not by any means low.   The
exploration of some ancient dwellings near Salisbury has established the fact of their acquaintance with wheat.   It is also
certain that they knew the arts of spinning and weaving, for
spindle whirls have been found in their tombs and habitations,
together with small curry-combs, which were probably used to
push the woof on to the weft.   They were also miners, as
shown by the flint pits of Sissbury and elsewhere, where vast
accumulations of their broken mining implements have been
found.   The lecturer when exploring at Sissbury was able to
decide where the miners sat at work, and actually succeeded
in finding the broken halves of one of their implements, which
is now preserved at Owens College.   Taking these things into
consideration, it was clear that they were considering the
claims not of an unimportant people, but of the introducers of
the very civilisation we now enjoyed.   That they were great

warriors could be proved by the multitudes of small village fortifications found throughout Wales. It is probable that they dwelt in small communities, something like those found by Mr. H. M. Stanley in Central Africa. They undoubtedly believed in a future state of existence, for the implements placed by the side of the dead were evidently intended for use in a future world. Sir John Lubbock, however, arguing from the fact that certain tumuli have been found without any traces of implements, doubts their belief in a future state. The lecturer was of opinion that the presence or absence of implements in the tumuli denoted the estimation in which the departed had been held during and after life.

The remains of a similar people as those already mentioned have been found on the Continent, *i. e.*, in the region west of the Rhine and north of the Alps. All over Gaul, Spain, Belgium, and Switzerland, traces are to be had of this ancient people, and owing to the larger area and to the remains found in the Swiss lakes, where their former habitations have been wonderfully preserved, the picture is more forcibly brought before us. They used to grow wheat, barley, millet, and hemp, and were in the habit of using linseed meal: they also possessed gardens, for we have their fruit preserved to us by the mere accident of being burnt. The cattle mentioned as appertaining to the ancient people of Wales have also been found on the Continent in the region already referred to, together with specimens of the large cattle which here we identify with the English invasion. All these facts go to prove the large area over which these people were scattered, and the uniform civilisation which prevailed among them.

The next question to decide was who were these people? The examination of their remains has shown them to be a short race, with long heads, delicately cut aquiline features, and oval face, with the lower portion devoid of the strength of that of the Cymry of the present day. The researches of Dr. Broca, Professor Huxley, and other ethnologists, seem to prove that this ancient neolithic people are most nearly represented at the present time by the Basques or Iberians, who are to be found in the western portion of the Pyrenees, *i. e.*, the small dark Basques as distinguished from the Goth element which wandered into that region. Who were the Basques? History unerringly tells us that they represent the ancient Iberian people which had a large population scattered over Western Europe at the beginning of history. A comparison of the historic and neolithic maps shows that at the period mentioned their area had been considerably contracted, that is to say, they had been pushed as far westward as possible by the pressure of invaders on their eastern borders. Dr. Broca in his admirable work, and the Anthropological Institute of Paris by its researches, have shown that the early inhabitants of Gaul during the neolithic age were invaded by a people differing from them as well in physique as in manners and customs. Specimens of these have also been found in the sepulchral chambers, proving them to belong to the Gauls or Ancient Celts who, standing in the vanguard of Aryan civilisation, had invaded Europe in the neolithic age, and driven the Iberians to the west. These were taller men with round or broad skulls, massive features, and the lower part of the face characterised by what is called "snoutiness". One of the new fashions introduced to Gaul by the Celts was that of disposing of the dead by cremation. Traces of the fashion have been found in France, but none in the neolithic tombs of this country. It is evident the Celts crossed over here in the neolithic age. For a considerable time "the silver streak", on which the Britons of to-day place such exaggerated importance, kept all invaders away. The discovery of bronze brought with it new implements and weapons, a higher mode of warfare, and a more advanced state of civilisation. It is a singular fact that this country does not appear to have been successfully invaded till the beginning of the bronze age. At that time, what happened in Gaul appears to have been repeated in Britain, i. e., the ancient inhabitants were for the most part driven westward; but one contrary fact seems to be established, viz., that during the bronze age there was an Iberic population in Yorkshire, showing that they were not then totally displaced. The tendency, however, was otherwise, and the Iberians had to move to the West, the Celts evidently following them, for their bronze implements and ornaments have been found over the whole surface of the country, and even in Wales and Ireland. Bronze implements are ever indissolubly connected with the Celtic invasion, though it should be remembered that the Iberians would use bronze tools and weapons when they came to know them. The Celts were undoubtedly a fair-haired people. Where their descendents are not so, the lecturer would attribute it to the mingling of the Celts with the Iberians, and as this took place everywhere, it is very difficult to draw any hard and fast line on this point.

When Cæsar conquered the West he found three sets of people, viz., the Iberians, the Gauls or Celts, and the Belgæ. Who were the Belgæ? Some authorities say they were Germans, others are contented to class them with the Celts. So far as the testimony of their bones go they are, without doubt, characteristic of the latter. In course of time iron was discovered, and along with it a higher civilisation sprang up. The lecturer felt bound to associate the Belgæ with the iron age, though he was unable to connect them with the introduction of iron into this country. When Cæsar arrived here he found the country inhabited by Belgæ, Celts, and Silurians, who, from Tacitus's description, bore a marked resemblance to the Iberians of Spain. Traces of the Belgæ have been found in Yorkshire as well as in Ireland, but, ethnologically speaking, the impression they left was unimportant, for they were as nearly related to the Celts as the Saxons were to the Jutes.

The influence of the Roman invasion, again, while it made a vast change in the civilisation of the country, made but little difference in its ethnology. But with the departure of the Roman legions came a turning point in the history of Wales. The Roman Empire broke down under a great combination of invaders of the German race, who, breaking through its military defences, overran Gaul and settled in extreme and remote parts of Europe, leaving traces of their names in Lombardy, Burgundy, and France. The Saxon invasion of Britain was a part of this dismemberment of the Roman Empire. For four centuries Britain had enjoyed profound peace under the shadow of the Roman eagle. In 449 A.D., the northern pirates, who had harried the eastern coast, made a descent on the island; others ere long joined them, and together they commenced a war of extermination against the Britons. They were, perhaps, the hardest fighters in the world, but they found the Britons worthy of their steel, and it took them two centuries to drive their opposers to the West. Driven, however, they were, and the eastern part of Britain became England. In the ethnology of Wales we now have three elements (two if Celts and Belgæ are joined), besides English and Danish elements. The descendants of the short dark ancient people are still to be found there; but now that the Welsh are proving themselves cosmopolitan, the old race is being rapidly crossed out. Even in the last twenty years the lecturer had noticed a great diminution among the small Iberic people in the neighbourhood of St. Asaph. The Welsh, with the Basques, the Southern Irish, and the Highlanders, are of the same ethnological family, but the small dark people must be looked upon as the most ancient. The main staple of the Welsh race are the Celts, but, among these, especially along the estuary of the Dee, and in the direction of the Menai

Straits, are many families of ancient English descent who are now, however, as much Welsh as the old stock. Having thus placed before the meeting as an archæologist and geologist the evidence of pick and shovel, and compared history and ethnology, the lecturer opined that his hearers would agree with him that the ethnology of Wales is an epitome of the ethnology of Western Europe.

In conclusion, he said the ancient Iberian language had curiously preserved traces of the neolithic age in the words used for various implements which were formerly made of stone, but now of steel; an interesting case of philological survival squaring with ethnological facts. Professor Rhys has been searching for Basque roots in the Welsh language, and without forestalling Mr. Rhys's discoveries, he might say that traces of Iberian roots have at last been found therein. As a Welshman who had wandered across the border, and remained so long that he had almost forgotten he was a Welshman, he thanked the Society for giving him an opportunity of being so pleasantly reminded of it that evening.

FIFTY MILLION YEARS AGO.

[*From the St. James's Gazette.*]

The discovery of the position of the planet Neptune by the independent researches of Adams and Leverrier is justly regarded as one of the most magnificent triumphs of mathematical reasoning. Its nature was such that the popular mind could grasp its meaning and appreciate its significance; and it is of course to this element of its character, no less than to the ocular demonstration of its truth, that it owes its notoriety. This will be at once clear when it is pointed out that, twelve years before, Galle found the planet close to the spot which had been assigned to it by calculation. Sir William Hamilton foretold the existence of the phenomenon commonly known by the name of conical refraction, and his conclusions were soon afterwards experimentally verified by Lloyd. As an example of what may be accomplished by a skilful manipulation of figures, this prediction was in no degree less remarkable than the detection of Neptune's place in the heavens: the result of Lloyd's test did, indeed, make a profound impression upon all who understood its importance; but the circle to which it appealed was necessarily limited in extent. Quite recently attention has been drawn to a theory which once more illustrates the increasing influence of mathematics as a help to the study of all sciences. It is true that an experimental demonstration of its truth or falsity, is from the nature of the subject-matter, impossible, so that it will lack one of the ingredients which have rendered the achievement of Adams and Leverrier famous and Hamilton's view convincing; yet, as it deals in a wonderful way with the history of the earth and moon, it naturally aroused more than ordinarily the curiosity of the public.

The hypothesis has its origin in a consideration of the work which has, in the course of time, been done by agents with which we are all familiar enough. For every one has watched the tides rise and fall; and centuries before any explanation was given of the relation which exists between them and the phases of the moon, the fact that there is a connection was too obvious to escape recognition; so that from a very early period the phenomena of the tides have been ascribed to the influence of the moon. Not long ago it was definitely shown that, although the tides are in part caused by the sun, they depend principally upon the moon's action: and, more recently, the increase which had been observed in the length of the day was attributed to their operation. This increase is of course due to a retardation in the rate of the earth's rotation about its axis; and, although extremely slow, thousands of years being required for the addition of a second, still it is continuous. For reasons which it is unnecessary to explain here, this change in the length of the day is accompanied by an enlargement of the orbit in which the moon revolves. It follows that the distance of the moon from the earth, as well as the length of the day, is constantly becoming greater; and it is equally apparent that there was a period when the day was much shorter and the moon much nearer than at present. Now Mr. George Darwin has traced back the effects of the tides upon the system of the earth and moon until an epoch is attained at which our planet and its satellite are almost in contact with one another; and he finds that the earth's period of rotation, or the day, was then from two to four hours in length, and corresponded with the moon's period of revolution round the earth, or the month, while the year remained virtually at its present value. The configuration of the system at this epoch, as estimated by Mr. Darwin, has led him to suggest that the moon owes its origin to a rupture, caused by the rapidity of rotation or some other agency, of a planet whose mass originally consisted both of the moon and the earth; and this view differs from the nebular theory of Laplace and

Kant in that it assumes that the rupture did not occur until the planet was partly consolidated and was approximately of its present size.

In order to appreciate the force of this suggestion it is necessary to bear in mind that at the time under consideration—computed to be at least fifty-four million years ago—the earth was of a very different character from the world with which we are acquainted : it was probably partly solid, partly liquid, and partly gaseous.   And we must further remember that the earth is not a sphere, but is flattened at the poles and bulges out at the equator.   This form, we all know, is a result of its rotation upon its axis, and the greater the velocity of rotation the greater will be the prominence at the equator.   So that if the earth spun round with sufficient speed, a stage in its history must be reached at which the attraction which bound together the portions at the equator and the rest of its mass would be obliged to yield to the centrifugal force, and the equatorial regions would be severed from the body of the planet.   It is estimated that this separation would occur when the rotation was completed in about three hours.   At the period, therefore, indicated by Mr. Darwin, the earth was extremely liable to rupture ; and at this point probably the solar tides—the effect of which is so small that at the present day it may be practically ignored—by a succession of impulses, played an important part.   It is plain that no lunar tides existed before the moon was formed ; the earth was therefore affected only by these solar tides, which were apparent as throbs in the materials of the earth.   The vibrations of the earth induced by the solar tides would by themselves even then be small ; but, owing to the synchronism of the earth's oscillation and the period of these tides, their amplitude would be gradually increased, and at last the cohesion of the mass would be overcome.   According to Dr. Ball, at this point "a separation took place ; one portion consolidated to form our present earth, the other portion consolidated to form the moon."   Mr. Proctor, on the other hand, considers that the rupture probably took place at a much later period than that which is calculated by Mr. Darwin ; and expresses strong disapproval of the notion that the moon was formed at a single effort, because small portions of the original planet would most likely be detached long before the disturbance was great enough to enable it to part with such a large body as that of the moon. Each portion so thrown off would move away from the earth directly it was freed from the original mass ; and in this way

a series of rings, making up a single flat ring-system like that
of Saturn, would be formed; then by mutual impact the bodies
would become less in number, until, perhaps, they accumulated
in centres, and, finally, a union of the masses of which those
centres were constituted would gather them into one spherical
body.

But whether the moon was formed suddenly or gradually,
it is easy to follow its history and that of the earth from the
time when they were close to one another. For it was inevitable that the moon should either retreat or be again
absorbed in the earth. Its present position indicates that it
began to move away; so that the month and day altered until
they reached their existing lengths of about twenty-seven days
and twenty-four hours respectively. But as the change in the
month was quicker than the corresponding variation in the
day, there was an epoch at which the month was composed of
twenty-nine days; since then the ratio has diminished, and the
month (measured by days) has decreased. This decrease in
the number of days per month will be attended by an increase
in the number of hours per day, and will continue until the
lengths of the month and day are once more identical, and
each consists of 1,400 hours. It is, moreover, well known
that the moon always presents the same region of her surface
to the earth; this is a result of the tides formerly raised in
the moon by the attraction of the earth. When the day is
1,400 hours long the earth will in like manner present the same
face to the moon; and, when this epoch has been reached, the
lunar tides will obviously have ceased, and the solar tides will
once more play an important role : they will create little disturbance upon the moon; but they will have power to dimi-
nish the rotation of the earth, so that ultimately the moon,
following the example of the interior satellite of Mars, will
revolve round the earth in much less than a day. Once again,
then, the earth will not present the same region to the moon,
and once again tides will be raised in the earth by her satellite. But the effect, under these circumstances, will be to
increase the rotation of the earth and to decrease the moon's
distance. The curtain may be drawn upon the earth and
moon intent upon once more renewing their embrace; and it
may be anticipated that the greeting, after so long a parting,
will be warm.

Dr. Ball has expressed his conviction that the former prox-
imity of the moon will sufficiently account for the disagree-
ment which exists between astronomers and geologists with
regard to the age of the earth. It cannot be disputed that

when the moon was much nearer to the earth than it is at present, the tides rose to a far greater height than they do now; and Dr. Ball contends that if their effect be recognised, geologists will no longer be forced to rely upon the agents of the present day for an explanation of the palaeozoic rocks. In support of his opinion he alludes to the work which would be accomplished by tides more than two hundred times as high as those which now rise and fall on our coasts. But Mr. Darwin does not himself admit the application of his theory in this direction to the extent which Dr. Ball desires; and has explained that when he pointed to the acceleration of geological action as a result of his speculations, he did not consider that even in the earliest geological times the tides were more than two or three times as high as at present. On the other hand, he thinks that, as the denuding effect of rain and air is far greater than that of the waves, the larger amount of rainfall which might reasonably be expected with only that increase in height would have as great an effect as direct tidal action. Professor Newberry supports Mr. Darwin's limitation by declaring that, so far from affording any indication of the action of such huge tides as those depicted by Dr. Ball, the whole geological record is opposed to the possibility of their existence during the period which is included in it. However, the dispute between the author of the theory and his interpreter is only as to the extent of the influence; and, undoubtedly, the speculation lessens the difficulty to a considerable extent.

VICTOR HUGO AND JEWISH PERSECUTION.

Refer to page 167.

The Paris newspapers of June 18, 1882, print the following appeal of Victor Hugo in relation to the persecution of the Jews raging in Russia:—

"This is the decisive hour. The moribund religious are betaking themselves to their last resources. What this moment is rearing its head is not merely something criminal, but something monstrous. A nation is being transformed into a monster; horrible spectre! A curtain is rent in twain, and a voice cries, 'Children of men, behold and choose; either of two solutions is open to you.' On one side man advances with measured but certain tread, towards an ever brighter horizon, leading by the hand a child. He steps forth, his head full of light; the child, its head full of hope. Labour does its grand work; science seeks God. The mind beholds him—God-truth, God-justice, God-conscience, God-love. Man blends with things belonging to earth, with Liberty, Equality, and Fraternity. God sought is philosophy; God seen is religion. There is nothing more—no more idle tales, no more dreams, no more dogmas. All the peoples are brothers. Frontiers disappear. Man perceives that yet the earth has not been possessed. Wars become rarer. Races have henceforth but one motive, and one goal—civilisation. Every throb of the human heart means progress. On the other side, man is seen receding. The horizon becomes blacker. Multitudes go about groping in the gloom. . The old religions, crushed under their two thousand years, have lost everything but their myths: once the illusion of the childhood of humanity, but now the scorn of its maturity; once accepted by ignorance, but now contradicted by science; leaving to the clinging believer, whose eyes are closed and ears stopped, no other refuge than the frightful ' *Credo quia absurdum.*' Errors devour one another. The Jews are martyred by the Christians. Thirty towns at this moment are the prey of pillage, and the inhabitants are massacred, are hunted forth from their homes. What is going on in Russia fills one with horror. The crime being committed there is colossal. But in truth it is no crime, for the populations engaged upon their work of extermination have lost all sense of crime. Their religions have plunged them into the depths of bestiality. Theirs is the terrible innocence of the tiger. The centuries of the past—the one with its Albigenses; another with its Inquisition; a third with its Holy Office; a fourth with its St. Bartholomew; a fifth with its dragonnades; a sixth with its Austria of Maria Theresa—are rushing in combination upon our nineteenth century, with intent to stifle it. The mutilation of man, the outrage upon woman, the burning of children, are all in the aim to suppress the future. The past has no mind to be annihilated; it is holding mankind in its deadly grasp. The thread of life is still between its spectral fingers; on one side the people, on the other the rabble; on one side light, on the other, darkness. Choose!" (See p. 165.)

THE DESTRUCTION OF ALEXANDRIA.
(*See p.* 167.)
THE LAW OF NATIONS AND EGYPT.

[*To the Editor of the Standard.*]

SIR,—To reason about the late events and present state of things in Egypt with any reference to International Law is almost impossible, for all is confusion, contradiction, and inextricable difficulty. A distinction has been asserted between International Law and common sense. Both are now utterly confounded in Egypt. But they ought to be identical. Let us consider facts.

The Prime Minister says :—" I do not admit that we are at war with any one." This is astounding. The British Fleet has been bombarding the forts of Alexandria and we are preparing to send an army. If this is not war, what is war? It is war; but we are told that it is war against nobody. We are in amity with the Khedive, whose life we have endangered, and the destruction of whose city we have caused; and with the Sultan, who has remonstrated against our violence. Our object, forsooth, is to remove Arabi. This is like the tame bear who, seeing a wasp on his master's nose, administered a crushing blow with all his weight, which killed the insect, but smashed his master's head. Then the Government says that we have acted in self-defence, because the forts endangered our Fleet. The forts did not go to the Fleet, but the Fleet went to the forts. The Fleet had only to move out of reach of fire. In the courts of law, if a man deliberately goes to a nuisance he is not allowed to complain of it. The Government rely on the example of Navarino. But we all know that Navarino was described at the time as an untoward event, and it was a *mauvais coup de tête*, instigated by rash words of the Lord High Admiral. It was an offence against the Law of Nations, and not a precedent. What would have been said if Guiteau had relied in his defence on the murder of the Emperor of Russia ?

And what right had we to intervene against Arabi, or to interfere with him, except so far as he injured our rights, if he did so ? It seems to be forgotten that within a fortnight the Sultan, who is the Sovereign of Egypt and the chief of the Mahometan religion, has decorated Arabi with the highest honour he can confer, equal to the Garter in this country. I do not justify Arabi's conduct; but he is the representative of Egypt for the Egyptians; and I believe the Mahometan world, including our fellow-subjects in India, look upon him as a champion of Islam.

Apart from all astuteness and subtle casuistry, of which Mr. Gladstone is a master, I want to know what we are fighting for? I ask for what has our Fleet been pouring death and destruction on the Egyptians, and our own men have shed their blood, and for what are we preparing an army to invade Egypt? We have caused the utter ruin, the destruction, of one of the finest cities in the East, a city of two hundred thousand souls, with massacres, outrages, and terrible slaughter, and incalculable destruction of property. These horrors are irreparable. They are the result of our policy, and they will always be remembered against us. During all this the Prime Minister says—" I do not admit that we are at war with any one." If we are not at war with any one, we are not lawful belligerents, and every man killed is murdered. If, as some papers tell us, the Law of Nations is a parcel of rubbish, we must fall back into the lawlessness of remote ages, and *Quod placet sanctum est.* Talk of " blood-guiltiness," we see it now, and we are responsible for every drop of blood that is spilt in an unlawful war and all its consequences.

" Hostes", says Florentinus, in the *Pandects,* " sunt qui nobis vel quibus nos publice bellum decrevimus, cæteri prædones et pirati sunt." " Prædones et Pirati !" We must say with Pseudolus, " Mea sunt cognomina."

I am, Sir, your obedient servant,

July 15, 1882.   GEORGE BOWYER.

———

THE PUBLIC LAW OF BELLIGERENCY.

[*To the Editor of the Standard.*]

SIR,—Some exposition of the Public Law regarding lawful war may be useful at the present time.

The text universally received on this subject is that Law of Florentinus, which I have cited—" Hostes sunt qui nobis vel quibus nos publice bellum decrevimus, cæteri prædones et pirati sunt." The words *publice bellum decrevimus,* do not signify that a formal declaration of war is necessary. It is an established principle that though this should be done as a general rule, there are many exceptions. War has sometimes to be commenced on an emergency, and if a formal declaration were necessary the object of the war would be frustrated.

Thus, in the case of Copenhagen, our Government had purchased for three thousand pounds the secret article by which the fleet of a State with which we were at peace was to be given up to our enemy, France. There it was necessary to act without any declaration of war.

The words *publice bellum decrevimus* mean that war must be commenced by public authority—by authority of the State, as war—and not as mere acts of violence in time of peace. In the case of Egypt, the Prime Minister, speaking with the authority of the Crown, has said—" I do not admit that we are at war with any one." Now war requires two belligerents, just as an action *in foro contentioso* requires contestation—a plaintiff and defendant. We are at peace with the Khedive and with the Sultan; therefore the Crown, to which alone belongs the prerogative of peace and war, is and was in a state of peace. We could not be at war with Arabi because he is not a lawful belligerent, being a subject of the Khedive and the Sultan.

Yet, in this state of peace, declared by the Prime Minister, we have resorted to the most warlike measures and all the horrors of war. We have bombarded the forts of Alexandria, and with our eyes open we have caused most terrible massacres and outrages, and the sacrifice of thousands of lives by fire and sword, with incalculable destruction of property belonging to the inoffensive natives and to foreign nations, for which we shall no doubt be held liable. And all this has taken place while we were not at war with any one. It is clear that we cannot claim the rights of lawful belligerents, and that we have been guilty of piracy.

With regard to Arabi, our only lawful course would have been to offer to the Sultan and the Khedive the assistance of so many regiments to bring him to obedience under their authority. We should have sent an auxiliary force to land and occupy Alexandria—under the authority of the Sovereign of the country—and to maintain order in Egypt. But now we have been worse than any of the plagues of Egypt.

I am, Sir, your obedient servant,

July 17, 1882.   GEORGE BOWYER.

———

ROME, MONDAY NIGHT.

The papers continue to write in a tone of bitter hostility to England. Great anxiety is shown to make out that the destruction of the city was due to the English, and not to the Egyptian soldiers or convicts. A letter in the *Fanfulla*, from

Paris, says large numbers of Greek firms have received telegrams assuring them that the conflagration was mainly caused by the English bombs. Many rich Egyptians at Paris have received similar information.

The *Diritto* publishes a summary of Egyptian history since the time of Ismail Pacha, which is intended to show that all the recent evils are due to the Anglo-French greed of usurious interest. "The Control ruined the Fellaheen and then persuaded the Khedive to separate himself from the true patriots represented by Arabi Pacha, and thus produced all that has followed. The *Diritto* accuses Sir Rivers Wilson and M. Blignières of acting for their personal enrichment.

The *Fanfulla*, after remarking that the telegraph is in the hands of Sir B. Seymour, says:—" If the Arabs, seeing the English begin the work of destruction, completed it in desperation, which are the greater barbarians?"—*Italian Correspondence of the " Standard."*

CANTREF UWCH NANT.—COMOT AND LORDSHIP OF MAELOR SAESNEG.

This comot contains the parishes of Y Gwrddymp, now called Worthympbury, or Worthenbury, containing the township of Y Gwrddymp; the parish of Hanmer, which contains the townships of Hanmer, Llys Bedydd, Bronington, Ty Broughton, Willington, and Halchdyn; the parish of Bangor Is y Coed, and the townships of Is y Coed in the parish of Malpas, the township of Penley in the parish of Ellesmere, the township of Merford in Gresford parish, the township of Maelor in the parish of Erbistog, and the township of Osley.

BANGOR IS Y COED.

This parish contains the townships of Bangor, Knoltyn, Overton Madog, and Overton Foreign in Maelor Saesneg; the townships of Picyllt, Rhwytyn, and Seswick, in Maelor Gymraeg.

Bangor was the Banchorium Statio of Richard of Cirencester, and in this township stood the celebrated monastery of Bangor Is y Coed, founded by Cadell

Deyrnllug, King of Powys, in the sixth century. This
Cadell Deyrnllug was the grandfather of Brochwel Ys-
gythrog, King of Powys, who was slain in 612. ·This
monastery contained 2,400 monks, who, dividing themselves into seven bands, passed their time alternately in
prayer and labour,[1] or, according to Camden, a hundred
by turns passed one hour in devotion, so that the whole
twenty-four hours were employed in sacred duties. The
first abbot was Dunawd. This monastery was destroyed,
and 1,200 of the monks were put to death, by Æthel-
frid, King of the Angles, for praying for the success of
their king, Brochwel Ysgithrog, against their enemies, as
previously stated (see vol. i). After this the monastery
fell to decay ; for William of Malmsbury, who lived in
the reign of King Stephen, says, "There remained only",
in his time, "the footsteps of so great a place, so many
ruinous churches, and such heaps of rubbish as were
hardly elsewhere to be met with."

I have given this account relative to the foundation of
the monastery of Bangor Is y Coed, as I have found it
given in the Welsh MSS., and very fully given in the
MS. of Iolo Morganwg. However, there is a different
account given in other histories. By them we learn
that a heresy broke out in the monastery of Bangor Is y
Coed which spread amongst the Christians of Britain.
This heresy was said to have been promulgated by a
monk of this monastery, whose name was Morien, and
his peculiar teachings were named after him, Morien
Ddysg. To oppose this heresy, Celestine II, Pope of
Rome in 424, sent St. Germanus, Bishop of Auxerre in
Gaul,[1] as his legate, to suppress it. When he came into
what was subsequently called Powys-land, the Prince of
that part of it called Iâl and Ystrad Alun, whose name
was Benlli Gawr, would have nothing to do with him,
and ordered him to be off. Upon which, we are told by
the monk Nennius, that, the anger of God fell upon the
king, and that "ignis de cœlo occidit et combussit
arcem, et omnes qui cum tyranno (i. e., Benlli) erant, nec

---

[1] Bede's *Ecclesiastical History*, ii, c. II, p. 80.

ultra apparuerunt, nec arx reædificata est usque in hodiernum diem." However, lest the country should be without a ruler, Germanus anointed a man, named Cadell Deyrnllug, a servant of King Benlli's, who had given him food and shelter, to be King of Teyrnllwg in his place. This must have occurred sometime previously to 448, for, in that year, Germanus left Britain with the Roman legions and went to Ravenna, where he died on the 25th July in the same year.

This story, therefore, proves that Pelagianism was prevalent in Britain previous to the middle of the fifth century, and that it was supposed to have emanated from a monk of the name of Morien, who subsequently took the Greek name of Pelagius in place of his Keltic name of Morien—which means the same thing, Mor being the Keltic name of Pelagos, the sea—and that this Morien was supposed to have been a monk of the monastery of Bangor Is y Coed, which, if such is the case, proves either that the Bangor monastery must have been in existence previous to the reign of Cadell Deyrnllug II, or, if it was really built and founded by him, as related in the account previously given in vol. i, then Morien or Pelagius must have belonged to some other monastery.

What we really do know, is, that in the beginning of the fifth century, a British monk, who had assumed the name of Pelagius, passed through Western Europe and Northern Africa, teaching that death was not introduced into the world by the sin of Adam; that, on the contrary, he was necessarily and by nature mortal, and had he not sinned he would nevertheless have died; that the consequences of his sins were confined to himself, and did not affect his posterity.

At Rome, Pelagius was received with favour: at Carthage, at the instigation of St. Augustine, he was denounced. By a synod held at Diospolis, he was acquitted of heresy, but, on referring the matter to the Bishop of Rome, Innocent I, he was, on the contrary, condemned. It happened that at this moment Innocent

died, and his successor, Zosimus,[1] annulled his judgment,
and declared the opinions of Pelagius to be orthodox.
These contradictory decisions are still often referred to
by the opponents of papal infallibility.   Things were in
this state of confusion, when the African bishops, through
the influence of Count Valerius, procured from the emperor an edict denouncing Pelagius as a heretic ; he and
his accomplices were condemned to exile and the for-
feiture of their goods.   To affirm that death was in the
world before the fall of Adam was a State crime.

In deciding whether death had been in the world before the fall of Adam, or whether it was the penalty
inflicted on the world for his sin, the course taken was
to ascertain whether the views of Pelagius were accord-
ant or discordant, not with nature, but with the theolo-
gical doctrines of St. Augustine, and the result has been
such as might be expected.   The doctrine declared to be
orthodox by ecclesiastical authority is overthrown by
the unquestionable discoveries of modern science.   Long
before human beings had appeared upon the earth, millions of individuals—nay, more, thousands of species and
even genera—had died ; those that remain with us are
an insignificant fraction of the vast hosts that have
passed away.[2]

That death came not into the world because of any
transgression by man of a commandment of God is certain ; for that the earth was peopled by myriads of animals which lived and died æons before man appeared
upon the scene, is certified to us by the remains of those
we find entombed in such profusion in the strata that
compose the crust of the globe.   The law of evolution,
of birth and death, instituted as it undoubtedly was
from the beginning of life on the earth, may without
irreverence be spoken of as a necessity in the nature of
things.   Were this not so, the law would not now exist ;

---

[1] This is the Pope Zosimus mentioned in the *History of St.
Curig.*

[2] *Conflict between Religion and Science.*   By J. W. Draper, M.D.,
LL.D.

for neither God nor the revelation He makes of Himself in His laws suffers essential change.

It is not true, therefore, according to the Hebrew tale itself, that death was brought into the world through man's infringement of an order not to eat of the tree of knowledge of good and evil ; but he was driven out of the garden of Eden lest he should take also of the tree of life, eat, and so like the Elohim—the gods—live for ever. The tale of Adam and Eve being driven out of Paradise may be explained in many ways, among others, is the following astronomical one. By turning to a celestial globe it will be seen that as Virgo (Eve), with the ears of corn or fruit-bearing bough in her hand, followed by Arcturus (Adam) sinks in the west, Perseus (the cherub armed with the flaming sword) rises in the east, and seems to drive the woman and the man from the sky.[1]

CHRISTIANITY.

The Jews are supposed to have had the most perfect conception of the Supreme Power, but the Hebrew Scriptures represent their God as walking in the garden of Eden in the *cool* of the evening ; and, on one occasion it is related of Moses, that he saw a portion of God's person like the hinder parts of a man. But not only do the Jews suppose themselves to be made bodily in the likeness of God, but they give to God the likeness of all their worst passions. He is proud, jealous, revengeful, the Commander-in-Chief of their armies, ordering whole towns to be levelled with the ground, and peoples to be put to death—men, women, children, and even the cattle—because they called *their* god by another name ; and ordered the sun and moon to stand still that the Jews might make a greater slaughter of their enemies ; but at the same time easily turned from His purpose by obedience and flattery. To these vices were certainly added all the human virtues, and some of the highest

[1] *The Pentateuch and Book of Joshua.* By a Physician. London : Williams and Norgate.

attributes which the human mind is capable of conceiving, and several that are beyond man's conception. The Christian God is all this. The ancient Hebrews, at least, believed that evil was confined to this world, not believing in a future state ; but the Christians make evil Absolute, as, according to them, the torture of the wicked and unbelieving, who are supposed to be the great majority, is to endure *for ever and ever.* The Creed of St. Athanasius says :—

" Whosoever will be saved : *before all things* it is necessary that he hold the Catholic Faith.

" Which Faith, except every one do keep whole and undefiled : *without doubt* he shall perish everlastingly. . . .

" He (Christ) suffered for our salvation : *descended into hell,* rose again the third day from the dead.

" At Whose coming all men shall rise again *with their bodies :* and shall give account for their own works.

" And they that have done good, shall go into life everlasting : and they that have done evil, into *everlasting fire.*

" *This* is the Catholic Faith, which except a man believe faithfully he cannot be saved.

" Glory be to the Father, and to the Son, and to the Holy Ghost : As it was in the beginning, is now, and ever shall be, world without end. *Amen.*"

According to the popular belief, all who differed from the teaching of the orthodox lived under the hatred of the Almighty, and were destined after death to an eternity of anguish in hell, " where their worm dieth not and the fire is not quenched, but the smoke of their torment goeth up for ever and ever", and no moral or intellectual excellence could atone for their crime in propagating error ; and, according to Pope St. Gregory, the elect Christians " will be *sated with joy as they gaze on the unspeakable anguish of the impious,* returning thanks for their own freedom .... The just man will rejoice when he shall see the vengeance." Nirvana is better than such pleasure as this.[1]

We learn from the Westminster Confession of Faith, which is the Creed of the Scotch Church, that :—

[1] Lecky's *Morals,* vol. ii. p. 241.

" By the decree of God, *for the manifestation of his glory,* some men and angels are predestinated unto everlasting life, *and others foreordained to everlasting death.*

" These angels and men, thus predestinated and foreordained, *are particularly and unchangeably designed;* and their number is so certain and definite, that it cannot be either increased or diminished.

" Those of mankind that are predestinated unto life, God, before the foundation of the world was laid, according to His eternal and immutable purpose, and the secret counsel and good pleasure of His will, hath chosen in Christ unto everlasting glory, out of His free grace and love, without any foresight of faith or good works, or perseverance in either of them, or any other thing in the Creature, as conditions, or causes moving Him thereunto : *and all to the praise of His glorious grace.*

" As God hath appointed the elect unto glory, so hath He, by the eternal and most free purpose of His will, foreordained all the means thereunto. Wherefore they who are elected, being fallen in Adam, are redeemed by Christ ; are effectually called unto faith in Christ by His Spirit working in due season ; are justified, adopted, sanctified, and kept by His power through faith unto salvation ; neither are any other redeemed by Christ, effectually called, justified, adopted, sanctified, and saved, but the elect only.

" The rest of mankind, God was pleased, according to the unsearchable counsel of His own will, whereby He extendeth or withholdeth mercy as He pleaseth, for the glory of His sovereign power over His creatures, to pass by, *and to ordain them to dishonour and wrath for their sin, to the praise of his glorious justice.*"

Of the state of men after death, the same Confession of Faith tells us :—

" The bodies of men after death return to dust, and see corruption ; but their souls (which neither die nor sleep), having an immortal subsistence, immediately return to God who gave them. The souls of the righteous, being then made perfect in holiness, are received into the highest Heavens, where they behold the face of God in light and glory, waiting for the full redemption of their bodies ; and the souls of the wicked are cast into hell, where they remain in torments and utter darkness, reserved to the judgment of the great day. Besides these two places for souls separated from their bodies, the Scripture acknowledgeth none."

Of the Fall of Man, this Confession states :—

" Our first parents being seduced by the subtilty and temptation of Satan, sinned in eating the forbidden fruit. This their
sin *God was pleased, according to His wise and holy council, to
permit, having purposed to order it for his own glory.*"

Can anything be more diabolical than this ? " Shall
there be evil in a city and I have not done it ?" says
Jehovah.[1]

The following is the horrible doctrine of St. Augustine
upon the dogma of " Original Sin".

" Hold thou, then, most firmly, nor do thou in any respect
doubt, that infants, whether in their mothers' wombs they
begin to live and there die, or when, after their mothers have
given birth to them, they pass from this life without the
Sacrament of Holy Baptism, will be punished with the everlasting punishment of eternal fire." (See Colenso on the
Pentateuch.)

The ancient Egyptians, Zoroastrians, Jews, Buddhists,
and the ancient Philosophers, hoped to obtain eternal
happiness, by working out their salvation by practising
virtue, and all good works, and by conscientiously doing
their duty. (See vol. i, p. 300.)

The Roman Catholic rests his faith on the supposed
infallibility of his *Pope* and his *Church*. He reads in
his catechism, or is told by his catechist, that *the Church
cannot err in what she teaches*, and then he is told that
this unerring Church is composed only of those who hold
communion with the Bishop of Rome, and believe pre-
cisely as he, and the Bishops who hold communion with
him, believe. From that moment reason is set aside ;
authority usurps its place, and implicit faith is the necessary consequence . . . . He dares not doubt ; for in
his table of sins, which he is obliged to confess, he finds,
doubting in matters of faith to be a grievous crime.

But, on the other hand, is the faith of a Protestant
better founded ? He rests it on a *Book*, called the
Holy Bible, which he believes to be the *infallible Word
of God*. . . . . He is taught to believe the Bible to be the

[1] Amos iii, 6.

infallible Word of God before he has read or can read it; and he sits down to read it, with this prepossession in his mind, that he is reading the *infallible Word of God.* His belief, then, is as implicit as that of the Roman Catholic, and his motives for believing even less specious.

On the whole, then, I think it may be laid down as an axiom, that the bulk of Christians, Roman Catholics or Protestants, cannot be said to have a rational faith; because their motives of credibility are not rational motives, but the positive assertions of an assumed authority, which they have never discussed, or durst not question. Their religion is the fruit of unenlightened credulity.[1]

EGYPTIAN RECORDS.

Sacred science, as interpreted by the Fathers of the Catholic Church, demonstrated these facts :—1. That the date of Creation was comparatively recent, not more than four or five thousand years before Christ; 2. That the act of Creation occupied the space of six ordinary days; 3. That the Deluge was universal, and that the animals which survived it were preserved in an ark, about 2,000 years after the supposed Creation; 4. That Adam was created perfect in morality and intelligence, that he fell, and that his descendants have shared in his sin and fall.

But in direct contradiction to all this, we learn from history, that Manetho assigns to the mythological era of Egypt 24,000 years, and Chabas, a distinguished Egyptologist, who is by no means intemperate in figures, ascribes to the united mythological and monarchical age of Egypt 10,000 years; 4,000 B.C. being the date of Mena or Menes, her first king.

According to Manetho, the age of Mena dates back to a period of 5,004 years before the Christian era, a date which is nearly equal to 7,000 years from the present day. Brugsch favours a somewhat less interval, namely,

[1] Rev. A. Geddes, D.D., *Critical Remarks on the Hebrew Scriptures.*

4,455 B.C.; Birch and Chabas adopt 4,000 B.C., which is
equivalent to 6,000 years backwards from the existing
time.

Lieblein gives full credit to the chronology of Manetho,
as recorded by the historian Africanus, as likewise did
the distinguished Mariette, and differs very little from
the standard adopted by Birch. He assigns to Mena, as
the pioneer of the first monarchy, a date in round numbers of 3,900 years, which he obtains by means of the
following calculation. The total of the years of reign
from Mena to the birth of Christ he assumes to be 5,672,
from which he deducts contemporary reigns 1,777, leaving
a balance of 3,895 B.C. This date corresponds very
remarkably with the epoch of Adam and Eve as computed by Rydberg, a Swedish philosopher, namely, 3,893
B.C. The Deluge, 2,432, must have happened in the
time of Usertesen I, the founder of the first colossal
obelisks.[1]

Professor Huxley says :—"The first traces of the pri-
mordial stock whence man has proceeded need no longer
be sought by those who entertain any form of the doctrine of progressive development in the newest ter-
tiaries; but they may be looked for in an epoch more
distant from the age of the *Elephas primogenius* than
that is from us."

RELIGION OF THE JEWS.

In the *Liber Landavensis*, p. 309, it is stated that the
Pelagian heresy broke out in the reign of the Emperor
Constantine, who commenced his reign in 306, and died
in 337. Pelagius denied Baptism and the Sacrifice of
the Body of Christ, whence arose great hatred, conten-
tion, and wars, in consequence of which Baptism and
Sacrifice ceased in Britain, whence the whole population
became unbaptised Jews." In later times the Jews wor-

[1] *The Egypt of the Past.* By Sir Erasmus Wilson, F.R.S. London:
Kegan Paul and Co. Price 12s.

shipped a Deity called Yahveh or Jehovah, who is constantly met with in the sacred writings of the Jews as a Deity appearing in the two aspects of Good and Evil; their God, whether called El or Jahveh, is still ONE only. Though held to be no more than the greatest among the Gods, he is ever to them the Supreme, Lord of the Dark as of the Light, source Himself of the Evil as of the Good that befals. "Shall there be evil in a city and I have not done it, says Jehovah."[1] "I form the light and create darkness; I make peace and create evil; I, the Lord, do all these things."[2] (See vol. i, p. 289.)

When, however, the Britons again became Christians, they must have accepted the Christian Devil as the Author of Evil, which doctrine contradicts the express statements of Jehovah, which we find in His own inspired volume, where he declares Himself to be the Author of Evil. In earlier times, however, we find from the speech of Joshua[3] that the Jews did not worship Jehovah. "Now, therefore", says the writer, "fear Jehovah and serve Him in sincerity and in truth, and put away the gods which your fathers served on the other side of the stream (the Jordan) and in Egypt, and serve ye Jehovah. And if it seem not good unto you to serve Jehovah, then choose you this day whom ye will serve—whether *the gods which your fathers served on the other side of the stream* (the Jordan), or the gods of the Amorites in whose land ye dwell; but as for me and my house we will serve Jehovah." The people having determined to take Jehovah for their God, Joshua took a great stone, and set it up there under an oak that was by the sanctuary of the Lord, and said unto all the people, "Behold, this stone shall be a witness unto us; for *it hath heard* all the words of the Lord which He spake unto us; it shall be, therefore, a witness unto you lest ye deny your God." Hosea[4] says, "When Israel was a child then I loved him, and called my son out of Egypt. As they called them, so they went from them;

---

[1] Amos iii, 6.
[2] Isaiah xlv, 7.
[3] Joshua xxiv, 14.
[4] Hosea xi, 1, 2.

they sacrificed unto Baalim, and burned incense to graven images." And again, "Have ye offered me sacrifices and offerings in the wilderness forty years, O house of Israel? but ye have borne the tabernacle of your Moloch and Chiun (or Chamos), your images, the star of your God which ye made to yourselves." In the Gospel of Matthew, by a marginal reference in the Authorised Version, this text is made to refer to Jesus Christ; if so, he must have worshipped Baalim.

THEISM.

I have given the ideas that Pythagoras and other Theists hold with regard to the Deity in my first volume, at p. 5, in connection with which I will here insert the following piece of poetry, entitled,

The Dying Buddist's Hymn.

I go to Him in Whom all is,
The self-existent Perfectness;
   Who knows not of finality,
   The only Being that can be;
Who, without motion can create,
Or, motionless, annihilate
A world whose cup is brimming high
With will, and self, and blasphemy.

Unto the All be honour given,—
I shall not see Him, even in Heaven;
   The outline of Infinity,
   The substance of Divinity,
Created spirit may not grasp;
Only by faith His knees I clasp.
My little rill draws near the sea,
Source of my soul, I come to Thee.—W.

According to Pindar,—

The body yields to death's all-powerful summons,
While the bright image of eternity, the Soul,
Survives.

This alone is from God; from heaven it comes, says Plutarch, and to heaven it returns; not, indeed, with the body; but when it is entirely set free and separate from the body, when it becomes disengaged from everything sensual and unholy. For, in the language of Heraclitus, the pure soul is of superior excellence, darting from the body like a flash of lightning from a cloud; but the soul that is carnal and immersed in sense, like a heavy and dark vapour, with difficulty is kindled and aspires. There is, therefore, no occasion against nature to send the bodies of good men to heaven; but we are to conclude that virtuous souls, by nature and the divine justice, rise from men to heroes, from heroes to genii; and at last, if, as in the mysteries, they are perfectly cleansed and purified, shaking off all remains of mortality, and all the power of the passions, then they finally attain the most glorious and perfect happiness, and ascend from genii to the Deity, by the just and established order of nature.

Milton, in his *Comus*, writes as follows (see vol. ii, p. 95, Plato's statement in the *Phædo*).

> "The lavish act of sin
> Lets in defilement to the inward parts;
> The soul grows clotted by contagion,
> Imbodies, and imbrutes, till she quite lose
> The divine property of her first being.
> Such are those thick and gloomy shadows damp
> Oft seen in charnel vaults and sepulchres,
> Lingering and sitting by a new-made grave,
> As loath to leave the body that it loved,
> And links itself by carnal sensuality
> To a degenerate and degraded state."

Hesiod was the first who distinguished these four natures—men, heroes, genii, and gods—and believed, as did the ancient Egyptians, in a perpetual progression and improvement in a state of immortality. (See *Serpent Myths of Ancient Egypt*, by Cooper.) And also before the last degree, that of divinity, is reached, these souls are liable to be replunged into their primitive state of darkness, as were the Titans, or fallen angels or genii.

In the New Testament we are told that after his Cruci-
fixion, Christ descended into Hell, and preached to the
Spirits in prison "which some time were disobedient".

" Yes, another era is already dawning upon earth, when it
shall be light, when man shall wake from high and lofty
dreams, and these dreams he shall find realised, and that he
has lost nothing but sleep.

" And at the sunset gate of this age stands written, 'Here
lies the way to wisdom and to virtue'; as at the west gate of
the Chersonese the proud writing, 'Here lies the way to Byzantium.'

" O eternal Providence, Thou wilt that it shall be light!"

Hymn of the Dying Warrior.

As the stream pauses ere it plunge below,
  So on the last dread verge my spirit stands—
  Thou Who hast guided me through earthly lands,
Eternal Love, lift me to Heaven now!

Thou gavest bitter grief and deep delight,
  The fiery trial and victorious wreath,
  And, now, a tomb with those I loved on earth ;
The lamps of Heaven gleam through death's dark night—
  Lord, I adore Thee with my latest breath !
  Receive my soul now freed at length by death !

On God.

Whate'er exists within this universe
Is all to be regarded as enveloped,
By the great Lord, as if wrapped in a vesture.
There is one only Being who exists
Unmoved, yet moving swifter than the mind ;
Who far outstrips the senses, though as gods
They strive to reach Him ; Who Himself at rest
Transcends the fleetest flight of other beings ;
Who, like the air, supports all vital action.
He moves, yet moves not ; He is far, yet near ;
He is within this universe. Who'er beholds
All living creatures as in Him and Him—
The universal spirit—as in all,
Henceforth regards no creature with contempt.
                 From the *Isa Upanishad.*

For the great difference of the account given of Jehovah in the Old and New Testament, and that given of the Deity by the ancient philosophers, the reader is requested to refer to vol. i, pp. 2, 3, 4, 5, 57.

On Death.

Daily perform thine own appointed work
Unweariedly; and to obtain a friend—
A sure companion to the future world—
Collect a store of virtue like the ants
Who garner up their treasures into heaps;
For neither father, mother, wife, nor son,
Nor kinsman, will remain beside thee then;
When thou art passing to that other home—
Thy virtue will thy only comrade be.[1]

Single is every living creature born,
Single he passes to another world,
Single he eats the fruit of evil deeds,
Single the fruit of good; and when he leaves
His body like a log or heap of clay
Upon the ground, his kinsmen walk away;
Virtue alone stays by him at the tomb,
And bears him through the dreary trackless gloom.

From the Precepts of Manu.

THE ASHERA OR GROVE.

I have just received from a Roman Catholic gentleman well known in the controversial world, the following remarks upon what I have stated on this subject in vol. ii, pp. 366, 367.

" I think, if you would allow me to say so, that if you would only permit your reason and common sense to carry you a little deeper below the surface, they would lead you back thither (*i. e.*, to the Catholic Church). I cannot think, for one example, why you should lay such stress on what you have called Jacob's making conditions with Almighty God. Under the Jewish Dispensation the temporal promises to man were put forth more prominently than the spiritual, and that for reasons which are obvious enough to us now, who live under

---

[1] See vol. i, p. 302.

the last and Christian Dispensation. Jacob merely claimed all that God had promised before to his fathers in the event of his fulfilling the covenant. He did not first propound the conditions, and then require God to accede to them as the terms of his serving Him, although the close condensation of the narrative may make it at first sight appear so. I should very much like you to read the argument for Christianity, as against these and similar notions, in Newman's beautiful little book, *The Grammar of Assent.* You will, I am sure, find it on reflection quite sufficiently satisfying for a reasonable man."

My sole reason for quoting the verses from the Bible at p. 367, was to prove that the Hebrews had the same reverence for the column or pillar that the other nations of the world had, and many still have. I refer my readers to the above-mentioned pages, and to p. 368.

EYTON OF EYTON ISAF.

(*See* vol. ii.)

The following additional particulars relative to this ancient and formerly distinguished family have been kindly sent me by the Rev. E. H. Mainwaring Sladen, of the Gore, Bournemouth, taken from Randle Holmes's and other manuscripts.

Sir Kendrick Eyton of Eyton, Knt., succeeded his father, Sir Gerard Eyton, Knight Banneret, who died in 1653. Sir Kendrick was Judge of North Wales, and died in 1682. He married, first, Eleanor, youngest daughter and co-heiress of Sir Peter Mutton[1] of Llann-erch, Knt., by whom he had issue, besides daughters, three sons—

I. Kendrick Eyton of Eyton, Attorney-General for Cheshire and Flintshire. He married, first, Rebecca, daughter of Abraham Johnson.

II. Gerard Eyton of Malaga in Spain. In the College of Arms is the copy of a certificate granted to the father on behalf of his second son, Gerard, described as of Malaga, declaration of his gentle birth, etc.

III. Sir James Eyton of Mortlake in Surrey, and of London, Knt. He died in 1728, aged eighty-eight, and left a legacy to the church of Bangor Isgoed. He married, first, Jane Baldwyn, by whom he had no issue; and, secondly, he married Elizabeth Cannon, who died in 1729, and left a charity to Mortlake, still called Lady Eyton's Charity.

Sir Kendrick Eyton married, secondly, Mary, daughter of Sir Francis Bickley, Bart., and relict of William Hoo of the Hoo,[2] Herts., by whom he had a daughter, Mary, ux. Sir Henry Bunbury of Standy, co. Cestriæ, Bart., who died in 1687, aged thirty.

Kendrick Eyton of Eyton, the eldest son and heir, married Anne, daughter of Edward Birch of Leycroft, co. Stafford, Serjeant-at-Law, by whom he had a son and heir,

Kendrick Eyton of Eyton, High Sheriff for co. Denbigh in 1753. He married, in 1756, Hannah Jones, by whom he had issue two sons—

I. Kendrick Eyton of Eyton, who married, in 1783, Sarah Rowlands, and died 19th January 1786, *s. p.*

II. Edward Eyton, who married Hannah Bey of the Isle of Wight, by whom he had a son and heir,

Kendrick Edward Eyton, who married, in 1808, Margaret Jones.

---

[1] This is the Welsh way of spelling Mytton, the Welsh "u" being pronounced like the English "y".

[2] Lineally descended from the Lord Hoo of Hoo, *temp.* Henry VI.

Kendrick Eyton of Eyton.⸺Elizabeth, d. of Richard Brooke of Norton.

Sir Gerard Eyton, knighted at⸺Elizabeth,[1] d. and heiress of Edward Brom-
Shrewsbury, 1642; *ob.* 1653.   field of Mortyn.

| Eleanor, dau. and co-heir of Sir Peter Mutton of Llanerch, co. Denbigh, Knight, and M.P. for co. Carnarvon; *ob.* 1637. | Sir Kendrick Eyton of Eyton,⸺Mary, d. of Sir Francis Knight, Chief Justice of North Wales, and one of the Council of the Court of the Marches; living 1674. | | Bickley, Bart., and relict of William Hoo of the Hoo, co. Herts. |

| Francis, only son; living 1674. | Mary, *ob.* Dec. 1637, æt. 32. See vol. ii, p. 162. ⸺Sir Henry Bunbury of Bunbury and Stanney, co. Cestriæ, Bart. | Amicia, ux. Jasper Peck. |

| 1 |
| Sir Henry Bunbury of Stanney, Bart.; *ob.* 1732. ⸺ Susanna, d. of William Hanmer of Bettisfield (Llys Bedydd); *ob.* 1744. |

| 2 |
| William Bunbury⸺Sarah, sole surviving child and heir of Sir James Eyton of Mortlake, co. Surrey, Knt.; baptised 24th Jan. 1685. |
of the Inner Temple, London. Admitted 1697; called to the Bar 1702; Bencher 1725; *ob.* 1748.

| 1 |
| Sarah Bunbury, eldest d. and co-heir; *ob.* at Bath, 1798, æt. 89. = Edward Mainwaring of Whitmore, co. Stafford; b. 1709; High Sheriff for co. Stafford, 1768; *ob.* 1795. |

| 2 | 3 | 4 |
| Mary. Isabella. Susanna. All died young and unmarried. |

| 5 |
| Elizabeth, first wife of Edward Fleming of the Inner Temple. She died in 1735, æt. 25. | Eleanor, ux. George Wilson of the Inner Temple, by whom she had a son, William Wilson, aged 17 in 1747. |

a | 1   *b* | 2   *c* | 3   *d* | 1   *e* |

---

[1] On a tablet set in the north side of the chancel of Bangor Church are these arms painted, Eyton impaling Bromfield.

"BARON.—1. *Ermine*, a lion rampant *azure*, Eyton of Eyton; 2. Llywarch ab Bran, Lord of Cwmmwd Menai; 3. Palii of eight pieces *gules* and *argent*, a lion rampant *sable*, for Gruffydd Maelor; 4. Rhirid Flaidd, Lord of Penllyn; 5. *Argent*, a lion rampant *gules*; 6. *Or*, a lion rampant in a border *gules*.

"FEMME.—Quarterly, 1st and 4th, Idnerth Benfras; 2nd and 3rd, Palii of eight pieces, *argent* and *gules*.

"In the vault beneath lyeth the body of Dame Elizabeth, daughter and heir of Edward Bromfield, Gen., and late wife to Sir Gerard Eyton of Eyton, Knight. She dyed on the last day of October 1642." (See vol. ii, pp. 161, 328.)

a	1	b	2	c	3					d	1	e

Ken-
drick
Eyton
of
Ey-
ton.

Gerrard
Eyton
of Mala-
ga in
Spain.
1674.

Sir James Ey-= Jane Elizabeth Eleanor, ux.
ton of Mort- Baldwyn Cannon of John Puleston
lake, co. Sur- of Lon- London. of Havod y
rey, and Lon- don, Married in Wern.
don. Knighted married 1674; ob.
in London 1670; 1729.
29th Oct. 1602. ob. s. p.
Ob. 3rd June
1728; æt. 88.

| 2 | 3
Eliza-   Dorothy, ux. Robert
beth, ux.   Power of Bersham,
Gilbert   and heir of Mascu-
Fownes   lus Henry Power of
of Lon-   Valentia in Ireland.
don.   She died in 1642.
               See p. 25.

Kendrick Eyton, ob.
15th Dec. 1675.
Buried in the great
vault at Mortlake
with seven other
children of Sir
James Eyton.

Eleanor Eyton,
bapt. 22nd January
1679. Buried in
the south aisle of
St. Magnus the
Martyr's, near Lon-
don Bridge, 19th
January 1702.

Sarah Ey- = William Bunbury
ton, sole V   of the Inner
surviving   Temple, second son
child and   of Sir Henry Bun-
heir; bapt.   bury of Bunbury,
24th Jan.   and of Stanney, co.
1685.   Cestriæ, Bart.; ob.
               1748.

The will of Sir James Eyton, dated 12 George I, June
3 (1726), proved 14th June 1728. His widow, Elizabeth, described as of St. Alphage parish. Administration
granted to Sarah, wife of William Bunbury, Esq., 17th May
1729. Sir James Eyton left his house at Mortlake, etc.,
to William and Sarah Bunbury; a legacy to Amicia
Peck, his half sister; and another legacy to the churchwardens of Bangor Is y Coed.[1]

Lady Eyton, his widow, left by her will, dated 1729,
the gift of £100 for annual distribution to four men and
four women of the age of sixty years and upwards,
of the parish of Mortlake; which legacy purchased
£81 12s. 10d. The annual interest thereof, £2 9s. 0d.,
is still distributed.[2]

"MY DEAR SIR,—It occurs to me to ask your acceptance of a
copy of the certificate I have before referred to. It
may have interest for you, though not really calculated
for use in your book. I imagine a document of the kind
to be far from common, and it seems likely that Gerard

[1] From the Heralds' College, London.
[2] *Charities of Mortlake.* Edited by Octavius Ommaney, Churchwarden. 1858.

Eyton was contemplating marriage in Spain, and was called
to show his lineage. Otherwise, the great expense of the certificate and illuminated Pedigree roll together would scarcely
have been incurred, the latter being no less than 17 feet in
length. There is one rather curious statement in the certificate, viz., that Tudor Trevor flourished shortly before (*paullo
ante*) the times of King Edward I, the Conqueror of Wales.
And yet the Records of Heralds' College make him husband of
Ankaret, daughter of King Howell Dha, contemporary with
King Athelstan in the tenth century; and the date of 924 is generally given with the name of Tudor Trevor, more than three
centuries previous to the conquest of Wales, too long a period,
far, one would think, to be expressed by the Latin words
aforesaid. The words suggest a mistake in the writer of the
certificate, that he misunderstood in the MS. authorities an
earlier King Edward (*e.g.*, the Confessor) who may have been
mentioned in connection with Howell Dha or Tudor Trevor,
for the better known Plantagenet king. And I have seen an
extract from the Record Office in which the last named is
described as Edwardus Rex Angliæ, *Primus a Conquestu*,
evidently to exclude the Edwards before the Norman Conquest, which would hardly have been necessary unless one of
the Anglo-Saxon Edwards had previously been styled " Primus." You will see that Sir K. Eyton, Gerard's father, is in
the certificate (1674) simply " Armiger", which makes the
date of his knighthood (1675) important, as given by Francis
Townsend, Pursuivant of Arms, in his *Catalogue of Knights*,
from 1660 to 1760, published in 1833, in which, by-the-by, Sir
Kendrick Eyton is called, "of Eyton, Kent." This may be merely
a clerical error, particularly as Neve's volume (*Harl. Society*)
describes him of " Denbigh." But he was knighted at
Whitehall, and he may have required a residence nearer
London than his distant home. The Edenbridge station on the
South Eastern Railway had the " d" in Eden changed into "t",
and Hasted, in his *History of Kent*, vol. i, published 1778,
writes Eaton, and speaks of the name as corrupted, as it is
situate on the river Eden. It would be curious if Sir K.
Eyton once lived there and gave his name to the place, a
practice of which there are instances at the time, *e.g.*, Sir J.
Wynn of Gwydir, on coming into possession of Rhuabon,
changing the name of the Eyton house at Watstay to Wynnstay, as I dare say you know. I remember, too, in my young
days, hearing of members of the Auckland family as resident
at Edenbridge or its neighbourhood, and it would be again
curious if they should have been instrumental in restoring the

name of Eden. It is the only place of the name in Kent known
to me. I find, in my continuation of the Eyton pedigree,
Kenric Edward Eyton, son of Edward Eyton, whom you
report to have sold the property, described " of Eyton Hall",
which must be an error, though I think I copied the statement from a MS. which came from Heralds' College. Few would
act as did Sarah Rowlands. I had heard the anecdote before.
You are probably aware that the two knights, Sir Gerard
Eyton, and his son, Sir Kendrick, had both of them to com-
pound for their estate during the Protectorate, and this I
believe had the result of impoverishing the family ; and I
have somewhere seen a Kendrick Eyton named as bankrupt,
but cannot recall the authority. No doubt there were other
causes at work necessitating the sale.

" Pennant, in the advertisement, dated 1778, to his *Tour in
Wales*, expresses his obligations to Kenrick Eyton, Esq., of
Eyton, amongst others, and in a note he speaks of him as
recently deceased. The work was published in 1784. This
must have been the father-in-law of Sarah Rowlands, and I
have his death as occurring 11th February 1780. He was
sheriff of Denbighshire in 1753.

" I do not know whether I have more worth communicating,
unless it be the heraldry of the family, of which I can furnish
something if you should care to have it. I will mention, by
the way, that the coat of Jestyn ap Gwrgant, contained in the
shield accompanying the certificate, does not occur in the
larger number of quarterings (in all 41, excluding repetitions),
ascribed to the family by Heralds' College. Dunn's *Welsh Visita-
tions* show that the coat in question appertained to Bromfield,
and it was doubtless brought to Eyton by Sir Gerard's marriage
with the coheiress of Edward Bromfield. There are other
things that I could state, but they are purely of heraldic interest.
Apologising for the length to which this note has grown,

" I am, my dear Sir, yours faithfully,

" *4th July*, 1882. " E. H. M. SLADEN."

Sarah Bunbury, the eldest daughter of W. Bunbury and
Sarah Eyton, was a belle in her day. There are two portraits
of her in existence, one in her youth, the other (a miniature)
in her old age. The latter, a side face, is a fine outline. In
both she is dressed in blue. E. H. M. S.

In his letter, Mr. E. H. Mainwaring Sladen alludes
to the noble act of Sarah, the widow of Kendrick Eyton,

who died in 1786. This lady was the daughter of John
Rowland, and Anne, one of the daughters of Edward
Lloyd of Plâs Madog ; and Mr. Kendrick Eyton, after
his death, was interred in the church of Bangor Is y
Coed. After the funeral party had returned to the house,
his will was read in the large hall, which had a fine
timbered roof, with galleries all round it. When the will
was opened, it was discovered that Mr. Eyton had left the
whole of the Eyton estates to his widow *absolutely*.
After the will had been read, it was given to Mrs. Eyton,
who, rising from her chair, deliberately walked to the fire-
place and threw the will on the blazing fire, and, notwithstanding the importunities of her friends, who besought
her not to do such a thing, she resolutely thrust it into
the fire and kept it down with the poker till it was all
consumed. (See vol. ii, pp. 163, 164.)

Omnibus ad quos præsentes pervenerint Reges Heraldi et
Pursuivandi Armorum Anglicorum Salutem.

Quoniam authoritate regia fulciti juramentoque ligati nos
sumus Nobilium Regni Angliæ et Walliæ genealogias tesserasque suas gentilitias Collegio nostro Armorum conscribere
et in Salvum custodire ut ex iisdem exemplaria toties quoties
rogati fuerimus petentibus retribuissemus Nos rogante claro
viro Kendrico Eyton armigero domino de Eytona ditissimæ ac
pervetustæ familiæ illius Eytonorum sede Walliâ Septentrio-
nali sitâ, vobis notum facimus Quod Gerardus Eyton, Genero-
sus, Malagâ Hispaniæ jamjam moram faciens filius est secundo
genitus præmemorati Kendrici ex dominâ Elinâ uxore ejus
unâ filiarum et cohæredum domini Petri Moton Equitis aurati,
domini de Llannerch Walliâ eâdem patrimonio suo peramplo,
Qui Kendricus filius est primogenitus et hæres domini Gerardi
Eyton Equitis aurati et dominæ Elizabethæ uxoris ejus filiæ
unicæ ac hæredis Edvardi Bromfield armigeri, domini de
Mortyn Walliâ sæpedictâ domino. Et Gerardus ille, Eques
auratus, filius fuit alterius Kendrici Eyton armigeri filio secundo geniti Jacobi Eyton Armigeri filii ac hæredis Hugonis
Eyton Armigiri filii et hæredis Oeni Eyton Armigeri filii et
hæredis Gulielmi Eyton Armigeri, filii et hæredis Johannis
Eyton Armigeri, filii et hæredis alterius Jacobi Eyton de
Eyton Armigeri, genus suum rectâ lineâ paternali ducentis a
Theodoro Trevor, uno Magnatum Walliæ, qui ibidem floruit

paulo ante ea tempora quibus Wallia ab Edvardo Rege Angliæ istius nominis primo, subacta Coronæque Angliæ annexa fuit; præmemorati etiam Gerardi Eyton insignia, tesserasque gentilitias, ad ipsum lege Armorum ritè et legitimè spectantia, latere præsentium delineari curavimus. Quæ omnia e registris Armorum conscriptis et aliis memorandis fide dignis, tum Anglicis, cum Wallicis, transumpta pro veritate perlucida ac indubia per præsentes vobis significamus ac declaramus, Rogantes ut præmissis fidem debitam adhibeatis. In quorum Omnium testimonium Sigillum nostrum commune his Tabulis apponi fecimus Datis Londini Decimo die Mensis Julii Anno Regni Serenissimi ac potentissimi domini nostri Caroli Secundi Dei gratiâ Magnæ Britanniæ Franciæ et Hiberniæ Regis, fidei Defensoris, etc., Vicessimo Sexto, Annoque salutis nostræ reparatæ, Millesimo Sexcentessimo Septuagesimo quarto.

Examined p.   HEN : ST. GEORGE, Richmond.

THOMAS LEE, Chester.

Extracted from the Register marked " L 2", pp. 122*b*, 123, now remaining in the Heralds' College, London, and examined therewith this 22nd day of September, 1868, by me.

(Signed)   G. W. COLLEN,

Portcullis Pursuivant of Arms.

Annexed is a Shield of Arms, in trick, containing six coats, viz. :—1. *Ermine*, a lion rampant *azure* (the coat of Elyder ap Rhys Sais)—Eyton of Eyton, Denbighshire ; 2. Party by bend sinister *ermine* and *ermines*, a lion rampant *or*—Tudor Trevor, Earl of Hereford and Lord of Bromfield ; 3. *Argent*, a chevron between three ravens, each with a queen of *ermine* in the bill, all proper—Llowarch ap Bran, Lord of Holyhead ; 4. *Argent*, a cross engrailed couped fleury *sable* between four choughs proper, on a chief *azure*, a boar's head couped close, of the first—Bromfield, of Mortyn, Denbighshire. (The coat of Lles ap Idnerth Benfrâs, Lord of Maesbrwg). 5. *Gules*, three chevronels *argent*—Jestyn ap Gwrgant, Prince of Glamorgan ; 6. *Argent*, a cinquefoil *azure*—Moton (Mytton), of Llannerch, Denbighshire.

E. HILLS.

TOWNSHIP OF Y GWRTHYMP.—BROUGHTON OF
BROUGHTON OR BROCHTYN.

Harl. MS. 4181.

Ednyfed, Lord of Brochtyn, second son of Cynwrig ab Rhiwallon ab⊤
    Dingad ab Tudor Trevor. *Ermine,* a lion statant gardant *gules,*
    armed and langued *azure.*—See vol. i, p. 309.

Tudor ab⊤Annest, d. of Llywelyn	Einion	Gruffydd	Gwenllian, ux. Rhi-
Ednyfed Eurdorchog, Lord of	ab Ed-	ab	rid Fychan ab
of Iâl and Ystrad Alun.	nyfed.	Edny-	Rhirid Flaidd.
Broch- *Azure,* a lion passant	See	ved.	See Chirk Castle.
dyn. gardent *or.*	Bers.		

Ednyved Grûg of Brochdyn.⊤Janet, d. of Rhys Fychan ab Rhys Grûg, Lord
                         of Llanymdoferi.

Llywelyn Goch⊤Lettice, dau. of Sir Richard Manley, Knight, of Cheshire.
 of Brochdyn.   *Argent,* a sinister hand, couped at the wrist in a border
         engrailed *sable.*

Gruffydd Goch of Brochdyn.⊤

Gruffydd Ddû of⊤Margaret, d. of Maredydd of Yr Hôb, second son of Gru-
 Brochdyn.   ffydd ab Llywelyn ab Ynyr of Bod Idris in Iâl. *Gules,*
        three pales *or,* in a border of the second charged with
        eight ogresses.

1	2
Madog ab ⊤Angharad, d. of Iorwerth Foel of	Iorwerth ab Gruffydd, an-
Gruffydd of Mortyn, ab Robert ab David	cestor of the Ellises of
Brochdyn. Goch ab David Hen ab Goron-	Alrhey and the Powels
wy of Mortyn and Llai.	of Alrhey.

Ednyved ab Madog of⊤Angharad, d. of Robert ab Gruffydd ab Madog ab
 Brochdyn.   Ednyfed Goch ab Cynwrig ab Gruffyd Fychan.
        Ermine, a lion statant gardant *gules.*

Iorwerth Goch⊤Alice, d. of Sir Randle Brere-	Morgan ab⊤Angharad, dau.
of Brochdyn; ∨ ton of Malpas, Knt., and	Ednyved. of Madog Pulc-
ob. 17th Oct. sister of Sir Randle Brere-	ston of Bers.
1496. ton, Knt. *Argent,* two	*s. p.*
bars *sable.*	

The above named Iorwerth Goch, had issue by his wife Alice, besides a daughter Jane, ux. Gruffydd Llwyd of Talwrne, seven sons—1, Randle Broughton, of whom presently ; 2, Thomas Broughton, *ob. s. p.;* 3, Edmund Broughton, who married and had issue two daughters— Elizabeth, ux. Stephen Goldsmith of London ; and Alice, ux. . . . . Norbury, a lawyer ; 4, John Broughton ; 5, Mathew Broughton ; 6, Morgan Broughton of Plâs Isaf in Marchwiail, ancestor of the Broughtons of Marchwiail in the manor of Rhiwabon ; and 7, Sir Edward, a priest.

Randle Broughton of Broughton or Brochdyn, married Margaret, daughter and heiress of David Eyton, second son of Elis Eyton of Rhiwabon, by whom he had issue two sons, 1, John, of whom presently ; and 2, Randle Broughton ; and two daughters, 1, Janet, ux. James Eyton of Pentref Madog in Tref Dudlyst (*ermine, a lion rampant azure*), *ob. s. p.;* and 2, Anne, ux. John Trevor of Trevalun.

John Broughton of Broughton, married Margaret, daughter of William Williams of Cwchwillan,[1] by whom he had issue four sons, 1, Randle, of whom presently ; 2, John Broughton ; 3, William Broughton ; and 4, Ralph Broughton ; and four daughters, 1, Alice, ux. Thomas Dimoch of Halchdyn ; 2, Lily, ux. Roger Eyton of Bodylltyn in Rhiwabon ; 3, Margaret, ux. Hugh Gwynn ; and 4, Anne.

Randle Broughton of Broughton, 1593, married Jane, daughter of Roger Puleston of Emrall, by whom he had issue two sons, 1, John, of whom presently ; and 2, Randle Broughton, an idiot ; and three daughters, 1, Magdalene, ux. John Edwards of Plâs Newydd yn Y Waun (Chirk) ab John Edwards, descended from Tudor Trevor ; 2, Dorothy ; and 3, Susan.

John Broughton of Broughton, who married Susan, daughter of Edward Billott of Mortyn or Burton, and Amy his wife, daughter and heiress of Anthony Gros-

---

[1] The arms of the Williamses of Cwch Willan were *gules*, a chevron *ermine*, inter three Englishmen's heads in profile, couped at the neck ppr.

venor of Tref Dudlyst (*argent*, on a chief *gules*, three cinquefoils of the field), by whom he had issue a son and heir,

John Broughton of Broughton, who married Awdrey, daughter of William Lovergage of Whelock in Cheshire, by whom he had a son Thomas, who died *s. p.*, and a daughter,

Elizabeth Broughton, heiress of Broughton, who married Rowland Whitehall of Lockwood, in the parish of Kinsley, co. Stafford, 1663 (*argent*, a fess chequey *gules* and *sable*), inter three helmets ppr., by whom she had a son and heir,

John Whitehall of Broughton, born 2nd April 1660, and married Mary, daughter of Sir Andrew Hacket of Moxhall Park, co. Warwick, Knt. (*sable*, three piles conjoined in base *argent*, on a chief *gules*, a lion passant gardant *or*), by whom he had a son and heir,

Broughton Whitehall of Broughton, who married Letitia, daughter of Robert Davies of Gwysanau and Llanerch Park, and Letitia his wife, sister of John Vaughan, first Viscount Lisburne, and daughter of Edward Vaughan of Trawsgoed, co. Cardigan, Esq. By this lady he had three daughters, co-heirs.

I. Elizabeth Whitehall, heiress of Broughton. She married Peter Davies, third son of Robert Davies of Llanerch and Gwysannau, by whom she had a son and heir, Whitehall Whitehall Davies of Broughton, who died unmarried 11 June 1824, aged sixty, and was buried at Worthenbury; and a daughter, Anne Elizabeth, heiress of Broughton and Llanerch, who married the Rev. George Allanson of Middleton Quernhow, co. York, by whom she had issue two sons, 1, George Allanson; and 2, Cuthbert, *ob.* 1817, aged thirteen; and two daughters, 1, Elizabeth, ux. John Whitehall Dod of Cloverley, M.P. for North Staffordshire; and 2, Dorothy, ux. Sir Digby Cayley, Bart., son and heir of Sir George Cayley of Brampton, co. York, Bart.

II. Mary, the second daughter and co-heir of Broughton Whitehall, married Robert Dod of Cloverley.

III. Letitia, the third daughter and co-heir, married Robert Davies of Llanerch Park and Gwysannau, by whom she had issue two sons and two daughters, eventually the co-heiresses of their brother. She died in childbirth, and was buried at Mold in 1745.

I. John Davies of Llanerch Park and Gwysannau, *ob.* 1785, and buried at Mold, *s. p.*

II. Robert Watkin Davies, *ob. s. p.*, and buried at Mold, 1739.

I. Letitia Davies, co-heir; she had Llanerch. She married Daniel Leo of Bath, and, dying *s. p.*, she devised her possessions to her cousin, Anne Elizabeth, daughter and heiress of Peter Davies, and wife of the Rev. George Allanson.

II. Mary Davies; she had Gwysannau for her portion of the estates, and married Philip Puleston of Havod y Wern, Chamberlain of North Wales. She died 22nd September 1802.

ELLIS OF ALRHEY.

Harl. MS. 4181.

Iorwerth of Alrhey, the second son of Gruffydd Ddu ab Gruffydd Goch of Brochdyn, married Janet, daughter of Madog Kynaston of Stoke near Ellesmere, ab Philip Kynaston ab Gruffyd Kynaston (*argent,* a chevron engrailed inter three martletts *sable*), by whom he had a son and heir,

Morgan ab Iorwerth of Alrhey, who married Catherine, daughter and heir of Madog ab Maredydd ab Llywelyn Ddu ab Gruffydd of Maelor Saesneg, second son of Iorwerth Foel, Lord of Chirk, by whom he had issue three sons.

I. Howel ab Morgan, of whom presently.

II. Edward ab Morgan, who by Angharad his wife, daughter of Richard ab Morgan of Halchdyn in Maelor Saesneg, had an only daughter and heiress, Margaret, who married Pyers or Peter Kynaston ab Jenkyn Kynaston, by whom she had a son and heir, Humphrey Kynaston, *jure uxoris* of Otely Park near Ellesmere, and ancestor of the Kynaston Mainwarings of that place.

III. Thomas, the father of Edward, who had three sons, 1, Thomas ab Edward ; 2, John ab Edward ; and 3, Elis ab Edward.

Howel ab Morgan of Alrhey, married Janet, daughter of Tudor Fychan of Pen Mynydd yn Môn, ab Gruffydd ab Gwilym ab Gruffydd ab Heilin ab Sir Tudor, Knt., ab Ednyfed Fychan, by whom he had issue three sons, 1, Richard ab Howel of Alrhey ; 2, Edward ab Howel, ancestor of the Powels of Alrhey ; and 3, Gruffydd ab Howel.

Richard ab Howel of Alrhey, married Margaret, daughter and heir by Parnel his wife, daughter of Sir Thomas Bulkeley, Knt., ab William Bulkeley of Shaklys in Cheshire, of Elis Eyton, third son of Elis Eyton of Rhiwabon, ab John Eyton of Eyton and Rhiwabon, and relict of Randle Goch Brereton of Borasham, by whom he had issue three sons, 1, Elis ab Richard ; 2, Richard, who by Mallt his wife, daughter of Philip ab Llywelyn, had a son Roger ab Richard ; and 3, James ; and three daughters, 1, Anne, ux. Ralph Broughton of Plas Isaf in Marchwiail ; 2, Margaret, ux. Edward ab Robert ab David ab Einion ab Madog Goch ab David Goch ab Iorwerth ab Cynwrig ab Heilin of Pentref Heilin ab Trahaiarn ab Iddon, Lord of Tref Dudlysh (*argent*, a chevron inter three boar's heads couped *gules*, tusked *or*, and langued *azure*) ; and 3, Catherine, ux. Elis ab Tudor.

Elis ab Richard of Alrhey, Standard-bearer to Owain Glyndwfrdwy. He married Jane, daughter of Sir Thomas Hanmer of Hanmer, Knt., by whom he had issue nine sons and four daughters, 1, Humphrey Elis, *ob. s. p.*; 2, Thomas Elis, *ob. s. p.*; 3, John Elis, of whom presently; 4, Elis Elis, who by Margaret his wife, daughter of .... Gwrling of North Flock, had a son and heir Sidney Elis of Picillt, who married Catherine, daughter of John Owain Fychan of Llwydiarth (*sable, a he-goat argent, attired or*), by whom he had two sons, Elis Elis and John Elis ; 5, Ralph Elis ; 6, Andrew ; 7, Randle ; 8, William ; and 9, Edward Elis ; and four daughters, 1, Mawd, ux. John Wynn Deccaf of Rhwytyn in the manor of Rhiwabon (*ermine, a lion rampant azure*) ; Ermine, ux. Thomas Hughes, son of Hugh ab William ab Gruffydd Fychan, eighth Baron of Cymer yn Edeyrnion (*argent, a lion rampant sable, debruised by a baton sinister gules*) ; 3, Elen, ux. Robert Wynn ab William ; and 4, Margaret, ux. Ieuan ab Maredydd ab Ieuan.

John Elis of Alrhey, the third surviving son, married Jane, daughter of John Edwards of Plas Newydd yn Y Waun (Chirk), and Jane his wife, daughter of Sir George Calverley of the Ley in Cheshire, Knt., by whom he had issue three sons, 1, Humphrey, of whom presently; 2, William Elis, *ob. s. p.*; and 3, Randle Elis; and three daughters, 1, Jane, ux. Francis Lloyd of Hardwick ; 2, Magdalene ; and 3, Margaret.

Humphrey Elis of Alrhey, married Dorothy, daughter of Edward Jones of Plâs Cadwgan, by whom he had issue, besides four daughters, 1, Margaret, ux. 1st, Edward Puleston of Hafod y Wern, and 2nd, Rhys Lloyd of Fern in Glyn Berbrwg in Ystrad Alun ; 2, Catherine, ux. Thomas Eyton ab Randle Eyton; 3, Susan, ux. John Roberts of Hafod y Bwch ; and 4, Magdalene ; a son and heir,

Roger Elis of Alrhey, 1620, who married Margaret, daughter of Sir Thomas Hanmer of Hanmer, Knt., and

Catherine his wife, daughter of Thomas Mostyn of Mostyn, by whom he had a son and heir,

Andrew Elis of Alrhey, *ob.* 1627. He married . . . . daughter of James Fiennes, eldest son of Lord Say and Sele, by whom he had a son and heir, Cecil Elis.

POWEL OF ALRHEY.

Harl. MS. 4181.

Edward ab Howel ab Morgan ab Iorwerth ab⊤Angharad, d. of John ab
  Gruffydd Ddû ab Gruffydd Goch of ·Alrhey. | Richard ab Madog ab
                                         Llywelyn of Halchdyn.

John ab Edward⊤..., d. of Pyers Hope of Broughton in   Thomas ab
  of Alhrey. | Merffordd. *Argent*, three storks *sable*.   Edward.

Roger ab John of Alrhey.⊤Jane, d. of John Griffith of Overton Madog.

John Powel of Alrhey.⊤..., d. of Edward Eyton of   Ermine.   Jane.
                   Bodylltyn.

Roger Powel of Alrhey, 1661. =

KENRICK OF NANTCLWYD.

Sir David ab Cynwrig ab Gruffydd Fychan ab Gruffydd ab Einion ab Ednyfed, Lord of Broughton, who bore *ermine*, a lion statant gardant *gules*, the second son of Cynwrig ab Rhiwallon, Lord of Maelor Gymraeg. *Ermine*, a lion rampant *sable* (see vol. iii, page 20). This Sir David was Standard Bearer to the Black Prince during his wars in France. On his return to England, he, with a number of men, lost his way in a forest in Shropshire. He stuck his spear into the ground, and vowed to the Virgin Mary that, if she would show him the way out, he would build a church in her honour. They got out, and he built a church at a place called Ashley in that county; and the history is substantiated by a painted glass window which still remains, and in this church he was buried.

John Kenrick of Apsle in the county of Stafford, was at the Battle of Blore Heath.

1		3	
John Kenrick.=..., d. of Ashley of Ashley.		James. = Alice, d. of John Bucknall.	Matilda, *ob. s. p.*

John Kenrick=Alice, d. of John of Asbley.	Tillesley.	Richard = Isabella, d. of Kenrick. ... Blackborne	William Kenrick.

1	2		
John Kenrick, *ob. s.p.*	William Kenrick, Groom of the Bedchamber to=Margaret King Henry VIII.		Morris.

2			1
Thomas Kenrick of Acton Burnell.=Mary, d. of Thomas Taylor.			Richard, *ob. s.p.*

Richard Kenrick of Acton Burnell, co. Salop.=Agnes, d. of Edward Norton of Shute.

John Kenrick of Ower, co. Salop;=Elizabeth, d. and sole heir of Jasper living 1623; buried at Ashley. | Lodge of Ower; *ob.* 1646.

a | 1   b | 2   c | 3   d |

a | 1	b | 2		c | 3	d |
Richard Kenrick, aged 26 in 1623; *ob.* 1642, *s p.*, and was buried at Ashley.	Andrew Kenrick; *ob.* 1650.	=Mary, d. of William Whitway of Dorchester.	Matthew = Kenrick of London.	Rebecca Percival.

James, 4.
George, 5.
Edward 6.
John 7.
Thomas 8.

Dorothy.

Bridgett.

Richard Kenrick, born 5th Feb. 1642; married 16th May 1664.	=Rebecca, d. and co-heir of Maurice Gethin of Plâs Cerniogau, in the parish of Caer or Cerrig y Drudion; High Sheriff for co. Denbigh, 1667.	Andrew. Mary. ux. Ralph Troplett.	Elizabeth.

Richard Kenrick of Over or Woore and=Dorothy Baker of Birchendew
Plâs Cerniogan. in Sussex.

Gethin Kenrick, 1684.	Andrew Kenrick of Woore and Plâs Cerniogau.	=Martha, d. and heiress of Eubule Thelwall of Nantclwyd.	Richard Kenrick.	John Kenrick.	William Kenrick.

| 1
Dorothy, ux. Randle Wilbraham of Rode Hill, M.P. and Deputy High Steward of Oxford, grandfather of Edward, Lord Skelmersdale.

Mary. Elizabeth. Sarah. Anne.

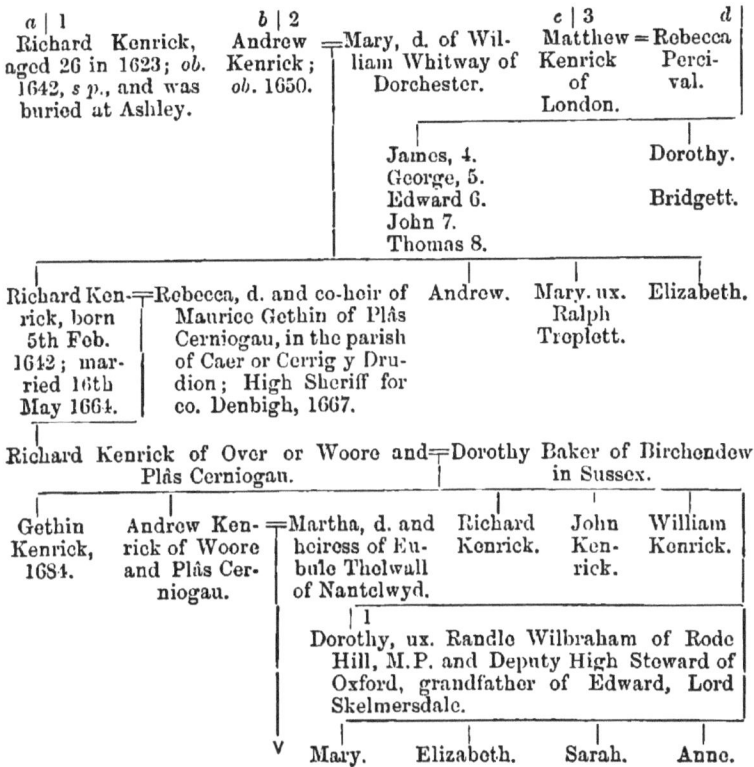

The above-named Andrew Kenrick, by his wife Martha, had issue three sons and five daughters, 1, Richard, of whom presently; 2, George Watkin, of whom presently; and 3, Charles Gethin of Cefn y Gadfa, who married Eliza, daughter of Butler Clough, Esq., and died *s. p.* The daughters were, 1, Elizabeth, ux. Richard Price, of Rhiwlas, Esq.; 2, Harriet, ux. Thomas Ikin, Esq.; 3, Sophia, ux. Sir George Farmer, Bart. ; 4, Maria, who married, first, Price Jones of Glynn, Crogen Iddon, Hendref Brys, and Plâs Iolyn, Esq., Lord of the Manor of Yspythy Ieuan, and, secondly, J. Nicholls, Esq.; and 5, Laura, *ob. s. p.*

1. Richard Kenrick of Nantclwyd, Plâs Cerniogau, and, *jure uxoris*, of Ucheldref, Maenan Abbey and Belmont. He married Ermine, daughter and co-heir of Sir Thomas Kyffin of Maenan Abbey and Belmont, Knt.,

by whom he had issue three sons, 1, Richard; 2, Thomas, *ob. s. p.*; and 3, Henry Kyffin of Belmont, *ob. s. p.*; and three daughters, 1, Margaret, *ob.* 1851; 2, Elizabeth, had Belmont and took the name of Kyffin; and 3, Harriet, ux. Henry Hawarden Fazakerley of Gillibrand Hall, co. Lancaster, Esq. The estates of Nantclwyd, Ucheldref, and Cyrniogau were all sold.

II. George Watkin Kenrick, who died in 1838. He married, first, Mary, daughter and co-heir of John Ffoulkes of Llanrhudd, Esq., by whom he had an only daughter, Mary Elizabeth, ux. Sir William Henry Clarke of Hitcham, co. Bucks, Bart. He married, secondly, Mary Isabella, daughter of James Ffaringdon of Worden, co. Lancaster, Esq., by whom he had issue two sons, 1, George Kenrick of Woore Manor, who married Louisa, daughter of W. Postlethwaite of Demerara; and 2, William Lloyd; and six daughters, 1, Isabella Harriet, ux. Holroyd FitzWilliam Way, Esq.; 2, Sophie Margaret Ford; 3, Charlotte Louisa Alexandrina, ux. William Gladstone of London, Esq.; 4, Mary Hannah Albina, ux. Rev. H. W. Bellairs; 5, Ermine Elizabeth, ux. Allan Edward, Esq.; and 6, Fanny Georgina Catherine, ux. James Edward, Esq.

The Kenricks became possessed of the Cyrniogau estate by the marriage of Richard Kenrick of Woore Manor, son of Andrew Kenrick, with Rebecca, daughter and heiress of Maurice Gethin of Cyrniogau, high sheriff for county Denbigh, in 1667,[1] son and heir of Maurice Gethin of Plâs Cyrniogau, son and heir of Robert Gethin, son and heir of Robert Wynn Gethin of Plâs Cyrniogau, second son of Maurice Gethin, second son of Rhys ab Meredydd ab Tudor of Foelas, lineally descended from Marchweithian, Lord of Is Aled, who bore *gules* a lion rampant *argent*. Maurice Gethin, the

---

[1] In the *Calendar of State Papers* for the year 1667, Jan. 9, is the following entry: "Whitehall. Dispensation for Maurice Gethin, High Sheriff for Denbighshire, to live out of the county, at his house at Islington, on account of his age (seventy years) and his ill health, he appointing sufficient deputy."

second son of Rhys ab Meredydd of Foelas, had an
elder son Cadwaladr, and to this Cadwaladr and his
younger brother, Robert Wynn Gethin, Henry VIII
granted, 16th March 1545, the lands of Foelas, Cyrniogau, and other lands, tenements, and hereditaments
in the parish of Llanwith (Llannefydd), county Denbigh,
being parcel of the township of Hiraethog, then lately
belonging to the monastery of Conway, dissolved by Act
of Parliament ; and among the rest of the tenements,
etc., that of Tyddyn y Foelas, late in the tenure and
occupation of Maurice ab Rhys ab Meredydd, to hold to
them for the consideration of £98 4s., to hold as of the
Manor of Hiraethog in free soccage by fealty only, and
not *in capite.*   On the 8th February 1546, a deed of
partition was executed between the brothers, whereby
Calwaladr took Foelas, and Robert Wynn Gethin took
Cyrniogau.   These estates had been granted to the Cis-
tercian monastery of Conway by Llewelyn ab Iorwerth,
Prince of Wales, by charter dated 7th January 1198.
Rhys ab Meredydd, the ancestor of these two brothers,
was one of the Welsh leaders at the battle of Bosworth
in 1485.   When Sir William Brandon was prostrated
by King Richard III, he was entrusted by the Earl of
Richmond, afterwards Henry VII, with the British
standard of the Red Dragon.   At his death, he was
buried in the church of Yspytty Ieuan, together with
his wife Lowry, daughter and heiress of Howel, one of
the sons of Gruffydd Goch, Lord of Rhos and Rhufoniog
(*argent,* a griffin passant *gules*), where their effigies still
remain.   Rhys, who with his descendants bore *gules* a
lion rampant *argent,* holding in its paws a rose of the
second seeded *or,* stem and leaves ppr., was the son of
Meredydd ab Tudor[1] ab Howel, ab Cynwrig Fychan ab

[1] Tudor ab Howel.=Susannah, d. and heir of Meredydd ab Madog ab Ithel
              ab Ionas ab Hwfa ab Ithel Felyn.

Meredydd ab Tudor.=Eva, d. of Ieuan ab Rhys Wynn ab David
(*Lewys Dwnn,* vol. ii, pp. 343-5;   Lloyd ab Goronwy Llwyd ab Y Penwyn.
Harl. MSS. 1971, 21977, fo. 54,   *Gules,* three boar's heads erased in pale
      65.   *argent.*

a | b |

Cynwrig ab Llywarch ab Heilyn Gloff ab Tyfid Farfog ab Taugno ab Ystrwyth ab Marchwystl ab Marchweithian of Llys Llywarch, Lord of Is Aled, who bore *gules*, a lion rampant *argent*. His lands were Carwed Fynydd, Din Cadfael, Prees, Berain, Llyweni, Gwytherin, and many other townships in Is Aled. Besides his son Maurice, Rhys ab Meredydd had a third son Sir Robert, chaplain and cross-bearer to Cardinal Wolsey, who obtained the lands of Cwm Tir Mynach, formerly belonging to the cell of Moch Rhaiadr or Boch Rhaiadr, and now comprised in the estate of Plâs yn Rhiwlas. These lands are situate in the parish of Llanycil, which was formerly a township in the parish of Llanfihangel in the comot of Migneint in Penllyn. Sir Robert, before he had a grant of these lands, held them on lease for 66s. 8d. He likewise held on lease various lands and tenements in Penllyn, which had been granted to the Abbey of Basingwerk in Tegeingl, by Llewelyn ab Iorwerth, Prince of North Wales, and confirmed by his son and successor, Prince David, in 1240. We find,

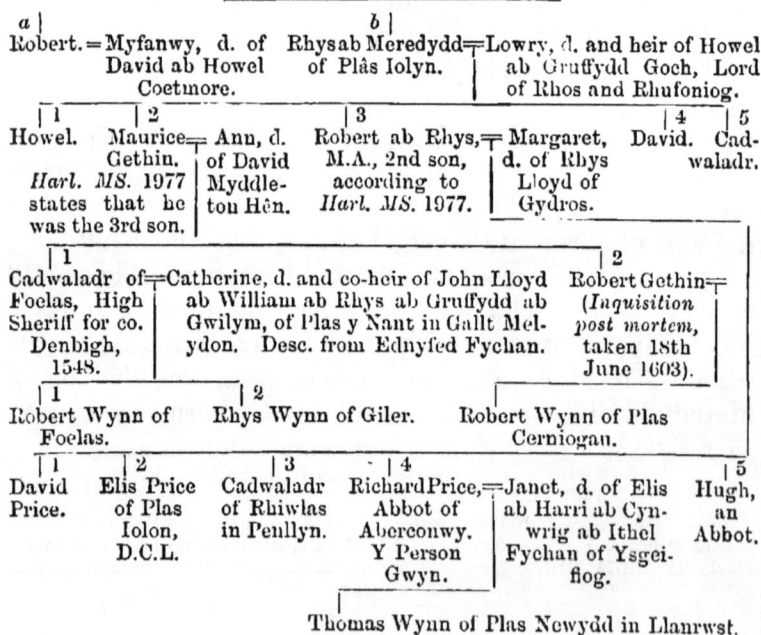

a Robert.=Myfanwy, d. of David ab Howel Coetmore.		*b* Rhysab Meredydd=Lowry, d. and heir of Howel of Plâs Iolyn.		ab Gruffydd Goch, Lord of Rhos and Rhufoniog.
1 Howel.	2 Maurice= Ann, d. Gethin. of David *Harl. MS.* 1977 Myddle- states that he tou Hên. was the 3rd son.	3 Robert ab Rhys,=Margaret, M.A., 2nd son, d. of Rhys according to Lloyd of *Harl. MS.* 1977. Gydros.		4 5 David. Cadwaladr.

1 Cadwaladr of=Catherine, d. and co-heir of John Lloyd Foelas, High ab William ab Rhys ab Gruffydd ab Sheriff for co. Gwilym, of Plas y Nant in Gallt Mel- Denbigh, ydon. Desc. from Ednyfed Fychan. 1548.	2 Robert Gethin= (*Inquisition* *post mortem,* taken 18th June 1603).

1 Robert Wynn of Foelas.	2 Rhys Wynn of Giler.	Robert Wynn of Plas Cerniogau.

1 David Price.	2 Elis Price of Plas Iolon, D.C.L.	3 Cadwaladr of Rhiwlas in Penllyn.	4 RichardPrice,=Janet, d. of Elis Abbot of ab Harri ab Cyn- Aberconwy. wrig ab Ithel Y Person Fychan of Ysgei- Gwyn. fiog.	5 Hugh, an Abbot.

Thomas Wynn of Plas Newydd in Llanrwst.

from the *Valor Ecclesiasticus*, 26 Henry VIII, that Robert ab Rhys paid for these lands £1 16s. 8d. per annum. He lived at Plâs Iolyn, and married Margaret, daughter of Rhys Lloyd of Gydros, by whom he had thirteen sons and four daughters. The second son was the notorious Ellis Price of Plâs Iolyn, LL.D., who was generally known during his lifetime as the "Doctor Goch". He obtained a grant from Queen Elizabeth in 1560 of the manor and lands belonging to the Knights Hospitallers of St. John, called from them Yspytty Ieuan, but formerly the name of the place was Dol Gynwal. Llewelyn ab Iorwerth, Prince of North Wales, endowed the hospital of St. John at Dol Gynwal with lands and privileges in 1190.

William Parry of Nantclwyd, whose daughter and heiress, Mary, married Eubule Thelwall, was the son of Thomas Parry of Nantclwyd, the son of Simon Parry of Pont y Gof or Nantclwyd, seventh son of Thomas Parry Wynn of Pont y Gof or Nantclwyd, second son of John ab Harri of Tref Rhuddin in the parish of Llanrhudd. The mother of William Parry was Grace, daughter (by Mary his wife, daughter of John Wynn Edwards of Cefn y Wern) of Robert Lloyd of Plâs Is y Clawdd in Chirkland, coroner of Denbighshire.

TREF RHUDDIN AND LLWYN YN.

Harl. MS. 2299 ; *Lewis Dwnn*, vol. ii, p. 337.

Cowryd ab Cadvan (Gwehelaeth Ceinmarch) ab Gaelawg Gawr ab Iddig, lineally descended from Cadell Deyrnllug, King of Powys. *Argent*, three boar's heads couped *sable*, tusked *or*, and langued *gules*, for Cowryd ab Cadvan.

David of Ceinmarch.

Iorwerth of Ceinmarch.

David of Ceinmarch.

Heilin.

Iorwerth.

Llewelyn.

David Fychan of Ceinmarch.

Iorwerth. Extant Dinbich. Villa de Bryn Lluarth.

..., d. of Bleddyn Llwyd ab Bleddyn Fychan of Hafod Un Nos in the parish of Llangerniw, ab Bleddyn ab Y Gwion ab Kadiach ab Alser ab Gwrgi ab Hedd Moelwynog, Lord of Uwch Aled. *Sable*, a hart *argent*, attired and unguled *or*.

Ieuan of Ceinmarch.

Eva, d. of David ab Philip Goch of Vaenor in Aber Rhiw, in Cedewain, ab Howel ab Llewelyn ab Meilir Grug, Lord of Tref Gynon and Westbury. *Sable*, three horse's heads erased *argent*.

Iorwerth Sais of Llanynys. *Or*, 3 lions couchant in pale *sable*.

Arddun, d. of Llewelyn Fychan ab Llewelyn ab Ynyr of Iâl.

Meredydd of Bryn Lluarth, ancestor of the Lloyds of Bryn Lluarth,[1] and the Pryses of Llawesog.[2]

a | b | c |

---

[1] John Lloyd of Bryn Lluarth, ab John Lloyd ab Ieuan Lloyd ab Rhys ab Llewelyn ab David ab Ieuan ab David ab Meredydd of Bryn Lluarth. This family is now represented by the Mostyns of Llawesog and Segroed.

[2] John Pryse of Llawesog, ab Robert Pryse, son of Rhys ab

a | b | c |
| Tudor, ances-   Elen, ux. Iolyn ab Ieuaf ab Madog ab Goronwy
| tor of the   ab Iorwerth ab Caswallawn ab Hwfa ab Ithel
| Lloyds of Plas   Felyn. She married, secondly, Ednyfed ab
| Llanynys.   Cynwrig Brawd ab Cynwrig Fychan ab Cyn-
                           wrig, third son of Ednyfed Fychan.

Gruffydd Goch of Pentref Coch near Rhuddin. He built the⊤Mali, d. of
church of Cyffylliog, in the comot of Llanerch, as a chapel- | Ieuan ab
of-ease to Llanynys, which parish lies partly in the comot of | Gruffydd
Llanerch, in the cantref of Dyffryn Clwyd, and partly in the | Llwyd.
comot of Ceinmeirch, in the cantref of Ystrad.

Sir John⊤ Mar-	David, ancestor	Lleicu, ux. Llewelyn	..., ux. David
Parson	garet, d.	of Ieuan Llwyd	ab Iolyn ab Ieuaf ab	Lloyd ab
of Llan-| of Cyn-	of Henblas in	Madog ab Goronwy	Gruffydd ab
ynys.	wrig ab	Cyffylliog, an-	ab Cynwrig ab Ior-	Cynwrig ab
	Einion	cestor of Wilson| werth ab Caswallawn	Bleddyn
	Gethin.	Jones of Harts-	ab Hwfa ab Ithel	Llwyd of
		heath and Gelli	Felyn. (*Arch. Camb.*,| Hafod Un
		Gynnon, Esq.[1]	Jan. 1875, p. 36.)	Nos.

Harri of Tref Rhuddin.⊤Janet, d. of Richard ab Jenkyn ab Gruffydd ab Rhys.

John ⊤Janet, d. of	Rich-⊤Elen, dau. of	Thomas	Robert, married,
ab	Edward	ard.	Alan Ash-	ab	first, Jane, dau. of
Harri	Thelwall ab		pool ab Wil-	Harri,	Rowland Egerton,
of	Eubule ab		liam ab Philip ab	Vicar of	by whom he had
Tref	Simon Thel-		Hugh Ashpool of	Llan-	a daughter Eliza-
Rhudd	wall of Plas		Llandyrnog. Party	ynys.	beth, who mar-
Din.	y Ward.		per fess *argent* and	*ob. s.p.*	ried, 1st, Hercules
			gules, three grif-		Raensffoi; and
			fon's heads coun-		2ndly, William Bwras of
			tercharged.		Dalton. Robert married,
					2ndly, a daughter of Pyers
					Hope, Esq., by whom he
					had a son William Parry
					of London.

5	6	7	1	2	3
Edward,	Lucy, ux. Harri	Alice, ux.	Dowse, ux. Richard ab
s. p.	Salusbury Goch,	John Wynn	Rhys ab John, by
Edward,	by whom she had	Ashpool of	whom she was mother
s. p.	a son, David	Llandyrnog.	of John Pryse of Der-
David,	Salusbury.		wen in the comot of
s. p.			Coleigion.

d | 1   e | 2   f | 3   g |

Llewelyn of Bryn Lluarth. Robert Pryse, who was " Sergeant o'r
Ewri" (?), married Catherine, daughter and heiress of Maurice Kyffin
of Macnan.

[1] Wilson Jones ab John Jones ab Maurice Jones ab Hugh Jones
of Gelli Gynan, ab John ab Thomas ab Hugh ab David ab Ieuan
Llwyd of Henblas in Cyffylliog, ab Elis ab Ieuan ab David ab Gruffydd Goch of Pentref Coch.

$d \mid 1$		$e \mid 2$		$f \mid 3$	g
Richard	Mary, d. of	Thomas	Margaret,[3] d. of	Harri.	Catherine, d. of
Parry	John	Parry	John Griffith of		Reignallt ab
of Tref	Pryse[2] of	Wynn of	Cichli in Tind-		Ieuan ab
Rhudd	Derwen.	Pont y	aethwy, son of		Einion.
Din.[1]	*Argent*, six	Gof or	Sir William		
	bees ppr.,	Nant-	Griffith of Pen-		
	3, 2, 1.	clywd.	rhyn, Knt.		

Richard.   Annest.   Margaret.

Jane, ux. Tudor Lloyd, third son of John
Lloyd of Plymog in Llanveris, and
wife also of Ieuan Lloyd of Henblas
in Cyffylliog.

$\mid 1$	$\mid 2$	$\mid 3$	$\mid 4$	$\mid 5$	$\mid 6$	$\mid 7$
John.	Thomas.	Richard, *s. p.*	James.	Edward.	William.	Simon.

$\lceil 1$	$\mid 2$	$\mid 3$
Joan.	Gwen.	Blanch, *s. p*

Simon Parry Gwr,	Jane, d. of	GabrielParry	Mary, eldest d. of Edward
o'r Gyfraith; *ob.*	John Thel-	Bach, D.D.[4]	Pryse of Llwyn Yn, near
7th July 1627.	wall of	(*Harl. MS.*	Ruthin, High Sheriff for
(*Harl. MS.* 2299.)	Llan-	2299.)	co. Denbigh, 1627; and
See p. .	rhudd.		co-heir of her brother,
			John Pryse, of Llwyn Yn.

$h \mid$ $i \lceil 3$ $j \mid 1$ $k \mid 3$ $l \mid 3$ $m \mid 4$

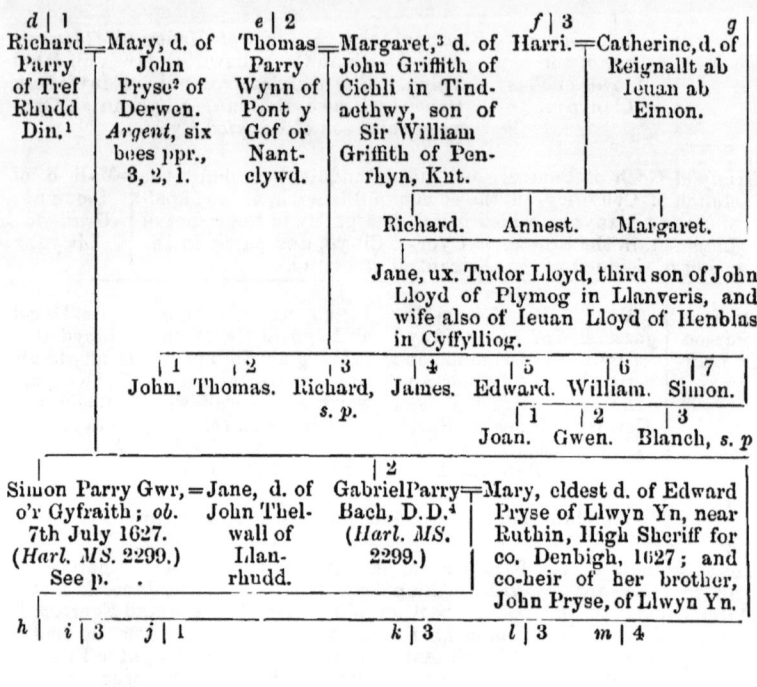

[1] The descendants of Richard Parry are given here according to
Lewys Dwnn; but all of Richard's children are stated in the *Harl.
MS.* 2299 to have been the children of Thomas Parry Wynn; and
the children of Thomas Parry Wynn, as given by Lewys Dwnn, are
not mentioned.

[2] John Pryse ab Richard ab Rhys ab John ab Maredydd ab Ieuaf
Llwyd ab Llewelyn Goch ab Ieuaf Goch ab Ieuaf ab Madog ab
Rhirid ab Adda ab Ieuaf ab Adda Fawr ab Adda Foel ab Llewelyn
ab Bleddyn ab Maredydd ab Trahaiarn Goch of Emlyn, who bore,
argent, six bees ppr., 3, 2, 1. John Pryse married Gwen, daughter
of Ffoulk Salusbury of Tref Rhuddin, third son of Pyers Salusbury
of Bachymbyd.

[3] Margaret married, secondly, William Lloyd of Tref Rhuddin,
son of Ieuan Llwyd Hynaf, illegitimate son of Tudor ab Robert
Fychan of Berain in Llanufydd, by whom she had two daughters,
coheirs, viz., Anne, ux George Langford, fifth son (by Elizabeth,
his wife, daughter of Richard Parry of Tref Rhuddin) of Richard
Langford of Tref Rhuddin and Trefalun, High Sheriff for co. Denbigh in 1640; and Barbara, the other coheir of William Lloyd, who
married John ab Robert Jones of Pont Gruffydd.

[4] "Gabriel Parry, A.M., Head Master of Ruthin School, 1607;
S. R. Llanrhaidr yn Mochnant, 1608; V. Henllan, 1609; V. Aber-

h |	i | 3	j | 1	k | 2	l | 3	m | 4
	Daniel Parry.	Elizabeth, ux. Rich- ard Langford of Tref Rhuddin and Tref Alun, High Sheriff for co. Denbigh, 1640. He died in 1643. *Gules*, a shoveler *ar-gent*, membered *or*.	Dorothy, ux. Robt. ab Richard of Bach Eirig.[1]	Grace, ux Pyers Mule of Ruthin. *Sable*, two lions rampt. in fess *argent*.	Jane, ux., 1st, John Wynn Jones of Plâs Newydd, near Rhuddin; 2nd, William Vaughan of Bron Haulog, in Llanfair Talhaiarn.

William Parry⹀Catherine, d. and heiress of Roger Holland of Hendref
of Llwyn Yn | Fawr, High Sheriff for co. Denbigh in 1634, who died in
and Llanrhudd, | 1640; son and heir of Daniel Holland of Hendref Fawr,
High Sheriff | and Elizabeth, his wife, daughter of Maurice Kyffin. She
for co. Denbigh| died in 1705, and was buried in Abergeleu Church, where
in 1668. | a monument is erected to her memory. *Azure*, semé of
Married, 1643. | fleurs-de-lys, a lion rampant gardant *argent*.

David Parry of Llwyn | Susannah, heiress⹀John Roberts of Hafod y Bwch
Yn, High Sheriff for | of Llwyn Yn and ∨ in the parish of Wrexham, and
co. Denbigh in 1695 | Hendref Fawr,   of Plas Newydd, High Sheriff
and 1697; *ob.* at | married in 1693;   for co. Denbigh, 1705, and M.P.
Llwyn Yn, 1706, *s.p.* | *ob.* at Plas New-   for the Denbigh Boroughs in
                       | ydd, near Ruthin,   1710-15. *Ermine*, a lion rampt.
                       | in 1721.   *sable*. Buried at Llanfair Dyf-
                       | fryn Clwyd, 9th Sept. 1731.
                       | See p. 42.

---

gele, 1613; S. R. Llansannan, 1616; S. R. Llansantffraid yn Mechain, 1617; R. Llangynhafal and Precentor of Bangor, 1632."—
Hist. of the Diocese of St. Asaph, by the Rev. D. R. Thomas, M.A.

[1] Robert ab Richard's mother was Annet, daughter and heiress
of John ab Gruffydd Lloyd of Bacheirig.

TREF RHUDDIN AND LLWYN YN.

Harl. MSS. 2299, 4181.

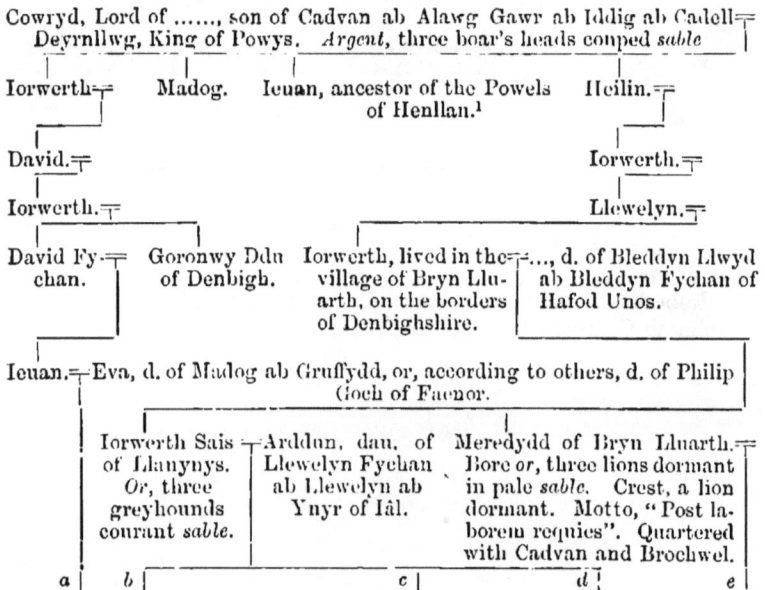

Cowryd, Lord of ......, son of Cadvan ab Alawg Gawr ab Iddig ab Cadell—
Deyrnllwg, King of Powys. *Argent*, three boar's heads couped *sable*

| Iorwerth— | Madog. | Ieuan, ancestor of the Powels of Henllan.[1] | Heilin.— |

David.—

Iorwerth.—

Iorwerth.—

Llewelyn.—

| David Fychan. | Goronwy Ddu of Denbigh. | Iorwerth, lived in the village of Bryn Lluarth, on the borders of Denbighshire. | ..., d. of Bleddyn Llwyd ab Bleddyn Fychan of Hafod Unos. |

Ieuan.—Eva, d. of Madog ab Gruffydd, or, according to others, d. of Philip
Goch of Faenor.

| Iorwerth Sais of Llanynys. *Or*, three greyhounds conrant *sable*. | Arddun, dau. of Llewelyn Fychan ab Llewelyn ab Ynyr of Iâl. | Meredydd of Bryn Lluarth.— Bore *or*, three lions dormant in pale *sable*. Crest, a lion dormant. Motto, "Post laborem requies". Quartered with Cadvan and Brochwel. |

| a | b | c | d | e |

---

[1] Richard Powell of Henllan in the commot of Cynmeirch, in the
cantref of Ystrad, ab Richard Powell ab Richard Powell ab John ab
Howel ab Alexander ab Howel of Henllan, ab Ithel ab Howel ab
Madog ab Ieuan ab Cowryd ab Cadfan. (*Harl. MS.* 4181.)

a	b	c	d	e
	Tudor, ancestor of the Lloyds of Plas Llanynys,[1] the Hugheses of Segroid and Ystrad,[2] and Robert Williams of Ysgeibion Elis.[3]	David, ancestor of Edward ab Thomas of Maes Maen Cymro,[4] and Ieuan ab John of Nant-glyn.[5]	Elen, ux. Iolyn ab Ieuaf ab Madog ab Goronwy ab Cynwrig ab Iorwerth ab Caswallawn. See Iâl.	

David, ancestor of the Lloyds of Bryn Lluarth and the Pryses of Llawesog.[6]

Gruff-=Gwladys or Mallt, d. ydd of Ieuan ab Llew- Goch. elyn ab Gruffydd Llwyd of Bodidris yn Iâl. Her mother was Mali, daughter of Tudor ab Gruffydd Llwyd ab Heilin Frych of Berain in Llannefydd.	Twna, ancestor of the Lloyds of Llanbedr in the comot of Llanerch.[7] He married Gwen, d. of David ab Howel ab Gruffydd ab Owain ab Bleddyd ab Owain Brogyntyn.	David Fwrddais, father of Gruffydd of Llangwyfan in the comot of Llanerch, ancestor of the Lloyds of Llangwyfan.

f	g	h	i

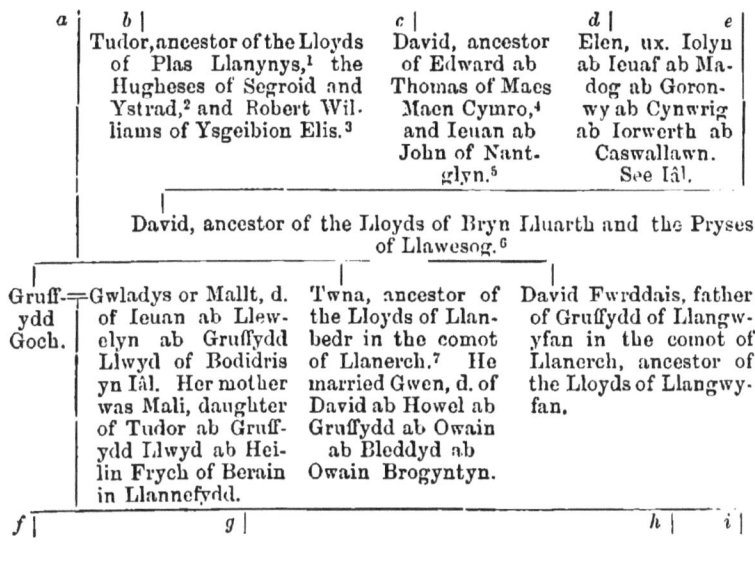

[1] Pyers Lloyd of Plas Llanynys ab John Lloyd ab Edward Lloyd ab Edward Lloyd, Archdeacon of Caermarthen, ab John ab Ieuan ab Tudor ab Iorwerth Sais. (*Harl. MS.* 4181.)

[2] Robert Hughes of Segroid in the parish of Llanrhaiadr, ab Sir Hugh, a priest, ab David ab Einion Fychan ab Tudor ab Iorwerth Sais. (*Harl. MS.* 4181.) Robert Hughes was ancestor of the present Thomas Hughes of Ystrad and Segroid, Esq.

[3] Robert Williams ab John ab William ab Ieuan ab Rhys ab Tudor ab Iorwerth Sais. (4181.)

[4] Edward ab Thomas of Maes Maen Cymro, ab Richard ab Edward ab John ab Robert ab David ab Iorwerth Sais. Edward ab Thomas married Jane, daughter of Humphrey Lloyd, fourth son of Edward Lloyd of Plas Llanynys, son and heir of Edward Lloyd the Archdeacon of Caermarthen. (*Harl. MS.* 4181.) Maesmaen Cymro is a township in the commot of Llanerch, and one of the six townships of the parish of Llanynys; the other five are Bryn Caredig, and Tref Fechan in the commot of Llanerch; Bach Ymbyd and Ysgeibion in the commot of Cynmeirch, in the cantref of Ystrad, and Rhyd Onen in the commot of Dogveilin.

[5] Ieuan ab John of Nantglyn (in the commot of Is Aled and cantref of Rhufoniog), ab Tudor ab David ab Iorwerth Sais. He married Janet, daughter of Rhys ab Llewelyn Boteroes, by whom he had a daughter and heiress, Lleuci, who married Rhys ab Llewelyn ab Ieuan ab David ab Maredydd of Bryn Lluarth.

[6] See note, p. 171.

[7] Edward Lloyd of Llanbedr, ab Ieuan Lloyd ab Gruffydd Lloyd ab David ab Twna.

f | *g* | *h* | *i*

Sir John Parson of Llanynys. = Margaret, d. of Cynwrig ab Einion Gethin.

David, ancestor of Rhys Gyffylliog ab Ieuan Llwyd ab Elis ab Ieuan ab David ab Gruffydd Goch. Rhys married Catherine, dau. of Rhys ab John Wynn of Llwyn Yn, descended from Edwin ab Goronwy (see p. 176) by whom he had issue five sons, viz., John Llwyd, Thomas, Robert, Hugh, and Maurice, and three daughters. See *Lewys Dwnn*, vol. ii, p. 315.

Sir Ieuan Parson of Derwen Anial.

Lowri, ux. David ab Howel Coetmor.

Leuci, ux. Llewelyn Fychan ab Iolyn ab Ieuaf ab Madog of Iâl, ab Goronwy ab Cynwrig ab Iorwerth ab Caswallawn.

..., ux. David Lloyd ab Gruffydd ab Cynwrig of Hafod Unos in Llangerniw, ab Bleddyn Llwyd ab Bleddyn Fychan.

Gwen, ux. David Llwyd ab Gruffydd ab Cynwrig.

Alice, ux. Howel ab Madog ab Cynwrig of Llanfwrog, ab Howel ab Madog ab Einion ab Maredydd ab Rhirid ab Iorwerth ab Madog ab Goronwy ab Owain ab Uchdryd ab Edwyn.

Margaret, ux. David ab Maredydd ab Llewelyn Chwith ab Gruffydd, descended from Edwin.

Harri ab Sir John. He had four illegitimate children, two sons, David and Edward; and two daughters, Elen, ux. Nicholas ab William, and Gwladys, ux. Tudor ab Robin. = Janet, d. of Richard ab Jenkin ab Gruffydd ab Rhys.

Gwenllian, ux. Llewelyn ab Llewelyn.

Angharad, ux. John ab Ieuan ab Tudor ab Iorwerth Sais of Plas Llanynys.

John ab Harri of Tref Rhuddin. = Janet, d. of Edw. Thelwall ab Eubule Thelwall of Plas y Ward.

Richard = Parry. See p. 171.

Robert = Parry. Jane, dau. of of Sir Philip Egerton of Ridley in Cheshire, Knt. = ..., d. of Pyers, Hope, 2nd wife.

Sir Thos., Vicar of Llanynys.

Gruffydd = Anne, d. of Gruffydd Parry. ab Elis ab Gruffydd ab Edward ab Llewelyn Fychan of Iâl.

Elizabeth, ux. Hercules Renford of Bliford in Warwickshire; and 2ndly, Mr. Barnes.

William Parry.

Edward. Edward. David.

Lucy, ux. Harri Goch ab Harri Salusbury.

Alice, ux. John Wynn Ashpool, Esq., ab Thomas ab Harri ab Simon Ashpool of Llandyrnog, Esq. Party per fess *argent* and *gules*, three griffon's heads countercharged.

Dows, ux. Richard ab Rhys ab John ab Thomas ab Rhys of Croes Oswald ab Maurice Gethin ab Ieuan Gethin ab Madog Cyffin.

Anne, ux. Thos. Llwyd ab Ieuan Llwyd ab Maredydd ab Howel ab Moris Gethin ab Ieuan Gethin ab Madog Cyffin.

j | 1	k | 2	l | 3	m
Thos. Parry = Margaret, Wynn married, first, Margaret, d. of John ab Harri Gervys ab John Gervys ab Thomas;Gervys abGerard Goch of Tref Rhuddin, Esq., who bore *sable*, an arming sword *argent*, hilt and pommel *or*, a buckle *argent*. She died *s. p.*	Richard = Margaret, d. of John Prys of Derwen. *Argent*, six bees ppr., 3, 2, 1.	Harri = Cathe-rine Wen, dau. of	

| Margaret, d. of John Gruffydd of Chichele, 2nd wife. See p. 172. | Parry of Tref Rhuddin, married, 1st, Catherine, d. of Moredydd ab Goronwy, *ob. s. p.* | Richard. Annest Margaret. | Reignallt ab Ieuan ab Einion. |

John Perry = Elizabeth, d. of John = 2nd wife, Grace, re-
of Llan- | Wynn Ffoulkes of | lict of Pyers Mul of
bedr. | Erifiad. *Gules*, three | Ruthin, and daughter
        | boar's heads erased | of Thos. Parry Wynn.
        | in pale *argent*.

		1 | 2		
John Parry = Jane, d. of of Llanbedr.	Pyers Mul of Ruthin.	Catherine. Elizabeth.	Richard.	Martha.

4			
John Llwyd Wynn.	Jane, ux. Ffoulk ab Ieuan Llwyd ab Elis ab David ab GruffyddGoch. 2nd, Tudor ab John ab John Llwyd of Llanferis.	Janet, ux. John ab Bedo ab David ab Gruffydd of Llanbychan.	Catherine, ux. John Llwyd ab David ab Richard of Maesmaon Cymro.

Dorothy, ux. Morys   Gwenhwyfar, ux. Edward Wynn ab
ab Llewelyn ab Howel   Robert ab Gruffydd ab Llewelyn ab
of Llanarmon.   Einion of Llangynhafal, desc. from
   Edwin, King of Tegeingl. See note,
   p. 175.

Simon Parry of Pont y Gôf, Esq., Councillor-at- = Jane, d. of John Thel-
Law; *ob.* July 7th 1627. He bought Pont y Gôf | wall of Llanrhudd.
from Peter Ellis. *Add. MS.* 9864. *Ob.* 7th July
1627.

1	2	3
Thomas = Grace, d. Parry. of He was Robert disin- Lloyd of herited. Plâs is y *Add.* Clawdd. *MS.* 9864.	William = Martha, dau. of Parry of Simon Thelwall Pont y Gôf of the Court of or Nant- Arches, ab John clwyd. Wynn Thelwall of Llanrhudd.	Richard = Anne, d. Parry, of Roger an At- Holland torney. of Hendref Fawr.

Mary, heiress of Pont y Gôf or Nantclwyd, married Eubule Thelwall, a
Barrister of Gray's Inn, second son of John Thelwall of Plâs Coch and
Bathafarn Park.

4 | 5	1	2	3	4 | 5 | 6
Gabriel. Samuel.	Margaret, ux. Hugh Wynn of Llanforda.	Jane, ux, Thomas Wynn of Bwlch y Beudy. *Sable*, a hart *argent*, attired and unguled *or*.	Martha, ux. John Wynn of Efynecht-yd.	Elizabeth, *ob. s. p.* Grace, *ob.* 1699. Mary, *ob.* 1701.

PLÂS CERNIOGAU.

Maurice Gethin of Y Foelas in Yspytty Ieuan, the third son of Rhys ab Maredydd of Plâs Iolyn (see p. 341), married Anne, daughter of Dafydd Myddleton Hên, Receiver of North Wales (see Chirk Castle), by whom he had issue three sons and five daughters.

I. Cadwaladr ab Maurice of Y Foelas, ancestor of the Wynnes of Foelas and the Prices of Giler.

II. Robert Gethin, of whom presently.

III. Sir John, a Priest.

The daughters were, 1, Elen, ux. Tudor Fychan of Rhyd y Garnedd ; 2, Margaret, ux. John ab Maredydd Llwyd ; 3, Golenbryd, ux. John Wynn ab Robert ab Ieuan ab Tudor ; 4, Lowri, ux. Dafydd ab Thomas of Llandecwyn ; and 5, Jane, ux. Gruffydd Lloyd ab Gruffydd.

Robert Gethin of Plâs Cernioge, the second son of Maurice Gethin, married Catherine, daughter of Owain ab Jenkyn ab Rhys ab Tudor ab Howel of Llandecwyn, descended from Llywarch ab Bran, Lord of Cwmwd Menai, by whom he had issue three sons, 1, Humphrey, *ob. s. p.;* 2, Robert Wynn Gethin, of whom presently ; and 3, Thomas Gethin.

The daughters were, 1, Margaret, ux. William Fychan, brother to Tudor ab Robert of Berain ; 2, Gwen, ux. John Lewis of Ffestiniog ; 3, Lowry, ux. first, Robert ab Ieuan, and, secondly, Geoffrey ab Hugh; 3, Catherine, ux. Hugh ab Rhydderch ab Thomas ; 4, Gwen, ux. Humphrey ab Howel Fychan ab Howel ab David Lloyd; and 5, Elizabeth, ux. John Wynn of Garth Meilio.

Robert Wynn Gethin of Plâs Cerniogau married Anne, daughter of Ieuan Lloyd ab Rhys of Bryn Lluarth, ab Llywelyn ab David ab Ieuan ab David ab Maredydd ab Iorwerth of Bryn Lluarth, ab Llywelyn ab Iorwerth ab Heilin ab Cowryd ab Cadvan ab Gaelawg Gawr ab Iddig, Lord of Ceinmarch, by whom he had issue two sons, 1, Robert Gethin, of whom presently ; and 2, Maurice Gethin ; and three daughters, Elizabeth, Alice, and Anne.

Robert Gethin of Plâs Cerniogau, married Dorothy, daughter of Simon Thelwall of Plâs y Ward. She died s. p. August 1649.

Maurice Gethin, a merchant in London, the younger brother of the above-named Robert Gethin, succeeded to the Plâs Cerniogau estates, and was High Sheriff for co. Denbigh in 1667. He married Elizabeth Juxon, by whom he had issue three daughters, of whom one, named Rebecca, had Plâs Cerniogau and married Richard Kenrick, son of John Kenrick of Woore Manor. The other daughters were Sarah, who married Edward Ffarringdon of London, and Elizabeth, the wife of John Kay of London.

From an old pedigree of the Gethin family, kindly lent me by Reginald Watkin Edward, Esq., whose mother was Miss Ermin Kenrick of Nantclwyd. This Richard Kenrick, who married the heiress of Plâs Cerniogau, was the son of John Kenrick of Ower, son of Richard Kenrick of Acton Burnel, son of Thomas Kenrick son of William Kenrick, who was Groom of the Bed-chamber to King Henry VIII, and son of John Kenrick of Ashley, son of John Kenrick of Ashley, son of John Kenrick of Ashley, who was slain at Blore Heath, and son of David ab Kenric, Standard Bearer and companion to the Black Prince at the battles of Crecy and Poitiers, who founded the Church of Ashley, co. Stafford, as before related.

MAES GWAELOD.
Harl. MS. 4181.

David Eyton of Eyton Uchaf, Constable of Holt Castle. See vol. ii.⊤

2nd son. Sir Robert Eyton, Priest of Overton Madog.⊤Anne Watson.

⌈ 1 ⌈ 2
John Eyton of Maes Gwaelod. James Eyton, had lands in Gwalian.⊤

Richard Eyton of Gwalian.⊤

Randle Eyton of Maes Gwaelod.⊤Jane, d. of Edward Trevor of Bryn Cunallt.

Thomas Eyton of Maes Gwaelod.=Catherine, dau. of Humphrey Ellis of Alrhey.

CASTLE OF OVERTON.

The Castle of Overton was built by Prince Madog ab Maredydd, and it was here that he chiefly resided; from this circumstance the place received the name of Overton Madog. In 1278, 7 Edw. I, it was in the possession of Robert de Crevecœur. In 1331, 5 Edw. III, it was granted, with other lands in this comot, to Eubule L'Estrange, Baron of Knockin. There are now no remains of this castle, which stood on the banks of the Dee, in a field called Maes y Castell.

The lordship or comot of Maelor Saesneg was granted by Henry IV to Sir John Stanley, Knt., and it continued in his family till the 41st of Elizabeth; when William, Earl of Derby, devised it to Sir Randle Brereton of Malpas, Knt., and it now belongs to the families of Hanmer and Gwern Haulod.

23 2

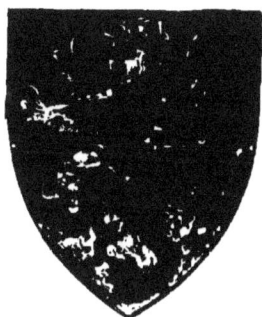

GWERN HAULOD.

Harl. MS. 2299.

Y Bady, *alias* Madog, *temp.* Hen. VII, second son of Howel ab Ieuan⹋ Fychan ab Ieuan Gethin ab Madog Cyffin of Moeliwrch, in Cyn- llaith. Party per fess *sable* and *argent*, a lion rampant counter- changed.

Philip of⹋Augusta, d and
Gwern | heir of John
Haulod. | Trevor Fawr.

Margaret, ux. Gruffydd ab David ab Iorwerth ab Hwfa ab Iorwerth ab Howel ab Owain ab Bleddyn ab Owain Brogyntyn. See Pen- tref Morgan.

Edward ⹋Elizabeth, d. and
ab Philip | heiress of David
of | ab Rhys ab David
Gwern | of Rhosbamty.
Haulod. |

Janet, ux. David ab Robert ab Jenkin ab Madog ab Ieuan ab Madog ab Iorwerth ab David ab Meilir ab Owain ab Edwyn ab Goronwy.

Edward Philips of⹋Jane Llwyd, full sister of Robert Lloyd of the Bryn, one
Gwern Haulod. | of the Guard to Queen Elizabeth (2nd wife).

Edward Philips of⹋Mary, d. of John Hanmer of Bradenheath, brother of Sir
Gwern Haulod. | Thomas Hanmer ab Sir Thomas Hanmer.

William Philips⹋Elizabeth. d. of Edward Eutyn of Gwrych Têg at Halch-
of Gwern Haulod. | dyn. *Gules*, on a bend *argent*, a lion passant *sable*.

Edward Philips of⹋Mary, d. of Thomas Overton ab John Overton of Overton
Gwern Haulod. | Madog.

William Philips of⹋Anne, dau. of Captain William Broughton, ab Morgan
Gwern Haulod. | Broughton of Plás Isaf in Marchwiail.
Married in 1660. |

Mary, heiress of Gwern Haulod; born 1661;⹋Thomas Lloyd of Halchdyn,
ob. 1728, aged 67. | Esq.

| *a* | *b* |

a		b	
Thomas Lloyd, = Alice, d. of ...		Mary Lloyd, heir-=The Rev. John Fletcher	
only son and	Cleveland of	ess of Gwern	of Struddabank, co.
heir; *ob. s. p.*	Liverpool.	Haulod.	Cumberland, rector of
			Hawarden and Bangor
			Is y Coed.

Phillips Lloyd Fletcher=Eleanor, d. of Owen Wynn of Llwyn, co. Denbigh,
of Gwern Haulod.   and Pengwern, co. Meirionydd, Esq.

Colonel Phillips = Mrs. Rid-	Capt. John,	Major Thomas = ..., dau.	**3**
Lloyd Fletcher	dle of	*ob. s. p.*	Lloyd Fletcher	of ...
of Gwern Hau-	Hampton		of Gwern Haulod.	Towers,
lod; *ob. s. p.*	Court.			Esq.

3	**1**	**2**	
Phillips Lloyd Fletcher	Thomas Han-	Fredk. Lloyd	Catherine
of Nerquis Hall,	mer Fletcher	Fletcher of	Wynn
Gwern Haulod, and	of Nerquis	Nerquis Hall;	Fletcher, ux.
Pengwern.	Hall; *ob. s. p.*	*ob. s. p.*	Rev. Doveton
			Philpot.

Charlotte.	Julia.	Harriet.	Frances.	Mary.	Henrietta, ux. Rev.
					William Elwes.

4					
Rev. Lloyd	Mary, ux.	Harriet,	Caro-	Eleanor =Captain Wil-	
Fletcher, took	Major	*ob. s. p.*	line,	Amelia.	liam Tring-
the name of	Walker, had		*ob. s. p.*		ham, R.N.,
Wynn on suc-	issue one d.,				nephew of
ceeding to	Mary Ellen,				the late Lord
Nerquis Hall,	who died *s.p.*,				Wrottesley.
ob. s. p.	Dec. 1881.				

William Lloyd Tringham,=Eleanora	George Wynn	Emily Mary, ux.
ob. April 1882. Howel.	Tringham.	Henry Sewell,
		Esq., R.N.

Llewelyn Watkin Howel Tringham.	Mostyn Frederick Lloyd Tringham.

WYNN OF LLWYN.

*For the commencement of this Pedigree, see Williams Wynn
of Llangedwyn and Wynnstay, vol. iv.*

Maurice Wynn=1st. Jane, d. of Sir=2nd. Catherine, d. and heir of Tudor
of Gwydir. | Richard Bulkeley | ab Robert Fychan of Berain in Llan
| of Beaumaris, | Nefydd (*gules*, a lion rampant *ar-*
| Knt. | *gent*), and relict of John Salusbury,
| | eldest son and heir of Sir John Salus-
| | bury of Lleweni, Knt.

Sir John Wynn of Gwydir. | Edward Wynn of Ys-=Blanche, d. of John
Created a Baronet in 1611. | trad. Buried at | Vaughan of Blaen y
Ancestor of the Wynns of | Llanrhaiadr in Cin- | Cwm, co. Carnarvon.
Gwydir, now represented by | meirch, 1640. He | Buried at Llan-
the Lord Willoughby D'Er- | had seven sons and | rhaiadr.
esby, and Sir W. W. Wynn | four daughters. |
of Wynnstay, Bart. | |

| 1 | | 2 | 3
Robert Wynn=Barbara, d. and | Thomas | Owain Wynn= The Lady
of Ystrad. He | heir of Richard | Wynn of | of Cilcain. | Mostyn,
had five sons | Williams of | Denbigh. | Buried at | relict of Sir
and two | Llwyn, co. | Buried at | Llan- | Thomas
daughters. | Denbigh. | Llanrba- | rhaiadr; *ob.* | Mostyn,
| | iadr, 1623. | *s. p.* | Bart.

| 4 | | 2
Captain Edward Wynn. He was | Mary, ux. Edward
Captain of a Company of Foot in | Williams of Pont
Denbigh Castle, in the Royal Army, | y Gwyddel. *Ar-*
was wounded in a sally made by the | *gent*, a chev. inter
garrison against the besiegers un- | 3 boar's heads
der Sir John Carter, and in three | couped *sable.*
days after died of his wounds, and |
was interred with military honours |
at Llanrhaiadr. |

a | 1　　　　　　b | 2　　　　　　　　　c | 3　 d | 4

a | 1	b | 2		c | 3	d | 4
Edward Wynn of Llwyn, Clerk of Green Cloth to Charles II; *ob. s. p.*	Owain Wynn=of Llwyn. Buried at Llanrhaiadr, 1701.	Anne, d. and heir of Maurice Lewys of Pengwern or Pen y Wern, co Meirion-ydd; *ob.* 1717, aged 67.	A son.	John Wynn. Buried at Llanrhaiadr, 1716.

Maurice Wynn of Llwyn.=Elizabeth, d. and heir of Francis Edwards of Pen Heskin in Môn and Plâs yn y Coed, co. Flint.

Owain Wynn of Llwyn.=Eleanor, d. of Thomas Seel, Esq.

Watkin Edward Wynn=Anna Maria, relict of Llwyn. Buried at of John Mostyn of Llanrhaiadr 1796, Segroed. Buried at aged 42, *s. p.* Llanrhaiadr 1828.		Owain Wynn,= Amelia *ob.* 1805, *s. p.* Maria Seel.

The Rev. Maurice Wynn of Llwyn, Rector of Bangor Is y Coed, and Vicar of Much Wenlock, co. Salop. *Ob.* 26th May 1835, aged 75. He devised his property to his nephew, the Rev. Lloyd Fletcher, who assumed the name of Wynn. Nerquis Hall was left to the Rev. Maurice Wynn by the two Miss Giffards of that place.	Eleanor.=Philip Lloyd Fletcher of Gwern Haulod. Rev. Lloyd Fletcher Wynn of Nerquis Hall; *ob. s. p.*

LLOYD OF HALCHDYN IN THE PARISH OF HANMER.

Harl. MS. 4181 ; *Cae Cyriog MS.*

Llywelyn of Halchdyn, the eldest son of Ednyfed Gam of Llys Pengwern in Nanheudwy, the fourth son of Ior-werth Foel, Lord of Chirk, Nanheudwy and Maelor Saesneg (see Vol. i. p. 316), married Anne, daughter of Sir Roger Puleston of Emrall or Emerallt ab Sir Richard ab Sir Roger Puleston of Emerallt, ab Sir Richard de Puleston in Cheshire, 1290, and relict of Ieuan ab Madog ab Llywelyn, by whom he had issue, besides two daughters, 1, Margaret, ux. Gruffydd ab Madog Pabo ab Ednyfed Goch ah Cynwrig of Bers (*ermine*, a lion statant gardant *gules*); and 2, Angharad, who, married, first, David ab David ab Ieuan ab Iorwerth ab David Hên ab Goronwy of Mortyn and Llai (*vert*, semé of broomslips, a lion rampant *or*), and, secondly, David ab Llywelyn ab Iorwerth Fychan (*sable*, three roses *argent*) ab Iorwerth ab David Hên ab Goronwy of Llai, a son and heir,

Madog ab Llywelyn of Halchdyn, who married Margaret, daughter of Goronwy ab Iorwerth of Llai (*argent*, on a bend *sable*, three mullets of the field). Iorwerth of Llai was the eldest son of David Hên ab Goronwy of Burton, or Mortyn, and Llai (see Plâs yn Horslli). By this lady, Madog had issue, besides a daughter, Lleuci, ux. Ieuan ab David Dymock of Penley, a son and heir,

Richard ab Madog of Halchdyn, who married Elen, daughter of Ieuan ab Einion ab Gruffydd ab Llywelyn, and sister of David ab Ieuan ab Einion, Constable of Harlech Castle under King Henry VI, by whom he had two sons, 1, Robert, *ob. s. p.*; and 2, John, of whom presently; and a daughter Angharad, ux. Edward ab Morgan of Alrhey.

John ab Richard of Halchdyn. He married Mawd, daughter of Madog ab David ab Madog Llwyd ab Gruffydd of Maelor Saesneg ab Iorwerth Foel, by whom he had issue, besides three daughters, 1, Margaret, ux. David ab Robert Sutton of Sutton and Gwersyllt; 2, Alice, ux. Philip Bird of Estwick; and 3, Angharad, ux Edward ab Howel ab Morgan of Alrhey, a son and heir,

William Lloyd of Halchdyn, who married Nest, daughter and co-heir of Elis ab Tudor of Ystrad Alun ab Gruffydd ab Ieuan ab Llywelyn ab Gruffydd Llwyd ab Llywelyn ab Ynyr of Iâl, by whom he had issue,

besides a daughter, Margaret, who married, first, John
Jeffreys of Acton, Justice of North Wales 1606;
secondly, she married Sir Thomas Ireland, Knt., Cham-
berlain of Chester; and, thirdly, Sir Edward Trevor, of
Bryn Cunallt, Knt., four sons, 1, William Lloyd of
Halchdyn, *ob. s. p.*; 2, Thomas Lloyd, who died in
France; 3, Randle Lloyd, who died in Spain; and 4,
Edward Lloyd.

Edward Lloyd, the fourth son, who married, first,
Margaret, daughter of . . . . Jeffreys of Acton, succeeded his eldest brother, William, at Halchdyn. He
married, secondly, Beatrice, daughter of Thomas Overton
ab John ab Gruffydd ab Gruffydd ab Jenkyn ab David
Foel ab Philip Hanmer,[1] by whom he had issue three
sons, 1, Thomas; 2, William Lloyd; and 3, John Lloyd
of Bryn Gnoltyn in Bangor parish; and three daughters,
1, Margaret, who married Thomas Mostyn of Rhyd; 2,
Anne; and 3, Ffrances. Edward Lloyd died in 1646,
and he and his wife are buried in the old chancel of
Hanmer Church.

Thomas Lloyd of Halchdyn, died in 1693. He married
and had issue a son and heir,

William Lloyd of Halchdyn, 1697, who married
Martha, daughter of John Edisbury of Erddig and
Pentref Clawdd, son of Cynwrig Edisbury, *alias* Wilkinson of Marchwiail. Wilkinson was the name of this
family when they first came to Maelor, from the Hundred
of Edisbury. And the Welsh gave them this surname
on account of their coming from that place (Cac Cyriog
MS.). Mr. Lloyd had issue a son and heir, Thomas
Lloyd of Halchdyn, who married Mary, daughter and
heiress of William Philips of Gwern Haulod, by whom
he had a son, Thomas, who died *s. p.*, and a daughter
Mary, who married the Rev. John Fletcher.

---

[1] Philip Hanmer of Hanmer was the son of Sir John Hanmer,
Knt., Constable of Caernarvon in the time of Edward I.

HALCHDYN.—LLOYD OF BRYN HALCHDYN.

Harl. MS. 4181.

Thomas, fourth son of Owain ab Bleddyn ab Tudor ab Rhys Sais.=
See vol. i, p. 312.

Madog ab Maelor =Alice, d. and heir of Philip Phycdan.

Iorwerth ab Madog Maelor.=..., d. and heir of Owain Fychan ab Owain ab
Goronwy ab Owain ab Edwin.

Ieuan ab Iorwerth.=Janct, d. of Madog ab　　Cynwrig ab Iorwerth, ancestor
Philip ab Gruffydd.　　of the Lloyds of Halchdyn and
the Pennants of Downing.

Madog ab=Gwenllian, d. of Maredydd ab Lly-　Annest, ux. Howel ab Go-
Ieuan.　｜　welyn Ddû of Abertanad.　　ronwy of Hafod y Wern.

Jenkyn ab Madog.=　Philip, living 9th Henry VI.=Margaret.
Other MSS. state that
this Jenkyn was the　David=Rose, d. of Gruffydd　Roger.　John.　Ed-
second son of David　Lloyd.｜Hanmer of Ffens, ab　　　　　ward.
Lloyd of Isgoed, ab　｜Edward ab Sir Jeu-
Madog Lloyd of Is-　｜kin Hanmer of Han-
goed, ab Gruffydd ab　｜mer.
Iorwerth Foel.
　　　　　Margaret, sole heiress, married Jasper Lloyd of Hal-
　　　　　chdyn, ab Thomas ab Jenkyn ab David.　See p.365.

David Lloyd of=Gwen, d. and co-heiress of John Lloyd ab Tomlyn Lloyd of
the Bryn.　｜　Oswestry, second son of Madog Lloyd of Llwyn y Maen.
　　　　　Argent, an eagle displayed with two necks *sable*.

John Lloyd of the Bryn.=Alice, dau. of Randle Lloyd ab Gruffydd Lloyd of
Tal y Wern.

a |　　　　　　　　*b* |　　*c* |　　*d* |　　*c* |　　　*f* |

a	b	c	d	e	f
Captain Robert Lloyd of the Bryn, one of the Guard to Queen Elizabeth. Buried at Hanmer, March 11th, 1589.	=Elen, d. of David Llwyd ab Elissau of Allt Llwyn Dragon, now Plâs yn Iâl. *Ermine, a saltier gules, a crescent or, for difference.*	Alice, ux. Roger Eyton.	..., ux. David ab Roger.	...,ux. Edward Llwyd ab Howel of Barlin.	Jane, ux. Edward ab Edward ab Philip of Gwernhaeled.

Rose, ux. David ab Roger ab David ab Jenkin ab David Fychan ab David Foel ab Philip Hanmer ab Sir John Hanmer, Constable of Caernarvon Castle.

Robert Lloyd of=Margaret, d. and heiress of   Dorothy, ux. Thomas Lloyd
the Bryn.   Robert Sefton of Molling-   of Plâs Uwch y Clawdd.
                   ton, co. Chester.

Captain Luke Lloyd of the=Catherine, dau. of Thomas Whitley of Aston in
Bryn. Baptised 22nd Oct.   Merffordd, and Dorothy, his wife, d. of Thomas
1608; *ob.* 31st March   Ravenscroft of Bretton in Merffordd. *Argent,*
1695, aged 86. He fought   on a chief *gules,* three garbs *or,* for Whitley.
under Cromwell in 1643.   She died January 12, 1701, aged 91.

Luke Lloyd=Esther, d. of James Betton of Shrewsbury, D.D., which lady
of the   (having eventually survived her two brothers, and all her
Bryn.   sisters, with her nephew, James Betton, and his sister, the
            children of her eldest brother James) became the sole heir of
            this branch of the Betton family. *Argent,* two pales *sable,*
            each charged with three crosslets, fitchee *or.*

Catherine Lloyd, Heiress of the Bryn,   Sarah Lloyd, second co-heir, married
married Thomas Kenyon of Peel   Samuel Lloyd of Plâs Madog. She
Hall, co. Lancaster, ancestor of the   died, and was buried at Rhiwabon,
Lords Kenyon.   7th June 1699.

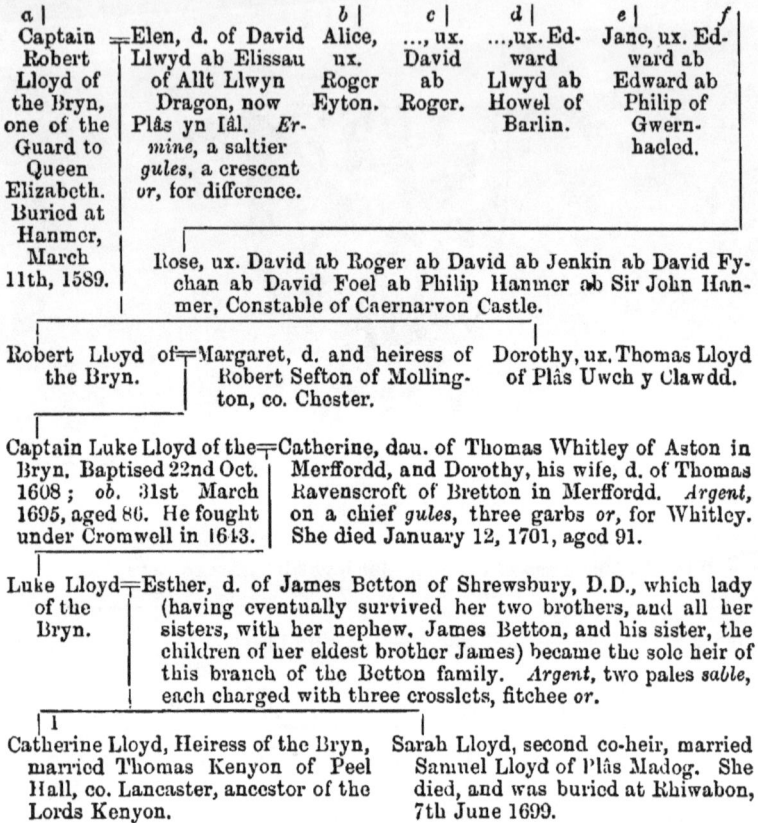

Philip Henry thus alludes to the death of Luke Lloyd the elder :--

"Luke Lloyd, Esq., of the Bryn, in Hanmer parish, my aged and worthy friend, finished his course with joy, March 31st, 1695, being Lord's day. He was in the 87th year of his age, and had been married almost 69 years to his pious wife (a daughter of Mr. Whitley of Aston), of the same age, who still survives him. He was the glory of the little congregation, the top branch in all respects of our small vine, and my friend indeed. When he made his will, under the subscription of his name, he wrote Job xxx, 25, 26, 27.

"Luke Lloyd had been, in his youth, a staunch Cromwellite, and had served with some distinction in the Revolutionary war.[1] His sword is kept at Gredington. The carved oak pulpit

---

[1] *Life of Lord Kenyon,* by G. K.

in Hanmer Church is noticed by the Duke of Beaufort in 1684, bearing these inscriptions in gold letters, '*Xtus est Agnus Dei qui tollit peccata mundi*, Be swifte to hear, Take heed how ye heare,' and the name 'JESUS,' with the date of its being given, 1627. The story told about it is that Luke Lloyd forbade the clergyman of that day praying for the king, and, when he persisted, threatened him with his stick. As compensation for his brawling in church he offered and gave the pulpit.[1]

"A.D. 1666, Aug. 15th, Mr. Luke Lloyd, jun., indited at the assizes at Flint for disturbing Mr. H (ylton), Vicar of Hanmer, in the time of the administration of ye Lord's Supper. Witnesse sworn deposed that Mr. H (ylton), refusing to give him the sacrament in his pew, as he had been used to do, after the blessing was pronounced, and the people dismissed and gone, he came up to him to know the reason, but that Mr. H., and some few of his friends, were then at the table, eating and drinking what was left of the consecrated elements; which (being appointed reverently to be done by the rubrick) the judge declared to be part of the sacrament, though the clerk deposed that Mr. H. was talking with R. E. when Mr. Lloyd came up to him. The jury brought him in not guilty, but were sent out again by the judge, and the second time brought him in guilty, and he was fined."

In Sir John Hanmer's *Memorials of Hanmer Parish*, p. 57, there is a letter from Sir Thomas Hanmer to Sir Job (Judge) Charleton on the subject, March 12th, 1665.

The following is the inscription on the tomb of Luke Lloyd :—

"Here lyeth the body of Luke Lloyd of the Bryn, gent., and Catherine, his wife, who lived in the marriage state together 68 years. He died the thirty-first day of March, 1695, being 86. She died January 12th, 1701, aged 91."

The following inscription is likewise in Hanmer Church :—

"Here lies in peace Mary, the wife of Roger Kenyon of Cefn, daughter and heiress of Edward Lloyd of Pen y lan, Esq., by Mary, daughter and co-heiress of Edward Lloyd of Plâs Madog, Esq. She was great-niece of Ellis Lloyd of Pen

---

[1] Rev. H. M. Lee, Vicar of Hanmer.

y lan, Esq., and to William Lloyd, Lord Bishop of Norwich,
one of those prelates who, having sworn fidelity to King
James II, refused taking the oath to his successor, choosing
rather to be deprived of his bishopric than let go his inte-
grity.

"Filial piety, connubial affection, parental tenderness, a
steady attachment to her friends and benevolence to all, were
eminently united in her character. She died in childbed,
leaving her disconsolate husband three sons and two daughters,
Feb. 4th, A.D. 1781, aged 30."

HALCHDYN.

Lewys Dwnn, vol. ii, p. 313.

Jenkyn ab David ab Cynwrig (ab Iorwerth ab═Gwen, d. of Gruffydd Han-
Ifor ab Cynwrig) ab Iorwerth ab Madog Mae- | mer of Hanmer, ab Sir
lor ab Thomas ab Owain ab Bleddyn ab | Jenkin Hanmer of Han-
Tudor ab Rhys Sais. See vol. i, p. 312. | mer.

Thomas ab Jenkyn.═Janet, dau. of William Brereton of Borasham, ab Sir
Randle Brereton of Malpas, Knt.

Jasper Lloyd of═Jane Fechan, sole d. and heir of David Lloyd ab Philip ab
Halchdyn. Madog ab Ieuan ab Iorwerth ab Madog Maelor, p. 377.

Edward═Margaret, d. of David John. Randal. Wil- Margaret, Elen.
Lloyd of | Randle Brere- Lloyd. liam. ux. John Janet.
Halch- | ton o Grun. Hanmer.
dyn. |

Randal Lloyd═Elen, d. of Brian Fowler of Llys William Eleanor. Jane.
of Halchdyn. Bedydd, now called Bettisfield, Lloyd. Elen. Mary.
who was the second son of
Roger Fowler of Broomhill, co.
Stafford, Esq.

FOWLER OF LLYS BEDYDD.

*Heraldic Visitation of Shropshire; Harl. MS. 157; Kimber's
Baronetage.*

Sir John Fowler of Foxley, co. Bucks,⫫..., d. and heir of ... Loveday. This Knt., lineal descendant of Sir Richard Fowler of Foxley, Knight, a Crusader, *temp.* Richard I. *Azure,* on a chev. *argent,* inter three lions passant gardant *or,* three crosses moline *sable.* — name occurs on the Roll of Battle Abbey. Party per pale *argent* and *sable,* an eagle displayed with two necks counterchanged, gorged with a ducal coronet *or.*

Sir Henry Fowler⫫..., sister and heiress of John Barton. *Ermine,* on a canton *gules,* an owl *argent,* crowned *or.*

Sir William Fowler⫫Cecilia, dau. and heir of Nicholas Englefield of Rycote of Rycote, co. Oxon., Knt. and Lanynton Gernon, co. Oxon. Barry of six pieces *gules* and *argent,* on a chief *or,* a lion passant *azure.*

Sir Richard Fowler of Rycote, Knt.⫫Jane, da. of Sir John D'Anvers of Colthorpe, co. Oxon., Knt.

Sir Richard Fowler of Rycote, Knt.   Thomas Fowler, esquire⫫Margarite, dau. and heir of ... of the Body to Edward IV.   Colville. *Or,* ten billets *gules,* 4, 3, 2, 1.

Edward Fowler of Twickenham.⫫1st. Alice. – 2nd. Edith. = 3rd. Margaret.

Roger Fowler⫫Isabella, d. and co-heir (by Isabella, his wife, d. and heir of of Broomhill, co. Stafford.   Sir Andrew Trollope, Knt.) of William Lee of Morpeth, Esq., Treasurer of Berwick, and sister of Rowland Lee, Bishop of Lichfield and Coventry, Lord President of the Marches of Wales, and of George Lee, the last Dean of St. Chadd's in Shrewsbury. *Azure,* two bars *argent,* over all a bend compony *or* and *gules.*

a | 1   *b* | *c* |

a | 1	b | 2	c | 3
Rowland Fowler. = .., d. of ... Bradshaw of Presteign, co. Radnor.	Brian Fowler of Stowe and St. Thomas's Abbey, co. Stafford, and *jure uxoris* of Llys Bedydd. Living in 1571. = Jane, dau. and heir of John Hanmer of Llys Bedydd, Esq. *Argent*, two lions passant gardant *azure*.	William Fowler of Harnage Grange, co. Salop, ancestor of the Fowlers of Harnage Grange & Abbey Cwm Hir; *ob.* 1597. = Maria, d. of Blythe, Esq., M.D.

Walter Fowler of Llys Bedydd and St. Thomas's Abbey. = Mary, d. of Ralph Sheldon of Boley, co. Stafford, Esq.

Elen, ux. Randle Lloyd of Halchdyn.

Walter Fowler of Llys Bedydd and St. Thomas's. =

Thomas Fowler, = Rector of Whitchurch.

Mary, buried at Hanmer, June 19th, 1589.

Thomas Ffowler, Esq. ; living 12th May 1703.[1]

The following information was kindly sent me by the Rev. M. H. Lee, Rector of Hanmer :—" The old house, Llys Bedydd, was built, I expect, by Brian Fowler (who married Jane Hanmer) with the spoils of the abbeys, which he got through his uncle, Rowland Lee, Bishop of Lichfield and Coventry, and Lord President of the Marches of Wales. In 1699, Edward Lhuid notices as living at Bettisfield (Llys Beddydd) .... Fowler, Esq. In or about 1714, Bishop Gastrell writes, "there are five ancient seats, Hanmer, Bettisfield .... Halghton, and Willington." In 1762, Candidus writes, in *The Gentleman's Magazine*: " Bettisfield Hall, a seat of the Fowlers, was mostly burnt down some years since, and it is not rebuilt ; the part which escaped the flames is inhabited by a tenant, and is the property of .... Fitzgerald, Esq., a Roman Catholic gentleman. There is a story told of old Madame Ffowler, after the fire, troubling the house until some magician got her into a bottle which was corked up and thrown into a pond. There she remained until the pond was mudded, when the inquisitive men must needs draw the cork, when out,

---

[1] In Cosin's *Rom. Cath. Non-Jurors in* 1715, p. 31, the following notice occurs :—" Com. Flint. John Fowler of St. Thomas in Com. Stafford, Esq., £260 8s. 0d." " This must be the Llys Bedydd property that is referred to."—Rev. M. H. Lee.

with a whiz, comes something like a humble bee, which
makes straight for Llys Bedydd, and in her flight assumes
the appearance of Madame Ffowler. Warned by experience she troubles them no more." The Fowler family
was one of great antiquity before the reign of Richard I,
when the then representative of the family, Sir Richard
Fowler of Foxley, co. Bucks, Knt., accompanied that
warlike monarch to the Holy Land, with a body of
archers raised among his own tenantry. At the siege
of St. Jean d'Acre, 1190, an attack of the Saracens
upon the Christian camp by night was frustrated by a
white owl, which, being disturbed by their approach,
flew into the tent of Sir Richard Fowler and awoke him.
He soon became acquainted with the threatened danger,
and hastily arousing his men, immediately engaged and
defeated the enemy. King Richard rewarded his fidelity
by knighting him upon the scene of the engagement,
and changed his crest, which was the hawk and lure, to
the vigilant owl. Subsequently, in the reign of Henry
IV, his descendant, Sir William Fowler of Foxley, Knt.,
became possessed of Rycote, co. Oxon, by his marriage
with Cecilia, daughter and heiress of Nicholas Englefield
of Rycote and Lanynton Gernon, co. Oxford, Esq., who
died in 1414, as we learn from his epitaph :—" Here
lieth the body of Nicholas Englefield, Esq., some time
Comptroller of the House to King Richard II, who died
1st April in the year of grace M.CCC.XIV, whose soul Jesu
pardon. Amen, Amen, Amen." He was the third
son of Sir Philip de Englefield, Lord of Englefield, the
head of an ancient family, which, according to Camden,
takes its name from the town of Englefield in Berkshire,
of which place they were stated to have been the pro-
prietors in the second year of Egbert's reign, 803. For
a full account of the Fowler and Englefield families, see
Wotton and Kimber's *Baronetage.*

ARMS.

1. *Azure,* on a chevron *argent,* inter three lions passant
gardant *or,* three crosses moline *sable.* Fowler.
2. Party per pale, *argent* and *sable,* an eagle displayed with

two necks counterchanged, gorged with a ducal coronet *or*.
Loveday.

3. *Ermine*, on a canton *gules*, an owl *argent*, crowned *or*.
Barton.

4. Barry of six pieces, *gules* and *argent*, on a chief *or*, a lion
passant *azure*. Englefield.

5. *Argent*, a chevron, inter three rooks *sable*. Clarke of
Rycote and Lanynton Gernon.

6. *Argent*, three wolf's heads erased *gules*, in a border *azure*,
charged with eight turrets *or*. Rycote of Rycote.

7. Vaire, *argent* and *azure*. Gernon of Lanynton Gernon.

8. *Azure*, two bars *argent*, over all a bend company *or* and
gules. Lee of Morpeth.

9. *Vert*, three goats rampant *argent*, attired *or*. Trollope.

10. *Argent*, two lions passant gardant *azure*. Hanmer.

Crest. On a wreath of the colours, an owl *argent*, crowned *or*.

LLOYD OF TALWRN OR TAL Y WERN, IN THE TOWNSHIP OF WILLINGTON.

Harl. MS. 4181.

Iorwerth Foel,[1] Lord of Chirk, Nanheudwy and Maelor
Saesneg (see vol. i, p. 313), married Gwladys, daughter
and co-heiress of Iorwerth ab Gruffydd ab Heilin of
Fron Goch in Mochnant ab Meurig ab Ieuan ab Adda
ab Cynwrig ab Pasgen, Lord of Cegidfa and Deuddwr
(1, *sable*, three horse's heads erased *argent*; 2, *argent*, a

---

[1] Iorwerth Foel is styled by Reynolds, "Baro de Halchdyn".

chevron *sable*, inter three Cornish choughs, each with
a spot of *ermine* in their bills, ppr.) Gwladys was buried
in Hanmer Church, where her tomb still remains with
this inscription : " HIC IACET WLADYS VXOR IERWERTH
VOEL, ORATE P.EA." round the verge of the coffin lid.
Within the inscription is a very fine floriated cross,
almost identical with that described by Camden (i. 12),
as being at St. Buriens, Cornwall. By this lady Iorwerth
Foel had issue five sons, 1, Madog Llwyd of Bryn
Cunallt yn Y Waun ; 2, Gruffydd of Maelor Saesneg,
of whose line we have to treat ; 3, Morgan, ancestor of
the Yonges of Bryn Iorcyn yn Yr Hôb, and the Yonges
of Sawerdee and Croxton ; 4, Ednyfed Gam of Llys
Pengwern in Nanheudwy ; and 5, Ieuan of Llanfechain.

Gruffydd of Maelor Saesneg, married Gwerfyl, daughter
and co-heiress of Madog ab Maredydd of Blodwel and
Abertanad ab Llywelyn Fychan ab Llywelyn ab Owain
Fychan ab Owain, Lord of Mechain Is y Coed, second
son of Madog ab Maredydd, Prince of Powys Fadog
(*argent*, a lion rampant *sable*, in a border indented
gules).[1] By this lady Gruffydd had issue, besides a
daughter, Eva, ux. Howel, fourth son of Madog ab
Llywelyn ab Gruffydd, Lord of Eyton, Erlys, and Bwras,
seven sons.

I. Madog Llwyd, of whom presently.

II. Llywelyn Ddû of Abertanad and Blodwel in Mechain Is y Coed.

III. David ab Gruffydd, who married and had issue a
son, Madog ab David, the father of Gruffydd Llwyd of
Talwrn, who married Jane, daughter of Iorwerth Goch
ab Ednyfed ab Madog of Brochdyn or Broughton (*ermine*,
a lion statant gardant *gules*), by whom he had an only
daughter and heiress Alice, ux. John ab David Llwyd
ab Jenkin ab Madog ab Ieuan.

IV. Madog Ddû.

V. Iorwerth Foel, the father of David Ddû, who
married Alice, daughter of David ab David ab Ieuan

[1] *Harl. MS.* 2299, f. 42.

ab Iorwerth, eldest son of David Hên ab Goronwy of Mortyn and Llai, by whom he had a son Icuan ab David, who married Cari, daughter of Ednyfed Goch ab Goronwy ab Owain of Gnoltyn, by whom he had an only daughter and heiress who married Richard ab Lawrence.

VI. Morgan Goch of Willington, who by Margaret his wife, daughter of Sir John Upton of Hanmer, Knt., had a son and heir, Gruffydd ab Morgan, who had two daughters co-heirs, 1, Margaret, who married, December 6th, 1487, Thomas Dimog ab Icuan ab David Dimog, and by her he had his lands in Willington; and 2, Maud, co-heir, ux. Madog ab David ab Madog Llwyd ab Gruffyd ab Iorwerth Foel.

VII. Goronwy Ddû of Abertanad and Treflodwel.

Madog Llwyd the eldest son of Gruffydd of Maelor Sacsneg, married three times; by his first wife Catherine, daughter of Owain Barton of Chester, he had a son and heir, David ab Madog, of whom presently. He married, secondly, Lleuci, daughter of Iorwerth Fychan ab Iorwerth ab Awr ab Icuaf ab Niniaw ab Cynwrig ab Rhiwallon (*ermine, a lion rampant sable*), by whom he had issue one son, David ab Madog (see Bodylltyn), and four daughters, 1, Cari, ux. John Hoord, Lord of Walverton, co. Salop (*azure, on a chief or, an owl sable*); 2, Annest, ux. Sir . . . . Roydon of Kent; 3, Dygoes, ux. Howel ab Gruffydd ab Iorwerth Fychan of Groes Foel; and 4, Margaret, ux. Thomas Roydon. Madog Llwyd married, thirdly, Gwerfyl, daughter of Ednyfed ab Gruffydd ab Llywelyn ab Gruffydd, by whom he had a son Icuan ab Madog of Rhuddallt, who married . . . . daughter of Madog ab Iorwerth ab Madog, by whom he had an only daughter and heiress, Gwenllian, ux. Jenkyn ab Llywelyn ab Ithel Goch ab Llywelyn ab Madog ab Einion ab Madog ab Bleddyn ab Cynwrig ab Rhiwallawn.

David, the eldest son of Madog Llwyd, married Gwenllian, daughter of Bleddyn ab Einion Fychan ab Einion ab Llywelyn of Ystrad Alun ab Cadwgan Ddû ab Cadwgan Goch ab Y Gwion ab Hwfa ab Ithel Felyn, Lord of Ial and Ystrad Alun (*sable*, on a chevron inter three goat's heads erased *or*, three trefoils of the field), by whom he had issue three sons, 1, Madog ab David, of whom presently ; 2, Jenkyn ab David, ancestor of the Lloyds of Willington, and according to some authors the Lloyds of the Bryn in the parish of Hanmer ; and 3, David ab Jenkyn.

Madog ab David of Tal y Wern in Willington, the eldest son, married Maude, daughter and co-heir of Gruffydd ab Morgan Goch of Willington, ab Gruffyd ab Iorwerth Foel, Lord of Chirk, by whom he had issue, besides a daughter Maude, ux. John ab Richard ab Madog ab Llywelyn of Halchdyn, two sons, 1, Gruffydd Lloyd, of whom presently ; and 2, Richard Lloyd, the father of John Lloyd, the father of William Lloyd, the father of William Lloyd.

Gruffydd Lloyd of Tal y wern or Talwrn, married Jane, daughter of Iorwerth Goch ab Ednyfed ab Madog ab Gruffydd Ddû of Brochdyn or Broughton, by whom he had issue, besides two younger sons, Edward Lloyd and William Lloyd, an elder son and heir,

Randal Lloyd of Tal y wern, who married and had issue, besides a younger son, John Lloyd, a son and heir,

Randal Lloyd of Tal y wern, who married Ermine, daughter of Sir Thomas Hanmer of Hanmer, Knt., and relict of William Lloyd of Halchdyn, by whom he had issue, besides a daughter Catherine, ux. Roger Eyton of Halchdyn, a son and heir,

Randle Lloyd of Tal y wern, who by Elin his wife, daughter of Edward Lloyd of Hersedd in Ystrad Alun (*argent*, a cross flory engrailed *sable*, inter four Cornish choughs, ppr.) had six sons and five daughters, 1, Randal, of whom presently; 2, William; 3, John ; 4, Roger ; 5, Edward ; and 6, Humphrey Lloyd ; and five daughters, 1, Ermine, ux. John Williams ; 2, Catherine, ux. John Milton of Shotlach ; 3, Dorothy ; 4, Jane, ux. Robert Davies ; and 5, Margaret, ux. John Evans of Bangor.

Randal Lloyd of Tal y wern, married Elen, daughter of

William Hanmer of Ffens, and Margaret his wife, daughter
and heiress of David Kynaston of Crickett or Crugaeth
in Shropshire, by whom he had issue two sons, 1, William,
of whom presently; and 2, John Lloyd; and two daughters,
Alice and Elen.

William Lloyd of Tal y Wern.

BODYLLTYN IN RHIWABON.

Harl. MS. 4181.

David, the second son of Madog Llwyd ab Gruffydd
of Maelor Saesneg, married Angharad, daughter of Ieuan
ab Madog of Rhuddallt ab Cadwgan Ddû ab Cadwgan
Goch ab Y Gwion ab Hwfa ab Ithel Felyn, Lord of Iâl
and Ystrad Alun (*sable*, on a chev. inter three goat's
heads erased *or*, three trefoils of the field), by whom he
had issue, besides four daughters,—1, Dugws, ux. Deicws
ab Y Badi ab David Goch ab Iorwerth Ddû ab Howel
Voel v. Ach Jenkyn Llwyd ab Ieuan; 2, Lleuci, ux.
first, Gruffydd of Rhuddallt ab Iorwerth ab Madog, and
secondly, Adda ab David ab Ieuan ab Adda; 3, Eva, ux.
first, Gruffydd Goch, and secondly, Richard ab Llywelyn
Gethin; and 4, Angharad, ux. first, Jenkin ab Ieuan ab
David Y Rhug, and secondly, Edmund ab David Fychan
of the Wern in the parish of Hanmer (*argent*, two lions
passant gard. *azure*),—two sons.

I. Madog ab David, who married Gwenllian, daughter

and heiress of Madog Llwyd ab Hwfa ab Ieuan ab Madog yr Athro, by whom he had a son and heir,

Edward ab Madog of Bodylltyn in Rhiwabon, who married Mec, daughter of Madog ab Einion ab David ab David ab Ieuan ab Iorwerth ab David Hen ab Goronwy of Mortyn and Llai (*vert*, semé of broomslips a lion rampant *or*), by whom he had an only daughter,

Gwenllian, heiress of Bodylltyn, who married Roger Eyton, son of John ab Elis Eyton of Rhiwabon.

II. Gruffydd, the second son of David second son of Madog Llwyd ab Gruffydd of Maelor Saesneg, married and had issue a son, Madog ab Gruffydd ; who married and had issue a son, Gruffydd ab Madog; who married Angharad, daughter of Griffith ab John ab Gruffydd ab Madog ab Hwfa, by whom he had a son Roger.

LLOYD OF WILLINGTON.

Harl. MS. 4181.

Jenkyn Fychan, second son of David,=..., d. of Maurice Yonge ab Jenkyn the eldest son of Madog Llwyd ab | of Bryn Iorcyn in Yr Hôb.
Gruffydd of Maelor Saesneg. |

| 2 | | 1 | |
David ab Jen-=Gwen, d. and heiress of John Lloyd   John.   Elen, ux. Gruff-
kyn of Wil- | of Oswestry, ab Tomlyn Lloyd of   ydd Llwyd ab
lington. | Oswestry, second son of Madog   Gwyn.
             | Lloyd of Llwyn y Maen.

a | *b* |

a |
Robert=Catherine, d. of William
Lloyd | Willascote of Willascote.
of
Wil-
ling-
ton.

b |
John Lloyd of Bryn=Alice, d. of Randle
in Halchdyn. | Lloyd of Tal y
Wern.

Captain Robert Lloyd of the Bryn, one of the Guard to Queen
Elizabeth; *ob.* 11th March 1589. See p. 363.

William Lloyd of=Catherine, d. of Robert Jones of Llwyn On, and relict of
Willington. | ... Brereton.

John Lloyd=Lili, d. of James Eyton   Elizabeth, ux. Mary, ux. Jane.
of | of Eyton.   Henry   Gruffydd
Willington. | Billing.   Gwynn.

Robert Lloyd=Margaret. d. of Sir Thomas Hanmer   Catherine, ux. Thomas
of | of Hanmer, Knt.   Lith.
Willington. |

John Lloyd=Sarah, d. of Sir Robert   Thomas   Jane, ux. Elen, ux. Ed-
of | Gerard Eyton Lloyd.   Lloyd.   Edward   ward ab
Willington. | of Eyton,   Phillips. Randal
         | Knight
         | Banneret.

John Lloyd of Willington,[1] 1676.

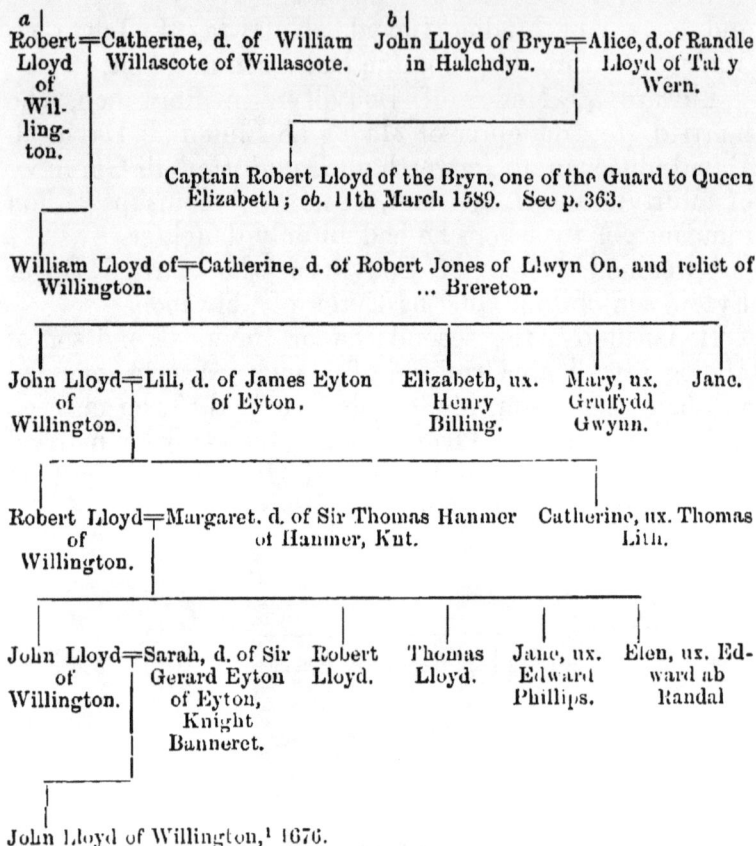

[1] In Cosin's *Roman Catholic Non-Jurors in* 1715, page 8, *sub*
"Cardigan", there is, "Katherine Palmer of Willington, in com.
Flint, widow, £743 : 11 : 6".

YONGE OF SAWARDEK, IN THE TOWNSHIP OF CROXTON.

Harl. MS. 4181.

Morgan of Maelor Saesneg, third son of Iorwerth Voel, Lord of Chirk,⊤ Nanheudwy, and Maelor Saesneg.

Iorwerth ab Morgan.⊤Margaret, d. and heir of William Yonge of Sawardek.

Morgan Yonge of Sawardek.⊤Gwenllian, d. and heir of Ithel ab Bleddyn ab Ithel Anwyl.

Jenkin Yonge of Sawardek.	⊤1st, Mallt, d. and heir of Deio ab David ab Madog Ddu ab Iorwerth ab Gruffydd of Caer Fallwch.	2nd, Gwladys, dau. and heir of Tudor ab Madog Voel of Bryn Iorcyn in Yr Hob, ab Gruffydd ab Llywelyn ab Ynyr of Iâl.	..., ux. Cwnnws, an illegitimate son of Ithel ab Cynwrig ab Bleddyn ab Ithel Anwyl.

1		2
Lewys Yonge of Sawardek.⊤Sibil, d. of Richard Spirstow of the parish of Bumbri, in Cheshire.		MauriceYonge of Bryn Iorcyn.

Gruffydd Yonge of Sawerdek.	⊤Angharad, d. of Gruffydd Gwyn ab Jenkyn Gwyn of Ystrad Alun ab Madog ab David Llwyd ab Gruffydd Goch ab David Goch Fychan.	Richard, *ob. s. p.*	Elin, ux. Howel ab David ab Ithel.	Margaret, ux. Randal ab Edward ab Ieuan ab Gruffydd.

John Yonge of Sawardek.	⊤Elizabeth, d. of Randle Dymock of Willington.	Gwen, ux. John ab Gruffydd ab Jenkin.	Margaret, ux. John Puleston.

Thomas Yonge of Sawardek.	⊤Margaret, d. of Ralph Broughton of Broughton or Brochdyn.	Humphrey Yonge.	Elen.

1	2	3	4	5	6	7
Thomas Yonge.	William Yonge.	Humphrey Yonge.	Ffrancis Yonge.	Randolph Yonge.	Thomas Yonge.	Edward Yonge.

Anne.	Jane.	Mary.

PENNANT OF DOWNING.
Harl. MS. 4181.

Thomas, fourth son of Owain ab Bleddyn ab Tudor ab Rhys Sais.⹋

Madog ⹋Alice, d. and heir of Philip Phychdan, and Margaret, his wife, d.
Maelor. | and co-heiress of David ab Rhirid ab Ynyr ab Jonas of Penley,
| Lord of Llancrch Banna.

Iorwerth ab Madog.⹋..., dau. of Owain Fychan ab Owain ab Goronwy ab
| Owain ab Edwin.

Cynwrig ab Iorwerth.⹋   Ieuan.

Ithel ab Cynwrig.⹋Margaret, d. of Llywelyn ab Madog Foel of Marchwiail.

Tudor ⹋Gwenllian, dau. of   Alice, ux. Deicws Goch   Agnes, ux. Gruffydd
ab | Llywelyn ab Edny-   of Marchwiail, ab   ab Bleddyn ab Robert
Ithel. | ved ab Maredydd.   Einion ab David.   ab David ab Goronwy.

David Pennant of Fichdan.⹋Agnes, d. of Jenkin Don.

| 1 | 2 | 3
Thomas Pennant, Abbot of   Roger Pen-   Hugh Pen-⹌Janet, d. of Robert
Dinas Basing.   nant.   nant.   ab Howel.

Thomas Pennant,[1] Abbot of Dinas Basing or Basingwerke, left his monastery and married Mallt, daughter
of Sir John Constable, Knt., by whom he had issue five
sons and five daughters, 1, Edward, of whom presently ;
1, Margaret ; 2, Anne ; 3, Catherine ; 4, Winefrid ; 5,
Dorothy ; 6, Elen ; 7, Ffrances ; 8, Elizabeth ; and 9,
Mary, *ob. s. p.*

---

[1] According to a poem by Guthyn Owain, who flourished about the
latter part of the fifteenth century, this Thomas Pennant, when Abbot,
greatly enlarged and improved the Abbey and its appurtenances, and
resided there in almost regal splendour.—*Lewys Dwnn*, vol. ii, p. 305,
note.

2, Thomas Pennant, Vicar of Tref Ffynon in Tegeingl;
3, Nicholas Pennant, Abbot of Dinas Basing; 4, David
Pennant, ancestor of the Pennants of Hendref Figillt;
and 5, John Pennant; and five daughters; 1, Gyenes;
2, Elen; 3, Margaret, *ob. s. p.*; 4, Margaret; and 5,
Catherine.

Edward Pennant, the eldest son, married Catherine,
daughter of Howel ab John ab David of Ysgeifiog in
Tegeingl ab Ithel Fychan ab Cynwrig ab Rotpert ab
Iorwerth ab Rhirid ab Iorwerth ab Madog ab Ednowain
Bendew, Chief of one of the Noble Tribes, who bore
argent, a chevron inter three boar's heads couped *sable*,
tusked *or*, and langued *gules*, by whom he had issue four
sons, 1, Henry, of whom presently; 2, Thomas Pennant,
ob. s. p.; 3, Nicholas Pennant, *ob. s. p.;* and 4, Maurice
Pennant; and one daughter, Jane, ux. Thomas Fychan
Conwy of Plas yn y Nant, in the parish of Meliden in
Tegeingl, ab Harri Wyn Conwy ab Reignallt ab Hyw
Conwy of Llys Bryn Euryn in Llandrillo in Rhos, son
of Robin ab Gruffydd Goch, Lord of Rhos and Rhiw-
fawniog (*argent*, a griffon passant, its wings erect, *gules*),
descended from Marchudd, Lord of Uwch Dulas.

Harri or Henry Pennant married twice. His first wife
was Margaret, daughter of Gruffydd ab John ab Gruffydd
Fychan of Pentref Llongad, descended from Ednowain
Bendew. His second wife was Elizabeth, daughter of
Robert Sonlli of Soulli, by whom he had one son, Peter
Pennant, and a daughter, Elen, ux. William Parry. By
his first wife, Margaret, he had issue one son, Nicholas, and
six daughters; 1, Jane, ux. John Davies of Kindlon; 2,
Catherine, ux. first, Randle Lloyd of Calcot, and secondly,
John Davies of Halkin or Helygen; 3, Alice, ux. Henry
ab Hyw of Fflint; 4, Elen, *ob. s. p.*; 5, Anne, ux. Hyw ab
Thomas of Chwitffordd ab Robert ab Ithel ab Icuan; and
6, Margaret, ux. Hyw Pennant ab Thomas of Llanasaff.

Nicholas Pennant, married Jane, daughter of William
Mostyn of Maes Glas Helygen, descended from Tudor
Trevor, by whom he had issue three sons, 1, Edward, 2,
Henry, and 3, Thomas Pennant; and nine daughters,

Edward Pennant married Elizabeth, daughter of Edward Giffard of Chillington, in Com. Stafford, by whom he had issue five daughters, 1, Ffrances ; 2, Anne ; 3, Elizabeth ; 4, Jane ; and 5, Mary.

PENNANT OF HENDREF VIGILLT.

Harl. MS. 4181.

David Pennant, fourth son of Thomas⊤Deili, d. and heir of John ab Deio
  Abbot of Dinas Basing.   ab Ieuan.

Elis Pen-⊤Catherine, d. of David ab   Edward Pennant of Derwen in Rhe-
  nant. | John ab Gruffydd of   lefnwyd, married Margaret, d. and
         | Tre'r Flynnon.   heir of Thomas ab John Wynn ab
                                      Ithel ab Gwyn of Rhelefnwyd.

John Pennant.⊤Jane, d. of Edward ab Rhys ab David ab Jenkin.

Peter Pennant of Hendref Vigillt.⊤Barbara, d. of John Eyton of Coed y Llai.

John Pennant of Hundref Vigillt. =   Edward Pennant of Caerwys.⊤

      Edmund Pennant, Parson of Llanarmon yn Iâl.   Margaret.

DAVIES OF DUNGREY.

Lewys Dwnn, vol. ii.

Sir John de Upton, Constable of⊤Hawys, dau. of Einion ab Gwilym ab
  Caernarvon Castle, had a grant of | Gwenwynwyn, and relict of Ieuaf
  lands in Hanmer. *Argent,* two lions | Fychan ab Ieuaf of Llwyn y Maen.
  passant gardant *azure.*

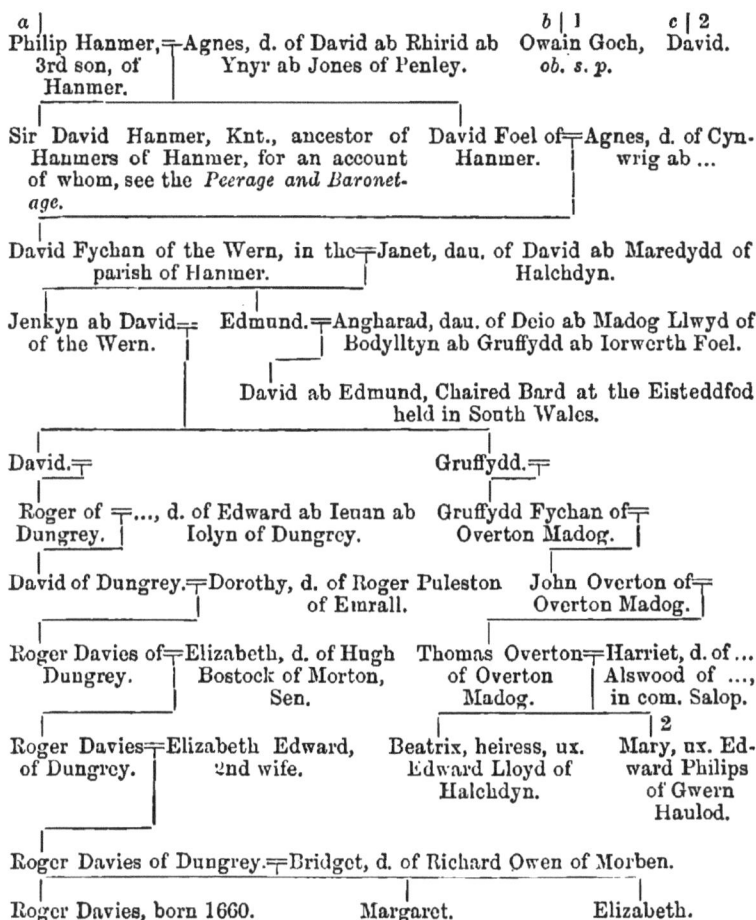

a |
Philip Hanmer,=Agnes, d. of David ab Rhirid ab
3rd son, of   Ynyr ab Jones of Penley.
Hanmer.

b | 1
Owain Goch,
ob. s. p.

c | 2
David.

Sir David Hanmer, Knt., ancestor of David Foel of=Agnes, d. of Cyn-
Hanmers of Hanmer, for an account   Hanmer. | wrig ab ...
of whom, see the *Peerage and Baronet-* |
age.

David Fychan of the Wern, in the=Janet, dau. of David ab Maredydd of
parish of Hanmer. | Halchdyn.

Jenkyn ab David== Edmund.=Angharad, dau. of Deio ab Madog Llwyd of
of the Wern. | | Bodylltyn ab Gruffydd ab Iorwerth Foel.

David ab Edmund, Chaired Bard at the Eisteddfod
held in South Wales.

David.=   Gruffydd.=

Roger of =..., d. of Edward ab Ieuan ab Gruffydd Fychan of=
Dungrey. | Iolyn of Dungrey.   Overton Madog. |

David of Dungrey.=Dorothy, d. of Roger Puleston   John Overton of=
| of Emrall.   Overton Madog. |

Roger Davies of=Elizabeth, d. of Hugh   Thomas Overton=Harriet, d. of ...
Dungrey. | Bostock of Morton,   of Overton | Alswood of ...,
| Sen.   Madog. | in com. Salop.
                                              | 2
Roger Davies=Elizabeth Edward,   Beatrix, heiress, ux.   Mary, ux. Ed-
of Dungrey. | 2nd wife.   Edward Lloyd of   ward Philips
| Halchdyn.   of Gwern
                                              Haulod.

Roger Davies of Dungrey.=Bridget, d. of Richard Owen of Morben.

Roger Davies, born 1660.   Margaret.   Elizabeth.

LORDSHIP OF Y DREWEN, OR WHITTINGTON.

Cae Cyriog MS.; Harl. MS., 4181; *Add. MSS.*, 9864-6.

The Lordship of Y Drewen, Blancheville, or Whittington, comprises the townships of Traian and the parish of Whittington, which contains the townships of Whittington, Welsh Francton, part of Old Marton, Bergheld, Daywell, Fernhill, Hindford, Henlle, Ebnall, and Halston; which last township, in which there is a chapel, formerly belonged to the Knights Hospitallers of St. John of Jerusalem.

This lordship, of which all the lands once belonged to Tudor Trevor, was given by his descendant, Tudor[1] ab Rhys Sais, who was Lord of Whittington, Chirk, Nanheudwy, and Maelor Saesneg, to his second son, Goronwy Pefr (the smart or handsome), sometimes also called Wrenoc. He married twice, his first wife being Maude, daughter of Ingelric, a noble Saxon ("who had previously had a son named William, of whom the Conqueror himself was the father");[2] and, secondly, he married Gwenllian, daughter of Reginald Broadspear.

By his first wife he had issue three sons,

    I. Sir William Befr, otherwise called Sir William de

---

[1] Tudor ab Rhys Sais was living in 1079 (13th William I), for in that year he, with his two brothers, Elidur and Iddon, slew Gwrgan, King of Powys.—*Brut y Tywysogion.*

[2] *Arch. Camb.*, 1852, p. 285.

Powys, Knight (*Llwyth Gwydd y Derwen*), Lord of
part of Whittington and Estwick.   He had an only
daughter and heiress, Gwen, who married Gwarine de
Meaux, or de Metz, a nobleman of Lorraine, and one of
the Lords Marchers, by whom he had a son, the celebrated Sir Ffulke Fitz-Warine.   As, however, by the
British laws, a female could not inherit the manors or
lordships of her ancestors, they went to the second son,
Sir Roger de Powys.

II. Sir Roger de Powys, of whom presently.

III. Jonas of Penley (*Llwyth Llanerch Banna*), or
Lord of Llanerch Banna, in the parish of Ellesmere
(*azure*, three boars passant in pale, *argent*).

Sir Roger de Powys, Lord of Whittington, Knight of
Rhodes.   He bore *vert*, a boar *or*, and married Cecilia,
daughter of Hwfa ab Iorwerth ab Gruffydd ab Ieuaf ab
Niniaf ab Cynwrig ab Rhiwallawn (*gules*, two lions
passant *argent*, for Iorwerth ab Gruffydd of Bers), by
whom he had issue four sons :

I. Sir Meurig or Sir Maurice Llwyd de Powys, Knight,
Lord of Whittington and Estwick, who was slain by his
kinsman, Sir Fulke Fitz Warine ; and thus, says Gutyn
Owain, the Lordship of Whittington went to Sir Fulke
Fitz Warine,[1] who had it confirmed to him in 1219 by
Henry III, King of England, and for which confirmation
he gave the King £262 and two coursers.[2]   Sir Maurice,
or Meurig, Llwyd, died without issue.

In an Anglo-Norman life of Sir Fulke Fitz Warine,
written in the time of Edward I, Iorwerth Drwyndwn,
it is said, "dona a Rogero de Powys, Blanche Ville e
Maylour"; and when he died, we are told that Llywelyn
ab Iorwerth, Prince of Wales, regretted his death "pur
ce qe Morys fuit son cousyn".[3]

In "Bye Gones" of the *Oswestry Advertiser*, October
6th, 1880, the following statement is made under the
heading of "Llan y Blodwell" :—

[1] *Cae Cyriog MS.*   [2] Pennant's *Tour*, vol. i, p. 323.
[3] *Lewys Dwnn*, vol. ii, p. 13.

"In the Escheat Roll, 56 Henry III (1272), the place now called *Blodwell* is written Bodewennan. Wennen (*i.e.*, Gwên) was one of the sons of Meirig de Powys, a descendant of Tudor Trevor. This Gwên, with his brother Greno—written in the grant, *Wrenoc* (Greno) and *Wennen* (Gwên)—had a grant from King John in the 2nd year of his reign, 1201, of the Lordship of Whittington, of which Fulk Fitzwarine had been temporarily deprived." Signed, "W. A. L." This statement does not agree with the pedigrees or other settlements made by Llywelyn ab Iorwerth, Prince of Wales, and confirmed by Henry III. Sir Meurig de Powys had no issue, but he left three brothers, Sir Roger, Goronwy (Wrenoc), and Owain, who may be the Wennen of the Charter.

II. Sir Roger Fychan, Knight, Lord of Estwick (*vert, a boar or*). He was declared to be the heir of his brother, Sir Meurig Llwyd, Knight, by a deed of settlement made by Llywelyn ab Iorwerth, Prince of Wales, and confirmed by Henry III, King of England. He left issue (besides a daughter named Gwerfyl, who married, first, Philip Kynaston of Stocks, ancestor of the Kynastons of Hardwicke, secondly, she married Pain ...... and thirdly, she married David Rwth) a son and heir, Maredydd of Estwick; whose only daughter and heiress, Gwerfyl, married Ieuan Foel ab Gwilym ab Cymrig Sais ab Cynwrig ab Owain ab Bleddyn ab Tudor ab Rhys Sais.[1]

III. Goronwy ab Sir Roger de Powys of Estwick married, and had issue a son, Llywelyn ab Goronwy of Estwick, the father of Llywelyn Fychan of Estwick, who married and had issue two sons,

1. Llywelyn Foel of Estwick, who married and had issue (besides two daughters, Dyddgu, ux. David Dod, by whom she had a son, Hugh Dod; and Tibot, ux. Iorwerth ab Gwilym, by whom she had a son, Bleddyn ab Iorwerth), a son and heir, Ednyfed ab Llywelyn Foel of Estwick, whose daughter and heiress, Dyddgu, mar-

[1] *Cae Cyrog MS.*; *Add. MSS.* 9864-6.

ried . . . . by whom she had a son and heir,
Jenkin Estwick of Estwick, the father of Lawrence
Estwick.

2. Gruffydd ab Llywelyn Fychan of Pentref Madog in
Tref Dudlysh yn y Waun. He married Elen, daughter of
Ednyfed Lloyd ab Iorwerth Fychan ab Iorwerth ab Awr
(see Plas Madog), by whom he was father of Llywelyn
of Pentref Madog, the father of Gruffydd of Pentref
Madog, whose daughter and heiress, Eva, married David
Bird Hên of Estwick, and, *jure uxoris*, of Pentref Madog.

IV. Owain ab Sir Roger de Powys. He married, and
had issue three daughters, co-heirs,

1. Gwerfyl, ux. Einion ab Gwilym, an illegitimate
son of Gwenwynwyn, Prince of Powys, by whom she
had an only daughter and heiress, Annest, who married,
first, Ieuaf Fychan of Llwyn y Maen, Constable of
Knockyn Castle, and, secondly, Sir John Upton of
Hanmer; 2, Gwen, ux. Rhys Goch ab Rhys Gochyn;
and 3, Eva, ux. Howel ab Madog ab Howel.

In 1220, the Castle of Whittington was dismantled
by the Welsh, as we may infer from Henry having
given Sir Fulke Fitz Warine permission to fortify it.
The memory of this is still preserved in 'a room in the
gateway, by a figure of a knight on horseback, coarsely
painted on the wall, with the following lines, now almost
obliterated, placed beneath :—

" This was Sir Ffoulke Fitz Warren, late a great and valiant
      knight,
  Who kept the Britons still in awe, and ofttimes put to
      flight.
  He of this castle owner was, and held it by command
  Of Henry, late surnamed the Third, and King of all this
      land.
  His grandfather, a Lorrainer, by fame was much befriended,
  Who Peverley's dau'r took to wife, from whom this Ffoulke
      descended.
  His ancient feats of chivalry in annals are recorded ;
  Our King of England afterwards, him baron made and
      lorded."[1]

---

[1] Pennant's *Tour*, vol. i, p. 327.

Y Dref Wen, or Whittington, was celebrated by Llywarch Hên as the place where Cynddylan, King of Powys, was slain in 613.[1]

TRAIAN.

Cae Cyriog MS.

Gutyn Owain, the historian of the Abbeys of Basingwerke, or Dinas Basing and Strata Florida, who was "Pencerdd" and bard to David ab Ieuan ab Iorwerth, Abbot of Valle Crucis,[2] and also to the Abbots of the two first-mentioned monasteries, lived at Traian in this lordship. He was a great herald and genealogist, and wrote an epitome of the British history, which was preserved in the Abbey of Dinas Basing, and from this circumstance was called *Llyfr Du Basing*. It is now in the possession of the heir of the late Thomas Taylor Griffith of Wrexham and Cae Cyriog, Esq. Gutyn Owain was nephew of John ab Richard, Abbot of Valle Crucis, the immediate predecessor of the Abbot David ab Ieuan ab Iorwerth.

His pedigree, according to Lewys Dwnn, and preserved in the *Cae Cyriog MS.*, is as follows :—

Gutyn Owain ab Huw ab Owain ab Iorwerth ab Hwfa Llwyd ab Gruffydd ab Adda ab Tegwared ab Iorwerth ab Trahaiarn ab Cynddelw ab Rhirid ab Pod ab Pasgen ab Helig ab Glanawg ab Gwgan Gleddyfrudd, son of

---

[1] *Arch. Camb.*, 3rd Series, vol. ix, p. 148.

[2] David, Abbot of Valle Crucis, was the son of Ieuan ab Iorwerth ab Ieuan Baladr ab Y Cethin ab Ieuan ab Iorwerth Fawr ab Iorwerth ab Heilin ab Madog ab David ab Howel ab Meurig, who had half of the lordship of Trevor in Nanheudwy, and fourth son of Tudor ab Rhys Sais, Lord of Chirk and Nanheudwy (*Harl. MS.* 4181). He was consecrated Bishop of St. Asaph, April 26th, in 1500. He died in 1503, as is supposed, at the Abbey, and was probably buried there ; where it is presumed he lived, on account of having no episcopal palace left standing in his diocese, since it was destroyed in the wars of Owain Glyndwr (Willis' *Survey of St. Asaph*).

Caradog Freichfras, King of Fferlis and Brycheiniog, and one of the Knights of King Arthur's Round Table, who bore *sable*, a chevron inter three spear's heads *argent*, the points imbrued proper.

According to the books of Thomas ab Ieuan, the above Hwfa Llwyd was the son of Gruffydd Goch ab David ab Tegwared.

David ab Teg-=Tangwystl, d. of Madog ab Cyfnerth ab Cubelyn ab Lly-
wared. | warch ab Llywarch Goch ab Llywarch Holbwrch, Lord
| of Meriadog. *Vert, a stag trippant argent, attired or.*
|
Gruffydd Goch =
|
Hwfa =Gwenllian, d. of Iorwerth ab Meilir   Madog   Tudur   Gruffydd.
Llwyd. | Goch ab Meilir ab Rhys Goch ab   Llwyd.   Llwyd.   Goch.
| Rhys Gethin, Lord of Llanymddy-
| fri. *Argent, a lion rampant sable*
| armed, langued and crowned *gules*.
|
Iorwerth.=Agnes, dau. of Gruffydd ab Cadwgan ab Meilir Eyton, Lord of
| Eyton, Erlys, and Bwras. *Ermine, a lion rampant azure.*
|
Owain ab Iorwerth.=Gwenllian, d. of Gruffydd ab Einion Bach.
|
Huw ab Owain.=..., d. of Richard ab...of Rhiwabon, and sister   David ab=
| of John ab Richard, Abbot of Valle Crucis   Owain. |
| Abbey.
|
David ab   Gruffydd ab Huw ab Owain, | Angharad, ux. Llywelyn,   Gwenllian,
Huw ab   *alias* Guttyn Owain, *ob.* ..., | 2nd son of Gruffydd ab   ux. Howel
Owain.   and was buried at Strata | Rhys ab Gruffydd ab   Fychan ab
     Florida Abbey, 14... | Madog Llwyd of Bryn   Howel of
                                Cunallt.   Croes Os-
                                                wald.
|
Goronwy[1] ab David=
|
Tudor ab Goronwy.

It is uncertain when Guttyn Owain died, but we find that " the first step" taken by the Earl of Richmond after his accession to the throne in 1485 was a commission issued to the Abbot of Llanegwestl, or Valle Crucis, Dr. Owain Pool, Canon of Hereford, and John King, Herald-at-Arms, " to make inquisition concerning Owain Tudor", his grandfather. Dr. Powel, in his *Historie of Cambria*, printed in 1584, mentions this com-

[1] *Harl. MS.* 1972.

mission, and states "that the commissioners, coming into Wales, travelled in that matter, and used the helps of Sir John Leiat, a priest, Guttyn Owain Bardh, and Gruffydd ab Llywelyn ab Ieuan Fychan of Llanerch in Dyffryn Clwyd, and others, in search of the Brytish or Welsh bookes of petigrees, out of which they drew his perfect genealogie".[1]

CHARTER ROLL, 2 EDW. I, No. 39 (1274).

P' ffulcone filio Warine.

R' Archiepis'[1] etc. sal't'm. Sciatis nos concessisse et hac carta n'r'a confirmasse d'i et fr' n'ro ffulconi fil' Warini q'd ip'e et h'edes sui imp'petuu' h'eant lib'am Warenna' in om'ib' d'nicis t'ris suis de Wytinton jux' Oswaldestr' dum t'n t're ille no' sint infra metas foreste n're. Ita' q'd nullus intret t'ras illas ad fugand' in eis u'l' ad aliquid capiend' quod ad Warrenna' p'tineat sine licentia et voluntate ip'ius fulcon' v'l h'edum suor' sup' forisf'c'uram n'ram decem librar'. Q're volum' et firmit' p'cipim' p' nob' et h'edibus q'd p'd'cus fulco et h'des sui imp'petuu' h'eant lib'am warenna' in om'ib' d'nicis t'ris suis p'dcis. Dum tamen etc. Ita' q'd, etc. sicut p'd'c'm est. Hiis testib' Edm' fre' n're, Joh' de Warrenn' Com' Suff. Henr' de Lacy Com Linc', Rob'o de Brus Com' de Kanck, Ric'o de Brus, Rob'o fil' Joh'is, Petro de Chaumpnent et aliis. Dat' p' manu' n'ram apud Ab' conway in Suandon xxvj die Marc'.

FULK FITZ WARREN OF WHITTINGTON.

Among the Records of ye Court of Chancery in the Tower of London, that is to say, the *Inquisitiones post mortem* of the 23 Edw. III, Part 1, No. 39, is thus contained. Ao. 1349.

EDWARD by the Grace of God King of England and France and Lord of Ireland, To his beloved John de Swinnerton his Escheator in ye county of Salop Greeting *Inasmuch* as Fulk fitz Warren held of Us in Capite on the day of his death as we are informed, We command you that without fail you take into our hands all the lands and tenements of which the said

---

[1] *Lewys Dwnn*, vol. i, XIV.

Fulk was seised in his demesne of as of fee of your Baliwick on the day on which he died and cause the same to be safely kept untill We shall thereupon otherwise command. And by the oath of good and lawfull men of your Baliwick by whom the truth of the matter may be better known you diligently enquire how much lands the said Fulk held of Us in Capite as well as in demesne as in Service in your Baliwick on the day on which he died and how much of others and by what Service and how much those lands are worth yearly in all issues, and on what day the said Fulk died and who is next heir and of what age. *And* the Inquisition thereupon distinctly and openly made, without Delay you send to Us under your Seal and the Seals of those by whom the same shall be made and this Writ. *Witness* myself at Westminster the 20th day of August in the year of our reign of England the 23 and of our Reign of France the tenth.

THE MARCHES OF WALES.

An Inquisition taken before John Swynnerton Eschaetor of the Lord the King in the County of Salop and the marches of Wales adjacent at Shrewsbury on Friday next after the Feast of St. Michael, in the 23rd year of the reign of King Edward the third after the Conquest that is to say according to the tenor of the Writ of the said Lord the King to this Inquisition served, by the oath of Madoc ap Zerward David ap Kenewrick, Howell ap David, Madoc ap David ap Howell Payn ap Ithel Ievan ap Ada, Ierwerth Vauchan, Ievan ap Ithell Ievan Meiller, Madoc ap David Payn ap Ierworth and Howell ap Heillez. *Who* say upon their Oath that Fulk fitz Warryn held in his demesne as of Fee on the day on which he died the Manor of Whytynton with the Appurt's in the Marches of Wales aforesaid of the Lord the King in Capite by service of one Knights fee. In which Manor there is a certain Castle which is worth nothing yearly beyond Reprises, because it wants every year for repairing of the Houses and Walls there 40s. And there is a certain Garden·which is worth yearly 6d. And there is a certain Dovehouse which is worth yearly 12d. And there is there two Water Mills which used to be worth yearly 40s. and now are worth only 20s. by reason of the Pestilence, because the tenants are dead in the present pestilence. And there is two Ponds, the fishery thereof is worth yearly 2s. And there is a certain Wood, the underwood whereof is worth yearly 2s. and the Past're thereof is common. And there is a certain Park in which there is no underwood and the Pasture thereof is worth nothing yearly beyond the sustentation of the wild beast there. And there is a certain Chase which the Jurors know not how to extend because there is no wood and Pasture there but in Common. And there is there two Carucates of land which used to be worth yearly 20s. and not more because the land could not be ploughed by reason of the Stones and now is worth only 10s. because no one would lease the same. And there is five Acres of Meadow which are worth yearly 20s. and they were mowed and taken away in the life of the said Fulk, there used to be rent of Assize of free (tenants) there 60s. and it was paid at the terms at the Birth of our Lord and the nativity of S't John the Baptist in equal Portions, and now there is only 20s. at the terms aforesaid and this by reason of the Pestilence. The Pleas and Perquisites of Courts there used to be worth nearly 40s. and now they are worth only 13s. 4d. Also they say that the said Fulk died on Wednesday before the feast of the Nativity of the blessed Virgin Mary last past. And they say that Fulk son of y'e said Fulk is the next Heir of the said Fulk and was of the age of 9 years at the feast of S't James the Apostle last Past. *In Testimony* whereof the said Jurors to this Inquisition have put their Hands and Seals.

LLANERCH BANNA.

Harl. MS. 4181.

Goronwy, Lord of part of Whittington, Llanerch Banna, and Estwick, the second son of Tudor ab Rhys Sais, gave the lordship of Llanerch Banna to his third son,

Ionas ab Goronwy of Penley (Llwyth Llanerch Banna)

Lord of Llanerch Banna, bore *azure*, three boars passant in pale *argent*, tusked and unguled *or*.   He married Gwladys, daughter of Jenkin ab Adam Herbert, Lord of Gwern Ddu, and Gwenllian, his wife, daughter of Sir Aaron ab Rhys ab Bledri, Knight of the Sepulchre, by whom he had issue five sons,

i. Ynyr ab Ionas, of whom presently.

ii. David ab Ionas.

iii. Gwilym ab Ionas.

iv. Rhirid ab Ionas, the father of David, the father of Tudor, the father of Goronwy, who married Margaret, daughter of Llywelyn Ddu of Abertanad, ab Gruffydd ab Iorwerth Foel.

v. Goronwy ab Ionas.

vi. Llywelyn ab Ionas, the father of David, the father of Llywelyn, the father of Ieuan Llwyd, whose only daughter and heiress, Eliw, married Gruffydd ab Madog ab Einion, ancestor of the Bromfields of Bryn y Wiwer in Rhiwabon.

Ynyr ab Ionas of Penley, in the parish of Ellesmere, Lord of Llanerch Banna, married Eleanor, daughter of Lison ab Ieuan of Neath, by whom he had issue three sons,

i. Gruffydd ab Ynyr, of whom presently.

ii. Rhirid ab Ynyr of Penley (see p. 391).

iii. Ithel ab Ynyr, who was the father of Howel, the father of David, the father of Howel ab David, who married Myfanwy, daughter of Maredydd ab Robert ab Howel of Cynllaith, by whom he had a son, Rhys ab Howel, who married Eva, daughter of Deio ab Iorwerth ab Ieuan Dlysswr.

Gruffydd ab Ynyr ab Ionas, the eldest son, married, and had issue four sons, 1, Rhirid, of whom presently ; 2, Minro Fychan ; 3, David ab Gruffydd ; and 4, Iorwerth Goch.

Rhirid ab Gruffydd married, and had issue two sons,

ii. Tudor ab Rhirid, whose only daughter and heiress, Tanglwyst, married Iorwerth Foel Ddu.

ii. David ab Rhirid, who married Gwenhwyfar, daughter of Ednyfed ab Iorwerth ab Einion Goch, Lord

of Sonlli, by whom he had issue four sons, 1, Tudor ab
David ; 2, Ednyfed ; 3, Rhirid Llwyd ; and 4, Cynwrig,
and one daughter, Gwenhwyfar.

LLANERCH BANNA.—PENLEY.

Harl. MS. 4181.

Rhirid of Penley, the second son of Ynyr ab Ionas of
Penley, Lord of Llanerch Banna, was slain in a sea-fight
at the relief of Rochelle, 46 Edw. III, 1373. He married Jane, daughter of Tudor ab Goronwy ab Ednyfed
Fychan, ancestor of the Royal House of Tudor, by whom
he had issue three sons,

I. David Goch, ancestor of Sir Matthew Goch, Knt.
(see p. 396).

II. Tudor ab Rhirid of Penley, who married . . . .
daughter of Ithel Anwyl ab Bleddyn, a younger son of
Ithel Llwyd ab Ithel Gam, Lord of Mostyn, son of
Maredydd ab Uchdryd ab Edwyn ab Goronwy, Prince
of Tegeingl. Ithel Anwyl lived at Ewlo Castle in
Merffordd, and was one of the Captains of Tegeingl to
keep the English from invading the country. He bore,
party per pale *or* and *gules*, two lions rampant addorsed
counterchanged, a sword pointed downwards *argent*, the
hilt *or*, between them. By this lady, Tudor had an only
daughter and heiress, Margaret, who married David ab

Madog ab Rhirid ab Cadwgan ab Owain Fychan, ancestor of the Dymocks of Penley Hall.

III. David ab Rhirid, who married Mali, daughter of Ednyfed ab Iorwerth ab Einion Goch, Lord of Sonlli and Eyton Uchaf (*ermine, a lion rampant sable*), by whom he had two daughters, co-heiresses,

I. Margaret, ux. Philip Phichdan, whose only daughter and heiress, Alice, married Madog Maelor ab Thomas, fourth son of Owain ab Bleddyn ab Rhys Sais, and ancestor of the Pennants of Downing and Penrhyn Castle.

II. Annesta, ux. Philip Hanmer ab Sir John Upton of Hanmer, Knt.

LLANERCH BANNA.—DYMOCK OF PENLEY.

Harl. MS. 4181.

Madog ab Rhirid ab Cadwgan ab Owain Fychan, 5th son of Owain ab⫤ Bleddyn ab Tudor ab Rhys Sais. See vol. i, p. 312.

David ab Madog.⫤Margaret, d. and co-heiress of Tudor ab Rhirid ab Ynyr ab Ionas of Penley in Llanerch Banna. *Azure*, three boars passant in pale *argent*, tusked and unguled *or*.

David Dymock⫤Margaret, d. of David Foel of Hanmer, ab Philip Hanmer
alias Dai ab Ma-│of Hanmer ab Sir John Upton of Hanmer, Constable of
dog of Penley. │Caernarvon Castle, *temp.* Edward I. *Argent*, two lions passant gardant *azure*.

Ieuan Dymock of⫤Lleuci, d. of Madog ab Llywelyn of Halchdyn, the eldest
Penley. │son of Ednyfed Gam of Llys Pengwern. Party per bend sinister *ermine* and *ermines*, a lion rampant *or*.

a │   b │

a |
Thomas Dy-⊤Margaret, d. and co-
mock of Pen- | heir of Gruffydd ab
ley, and of | Morgan Goch of Wil-
Willington, | lington, 6th son of
jure uxoris. | Gruffydd of Maelor
| Saesneg, ab Iorwerth
| Foel.
|
|
Thomas Dymock of Pen-⊤Margaret, d. of Sir Randle Brereton of Malpas, in
ley and Willington.   v   Cheshire, Knt. *Argent, two bars sable.*

b |
David Dymock, living⊤Cadwen, d. of
17 Henry VI. | Howel ab
| Ithel.
|
Llywelyn Dymock,   Robert Dy-
Chaplain, 13 Henry   mock, 29 Henry
VII.   VI.

The above-named Thomas Dymock had issue by Margaret Brereton, his wife, besides two daughters, Mary, ux. Jenkin Hanmer of Ffens, ab Gruffydd Fychan Hanmer ab Edward Hanmer of Y Ffens, fourth son of Sir Jenkin Hanmer of Hanmer, Knt., and Alice, ux. Humphrey Hanmer, nine sons,

I. Randal Dymock, of whom presently.

II. Thomas Dymock of Halchdyn, who married Janet, sister and heir of John ab Owain ab Roger Puleston, by whom he had issue four sons, 1, John Dymock, *ob. s. p.* ; 2, Thomas Dymock, 1595, who married Alice, daughter of John Broughton, and had issue a son Thomas ; 3, William Dymock, *ob. s. p.* ; 4, Richard Dymock ; and three daughters, 1, Margaret, ux. Pyers Griffith of Warwickshire ; 2, Christian, ux. John Gee of Warwickshire ; and 3, Elizabeth, ux. Robert Puleston of Wrexham.

III. Humphrey Dymock, who married a daughter of the Lord Hussey, by whom he had issue, besides two daughters, Mari and Catherine, ux. Thomas Tresso, three sons, 1, Francis Dymock, who, by Margaret, his wife, daughter and heir of . . . had issue a son, George, and a daughter ; 2, Harri ; and 3, Thomas Dymock.

IV. Jenkyn Dymock, the father of William Dymock.

V. Urien ; VI. Edmund ; VII. Charles ; VIII. Edward ; and IX. Philip.

Randal Dymock of Penley and Willington married Elizabeth, daughter of Gruffydd Hanmer of the Ffens, ab Edward Hanmer of the Ffens, ab Sir Jenkin Hanmer, Knt., ab Sir David Hanmer of Hanmer, Knt., Chief

Justice of England in 1383 (*argent*, two lions passant gardant *azure*), by whom he had issue, besides four daughters, 1, Elizabeth, ux. John Yonge of Croxton ; 2, Alice, ux. Thomas ab Owain of Willington ; 3, Margaret, ux. Richard Gillam of Coventeri ; and 4, Elen, ux. John Wynn Lake, two sons,

i. Edward Dymock, of whom presently.

ii. Humphrey Dymock, who married Elen, daughter and heir of William Davison ab Jenkin ab David ab Ednyfed ab Goronwy ab Owain of Penlees, by whom he had issue one son, Randal, who died *s. p.*, and four daughters, 1, Elizabeth, ux. John Wynn Roberts of Hafod y Bwch ; 2, Anne, ux., first, Thomas Bird of Estwick, secondly, ux. Robert Tunbridge ; 3, Eleanor, ux., first, Edward Broughton of Marchwiail, in the manor of Rhiwabon, secondly, ux. Thomas Sherer ; and 4, Catherine, who married, first, John Lutley, and, secondly, William Knight of Chester.

Edward Dymock of Penley and Willington married four times. His first wife was Catherine, daughter of Richard Conwy, by whom he had issue two sons, Humphrey and Randal, who both died *s. p.*, and five daughters, 1, Elen, ux., first, Pyers Salusbury, secondly, Hyw Gwyn ab Humphrey; 2, Jane, ux. Richard ab David ab Maredydd of Pentref Sianet ; 3, Catherine, ux. George Wynn of Croes Oswald ; 4, Rose ; and 5, Margaret, ux. William ab Thomas Bedo.

His second wife was Mawdlin, daughter of Roger Puleston, by whom he had issue two sons, 1, William, of whom presently ; and 2, Edward Dymock ; and two daughters, 1, Eleanor, ux. Sir William Hanmer of Ffens, Knt., who was knighted 23rd July 1603, and died in 1621 ; and 2, Dorothy, who married, first, Robert Wynn of Conwy, and secondly, Sir William Williams of Vaenol, co. Caernarvon, Bart.

His third wife was Catherine, daughter of William Mostyn, by whom he had no issue.

His fourth wife was Margaret, daughter of Thomas Kynaston, by whom he had issue a son, Thomas, and a daughter, Anne.

William Dymock of Penley and Willington, married Margaret, daughter of William Hanmer of Ffens, by whom he had issue two sons, 1, Humphrey Dymock, who married Anne, daughter of Sir Thomas Hanmer of Hanmer, Knt., and Catherine, his wife, daughter of Thomas Mostyn of Mostyn, Esq. He died in 1650, and was the father of nine children, who all died *s. p.*; 2, Edward Dymock, of whom presently; and four daughters, 1, Magdalene, ux. William Lloyd of Penley; 2, Elizabeth, ux. Lapthorn Clarke; 3, Mary; and 4, Elen, ux. . . . . Touchet of . . . . in co. Chester.

Edward Dymock of Penley succeeded his brother, and married Mary, daughter of John Davenport, and had issue a son and heir,

Edward Dymock of Penley, who died in 1705, and was buried at Hanmer, married Mary, daughter of David Jones of Oakenholt, and had, besides a daughter, Elizabeth, ux. Edward Morral of Plâs Iolyn, three sons,

I. Edward Dymock of Penley died unmarried, and left the Penley estate to his great nephew.

II. William Dymoke, father of John Dymock, who by Elizabeth, his wife, was the father of Edward Dymock, the inheritor of Penley.

III. John Dymock, *ob. s. p.*

Edward Dymock of Penley, who was born in 1730, married Elizabeth, daughter of Humphrey Brown, by whom he had issue three sons, 1, Edward, his successor; 2, John; and 3, William.

Edward Dymock of Penley, born in 1752. He married, 8th January 1774, Mary, daughter of Edward Edwards of Pentref Heilin, and, dying in 1784, left, besides four daughters, 1, Christian; 2, Elizabeth; 3, Frances; and 4, Anne; a son and heir,

Edward Dymock of Penley Hall and of Ellesmere, J.P. and D.L., born 16th December 1774, married in 1804 Mary, daughter of John Jones of Coed y Glyn in Maelor Gymraeg, by whom he had issue, besides a daughter, Mary Anne, who married in 1825 Robert Darwin Vaughton of Whitchurch, four sons,

I. Edward Humphrey, born 1809.
II. John, born in 1816.
III. Robert Myddleton, born in 1817.
IV. Thomas Biddulph, born in 1828.

GOCH OF MAELOR,

AFTERWARDS OF THE FOREST OF DEAN.

Harl. MS. 4181.

David Goch of Maelor, the eldest son of Rhirid ab Ynyr of Penley, married Catherine, daughter of Howel ab David, lineally descended from Owain Gwynedd, King of North Wales, by whom he had issue a son and heir,

Sir Matthew Goch of Maelor, Knight, who was born there in 1386 (10 Richard II), a most valiant and renowned soldier, Captain to King Henry V and King Henry VI, Governor of Tanceaux, Le Hermitage, Tanqueville, and Liscaux. It appears, from a poem by Guto'r Glyn, that he was at one time a prisoner in France. Having obtained his release, he returned to Maelor. In 1439, however, he appears to have settled in the Forest of Dean in Gloucestershire. Being at last sent by the Lord Scales to assist the Lord Mayor and the Londoners against that arch-rebel, Jack Cade, he was slain upon London Bridge, valiantly fighting in defence of the

King and City, July the 4th, 1450, in the sixty-fourth year of his age, and 29th Henry VI.

He married Margaret, daughter (by Margaret, his wife, daughter of Sir Bryan de Harley, Knight, Lord of Brampton Bryan, in the county of Hereford, the ancestor of the Harleys, Earls of Oxford) of Rhys Moythe, Lord of Castell Edwin, ab Rhys Moythe or Mowdde ab David Mowdde, ab David ab Gruffydd Foel, Lord of Castell Edwin, son of Ifor ab Cadifor ab Gwaethfoed, Lord of Ceredigion (*or*, a lion rampant regardant *sable*), by whom he had issue three sons, 1, Geoffrey Goch ; 2, Matthew Goch ; and 3, David Goch ; and a daughter, Margaret.

Geoffrey Goch of the Forest of Dean was born when his father was fifty-three years of age, and was the first of this family that was born in England. He was born May 17th, 1439, 18 Henry VI, and aged eleven years at the death of his father. He married Elizabeth, daughter and sole heir of Avery Traherne, Esq., ab William Traherne ab John ab Traherne ab Suan ab Suich, who bore, 1, *argent*, a griffon rampant *sable*, his fore legs, wings, and beak *or*, armed *gules;* 2, *argent*, a lion rampant *gules*, crowned *sable;* 3, *gules*, three towers triple turreted *or;* 4, Rhys Goch ; 5, Caerlleon ; 6, *vert*, a chev. inter wolves' heads erased *argent*. Her mother was Maud, daughter of Thomas ab Gwilym ab Jenkin of Gwerndu. Elizabeth died in 1493, and Geoffrey followed her, November 28th, 1512, 4 Henry VIII, aged seventy-three, leaving issue a son and heir,

John Goch, who married Jane, daughter and heir of James Bridges, Esq., and died July 23rd, 1538, aged sixty-eight, leaving issue a son and heir,

Robert Goch, who married, first, Margaret, daughter of Sir Walter Mantell of Heyford in Northamptonshire, Knight. She died July 24th, 1540, leaving issue a son and heir, Barnaby Goch. Robert married, secondly, Helen Gadbury, by whom he had issue a second son, Robert Goch, and at his death, which occurred May 5th, 1557, in the fifty-seventh year of his age, he was succeeded by his eldest son,

Barnaby Goch, who married Mary, daughter and co-heir of Thomas Darell of Scotney Castle in Sussex, by Mary, his wife, daughter and co-heir of Thomas Roydon of Fortune House, in Peckham in Kent (*azure*, a lion rampant *or*, crowned *argent*, the shoulder charged with a cinquefoil, armed and langued *gules*), by whom he had six sons, 1, Matthew Goch ; 2, Thomas Goch ; 3, Barnaby Goch, Doctor of Canon and Civil Law ; 4, William, *ob. s. p.* ; 5, Henry Goch, Fellow of Trinity College, Cambridge ; and 6, Robert Goch, Fellow of All Souls' College, Oxford.   Of the daughters, Mary, the eldest, was the first Lady Abbess of the Poor Clares in Gravelines.

Matthew Goch of Alvingham married Alice, third daughter of Thomas Coney of Basingthorpe, in Lincoln-shire, and Alice, his wife, daughter of Sir Thomas Leigh of Stone Leigh in Warwickshire, Knt., (barry of eight, *argent* and *azure*, on a bend between two cotises *or*, three tortoises), by whom he had issue eight sons, of whom the eldest, Barnaby Goch, was born in 1591, and seven daughters.

The crest of this family is an arm erected in armour, holding up a dragon's head erased *vert*.   Motto, "Post Tristia Leta".

A POEM BY GUTO'R GLYN[1] IN PRAISE OF SIR
MATTHEW GOCH, KNT.

Translated by Howel W. Lloyd, Esq., M.A.

> When in our day is known to fame,
> In Normandy, a hero's name,
> To Matthew will the boast belong,
> Yclep'd " The Red", by wine made strong,
> Of valiant captains all the soul,
> Chiefest of all the muster-roll.
> O'er all the youth, an eagle he,
> Rolando's twin in chivalry,

---

[1] Guto' Glyn was a native of the comot of Nanheudwy.

Shows Arthur's front to those of France,
Fells countless foes with crimson'd lance.
Red Matthew's lance o'erthrows a host,
He charges—and the battle 's lost.
Lo, Matthew here, and England all
Rushes to Matthew's rousing call.
From childhood hath he learnt to bear
The bell in battle with his spear.
His valour stood in sooth confest,
When on Rhone's bank, his lance in rest,
Like some stone ball from gun propell'd,
A fort's fierce opposition quell'd.
Gallant the feat—he led his band
A dance thro' Maine's and Anjou's land,
By all the saints ! a glorious sight,
Rolando tearing through the fight.
Their gift to us in him we hail
The shepherd[1] of men clad in mail.
Of purpose pure—the praise is rare—
This man of force from Maelor fair.
The branch of some widespreading tree
Hath just his stately dignity.
No vantage 'scapes his ken, a wall
Steel-proof is Matthew, ne'er to fall.
The men by his command controll'd
For daring deeds as bulls are bold.
Like mangonels his warrior bands
Range Maine's and Anjou's ravaged lands.
Tho' pitiless their onward pace,
Like flowers of war, they tread with grace,
The highways and the forests clear
With hue and cry, like hunt of deer.
For Matthew's guerdon, Mary ! give
Long Matthew and his men to live.
That he was ta'en, when 'twas heard tell,
Fear on the afflicted minstrels fell ;
Cities, while he a captive lay,
For news frequented were each day ;
Keen to the Cymru is the blow,
Tears for their kinsman freely flow,
For him let not their fright increase,
For Matthew's bondage soon will cease,

---

[1] Cf. the Homeric "Ποίμενα λαῶν".—H. W. Ll.

The cost contributed conclude
His shorten'd term of solitude.
Bring all your gifts—a double grief
At double cost deserves relief.
His strength and stature none gainsay,
The Dauphin's people we must pay ;
'Tis not that Matthew loves the gold,
Tho' greed be rife, and worldlings cold ;
The coin that buys from prison-cell
Our kin, doth other hoard excel ;
He is not emulous of strife,
Nor yet for office loves his life.
Not one is he to barter fame,
Or for Job's wealth belie his name ;
The world on praise sets mighty store,
Her Melwas[1] still is Maelor's lore.
To the Cymraeg this Cymro good
Be honoured by proud Cymru's brood :
Let England his renown enhance,
And—where he frets for freedom—France !

H. W. Ll.

---

[1] *I.e.*, to Maelor, Matthew in glory is equal to Melwas. A strange comparison, as the Melwas of Cymric legendary lore eloped with Gwenhwyfar, Arthur's queen, whose suite he surprised by starting up arrayed in leaves like a " Jack in the Green", as she went a-Maying. But the temptation involved in the alliteration of Maelor and Melwas bore down the judgment of our bard.— H. W. Ll.

EYTON OF PENTREF MADOG IN DUDLYSTON.

Cae Cyriog MS.; Harl. MS. 4181; *Lewis Dwnn,* vol. i, p. 324.

Sir Roger de Powys, Lord of Whittington and Knight of Rhodes, who bore *vert* a boar *or*, settled this estate and the manor of Estwick upon his fourth son, Goronwy, Lord of Estwick, who was the father of Llywelyn, the father of Llywelyn Fychan, who had two sons, Llywelyn Foel of Estwick, ancestor of the Estwicks of Estwick, and Gruffydd ab Llywelyn, who had Pentref Madog. Gruffydd married Elen, daughter of Ednyfed Llwyd ab Iorwerth Fychan ab Iorwerth ab Awr, ancestor of the Lloyds of Plâs Madog, by whom he was father of Llywelyn, the father of Gruffudd ab Llywelyn, who had an only daughter, Eva, heiress of Pentref Madog, who married David Bird or Bride Hên of Estwick.

David Bird Hên, *jure uxoris* of Pentref Madog, was the son of Ieuan ab David of Estwick, ab Ieuan ab

Llywelyn ab Cynwrig ab Rhiwallawn (*ermine*, a lion rampant *sable*, armed and langued *gules*). By his wife, Eva, he had a son and heir,

Philip Bird of Pentref Madog, who married Alice, daughter of John ab Richard ab Madog ab Llywelyn of Halchdyn in Maelor Saesneg, by whom he had three daughters, co-heirs,

1. Margaret, heiress of Pentref Madog, who married James Eyton of Dudleston.

2. Mawd, ux. David Kynaston of Groicot.

3. Anne, ux. Edward Yonge of Bryn Iorcyn yn Yr Hôb.

James Eyton, *jure uxoris* of Pentref Madog, was the son and heir (by Elizabeth, his wife, daughter and heiress of Owain, by Gwenllian, his wife, daughter and heir of Einion Fychan, ab Gruffydd ab Owain ab Howel ab Madog of Dudlyston, descended from Madog, Lord of Yr Hendwr in Edeyrnion, who bore *argent*, on a chevron *gules*, three fleurs-de-lys *or*) of John Eyton of Dudlyston, youngest son of William Eyton of Eyton Isaf (*ermine*, a lion rampant *azure*, armed and langued *gules*).

James Eyton of Pentref Madog, had issue by his wife Margaret a son and heir,

William Eyton of Pentref Madog, who was living in 1592, and married Dorothy, daughter of James Eyton of Eyton (*ermine*, a lion rampant *azure*), by whom he had issue a son and heir,

James Eyton of Pentref Madog, who died 9th February 1630, and was buried at Dudlyston, married Mary, daughter of Sir Richard Bulkeley of Baron Hill, in Môn, Knt., by whom he had a son and heir,

Sir Robert Eyton of Pentref Madog, Knt. This gentleman was taken prisoner, with Sir Gerard Eyton of Eyton, Knight Banneret, and Mr. Edisbury of Erddig, at Eyton, by the Parliament troops under Colonel Mytton in 1643. He married Joyce, daughter and heiress of Francis Lloyd of Hardwick, by whom he had issue three sons, 1, Robert Eyton; 2, James; and 3, Gruffydd Eyton; and two daughters, Penelope and Arabella.

WYNN OF PENTREF MORGAN.

Add. MS. 9865.

Hwfa ab Ieuaf ab Iorwerth ab Howel ab Owain ab Bleddyn ab Owain⊤
⠀⠀⠀⠀⠀Brogyntyn, Lord of Dinmael and Edeyrnion.⠀⠀⠀⠀⠀⠀⠀⠀|

Iorwerth⠀ab⊤Gwerfyl, d. of Madog ab Iorwerth ab Madog ab Rhirid Flaidd.
⠀Hwfa.⠀⠀|⠀⠀*Vert*, a chevron inter three wolf's heads erased *argent*,
⠀⠀⠀⠀⠀⠀|⠀⠀langued *gules*.

David ab Ior-⊤Margaret, d. of Madog Goch ab Madog ab Cynwrig ab Heilin
⠀⠀werth.⠀⠀|⠀⠀ab Trahaiarn ab Iddon ab Rhys Sais. *Argent*, a chevron
⠀⠀⠀⠀⠀⠀|⠀⠀inter three boar's heads couped *gules*, tusked *or*, and lan-
⠀⠀⠀⠀⠀⠀|⠀⠀gued *azure*.

Gruffydd⠀ab⊤Margaret, d. of Y Badi ab Howel ab Ieuan Fychan ab Ieuan
⠀⠀David.⠀⠀|⠀⠀Gethin ab Madog Cyffin. Party per fess *sable* and *argent*,
⠀⠀⠀⠀⠀⠀|⠀⠀a lion rampant counterchanged.

Madog, *jure*⊤Isabel, d. and heiress of David ab Einion ab Ednyved Ddu
⠀*uxoris* of⠀|⠀ab Iorwerth ab Goronwy Ddu ab Morgan of Pentref Mor-
⠀⠀Pentref⠀⠀|⠀gan, ab Iddon ab Rhys Sais. *Argent*, a chevron inter three
⠀⠀Morgan.⠀|⠀boar's heads couped *gules*, tusked *or*, and langued *azure*.

David ab Ma-⊤Margaret, d. of David ab Llywelyn⠀⠀John ab Madog, ances-
⠀dog of Pen-⠀|⠀⠀⠀ab Maredydd Fychan.⠀⠀⠀⠀⠀tor of the Lloyds of
⠀tref Morgan.|⠀⠀⠀⠀⠀⠀⠀⠀⠀⠀⠀⠀⠀⠀⠀⠀⠀⠀⠀⠀Ebnall.

John Wynn of Pentref Morgan.⊤Elizabeth, dau. of William Leigh ab John
⠀⠀⠀⠀⠀⠀⠀⠀⠀⠀⠀⠀⠀⠀⠀⠀⠀|⠀⠀⠀⠀⠀⠀⠀⠀⠀Leigh.

Thomas Wynn of Pentref Morgan.⊤Ermine, d. of David ab Roger ab David
⠀⠀⠀⠀⠀⠀⠀⠀⠀⠀⠀⠀⠀⠀⠀⠀⠀⠀⠀|⠀⠀⠀⠀⠀ab Jenkyn ab David Fychan.

Morgan Wynn of Pentref Morgan. = Lettice. d. of ...

LORDSHIP OF WHITTINGTON.—LLOYD OF EBNALL.

Harl. MS. 9865.

Hwfa ab Ieuaf ab Iorwerth ab Howel ab Owain ab Bleddyn ab Owain⹻
Brogyntyn.   *Argent*, a lion rampant *sable*, debruised by a baton
sinister *gules*.

Iorwerth ab⹻Gwerfyl, d. of Madog ab Iorwerth ab Madog ab Rhirid
  Hwfa.   │   Flaidd.

David ab Ior-⹻Margaret, d. of Madog Goch ab Madog ab Cynwrig ab Heilin
  werth.   │   ab Trahaiarn ab Iddon, Lord of Tref Dudlysh. *Argent*, a
           │   chevron inter three boar's heads couped *gules*, tusked *or*,
           │   and langued *azure*.

Gruffydd ab⹻Margaret, d. of Y Badi ab Howel ab Ieuan Fychan ab Ieuan
  David.   │   Gethin of Moeliwrch. Party per fess *sable* and *argent*, a
           │   lion rampant counterchanged.

Madog ab ⹻Isabel, d. and heiress of David ab Einion ab Ednyfed Ddû of
Gruffydd of │   Pentref Morgan in Tref Dudlysh, ab Iorwerth ab Goronwy
Pentref Mor- │   Ddû ab Morgan ab Iddon, Lord of Tref Dudlysh yn y
  gan.   │   Waun. *Argent*, a chevron inter three boar's heads couped
           │   *gules*, tusked *or*, and langued *azure*.

John ab Madog⹻Catherine, d. of John Wynn Kynaston of Pant   David of
  of Ebnall. │   y Burslley, ab Jenkyn Kynaston of Stokes,   Pentref
             │   ab Gruffydd Kynaston. *Argent*, a chevron   Morgan.
             │   engrailed inter three martletts *sable*.

David Lloyd⹻Sina, d. and heir of David Glyn ab John ab William of Garth
  of Ebnall. │   Eryr in Mochnant, ab Maurice of Garth Eryr, ab Ieuan
             │   Gethin ab Madog Ceffin. Party per fess *sable* and *argent*,
             │   a lion rampant counterchanged.

Edward   ⹻Catherine, d. of John ab William ab Maredydd of Plas y Bol
Lloyd of Eb- │   in Maes Mochnant, ab Iolyn ab Ieuan Gethin ab Madog
  nall.   │   Cyffin.
  │ a

| a

Philip Lloyd=Angharad, d. of William ab Maredydd of Westyn Rhyn.
of Ebnall. |

Edward   =Elizabeth, d. of Rhys Lloyd of Fferme in Glyn Berbrwg in
Lloyd of Eb-   Ystrad Alun, and Margaret, his wife, d. of Roger Ellis
nall.   of Alrhey.   Other MSS. state that Edward Lloyd married
        Anne, d. of Philip ab John of Berghill.

Richard Lloyd of Ebnal.=

Edward Lloyd=..., d. of Ffoulk Morgan.

Mary Lloyd, the heiress of Ebnal, married Edward
Lloyd of Llwyn y Maen.

LORDSHIP OF WHITTINGTON.—POWEL OF PARK.

Howel, second son of Gruffydd of Abertanad, ab Ieuan Fychan=..., dau. of
ab Ieuan Gethin ab Madog Cyffin of Moeliwrch. Party per | ...Strange.
fess *sable* and *argent*. a lion rampant counterchanged.

Robert=Catherine, relict of Tudor Lloyd of Bodidris yn Iâl, and eldest
Powel.   daughter of John Edwards Hen of Plâs Newydd, Receiver of
    Chirkland, and Gwenllian, his wife, daughter of Elis Eyton of
    Rhiwabon. Party per bend sinister *ermine* and *ermines*, a lion
    rampant *or*.

| Thomas Powel of Park,=Mary, dau. of | Marga- | Blanche, ux. Thomas Wil-
| *ob*. 1588. He obtained | Sir Robert | ret, ux. | liams of Willaston, ab
| Park from Henry Fitz | Corbet of | William | Reignallt ab William,
| Alan, Earl of Arun- | Moreton | Mostyn. | Lord of Willaston. *Sable*,
| del, in 1563.' | Corbet. | | three horse's heads erased
| | | | *argent*.

| a | b

[1] *Shropshire Archæological Transactions*, vol. iii, Part I, p. 70.

a			*b*
Robert Powel of=Anne, d. of Robert Needham of		..., ux. Robert Lloyd of	
Park.	Shavington.	Ashton.	

Thomas Powel of=Mary, dau. of   Edward Powel of=Mary, d. of William
Park, *ob*. 1618. | Thomas At-   Park. | Barnham of Lon-
kins. | don; *ob*. 1674.

Robert Powel of Park,   Margaret,   Rev. Robert Powel of Park, D.D., Rector
High Sheriff for co.   ux. Andrew   of Whittington and Hodnet; *ob*. 1680.[1]
Salop, 1647; *ob*. 1653, Lloyd of   This line ended in an heiress, Jane
s. p.   Aston.   Powel, who sold the Park Estate to
                                          Sir Francis Charlton of Ludford, Bart.

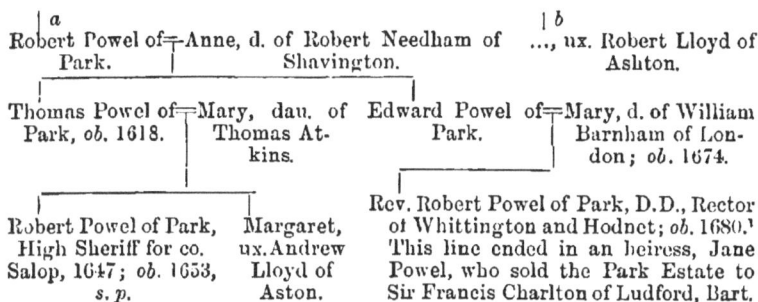

Sir Francis Charlton of Ludford, Bart., had a son, Job
Charlton of Park, High Sheriff for co. Salop in 1748;
and a daughter, Emma, heir to her brother; who married
John Kinchant, Esq., Captain in the 32nd Regiment of
Infantry, by whom she had issue three sons, 1, John
Charlton Kinchant of Park, High Sheriff for co. Salop, in
1775—*ob. s. p.*, 1832; 2, Francis; and 3, Richard, father
of Richard Henry Kinchant of Park, Esq., J.P. and D.L.,
and High Sheriff for co. Salop in 1846.

Y DREF NEWYDD, IN THE LORDSHIP OF WHITTINGTON.

Add. MS. 9864.

John Lloyd of Dref Newydd, second=Eleanor, d. of John Pryse, Parson of
son of Edward Lloyd of Llwyn | Whittington, Llandderfel, and Vicar
y Maen, second son of Richard | of Oswestry, son of John ab Thomas
Lloyd ab Robert Lloyd. | ab Rhys of Oswestry, ab Maurice Ge-
                                   | thin ab Ieuan Gethin ab Madog Cyffin.

a

---

[1] His son Thomas was High Sheriff for co. Salop in 1717, and his
daughter Jane sold the estate.—*Shropshire Archæological Transactions*, vol. iii, Part I, p. 70.

| a

Edward Lloyd of=Catherine, d. and co-heir of John Trevor Fychan of Os-
Dref Newydd. | westry, and Margaret, his wife, daughter and heir of
| Richard Stanney of Oswestry, and relict of Thomas
| Kynaston of Vorhen.

| 1 | 2 | | |

John   Marmaduke=Penelope, d. and heir (by Rebecca,   George   Four
Lloyd,   Lloyd of | his wife, d. of Richard Langford   Lloyd.   daugh-
ob. s.p.   Dref New- | of Trefalun, High Sheriff for co.   ters.
              ydd. | Denbigh in 1640) of Charles Goodman
                        | of Glanhespin, High Sheriff for co.
                        | Denbigh in 1666.

Edward Lloyd of Dref Newydd,   Charles Lloyd=Anabella   John.   Cathe-
the Shropshire historian, whose   of Dref New- | Kingston   rine.
valuable collections were at one   ydd, ob. Jan. | of Ciren-
time at Halston, but are now pre-   1749-50. | cester, ob. 1728.
served at Hawkestone. Buried
at Whittington 5th November
1715, s. p.

Anabella, heiress of Dref Newydd, third wife of Richard Williams of
Penbedw, M.P. for Flint, youngest brother of Sir Watkin Williams Wynn, the third baronet of that house.

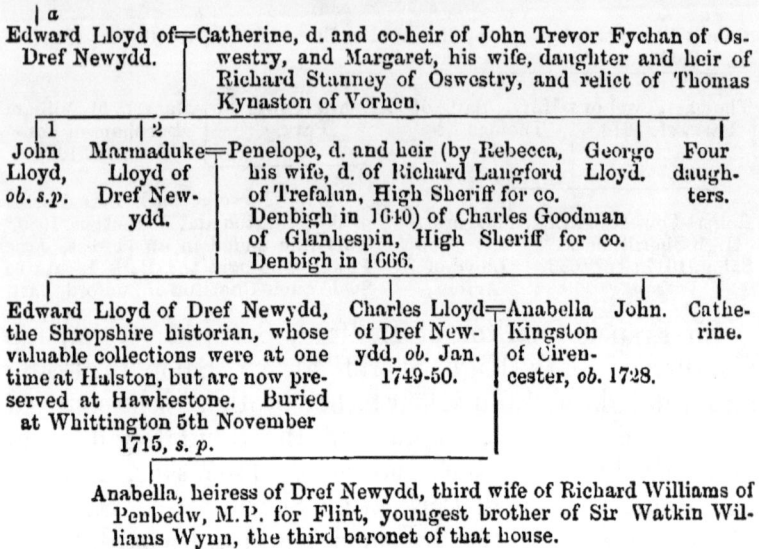

Dref Newydd was sold about the year 1830, by Ana-
bella Williams of Penbedw (granddaughter of Richard
Williams), and her nephew, W. W. E. Wynn of Peniarth,
Esq., to the late W. Ormsby Gore of Brogyntyn, Esq.,
M.P.

ADDENDA.

HOLT CASTLE.

In the reign of Richard II, this Castle was in the hands of the Crown. That unfortunate sovereign stayed there for a time on his Irish expedition, and deposited there jewels to the amount of 200,000 marks, and 100,000 marks in specie, which afterwards fell into the hands of Bolingbroke.

Henry VII made a grant of it to Sir William Stanley, but resumed it on Sir William's execution, with all its treasures, the spoils of Bosworth field, valued at £40,000 in money and plate, besides jewels, household furniture, and cattle on his grounds, and all his real estate, worth £3,000 per annum (see volume i, p. 340).

Henry VIII made a grant of the Castle and Lordship to Henry Fitz Roy, Duke of Richmond, his natural son by a Shropshire lady ; and he, in 1535, coming to take possession, accompanied by two other Dukes and a large retinue, stopped a night at Shrewsbury.

In the reign of Edward VI the Castle was held by Thomas Seymour.

In 1643 it was in the hands of the Crown, but was seized by the Parliamentary forces under Sir William Brereton and Sir Thomas Myddleton. The Royalists regaining it, it was again besieged and razed by the Republicans, under Major General Mytton, but not till the Governor, Sir Richard Lloyd of Esclusham (see p. 35), had secured, by his gallant defence, and honourable capitulation, permission for himself to retire beyond the seas, with £300 per annum, and the enjoyment of his estates, value £300 per annum, to his wife. The surrender, however, was made to Colonel Pope in the absence of Mytton, who that morning, having come to Wrexham, had a narrow escape for his life ; for the Parliamentary soldiers, exasperated for want of pay, broke out in a mutiny, and fired upon Mytton as he was hurrying off to seek protection amongst his own men at Holt.

A passage in the Charter permits the Burgesses of Holt to dig for coals in the wastes of Brynbwa and Coed Poeth; but subject to this right, which is never asserted, the minerals of Bromfield belong to the Grosvenors, by grant from Charles II, and form a great revenue.[1]

---

[1] *History of Wrexham.*

ELLIS OF CROES NEWYDD, NEAR WREXHAM.
(See p. 68.)

Peter Ellis, of Groes Newydd, Esq., Attorney at Law, Deputy Steward for Maelor and Iâl, and Justice of the Peace, 1697, son and heir of Robert Ellis, Colonel in the Royal Army of Charles I. This Colonel Robert Ellis bought Groes Newydd, and was son of Peter Ellis, a learned lawyer in Wrexham ("Hen achwr mawr cyfarwydd a dyscedig"), son of Richard ab Ellis ab Gruffydd ab Gwyn ab Goronwy ab Gwilym ab Meredydd ab Gruffydd ab Llywelyn ab Howel ab Gruffydd ab Sanddef Hardd.

Colonel Robert Ellis of Croes Newydd had served under Gustavus Adolphus. He was highly esteemed by Charles I, who gave him a commission, dated November 1643, for raising 1,200 men. Lord Capel appointed him Commander-in-chief (under himself) of the counties of Denbigh and Flint.

Croes Newydd passed into the possession of F. R. Price of Bryn y Pys, Esquire, by whom it was exchanged for other property with the Fitz Hughe of Plâs Power.[1]

FOWLER OF ABEY CWM HIR AND HARNAGE
GRANGE. *(See p. 366.)*

Roger Fowler of Broom Hill, Co. Statford, Esq., had issue by his wife Isabella, daughter and heir of William Lee of Morpeth, Treasurer of Berwick, and Isabella his wife, daughter and heiress of Sir Andrew Trollope, Knt. (*Vert* three goats rampant *argent*, attired *or*, for Trollope), a third son, William Fowler, of the Middle Temple, and of Harnage Grange, Co. Salop. In the year 1565 a license was granted to Nicholas Williams, by Queen Elizabeth, to alienate to William Fowler and Edward Herbert the manor of Golon, the site of the Monastery of Cwm Hir, and certain messuages, lands, etc., in Golon, Llanbistair, Llanddewy, Llananno, Llanbadarn, St. Harmon's, Nantmel, Karnaff and Clirow in the county of Radnor. (*Record in the Chapel of the Rolls.*)

In the same year Nicholas Williams executed a deed of conveyance with William Fowler, conveying to him the manor of Golon, the site of the Monastery, with all the lands, etc. in the aforesaid parishes, to it belonging. (*Record in the Chapel of the Rolls.*)

William Fowler died in 1597, leaving issue by Maria his wife, daughter of John Blythe, Esq., M.D. (*ermine*, on a fess *gules*, three goats rampant *or*), three sons, 1, Richard, of whom presently; 2, Peter; and 3, Thomas; and three daughters, 1, Mary; 2, Alice, ux.

---

[1] *History of Wrexham.*

Robert Sontley of Sonlle, Esq. ; and 3, Margaret, ux. Thomas Vaughan of Pant Glâs, co. Caernarvon, Esq.

Richard Fowler of Harnage Grange, and Abbey Cwm Hir, was High Sheriff for Radnorshire in 1601, 1615, and 1626, and died in 1667. He married Mary, eldest daughter of Sir Edward Littleton of Pillaton Hall, Co. Stafford, Knt., and Margaret his wife, daughter and co-heiress of Sir William Devereux, Knt., youngest son of Walter, Lord Viscount Hereford, K.G., who died in 1558. By this lady he had issue five sons, 1, William ; 2, Edward ; 3, John ; 4, Richard ; and 5, Thomas. He garrisoned Abbey Cwm Hir for the King in 1644 ; early in December Sir Thomas Myddleton appeared before the place and summoned it to surrender. The answer was a flat denial. Whereupon it was taken by storm, and in it were taken prisoners Colonel Barnard the Governor, Mr. Hugh Lloyd, the High Sheriff, two Captains of Foot, one Captain of Horse, 1 Captain-Lieutenant, three Lieutenants, two Foot Colours, 1 Cornet of Horse, four Sergeants, eight Corporals, two trumpeters, four drums, sixty common soldiers, three barrels of powder, sixty fire locks, forty horses, forty horse arms, besides 200 musketeers, many arms and other ammunition.

After Sir Thomas Myddleton had taken and burnt to the ground the ancient mansion of Mathafarn, the seat of Rowland Pugh, Esq., Lord of Cyfeiliog, he received intelligence " that the enemy had made them a garrison at Abbey Cwm Hir, a very strong house, and built of stone of great thickness, and the walls and outworks all very strong, the house having been in former times an Abbey of the Papists. We arrived at the Abbey on Wednesday last with our old forces, and Colonel Beales, and Lieut.-Colonel Carter.[1] Our General having resolved to do his utmost for the gaining of it, summoned the Castle, but the Governor returned a flat denial, and said that he would not deliver up the said garrison to us ; whereupon we immediately stormed it, and that with such violence that we soon took it by force. This garrison of theirs is Master Fowler's house, which began to be a great annoyance to us. Since which, our General, having thrown down the enemy's works, made the garrison unserviceable for the future."[2]

William Fowler of Harnage Grange and Abbey Cwm Hir, who was High Sheriff for Shropshire in 1650 (see the *Sheriffs of Shropshire*, by Owen and Blakeway), married Anne, daughter of Thomas Perks of Willingworth, co. Stafford, Esq., by whom he had issue eight sons and one daughter, and was succeeded by his eldest son.

---

[1] Colonel Sir John Carter died 25th November 1676. He bore *azure*, a Talbot passant inter three buckles *or ;* and married Elizabeth, daughter and co-heir of David Holland of Kinmael, Esq., by Dorothy, his wife, one of the daughters of Jenkyn Lloyd of Berth, near Llanihloes, Esq., and sister of Sir Edward Lloyd, Knt.

[2] *Civil Wars in Wales.* By S. Rowland Phillips, Esq.

Richard Fowler of Harnage Grange and Abbey Cwm Hir, who was born in 1618, was High Sheriff for Radnorshire in 1655. Richard Fowler married Margaret, daughter of Richard, Lord Newport of High Ercall, co. Salop, and Rachel his wife, daughter of John Levison of Haling, in Kent, Esq., and sister of Sir Richard Levison of Trentham, co. Stafford, Knt., by whom he had besides other issue, three sons—

I. Francis Levison Fowler, who by Anne his wife, daughter of Peter Venables, Baron of Kinderston, had issue an only daughter and heiress Frances, who married, first, Thomas Needham, Lord Viscount Kilmorey; secondly, she married Theophilus Hastings, Earl of Huntingdon; and thirdly, she married the Chevalier de Ligonday, of the house of Auverne, Colonel of Horse, one of the French prisoners taken with Count Tallard at the battle of Hocksted, by whom she had a daughter and heiress who married the Honorable — Beresford, son of the Earl of Tyrone.

II. Sir William Fowler of Harnage Grange, who was created a Baronet by Queen Anne in 1704, and died in 1717 (see *Extinct Baronetage*). He married Mary, daughter of Sir Richard Cotton of Combermere Abbey, Bart.

III. John Fowler of Bron Dref Fawr, had Abbey Cwm Hir for his share of the estate. He built the chapel at the Abbey, where he and his wife, his only son Edward, and his second daughter Jane are buried. He was High Sheriff for co. Radnor in 1690, and died in 1696 (see "Clochfaen", in vol. ii, p. 250). I have been unable to find out whom John Fowler married, but, from the escutcheons on the plate, she bore . . . . a sword pointed downwards between two wolf's head couped at the shoulders . . . . on a chief . . . . a lion passant . . . .

TREF GAIAN.

The Arms of Tegwared y Bais Wen, were, *argent*, on a chevron *sable*, three mullets of the field (see vol. ii, p. 135).

GERVYS OF RHUDDIN.

Sable, a sword in pale pointed downwards, with the scabbard and belt *argent*; on the sinister side a Catherine wheel of the second (see pp. 46, 252).

WREXHAM.

About 9th November 1643, in his advance into Wales, Sir William Brereton is charged that he "did pull down the organs, defaced the windows in all the Churches, and the monuments." In Wrexham they broke in pieces one of the best pair of organs in the King's dominions, and pulled down the arms and hatchments in all the Churches.

LLANGURIG.

This extensive parish lies in the comot of Gwarthrynion, in the Cantref of Arwystli, Uwch y Coed.

CANTREF MEIRION.

This Cantref contains the Comots of Tal y Bont, Pennal, and Ystum Anner.

Tal y Bont contains the parishes of Dolgelli, Llanfachreth, Llangelynin, and Llanegryn.

Pennal contains the parishes[1] of Tywyn, Pennal, and Aberdyfi.

Ystumaner contains the parishes of Tal y Llyn, Meingul, and Llanfihangl y Pennant; in the centre of which last parish are the ruins of an old Castle, called Castell yr Aberydd.

---

[1] *Harl. MS.* 2155, fol. 135.

INDEX.

A.

ABBEY CWM HIR, 409, 410
Abbot David, 385
Aberdyfi, 411
Abergavenny, Lord of, 111
Aber Rhiew, 46
Aberystwyth, 271
ACTON, 68
Adam and Eve, 313
Adda ab Awr, 3
Adda Goch, 196
Addison, 168
Aelhairn, 193
Alexandra, 306
Allt Llwyn Dragon, 91, 226
Almor, 192, 194, 209
ALRHEY, 335
ALUNTON, 220
Apparition of Madame Fowler, 367
Ariconium, 262
Arwystli, Hugh, 270
Arwystli Uwch y Coed, 411
Ashera, the, 323
Ashpool, 346
Athanasian Creed, 314
Aylmar, William, 151
AYLMOR OR ALMOR, 216

B.

Bachymbyd, 49, 105
Badenoch, 92
BADY, 123
BANGOR IS Y COED, 309
Bardsey Island, 29
Barnard, Colonel, 410
Baron, Lewys Owain, 49
Bathafarn Park, 37, 47
Beli ab Bennlli Gawr, 270
Belyn of Y Nercwys, 99
Berain, 46, 94, 100
BERS, 21, 22, 23
BERS, LLOYD OF, 26
BERS, WYNN OF, 20
BERSHAM, 18
Berth, Lloyd of, 67
Berth Lloyd, Lloyd of, 410
Bettws, Wyrion Iddon, 33, 44, 103
Bettws y Coed, 33, 44, 103

BETTWS Y MHERS, 23
BILLOTT, 232
Blodwell, 249
Blythe, William, 409
Bodfel, 29
Bod Idris, 46, 62, 90, 91, 95
BODYLLTYN, 373
Bodylltyn, 21, 23
Bold, Sir Richard, 37
BORASHAM, 91, 106
Boscawen, 204
Bosworth, battle of, 408
Bowyer, Sir George, 307, 308
Boyd Dawkins, 195
BRERETON, 92
Brereton, 91
Brereton, Owain, 132, 136, 143, 154
Brereton, Sir William, 411
BRITISH KINGS, 264
Bromley, 133, 142, 162
Bron Haulog, 348
Bruer of Bruer, 211
BROUGHTON, 332
BRYNBWA, 36
Brynbwa, 5
Bryn Cunallt, 43, 101
Bryn Ffanigl, 103
Bryngwyn, 7, 9
BRYN HALCHDYN, 362
Bryn Iorcyn, 21, 39, 376
Bryn Lluarth, 8, 38, 345, 349
Bryn Owain, 16
Bryn Tangor, 151
Bryn y Ffynnon, 35
Bryn y Wiwair, 13, 25
BURTON, 173, 228
BWRAS, 90

C.

Cadair Benllyn, 41
Cadell Deyrnllwg, 11, 192
Cae Cyriog, 11
Cae Madog Coch, 67
Caer Dilinog, 19
Caer Fallwch, 95, 105, 376
Caer Gilor, 193
Caerwys, 101, 104

Calverley, Sir George, 218
Camber or Cambrey, 198
Cantref Meirion, 411
Caradog Ffreichfras, 34
Carter, Sir John, 410
Castell Cefel Ynghoedmor, 33
Castell Dulyn, 108
Castell yr Aberydd, 411
Castle of Holt, 408
Castle of Overton, 355
Castle of Whittington, 384
Catherine of Berain, 94
Cayley of Brampton, 334
CEFN Y BEDW, 5, 6
Cefyn y Bedw, 60
Cefyn y Carneddau, 6, 7
Ceinmarch, 345
Cemaes, Baron of, 20
Chabas, 317
Charlton, 406
Chester, Earl of, 92
Christianity, 313
Churchyard, poet, 171
Cicero, 170
Cilmin Droedtu, 28
Clochfaen, 257
Clynog Fawr, 33
COBHAM, 88
Coed Abynt, 198
Coed Cristionydd, 3, 13
Coed Helen, 247
Coed Marchan, 51
Coed y Cra, 67
Coed y Llai, 37, 68, 108
Collwyn ab Tangno, 29
Combermere Abbey, 411
Comyn, the Black, 92
Confession, Auricular, 165
Conwy, 102
COOKE, 122
Copa'r Goleuni, 49, 81, 99
Corbet, 99
Cotton, 65, 411
Cowryd ab Cadvan, 43, 45, 210, 345
Cowydd i John ab Rhys, 265
Cristionydd, 3, 4, 5
CROES FOEL, 38
Croes Foel, 19, 31
Croes Iocyn, 35
CROES NEWYDD, 409
Croes Wladys, 181
Croft of Croft Castle, 196
Cwmwd Menai, 22
Cwrt Plâs yn Dref, 49
Cyfeiliog, Hugh, 92
Cyffylliog, 346
Cynllaith Owain, 106
Cynmeirch, 63
Cynwrig Efell, 20, 63, 195, 217
Cynwrig Fychan of Wepra, 101

D.

Dacre, Lord, 204
David, Abbot, 385
David, Lord of Denbigh, 32, 44, 64
Davies of Dungrey, 379
DAVIES OF ERLYS, 103
Davies of Llanerch, 334
DAVIES OF TREFALUN, 222
Death, Ode on, 323
De Baliol, 92
De Becke, 99
DE BRERETON, 92
De Grey of Ruthin, 208
De Laci, 20
De Ligonday, 411
De Mety, 382
De Monte Alto, 220
De Powys, 18, 381, 383
De Sancto Petro, 93
De Swinnerton, 99
De Thornton, 92
De Upton, 379
Devereux, 410
De Vernon, 93
DE WEILD, 91, 93, 99
Derwen Anial, 67
Dinas Basing, 377
Dinbryn, 1
DINHINLLE, 17
Diodorus Siculus, 259
Dolgelli, 411
Dol Gynwal, 344
Dref Newydd, 49
Dyffryn Aled, 37, 45
Dyffryn Clwyd, 192
Dyffryn Erethlyn, 44
DYMOCK, 392
Dulassau, 34
Dutton, 208
Dynevor Castle, 204

E.

EBNALL, 404
Edisbury, 59
EDISBURY, 60
Ednowain ab Bradwen, 101
Ednowain Bendew, 18, 43
Edwards, John, of Plâs Newydd, 137
Edwards, of Caer Fallwch, 105
EDWARDS OF STANSTI, 81
Egerton of Egerton, 81, 93, 122
EGLWISEGLE, 51
EGYPTIAN RECORDS, 317
Einion Efell, 133
Einion Sais, 34
Eleazar, priest, 166
ELIS OF MAELOR, 125
Ellis, Colonel, 109
Ellis, Dr., 146
ELLIS OF ALRHEY, 335

ELLIS OF GROES NEWYDD, 68, 409
Elystan Glodrhudd, 30
Englefield Family, 368
Erbistog, 25
Eriviat, Ffoulkes of, 31, 46
ERLYS, 108
Erddig of Erddig, 31
ERDDIG, 60
ERDDIG OF ERDDIG, 62
ERLYS OF ERLYS, 109, 110
Esclusham, 3, 5, 17, 32
Esclys, 3, 32
Esgair Clochfaen, 257
Estwick, Lords of, 383, 401
Estwick of Estwick, 384
Ethnology, Welsh, 295
ECNYDD, 192
EVANS OF PLAS LLANEURGAIN, 100
EWLO CASTLE, 241
Ewlo Castle, 101, 106, 120, 245
Eyton, Gerard, 330
Eyton of Coed y Llai, 37
Eyton, Mrs. Sarah, 329
Eyton of Eyton Isaf, 26, 95, 122
EYTON OF EYTON ISAF, 324
EYTON OF MAES GWAELOD, 355
EYTON OF PENTREF MADOG, 401

F.

Faenor, 46
Fairdref, Holland of, 103
Falmouth, Viscount, 204
Ffachnallt of Ffachuallt, 94, 104
Ffynogion, Wynn of, 44
Fifty Million Years Ago, 300
Fitz Roy, Henry, 408
Fitz Warine, 382, 384, 387
FLETCHER WYNN, 357
Foelas, Wynn of, 342, 343
Fowler, 220
FOWLER OF ABBEY CWM HIR, 409
FOWLER OF LLYS BEDYDD, 366
FRONDEG, 18, 83
FRONDEG, JONES OF, 66, 124
Fron Dêg, 16, 39
Fron Gôch, 368
Frontinus, 262

G.

Gaerddin, 7
Garth Aiarn, 193
Garth Eryr, 197
Gelli Gynan, 62
Gentleman, the true, 172
Gerard, Sir William, 218
Gervys of Rhuddin, 46, 208, 209, 352
GETHIN OF PLAS GERNIOGAU, 353
GLAN Y PWLL, 104
Clegg of Gayton, 102
Glyn Berbrwg, 38, 81

Glyn Dyfrdwy, 196, 197
Glyn Llufon, 28
Glyn Llugwy, 33
GOCH OF MAELOR, 396
Goch, Sir Matthew, 396, 398
God, His Nature, 322
Golon, Manor of, 409
Goodman, 49, 131, 135
Goronwy of Llai, 281
Goronwy Pefr, 381
Green of Stapleford, 211
Grey de Ruthin, 208
Griffith of Caerwys, 104
GRIFFITH OF TREF ALUN, 222
GROES NEWYDD, 68
Gruffydd ab David Goch, 33, 44
Gruffydd Goch, 209, 346
GRUFFYDD OF BRYNBWA, 36
GUTYN OWAIN, 385
Gwarthrhynion, 411
GWERN HACLOD, 356
GWERSYLLT ISAF, 186, 187, 188
GWERSYLLT UCHAF, 187, 188
Gwerystan ab Gwaethfoed, 192
Gwydir, 8, 33
Gwyn of Llanidloes, 128
Gwysannau, 122, 334
Gyffylliog, 46, 209

H.

HAFOD UN NOS, 42, 43
Hafod Un Nos, 345
HAFOD Y BWCH, 41, 90
HAFOD Y BWCH, ROBERTS OF, 348
HAFOD Y WERN, 119, 120
Hafod y Wern, 110
Halchdyn, 186
HALCHDYN, 359, 365
Hampden, Viscount, 201, 203, 204
Hanmer of Caer Fallwch, 95
Hanmer, Sir David, 380
Harlech Castle, 106, 187
HAWARDEN CASTLE, 237
Hedd Moelwynog, 43
HEIM, 88
Henblâs, 346
HENDREF FAWR, 50
Hendref Fawr, 43, 47, 348
Hendref Rhys Gethyn, 44
Henglawdd, 103
Herbert, Edward, 409
Hereford, Viscount, 410
Hersedd, Lloyd of, 81, 102
Huckleton, 209
Hocksted, battle of, 411
Holland, 22, 410
HOLLAND, 50
Holt, 91, 101, 409
HOLT CASTLE, 408
Hope, 37

Hope of Broughton, 227, 246
Howel Coetmor, 33, 64
HOWEL MAELOR, 126
Howel Wyddel, 215
Howel y Gadair, 41
Hugh Lupus, 105
Hughes of Segroed, 350
HUGHES, 55
Hughes of Ystrad, 350
Huntingdon, Earl of, 92, 410
Huxley, Professor, 318

I.

Iestyn ab Gwrgant, 3
Inquisition, Roman, 165
Iorwerth Sais, 345
Ipstone, 93
IPSTONE OF IPSTONE, 99
Iremonger, 247
Isabella, Queen, 166
ISGOED, 84
Ithel Anwyl, 101, 106, 245
Ithel Felyn, 20, 29

J.

JEFFRIES OF ACTON, 68
Jehovah, 166, 167, 260
Jesus Christ, 167, 260
Jews, Persecution of, 166, 304
Jews, Religion of, 318
Job, 168, 169
JONES, 38, 39, 42, 346

K.

Kaer Estyn, 173
Kenrick of Nantclwyd, 47
KENRICK OF NANTCLWYD, 339
Kenyon of Cefn, 364
Kilmorey, Viscount, 410
Kinchant of Park, 406
Kinderton, 93, 410
Kinmael, 51, 103, 410
Kyffin of Maenan, 109, 340
Kynaston, 7

L.

Langford, 193
LANGFORD, 207
Lateran Council, 165
Lee of Morpeth, 409
LEEDS ABBEY, 82
Legend of S. Curig, 271
Levison, 410
Lewys, Capt. Anthony, 228
LEWYS OF BURTON, 228
Littleton, Sir Edward, 410
Litton, 96
Llai, Lloyd of, 209
Llanarmon yn Iâl, 67
Llandderfel, 193

Llanegryn, 411
Llanegwestl, 197
LLANERCH BANNA, 389
Llanerch Park, 122
Llanerch Rugog, 19, 41
LLANERCH RUGOG, 55
Llaneurgain, 95, 101
Llanfachraeth, 411
Llanfair, D. Clwyd, 67
Llanfihangl y Pennant, 411
Llanganafal, 65
Llangedwyn, 18
Llangelynin, 411
Llangurig, 55, 257, 265, 267, 411
Llangyrniew, 42
Llangwyfan, 210
Llangwyfan, Lloyds of, 350
Llanidloes, 128
Llan-Uwchllyn, 227
Llanynys, 63, 345
Llanrhaiadr, 43
Llanrwst, 33
Llawesog, 345
Lleprog, 192
Lleyn, Griffith of, 95
Lloran, Uchaf, 113, 114
Llorente, 166
Lloyd, Evan of Iâl, 136, 143, 145
Lloyd, Hugh, 410
Lloyd, Jenkyn, 410
Lloyd, Capt. Luke, 363
LLOYD OF BERS, 26
Lloyd of Bryn Lluarth, 359
LLOYD OF COED CRISTIONYDD, 13
LLOYD OF DREF NEWYDD, 406
LLOYD OF EBNAL, 404
LLOYD OF ESCLYS, 32
LLOYD OF HALCHDYN, 359
Lloyd of Llai, 209
Lloyd of Palau, 44
LLOYD OF PENTREF CLAWDD, 59
LLOYD OF PENTREF HOBYN, 243
LLOYD OF PLAS UWCH Y CLAWDD, 58
Lloyd of Plâs Llanynys, 346, 350
LLOYD OF TAL Y WERN, 369
LLOYD OF THE BRYN, 362
LLOYD OF WILLINGTON, 371
LLOYD OF YR ORSEDD GOCH, 215
Lloyd of Ysgeifiog, 104
Lloyd, Sir Edward, 410
Lloyd, Sir Richard, 408
Llygadog, 193
Llwyn Dyrus, 44
Llwyn Egryn, 245
Llwyn On, 196
Llwyn y Cnotiau, 198
Llwyn y Maen, 113
LLWYN YN, 42, 45, 48, 49, 345, 349
Llwyn Yn, 347
Llys Bedydd, 100, 112

Llys Bradwen, 101
Llys Coed y Mynydd, 48
Llys Edwin, 105
Llys Pengwern, 7, 8, 20, 109, 186
Llys Trevor, 3, 4, 14, 66, 246
Llywarch ab Bran, 22
Llywelyn ab Ifor, 227
Llywelyn Eurdorchog, 192
Llywelyn Holbwrch, 245

M.

Madog Danwr, 55
Madog Gloddaeth, 110
Madog Llwyd, 43, 371
Madog Maelor, 365
Madog Pabo, 21
Madog Voel, 376
Maelgwn ab Rhyswallawn, 287, 292
MAELOR SAESNEG, 309
Mears, 14
Maenan Abbey, 109
Maen Gwynedd, 62
Maes Maen Cymro, 63, 64, 350
MAES MAEN CYMRO, 65, 66
Maes y Pandy, 34
Malpas, Barons of, 93
Manetho, 317, 318
Manley, 25
Marchudd, 45
Marchweithian, 341
Marchwiail, 110, 111
MAREDITH OF STANSTI, 82
Maredith, Sir William, 193
MAREDYDD OF TREFALUN, 224
Martin, William, 20
MARTYRDOM OF RICHARD GWYNN, 128
Mathafarn, 101, 410
Maurice Gethin, 341
Meini Hirion, 270
Meirion, Cantref of, 411
MERFFORDD, 236
Middleton, Dr. Conyers, 170
Midianites, 166, 167
MINERA, MANOR OF, 180
MONUMENTS, ANCIENT, 257
Moreton Corbet, 99
Morgan of Gwylgre, 245
Morley of Glynde, 201
Moses, 166, 167
Mostyn, 7, 18
MOSTYN, 8, 105
MORTON ANGLICORUM, 180
MORTON OF MORTON, 233
Mule of Rhuddin, 348
Mwssoglen, 22
Myddleton, 37
MYDDLETON, 40, 41
Myddleton, Sir Thomas, 408, 410
Mynachlog Rhedyn, 101
MYNACHLOG RHEDYN, 105
Mytton, Major-General, 408

N.

NANTCLWYD, 47, 339, 344
Nant Conwy, 32, 44, 64
Nercwys Hall, 359
Newport, Lord, 410
Norris of Speke, 81

O.

Ode to John ab Rhys, 267
Ostorius, 262
OVERTON OF OVERTON, 380
Owain Glyndyfrdwy, 90
Owen of Garth y Medd, 143, 153
Owen of Talwrn, 33
OWSTON, 122

P.

Palmer of Wingham, 82
Pant Iocyn, 41
PANT IOCYN, 216
Pant Meugan, 192
Pant y Llougdu, 68
PARKINS TREVOR, 205
Parry, Dr. William, 102
Parry of Llwyn Yu, 42
PARRY OF LLWYN YN, 45
PARRY OF NANTCLWYD, 344, 352
Parry of Pwll Halawg, 43
PARRY OF TREF RHUDDIN, 45, 349
PELAGIUS, 311
Penllyn, Lord of, 227
PENARTH HALAWG, 237
Pengwern, 8
Peniarth, 36
PENLEY, 391
PENLEY, JONAS OF, 382, 389
Pen Machno, 32, 33
Pennal, 411
PENNANT, 377, 379
Pentref Bychan, 193
PENTREF CLAWDD, 59
Pentref Cristionydd, 16, 17
Pentref Cuhelyn, 67
Pentref Goch, 43, 46, 209, 346
PENTREF HOBYN, 243
Pentref Madog, 384
PENTREF MADOG, 401
PENTREF MORGAN, 403
Penrhyn, 35, 46
PEN Y BRYN, 9
PEN Y LAN, 17
Pen y lan, 364
Philip Phychdan, 377
PICKHILL, 181
Pillaton Hall, 410
Pindar, 320
Plâs Cadwgan, 37
PLAS CADWGAN, 40
Plâs Cerniogau, 341
PLAS CERNIOGAU, 353
Plâs Coch, 47

Plâs Iolyn, 344
Plas Isaf, 15
Plas Kynaston, 7, 8
Plas Llaneurgain, 100
Plâs Llanynys, 346
Plâs Madog, 4, 9, 14, 21, 364
Plas Newydd, 42, 47
Plas Power, 25
Plas Teg, 201
Plas Uchaf, 14
Plas Uwch y Clawdd, 89
Plâs y Bada, 38
Plâs y Drain, 60
Plâs y Bold, 37, 40
Plas y Mhers, 27
Plâs ym Machymbyd, 62
Plas ym Machymbyd, 63
Plas yn Horslli, 214, 248
Plas yn Iâl, 91
Plas y Ward, 46, 211
Pleydell, 69, 77
Pont y Gôf, 347
Pont y Gôf, 47, 352
Pope, Colonel, 408
Portland, Earl of, 234
Powel of Alrhey, 338
Powel of Glan y Pwll, 104
Powel of Henllan, 349
Powel of Park, 405
Powel of Plas Yn Horslli, 248
Powel, 25
Price, Dr. Ellis, 344
Pryse of Derwen, 347
Pryse of Llawesog, 345
Pryse of Llwyn Yn, 49
Pugh, Rowland, 410
Puleston, 5, 14, 16, 21, 131
Puleston of Hafod y Wern, 120
Puleston of Trefalun, 219
Pulford of Pulford, 101

R.

Races, Ancient, 257
Ravenscroft, 36
Rhagad, Lloyd of, 67
Rhelefnwyd, 379
Rhirid Flaidd, 227
Rhirid Foel, 249
Rhiwlo, 31, 38
Rhuddin, 193
Rhôs, Cantref of, 103
Richmond, Duke of, 408
Rhual, 105
Rhuddallt, 5, 6, 25
Rhydonen, 63
Rhys ab Marchan, 192
Rhys ab Maredydd, 342
Rhys Gethin, 33
Robert ab Rhys, Sir, 343
Roberts, 17

Roberts of Hafod y Bwch, 41
Robinson, Colonel, 187
Robinson of Gwersyllt, 41
Robinson of Gwersyllt Uchaf, 188
Rogers of Bryn Tangor, 151
Rosendale, 228
Roydon, 19, 93, 100, 189, 227
Roydon, 111

S.

Salusbury, 94, 100
Sanddef Hardd, 248
Sandief of Mortyn, 227
Scotland, King of, 92
Segrwyd, 64
Seswick, Manor of, 181
Shackerley, Sir George, 187
Sir Fulk Fitz Warine, 382
Sir Roger de Powys, 383, 401
Sir Roger Fychan de Estwick, 383
Sir William de Powys, 381
Sladen, Rev. Mainwaring, 324, 329
Soulli, 15, 16, 41
Soulli, Hugh, 136, 153, 161
Stanley of Ewlo, 121
Stanley of Ewlo Castle, 242
Stanley, Sir William, 408
Stansti, 81, 123
Stansti, 193
St. Augustine, 316
St. Clears, 227
St. Curig, 274
St. Elidan, 288
St. George, 92
St. Germanus, 310
St. Gregory, Pope, 314
Sutton of Sutton, 185
Sychdin, 102
Symon of Coed y Llai, 223

T.

Tacitus, 262
Tallard, Count, 411
Tal y Bont, 101, 411
Tal y Llyn, 411
Tal y Wern, 369
Tegin of Frondeg, 83
Tegwared y Bais Wen, 411
Teirdan, 37, 51
Teynham, Lord, 204
Thelwall, 37, 47, 211, 344
Thelwall, Simon, 131, 143, 147, 148, 149, 163
Theism, 320
Thomas of Coed Helen, 30
Tir y Cellach, 6
Torquemada, 166
Trafford, 31
Trahairn Goch of Emlyn, 347
Trahairn Goch of Lleyn, 18

Traian, 385
Trawst, the Lady, 239
Trefalun, 192, 195, 196, 207, 212, 219, 220, 221, 222, 224
Tref Eyarth, 49
Tref Fechan, 16
Tref Gaian, 29, 411
Tref Garnedd, 44
Tref Nant Bychan, 44
Trefnant y Rhiw, 192
Tref Pen y Coed, 192
Tref Rhuddin, 45, 345, 349
Trentham, 410
Trevor Hall, 246
Trefor John, 206
Trollope, Sir Andrew, 409
Twiss, Sir Travers, 212
Ty Bellots, 23, 25
Ty Cerrig, Lloyd of, 13
Ty Cerrig, Roberts of, 25
Tywyn, 411

U.

Uchdryd, 105
Ucheldref, 193

V.

Valentia, Viscount, 25, 26
Valle Crucis Abbey, 3, 115, 197, 246, 385
Venables, 93, 410
Vaughan of Pant Glâs, 410
Virgin Mary, 239

W.

Warfield Hall, 43
Wattlesborough, 99
Wepra, 101, 106
Westminster, Creed of, 315
White, Richard, 128
Whitchall, 334

Whitney, 27, 28, 121
Whittington, 381, 405
Wigfair, Wynn of, 94
Williams, Nicholas, 409
Willington, 374
Wood, 210
Woodhouse, 8
Worslley, 254
Wrexham, 132, 411
Wrexham Abad, 115
Wrexham Gentry, 171
Wrexham Manor, 115
Wynn, 16, 19, 20, 33, 42, 108, 141
Wynn Jones, 348
Wynn of Bodfel, 29
Wynn of Frondeg, 18
Wynn of Llwyn, 358
Wynn of Pentref Morgan, 403
Wynn of Wigfair, 94
Wynn of y Groesffordd, 226

Y.

Y Dref Newydd, 406
Y Dref Wen, 381, 385
Y Fynechtid, 192
Y Glwysegl, 55
Y Groesffordd, 192, 193
Y Groes Llwyd, 192
Ynys Enlli, 29
Yonge, 21, 39
Yonge, 376
Yr Orsedd Goch, 215
Y Saeth Marchog, 193
Ysgeifiog, 104
Yspytty Ieuan, 342, 344, 353
Ystum Anner, 101, 411
Ystum Cegid, 101
Y Têg Fadog, 62

Z.

Zimri, 167
Zosimus, Pope, 274, 312

T. RICHARDS, PRINTER, 37, GREAT QUEEN STREET.

www.ingramcontent.com/pod-product-compliance
Lightning Source LLC
Chambersburg PA
CBHW032307280326
41932CB00009B/727